EDGAR ALLAN POE

EDGAR ALLAN POE

Reproduced from the original portrait by Samuel S. Osgood, through the
courtesy of the New York Historical Society. It represents Poe at about
thirty-five years of age.

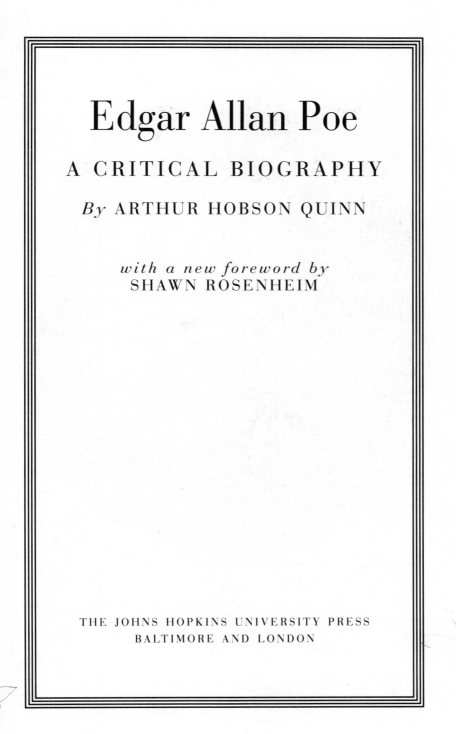

Edgar Allan Poe

A CRITICAL BIOGRAPHY

By ARTHUR HOBSON QUINN

with a new foreword by
SHAWN ROSENHEIM

THE JOHNS HOPKINS UNIVERSITY PRESS
BALTIMORE AND LONDON

Originally published in 1941 by Appleton-Century-Crofts, Inc., New York
Foreword © 1998 The Johns Hopkins University Press
All rights reserved
Printed in the United States of America on acid-free paper

Johns Hopkins Paperbacks edition, 1998
9 8 7 6 5 4 3

The Johns Hopkins University Press
2715 North Charles Street
Baltimore, Maryland 21218-4363
www.press.jhu.edu

Library of Congress Cataloging-in-Publication Data
Quinn, Arthur Hobson, 1875–1960.
    Edgar Allan Poe : a critical biography / by Arthur Hobson Quinn ; with a new
foreword by Shawn Rosenheim.
        p.   cm.
    Previously published: New York : Cooper Square, 1969.
    Includes bibliographical references and index.
    ISBN 0-8018-5730-9
    1. Poe, Edgar Allan, 1809–1849.   2. Fantastic literature, American—History and
criticism.   3. Authors, American—19th century—Biography.   I. Title.
PS2631.Q5   1998
818′.309—dc21
[B]   97-18240
                                                                                    CIP

A catalog record for this book is available from the British Library.

To

C.Q.H.

A.H.Q.,Jr.

K.C.Q.

F.Q.S.

J.H.Q.

Contents

CONTENTS

Illustrations

Foreword

Like Americans more generally, scholars of American literature have long been obsessed with biography. Besides the abiding readerly interest in the lives of American authors, new modes of biographical writing and new standards for what it is permissible to reveal have led to a flood of studies. Some of them, like *Dearest Beloved*, T. Walter Herbert's portrait of the Hawthorne family, are works of abiding interest. Of all American writers' lives, probably none has sparked so many versions as that of Edgar Allan Poe. Although Poe's critical esteem rises and falls, there has been an unbroken fascination with his curious, tormented life. At least three new biographies of Poe have appeared in the last few years, one of which (Kenneth Silverman's *Edgar A. Poe: Mournful and Never-ending Remembrance*) met with justified commercial success. In the face of these new studies, readers unfamiliar with Arthur Hobson Quinn's masterly work might be forgiven for wondering at the rationale for publishing yet another Poe biography, and that a reprint to boot.

Poe biography is an odd business, to be sure. Even the earliest accounts of Poe's life, such as that written by James Russell Lowell for *Graham's Magazine* in 1841, adulterate Poe's history, mixing actual events with Poe's exaggerated or distorted recollections. Lowell—who unwisely took most of his information from Poe himself—begins well enough, correctly describing Poe as "the offspring of a romantic marriage" who was left an orphan at an early age. He was then informally adopted by John Allan, "a wealthy Virginian whose barren marriage-bed seemed the warranty of a large estate to the young poet." But Lowell's claims effervesce into Byronic fantasies of what Poe *wished* had happened in his life: "Having received a classical education in England, he returned home and entered the University of Virginia, where, after an extravagant course, followed by reformation at the last extremity, he was graduated with the highest honors of his class. Then came a boyish attempt to join the fortunes of the insurgent Greeks, which ended at St.

Petersburg, where he got into difficulties through the want of a pass-port, from which he was rescued by the American consul and sent home" (February, 1845).

Poe's death in 1849 only made the task of illuminating his life more difficult. Again, it was Poe who complicated the situation by entrusting his literary estate to the Rev. Rufus Griswold, a would-be litterateur whom Poe had insulted in print and who had been his rival for the af-fections of the poet Fanny Osgood. It was as if Mozart had left his scores to Antonio Salieri. Griswold wholeheartedly exploited his posi-tion of power, publishing a memoir so chock-full of distortions and out-right lies (for example, Griswold rewrote Poe's letters to paint himself as Poe's beneficiary) that Poe has never fully recovered from Griswold's portrait of him as a drunken, amoral, death-obsessed wretch.

Not that subsequent biographers haven't tried to amend Griswold's slanders. Indeed, their number approaches legion. In the library at the small college at which I teach one can find, among fifty or sixty other titles, *Edgar Allan Poe: A Biography*; *Edgar Allan Poe: A Critical Biog-raphy*; *Edgar Allan Poe: A Memorial Volume*; *Edgar Allan Poe: A Study in Genius*; *Edgar Allan Poe: His Life and Legacy*; and *Edgar Allan Poe: The Man, the Myth, and the Legend.* There are works on *The Mind of Poe*; *The Life of Poe*; *Poe in Northlight*; *The French Face of Edgar Allan Poe*; *The Histrionic Mr. Poe*; *Poe, Journalist and Critic*; and—one of my favorites—*Edgar Allan Poe: How to Know Him* (by C. Alphonso Smith, head of the Department of English at the United States Naval Academy, and author of *What Can Literature Do for Me?*).

How to know him, indeed: biographers have idealized his genius, de-monized his behavior, debunked his literary pretensions, made him a patron saint for high modernism, and sought to explain his psyche through a variety of Freudian approaches. First came Princess Marie Bonaparte, who in 1933 published *Edgar Poe: Etude psychanalytique*, with a foreword by Sigmund Freud himself. Despite their various ap-proaches and interpretations, however, a remarkable number of Poe's biographers share a pathological identification with their subject. John Henry Ingram, Poe's second biographer, was so inspired by Poe's writ-ing that he spent years trying to become a poet, quitting only after one of his thoroughly imitative poems, "Hope: An Allegory," was reprinted in Walter Hamilton's *Parodies* as an unintentionally comic knock-off of "Ulalume." Ingram's poetic failure was Poe's good fortune, because In-gram devoted a half-century of his life to rescuing Poe's name, publish-ing ten volumes of editions and biographies, writing fifty articles, and creating a collection of primary evidence about Poe's life that runs to one thousand items. Even Griswold remained permanently fixed on Poe's image; when he died in 1857, after a run of disasters that included divorce, terrible scarring from fire, and impoverishment, the sole decorations in his New York room were portraits of himself, Fanny Osgood, and Poe, as if their literary-romantic triangle had been *the* salient fact of his life.

The intensity of such biographical identification suggests that there is something symptomatic about the relation of Poe's life to his writing, as if that life were under pressure to explain something about his texts. In part, this is due to the intimate, insinuating voice of Poe's first-person narrators, those unnamed figures whose fierce desire to maintain their rationality ("True!—nervous—very, very dreadfully nervous I had been and am; but why *will* you say that I am mad?") propels so many of his tales and whose erudition and literary grace they share with their creator. Indeed, Poe's fiction aggressively muddies distinctions between life and art. In the preface to *The Narrative of Arthur Gordon Pym*, Pym insists that his memoirs were originally published under Poe's name because of Pym's fears that his adventures would not be believed. As "Pym" recounts the story, "finding that I would not stir" in the matter of writing, Poe

> afterward proposed that I should allow him to draw up, in his own words, a narrative of the earlier portion of my adventures, from facts afforded by myself, publishing it in the *Southern Messenger* under the garb of fiction. . . . This exposé being made, it will be seen at once how much of what follows I claim to be my own writing; and it will also be understood that no fact is misrepresented in the first few pages which were written by Mr. Poe. Even to those readers who have not seen the *Messenger*, it will be unnecessary to point out where his portion ends and my own commences; the difference in point of style will be readily perceived.

Since Poe was the author of both parts, it's hardly surprising that no "difference in point of style" can, in fact, be perceived. To the contrary, *Pym*'s preface confuses the very thing it claims to explain, interweaving Poe's life and art in such complex arabesques that the temptation to read Poe's biography out of his fiction is rendered almost fatally attractive. Such doubling is a familiar motif in Poe's work, ranging from the psychic splitting of "William Wilson," to the relation between Dupin and "the Minister D——" in "The Purloined Letter," to Poe's habit of reviewing his own work under assumed names. Such confusion poses problems for biography, which depends on fidelity to the known facts

at hand; but as the preface to *Pym* indicates, Poe's life brooks no absolute distinction between *what happened* and *what was written*. As a
consequence, biographers have often been seduced by the parallels between Poe's life and his fiction. (As Mary Newton Stanard writes in *The
Dreamer: A Romantic Rendering of the Life-Story of Edgar Allan Poe,*
"more than to any one of his biographers, I am indebted to Poe himself
for the revelations of his personality which appear in his own stories
and poems, the most part of which are clearly autobiographic.") What's
ironic is that this image of Poe as a figure of gothic romance doomed by
the accidents of his childhood to self-frustration and tragic love is cast
by the texts themselves, an oversized authorial projection much like the
shade that rises up at the end of *Pym*. It is not merely that Poe's life is
structured like one of his tales, but that our ability to appreciate his life
is predicated upon our prior knowledge of his fiction.

What, then, can we as readers get from *any* biography of Poe that we
couldn't experience more powerfully in the fiction itself? Above all, we
get a thoroughly convincing account of Poe's life within the American
culture of his day. *Edgar Allan Poe: A Critical Biography* is a remarkably well-researched book—one that has never been equaled before or
since in the canon of Poe biography. Not content merely to interpret
Poe's life, Quinn provides his readers with a compendium of documentary sources, making extensive use of bills, newspaper records, and
Poe's correspondence, much of which had never before been published.
Nor does Quinn limit his evidence only to material that confirms a particular interpretation of Poe's life. *Edgar Allan Poe* is full of casual in-
sights and throw-away moments of considerable wit. Writing of Poe's
professors at the University of Virginia, he records that George Blaettermann, the professor of modern languages, "was an irascible person,
who went so far as to cowhide his wife on the street, and he was dismissed in 1838 at the request of the undergraduate body." But, Quinn
drolly adds, "he seems to have been a competent linguist nonetheless"
(99). Challenging the much-later recollections of some of Poe's female
acquaintance, Quinn notes that "far from being a philandering young
poet, wasting his time in harrowing up the emotions of young women,
Poe was a hard-working writer of fiction, probably also of unidentified
hack work for newspapers, and was self-respecting in habits and appearance. . . . That he was desperately unhappy, his letter shows, and
that he resented his fate is equally clear. It is the appeal of a normal
young man who wishes to work and can find no one to employ him"
(198–99). Interpreting Poe's curious marriage to his cousin Virginia,
Quinn quotes a letter from newspaperman Lambert Wilmer in which

Wilmer remembers once finding Poe engaged, "on a certain Sunday, in giving Virginia lessons in Algebra." Although "Wilmer's account is evidently at times unreliable," Quinn finds a quotidian reality about the algebra lessons that helps to verify Wilmer's picture of Poe's domestic relations (198).

Most crucially, Quinn exposes many of Griswold's forgeries, redressing his slanders with a rather charming moral clarity (of Griswold's attempts to disrupt Poe's relations with the publishers Graham and Godey, he observes, "There is something especially dastardly in attempting by a forgery to deprive a dead man of his friends" [671]). Consider, too, how cleverly Quinn explodes the belief, still common today, that Poe was drummed out of the University of Virginia after his freshman year for nonpayment of gambling debts. Poe doesn't exactly deny the charge (so much for being graduated "with the highest honors of his class"), but insists that the gambling was merely a by-product of having been sent to college without money to survive. Poe's letter to his informal adoptive father, John Allan, written around this time, sounds awfully self-serving. Despite his poverty, Poe maintains, "books must be had . . . and they were bought accordingly upon credit."

> In this manner debts were accumulated . . . for I was obliged to hire a servant, to pay for wood, for washing, and a thousand other necessaries. It was then that I became dissolute, for how could it be otherwise? I could associate with no students, except those who were in a similar situation with myself—altho' from different causes—They from drunkenness, and extravagance—I, because it was my crime to have no one on Earth who cared for me, or loved me. . . . I then became desperate and gambled—until I finally involved myself irretrievably. (111)

Poe's letter slips all too easily from the purchase of course books to the hiring of a servant to "a thousand other necessaries," before attributing his whole financial crisis, in a burst of self-pity, to the fact that he had "no one on Earth who cared for me, or loved me." Only then, he claims, does gambling enter the picture. Seeing here the self-exculpating half-truths so familiar from Poe's later letters, in which he explains away his drunkenness as the unavoidable result of fatigue or poverty or despair, one would be pardoned for siding with Allan.

Yet as Quinn proves, Poe's statements about the university charges "are correctly given and indeed are understated" (111). Having taken the time to rummage through obscure and decaying correspondence, Quinn unearths bills sent to "Mr. Edgar A. Powe" and forwarded to

Allan for such minutiae as "3 yds Super Blue Cloth" at $13.00 a yard, "1 doz. Buttonmoulds," and "1 pr. Drab Pantaloones and Trimmings," thereby demonstrating that Poe's debts were not merely incurred in gambling. Although students were expected to deposit funds with the university for clothes and incidental expenses, Allan "evidently failed to send any pocket money at all. To a college where the proctor estimated that the great majority of the young men spent at least five hundred dollars in one session, Poe was sent by John Allan deliberately, without a decent allowance, or even the minimum charges of the institution. . . . Allan was in easy circumstances, and yet he refused to contribute for a year's expenses less than a third of the amount he had paid in England when he was not by any means so well off" (113).

Quinn's point isn't to acquit Poe of charges of immorality, but to get the facts of his life right. Almost alone of Poe's biographers, Quinn prefers to detail the moments of Poe's daily life as accurately as possible, rather than to identify Poe with his fictional characters. Though it sounds like a simple thing, this ability to see Poe primarily as a working writer has been the rarest of gifts in Poe's biographers. Quinn himself—poised, thorough in matters of fact, trustworthy in his presentation—is fundamentally so *unlike* his subject that he is able to recount Poe's life without falling into the polarities represented by Griswold and Ingram. What Quinn does share with Poe is an encyclopedic knowledge of, and passion for, American writing. As the author or editor of a dozen wide-ranging studies of American drama, fiction, and verse, Quinn has something both of Poe's encompassing absorption in the national literature and of his sometimes desperate relation to a culture that often seemed indifferent to its claims.

Not that Quinn is indifferent to Poe: far from it. One need only read his concluding paragraphs to hear his deep admiration for Poe's life-long dedication to writing in the face of mercenary publishers, philistine reviewers, and readers who often preferred cheap, pirated British novels to their American counterparts: "Even the specter of want could not force him into the prostitution of his genius as a poet and a writer of romance. . . . It is for this great refusal, for his willingness to lay all things upon the altar of his art, that Poe is most to be respected. He could hardly have done otherwise. A patrician to the fingertips, the carefulness of his dress, even in his poverty, was but an index to his devotion to those fields of effort in which he knew he was a master."

Quinn refuses to insist on the pathos of Poe's life at the expense of the thousand details of life and business that give *Edgar Allan Poe* its authority and texture. Instead, over the course of hundreds of pages,

Quinn builds a drama out of Poe's determination to survive as a writer at a time when most of his peers (including Nathaniel Hawthorne and Herman Melville) eventually abandoned writing for the security of more settled careers. "In biography the truth is everything," Poe wrote, perhaps as much in provocation as for any other reason. Although Poe's biographers will never fully resolve the tangled web of his writing and his life, it is Poe's good fortune, and ours, that in Arthur Hobson Quinn Poe found a biographer who recognized that the deepest interest of Poe's life is not the way it repeated the themes of his fiction, but the high ambition and persistence Poe showed in pursuing the profession of authorship throughout the course of that life.

SHAWN ROSENHEIM

Preface

A biography of Edgar Allan Poe becomes at once an exercise in discrimination. Around his name has accumulated a mass of rumor, conjecture, psycho-analysis, and interpretation based upon imagination rather than fact. To picture Poe as he really was, it is necessary for a biographer to examine all these speculations but it is not necessary to trouble the reader with them.

I have tried to tell the story of Poe the American, not the exotic as he has so often been pictured, especially by European critics. He is best understood in contrast but not in conflict with his environment. His great achievement needs no reflected glory from the mirror of an America depicted as a barren waste of spiritual vacancy. In order to establish his place as one of the pioneers of the sterling group of American writers who dignified our literature during the period before the Civil War, it is necessary to clarify his relations not only with these authors but also with the critics, editors, and publishers who determined the conditions under which a creative artist of that time must live. Only in this way may we understand how vitally Edgar Poe was a part of that life. How keen was his desire to present the best literature America was producing, in the pages of a magazine edited and owned by himself, how he might have succeeded if he had been given the necessary capital, how undaunted he was by failure, will be apparent, I trust, in this biography. If this hope of his was only a dream, it was at least a noble dream.

There is a mass of evidence, based upon contemporary personal knowledge of Poe or later scholarly research, which must be weighed carefully before it is accepted or rejected. In these cases it is obvious that final conclusions must be supported by first-hand documentation. I have usually placed this documentation in footnotes or appendices, in order that the flow of narrative shall not be impeded. I have not, however, been a slave to uniformity, and I have been guided as to my inclusion in the text of original evidence by its importance rather than by its form.

In accepting evidence, I have followed no mere chronological formulae. Even the earliest biographers have still something to contribute. My sole test is that of credibility—and their own ability to judge evidence that has now disappeared. A modern biography would be a much easier task if it were possible to classify sharply witnesses who knew Edgar Poe, as either reliable or unreliable. But some of our most interesting descriptions of him come from writers like Susan Talley Weiss, who is quite competent when she is treating of his personal character and equally incompetent when she is transmitting tradition which she received at second hand.

Poe's own letters are so interesting and reveal his nature so clearly that it seems to me impertinent to paraphrase them, or to present mere abstracts except in those cases where they are concerned with matters of transitory interest. It is my good fortune to be able to present some of the most significant of these letters either for the first time, or, what is often quite as important, for the first time as Poe wrote them.

It is the obvious duty of a biographer to spare no pains to reproduce Poe's letters only from their originals, where this is possible. Indeed it would seem unnecessary even to mention such a matter, but in the case of Poe, there are especial reasons for this care. It has been known that Rufus W. Griswold tampered with the correspondence entrusted to him, but the reader of this volume will, I believe, be amazed at the revelation of the forgeries in which Poe's first editor indulged, not only in the letters written by Poe but also in those written to him. For the first time some of the most persistent slanders are thus stripped of their foundations. Under these circumstances, I have felt it necessary to give the present location of the autograph material in all cases where it is known to me.

I trust that I have avoided an infection which has attacked in singular measure the investigators of Poe's career, and which breaks out in the form of an acute desire to expose the inaccuracies or omissions of their predecessors. Many of mine worked before the days of photostats or other devices which now make accuracy of transcription easy as well as obligatory. Only in those cases where unwarranted interpretations of evidence have become widespread, as in that of the supposed "secret marriage" of Poe and Virginia, has it been absolutely necessary to refer to the statements of earlier biographers, in order to disprove their validity.

So much generous help has been given to me and so much new material has been placed at my disposal that even the record of my gratitude becomes a roll-call of scholars, collectors, and libraries associated with Poe. Dean James Southall Wilson, Edgar Allan Poe Professor of American Literature at the University of Virginia, has generously given me permission to print in complete form for the first time certain letters of Poe to "Annie," which he has been preserving for his biography of Mrs. Richmond. His constant advice and that of his colleague, Mr. John Cook Wyllie, have helped me in many ways. Dr. Thomas O. Mabbott has not only read the proofs, but has also given me valuable information in advance of the much needed critical edition of Poe's works, which I trust will soon appear under his editorial care. Dr. John C. French, Dr. Milton Ellis, Dr. J. B. Hubbell, Dr. R. A. Law, and Dr. Stanley T. Williams have been helpful in giving me counsel drawn from their special knowledge of Poe.

In Richmond, Mr. Granville Valentine not only gave me permission to quote freely from the published correspondence of Poe and John Allan (now known as the "Valentine Letters") but also gave me free access to the unpublished manuscripts in his possession. To the skill in research and the unfailing courtesy of Mrs. Ralph T. Catterall, Honorary Curator of Prints and Manuscripts of the Valentine Museum, I owe the accounts of T. H. Ellis, of Charles Ellis, and of Mrs. Shelton, recorded by Edward V. Valentine, which not only establish dates of vital importance in the lives of Poe and John Allan in Richmond, but correct much that has been published concerning their English and Scottish days. Miss Mary Gavin Traylor, Secretary of the Poe Shrine in Richmond, has spared no pains to aid me in the solution of special problems. Dr. Joseph Wheeler and Mr. Richard H. Hart of the Pratt Library in Baltimore have made it possible for me to print the letters from the Amelia Poe Collection which alter completely our knowledge of the relations of Poe and Virginia. Mr. Louis H. Dielman, Secretary of the Peabody Institute, has been of invaluable service in tracing Poe's life in Baltimore, and in searching the original church records of the Poe and Clemm families. Miss May G. Evans has also sent me the results of her researches in Baltimore.

I am under special obligation to Major General E. S. Adams, of the War Department, and Dr. P. M. Hamer, Chief of the Division of Reference in the National Archives in Washington, who enabled me to publish the complete army record of Poe, for the first time. Dr. St. George L. Siousatt, Chief of the Manuscript Division of the Library of Congress, aided invaluably in my study of the *Ellis-Allan Manuscripts,* and to Mr. Alanson Houghton and Miss Alice Lerch of the Rare Book Collection I owe the unusual opportunity of obtaining a complete photostat of the *Prose Romances* of 1843. For permission to use as a frontispiece the Osgood painting of Poe, I am indebted to the New York Historical Society.

Private collectors of Poe material have literally overwhelmed me by their courtesies. Mr. Josiah K. Lilly, Jr., of Indianapolis, has sent me photostat copies of the original letters from Poe to Mrs. Whitman, and of correspondence between Mrs. Whitman and many others, which enable me to depict her relations with Poe fairly and without sentimentality. Mr. William H. Koester, of Baltimore, has not only welcomed my visits to his Poe Collection, which now includes the collection of the late J. H. Whitty, but has also sent me photographs of every item I needed. To Mr. H. Bradley Martin of New York I owe the opportunity of examining some of the rarest of all Poe items, including the unique copy of the *Phantasy Pieces,* a facsimile of which I owe to the generosity of the late George Blumenthal. Mr. H. M. Lydenberg has not only placed the resources of the New York Public Library at my disposal but has secured through Dr. Victor H. Paltsits invaluable judgments upon the forgeries which make Poe study a series of pitfalls. Dr. Zoltán Haraszti and Miss Elizabeth L. Adams of the Boston Public Library have welcomed my researches among the Griswold Manuscripts and have given me valuable expert advice in connection with my discoveries of the forgeries of Griswold. Dr. Max Farrand, Captain Reginald B. Haselden, and Mr. H. C. Schulz, of the Huntington Library, have been as always helpful in my examination and reproduction of their Poe material. Director K. D. Metcalf, Mr. R. H. Haynes, and Mrs. Lillian Hall of the Harvard College Library, Mrs. Belle da Costa Greene of the Pierpont Morgan Library, Mr. Clarence Brigham of the American Antiquarian Society, Miss Viola C. White of the Middlebury College Library, Mr. Lyman B. Stowe of the Authors' Club in New York, have not only permitted the printing of the manuscript material in their possession but have spared no efforts to aid me with authentic information. Among the collateral relatives of Poe, I am under special obligations to Mrs. Josephine Poe January, Miss Margaret Cheston Carey, and Mr. Harry T. Poe, Jr. For valuable help in tracing Poe's background in Charleston, I am indebted to Miss Laura Bragg and to Miss Helen Mac-Cormack, and for information concerning Poe's relations to his friends at Lowell, Massachusetts, to Mr. F. W. Coburn. Mr. Arthur G. Learned has generously permitted the reproduction of his charming sketches, and Dr. Mary Bennett, of Columbia University, has been of great service in searching newspaper files in New York City.

In my home city I owe to Dr. Marie H. Law, of the Drexel Institute, permission to publish for the first time Poe's early letter to Isaac Lea, explaining the meaning of "Al Aaraaf." To Dr. A. S. W. Rosenbach and Mr. Percy Lawler, Dr. A. K. Gray of the Library Company, Mr. Franklin Price of the Free Library, Dr. William Reitzel of the Historical Society of Pennsylvania, Mr. Joseph Jackson and Mr. Guido Bruno, I owe many courtesies. Mr. Richard Gimbel and his curator, Mr. Anthony Frayne, have been helpful in loaning me Poe material now in the Poe House. I regret that owing to Mr. Gimbel's long absence from Philadelphia I have been unable to see all his autograph material.

It is with special pleasure that I record the assistance of my associates at the University of Pennsylvania. To President Thomas S. Gates and Provost George W. McClelland, who arranged a year's leave of absence, without which I am afraid the book might never have been completed, and to the Faculty Research Committee, which provided funds to aid me in travel and investigation, I am greatly indebted. Mr. Edward H. O'Neill and Mr. E. B. Heg have generously read the proofs, and other colleagues in the Department of English, especially Dr. Paul Musser, Dr. A. C. Baugh, Dr. E. S. Bradley, Dr. R. D. James, Dr. W. J. Phillips, and Mr. D. P. Dow have helped me in many ways. Dr. Albert Gegenheimer spared the time from his own researches to bring me photographs of scenes in England and Scotland associated with Poe and to search records for the careers of his English ancestry. If I were to mention everyone of the force of the University Library who has assisted me, I would simply be reprinting that part of the University Catalogue. Mr. Seymour Thompson and his associates have been untiring in their efforts to build up an adequate Poe Collection and to make it available to me.

I beg to acknowledge the following courtesies from publishers. To D. Appleton-Century Company for permission to reprint letters of Poe, edited for the *Century Magazine* by G. E. Woodberry, in 1894 and again in 1903, in those instances in which I was unable to find the original manuscripts. Similar acknowledgments are due to the Thomas Y. Crowell Company, publishers of the Virginia Edition of Poe; to Houghton Mifflin Company, publishers of Woodberry's *Life of Poe* and of the *Letters of James Russell Lowell;* to J. B. Lippincott Company, publishers of the *Valentine Letters;* to Charles Scribner's Sons, publishers of the Stedman-Woodberry Edition of Poe's Works; to Harper and Brothers, publishers of *New Letters of James Russell Lowell;* to Jacob E. Spannuth, publisher of the *Doings of Gotham;*

and to the Editors of the *Yale Review*, for permission to quote from the material controlled by them.

My wife and children have criticized with patience the work as it progressed and have helped me as always. To my daughter Kathleen, who made the Index, with the assistance of our colleague, Mrs. John P. Jones, I am under special obligation.

A.H.Q.

University of Pennsylvania

EDGAR ALLAN POE

CHAPTER I

The Heritage

On April 15, 1796, at the end of the second act of Andrews' Gothic melodrama, *The Mysteries of the Castle,* a little girl of nine came out on the stage of the old Boston Theatre and sang the popular song of "The Market Lass." It was the first appearance of Elizabeth Arnold on any stage, and her mother, who had come from England in January to strengthen the Boston Company, undoubtedly sent her out as a tribute to the friendly audience who had honored her on her benefit night.[1]

From that moment the life of Elizabeth Arnold was the life of the American theatre. Fortunately, perhaps, the little girl could not look into the future. She could not foresee that day on January 19, 1809, when, again in Boston, struggling against anxiety and uncertainty, she had left the stage of the same theatre for a brief respite, to become the mother of Edgar Poe. To some women the joy of watching the genius of their sons develop and the recognition of their achievements have been given in full measure. But Elizabeth Poe, dying in Richmond in 1811 under distinctly miserable circumstances, could leave her two-year-old boy only her high heart, her unremitting industry, and that indefinable charm which made her a favorite from Boston to Charleston among the theatre-goers of that day.

Since we know so little of Edgar Poe's parents in their personal histories, the records of their careers in the theatre become of unusual significance. What was their professional standing, what characters did they portray, and above all, how did the circumstances of the actors' life affect the lives of their children? As we shall see later, a close search of the theatre records has revealed for the first time the date and circumstances of their marriage.

It was indeed a hard life that little Elizabeth Arnold entered in 1796. To a large section of the public, especially in New England, the theatre was an immoral institution, the resort of the vicious and the extravagant, and the actors were without the pale. Four years before, the legislature of Massachusetts had refused to repeal the laws pro-

[1] *Massachusetts Mercury,* April 15, 1796.

hibiting theatrical productions, and among those protesting against this repeal was that staunch old advocate of personal liberty, Samuel Adams. When the actor Morris and his wife made an attempt to evade the law by playing *The School for Scandal* as a "moral lecture," another noted liberal, John Hancock, then Governor, took pleasure in punishing the offenders.

The first record of Edgar Poe's maternal ancestry that is based on more than rumor [2] is an entry in the marriage records of St. George's Church, Hanover Square, London, which may refer to the wedding of his grandparents:

> Henry Arnold and Elizabeth Smith, both of this Parish were Married in this Church by Banns, this 18th Day of May, 1784 by me the R^d Pitt, Curate.
>
> in the   Thos. Topson
> Presence
> of   Calbeb [?] Greville [3]

Although the witnesses wrote their names, both husband and wife only made their marks, their names being written by the clerk who entered the record. This may indicate illiteracy on their part, and invalidate the entry as referring to two actors, who must have been able to read and write. The custom of making a cross instead of a signature on a religious document may, on the other hand, have accounted for the form of the entry. But such a custom was rare as late as 1784.

If Henry, or William Henry, Arnold was the father of Elizabeth Arnold, he does not appear in any records of which I feel sure. [4]

But of Mrs. Arnold there is definite information. [5] She first appears

[2] The speculations concerning the ancestry of Henry Arnold and Elizabeth Smith in Mary E. Phillips' *Poe the Man* are interesting, but I cannot see that they are conclusive. She and her informant, R. M. Hogg, however, are entitled to credit for the first discovery of the marriage record, at Hanover Square, although he failed to notice that the principals made their marks.

[3] Entry 245 of the year 1784. Copy made for me by Dr. A. F. Gegenheimer, Harrison Fellow in English, University of Pennsylvania.

[4] Under Dr. Gegenheimer's direction research was made of the London directories and all printed Church Registers in London, the index of the *Gentlemen's Magazine*, etc., and no actor of that name was found at the time in question. Registrations of births, deaths, and marriages did not begin until 1839 and were not compulsory until about 1864, so Somerset House was not helpful.

[5] The information concerning Mrs. Arnold's theatrical career is based on photographs of the playbills in the Gabrielle Enthoven Collection, Victoria and Albert Museum, London.

on the stage at Covent Garden Theatre, February 28, 1791, in a "vocal part" in the comic opera of *The Woodman*, which must have been popular for it was given thirty-one times during the season. Mrs. Arnold was announced to sing "A sailor's life's a life of woe" as part of *A Rural Masquerade* on September 19, 1791, and she sang several times in Juliet's funeral procession, as her daughter was to do some years later. She was "an Aerial Spirit" in the pantomime of *Blue Beard* in January, 1792, and was one of "the Principal Shepherdesses, Furies and Shades of Departed Heroines," a sufficiently versatile part, in *Orpheus and Eurydice*, on March 6, 1792.

On May 11, 1792, she is featured for the first time in large type on the program as Pallas in the burletta of *The Golden Pippin*. There is no record of her performance in 1793, but on October 3, 1794, she played Catalina, the rather frisky servant maid in *The Castle of Andalusia*, a part which her daughter was to play in Baltimore in 1799.

On January 14, 1795, she was cast for Theodosia, the young gentlewoman and second lead in Bickerstaffe's popular opera, *The Maid of the Mill*, and she repeated this part on June 13th, the last night on which her name appears. On May 29, 1795, she had taken the part of Laura, the grasping courtesan in Mrs. Cowley's *Bold Stroke for a Husband*. She was evidently progressing from minor rôles and soon she determined to try her fortune in America.

A friendly notice in the *Massachusetts Mercury* for January 5, 1796, tells the story of her arrival in America:

> On Sunday [January 3rd] arrived in this Port in the Ship *Outram*, Capt. Davis, from London, Mrs. Arnold and Daughter from the Theatre Royal, Covent Garden, and Miss Green. Both engaged by Mr. Powell, for the Boston Theatre, Each of the Ladies are tall and genteel—have an expressive Countenance— And Move with a Symetry [sic] unequalled. Mrs. Arnold is about in her four and twentieth year.... Miss Green apparently 20. They will be valuable acquisitions to our Theatre, and we anxiously hope they will be engaged.
>
> ———
>
> Other passengers by Captain Davis, Mr. Tubbs, ...

It is to be noted that the line separating the theatrical notices from the record of his arrival indicates that Mr. Tubbs, who was soon to marry Mrs. Arnold, was not yet an actor!

Mrs. Arnold made her American debut at the Boston Theatre on

February 12, 1796, as Rosetta in *Love in a Village*.[6] During that season she sustained twenty-one parts, varying from romantic noblewomen of melodrama like Alinda in *The Sicilian Romance,* Constantia in *The Mysteries of the Castle,* or Lady Alford in *The Children in the Wood* to lighter fare like Rosetta, or Caroline in *The Prize*.[7]

After the close of the Boston season on May 16, 1796, Mrs. Arnold gave concerts at Portsmouth, New Hampshire, and other New England towns, assisted by her daughter. About this time she married Mr. Tubbs,[8] or indeed she may have married him in England. No data are available.

On November 17, 1796, the Portland *Eastern Herald and Gazette of Maine* announced that "Mrs. Tubbs, late Mrs. Arnold of the Theatre Royal, Covent Garden, who arrived from England last January . . . proposes having a CONCERT OF VOCAL AND INSTRUMENTAL MUSICK on Monday Evening next, November 21st, at the Assembly Room . . . after which Mr. Tubbs intends setting up a THEATRE and performing some of the most admired PLAYS AND FARCES, having engaged a few able and eminent performers for that purpose. The day of arrival of the other comedians is uncertain."

The hall in which they played was a modest two-story building in which the arrangements of the stage must have been primitive, and to those acquainted with the history of the theatre, the last sentence of Mr. Tubbs' announcement tells a familiar story. Evidently the company of Mr. Tubbs was a family venture, and while the advertisements give no casts, we may glean from the infrequent criticisms that Elizabeth Arnold was an important asset to the company. In fact, I suspect that she and Mrs. Tubbs were the only women in the plays. We may be sure she sang at the concert on November 21st, and we know that on the opening night of the Portland Theatre, November 25, 1796, she played Biddy Bellair in Garrick's farce, *Miss in Her Teens.*

Elizabeth Arnold was, like her famous son, a precocious child. To

---

[6] "THEATRE. TO-MORROW EVENING Feb. 11th [evidently error for Feb. 12th] will be presented the COMIC OPERA, called LOVE IN A VILLAGE. (The part of Rosetta, by Mrs. Arnold, from the Theatre Royal Covent-Garden, being her first appearance in America.) To which will be added, an ENTERTAINMENT called, THE DEUCE IS IN HIM." [Boston] *Independent Chronicle and the Universal Advertiser,* February 11, 1796.

[7] For complete list of her rôles during the season, see G. O. Seilhamer, *History of the American Theatre,* III, 307-311.

[8] Seilhamer, III, 313.

Theatre Royal, Covent Garden,

This prefent SATURDAY, June 13, 1795,

Will be prefented the Comic Opera of

The Maid of the Mill.

Lord Ain.worth by Mr DAVIES,
Sir Harry Sycamore by Mr POWEL,
Ralph by Mr MUNDEN,
Mervin by Mr TOWNSEND,
Fairfield by Mr RICHARDSON,
Farmer Giles by Mr HAYMES,
Fanny by Mrs MARTYR,
Theodofia by Mrs ARNOLD,
Lady Sycamore by Mrs DAVENPORT,
Patty by Mrs MOUNTAIN.

To which will be added the Farce of

Two Strings to Your Bow.

Lazarillo by Mr MUNDEN,
Borachio by Mr DAVENPORT,
Octavio by Mr DAVIES,
Ferdinand by Mr MACREADY,
Don Pedro by Mr POWEL,
Don Sancho by Mr THOMPSON,
Drunken Porter by Mr FARLEY,
Waiters, Meff. CROSS and LEDGER,
Leonora by Mifs Stuart, Maid by Mifs Leferve,
Donna Clara by Mifs HOPKINS.
No Money to be Returned.

On Monday (by Particular Defire) the new Comedy of the Deferted Daughter, with the new Mufical Farce
of the Poor Sailor, or, Little Bob and Little Ben, and the Tythe Pig.
Tuefday the Woodman, and Harlequin & Faufus, for the Benefit of Meff. TOWNSEND and FOLLETT.
And on Wednefday the Theatre will CLOSE for this SEASON, with the Comedy of the Sufpicious Hufband.

PLAYBILL FEATURING POE'S GRANDMOTHER, ELIZABETH ARNOLD,
ON THE LAST NIGHT OF HER APPEARANCE AT
COVENT GARDEN THEATRE

From the Gabrielle Enthoven Collection, Victoria and Albert Museum,
London.

maintain this leading part of Biddy she had to flirt with three lovers, with a dexterity that seems extraordinary. Of her performance, "a correspondent who was present at the exhibition on Friday evening" [November 25th], after commenting favorably on the acting of Mrs. Tubbs, "in Le [o] nora and Tag," continues, "But Miss Arnold, in Miss Biddy, exceeded all praise. Although a Miss of only nine years old, her powers as an Actress would do credit to any of her sex of maturer age. It is hoped that Gentlemen of the town will attend once more. But the Ladies, perhaps ought not to attend till it is known whether their ears are again to be offended with expressions of obscenity and profanity." [9]

Of the performance on November 28th when Murphy's *The Citizen* and Yarrow's farce, *Trick upon Trick, or The Vintner in the Suds* were given, the same correspondent remarks: "Mrs. Tubbs and her daughter, Miss Arnold, received and certainly deserved the warmest marks of approbation." [10] Elizabeth must have played Solomon Smack, a young boy, in the farce, for she played it later in Newport. Since the criticisms make no mention of actresses besides Mrs. Tubbs and Miss Arnold, it is reasonable to assume that she played regularly. Indeed, with a knowledge of the later history of Elizabeth Arnold, it would not be hard to indicate her probable parts in the nineteen performances which took place in her first season as an actress. But judging only from those plays in which there is definite criticism of her acting, it was a distinct personal success. On December 20th, the opera of *Rosina* and the farce of *The Spoiled Child* were selected for her benefit. Rosina became later one of her favorite parts, and she may have played it here, but of Little Pickle in *The Spoiled Child* we are sure.[11] The correspondent grows eloquent upon this performance: "... Mrs. Tubbs always does well. Her vocal powers we believe are equal to any of her sex who have appeared in this country. But the powers of her daughter, Miss Arnold, astonish us. Add to these her youth, her beauty, her innocence, and a character is composed which has not, and perhaps will not again be found on any Theatre.—Lovely

[9] *Eastern Herald and Gazette of Maine*, Monday, November 28, 1796. See issue of November 24th, announcing opening on the 25th—usually given by biographers as the 21st. See especially James Moreland's "The Theatre in Portland in the Eighteenth Century," *New England Quarterly*, XI (June, 1938), 331-342.

[10] *Eastern Herald and Gazette of Maine*, December 1, 1796.

[11] See Epilogue, p. 7, and she is recorded in the part at Newport, April 12, 1797. Seilhamer, III, 374-375.

child! thy youth we know will not long continue; thy beauty soon must fade; but thy Innocence! may it continue with and support thee in every character while on the theatre of this world." [12]

The season, however, was not proving too profitable, for on January 12, 1797, Elizabeth took another benefit, apologizing in her announcement for doing so. Charles Dibdin's *The Deserter,* a musical drama, would have afforded her an opportunity to sing, either in the parts of Louisa or Jenny, and in Foote's *The Mayor of Garratt* she would have had to assume the more mature parts of a shrew or of an ill-treated wife. When the theatre closed, on January 17th, a farewell Epilogue, written "by a gentleman of Portland," was spoken by Elizabeth. In it we have definite proof of her versatility. After the usual compliments, she continues:

> Accept my warmest thanks for favours shown;
> I claim no merit—candour is your own.
> But tho to merit I can lay no claim,
> To please has been my never-ceasing aim;
> And to effect this end, to me you find
> What various characters have been assigned,
> A miss just in her teens, a rigid nurse,
> A boy to please old maids, O lud! that's worse;
> Sometimes I have appeared a ghost, 'tis true,
> But yet—I'm flesh and blood—as well as you;
> A sailor too—"O pity, pity" Jack—
> Sun in a cloud, and taken all aback;
> A lover I have been—but how perplexing!
> And to our sex the thing is always vexing!
> But, Ladies, pardon me, 'twas by direction,
> And nothing—nothing—nothing—but a fiction.

Here are clearly reflected Biddy Bellair in *Miss in Her Teens,* and Little Pickle in *The Spoiled Child,* for in the latter she played the part of a boy who is disguised both as a sailor and the lover of his own aunt! The "ghost" would seem to point to Mrs. Centlivre's *The Ghost; or the Dead Man Alive,* which was played for Mr. Tubbs' benefit on January 13th, but it is hard to imagine Elizabeth as Sir Jeffrey Constant. The "rigid nurse" is even harder to identify. But the impression she made upon Portland is unquestionable.

After a brief association with the Harper Company, first in Newport where she played Little Pickle again in April for her mother's

[12] *Eastern Herald and Gazette of Maine,* Thursday, December 22, 1796.

benefit, and was announced as "a young girl of ten years," [13] Elizabeth Arnold accompanied her parents South.

Elizabeth Arnold's first appearance in New York City was due to the war of the theatres that raged between the Old American Company, under the management of Dunlap and Hodgkinson, now entrenched in New York, and the company which the great low comedian Wignell had started in Philadelphia. John Sollee, the manager of the City Theatre in Charleston, formed an alliance, defensive and offensive, with Hodgkinson and Dunlap, and on his way to open a rival to Wignell's New Theatre in Philadelphia, he stopped for two nights at the old John Street Theatre in New York. With him were Mrs. Tubbs, and her little daughter, who played Maria, the sister of Little Pickle, on August 18, 1797. It was apparently her only appearance at this time.[14]

Sollee had planned to invade Philadelphia, but the yellow fever, which interfered so often with theatrical plans, prevented him. So Elizabeth and her mother began the season of 1797-1798 at Charleston. They must have been pleased with the difference in the atmosphere. Charleston had been friendly to the theatre since 1736, when its first season opened. Life was easier in the South than in New England and amusement was welcome. Elizabeth's first appearance was on November 18, 1797, when she sang her song of "The Market Lass." [15]

At first she played such parts as "The Child" in *The Adopted Child,* or as "a Dancing Nymph" in that remarkable musical and allegorical Masque, *Americana and Eleutheria,* which, when read today, excites our wonder at the energy of John Sollee. Elizabeth had a fair opportunity in the part of Julia in *The Sicilian Romance,* for while the part is a minor one, Julia is the one natural character in an absurdity. On December 6, 1797, she played her first Shakespearean character as the Duke of York in *Richard III.* This character as represented by Shakespeare is that of a rather pert boy who has a ready answer to all questions, and it probably suited Elizabeth Arnold. Trouble, however, was brewing in Sollee's Company, and after a "secession" in which Mr. Tubbs figured prominently, and a visit to Wilmington, North Caro-

---

[13] Seilhamer, III, 374-375.

[14] J. N. Ireland in his *Records of the New York Stage* gives Elizabeth Arnold as Agnes in *The Mountaineer* on August 20th. G. C. D. Odell, however, in his *Annals of the New York Stage* gives Mrs. Williamson in the part on August 21st. Where there is a conflict Odell is always to be preferred, especially in this case, since August 20, 1797, fell on Sunday!

[15] For complete list of parts played by her in this and succeeding seasons, with supporting references, see Appendix.

lina, they were reorganized under the management of Mr. Edgar, one of the Company, as the "Charleston Comedians." This group included Mr. and Mrs. Tubbs and Miss Arnold. Elizabeth now had an opportunity to revive parts like Biddy Bellair or Little Pickle, to act young gentlewomen like Nancy in Murphy's *Three Weeks After Marriage,* or Sophia in Holcroft's *The Road to Ruin;* rustic maids like Phoebe in *Rosina,* besides less important rôles. At the close of the season of the Charleston Comedians, she delivered the Farewell Address "written by an American Gentleman for and to be spoken by Miss Arnold." [16]

Into the bitter feelings caused by this Charleston "secession" it is not necessary to go.[17] But is it not within the range of possibility that Elizabeth Poe, looking years later for a name for her second son, should remember the first manager outside of her own family who gave her an opportunity to develop her powers as an actress? Sollee had no time for Edgar, but as he had helped to break up Sollee's Company, the former manager may have been a bit prejudiced. The newspapers give a different impression of Edgar.[18]

After a reading and concert on May 2, 1798, at which Mr. and Mrs. Tubbs and Miss Arnold performed, her mother disappears from the record. The yellow fever may have claimed her, but not in Charleston, for the city was unusually free from an epidemic during the summer and winter of 1798, and even sent aid to the sufferers in Philadelphia,[19] where it was raging. Since it was with the New Theatre Company in Philadelphia that Elizabeth Arnold next appears, her mother may have fallen a victim there. The young girl was apparently under the protection of Mr. Tubbs and of an actress, Miss L'Estrange, in real life Mrs. Snowden, and later Mrs. Usher, who had joined Wignell's Company in December, 1796, with her father and mother. The New Theatre was closed from May 5, 1798, to February 5, 1799, on account of the yellow fever. On March 18, 1799, Elizabeth Arnold is announced as Miss Biddy Bellair, and as "from the Charleston Theatre, being her first appearance on this stage." [20]

[16] *City Gazette and Daily Advertiser,* April 30, 1798.

[17] See Eola Willis, *The Charleston Stage in the XVIII Century,* pp. 384-412.

[18] *The City Gazette and Daily Advertiser* of November 23, 1797, states that George Barnwell "was given with all that ability which so highly distinguishes the performance of Edgar." The same journal praises his acting as young Norval on November 18th, and speaks generally of him with respect.

[19] *City Gazette and Daily Advertiser,* October 1, 1798.

[20] Claypoole's *Daily American Advertiser,* March 18, 1799.

During this season, Elizabeth Arnold acted in afterpieces, in which her qualities as a singer were in demand. In several of the parts, like Moggy McGilpin in *The Highland Reel*, Fanny in *The Shipwreck*, or Nina in *The Prisoner*, she disguised herself as a soldier or a sailor, and played a rôle which required agility at least. In her last appearance for the season on May 27, 1799, she acted Beda, a singing attendant, in Colman's *Blue Beard*, a play in which she was to take the leading rôle of Fatima, in Baltimore in 1802.

May 31, 1799, found her making her first appearance at the New Theatre in Baltimore, in her favorite character of Biddy Bellair. Mr. Tubbs was still looking after her, for on June 7th he played the "Master of the Hotel," a very minor part in Holcroft's farce, *He's Much to Blame*, for her benefit night.

In the Baltimore season of Wignell's Philadelphia Company, Miss Arnold played for the first time on October 4, 1799, the rural maid, Molly Maybush, in O'Keeffe's *The Farmer*. Her principal part was that of Prince John in *First Henry IV*, in which she represented a gallant young soldier, who, however, is not required to fight on the stage. We would like to have been present on October 9th, when she took part in a ballet as a portion of a celebration of the victory of the *Constellation* over *L'Insurgente*—dim echoes of the abortive war with France. The modern dance as representative of national ideas and impulses has a long ancestry. On October 30th she played Catalina in *The Castle of Andalusia*, a rôle her mother had sustained at Covent Garden in 1794. Other new parts were the "Little Midshipman" in *The Rival Soldiers; or, Sprigs of Laurel*, by O'Keeffe, and Annette, the page, in *Robin Hood*.

Tryout towns were not unknown even in those days, and Miss Arnold repeated a number of parts which she had just offered Baltimoreans, when she returned to the regular season in Philadelphia. This lasted until May 17, 1800. On December 26 and 30, 1799, she assisted in a monody on the death of Washington.

It was during this spring season in Philadelphia that she met her future husband, Charles Hopkins, who made his debut on March 14, 1800, as Tony Lumpkin.[21] He seems to have been a successful comedian and even to have attempted Hamlet at his benefit in Philadelphia. During the theatrical season of the Philadelphia Company in Baltimore from May 27 to June 10, 1800, Elizabeth Arnold was industrious, as usual. On June 3rd she not only played Nancy in *The Naval Pillar*, but also appeared as "one of the Females" in *The Moun-*

[21] *True American Commercial Advertiser*, March 14 and 28, 1800.

taineers, and danced in the ballet! On June 5th she shared a benefit with Messrs. Blissett and Hopkins, in which she repeated her part of Nancy in *The Naval Pillar.*

Elizabeth Arnold next took part in an auspicious event, the opening of the first theatre in Washington. Thomas Wignell, the manager of the Philadelphia Company, brought to it the full strength of his corps, and the United States Theatre, as it was called, was dedicated on August 22, 1800, by a splendid production of *Venice Preserved.* In the afterpiece, Elizabeth Arnold was selected to lead in her popular part of Little Pickle in *The Spoiled Child.*[22] On September 5th she danced a "Minuet de la Cour" and a new Gavotte during the first act of *Romeo and Juliet.* The season closed on September 19th.

On October 8, 1800, the Chesnut Street Theatre Company opened its season in Philadelphia, among the newcomers being Mr. Usher. He seems to have joined Mrs. Snowden, whom he married, in looking after Elizabeth Arnold, and his name in all probability suggested the title of one of Poe's greatest short stories. Miss Arnold appeared regularly through the season, which lasted until April 11, 1801. Again her singing and dancing were in demand. On nineteen occasions she took parts of priestesses, villagers, and even an Indian woman in *Columbus,* without counting repetitions, and at least ten times was cast for a fairly important rôle, such as Irene, the sister of Fatima in *Blue Beard,* Cupid in *Cymon and Sylvia,* or Celia in *A Trip to Fontainbleau.* In each of these she was supporting actresses in major rôles, to which she afterwards attained. She played the lead, Priscilla Tomboy, in *The Romp,* which Mrs. Jordan had made noteworthy at Drury Lane. On January 2, 1801, she played Prince Edward in *Richard III,* a promotion from her earlier part of the Duke of York. In March she was the charming child Rosina in *The Corsicans,* playing a girl of thirteen. In May and June, 1801, she visited Baltimore with the company, where she was employed constantly, being promoted from Dolly to Laura in *Lock and Key.*

It was in the summer season of 1801, in Philadelphia, however, that she assumed her first important Shakespearean part. The old Southwark Theatre, built in 1766 and superseded by the Chesnut Street Theatre, was reopened, and here on September 23rd she appeared as Ophelia,[23] a fact hitherto unnoted by her biographers. It would have been interesting if we could have had a contemporary criticism of the manner in which this girl of fourteen sustained this difficult rôle. In

[22] *Georgetown Centinel of Liberty,* August 22, 1800.
[23] *American Daily Advertiser,* September 23, 1801.

this new season of 1801-1802 she did not add many new parts. Her performance of "a fair Quaker" in *The Wags of Windsor* did not seem to be an improvement, according to the sage critic in the *Portfolio*— as though the part of Grace Gaylove were likely to be! On April 7, 1802, she shared a benefit with Mr. Usher and Mrs. Snowden, in *Speed the Plough,* and the season closed.

Miss Arnold's growing importance in the Philadelphia Company was shown on the opening night of the Baltimore season, April 22, 1802. She was first advertised as "one of the Reapers" in *Rosina,* but later was announced as playing Phoebe, in place of Mrs. Oldmixon, one of the leading actresses of the time. She had been given the part by Edgar in Charleston in 1798, an illustration of his belief in her ability. She was promoted in *Blue Beard,* also, from Beda to Irene and Fatima. For her benefit, June 4th, she played Irene. She was still announced as "Miss Arnold" when she sang "Moggy, or the Highland Bell," on the last night of the season, June 12th. Her experience with the Philadelphia Company had given her opportunities to strengthen her stage equipment through contact with the foremost group of players in the United States, and to play in her first great part.

Sometime between June 12 and August 11, 1802, she was married to Charles Hopkins,[24] and joined Green's Virginia Company, with which Hopkins had acted in the spring of 1802. Green opened his season at Alexandria, Virginia, on August 2nd, and Hopkins played on August 6th. But the first mention of "Mrs. Hopkins" is her appearance in her old part of Fanny in *The Shipwreck*[25] on August 11th. She played farcical parts and was employed mainly for singing and dancing until the season closed on September 16th with "a grand concert."

On March 9, 1803, when the new season of Green's Virginia Company opened at the New Theatre on Fenchurch Street in Norfolk, Virginia, Hopkins played Tilman Totum, and Mrs. Hopkins took the leading part of Louisa, in the Prince Hoare adaptation of Kotzebue's *Sighs; or, Poverty and Honor.* She was announced as "Late Miss Arnold, of the Philadelphia Theatre, being her first appearance here."[26] She also sang Rosina in *Rosina.* The editorial comment was only mildly appreciative: "She appeared at the commencement of the play much abashed, and we were sorry to perceive that in some respects

[24] Marriage records of Baltimore show no listing of a marriage between March 1st and August 15th.

[25] *Columbian Advertiser* of Alexandria, August 11, 1802. The files are not complete, nor are the casts always given.

[26] *Norfolk Herald,* March 8, 1803.

she was badly supported...however, towards the conclusion she seemed at home and gave general satisfaction." [27]

It was evidently a rough life, for "one of the audience" wrote protesting against the disorders incident upon an obnoxious critic being kicked downstairs by one of the actors and the doorkeeper. He remarks, "With the solitary exceptions of Mrs. Hopkins in Moggy McGilpin [in *The Highland Reel*] and Mr. Sully in Shelty, who kept alive the drooping spirits of the audience, the rest were 'weary, stale, flat and unprofitable' in the extreme." [28]

The girl of sixteen was, as usual, doing her best in discouraging circumstances. Notwithstanding these drawbacks, during the season, which lasted until July 13, 1803, she appeared in twenty-one different parts, not including repetitions, and on five other occasions she was clearly playing, although her part is not given. Her talent for singing was in demand, the part of Mary Tactic in *The Rival Soldiers*, which she was to play as late as 1808, being repeated. Recognition came to her in the assignments of romantic parts like Elmira in *The Sultan*, which Mrs. Inchbald had played at Drury Lane in 1787; gentlewomen, like Rose Sydney in Morton's *Secrets Worth Knowing*, and, most important, Constance Neville in *She Stoops to Conquer*.

In the meantime David Poe, Jr., the father of Edgar, had also begun his career in the theatre. Unlike Elizabeth Arnold, however, there was no theatre in his blood. Dismissing as without foundation the mythical tales which connect Edgar Poe with noble families of Europe, it seems certain that his great-great-grandfather was David Poe, a tenant-farmer in Dring, in the parish of Kildallon and County Cavan, Ireland, who died in 1742. David's son, John Poe, emigrated to Pennsylvania in 1749 or 1750,[29] having married Jane McBride, daughter, it is

[27] *Herald,* March 12, 1803.

[28] *Herald,* April 14, 1803. See also editorial comment dwelling on the same disorders, which seemed to be caused quite as much by some of the actors as by the audience.

[29] Sir Edmund T. Bewley, *The Family of Poe or Poë* (Dublin, 1906). Bewley searched the baptismal records of the Presbyterian Church at Croghan, near Dring, and found no baptismal records after February, 1748/9, of any member of the Poe family. Bewley's dates may be accepted so far as the Irish ancestors of David Poe, Sr., are concerned. I do not follow, however, his attempt to provide them with an ancestry dating from 1665 on the basis of the similarity of "Poe" to "Powell." Curiously enough, Dr. Leonard Poe—d. 1630—a distinguished English physician, whose first name might seem to be the origin of William Henry Leonard Poe's third name, seems to have no connection with the Poes of Dring.

possible, though not certain, of a clergyman, Reverend Robert Mc-
Bride, and sister of an admiral of the Blue, John McBride. After living
for a time in Lancaster County, Pennsylvania, John Poe moved to
Baltimore, where he died in 1756.

John's eldest son, David, had been born in Ireland in 1742 or 1743.
He carried on his business of making spinning wheels and clock reels,
on Market Street in Baltimore from 1775.[30] He was one of the "Whig
Club" who, in 1777, attacked William Goddard, the editor of the
Maryland Journal, and drove him out of town. The article, signed
"Tom Tell Truth," which excited the ire of the "Whig Club," was in-
tended by Goddard to be ironical, and read today, it seems that the
Club had little sense of humor. Goddard appealed to the House of
Delegates for protection and the Club was rebuked. According to his
pamphlet, *The Prowess of the Whig Club* (1777) he was a martyr to
the cause of the freedom of the Press. In a "postscript" to this pamph-
let he gives a list of thirty persons who belong to the Club, "David
Poe, Spinning Wheel Maker" being the last named.[31] Goddard was not

---

[30] An advertisement in the *Maryland Journal and Baltimore Advertiser*
for June 3, 1776, announces:
"The Subscriber takes this method of acquainting the public, that he has
removed from where he formerly lived, near the upper end of Market St.
to a house next door to where Doctor John Boyd lately lived, a few doors
below Calvert street, in Market st. aforesaid, where he continues as usual
to make and repair all sorts of Spinning Wheels, Clock Reels, Weavers'
Spools, &c. He would also express his Gratitude to those Gentlemen and
Ladies who have hitherto favoured him with their custom, presuming he
has, and still means to give general Satisfaction, being well provided with
every material necessary for carrying on said business.—Gentlemen at a
distance, giving a few days Notice, by Letter or otherwise, may be supplied with a Quantity, on reasonable Terms, by the Public's very humble
Servant

"David Poe"

[31] Goddard prefaces this list by the following paragraph, which includes
the manuscript notes made by him in the printed copy now in the possession of the American Antiquarian Society.
"[Who these Gent⁸ are is not *yet* known, but] The under-mentioned
Personages, it is said, have been the most *renowned* for their *Prowess* and
Legionary Manoeuvres in [and out of] WHIG-CLUB; but having, alas!
become wretchedly *brainsick,* (not by too much *Learning*) *Humanity* be-
speaks *suitable Apartments* for them in an AMERICAN BEDLAM, *proposed* to be instituted for the Reception of *mad Whigs, mad Heroes,* and
mad Politicians!"
The manuscript now in the John Carter Brown Library, of the second
and unpublished part of the *Prowess of the Whig Club,* contains a small

a Tory, but judging from the "Queries, Political and Military,"[32] reflecting on Washington's honesty and conduct of the war, which he published in 1779, he was playing a dangerous game. It is, moreover, interesting that David Poe, Sr., was the first of three generations to answer the criticisms of objectionable editors by force!

David Poe was a member of Captain John McClellan's Company of Baltimore troops in 1778 and 1779, and was commissioned Assistant Deputy-Quartermaster General for the City of Baltimore[33] with the rank of Major on September 17, 1779. He was a patriot who took responsibility cheerfully. His published correspondence with Governor Lee, of Maryland, shows that he purchased supplies with his own money in 1780, when his license was delayed. In another letter, to General Smallwood, March 20, 1782, he says:

"I received your favor, of the 17th instant, by Colo. Gunby; at present I am almost out of forage, but rather 'han the public property should suffer, I shall struggle hard, as it has ever been my inclination, to endeavour by all means in my power to preserve it, and will, therefore, once more try my credit, in order to procure forage to preserve the horses from perishing."[34]

An unpublished letter[35] of September 14, 1782, proves that he was entrusted with the responsibility of transporti g a large portion of the French Allies from Baltimore by sea and across the Susquehanna River. So well known were Major Poe's services that he became brevetted in the eyes of the public and was known for many years as "General" Poe.[36] His wife, Elizabeth Cairnes, born in 1756 in Lancaster County, Pennsylvania, also of Irish descent, shared in his energy and patriotism. When LaFayette passed through Baltimore in 1781 with the ragged Colonial troops, Mrs. David Poe was one of the women who furnished clothing for them. It was due to these services that LaFayette, during the ball given in his honor when he visited Baltimore in 1824, turned to one of the committee and said, "I have not seen among these [the surviving officers of the Revolution who were present] my friendly and patriotic commissary, Mr. David Poe,

broadside, in which Goddard specifically mentions David Poe as one of those who had assaulted him.

[32] J. T. Scharf, *The Chronicles of Baltimore*, (Baltimore, 1874), pp. 159, 172-175.

[33] *Maryland Journal*, September 28, 1779, p. 3, col. 2.

[34] *Papers Relating Chiefly to the Maryland Line During the Revolution*, ed. by Thomas Balch (Philadelphia, 1857), p. 171.

[35] In the E. J. Wendell Collection, Harvard College Library.

[36] Scharf, p. 186.

David Poe, m. Sarah—
of Dring, Cavan Co., Ireland. d. 1742.

John Poe, m. Jane McBride		Alexander, m. Margaret	Anne,
Came to Penna., 1749-50. d. circa 1756, Baltimore.	b. 1706[?] m. Sept. 1741. d. July 17, 1802.		

David Poe, m.	Elizabeth Cairnes	George, m.	Catharine Dawso
b. Ireland, 1743[?] d. Oct. 17, 1816, Baltimore.	b. 1756, Lancaster Co., Pa. d. July 7, 1835, Baltimore	b. July 31, 1744. m. cir. 1775. d. Aug. 27, 1823, Frederick Co., Maryland.	b. Cecil Co., I May 13, 1742 d. Aug. 14, 18 Havre-de-Grac

John Hancock	William	George Washington	David, jr. m.	Elizabeth Arnold Ho
b. Aug. 25, 1776.	b. March 2, 1780.	b. Aug. 21, 1782.	b. July 18, 1784. m. March 14- April 9, 1806. d.[?]	b. England, 1787 d. Dec. 8, 1811.

William Henry [Leonard?]	Edgar Allan, m. Virginia Eliza Clemm		Rosalie
b. Jan. 30, 1807, Boston. d. Aug. 1, 1831.	b. Jan. 19, 1809, Boston. m. May 16, 1836. d. Oct. 7, 1849, Baltimore.		b. Dec. 20, 18 d. July 21, 187

bald Scott   Mary [?]

Children *   William   m.   Frances Winslow

b. 1755, Lancaster, Pa.   d. July 22, 1802
Moved to Georgia,
1789-90.
d. Sept. 13, 1804.

el	Maria m.	William Clemm, Jr.	Elisabeth m.	Henry Herring
c. 21, 1787.	b. March 17, 1790.	b. May 1, 1779.	b. Sept. 26, 1792.	
	m. July 12, 1817.	d. Feb. 8, 1826.	m. Nov. 17, 1814.	
	d. Feb. 16, 1871.		d. Dec. 8, 1822.	

	Henry Clemm	Virginia Maria	Virginia Eliza	
	b. Sept. 10, 1818.	b. Aug. 22, 1820.	b. Aug. 15, 1822.	
		buried Nov. 5, 1822.	baptized Nov. 5, 1822.	
			d. Jan. 30, 1847.	

Mrs. Clemm mentions also Robert, Samuel, Jane, Hester, John, Mary, and James—letter to William Poe, Jr., tober 7, 1835.

who resided in Baltimore when I was here, and out of his own very limited means supplied me with five hundred dollars to aid in clothing my troops, and whose wife, with her own hands, cut five hundred pairs of pantaloons, and superintended the making of them for the use of my men."

When LaFayette was told that David Poe had died in 1816, but that his widow was still alive, he expressed an anxious wish for a meeting, at which he paid an eloquent tribute to the memory of his friend.[37] In the Baltimore Directories of 1810 and 1812 David Poe, Sr., is entered as "a gentleman," at his residences, 19 Camden Street and Park Lane. "General" Poe seems also to have taken part in the defence of Baltimore in 1814 against the British attack. He died October 17, 1816.[38] His widow survived him until 1835.

Whether the Irish strain in Edgar Poe was responsible for any imaginative quality would be difficult to establish. The Celtic flame in literature does, however, kindle into a mysticism which concerns itself with those dim regions in which the relations of man and the supernatural are depicted. Symbolism, too, is the air which the Celt has always breathed, and in symbolism Poe revelled. One Irish trait—of a more tangible quality—may more certainly be attributed to his Poe ancestry. As any descendant of that race knows, there is a tendency to refuse to conform to what appears to be one's best interests at the moment in favor of another course which will provide more spiritual, or emotional, satisfaction at a later time. This quality is spoken of as perverseness. Edgar Poe described one phase of this quality in his story "The Imp of the Perverse," but that tale deals with the soul driven to do the very thing he knows is to his disadvantage. As we shall see, the younger David Poe seems to have been animated by that unfortunate tendency at times, when he threatened with physical violence the theatrical critics upon whose favor his very livelihood depended. How often the career of his gifted son has to be explained by this apparent perversity will appear in the records of his life. Certainly his father's choice of a profession seems to have been dictated by it. To enter the actors' career without training at a time when almost no native Americans had preceded him, when reputation from success on the English stage was a necessity, whose lack forced even such a skilled actor as John Howard Payne to leave his native country,

[37] Scharf, p. 415.
[38] "Died yesterday, in his 74th year, David Poe, a native of Ireland, and for the last 40 years a resident of Baltimore." *Federal Gazette*, October 18, 1816.

certainly calls for an explanation which no biographer has been able to offer. He had probably been a member of an amateur group in Baltimore about which little is known, and there seems no reason except sheer love of the theatre and perhaps distaste for the law, which he was studying, to urge him to seek the stage. The old stories about his joining the profession on account of Elizabeth Arnold are disproved by the records of the stage.

Perhaps another brilliant American of Irish descent, Philip Barry, has best described this quality in his novel, *War in Heaven:* "You can usually tell them by their eyes, which like his, have a way of looking past the instant day, the immediate objects in it, the present quick concerns of it, and past the night of the day as well. As a rule they are not happy people."

David Poe, Jr., was born in Baltimore, July 18, 1784, and baptized on September 21st.[39] He was therefore only nineteen when he made his debut on the stage of the Charleston Theatre, on December 1, 1803, as an officer in the pantomime, taken from Kotzebue's *La Peyrouse.* On December 5th he played Laertes, a young Danish nobleman attending upon Christina in Brooke's *Gustavus Vasa,* announced as "his second appearance on any stage."[40] On December 7th he was advanced to the part of Harry Thunder in *Wild Oats,* the second lead, a part in which he probably felt at home, for Harry runs away from his father to join a group of strolling players. On December 9th David Poe played his first Shakespearean rôle, Donalbain in *Macbeth.* The company left for Savannah on December 23rd, and from its return on January 31, 1804, to the end of the season in April, Poe was given a variety of parts. Criticism was divided as usual. "A Friend of the Drama," (Dr. John B. Irving) calls attention to an apparent defect in pronunciation which was to cause the less friendly critics of New York in 1809 to literally hound Poe off the stage: "He is also extremely diffident; indeed so much so, that the slightest lapse in his speech throws him from the little confidence he has acquired, back into his first night's trepidation. We hope he will excuse our suggesting to him,

---

[39] Records of First Presbyterian Church, Baltimore.

[40] *City Gazette and Daily Advertiser,* of Charleston, December 1 and 5, 1803. Miss Eola Willis in *The Bookman,* LXIV (November, 1926), 289, quotes a lengthy criticism from the *Courier* concerning the advent of "a young gentleman" in the part of Belmour in *Jane Shore,* and assumes that it was David Poe. Since the only performance of *Jane Shore* during that season was on November 19, 1803, it must have been some other young gentleman.

that speaking slower will not only help him to get rid of those fears more quickly, by making him less subject to lapses, but will improve his delivery, and give meaning and effect to his words. He ought to practise before some judicious friends, and beg of them candidly to set him right, when he is wrong." [41]

David Poe was evidently by stature and appearance qualified to play a young lover, especially a patrician. "Thespis," probably Stephen Cullen Carpenter, tells us that he performed the character of Stephano in Holcroft's *A Tale of Mystery* handsomely. "He looked it well." [42] Again, "Young Poe in the character of Tressel [in *King Richard III*] did more to justify our hopes of him than he has done in any character since his return from Savannah." [43] When he played Don Pedro, in *Much Ado About Nothing*, "Thespis" remarks, "Young Poe being less than usual under the dominion of that timid modesty which so depresses his powers, acted Don Pedro so respectably as to animate the hopes we have entertained of his future progress." [44] One significant fact emerges from the criticisms. Poe was best in his Shakespearean parts and he was given better ones as the season progressed. On April 12th he played Hortensio in *Catharine and Petruchio*, and while the part of Bianca's husband is less prominent in this abridgment of *The Taming of the Shrew*, it is still an important rôle.

During this first season, David Poe sustained twenty-four rôles varying from important parts like Hortensio or Harry Thunder to minor characters like Don Antonio Gaspard in *Liberty in Louisiana*.

Mr. and Mrs. Hopkins were with Green's Virginia Company in Richmond early in 1804. While the casts are not always given, Hopkins was playing Sir Simon Rochdale in *John Bull* on January 18th, and while his wife is not mentioned until March 21st, when her benefit occurs, the fact that she was given one proves she was acting regularly. For her benefit *The Point of Honor* and *The Agreeable Surprise* were given, but there is no indication of her rôles. If it was Charles Kemble's *Point of Honor*, based on Mercier's *Le Déserteur*, she must have played Bertha, the young lead; and Laura, in *The Agreeable Surprise*, became later one of her favorite parts. Green evidently kept his Company on at Richmond until May, but Mr. and Mrs. Hopkins are not mentioned in the infrequent casts. The great fire in Norfolk may have kept them from playing the usual spring season there. The

[41] *Charleston Courier*, December 10, 1803.
[42] *Courier*, February 4, 1804.
[43] *Courier*, February 13, 1804.
[44] *Courier*, February 29, 1804.

Virginia Gazette of June 30, 1804, announced that the "Temporary Theatre" in Richmond was opened "for the season" and "Mr. Poe from the Charleston Theatre, will (likewise) make his first appearance on our boards this evening." He played Henry, and Mrs. Hopkins, Susan Ashfield, in *Speed the Plough,* possibly for the first time.

There was evidently some trouble in the Company, for on July 18th the proprietress and manager of the theatre relinquished their interest and a new management headed by Hopkins was given control.[45] All three were constantly employed, either repeating former rôles or attempting new ones. Poe was given Henry Morland in Colman's *The Heir at Law,* Charles Kemble's well-known part, and Mrs. Hopkins, Caroline Dormer, while Hopkins played Dr. Pangloss. Poe delivered "an original Epilogue." At the benefit of Mr. and Mrs. Hopkins on August 11th, Poe played Lindorf and Mrs. Hopkins, Stella, the two leads in Boaden's *Maid of Bristol,* while Hopkins was cast for Cranium. Several of Poe's new parts were minor ones like Jacob in *The Road to Ruin,* or Nat Putty in *The Flitch of Bacon.* At his benefit on August 15th, however, when *George Barnwell* was offered, he probably played the title rôle, as he certainly did on December 26th, and he played the important part of the Duke of Buckingham in *Jane Shore* on August 25th. In Colman's *John Bull* on December 19, 1804, Poe played Frank Rochdale, the charming young hero-villain, and Mrs. Hopkins, Mary Thornberry, the heroine who has loved him too well.

In January, 1805, Mrs. Hopkins was given the part of Emily Worthington in Colman's *The Poor Gentleman,* which she was to repeat in Boston on April 15, 1807. Poe played Sir Charles Cropland.

Unfortunately, the *Norfolk Herald* gives few casts in the season of 1805, when the Virginia Company played in that city. David Poe played the minor part of Joey, speaking a rural dialect, in Allingham's *Hearts of Oak* on April 6th, Hopkins having the lead as Argent. On April 15th Poe took part in a "Strathspey" with Mrs. Hopkins. Many of the other plays put on were in their repertoires, but in the absence of definite information, we may not chronicle their parts.

On June 7, 1805, David Poe made his first appearance on the stage of Baltimore, his home town, in the leading part of young Norval in Home's *Douglas.* On August 28, 1805, Mrs. Hopkins and three friends gave a vocal and instrumental concert at the Haymarket Gardens at Richmond, but Hopkins is not mentioned.[46]

[45] *Virginia Gazette,* July 18, 1804.
[46] *Virginia Gazette,* August 28, 1805.

In 1805 the Washington Theatre was located at 11th and C Streets, N. W., and here on September 9th Mr. and Mrs. Hopkins began together his last season on the stage. He played Lord Priory in *Wives as They Were and Maids as They Are*. In the afterpiece of Colman's *Ways and Means, or A Trip to Dover*, Elizabeth was Kitty Dunder, a rather charming if flighty young gentlewoman, one of the leading parts. She was to play it again in Charleston in 1811, the year of her death. On September 26th David Poe played Joseph Surface and Hopkins Sir Peter Teazle in *The School for Scandal*.[47] Green, the manager of the Virginia Players, was having trouble in this season, and bolstered up his productions with recitations, of which David Poe gave one on October 2nd. At Hopkins' benefit on October 7th on which occasion the play, ironically enough, was *The Wife of Two Husbands*, the *Intelligencer* gives us three songs and recitations by him, but no indication of the parts he or Elizabeth took. Hopkins died on October 26th,[48] and his widow was given a benefit on November 6th. She probably played Orilla, the lead, in *Adelmorn the Outlaw*, since she had taken the part in Norfolk, but we cannot be sure. Newspaper criticism is friendly but general. We learn, too, that owing to the unfortunate deaths of Mr. Hodgkinson, Mr. Hopkins, and Mrs. Douglass, the Company was much weakened. The theatre closed on December 21, 1805.

During the Richmond season, from January to May, 1806, both Poe and Mrs. Hopkins added some interesting rôles to their repertoires. Mrs. Hopkins played the trying part of Sophia Woodbine and Poe the equally difficult rôle of Villars, suspected but innocent of evil, in *The Blind Bargain*. Poe was to appear later as Jack Analyze and as Tourly in the same play. On January 25th Mrs. Hopkins played Anna the confidante, and for her benefit on March 29th, the leading part of Lady Randolph in Home's *Douglas*, "for the first time and that night only." On February 26th Poe and Mrs. Hopkins took the leading parts of Harry Harebrain and Harriet Manly in Dibdin's comedy, *The Will for the Deed*, announced as "performed for the first time in America." [49] Since Harry runs away from his father to join a troupe of actors, the part was probably once more appealing to Poe.

On March 14, 1806, a fact which has escaped the research of biographers, a marriage bond was executed between David Poe, Jr., and Mrs. Eliza Hopkins. It was filed in the County Court House of

[47] *National Intelligencer and Washington Advertiser*, September 25, 1805.
[48] *Virginia Gazette* of Richmond, November 6, 1805.
[49] *Virginia Gazette*, February 22, 1806.

Know all men by these presents that we
David Poe jr and
are held and firmly bound unto William H.
Cabell Governor of the Commonwealth of
Virginia in the sum of one hundred and fifty
Dollars for the payment whereof well and
truly to be made to said Governor and his
successors for the use of said Commonwealth
We bind ourselves our heirs exors and admrs
jointly and severally firmly by these presents
sealed with our seals and dated this 14th
March 1806

The Condition of the above obligation
is such that whereas a marriage is
intended to be had and consummated between
the above bound David Poe jr and Mrs Eliza
Hopkins widow of Charles D Hopkins
decd of the City of Richmond If
therefore here be no lawful cause
to obstruct the said marriage then this
obligation to be void else to remain
in full force and virtue

Executed in presence of   David Poe jr

Geo Chisman   Jac Whitlaw

MARRIAGE BOND OF DAVID POE JR. AND ELIZABETH ARNOLD
HOPKINS

Reproduced for the first time from the original in the Henrico County
Court House, Richmond, Virginia.

Henrico County, Virginia, in which Richmond is located. The bond is still there, in one of the dusty packages in which the legal records of the County are preserved. By a curious chance, the bond was filed with those of 1800 instead of 1806, probably due to the endorsement of the original clerk who wrote 180ô on the outside of the document. It contains the only fully authenticated complete signature of David Poe, Jr.

On April 5, 1806, "Mrs. Hopkins" is announced for April 7th, Easter Monday, as Irene in *Blue Beard,* while on April 9th, the advertisement, in speaking of the benefit of Mrs. Green, on April 10th, gives the two leading parts of Malford and Mrs. Malford in *The Soldier's Daughter* to "Mr. and Mrs. Poe." [50] The marriage therefore took place certainly between March 14 and April 9, 1806, and probably between April 5th and April 9th, in Richmond. Since Easter fell on April 6th, it is not improbable that the young actors took a brief honeymoon on that day.

Criticism, definite or implied, in certain biographies of her son, concerning the interval that elapsed between the death of Charles Hopkins and the marriage of his widow to David Poe, proves to be unwarranted.[51] The conditions of theatrical life at that time made the lot of a widowed girl of eighteen difficult if not impossible, and there need be no speculation concerning her acceptance of David Poe's protection.

The New Theatre in Philadelphia was opened for eight nights beginning June 18, 1806, and Mr. and Mrs. Poe were engaged. Poe made his first appearance in Philadelphia on June 20th as Young Norval, and played other important parts such as Jack Analyze in *The Blind Bargain* or Captain Loveit in *Miss in Her Teens.* Mrs. Poe gave Philadelphians an opportunity to compare her performance of Priscilla Tomboy in *The Romp* with that of 1801, and played her old favorites like Biddy Bellair and a new part, Miss Kitty Sprightly, in *All the World's a Stage.* On July 16, 1806, the Poes were at the Summer Theatre at Vauxhall Garden in New York City. Mrs. Poe repeated her

[50] *Virginia Gazette* of Richmond, April 5 and 9, 1806.

[51] Woodberry (*Life of Edgar Allan Poe,* 1909, I, 9) states, "Within a month [of Hopkins' death on October 26, 1805], Mr. Poe, with some pecuniary aid from a friend, married Mrs. Hopkins, and early in February they were already playing in Richmond." Mr. Hervey Allen (*Israfel, the Life of Poe,* 1926, I, 10), after paraphrasing this sentence, adds, "Whether the young widow's haste was due to the natural ardor of her temperament or the failure of the deceased to engage her affections, must remain in those realms of speculation sacred to the theologians." Mr. Allen states also in his Appendix (II, 853) that the marriage took place "in January, 1806."

favorite parts like Priscilla Tomboy and Rosina. Poe played Captain Belleville, the handsome villain in *Rosina* on the 18th, and Frank, the young farmer, in *Fortune's Frolic.*

It was probably with high anticipations that the young actor and actress looked forward to October 13, 1806, when they took part in the opening night of the season at the Federal Street Theatre in Boston. The rapid flittings of the Virginia Company, the rough crowds, the insufficient support, were, they hoped, to be over. They were to be integral members of a well-organized company, not as good, to be sure, as Wignell's Company in Philadelphia, but perhaps on the other hand there would be more opportunity for leading rôles. To Mrs. Poe, at least, it must have seemed like coming home, to the stage on which she had sung her first song in 1796. For the next three years they were to remain in Boston and here two of their children were to be born. Their apprenticeship was over, and if they were to succeed upon the stage, they must win a secure place with the public and the critics. That they were reëngaged for three successive seasons may be looked upon as testimony to their merits.

The Poes began their Boston career with Thomas Morton's *Speed the Plough,* a melodramatic comedy in which David played Henry, the noble youth whose parentage is doubtful, and who saves the heroine, Miss Blandford, from the fire, and unmasks the villain. Elizabeth played Miss Blandford. The *Polyanthos,* a monthly journal edited by J. T. Buckingham, and devoted largely to the theatre, received the newcomers calmly:

> Morton's favourite comedy of *Speed the Plough* was selected for the first night's performance. The parts of Henry and Miss Blandford were filled by Mr. and Mrs. Poe from the Virginia theatres, their first appearance in Boston. Estimating the talents of this couple by comparison, we might say the same characters have been more ably sustained on our boards. A first performance however does not always afford a criterion by which merit may be estimated. Mr. Poe possesses a full manly voice, of considerable extent; his utterance clear and distinct. The managers will undoubtedly find him a useful, and the town a pleasing, performer in the Henrys, Charles Stanleys, &c.—Of the talents of Mrs. Poe we are disposed to judge favourably.[52]

During the season they were given important parts, sometimes in the same play. He was Frederick to her Amelia in *Lovers' Vows;* he was cast for Charles Stanley, the handsome young lover, while she was

[52] Vol. III, p. 205.

Jessy Outland, the charming country girl, in *A Cure for the Heartache*.
He played George Barnwell in that tragedy on October 22nd, and notwithstanding the unfavorable criticism, was chosen to repeat it in
March, 1807. He sustained the difficult part of Sir George Touchwood
in *The Belle's Stratagem* and even the critic of *The Emerald*, a weekly
journal, had a grudging word of praise:

"No objection is made to the appearance of Mr. Poe in Sir George
Touchwood. The character is certainly not a bustling one; we think
it susceptible of more life than he infused into it. We were however
sometimes gratified with displays of correct spirit; we hardly expected
it, and the audience appreciated and rewarded it as a novelty." [53]

On November 14, 1806, Poe played the character part of Maurice,
the blind father of the Countess Belflor in *The Wife of Two Husbands*.
Even the critic of the *Polyanthos* said, "Of Mr. Poe's Maurice justice
compels us to speak the language of approbation." [54]

On November 19th they played Frank Rochdale and Mary Thornberry, the two leads in *John Bull*, and in December Count Basset and
Miss Jenny in Vanbrugh's *The Provoked Husband*, which drew an
encomium for her, at least. Poe was the hero, Altamont, in Rowe's
The Fair Penitent in January. They had the two leads, Frederick and
Mariana, in Fielding's *The Miser*, two good high comedy parts. Mrs.
Poe was constantly used for singing parts and on January 12, 1807,
she sang Clorinda, the lead in McNally's opera of *Robin Hood*. On
the same evening David played Harry Torrid in *The Secret* and a
newspaper critic remarked: "The claims of Mr. Poe were never more
strongly urged than on this evening. He certainly possesses talent,
which merits cultivation. He wants however a deliberation and a
temperance of speech without which his articulation must ever be too
rapid to be discriminate." [55] On January 16, 1807, Poe played Beauchamp, the young, attractive soldier, and Elizabeth was Sophy
Pendragon, the low comedy part, in Mrs. Cowley's *Which Is the Man?*
These were the parts which had been entrusted to Hodgkinson and
Mrs. Hodgkinson, two of the most talented actors of our early stage.

From January 16 until February 25, 1807, Mrs. Poe is not mentioned in the announcements. William Henry Poe was born on January 30, 1807.[56] David Poe, however, was constantly on the stage,
sustaining parts like Laertes in *Hamlet*, Malcolm in *Macbeth*, Tressel

[53] Vol. I, p. 329.
[54] Vol. III, p. 278.
[55] *The Centinel*, January 14, 1807.
[56] T. H. Ellis Ms., Valentine Collection.

in *Richard III,* the Duke of Medina in *Rule a Wife and Have a Wife.* One of the difficulties of an actor in those days was the sudden change of bill. On February 16th *The School for Scandal* was substituted for the play announced and Poe was assigned to Charles Surface. A distinctly unfriendly critic remarked: "We are ready to make allowances for Mr. Poe's deficiency in Sir Charles Surface, in manners, spirit and orthoepy. The suddenness with which the character must have been assumed is a mantle, which like charity, covers a multitude of sins." [57]

On February 25th the Poes were together once more in *The Poor Soldier.* Elizabeth was announced to support Fennell in *King Lear* on March 2nd, but as the great tragedian was ill, *George Barnwell* with Poe in the lead was substituted, a sufficient indication of the opinion of the management concerning him. Elizabeth, however, did play Cordelia to Fennell's Lear on the 11th. A criticism in *The Centinel* reveals the writer's feeling that she was not up to the part, but it shows also the recognition of her personal character: "Of Mrs. Poe in Cordelia we would speak with the strictest delicacy and tenderness. Her amiable timidity evidently betrayed her own apprehension, that she had wandered from the sphere of her *appropriate* talent; while her lovely gentleness pleaded strongly for protection against the rigid justice of criticism. She was so obviously *exiled* from her own element by the mere humor of *authority* that we cannot in charity attempt any analysis of her performance. . . . —Mrs. Poe has one credit and that of no mean value:—she did not mutilate the *language* of Shakespeare." David was cast for the Duke of Albany in *Lear,* and for the Duke of Austria in *King John* when Elizabeth played Blanch. On March 25th she was selected to play the leading part of Cora, the priestess of the sun, while Poe was Orozimbo, the Indian ruler, in Morton's *Columbus; or, America Discovered.* On Mrs. Poe's benefit, she played Sophia with Poe as Young O'Donovan in O'Keeffe's *The Lie of a Day,* and she also sang the part of Sylvia in *Cymon and Sylvia.* On April 24th, David played Ferdinand, and Elizabeth was cast as Ariel, in *The Tempest.* On May 22nd, their joint benefit, Poe played Bertrand in Tobin's *The Curfew,* which he had already presented on May 6th, and Elizabeth acted the queer but amusing Queen Dollalolla in Fielding's *Tragedy of Tragedies.* The season closed on May 25th, 1807.

Mrs. Poe began the season of 1807-1808 on September 18th with two of her favorite parts, Rosina in *Rosina* and Clorinda in *Robin Hood.* Both David and Elizabeth repeated many of their earlier characters. Among her new parts were Donna Clara in Sheridan's *Duenna*

[57] *The Emerald,* II (February 21, 1807), 90.

and Rosalie Somers in Morton's *Town and Country.* She played Ophelia and Jessica during Fennell's engagement and Poe played Sir Richard Vernon in *Henry IV.* He was sometimes in the lead, but more often in supporting parts like Milford in *The Road to Ruin.* When Cooper, the leading Shakespearean actor, came to Boston in January and February, 1808, Elizabeth played Ophelia to Cooper's Hamlet. She also played Cordelia, and David, the Duke of Albany to his Lear; David was Volusius, the Volscian leader in *Coriolanus,* and Malcolm to Cooper's Macbeth. At their joint benefit on March 21, 1808, Elizabeth played Cora, the heroine, in Kotzebue's *Virgin of the Sun,* while David was cast in the important rôle of Ataliba, the King of Quito. On the same night she played Selina in Holcroft's *A Tale of Mystery.* They were the leads in Mrs. Inchbald's version of Kotzebue's *The Wise Man of the East,* Poe playing the rich young man, Claransforth, whose changes of character would have called for some good acting. On April 18, 1808, Mrs. Poe played Amelia, and Poe, Francis, the villain, in *The Robbers,* Schiller's famous melodrama. Having been killed as Amelia, Elizabeth came to life to play on the same night the intensely emotional part of Ella Rosenberg in Kenney's play of that name, in which she suffers almost every kind of persecution. Poe, having hanged himself in *The Robbers,* was revived to play the Elector of Brandenburg, who turns the tragedy into melodrama. Pursuers of psychoanalysis might have made much of the fact that just nine months later Edgar Poe was born, and that pride, love, and death, three of his favorite themes, are found within these two turgid plays. But whether or not their themes can have had any prenatal influence upon Edgar Poe, the anxiety under which his parents were struggling may well have had its effects. In announcing their second benefit, they felt it necessary to make a strong appeal to the public:

"Mr. and Mrs. Usher and Mr. and Mrs. Poe present their respects to the town of Boston and its vicinity, and beg leave to inform them that from the great failure and severe losses sustained by their former attempts, they have been induced, by the persuasion of friends, to make a joint effort for public favor, in hopes of that sanction, influence, and liberal support, which have ever yet distinguished a Boston audience."[58]

Even the critic of *The Emerald,*[59] in a similar appeal, speaks of Poe as "an improving performer" and of Mrs. Poe "as the favorite of the public, and the delight of the eye." Their first benefit on March 21st

[58] *Boston Gazette* and *Columbian Centinel,* April 16 and 18, 1808.
[59] New Series, I (April 16, 1808), 311.

had apparently resulted in a loss rather than a gain, notwithstanding the editorial appeal in their behalf:

If industry can claim from the public either favor or support, the talents of Mrs. Poe will not pass unrewarded. She has supported and maintained a course of characters, more numerous and arduous than can be paralleled on our boards, during any one season. Often she has been obliged to perform three characters on the same evening, and she has always been perfect in the text, and has well comprehended the intention of her author.

In addition to her industry, however, Mrs. Poe has claims for other favors, from the respectability of her talents. Her *Romps* and *Sentimental* characters have an individuality which has marked them peculiarly her own. But she has succeeded often in the tender personations of tragedy; her conceptions are always marked with good sense and natural ability....

We hope, therefore, that when the united recommendations of the talents of both Mr. and Mrs. Poe are put up for public approbation, that that public will not only not discountenance virtuous industry and exertion to please, but will stretch forth the arm of encouragement to cheer, to support and to save.[60]

During the long vacations, Mr. and Mrs. Poe were not idle. On Friday, July 8, 1808, "the public [of Richmond] are respectfully informed that Mr. and Mrs. Poe, Mr. Burke and Mrs. Shaw from the Boston Theatre intend to give an Entertainment at the Hay Market Theatre on Monday evening next. Particulars made known in future advertisements." [61] The "particulars" do not appear, but it is evident that the Poes were in the South, and earned what they could.

The Boston season of 1808-1809 opened on September 26th, but the first mention of the Poes occurs on October 19th, when Mrs. Poe played Cordelia and Poe Edmund in *King Lear,* supporting Fennell. In November Elizabeth repeated her performance of Arabella in Mrs. Cowley's *More Ways than One,* which she had played in March, 1808, but this time David was in the cast also as Carlton, a rather difficult "straight part," in a social comedy. Among his other important parts were Ennui, the affected young man of Reynolds' *The Dramatist,* and Virolet, the second male lead of *The Mountaineers.* On December 23,

---

[60] *Boston Gazette,* March 21, 1808. The system of "benefits" provided that the players received the profits for the performance after all the expenses had been paid. The managers evidently required those actors for whom the benefit was arranged to make up any losses, if the receipts did not equal the expenses.

[61] *Virginia Gazette,* of Richmond, July 8, 1808.

1808, David Poe took the part of Captain Miles Standish in a production "written by a gentleman of Boston," entitled *The Pilgrims; or, The Landing of Our Forefathers on Plymouth Rock.* During November and December Mrs. Poe is not frequently mentioned. She repeated Queen Dollalolla on November 18th, but obviously it must have been ill health which kept her off the stage. On January 4, 1809, Fawcett's pantomime ballet of *The Brazen Mask* was announced with Poe as Leczinsky, and Mrs. Poe's voice was useful as one of the peasants. This notice was repeated on January 6th, 9th, 13th, and 20th, obviously incorrectly, if, as we believe, Edgar Poe was born on January 19, 1809.[62] The *Gazette* welcomed Mrs. Poe back on February 9th: "We congratulate the frequenters of the theatre on the recovery of Mrs. Poe from her recent confinement. This charming little Actress will make her reappearance tomorrow evening as Rosamonda in the popular play of *Abaellino the Great Bandit,* a part peculiarly adapted to her figure and talents." [63]

[62] New confirmation of this date has been found in the Valentine Museum of Richmond in the handwriting of Charles Ellis, son of Charles Ellis, the partner of John Allan:

"Ed. V. Valentine, Esq

Dear Sir   I enclose you a copy of the extract I made from the family bible of the late John Allan, decd—which you will find on the opposite sheet—

Very truly yours
CHARLES ELLIS"

Enclosure:

"William Henry Poe was born on the 30th day of January, 1807—
Edgar Allan Poe was born on the 19th day of January, 1809—
Jno Allan married 5th Oct. 1830 L. G. Allan, (Mrs. Allan was Miss Louisa G. Patterson of Elizabethtown, New Jersey—   C. E.)
John Allan,   son of above, born 23d Aug 1831
Wm. G. Allan,   "   "   5th Oct. 1832
Patterson Allan,   "   "   26th Jan. 1834
Jno Allan Sr died 27th March, 1834—"

[63] *Boston Gazette,* February 9, 1809. There is in the Library of the University of Virginia a program of the Boston Theatre, dated February 8, 1809, which states after giving the principal play, *False Alarms; or, My Cousin,* in which the Poes do not appear, "To which will be added, for the 9th time, a new Grand Serious Pantomime called *Brazen Mask; or, Alberto and Rosabella. . . .* Lechinsky [sic] Mr. Poe," and among the peasants, Mrs. Poe. As the *Gazette* would hardly have announced her return on February 10th in the issue of February 9th if she had really appeared on the 8th, the playbill is probably in error. She would hardly have chosen to "reappear" in such a minor rôle. The names of the peasants were prob-

ELIZABETH ARNOLD POE
From a miniature sent by Mrs. Shew to John H. Ingram.

At the time of Edgar Poe's birth, his parents were living in a section of Boston south of the Common and near the Charles River. As usual, there is a dispute among antiquarians as to the exact location of their home, whether it was in a house then on Haskins Street and afterwards No. 62 Carver Street, or at No. 33 Hollis Street. I am inclined to the first theory, but since the streets were close together, it is quite possible that actors like the Poes moved from one house to the other. Neither house has survived and local tradition is shadowy.[64]

Meanwhile David Poe was constantly employed, among his important rôles being Belville in *The Country Girl*, Garrick's alteration of *The Country Wife*. On Mrs. Poe's return, however, while she is given leading rôles, like Charlotte in *The Apprentice*, David drops for a time out of the picture. He had gone South, probably to borrow money to meet the expenses attendant upon Edgar's birth. A letter kept until recently from publication illuminates not only the character of David Poe, Jr., but also his relations with his family and his own attitude toward his profession. The letter, while long, is not completed, signed, or fully addressed, and as it presents several problems, it is given so far as it relates to our interest:

Stockerton, March 6, 1809.

My dear Bill,

I am mortified by the reflection of my want of even *civility* which alone ought to have induced an answer to your first letter— I entreat you to think it did not spring from any lack of friendship, but to attribute to the right cause, which is that I did not then feel exactly in that frame of mind which is indispensibly necessary to me when I would write you a letter—I confess I wrote John two or three letters since I have written you *one*, but then you must recollect they were mere letters of *business* full of mercantile phrases, technical terms & prices current that would ill suit the ears of a Pastoral swain surrounded by his flocks & herds purling streams and murmuring rills &c as you are.—Therefore having as I hope made a sufficient apology for my seeming forgetfulness we will drop the subject—I am really very glad to find Catharine & William have recovered and hope they may enjoy perfect health—

As for the note we'll say nothing about that—I am convinced

ably kept standing by the printer. In the printed play (1809) the character Poe played is given as "Leczinsky (the Baron's officer)." It is a very minor part. The "peasants" had singing parts.

[64] See Appendix III, for a summary of the arguments for the two locations.

you will as soon as you can & sooner you know you cannot—only
remember that the *sooner* the more to my advantage—I have been
somewhat troubled within the last few days by a couple of Baltimoreans, connexions of *ours*—You may have heard my Father
speak of a visit I had a few days ago from young Roscius. well,
he is one of the Gentlemen alluded to; the other "tho' last not
least" in my estimation for respectability in society, is Mr. Thomas
Williams, familiarly called by those well acquainted with him
Yellow Tom, alias Tom Gibson or by others who take pleasure
in reversing the order of "things" (as old Whelan used to say) Gib-
sons Tom—

[A portion dealing with "Tom" but of no interest to us is omitted. Then comes a sentence which helps identify the writer.]

I persuaded Tom that Philadelphia was far enough from his wife
& quite as good a place as New York; it seemed to strike him that
it was so, and then you know Master George, said he, if she was
to come here she couldn't run me in debt.

[Resuming the letter after some irrelevant details]

The first mentioned Gentleman [David Poe] did not behave so
well. One evening he came out to our house—having seen one of
our servants (that is one of the two we keep) he had me called
out to the door where he told me the most awful moment of his
life was arrived, begged me to come and see him the next day at
11 o'clock at the Mansion house, [s]aid he came not to beg, &
with a tragedy stride walked off after I had without reflection
promised I would call—in obedience to my promise I went there
the next day but found him not nor did I hear of him until yesterday, when a dirty little boy came to the door & said a man down
at the tavern desired him to bring that paper and fetch back the
answer—it is only necessary for me to copy the note here that
you may see the impertinence it contains

Sir, *You* promised *me* on your honor to meet me at the Mansion
house on the 23d—*I* promise *you* on *my* word of honor that if you
will lend me 30, 20, 15 or even 10$ I will *remit* it to you *immedi-
ately* on my arrival in Baltimore. Be assured I will keep *my*
promise at least as well as you did yours and that nothing but
extreem [sic] distress would have *forc'd* me to make this application—Your answer by the bearer will prove whether I yet have
"favour in your eyes" or whether I am to be despised by (as I
understand) a rich relation because when a *wild boy* I join'd a
profession which I then thought and now think an honorable one.
But which I would most willingly quit tomorrow if it gave satis-

faction to your family provided I could do *any thing* else that would give bread to mine—Yr. politeness will no doubt enduce you to answer this note from Yrs &c

D. POE JR.

To this impertinent note it is hardly necessary to tell you my answer—it merely went to assure him that he [need] not look to me for any countenance or support more especially after having written me such a letter as that and thus for the f[uture] I desired to hear not from or of him—so adieu to Davy—

The writer of this letter is evidently named "George." He was George Poe, Jr.,[65] son of George Poe, Sr., and nephew of David Poe, Sr. He was, therefore, first cousin of David Poe, Jr. The "Dear Bill" was William Clemm, Jr.,[66] who had married George Poe's sister, Harriet Poe. Their two eldest children, Catherine and William, are probably those whose recovery is mentioned in the letter. George Poe, Jr., was accustomed to write to William Clemm, Jr., for a letter from Curaçoa March 17, 1806, to him is extant. The handwriting is the same as that of the "Stockerton" letter.[67]

This is the only letter known to be written by David Poe, Jr. It reveals clearly the dislike of the family concerning David Poe's career as an actor, and his resentment at that attitude. In its appeal for money and its prophecy of dire distress if the loan is not forthcoming, it is strangely like some of the epistles Edgar Poe wrote. If George Poe related the circumstances accurately, David was unreliable in

[65] George Poe, Jr., was born in Baltimore, November 12, 1778. He was supercargo (1799-1806) to South America, and a banker in Pittsburgh and Mobile. He was well off and as the letter indicates was accustomed to requests for aid from his family. He married Anna Maria Potts in December, 1808. She was the daughter of James Potts of the well-known Pennsylvania family. Her mother, Anna Stocker, was also a member of a prominent family which gave its name to Stockerton, a town in Lehigh County, northeast of Easton, Pennsylvania.

[66] William Clemm, Jr., was born in Baltimore, May 1, 1779. He married first in 1804, Harriet Poe, by whom he had four children. His third child, Josephine Emily, married her cousin, Neilson Poe. Harriet Poe Clemm was buried, according to St. Paul's Church records, January 8, 1815. William Clemm married on July 12, 1817, Maria Poe, and was therefore the father of Virginia Clemm.

[67] Permission for the publication of this letter has been given through the courtesy of Dr. Joseph Wheeler, Librarian of the Enoch Pratt Library of Baltimore. The complete letter is published in *Edgar Allan Poe Letters and Documents in the Enoch Pratt Library,* edited by A. H. Quinn and R. H. Hart (New York, 1941).

keeping his appointments. While there is danger in reading too much into one letter, there is an indication of habits which Edgar Poe may have inherited from him. In any final judgment upon the frailties of his son, this letter of David Poe must be an important witness.

In April, 1809, when John Howard Payne, at the beginning of his career, but already well known, came to Boston, Mrs. Poe was selected to support him. On April 5th she was Palmyra to Payne's Zaphna in *Mahomet,* the only woman in the cast; on April 7th, Juliet to his Romeo; on April 10th, Irene to his Selim in John Brown's *Barbarossa;* on April 14th, Sigismunda to his Tancred in Thomson's *Tancred and Sigismunda,* a part played by Mrs. Henry Siddons at Drury Lane. On April 17th, when Payne had his benefit, Mrs. Poe played Ophelia and David Poe Laertes to Payne's Hamlet. According to *The Patriot* of April 19th, "Mrs. Poe respectfully informs the public that in consequence of repeated disappointments in obtaining places during Master Payne's engagement he has consented to play one night longer at her benefit." She selected Kotzebue's *Pizarro; or The Death of Rolla,* in which she played Cora to Payne's Rolla and David took the important part of Alonzo, the Spaniard loved by Cora, the Priestess of the Sun. On the same night she sang Darina in Dibdin's *Il Bondocani* with Poe as Abdalla. On May 5th she played Cordelia in *Lear,* and on May 12th she closed her season in the difficult part of Miss Marchmont in Kelly's comedy of manners, *False Delicacy.*

Illness and other difficulties of Mr. and Mrs. Poe must have been augmented by the severe criticism which their efforts met. If the more favorable criticism of David Poe has been preferred for quotation, it is evidently based on more careful observation, undisturbed by personal dislikes. One of the most severe critics wrote many years later a more sober judgment than he had expressed in 1806-1809:

> The theatrical criticisms are all *my own.* Some of them are severe, but I am not aware that any were unjust. The players, however, at least some of them, were of a different opinion. One of them, during a representation of Sheridan's farce,—*The Critic—* paid off the score, by invoking the mercy of the editor of the *Polyanthos!* Mr. Poe—the father of the late Edgar A. Poe,—took offence at a remark on his wife's acting, and called at my house to chastise my impertinence, but went away without effecting his purpose. Both he and his wife were performers of considerable merit, but somewhat vain of their personal accomplishments.[68]

[68] Joseph T. Buckingham, *Personal Memoirs and Recollections of Editorial Life* (Boston, 1852), I, 57.

If the visit of David Poe was prompted by the criticism of his wife's performance as Little Pickle in *The Spoiled Child*—"We never knew before that the Spoiled Child belonged to that class of beings termed hermaphroditical, as the uncouthness of his costume seemed to indicate" [69]—we can only sympathize with the natural resentment of a gentleman. It did not endear him, however, to the most influential critic in Boston.

The Poes were to leave Boston for New York. It was a professional advance, but it was to bring them both into a fiercer competition and to personal attacks besides which the strictures of the *Polyanthos* were mild indeed. Professionally, the three years in Boston were successful ones. Both David and Elizabeth Poe were recognized as important and valued members of the Company. Their personal lot could hardly have been a very happy one, and the absence, at times, of their names in the announcements, followed by their reappearance in important rôles, indicates illness or absence from Boston. Yet at her death Mrs. Poe left a sketch of Boston Harbor, entitled "Morning, 1808," made by herself. On the back of this she afterwards wrote, "For my little son Edgar, who should ever love Boston, the place of his birth, and where his mother found her best, and most sympathetic friends." [70]

A notice in the *Commercial Advertiser* of New York indicates again illness or other difficulty in the Poe family. Caulfield, with whom Mrs. Poe had played in Boston, was announced to provide entertainment for June 6, 1809, at Mechanics' Hall and Mrs. Poe was to sing. But on that day Caulfield had to postpone the event "on account of the sudden disappearance of Mrs. Poe." [71]

To the Poes, their engagement at the Park Theatre in New York, which began its season on September 6, 1809, under Price and Cooper, must have seemed a promotion. Elizabeth played Angela, the leading part, and a strenuous one, in M. G. Lewis's *Castle Spectre*, in which she baffled ghosts and villains through five full acts. Notwithstanding the demands of this part which had taxed the powers of Mrs. Jordan so greatly in the London performance that she had to omit her song,[72] Elizabeth also played Priscilla Tomboy in the afterpiece, in which David was Captain Sightly. He played a Negro, Hassan, in *The Castle Spectre*.

[69] *Polyanthos*, IV (March, 1807), 282.
[70] Mrs. Shew to Ingram, copying this letter of Mrs. Poe from Mrs. Shew's *Journal*. Autograph Ms., Ingram Collection, University of Virginia.
[71] Odell, *Annals of the New York Stage*, II, 324.
[72] Introduction to London, 1818, ed. of play.

Cooper, whom Mrs. Poe had supported in Boston, must have brought her to New York. During September she played Cora to his Rolla, Ophelia to his Hamlet, Rosamonda to his Abaellino, and Desdemona to his Othello. On September 22nd she sustained the intensely tragic part of Imma in *Adelgitha*. She was also repeating her lighter parts in the afterpieces, and David was cast for good parts in them, and even took Eugene to her Laura in *The Agreeable Surprise*. But evil days were coming for David Poe. The critic of *The Ramblers' Magazine and New-York Theatrical Register* did his best to hound him off the stage. As Falieri in *Abaellino* Poe had apparently mispronounced "Dandoli" and from that time on he was "Dan Dilly" to this critic. The very violence of the personalities bear evidence to the unfairness of this critic's judgment. The following shows how even the editor felt called upon to protest:

> By the sudden indisposition of mr. Robertson, the entertainments announced for the evening (Pizarro and Princess or [sic] no Princess) necessarily gave place to the preceding. Mr. Poe was mr. R's substitute in Alonzo; and a more wretched Alonzo have we never witnessed. This man was never destined for the high walks of the drama;—a footman is the extent of what he ought to attempt: and if by accident like that of this evening he is compelled to walk without his sphere, it would bespeak more of sense in him to read the part than attempt to act it;—his person, voice, and non-expression of countenance, all combine to stamp him— *poh! et praeterea nihil.**
>
> * Here, as well as in some other passages of the Theatrical Register, our correspondent it [is] too acrimonious; and I must take the liberty to differ from him, in some measure, respecting mr. Poe's talents, who, *if he would take pains,* is by no means contemptible. [73]

Notwithstanding this opinion, the management gave Poe the important part of the prince Almarick in Thomas Dibdin's *Princess and No Princess* on September 29th, Mrs. Poe playing Elisena.[74] On October 2nd he played his last Shakespearean part, that of Sir Richard Ratcliff in *Richard III*, one of the last of the King's retainers to remain true to him, while Mrs. Poe played the Prince of Wales. But another blast from *The Rambler* indicates that David Poe may have threatened the

[73] *Ramblers' Magazine*, I, 27.
[74] See *Ramblers' Magazine*, I, 28-29.

critic. He had been cast for Amos, a black servant in *To Marry or Not to Marry*, on October 6th.

Dan Dilly played *Amos,* and in spite of the coat of lampblack that covered his muffin face, there was no difficulty in penetrating the veil and discovering the worthy descendant of the illustrious Daniel. By the by, it has been said, that this *gentleman* has taken some of our former remarks very much in dudgeon; but whether this be true or not, we entertain very great doubts, for certainly we have said nothing but the truth, and that should give no man offence. If it is the case, however, we are sincerely sorry for it; for from his amiable *private character,* and high *professional standing,* he is among the last men we would justly offend. We owe this to our friend Dan from having heard much of his *spirit;* for, for men of high spirit, we have a high respect, though no *fear.* This we beg to be explicitly understood; for as there are men who will sometimes mistake motives, it may happen that this conciliatory conduct on our part be imputed to causes foreign from the truth.[75]

On October 16th he was cast for the second lead, the romantic young lover, Virolet, in *The Mountaineers.* On October 18, 1809, David Poe made his last appearance on the stage. He played Captain Cypress in Richard Leigh's *Grieving's a Folly,* the part of a young officer who is the villain of the piece and tries to seduce the heroine. The play was announced for repetition, but a note in *The Rambler* tells us: "Friday [October] 20th. *Castle Spectre—Blue Devils—*and *Don Juan.* It was not until the curtain was ready to rise that the audience was informed that, owing to the sudden indisposition of *mr. Robertson* and *Mr. Poe,* the *Castle Spectre* was necessarily substituted for *Grieving's a Folly.*" [76]

Two points in this note are significant in their implications. The absence of David Poe was important enough to warrant, in part at least, a change of play. But it is even more significant that his "indisposition" caused his non-appearance. From that date his name does not appear in any theatrical notice. "Indisposition" is a term used often in theatrical notices of that day to cover intoxication, which would support the theory that accounts by heredity for Edgar Poe's infirmity. It is likely that the combination of drink, ill health, and unfavorable criticism brought on despair. *The Rambler* even descended to personal abuse, by the publication of these verses:

[75] *Ramblers' Magazine,* I, 92-93.
[76] *Ramblers' Magazine,* I, 100.

Sur un POE de Chambre

Rendons hommage au rédacteur
Du Ramblers' Magazine;
Il juge bien de chaque acteur
Les talens à la mine:
Suivant lui surtout,
Jamais du bon goût,
Monsieur Poh n'eut l'empreinte,
Son père était pot,
Sa mère était broc,
Sa grand mere était pinte.[77]

How severe also was the ordeal from the temper of the audiences of that day may be gleaned from the tragic account of the suicide of the actor Fullerton, who threw himself into the Delaware River, owing to the pitiless hissing which drove him from the stage.[78] That there were differences of opinion concerning Poe's ability is shown by a passage in a magazine, *Something,* edited by "Nemo Nobody, Esquire" in Boston. Under date of December 14, 1809, he addressed a letter:

To our brother Editors of New-York.

Gentlemen,
We strongly and feelingly recommend to your encouragement and protection, the talents of Mr. Poe.—He *has* talents, and they may be improved or ruined by your just or incautious observations. We think, that the duty of an editor is first to feel, next to weigh, and lastly to determine.—We are well aware of the errors of this gentleman, but we know that such errors have frequently been introduced by unfeeling criticism. It is disgraceful in any editor to make actors on the stage a mere mark to shoot at.—If your intentions are to do good, encourage; If after you have done your duty, they do not improve—censure freely.

N. N.

If, as is possible but not certain, "Nemo Nobody" was the actor James Fennell, his opinion is worth more than that of an unfriendly critic. But perhaps it is not necessary to indulge in any more speculations concerning David Poe's disappearance from the casts. On October 25, 1810, Edmund Simpson, later to be the co-manager of the theatre,

---

[77] *Ramblers' Magazine,* I, 88. The meaning is not clear. *Broc* means "pitcher" and *pinte* may mean "pint." The reference is probably to David Poe's drinking.

[78] See *Mirror of Taste and Dramatic Censor,* Philadelphia, I (1810), 505.

arrived from England. He was admirably fitted for the parts for which David Poe had been cast, and he was a better actor.

Notwithstanding the care of a husband, either an invalid or out of work, and of her two little children, Mrs. Poe kept up her valiant struggle. In November she played Jessica in *The Merchant of Venice*, and *The Rambler* notes that while the *Mock Doctor* of Fielding was badly put on, "Twaits, Mrs. Poe and Mrs. Young did their best." [79] The critic also praises her performance of Zamora in her disguise as Eugenio in *The Honeymoon*, and of Rosabelle in *The Foundling of the Forest*. Other important parts were Parisatis in *Alexander the Great* and the Prince of Wales in *Richard III*. When she played Cora in *Pizarro* and Dolly Bull in *John Bull at Fontainbleau* on December 11, 1809, the critic was again pleased: "In the afterpiece, *mrs. Poe* was excellent. It is in this line of characters she particular [sic] delights and to which she should bend her chief attention. It is difficult to be sprightly without being fantastic, and to act the hoyden, without being gross and mawkish. Mrs. Poe has hit the happy medium; and let her cultivate it with assiduity. It is one of the most difficult and most important departments of female comedy." [80]

The Park Theatre was closed from January 16 to February 22, 1810, owing to the poor business. Payne came in March and Mrs. Poe played Ophelia and Juliet in his support. She had the lead, the Widow Bellair, in *The Widow or Who Wins*, a part Mrs. Charles Kemble had taken at Covent Garden. In April she played Catherine in *The Exile*, a leading part in what seems to have been a great success. In May she repeated Imma in *Adelgitha* and played Regan in *Lear*, and had second leads in comedy. In June she sang Ulrica in a melodramatic part in *The Free Knights*. For her benefit on July 2nd she selected Rosamonda in *Abaellino* and Narcissa in Colman's *Inkle and Yarico*, the English girl who has a singing part. On her last appearance in New York, July 4, 1810, she repeated Ulrica in *The Free Knights* and Rosa in *The Caravan*.[81]

The assumption that Mrs. Poe was not reëngaged because of failure on her part is not a necessary one. As Odell remarks: "The four years [1806-1810] were among the most pointless in the whole history of the New York stage." She turned her attention again to the South, where the Placide family were managing the theatres. Whether David

[79] Vol. I, p. 185.
[80] *Ramblers' Magazine*, I, 211-212.
[81] *New York Post* and *Commercial Advertiser*, July 3, 1810.

Poe was still with her is uncertain. He apparently did not die in New York City.[82]

Mrs. Poe opened the season of the Richmond Theatre on August 18, 1810, as Angela in *The Castle Spectre* and Maria in *Of Age To-morrow*. She played leading parts like Florence in *The Curfew*, in which, disguised as a youth, she baffled an energetic band of robbers. For her benefit on September 21st, she sang and danced, and probably played Letitia Hardy in *The Belle's Stratagem*, a charming and effective lead in a comedy of manners. A correspondent of the *Richmond Enquirer* of September 21st writes a long letter, a portion of which must suffice: "From an actress who possesses so eminently the faculty of pleasing, whose powers are so general and whose exertions are so ready, it would be unjust to withhold the tribute of applause. Were I to say simply that she is a valuable acquisition to the Theatre, I should dishonor her merit, and do injustice to the feeling of the public. . . . On her first moment of entrance on the Richmond Boards she was saluted with the plaudits of admiration, and at no one moment since has her reputation sunk."

After September 21st, she is not mentioned in the casts which, indeed, were infrequently given. The season in Richmond lasted until November 13, 1810. This period of inaction for Mrs. Poe was probably caused by the birth of Rosalie Poe.[83]

In January, 1811, Mrs. Poe joined Placide's Company at Charleston, where she had played last in 1798. On her first night, January 23rd, owing to Mrs. Young's "indisposition" she sustained again the arduous rôles of Angela and Priscilla Tomboy. There were many new parts to learn, among them Jacintha in *The Suspicious Husband*, Lydia Lan-

---

[82] Searches of the burial records of every Protestant church then existing in New York City, made by the courtesy of the present rectors, produced no evidence of David Poe's death. No records of deaths were kept by the City of New York in 1810.

[83] This has been given on very uncertain evidence as December 20, 1810, at Norfolk, Virginia, at the Forrest home. This date originated, apparently, with J. H. Whitty on the authority of "the Mackenzie Bible." I have made a vain search in Richmond for any trace of this Bible, or any documentary evidence concerning the birth date. Rosalie was baptized in Richmond, September 3, 1812 (see p. 58), but the Church records for that date have been lost or destroyed. There are no vital statistics in Norfolk for the period, and the newspapers did not carry birth notices. The Forrest house on 16 Brewer Street, Norfolk, was owned in 1810 by Andrew Martin, who, from court records, apparently maintained a boarding house on the premises.

guish in *The Rivals*, Lady Eleanor in *Everyone Has His Fault*, Lady Teazle in *The School for Scandal*. These, it is to be noticed, were comedies of manners. She took also two leading parts in the rôle of Floribel in *The Doubtful Son* and Flora in *The Midnight Hour*, those managing maids which she knew so well how to play. She must have been charming as Donna Clara in *Two Strings to Your Bow*, in her mingled bravery and confusion, in which, disguised as her brother Felix, she has to fight a duel.

That she was given less important parts in Shakespeare's plays was due to the presence of Mrs. Beaumont, a "star" from Covent Garden. If she had to content herself with parts like Nerissa in *The Merchant of Venice* and Mopsa in *The Winter's Tale*, she may at least have appeared in the first American production of the latter in its una-bridged form. In April she played Sally in *The Purse*; it must have carried her back to the night in Charleston in 1797 when she played a page in the same play.

For her benefit on April 29th, she played Violante in Mrs. Cent-livre's *The Wonder; or, A Woman Keeps a Secret*, the part of a generous woman who keeps her friend Isabelle's secret at the risk of her own happiness. She also repeated her old part of Moggy McGilpin and took part in the "Comick Pantomical [sic] Ballet, Hurry Scurry," besides singing a song! For one evening this was a full program. Con-stant postponements indicate that the business was not good, and Placide was driven to spectacles and pantomimes, in which Mrs. Poe did her share. On one night she played Nancy Joblin in W. C. White's *Poor Lodger*, sang Maria in *Of Age To-morrow*, and was Columbine in the pantomime of *Harlequin's Restoration*. The season closed May 20, 1811, with another triple bill, in which she played Emma in *The Birthday*, sang Lucy in *The Review*, and played Almeida, a Moorish princess, in *Blackbeard!* She was, as usual, doing her full share. She had acted sixteen new parts, nearly all leads.

The visit of the Company to Norfolk was prefaced by the sale of the theatre there at public auction, an ominous prologue. Absence of information in the advertisements concerning the casts makes the parts Mrs. Poe played at Norfolk uncertain. On July 24th she probably repeated Fanny Growse in Arnold's comedy *Man and Wife*, which she had just played in Charleston, and she almost certainly repeated Donna Violante in *The Wonder* and Leonora in *The Padlock* for her own benefit on July 26th. A letter to *The Herald* on July 26, 1811, ex-presses the feelings of a correspondent, "Floretta," who, despite her emotional language, paints an interesting picture of the situation:

And now, Sir, permit me to call the attention of the public to the Benefit of Mrs. Poe and Miss Thomas for this Evening, and their claims on the liberality of the Norfolk audience are not small. The former of those ladies, I remember, (just as I was going in my teens) on her first appearance here, met with the most unbounded applause—She was said to be one of the handsomest women in America; she was certainly the handsomest I had ever seen. She never came on the Stage, but a general murmur ran through the house, "What an exchanting Creature! Heavens, what a form!—What an animated and expressive countenance!—and how well she performs! Her voice too! sure never anything was half so sweet!" Year after year did she continue to extort these involuntary bursts of rapture from the Norfolk audience, and to deserve them too; for never did one of her profession, take more pains to please than she. But now "The scene is changed,"—Misfortunes have pressed heavy on her. Left alone, the only support of herself and several small children—Friendless and unprotected, she no longer commends that admiration and attention she formerly did,—Shame on the world that can turn its back on the same person in distress, that it was wont to cherish in prosperity. And yet she is as assiduous to please as ever, and tho' grief may have stolen the roses from her cheeks, she still retains the same sweetness of expression, and symmetry of form and feature. She this evening hazards a Benefit, in the pleasing hope that the inhabitants of Norfolk will remember past services, And can they remember and not requite them generously?—Heaven forbid they should not.

Floretta also remarks that *The Wonder* has been played in Charleston in April for Mrs. Poe's benefit and "the result answered the lady's most sanguine expectations." That she was not without friends in Norfolk is revealed by the one note in her handwriting that has been preserved:

Mrs. Poe's respectfull [sic] compliments to Mrs. Taswell [sic] *returns* Mrs Liverne thanks for her great kindness—Mrs. P—being to sail this Eve Mrs. T will excuse the haste with which this is written
Tuesday Eve [84]

Mrs. Tazewell was the wife of Littleton W. Tazewell, Governor of Virginia, who resided in Norfolk from 1802.

Where David Poe was during this period is still uncertain, but he

[84] Original autograph Ms., J. K. Lilly Jr. Collection.

Mrs Poe; respectfull compliments to Mrs
Allan returns Mr Lionne thanks for her great
kindnes — Mr P. being to fail this Eve
Mrs P. will cover the task with which this
is wintthen —

Amusing Eve —

was evidently not with his wife and family. No contemporary account gives the date of his death.[85]

Mrs. Poe played her last season in Richmond. The company opened on August 16, 1811, but she is first mentioned on September 20th as one of the three graces in *Cinderella*. On September 27th she played the leading part of Emily Bloomfield in William Ioor's *Battle of Eutaw Springs*. When her benefit came on October 9th, with *Alexander the Great* and *Love Laughs at Locksmiths,* her name does not appear in the notices, but on October 11th, at the benefit of Miss Thomas, Mrs. Poe played the Countess Wintersen in *The Stranger,* the gentlewoman who helps to reconcile Mrs. Haller and her husband in that popular melodrama. It was her last appearance on the stage.

A letter from Samuel Mordecai, later to be the social historian of Richmond, sent to his sister Rachel and dated "2 November, 1811," gives us the only authoritative picture of the last days of Elizabeth Poe:

"A singular fashion prevails here this season—it is—charity. Mrs. Poe, who you know is a very handsome woman, happens to be very sick, and (having quarreled and parted with her husband) is destitute. The most fashionable place of resort, now is—her chamber—And the skill of cooks and nurses is exerted to procure her delicacies. Several other sick persons also receive a portion of these fashionable visits and delicacies—It is a very laudable fashion and I wish it may last long." [86]

When another benefit was announced for her on November 29th, the managers stated that it was given because of the "serious and long continued indisposition of Mrs. Poe and in compliance with the advices and solicitations of many of the most respectable families." [87] On the same day, the *Enquirer* contained this notice:

"To the Humane Heart

"On this night, *Mrs. Poe,* lingering on the bed of disease and sur-

[85] A press clipping without date or place stating that he died October 19, 1810, at Norfolk, is on the authority of Dr. T. O. Mabbott, printed on paper that proves it to be of much later origin. A careful search of wills, inventories, and audits of estates for the Borough and County of Norfolk and of the City and County records at Richmond discloses no record of the death of David Poe. The Charleston Bureau of Vital Statistics has no death records prior to 1821. See Appendix for discussion of Mrs. Weiss's account of the Poes in Norfolk.

[86] Mordecai MSS., Duke University Library. See J. B. Hubbell, "Poe's Mother," *William and Mary Quarterly,* XXI (July, 1941), pp. 250-54.

[87] *Virginia Patriot,* November 29, 1811.

rounded by her children, asks your assistance and *asks it perhaps for the last time*. The Generosity of a Richmond Audience can need no other appeal. For particulars, see the Bills of the day."

The brief announcement of her death came soon after: "Dec. 10, 1811—Tuesday. Died, on last Sunday morning, [December 8] Mrs. Poe, one of the Actresses of the Company at present playing on the Richmond Boards. By the death of this lady the Stage has been deprived of one of its chief ornaments. And to say the least of her, she was an interesting Actress, and never failed to catch the applause and command the admiration of the beholder."

Notwithstanding the dramatic accounts of Mrs. Poe's death in a little house, now numbered 2220½ Main Street, and shown in all its unsavory surroundings to visitors as the spot where she spent her last days, it is practically certain that she never lived there. By an admirable piece of research,[88] Mrs. Elizabeth Valentine Huntley of Richmond has proved through the investigation of the tax records, the deed books, and the insurance records of the Mutual Assurance Society of Virginia that the land on which the supposed death scenes of Mrs. Poe took place, was, in 1811, a portion of a vacant lot. The first appearance of this building on an insurance plat was in 1830.

Moreover, the second Indian Queen Tavern, so often referred to by biographers as standing next to this "last residence" of Mrs. Poe, and, therefore, on the north*west* corner of Twenty-third and Main (or E Street as it was then called), was not located on that spot. From 1806 to 1821, when it burned down, the Indian Queen Tavern was located on the north*east* corner of Twenty-third and Main Streets. The relation of the "little house" to the so-called "actors' boarding houses" of "Mrs. Phipps" is equally discredited, for the records seem to prove conclusively that these buildings were put up for the first time in 1816. Again, unfortunately for romantic biography, Mrs. Phipps herself becomes a very uncertain figure, for no advertisements give any woman by that name a shop on Main Street between Twenty-second and Twenty-third Streets. Finally, it seems unlikely that Mrs. Poe, who must have been in ill health for some time before her death, should have chosen to live fifteen blocks from the Richmond Theatre. This theatre stood on Broad Street, east of Twelfth Street, where the Monumental Church now stands, and in order to reach it, Mrs. Poe

---

[88] Since the detailed statement, prepared for this biography by Mrs. Ralph T. Catterall, Honorary Curator of Prints and Manuscripts of the Valentine Museum, on the basis of Mrs. Huntley's notes, is printed in Appendix V, I have given here only a brief résumé.

would have had to climb a steep hill both in going to and returning from what is now 2220½ Main Street.

Mrs. Huntley has suggested another location for the hard-working actress. From advertisements in the *Virginia Patriot* and the *Enquirer*, it is clear that Placide, the manager of the Virginia Company, as well as others in the Company, lived in or near the Washington Tavern, which had been known up to 1797 as the Indian Queen, and that the Tavern was used as a meeting place for the people of the theatre. From this Tavern, which stood at the northwest corner of Ninth and Grace Streets, the site of the present Hotel Richmond, Mrs. Poe need walk only one block to Broad Street and three blocks to Twelfth Street, and would have been near her children in any emergency. That Mrs. Poe should have brought Edgar, a child under three years of age, the long distance from Twenty-second Street, and by some accident, have passed by Mrs. Allan's home and attracted her attention to Edgar, is distinctly unlikely. It is easy to see, therefore, how rumor, confusing the old "Indian Queen" with the newer one, and transferring it from Ninth and Grace Streets to Twenty-third and Main Streets, collecting on the way "Mrs. Phepoe," who had a millinery shop at Turner's Tavern, on the corner of Fourteenth and Main Streets, and turning her into "Mrs. Phipps," should finally locate Mrs. Poe in a tenement that did not exist in 1811! Unfortunately, there is no house now standing at Ninth and Grace Streets which we can dramatize, as all the former buildings have been torn down to make way for larger edifices.

On December 26, 1811, the Richmond Theatre, a brick building which had been erected in the rear of the Old Academy or Theatre Square, was burned. Seventy-two persons perished, and the whole city went in mourning. But this tragic event could have had little effect on the two children whom Mrs. Poe left unprotected, since they were already provided for. Within a few days after Mrs. Poe's death, Edgar was taken by Mrs. John Allan, and Rosalie by Mrs. William MacKenzie, matrons of Richmond. Mr. and Mrs. Allan and Edgar were staying during the Christmas holiday with Bowler Cocke, a planter living at Turkey Island, and thus escaped the fire or its aftermath.[89]

The reaction of the city may be read in "The Players' Address to the Citizens of Richmond," which evidently refers to Mrs. Poe:

"In this miserable calamity we find a sentence of banishment from your hospitable city.—No more do we expect to feel that glow of

[89] T. H. Ellis Ms., Valentine Collection.

pleasure which pervades a grateful heart, while it receives favours liberally bestowed. Never again shall we behold that feminine humanity which so eagerly displayed itself to soothe the victim of disease; and view with exultation, the benevolent who fostered the fatherless, and shed a ray of comfort to the departed soul of a dying mother." [90]

A summary of the parts played by Elizabeth and David Poe reveals in a striking fashion the variety and the extent of their repertory. When Mrs. Poe died at twenty-four, she had to her credit, disregarding mere chorus, vocal, or dancing parts, two hundred and one different rôles.[91] Of these, fourteen were Shakespearean: Ariel, Ophelia, Cordelia, Juliet, Desdemona, Regan, Nerissa, Jessica, Prince John in *First Henry IV*, Blanch in *King John*, Prince of Wales and Duke of York in *Richard III*, Mopsa in *A Winter's Tale*, Valeria in *Coriolanus*.

She sustained leading tragic parts like Palmyra in *Mahomet*, Sigismunda in *Tancred and Sigismunda*, Laura in Lewis's *Adelgitha*, Lady Randolph in *Douglas*. In the romantic melodrama, often verging on tragedy, which was then so popular, she played twenty-four parts, mostly leads, like Cora in *The Virgin of the Sun*, in *Pizarro*, and in *Columbus*, Amelia in *The Robbers*, Rosamonda in *Abaellino*, Christina in *Gustavus Vasa*, Angela in *The Castle Spectre*, and Parisatis in *Alexander the Great*. She had a few good parts also in romantic farces, like Donna Clara in *Two Strings to Your Bow*. In her largest number of rôles she represented the gentlewoman of comedy, social or domestic. Among her eleven parts in the comedy of manners were Lydia Languish in *The Rivals*, Lady Teazle in *The School for Scandal*, Letitia Hardy in *The Belle's Stratagem*, Miss Marchmont in *False Delicacy*, Constance Neville in *She Stoops to Conquer*, and Louisa Courtney in *The Dramatist*.

In that indeterminate dramatic sphere where the social and domestic comedy blend, Mrs. Poe sustained forty-three parts. She could play both the gentlewoman, Miss Blandford, and the country girl, Susan Ashfield, in *Speed the Plough*. She often portrayed the gentlewoman in distress, like Caroline Dormer in *The Heir at Law*, Emily Worthington in *The Poor Gentleman*, Lady Eleanor in *Everyone Has His Fault*, or Stella in Boaden's *Maid of Bristol*. She seems to have

[90] *Particular account of the Dreadful Fire at Richmond, Virginia, December 26, 1811* (Baltimore, 1812), p. 30, see J. B. Hubbell, "Poe's Mother."

[91] See Appendix for list, as complete as possible. If casts had always been printed in the notices, the total would be still larger.

appealed strongly in those emotional parts, often of an orphan, poor but proud, who ultimately marries a gentleman, after incidental persecutions, of which Mary Thornberry in *John Bull* is an example. She also represented those extraordinary heroines, adapted from Kotzebue, like Ellen Metland in *The Wise Man of the East*. While she was popular in the light farcical parts like her first, Biddy Bellair, only nine can be so classified. They resemble the pert hoydenish characters in musical afterpieces like Little Pickle in *The Spoiled Child,* or Priscilla Tomboy in *The Romp,* in both of which she sang, but their constant repetition has caused them to be overstressed. In reality there are only eight of her singing parts in which she played a hoyden. In twenty-six of these afterpieces she sang, and often was disguised as a boy or a soldier, once even as a Negro servant! But it seems to have been her charming figure and pleasant voice rather than any buffoonery that made her popular as Moggy McGilpin in *The Highland Reel,* or Rosabelle in *The Foundling of the Forest,* when her "sprightly characteristic performance" was praised by *The Rambler.* Twenty-two of her singing parts were in romantic opera like *Rosina,* or in poetic drama like *The Honeymoon,* in which she played Eugenio, the page. Her remaining parts were those of maids, some of which were quite important, and there were several minor characters which need not be classified.

During his six years on the stage, David Poe played one hundred and thirty-seven parts. Nineteen of these were Shakespearean: Don Pedro in *Much Ado,* Tressel in *Richard III,* Duncan, Malcolm, and Donalbain in *Macbeth,* Laertes, Rosenkranz, and Bernardo in *Hamlet,* Decius Brutus in *Julius Cæsar,* Sir Richard Vernon in *Henry IV,* Montano in *Othello,* Duke of Austria in *King John,* Ferdinand in *The Tempest,* Edmund and Duke of Albany in *King Lear,* Volusius in *Coriolanus,* Salanio in *The Merchant of Venice,* Hortensio in *Catharine and Petruchio,* Ratcliff in *Richard III.* Forty of David Poe's parts were those of gentlemen, often soldiers, in social or domestic comedy, such as Colonel Raymond in *The Foundling,* Harry Harebrain in *The Will for the Deed,* Charles Stanley in *A Cure for the Heartache,* Harry Thunder in *Wild Oats,* Henry Morland in *The Heir at Law.* In the comedy of manners, he played Joseph Surface in *The School for Scandal,* and Sir George Touchwood in *The Belle's Stratagem.* In domestic drama of a more serious, even tragic, nature, he was cast in eleven parts, the principal ones being George Barnwell, Villars in *The Blind Bargain,* Malford in *The Soldier's Daughter,* and Frederick in *Lover's Vows.* In the romantic play, in verse or prose, his thirty rôles were frequently important ones like Ataliba in *The Virgin of the Sun*, Alonzo in *Pizarro*, Altamount in *The Fair Penitent*, the Duke of Buckingham in *Jane Shore*, Norval in *Douglas*, Bertrand in *The Curfew*, or the Duke of Medina in *Rule a Wife and Have a Wife*. He was also cast for character parts like Ennui in *The Dramatist*, Le Gout in *More Ways Than One*, Sir Larry MacMurragh in *Who Wants a Guinea?*, Negro parts like Hassan in *The Castle Spectre*, old men like Maurice in *A Wife of Two Husbands*. His other parts were less important.

In the light of these facts, we must reconstruct the traditional figure of David Poe as a negligible actor. Managers were not so lacking in talent that they could afford to risk failure by constant employment of a nonentity. The nature of the unfavorable criticism, resting evidently upon personal hostility, makes it of less value than the undeniable record of employment. But if the new light thrown upon David Poe by his complete stage record raises his stature as an actor, it makes clearer the unstable nature which he transmitted to his son. If Edgar Poe inherited from his father a handsome presence and that quality of impetuous chivalry that disturbed the critics of New York and Boston, he owed to him also that perverse tendency to hurt his own prospects and that weakness for drink which brought to the surface the bitterness revealed by David Poe's letter to his cousin George. Years later, Edgar Poe, in his reply to Dr. English, must have had his father in mind when he wrote:

"The errors and frailties which I deplore, it cannot at least be asserted that I have been the coward to deny. Never, even, have I made attempt at *extenuating* a weakness which is (or, by the blessing of God, *was*) a calamity, although those who did not know me intimately had little reason to regard it otherwise than as a crime. For, indeed, had my pride, or that of my family permitted, there was much —very much—there was everything—to be offered in extenuation. Perhaps, even, there was an epoch at which it might not have been wrong in me to hint—what by the testimony of Dr. Francis and other medical men I might have demonstrated, had the public, indeed, cared for the demonstration—that the irregularities so profoundly lamented were the *effect* of a terrible evil rather than its cause.—And now let me thank God that in redemption from the physical ill I have forever got rid of the moral." [92]

The qualities Edgar Poe inherited from his mother were quite different. There was evidently a spark of genius in that sprite-like figure,

[92] J. A. Harrison, *Virginia Ed.*, XVII, 242, quoting the *Philadelphia Spirit of the Times*, July 10, 1846.

and that her courage and charm descended to her son there need be little doubt. In 1845 when Edgar Poe was speaking of the Evangelical prejudice against the stage which Mrs. Mowatt had to combat, he paid a tribute to his mother:

"The writer of this article is himself the son of an actress—has invariably made it his boast—and no earl was ever prouder of his earldom than he of his descent from a woman who, although well born, hesitated not to consecrate to the drama her brief career of genius and of beauty." [93]

We may think of her also as the friend of people of breeding who remembered her with pleasure. Years later Beverley Tucker wrote of the beauty of Elizabeth Poe, and introduced himself to Edgar Poe as one who had known her.[94]

There is unfortunately another side to the picture. In the year of Edgar Poe's birth, Anne Holbrook, an English actress, put the case briefly but forcibly.[95] "An actress can never make her children comfortable.... The mother returning with harassed frame and agitated mind, from the varying passions she has been pourtraying, instead of imparting healthful nourishment to her child, fills it with bile and fever, to say nothing of dragging them long journies, at all seasons of the year." It would seem as though she were describing Elizabeth Poe's career. Is it any wonder that Edgar Poe was born with that physical handicap which made his life a struggle not only against a civilization as yet unaccustomed to genius, but also against a weakness, which was constantly "wearing its own deep feeling as a crown?" But, on the other hand, is it hard to believe that these two young actors, who lived among the symbolic figures of the stage, transmitted to their son that capacity to create those marvellous symbols of love, of pride, of death, and of beauty, which animate his poetry and his prose, and are his great gift to the literature of the world?

[93] *Broadway Journal,* II (July 19, 1845), 29.
[94] Letter of Beverley Tucker to T. W. White, November 29, 1835.
[95] *The Dramatist or Memoirs of the Stage* (Birmingham, 1809), p. 60.

CHAPTER II

Richmond — The Early Years

If Elizabeth Poe had any intimation from Mrs. John Allan and Mrs. William Mackenzie that they would take care of Edgar and Rosalie, she must have died with her greatest dread removed. Their grandfather, David Poe, was still living in Baltimore, it is true, but he was not well-to-do, and he had assumed the responsibility for William Henry Poe, his eldest grandson. On the other hand, John Allan was a partner in the firm of Ellis and Allan, exporters of tobacco and general merchants, and was in comfortable, if not in affluent, circumstances. The Allans were childless and the little boy, whose early charm had attracted Mrs. Allan, was apparently sure not only of material advantages, but also of that love and sympathy which foster-parents owe to a child for whom they voluntarily assume the responsibility. So much that is incorrect has been written concerning the relationship between Poe and John Allan, and so important was that relationship in shaping Poe's career, that it becomes necessary to try to understand the character of the two persons who were to guide Edgar Poe during his formative years.

Fortunately for our purpose, John Allan was one of the most voluminous correspondents of his time. In the hundreds of letters which he wrote, or received, and of which, with true Scottish caution, he preserved copies, we see a man exact in his business relations, anxious naturally to buy cheaply and sell at a good price, competent, and reasonably progressive in his methods. Many of these letters have been preserved in the papers of the Ellis-Allan firm, now in the Library of Congress and in the Edward V. Valentine Collection in the Valentine Museum in Richmond. A selection from the Valentine Collection, including the letters from Poe to John Allan, edited in 1925 by Mrs. Stanard, threw a new light upon Poe's life in a previously obscure period. New facts are also recorded in the manuscript by Thomas H. Ellis, the son of John Allan's partner, which has apparently not been available to biographers.[1]

[1] The Ellis-Allan papers, in the Manuscript Division of the Library of

51

John Allan was born in Cresland House in 1780,[2] in the parish of Dundonald, Ayrshire, Scotland, and came to Richmond before January, 1795, living at first with his uncle, William Galt, who had preceded him by twenty years, and who was one of Richmond's leading merchants. By articles signed on November 23, 1800, Charles Ellis and John Allan, clerks in William Galt's employ, entered into partnership as merchants, the business to commence on the first of September following.[3] Each contributed £1,000 sterling.

On June 4, 1804, John Allan was naturalized in the United States Circuit Court for the Fifth Circuit at Richmond, Virginia, and took the oath before Chief Justice Marshall. On this occasion he proved that he had lived within the United States since before January 29, 1795.[4]

Congress, to which the late Killis Campbell first called attention in 1910, were arranged in 1929 in 437 volumes, containing letters and other material from 1795 to 1856. There are also 27 volumes of Letter Books and 151 volumes of Journals, Ledgers, etc These will be referred to as "Ellis-Allan Papers, L. of C." Some, but not by any means all, of the more important items relating to Poe have been separated from their chronological order and placed in one volume. This will be referred to as "Ellis-Allan Papers, L. of C., Poe Volume." The letters edited by Mary Newton Stanard as *Edgar Allan Poe Letters Till Now Unpublished in the Valentine Museum, Richmond, Virginia* (Philadelphia, 1925), contain twenty-eight letters from Poe to John Allan, two from John Allan to Poe, and one from Mrs. Clemm to Allan. These have become known as "The Valentine Letters" and will be referred to under that title. Other letters of value, written to or by John Allan and members of his family, especially during his stay abroad, are in the Valentine Museum. Only a portion of these have been published in the Introductions to the "Valentine Letters." They will be referred to as "E. V. Valentine Collection." Other letters are in the Koester Collection. Much valuable material is also contained in "A paper prepared for Mrs. Margaret K. Ellis, in the 85th year of her age; from old letters in the possession of her son, T. H. E[llis], 1875." This Ms., dated Richmond, Virginia, May 11, 1876, forms part of the E. V. Valentine Collection. It contains, as will be seen, copies of some highly interesting letters by John Allan, and also information concerning family matters. It is in the handwriting of Edward V. Valentine, who evidently copied or organized T. H. Ellis' manuscript, which seems to have disappeared. It will be referred to as the "T. H. Ellis Manuscript, Valentine Collection."

[2] His tombstone in Shockoe Hill Cemetery reads, "John Allan who departed this life, March 27, 1834, in the 54th year of his age."

[3] T. H. Ellis Ms., Valentine Collection. The full articles of agreement are given in Vol. 13 of the Ellis-Allan Papers, L. of C.

[4] Order Book 4, p. 469, U. S. Circuit Court, Fifth Circuit. The order is signed by Marshall, who, though Chief Justice of the Supreme Court at

John Allan married Frances Keeling Valentine, daughter of the late John Valentine, of Princess Anne County, on Saturday, February 5, 1803. *The Virginia Gazette and General Advertiser* of February 9th announced the marriage of John Allan, merchant, "to the much admired Miss Fanny Valentine, both of this city." When Poe became a member of the household, Mr. and Mrs. Allan and Ann Moore Valentine, her sister, were living over the store of Ellis and Allan, on the northeast corner of Main and Thirteenth Streets.[5]

The fact that the Allans lived over the store had no such significance as it would today, for it was not an unusual custom in Richmond at that time. The neighborhood, however, was rather on the outskirts of fashion, being southeast of Capitol Square. They did not live on Fourteenth Street near "Tobacco Alley," at this time, as usually stated in the biographies, since the houses mentioned were not built until 1817. William Galt bought the lots in 1815.[6]

The Richmond to which John Allan came as a young man was a town in transition and his position, financial and social, developed with it. Samuel Mordecai, whose reminiscences[7] are accepted by modern Richmond antiquarians, describes it as made up in these early days of wooden houses, usually of two stories. No portion of Main Street in the carriage way, and only a few sidewalks, were paved. But its situation determined its future.

Founded in 1733 by Colonel William Byrd, of Westover, Richmond, through its location at the head of the navigation of the James River, was destined to be an important commercial city. In 1779 the seat of State government was transferred from Williamsburg and in 1782 it became a city in law as well as in fact. In 1800 it had a population of 5,300, about equally divided between whites and Negroes.

It was, and is, a city of hills. On the southeast rises Church Hill,

the time, had also from time to time to preside over the lower Federal Court in Richmond.

[5] There has been some doubt concerning the exact location of this first house in which the Allans lived. T. H. Ellis, who should have known where his father did business, states definitely in his manuscript—"She (Margaret Nimmo) was staying with Mr. and Mrs. John Allan, whose residence was at the N. E. Cor. of Main and 13th Street, over the store of Ellis and Allan."

[6] Mary Wingfield Scott, "Old Richmond Houses," *Richmond News Leader* (January 23, 1941), p. 20. Complete notes on the Richmond houses associated with Edgar Poe are to be found in the Valentine Museum.

[7] *Richmond in By Gone Days, Being Reminiscences of An Old Citizen.* (Richmond, 1856).

whose name still reflects its chief attraction, the old Church of St. John. Capitol Square, in the heart of the city, overlooks the James River to the south and Shockoe Hill and Cemetery to the north. When John Allan came to Richmond, there was an ugly old guard house on the Square, and the Governor's House adjoining was a plain wooden building of two stories, "unconscious of paint... With goats grazing on his Excellency's grounds." This crudity was redeemed, however, by the Capitol Building, designed by Thomas Jefferson along the lines of the Maison Carrée at Nîmes, and built in 1792. Its Greek simplicity and dignity made it a landmark, visible for miles. Even today it is a noteworthy building, hardly improved by the later wings. Houses like that of John Marshall, dating from 1780, still remain to mark this earlier period of Richmond as not entirely lacking in stately homes.

By one of those curious movements of fashion so common to American cities, the social center of Richmond moved from Church Hill to the neighborhood of the Capitol and to Shockoe Hill. A period of building began about 1810 when an architectural order of a modified late Georgian came into favor. The typical house was a square building, usually of two lofty stories, and a basement, with Greek porticoes in front and Doric pillars in the rear. The Wickham-Valentine house, built in 1812, now the Valentine Historical Museum, is a fine example of the residence of a prominent citizen. It was during Poe's childhood that this architectural renaissance was beginning, and it is quite possible that the prevailing classical tone may have had its effect upon him in developing a love of ordered beauty. In any event, of much greater importance were the character of the people he met at John Allan's home, and the influences of that household upon him. If there were varying degrees of affection shown him by John Allan and his foster-mother, this difference would have had its influence upon a sensitive child.

John Allan belonged, naturally, to that group of English, Scottish, and Irish merchants, usually younger sons, who came over before and after the Revolution. According to Mordecai, these young men were often requested by their employers not to marry in America, so that their interests would remain undivided, and he indicates that this prohibition prevented that social intercourse between merchant and planter which the hospitable disposition of the latter would have encouraged. If this were true in general, John Allan was a decided exception. In the first place, he came not as a representative of a British house, but as a man who identified himself with his adopted country.

Later, he reversed the usual process and went to England to establish a branch there of an American firm.

Certainly the letters which make up the Ellis manuscript reveal a distinctly active social life for the Allans, not only in the so-called "merchant set" but also with the planter group of which men like Bowler Cocke was an example. The first group of these letters, from 1808 to 1812, from Margaret Keeling Nimmo, a cousin of Mrs. Allan, whom she was visiting in Richmond, tell of many entertainments in which her hosts took part. A typical postscript in a letter to her brother, James Nimmo, on February 4, 1811 reads: "If you can meet with some good oranges, I wish you would bring up a dozen or two, as Cousin (Mrs. Allan) is to have a large party next week."

Of even greater interest are the letters from John Allan himself. Those whose reading has been limited to the business letters found in the Library of Congress, will be surprised at the lightness of touch, the gallantry and even raillery to be found in his letter of February 26, 1811, to Margaret Nimmo when she has left their home in Richmond to return to Norfolk. He begins with a quotation from Scott's verse— then writes a Preface:

My text will not fail to make you smile, if not laugh, for then you will fancy you see me strutting, with extended arm, relating the fight between Snowden's knight and my hero—stop! stop! Let me see: I think I have read somewhere, that the beauty of letter writing consists generally in using exactly that kind of freedom which a person might be supposed to do to another in common conversation; at all events, I have a mighty desire to try what stuff my brain will jumble together in the experiment. Hitherto, you see, I have not said anything to much purpose, and yet I have already written full eleven lines. Gracious God! as Bowler Cocke says; and if it be really true that in eleven lines, I have said nothing, how many more must I write before I come to my purpose? Now, curse me, if I can tell. I was going to tell you a long story; but I know you don't like long stories, and so I will e'en shorten it as much as possible. Pray, how do ye do? how did you get home? and where is my cloak? All these are important inquiries to "a man of my talents" as Swift says in a letter to—Oh the Devil! I forget, God forgive me! how fast I am consuming these most valuable items both to myself and others—Time, Candle, and Patience. I mean yours,—not to say anything of the minor objects—Pen, Ink and Paper. But just let me trespass a little farther; I shall run out presently, unless it should happen with this letter, as with most concerns in life, and that is, we generally say more about nothing, than when talking of Somebody, because in the latter case our ideas are fixed by a sort of imaginary boundary line, but in the former it's like the immensity of space, the subject is really inexhaustible, as you will see most amply illustrated by the preceding example! Now only consider, how I began, what I began about, how I have continued, and fancy where I should end if I did not here make a full (stop)

The Letter.

I really thought it probable we might have had a few lines from you on arriving safe at home, just to let us know the Gulf of Hampton Roads spared you for creating so many aching ♡'s in Richmond. Fitz James bears his misfortunes nobly: he feels, whilst he struggles—I hope successfully; Rhoderic is the same as ever; and Doctor Biscuit is almost restored to his senses. In fact, we begin to move on regularly and systematically as usual. Fitz spends the greatest part of his leisure hours with the family. Poor Frances has really been quite ill, and though by no means well now, yet she has much recovered. Nancy sticks to the old thing, Caroline has been unwell, but has recovered. So that we consider ourselves nearly fit for a frolic, as Davie says. I dreamt I heard there was a Lieutenant in your head, but I dreamt wrong. Peter has not been in our doors since you went away. Write Fanny and tell her all the news of Norfolk. How goes the report about you there? They will have you engaged, I doubt not. I have no more news at this time; so God bless you and all the family.

Your sincere Friend

But the most significant revelation comes in a letter from Allan to James Nimmo, dated October 14, 1814:

I have great pleasure in informing you of the return of my family to our own fireside, after a pleasant trip to the mountains, not, as you well know, from choice, but compulsion. Frances has caught a bad cold, but is not confined by it. Nancy has seen one of the wonders of the world—the Blue Ridge Mountains; she experienced much satisfaction in contemplating these prodigious works of nature, whose cloudcapped summits appear to aspire to the very heavens. To the stranger, their first appearance is awfully grand and interesting; but it by no means equals the view from their summit; which is extensive, various, and delightful. Mrs. Nimmo will be able to give you a pretty good account of the upper country for, as I am informed, she wanted to know everything by inquiring about all that she saw.... Margaret and your grandson are hearty; she is beginning to recover her flesh. Thomas H. Ellis is a wonderful fellow; I can't distinctly comprehend him yet, but in a short time I have no doubt he will be an equal match for little Margaret. I suspect he will be a perfect wonder, and I may have occasion in six or seven months more to relate such exploits of his performance, that you will be obliged to come up here (with Mrs. Nimmo, who I have no doubt was much pleased with Richmond,) to witness them.

I hope you have perfectly recovered your health, and see things with a more cheerful eye. Philosophy you must invite, which, aided by a hearty pinch of snuff, will work wonders. Try the experiment—for this is the age of experiments, both public and private. It's true, publickly, I cannot say much in their favour, privately, though not very fully informed, yet I know some folks who have learned to do without many comforts and conveniences which they once thought indispensable to their existence, (I leave enjoyment out of the question,); many others have found out that they can live on bacon (middling too) and not starve, can lay on straw (if to be had) in place of a feather bed and do pretty well. Now, my dear Sir, these things called privations—starvations—taxations—and, lastly, vexations, show the very age and figure of the times—their form and pressure, as Shakespeare says,—and he was a tolerable judge. Gods! what would I not give, if I had his talent for writing! and what use would I not make of the raw material at my command!

John Allan had ambitions then to write creatively! He was not, as is pictured, a man whose only interest lay in a ledger. Should not this dream, cherished but not followed, have made him sympathize with Poe? Or did it make him harder in his dealing with one who was bent on realizing an ambition to which John Allan knew he could never attain?

That John Allan was fond of children is revealed in a letter from Rosanna Dixon, a daughter of John Dixon, who had married a half sister of Mrs. John Allan. The letter also gives interesting information concerning Rosalie Poe:

Richmond,
September 6th, 1812

Dear Uncle, I received your affectionate letter from the Sweet Springs, and it gave me pleasure to find that you and Aunt Fanny were both pleased with my writing; indeed I will endeavour to improve, and follow the good advice you gave me in your letter. I now go to school to Mr. Taylor, who has lately come from Norfolk; I like him very much, altho' he is very strict. I am very sorry to inform you that poor little Rosalie is not expected to live, altho' she is much better now than she has been for two weeks past; she was christened on Thursday last [September 3, 1812] and had Mackenzie added to her name.—Uncle Richard was very much disappointed at not receiving a letter from you; he wrote to you at the Sulphur Springs and told you a great deal of news. Aunt Nancy is spending a week at Uncle Lambert's she sends her love to you and Aunt Allan. Tell Edgar, Tib is very well, also the Bird and Dog.—Commodore Rogers has arrived in Boston with four Prizes.—Uncle, Aunt, Caroline and the Doctor and myself send their love to you and Aunt Fanny. Kiss Edgar for me.—

T. H. Ellis adds a footnote which partly explains the problem of Rosalie's support:

Rosalie Mackenzie Poe, the sister of Edgar Allan Poe; who was adopted by Mr. William Mackenzie at the same time that Edgar was adopted by Mr. Allan, to wit, on the death of their mother, whose obituary appears in the Richmond *Enquirer* of the 10th of December 1811. Mr. Gallego by his will leaves to Mr. Mackenzie "for the benefit of Rosalie Poe (the orphan child that he and his good wife have taken charge of) $2,000." She died last year [1874] at the charitable "Home" founded by Mr. William W. Corcoran in Washington.

This letter of Rosanna Dixon does away with the statement made by Mrs. Weiss, that Edgar and Rosalie Poe were baptized on the same day, since the letter was sent to Staunton, Virginia, where Edgar was visiting with his foster-parents.

Of Frances Valentine Allan we know comparatively little. Her portrait by Sully reveals her as a woman with some claims to beauty. She was evidently fond of amusement, and ambitious to take a prominent part in Richmond social life. How competent she was to bring up a boy like Edgar Poe is an open question. One of the rare letters which have been preserved indicates a nervous temperament, easily disturbed and apprehensive. It was written from Staunton, Virginia:

sunday Septr 11th [1814]

My Dear husband

I received your kinde epistle of the 6th and was pleased to heare my dear friends were well also that our City is safe from the enemy   I trust in god it may continue so—you refered me to the paper for news. I have not recived them yet   Im anxious to heare a true statement of the conduct of the enemy in alexandria— thire are various reports we are at a lose to know what to believe. I am at present with uncle Ned—I came out last evening and intend returning to morrow   I have declined going to the springs

you know my reason   judge Coalter has been so polite as to call
on me and invite us to dine with him we accepted the invitasion
and spent a very agreable day it is probable this will go by him
do my Love write by every opportunity and let me know when
you will be able to come up I shall endevour to take you advices
as to my fears you see how badly my trembling hands perform
give my love to all my friends and accept the same from
yours affectionnately

FRANCES K. ALLAN

P S   I have just returned and thire is a report that the British have
landed at York   I shall be very unhappy until I know the trueth [8]

It will be best before attempting any final judgment upon the relations of Edgar Poe and his foster-parents to let the actors in the domestic drama speak for themselves.

Edgar Poe seems to have been accepted quickly into the household.
On January 7, 1812, John Allan paid Hobday and Seaton a bill of
$8.00 for "1 crib," evidently for the little boy.[9] It seems to be the first
recorded expense John Allan incurred for him. On May 14, 1813, John
Allan writes to Charles Ellis that "Edgar has caught the whooping
cough. Frances has a swelled face." [10] By May 18th they "are getting
better." On July 26th Edward Valentine, Jr., tells John Allan, "I am
happy to hear that Edgar has recovered from an attack of the
meazels." [11]

Amid the many details of business, there come at times sentences
which throw light on Allan's character. On June 2, 1813, in connection
with the blockade of American shipping, he remarks to Charles Ellis,
"I am not one of those much addicted to suffer by unavailing regrets." [12] In a long letter from Charles Ellis to Allan on August 10,
1813, telling of his engagement to Margaret Nimmo, Ellis, who writes
with an ardor and a delicacy of feeling which he assumes that John
Allan will appreciate, pays a tribute to the married life of his friend.
"You, I well know, long ago possessed something which I would have
given worlds to have known." [13]

[8] Ellis-Allan Papers, L. of C., Vol. 137.
[9] Ellis-Allan Papers, L. of C., Vol. 115. Hobday and Seaton were "chair
makers" according to the Richmond Directory of 1819, with stores on 13th
Street, near E or Main Street.
[10] Ellis-Allan Papers, L. of C., Vol. 127.
[11] Ellis-Allan Papers, L. of C., Vol. 129.
[12] Ellis-Allan Papers, L. of C., Vol. 128.
[13] Ellis-Allan Papers, L. of C., Vol. 130.

There are frequent bills to be found among the papers for the services of tailors "for cuting [sic] a suit for Edgar," and on January 15, 1815, among other items, James Hetherton charges Allan with $5.00 for "making a suit of Cloaths for son."[14] There can be little doubt that Edgar was looked upon by others, if not by John Allan, as his adopted son. Thomas H. Ellis, both in his manuscript in the Valentine Museum and in a letter published in the *Richmond Standard,* May 7, 1881, speaks of Poe as "the adopted son" of John Allan.

Poe's early schooling has been colored by romantic stories, based on insecure tradition. The first actual document I have found reads:

Mr. John Allen [sic]
To Clotilda Fisher, Dr.

1814. Jan[ry] the 20th To 1 quarters Tuition of
Edgar A. Poe $4.00
Received Payment
Clotilda Fisher.[15]

Who Clotilda Fisher was, I have been unable to discover. Her name does not appear in the earliest Richmond Directory of 1819—or in newspaper advertisements. She was probably the mistress of a "dame's school."

The only other school of which we may be certain, at this time, was kept by William Ewing, probably on Seventh Street between Franklin and Main Streets. In a letter sent to John Allan in London on November 27, 1817, Ewing says, "I trust Edgar continues to be well and to like his School as much as he used to do when he was in Richmond. He is a charming boy and it will give me great pleasure to hear how he is, and where you have sent him to school, and also what he is reading. ... Let me now only beg of you to remember me respectfully to your lady Mrs. Allan and her sister, who I hope are well, and also do not forget to mention me to their august attendant Edgar."[16]

It is a matter of regret that John Allan did not answer Ewing's question concerning Poe's reading. He did, however, on March 21, 1818, reply, "Accept my thanks for the solicitude you have so kindly expressed about Edgar and the family. Edgar is a fine Boy and I have no reason to complain of his progress."[17] The rest of John Allan's reply

[14] Ellis-Allan Papers, L. of C., Vol. 139. See other items in Vol. 141.
[15] Ellis-Allan Papers, L. of C., Vol. 133.
[16] Ellis-Allan Papers, L. of C., Poe Volume.
[17] Ellis-Allan Papers, L. of C., Poe Volume.

was brief and was mainly concerned with the substance of Ewing's letter, which was a request to pay the balance of the tuition fees of a boy, Edward Collier, from March 15, 1815, to March 14, 1818, at $42 per annum. Allan had evidently paid only one year's bill, and while he arranges for the payment of the remainder he quite definitely declines to provide any more education for the Collier boy. In fact, he wrote so hastily that he misspelled Ewing's name.[18]

There are other bills for Collier's education,[19] one to a Daniel Ford, on February 2, 1814, for one term, five dollars, and another, dated vaguely "Jan. 1," but certainly earlier, from a William Richardson for the same amount.[20] Since Ewing made his demand at the request of Mrs. Collier, it seems reasonable to assume, especially in the light of later acknowledgments of John Allan concerning the Wills twins, that Edward Collier was John Allan's son. Since Collier was going to a man's school while Poe was attending the dame's school of Clotilda Fisher, it is clear that Edward Collier was older than Edgar Poe, and therefore that John Allan's infidelities began before the latter was made a part of his household. The date of the Fisher receipt shows that Poe could hardly have been at William Ewing's school more than a year at the utmost, and that it is extremely unlikely that he attended any other school.

Why John Allan did not legally adopt Edgar Poe has been made the subject of much speculation. It could hardly have been due to a doubt concerning the possible demand from General David Poe, to give up his grandson, for a letter from Eliza Poe, David's daughter, makes clear both her interest in Edgar and her gratitude to Mrs. Allan:

Baltimore,
February 8th, 1813.

Tis the Aunt of Edgar that addresses Mrs. Allen [sic] for the second time, impressed with the idea that A letter if received could not remain unacknowledged so long as from the month of

[18] The signature of Ewing's letter is not very legible, and Allan's reply is clearly to "Mr. William Ervin," which has caused one biographer, at least, to embalm his error. But the advertisements in Richmond newspapers prove clearly that William Ewing is the correct name. See the *Virginia Patriot* for February 21, 1816, in which Ewing gives notice of the removal of his school "from Mr. McKechnies, to a brick tenement at the intersection of 8th with H St."

[19] Ellis-Allan Papers, L. of C., Vol. 134.

[20] Ellis-Allan Papers, L. of C., Poe Volume.

July; she is induced to write again in order to inquire in her family's as well as in her own name after the health of the Child of her Brother, as well as that of his adopted Parents. I cannot suppose my dear Mrs. Allen that A heart possessed of such original humanity as your's must without doubt be, could so long keep in suspence, the anxious inquiries made through the medium of my letter by the Grand Parents of the Orphan of an unfortunate son, surely e're this allowing that you did not wish to commence A correspondence with one who is utterly unknown to you had you received it. Mr. Allen would have written to my Father or Brother if it had been only to let them know how he was, but I am confident you never received it, for two reasons, the first is that not having the pleasure of knowing your christian name I merely addresed it to Mrs. Allen of Richmond, the second is as near as I can recollect you were about the time I wrote to you at the springs where Mr. Douglas saw you, permit me my dear madam to thank you for your kindness to the little Edgar—he is truly the Child of fortune to be placed under the fostering care of the amiable Mr. and Mrs. Allen, Oh how few meet with such A lot—the Almighty Father of the Universe grant that he may never abuse the kindness he has received and *that* from those who were not bound by any ties except those that the feeling and humane heart dictates—I fear that I have too long intruded on your patience, will you if so have the goodness to forgive me—and dare I venture to flatter myself with the hope that this will be received with any degree of pleasure or that you will gratify me so much as to answer it—give my love to the dear little Edgar and tell him tis his Aunt Eliza who writes this to you. my mother and family desire to be affectionately remembered to Mr. Allen and yourself —Henry frequently speaks of his little Brother and expresses A great desire to see him, tell him he sends his very best love to him and is greatly pleased to hear that he is so good as also so pretty A Boy as Mr. Douglas represented him to be—I feel as if I were wrighting to A sister and can scarcely even at the risk of your displeasure prevail on myself to lay aside my pen—with the hope of your indulgence in pardoning my temerity I remain my Dear Mrs. Allen yours with the greatest respect

ELIZA POE

Mrs. Allen the kind Benefactress
    of the infant Orphan Edgar, Allen, Poe.[21]

It may have been Allan's prejudice against the child of strolling players, or it may have been his doubt as to the feeling of his uncle,

[21] Ellis-Allan Papers, L. of C., Poe Volume.

JOHN ALLAN, POE'S FOSTER-FATHER
Courtesy of the Poe Shrine, Richmond, and of the *Century Magazine*.

FRANCES VALENTINE ALLAN, POE'S FOSTER-MOTHER
From an oil painting by Thomas Sully. Courtesy of the Valentine Museum of Richmond.

William Galt, which made him hesitate to adopt Edgar Poe. There were also the claims of his kindred in Scotland.

William Allan, John's father, a seafaring man who had married a sister of William Galt, was the father also of Nancy—who married Allan Fowlds—Mrs. Jane Johnston, Mrs. Elizabeth Miller, and Miss Mary Allan. Their letters to John Allan, both before and after his visit to Great Britain, show clearly that they had that dependent attitude toward him so characteristic of sisters toward a brother who is or will be prosperous, and who has the ear of their uncle, the ultimate source of wealth. In one of these letters, from Jane Johnston, on February 19, 1814,[22] after expressing her joy that her marriage had been approved by her uncle and her brother, she speaks of "Mrs. Allan's family, on the Halfway," and sends their greetings. They are referred to in other letters and it may be that Mrs. John Allan's family were also originally Scottish, or it may simply be a reference to another one of John Allan's clan.

There is no evidence that Allan visited Great Britain for family reasons. He had been to Lisbon in 1811 on business, but had not taken the opportunity to see his family. It was rather his sense of growing opportunities for trade that animated him. The earlier letters [23] indicate that he had thought of establishing a branch house in London in 1812, but the embargo put an end to this project. The business of Ellis and Allan was expanding. There is a statement, not dated, but placed among the papers in Volume 138, which includes November and December, 1814, which shows that the firm had assets of $223,133 and liabilities of $182,494. They were being recognized as solid citizens by the planters. James Penn, of New London, Caroline County, Virginia, who owed them £1,470, writes on February 7, 1814, that he would soon be with them and "in all spirit of friendship accede to those terms proposed." [24] During the war John Allan offered his services to General Cocke, but warns him that he "is not a military man." Charles Ellis, however, volunteered as a private in the Nineteenth Regiment of Richmond City.

In 1812 there began what Mordecai calls the "Flush Times in Richmond." Speculation was rife, and John Allan was caught with its spirit. Consequently, preparations were made in the spring of 1815 for the invasion of England, including the making by Hetherton of

[22] Ellis-Allan Papers, L. of C., Vol. 134.
[23] See letter from Margaret Nimmo to James Nimmo, T. H. Ellis Manuscript, Valentine Collection, April 10, 1812.
[24] Ellis-Allan Papers, L. of C., Vol. 134.

"a great coat for son." Allan writes to Ellis on June 22, 1815, from Norfolk, to sell Scipio, one of his slaves, for $600, and to hire out others at $50 a year, and continues:

> The Lothair & Steam Boat went off together today at 10 AM, the Boat moved off handsomely and with the tide, think she must have reached the Halfway House in an hour or a little better—to-morrow at 9 A. M will all go down to the Road to take our departure. I shall write by the Pilot Boat we have every thing comfortable. Frances & Nancey evince much fortitude; it has been a severe trial to them, their Spirit is good, Ned cared but little about it, poor fellow.

In a postscript he adds:

> Friday, June 23d 1/2 P. 3 P. M. off the Horse Shoe. Inclosed you have $8.63 which to my Credit—we are trying to Beat out, I hope to succeed. Frances & Nancy rather qualmish Edgar and myself well.[25]

Edgar Poe's first Richmond period was over.

[25] Ellis-Allan Papers, L. of C., Poe Volume.

CHAPTER III

The School Days in England

Poe is unique among the great American writers of his generation in having spent a portion of his childhood in England. This period of his life is important because for the first time we are able to trace a definite influence in his later fiction from the scenes in which he moved and thought and felt. The first essential, of course, before any analysis of the influences of his early schooling can be made, is to dispel at least one of the myths which tradition and the industry of his previous biographers have created. Fortunately, I have been able, through certain letters of John Allan to his Scottish relatives, and their replies, which had remained unpublished in the Valentine Museum, to trace more clearly the movements of Poe during the first year of his stay in Britain. As before, it is best to let these letters, combined with those in the Library of Congress, tell their own story.

On July 29, 1815, John Allan wrote to his partner in Richmond, "I am now on English ground after an absence of more than 20 years. After a passage of 34 days all well—Frances and Nancey were very sick but are now perfectly Hearty. Edgar was a little sick but soon recovered.... We got here yesterday at 5 P. M. I took our abode at Mr. Lillymans Hotel today." [1]

Edgar Poe's first experience of travel was evidently made very unpleasant by the penurious attitude of the Captain, and John Allan wrote to the owners in Norfolk, protesting that he had to sleep on the floor and "the Females of my Family were denied the privileges of Fire to broil a slice of Bacon." They evidently provided their own stores, and wood was short.[2] Allan was still at Liverpool on August 6th when he writes to R. F. Gwathmey, who was shipping guns to America, and Gwathmey writes to Allan at Kilmarnock in Scotland in care of his brother-in-law, Allan Fowlds, on August 11th.[3]

The family of four seem to have gone first, however, to Irvine,

[1] Ellis-Allan Papers, L. of C., Vol. 144.
[2] Ellis-Allan Papers, L. of C., Vol. 144.
[3] Ellis-Allan Papers, L. of C., Vol. 144.

where Allan's sisters, Mary and Jane, were living, but their stay must have been brief. For on August 22nd Allan writes to Ellis from Kilmarnock.[4] If Poe went to school at Irvine, as has been asserted, it could have been at this time little more than a few days. Allan writes Ellis from Glasgow on August 24th,[5] and again on September 11th,[6] from Kilmarnock. He probably went on business visits and the family remained at Kilmarnock as headquarters. It is naturally hard to say what influence this visit to Scotland had upon Poe. The poem *To the Lake* may have been inspired by memories of Scottish scenery, and there were, of course, romantic stories to hear. For example, there is said to have been a "Lady's walk" on which the wraith of Lord Kilmarnock, executed for participation in the Stuart uprising of 1745, took occasional strolls. But this form of influence is, of course, very tenuous.

From Greenock, on September 21st, Allan writes to Ellis that he will be in Glasgow the same day, then gives messages which indicate that Mrs. Allan was much impressed by the Scottish visit and reveal a very human and paternal relationship between John Allan and Poe. "Thomas" is, of course, Thomas H. Ellis, Charles Ellis's little son: "Frances says she would like the Land o' cakes better if it was warmer and less rain. She bid me say she will write Margaret as soon as she is settled but at present she is so bewildered with wonder that she cannot write. Her best Love to Margaret and a thousand kisses to Thomas. Nancy says give my love to them all—Edgar says Pa say something for me say I was not afraid coming across the Sea. Kiss Thos. for him. We all write in best Love to my uncle & our old friends. . . . Edgars Love to Rosa and Mrs. Mackenzie."[7]

Poe had an opportunity to see some of the historic spots in Scotland, for Allan's letter to Ellis from London on October 10th tells him, "I arrived here on the evening of the 7th from Kilmarnock by way of Greenock, Glasgow, Edinburg, New Castle, Sheffield." Then after expressing his dissatisfaction with the commercial situation, he continues, "Frances has been confined to her room with a bad cold—sore throat—the rest of us are well but cursedly dissatisfied."[8] Though Allan does not mention Edgar here, a letter from Allan Fowlds to

[4] Ellis-Allan Papers, L. of C., Vol. 145.
[5] Ellis-Allan Papers, L. of C., Vol. 145.
[6] Ellis-Allan Papers, L. of C., Vol. 146.
[7] Ellis-Allan Papers, L. of C., Poe Volume.
[8] Ellis-Allan Papers, L. of C., Vol. 147.

John Allan from Kilmarnock on October 24th [9] shows that Poe was with his foster-parents in London. On October 30th Allan gives Ellis a lively picture of the household at Southampton Row: "by a snug fire in a nice little sitting parlour in No. 47 Southampton Row, Russel [sic] Square where I have procured Lodgings for the present with Frances and Nancy Sewing and Edgar reading a little Story Book. I feel quite in a comfortable mood for writing. I have no acquaintances that call upon me and none whom as yet I call on. 6 Guineas a week furnished lodgings is what I have agreed to for 6 months until I can find a more convenient and cheaper situation. I have no compting Room yet of course, I cannot copy the Letters which I am obliged to write—every thing is high it alarms Frances she has become a complete economist and has a most lively appetite. I begin to think London will agree with her." [10]

Allan's letters continue to tell of Mrs. Allan's illness, and it was probably not a happy time for anyone. There is a tradition [11] that Edgar was sent back to Irvine to the Grammar School late in 1815, but it rests on very slim evidence. On November 11th John Allan's niece, Mary Fowlds, writes from Kilmarnock, and sends her love to "little Edgar" in London.[12] John Allan in a letter to Charles Ellis on November 15th, says, "Glad to hear my little Thomas is getting better and none more delighted than Edgar." [13] Again on November 21st, John Allan, writing to William Holden, speaks of Mrs. Allan as almost recovered, adding "and all the rest of us are well." [14] If Edgar had not been there with them, Allan would have simply said, "Miss Valentine." From Kilmarnock, on January 7, 1816, Allan Fowlds in writing to Allan in London, and rebuking him for his "long silence," sends regards to Edgar.[15] Not only do these letters leave insufficient time for a term at school in Irvine, but if all the details which some recent biographers have accepted or imagined concerning Poe's insubordina-

---

[9] E. V. Valentine Collection, Richmond.

[10] Ellis-Allan Papers, L. of C., Vol. 147.

[11] The foundation of this account is J. H. Whitty's interpretation of Major John Allan Galt's reminiscences of his father, James Galt, who came from Scotland to Richmond later. The article by Lewis Chase on "Poe's Playmates in Kilmarnock," *Athenaeum*, 4611 (November, 1916), 554, containing the statement of John Haggo concerning the memories of the late James Anderson, who knew Poe, refers clearly to the first visit.

[12] E. V. Valentine Collection.

[13] Ellis-Allan Papers, L. of C., Vol. 148.

[14] E. V. Valentine Collection.

[15] E. V. Valentine Collection.

tion at being sent back to Scotland had any basis, Allan Fowlds would certainly have spoken of Edgar's trip if it had occurred. That none of the letters mention it is final negative proof which may dissolve another myth concerning Poe's British stay. In fact, the whole Scottish episode has been overemphasized. If Mr. Whitty or his adaptors had seen all the unpublished letters in the Valentine Museum, they would have realized that the one month of December, 1815, was hardly sufficient for the establishment of so much speculation.

Allan evidently had made definite plans for his London branch of "Allan and Ellis," with its inversion of the firm's name. On November 20, 1815, he wrote to Ellis, "I told you I should stay here three years—this I gave you to understand was to remove Mrs. Allan's reluctance. You may count upon five years without an accident—the expense of making an establishment is too heavy for a shorter period. ... I would not stay longer on any account." [16]

From the home correspondence of the women comes continued complaint. In a letter from Margaret Ellis in Richmond to James Nimmo, January 19, 1816, occurs the sentence, "We had a letter from Nancy Valentine a few days ago; she says they are all miserably dissatisfied with London." [17] March in London did not help matters apparently, for Frances Allan did not "enjoy good health," but when Edgar is mentioned, as in the letter of March 27th, he is always well.[18] Allan writes Ellis in May, 1816, "If get through the year I hope I shall not see such another." [19] He had evidently, however, his private charities, for there is a note from a widow named Anne Bracken thanking him for his benevolence.[20]

Edgar's playmates in Richmond had not forgotten him. A little girl, C. W. Poitiaux, sends love to Edgar, on May 18, 1816. "Tell him I want to see him very much. ... Tell him Josephine and all the children want to see him very much." [21] Sometimes the usual remembrances from John Allan to his friends are a bit more definite. On August 31, 1816, we learn that "Nancy weighs 146, Frances 104, myself 157 of good hard flesh—Edgar thin as a razor." [22] He is mentioned as being with them in September and October, also.

[16] Ellis-Allan Papers, L. of C., Vol. 148.
[17] T. H. Ellis Ms., Valentine Collection.
[18] E. V. Valentine Collection.
[19] Ellis-Allan Papers, L. of C., Vol. 158.
[20] Ellis-Allan Papers, L. of C., Vol. 158.
[21] Ellis-Allan Papers, L. of C., Vol. 158.
[22] Ellis-Allan Letter Books, 1815-1817, L. of C.

The discouraging commercial conditions evidently did not keep Allan from attending to Edgar's education. In London he was sent first to a boarding school, kept by the Misses Dubourg, at 146 Sloane Street in Chelsea. The first bill for tuition, dated July 6, 1816, shows not only that he was granted the privilege of a "separate bed," but also proves that he was studying Geography, Spelling, and History. It is noteworthy, also, that he is known as "Master Allan," which surely indicates that John Allan looked upon him at that time as a son.

Masr. Allan's School Acct. to Midsr. 1816.

Board & Tuition ¼ year	7	17	6
Separate Bed	1	1	0
Washing	0	10	6
Seat in Church	0	3	0
Teachers & Servants	0	5	0
Writing	0	15	0
Do. Entrance	0	10	6
Copy Book, Pens &c.	0	3	0
Medicine, School Expences	0	5	0
Repairing Linen, shoe-strings &c. . . .	0	3	0
Mavor's Spelling	0	2	0
Fresnoy's Geography	0	2	0
Prayer Book	0	3	0
Church Catechism explained	0	0	9
Catechism of Hist. of England . . .	0	0	9
	£12	2	0 [23]

The Cash Books of the firm show that the bill was paid promptly, the receipt being signed by George Dubourg, a brother of the Misses Dubourg and a clerk in the employ of Allan and Ellis, at 18 Basinghall Street. Allan is charged with "£23 16 sh. for Miss Dubourg's a/c for Edgar" on December 28, 1816. On August 28, 1817, he is charged with £24 16 s. "for Edgar's School," and while the name Dubourg is not given, the similar amount indicates that he was still there.[24]

That the school made some impression we may be sure, for Poe used the name of "Pauline Dubourg" years afterward as a laundress and one of the witnesses in the story of "The Murders in the Rue Morgue."

That Edgar was not completely separated from the family is shown

[23] Cash Books, 1815-1817, L. of C.
[24] The late Killis Campbell first discovered these accounts, which I have checked with the Cash Books for 1815-1817 in the Library of Congress. See *The Dial*, 60 (February 17, 1916), 143, for Campbell's account.

by his inclusion in messages by Allan to John Galt on January 30, 1817,[25] and to James Fisher on February 3rd.[26] In "a sketch of a letter intended for Mrs. Galt," dated May 6, 1817, however, Allan states that "Edgar is at school." [27] This may indicate intermittent attendance, return at weekends, or simply holidays.[28] This letter apparently was not sent, but it is illuminating in its revelation of the relations of John Allan and his family in Scotland. He addresses his sister as "Dear Madam," denies that he is mean, and resents her letter which had evidently stated that he begrudged "the trifle they would have consumed during their stay." [29] Had a proposed visit of his sister, Elizabeth, to London been avoided by John Allan? His resentment was probably justified, for a letter from Allan Fowlds on May 27, 1817, thanks him and Mrs. Allan for a box of clothes sent to the young ladies of his family. Fowlds writes also on July 28, 1817,[30] about the passage of young William Galt, who is departing for Richmond. The other branches of the family did not intend to leave the rich uncle entirely to John Allan's influence.

There is a constant temptation to quote from John Allan's correspondence concerning the state of England at that time, and indeed it had its definite bearing upon his own circumstance. The following passage from a letter to General John H. Cocke paints a vivid picture of a "depression" of 1817—"you can have no idea of the distresses of this country since the termination of that long Contest which in its continuance had drenched Europe with Blood, every nation is endeavouring by salutary restrictions & in many cases interdictions to encourage their own manufactories which operates severely on this great Manufacturing Kingdom . . . thousands that depended upon this work for support are thrown out of employ or are working for wages barely sufficient to keep soul & body together. Taxes heavy, debt large, People discontented & desperate, Revenue falling off & scarcely

[25] E. V. Valentine Collection.
[26] E. V. Valentine Collection.
[27] E. V. Valentine Collection.
[28] Ingram, I, 12, states on authority of Mrs. Clemm via Neilson Poe that Edgar came home on Fridays, returning to the school on Mondays. Ingram believed this statement to refer to Bransby's School, but it is more likely to refer to the Dubourg School, which was nearer to 47 Southampton Row.
[29] E. V. Valentine Collection. The letter, in John Allan's hand, is not signed. It is evidently a draft of a letter which was not sent, or, possibly, a copy of one really forwarded.
[30] E. V. Valentine Collection.

a hope left of relieving the one or providing for the other. The Prince's Carriage was attacked with stones...." [31]

There is an indication in Allan's letters to Ellis that they should take account of stock. On January 15, 1817, he speaks of their property being worth $140,000, including Elkwood. There was some trouble at Richmond which is not made clear. [32]

Mrs. Allan continued unwell, and her husband took her to Cheltenham for the waters. Edgar was left at the school, for in a letter to George Dubourg, dated August 6, 1817, John Allan adds in a postscript, "Mrs. Allan desires her love to Edgar, she has derived great benefit from the use of the waters." [33] A few days later Allan writes, "Enclosed is a letter for Edgar who if he writes at all, must direct his Mama as I do not think she will return with me." [34] Mrs. Allan desired to give the waters a longer trial. The implication is clear that Edgar had been in the habit of addressing his letters to his foster-father, otherwise there would have been no occasion for John Allan to mention the matter.

It must be laid to Allan's credit that in this gloomy time he sent Edgar to a better and more expensive school. This Manor House School was conducted by the Reverend John Bransby at Stoke Newington, then in the country, but near London. The earliest information comes from a student of the Manor House School at a later time. [35] According to Mr. Hunter, Poe profited by a friendly atmosphere, then he added: "when he left it he was able to speak the French language, construe any easy Latin author, and was far better acquainted with history and literature than many boys of a more advanced age who had had greater advantages than he had had. I spoke to Dr. Bransby about him two or three times during my school days, having then, as now, a deep admiration for his poems, a copy of which I had received as a prize for an effort in English verse. Dr. Bransby seemed rather to shun the topic, I suppose from some feelings with regard to his name being used distastefully in the story of 'William Wilson.' In answer to my questions on one occasion, he said, 'Edgar Allan' (the name Poe was known by at school) 'was a quick and clever boy and would have been a very good boy if he had not been spoilt by his parents,' meaning the Allans; 'but they spoilt him, and allowed him an extravagant amount of pocket-money, which enabled him to get into all manner of mischief—still I liked the boy—poor fellow, his parents spoilt him!' At another time he said, 'Allan was intelligent, wayward, and wilful.' This was about all that I could ever learn from him with regard to his former pupil."

The Reverend John Bransby was born in 1784, and was educated at St. Johns College in Cambridge, where he received an M. A. in July, 1808. He was married in 1805. He seems to have begun his career in Stoke Newington in 1806, and was Lecturer of the Parish from October 27, 1814, until July 13, 1825. He was an active student of botany and a member of the Horticultural Society of Stoke Newington. He was fond of field sports, and, as the most definite account of his life indicates,[36] he had the reputation of being a good classical scholar, possessing also a fund of miscellaneous information. It is quite within the bounds of possibility that Edgar Poe, noticing how effective "miscellaneous information" may be when given offhand, took Mr. Bransby as his model later in the acquiring of all kinds of valuable odds and ends of literary and scientific knowledge.

By combining the charges recorded in the office-books of the firm, now in the Library of Congress, with actual bills in the Valentine Museum, we find a list of payments for tuition at the Manor House School as follows:

July 24, 1818	£16	14s	3d
Xmas, 1818	33	2	11
(paid Jan. 26, 1819)			
Jan. 15, 1819	69	16	11
Feb. 1, 1820	70	9	6
May 26, 1820	35	4	10

The irregular amounts and the two bills in January, 1819, indicate that some of these payments were made on account. There are, also, smaller bills, for medical care due to an injury to Edgar's hand, and for frequent mending of his shoes. Altogether, John Allan seems to have spent over £230 for the boy's education from July, 1818, to May, 1820. Considering the comparative purchasing power of money then and now, it would represent today an expenditure of about $1000 a year.[37] The only detailed bill is that sent at Christmas, 1818:

[36] For the facts concerning John Bransby, see Lewis Chase, "John Bransby, Poe's School Master," *Athenaeum*, 4,605 (May, 1916), 221-222.

[37] There is a gap between the last payment for Dubourg's School in August, 1817, and the first for Bransby's in July, 1818, so that the estimate

Manor House School
Stoke Newington, Xmas, 1818.

J. Allan Esqr
  for Masr Allan
    To the Revd John Bransby

	L	S	D
Board & Education	23.	12.	6.
Washing £1:11:6 Single Bed £2:2:0	3	13	6
Allowance £0:5:0 Pew & Char^y Sermon £0:3:6	—	8	6
Books, Stationary &c.	—	14	11
French	—	—	—
Dancing £2:2:0 Drawing £— Music £—	2	2	—
Shoemaker £1:15:6 Taylor £— Hairdresser £0:2:0	1	17	6
Sundries	—	1	—
Apothecary	0	13	0

Please to Pay Messrs. Sikes Snaith &
  Co. Mansion House St £33.   2.   11
The vacation will terminate Jany. 25th 1819.

The significant items are those which prove that Poe was taught dancing, but not music and drawing, at least during that term; that he had a rather small allowance, which does not agree with Mr. Bransby's remarks about his being spoiled by his parents, and that there is no charge for French, which implies that he did not take it, at least at that time. Unfortunately, the bill gives no indication of his actual studies.

The Manor House School was not the manorial building usually given in the biographies, but a more modest structure, here reproduced for the first time, from an old print.[38] The building which is

is not excessive. Probably at least one bill has been lost. I have had to depend on Killis Campbell for the charges derived from the "office books" in the Library of Congress as given by him in *The Sewanee Review* article, p. 206. A diligent search among the office books fails to find these items. However, since Dr. Campbell is one of the Poe scholars on whose accuracy one may depend, the figures may be taken as correct. The bills from the Valentine Collection are contained in an envelope in the possession of Mr. Granville G. Valentine, and have been checked. They have been published in the Valentine Letters, pp. 319-329.

[38] Dr. Gegenheimer secured in 1938 from Mr. Charles Blackmore, antiquarian in Stoke Newington, a photograph made while the old building was

usually reproduced stood opposite and was known as "The Laurels."

The Manor House School is of singular interest. In his story of "William Wilson" Poe described in terms of fiction not only the place, but also its master, to whom he gave his right name of Bransby, with the addition of a "Doctor" to which the reverend gentleman seems not to be entitled. Since our interest in the school lies entirely in Poe's connection with it, William Wilson's own words are better than any paraphrase:

> My earliest recollections of a school-life are connected with a large, rambling, cottage-built, and somewhat decayed building in a misty-looking village of England, where were a vast number of gigantic and gnarled trees, and where all the houses were excessively ancient and inordinately tall. In truth, it was a dream-like and spirit-soothing place, that venerable old town. At this moment, in fancy, I feel the refreshing chilliness of its deeply-shadowed avenues, inhale the fragrance of its thousand shrubberies, and thrill anew with undefinable delight, at the deep, hollow note of the church-bell, breaking each hour, with sullen and sudden roar, upon the stillness of the dusky atmosphere in which the old, fretted, Gothic steeple lay imbedded and asleep.
>
> It gives me, perhaps, as much of pleasure as I can now in any manner experience, to dwell upon minute recollections of the school and its concerns. Steeped in misery as I am—misery, alas! only too real—I shall be pardoned for seeking relief, however slight and temporary, in the weakness of a few rambling details. These, moreover, utterly trivial, and even ridiculous in themselves, assume, to my fancy, adventitious importance as connected with a period and a locality, when and where I recognise the first ambiguous monitions of the destiny which afterwards so fully overshadowed me. Let me then remember.
>
> The house, I have said, was old, irregular, and cottage-built. The grounds were extensive, and an enormously high and solid brick wall, topped with a bed of mortar and broken glass, encompassed the whole. This prison-like rampart formed the limit of our domain; beyond it we saw but thrice a week—once every Saturday afternoon, when, attended by two ushers, we were permitted to take brief walks in a body through some of the neighbouring fields—and twice during Sunday, when we were paraded in the same formal manner to the morning and evening service

still standing. It was originally surrounded by extensive grounds, but had been encroached upon by more recent structures. The error arose in part through Poe's inclusion in "William Wilson" of some features of the house across the way.

The Reverend John Bransby, Poe's School-
MASTER

From a photograph of an old painting. Courtesy of Mr. Charles Blackmore of Stoke-Newington.

Poe's School at Stoke-Newington, England
From a print made about 1860.

in the one church of the village. Of this church the principal of our school was pastor. With how deep a spirit of wonder and perplexity was I wont to regard him from our remote pew in the gallery, as, with step solemn and slow, he ascended the pulpit! This reverend man, with countenance so demurely benign, with robes so glossy and so clerically flowing, with wig so minutely powdered, so rigid and so vast—could this be he who of late, with sour visage, and in snuffy habiliments, administered, ferule in hand, the Draconian laws of the academy? Oh, gigantic paradox, too utterly monstrous for solution!

At an angle of the ponderous wall frowned a more ponderous gate. It was riveted and studded with iron bolts, and surmounted with jagged iron spikes. What impressions of deep awe it inspired! It was never opened save for the three periodical egressions and ingressions already mentioned; then, in every creak of its mighty hinges we found a plenitude of mystery, a world of matter for solemn remark, or for more solemn meditation.

The extensive enclosure was irregular in form, having many capacious recesses. Of these, three or four of the largest constituted the play-ground. It was level, and covered with fine, hard gravel. I well remember it had no trees, nor benches, nor anything similar within it. Of course it was in the rear of the house. In front lay a small parterre, planted with box and other shrubs; but through this sacred division we passed only upon rare occasions indeed, such as a first advent to school or final departure thence, or perhaps, when a parent or friend having called for us, we joyfully took our way home for the Christmas or Midsummer holydays.

But the house—how quaint an old building was this!—to me how veritably a palace of enchantment! There was really no end to its windings, to its incomprehensible subdivisions. It was impossible, at any given time, to say with certainty upon which of its two stories one happened to be. From each room to every other there were sure to be found three or four steps either in ascent or descent. Then the lateral branches were innumerable—inconceivable—and so returning in upon themselves, that our most exact ideas in regard to the whole mansion were not very far different from those with which we pondered upon infinity. During the five years of my residence here I was never able to ascertain with precision, in what remote locality lay the little sleeping apartment assigned to myself and some eighteen or twenty other scholars.

The school-room was the largest in the house—I could not help thinking in the world. It was very long, narrow, and dismally low, with pointed Gothic windows and a ceiling of oak. In a remote and terror-inspiring angle was a square enclosure of eight or ten feet, comprising the sanctum, "during hours," of our principal, the Reverend Dr. Bransby. It was a solid structure, with massy door, sooner than open which in the absence of the "Dominie," we would all have willingly perished by the *peine forte et dure.* In other angles were two other similar boxes, far less reverenced, indeed, but still greatly matters of awe. One of these was the pulpit of "the classical" usher, one of the "English and mathematical." Interspersed about the room, crossing and recrossing in endless irregularity, were innumerable benches and desks, black, ancient, and time-worn, piled desperately with much-bethumbed books, and so beseamed with initial letters, names at full length, meaningless gashes, grotesque figures, and other multiplied efforts of the knife, as to have entirely lost what little of original form might have been their portion in days long departed. A huge bucket with water stood at one extremity of the room, and a clock of stupendous dimensions at the other.[39]

This passage is, of course, fiction, and adds elements not to be traced to the Manor House School. Certainly Bransby seems to be unfairly represented, and the portrait of the clergyman is probably an imaginary one, or at least a composite of the rectors under whom Poe sat during his boyhood. The gloom and mystery are also, of course, exaggerated, but it is important to note that his method of creating mystery by the denial of the ordinary and the normal, has its roots in these school days in the atmosphere of a town long established and fairly rich with tradition. "William Wilson" was not published, it is true, until 1839, but there is a reality in the picture Poe paints of his early sensations which convinces us that these spiritual and intellectual echoes arise from impressions made so deeply in his childhood that they lay ever ready for his call. "There was really *no end* to its windings.... It was *impossible* ... to say with certainty upon which of its two stories one happened to be—I was *never* able to ascertain with precision, in what remote locality lay the little sleeping apartment assigned to myself ..." The italics are mine, but the method is clear, even without them. It does not need an earlier sentence in the story to tell us that it was "in this period and locality" that Poe first recognized the destiny which was to be his.

It is not hard to visualize the boy, eager, receptive to the overtones

---

[39] *Tales of the Grotesque and Arabesque,* I, 29-33. This text is, in my judgment, to be preferred to later ones for the purposes of this quotation, as Poe changed the description slightly in later versions.

that pass others by, letting his mind wander from the Latin or mathematics, to dramatize the rooms and corridors of the old building until their outlines faded and he entered them not as they were, but as his fancy endowed them with the colors of romance. William Wilson remarks himself how little there really was to remember, but how these trivial incidents "by a mental sorcery long forgotten, were made to involve a wilderness of sensation, a world of rich incident, an universe of varied emotion, of excitement the most passionate and spirit-stirring. 'Oh, le bon temps, que ce siècle de fer!' "

The years from six to eleven of a boy's life are also those in which the conscience begins its activity. The finer the nature, the keener will be the self-accusations, the more exaggerated the sense of guilt for the peccadilloes of childhood. It is just at that age that a boy needs the sympathetic understanding of a father, and even more, that of a mother. It is not unreasonable to believe that Poe, looking back upon these days, should remember how little help was given him in this regard. In any event, he chose for the theme of one of his greatest stories the career of a boy whose conscience was so active that it became a living human figure, sent to combat the progress of evil in a human soul.

On September 20, 1817, John Allan returned from Cheltenham to London and engaged lodgings until he could obtain possession of 39 Southampton Row,[40] a number used by Poe in his story "How the Little Frenchman Wears His Hand in a Sling." The family is not frequently mentioned in his letters to Ellis, but on June 23, 1818, Allan tells his partner that "Frances has had an attack of catarrh. Nancy is so attentive a nurse, she hasn't time to visit her friends." [41] Yet on June 25th he sends another letter describing "a grand dinner party on board the 'Philip Tabb.' Mrs. Allan was in great spirits and received the ladies up and down the decks." [42] Edgar, who was at Bransby's School, is not often mentioned. On September 28, 1818, however, Allan, in writing to his uncle, says: "Edgar is growing wonderfully and enjoys a good reputation as both able and willing to receive instruction." [43]

Mrs. Allan's health continued apparently to be the prime concern of all. One of the two letters from her that are extant and one that has only recently become available, is sent from her to her husband, from

[40] Autograph Ms. Letter, John Allan to George Dubourg, September 12, 1817. W. H. Koester Collection.
[41] Ellis-Allan Papers, L. of C., Vol. 196.
[42] Ellis-Allan Papers, L. of C., Vol. 196.
[43] Letter Books, 1817-1820, L. of C.

Dawlish, in Devonshire, on October 15, 1818, addressed curiously enough, to 16[sic] Basinghall Street, instead of to Southampton Row. I have not attempted to modify her spelling:

Dawlish, Octr 15 [1818]

My dear hubby

Your kind letter of the 13 was received this morning and you will perceive I have lost no time in replying to it, however pleasant a duty it may be I fear it will be long ere I shall write with any facility or ease to myself, as I fiend you are determined to think my health better contrary to all I say it will be needless for me to say more on that subject but be assured I embrace every opportunity that offers for takeing air and exercies but at this advanced seasons of the year we cant expect the weather to be very good I am this moment interupted with a message from Mrs. Dunlop requesting I would accompany her in a ride which I shall accept the Carriage is now at the door

Friday morning Octr 16

we had a very long and pleasant ride we started at two o'clock and did not return until six the day was remarkably fine we had a beautyfull view of the surrounding Cuntry we had a smart Beau with us who arrived here from London a few days ago I was very much pressed to go to the ball last night and nothing prevented me from going but the want of a little finery so you and the Doctr may lay aside some of your consequence for I really think you have a great deal of Vanity to immagien you are the cause of all my misery, I only wish my health would admit of my entering into all the gaieties of this place I would soon let you see I could be as happy and contented without you as you appear to be in my absence as I hear of nothing but partyes at home and abroad but long may the Almighty grant my dear husband health and spirits to enjoy them

now I must request my dear hubby to get me a nice piece of sheeting and a piece of shirting Cotton as they will be much wanted when I return tell Nancy she must get Abbatt to put up the tester and drapery to my bed and the parlour window Curtains to have the bedroom floors well cleaned before the Carpets are put down Miss G is very well and joins me in kind love to you the girls the Doctr Mrs Rennolds & all friends and believe me my dear old man yours truely

FRANCES K. ALLAN

(Endorsed on back: "F. K. Allan
        Octr 15, 1818.") [44]

[44] E. V. Valentine Collection.

Edgar is not mentioned in her remembrances. It seems, not to be unjust to Mrs. Allan, to be the letter of a woman whose main concern is with her own feelings. Another letter from Dawlish on October 24th, from Jane Galt to Mary Allan, who was visiting her brother in London, tells about the same story: "Mrs. Allan seems to dread very much the returning to London as she will enter it about the first of Nov. I think she regrets leaving this part of the country. Mr. Dunlop has been persuading her to remain here for some time. he will leave her in charge of two beaus who winter here, Major Court and Captain Donnell who he is sure will take good care of her and he would take a nice little cottage for her. What do you think of that arrangement   dont you think we plan very well?" [45]

They were in Tydemouth, Devonshire, on October 27th, according to Jane,[46] and Mrs. Allan was apparently back in London on November 28, 1818,[47] but there is no mention of Edgar. A Mr. Birch, who may have been their landlord, writes to urge payment for the rent, and usually the letters are purely business ones throughout the first part of 1819. Mrs. Allan was evidently planning another flight, for a letter to Allan on November 21, 1819, from Brighton tells of an agent searching for a house "for Mrs. Allan and another lady to stay." At last, after a long silence concerning his son, John Allan writes to his uncle, "Edgar is in the Country at School, he is a verry fine Boy and a good scholar." [48]

Business grew worse and on November 29, 1819, Allan writes to "Messrs. Ellis and Allan": "Please to bear in mind that I have only about £100 here in the world, and I depend upon you." [49] Allan was thinking about his return as early as December, for he tells Ellis, "Frances has the greatest aversion to the sea and nothing but dire necessity and the prospect of a reunion with her old and dear Friends could induce her to attempt it." He also tells Ellis that he cannot return until he receives some cash.[50] On December 4, 1819, Ellis and Allan write to Ewart Myers and Company from Richmond, speaking of their suspension and of their efforts to pay their creditors. Apparently the firm did their best to meet their obligations honorably.[51]

[45] E. V. Valentine Collection.
[46] E. V. Valentine Collection.
[47] Ellis-Allan Papers, L. of C., Vol. 203.
[48] Letter-Books, 1819-1820, L. of C.
[49] Ellis-Allan Papers, L. of C., Vol. 219.
[50] Ellis-Allan Papers, L. of C., Vol. 219.
[51] Ellis-Allan Papers, L. of C., Vol. 219.

On writing to his uncle on January 28, 1820, Allan tells him that "you are among the few that Edgar recollects perfectly." [52]

The family arrived in Liverpool on their return journey, June 8, 1820. From Liverpool Allan writes to Ellis:

I arrived here last Evening and I am told that the Courier with about 40 Sail of other vessels are detained at the Black Rock & supposing she may get off tomorrow I will try to get this on board. ... The arrival of the Queen [53] produced an unexpected sensation few thought she would return, but the bold & courageous manner by which she effected it has induced a vast number to think her not guilty. She was received with immense acclamations & the Populace displaced her horses drew her past Carlton House & thence to Alderman Wood's House. South Audley. The Same day the King made a Communication to the House of Lords charging her with High Treason (adul[ter]y) some said she had been arrested on Wednesday & sent to the Tower but I think this report *then* premature though equally certain in a few days;

The Martha Capt. Sketchly will not sail before Wednesday next the 14th int. I have made arrangements for all the Goods you ordered. In consequence of the Tariff Bill being rejected many purchasers have ass'd had it passed it would have ruined the trade. Mrs. Allan is in better Health than usual Ann is quite well so is Edgar. I for myself never was better."

It was probably on this boat, the *Martha,* that John Allan brought his family home.[54]

On the whole, it was fortunate for Poe that he had the experience of the English visit. It tended later to remove the provinciality which is the inevitable handicap of those whose vision has been limited to their native land. If the English education was limited in scope, it was probably thorough, and it may have contributed to that quality of Poe's mind which is best described as disciplined. Less tangible, of course, is the effect produced by the architecture, the public monuments, the survivals of past ages, which cannot have passed unnoticed by a boy like Edgar Poe.

[52] E. V. Valentine Collection.
[53] Queen Charlotte, the wife of George IV.
[54] Ellis-Allan Papers, L. of C., Vol. 224.

CHAPTER IV

Richmond Again, 1820-1826

With this second Richmond period in Poe's life, he enters a time of emotional stress, complicated by events in the Allan household, by his first ideal passion, and by his first love story. It is necessary, as always, to resist the temptation to read more into Poe's later references to his early life than the facts justify. Other boys have had similar adventures and hardly any have reached the age of seventeen without a youthful love affair. What makes Poe's nature more of a problem is his greater capacity for feeling both happiness and unhappiness. To this capacity, of course, we owe his poetry and prose. If the English sojourn gave him the locale for "William Wilson," this boyhood in Richmond gave him the inspiration for one of the world's greatest lyrics.

After a voyage of thirty-six days, John Allan and his family arrived in New York City on July 21, 1820. On July 27th Allan writes from New York: "Intended leaving the place today but Mrs. Allan was so unwell yesterday that we were obliged to call in Dr. Horrock—She is better & I intend starting tomorrow in the SteamBoat—by way of Norfolk." [1] By August 2nd [2] they were in Richmond, and in good health.

Allan and his family lived at the home of his partner, Charles Ellis, at the southwest corner of Franklin and Second streets, for nearly a year. [3] Mordecai speaks of this house in 1856 as "an unpretentious resi-

[1] Ellis-Allan Papers, L. of C., Vol. 225.

[2] The July 21st date and that of August 2nd are based on the statement of T. H. Ellis, quoted by Woodberry, II, 361. This checks approximately with letters of Charles Ellis on July 31st and August 10th, Vol. 225, L. of C., and with a letter from John Allan to London, August 5th, Letter Books, L. of C.

[3] Statements concerning the houses are based on the T. H. Ellis Manuscript and a later article by him entitled "Edgar Allan Poe," *Richmond Standard*, May 7, 1881, both in the E. V. Valentine Collection. He afterward repeated some of this information in letters to Woodberry and Harrison. His statements have been checked with Mary Wingfield Scott's "Notes on Poe's Houses in Richmond" in Ms. in the Valentine Museum.

dence now overtopped by those around it. . . . The square opposite to
it was Mr. Ellis's garden embellished by a row of fine linden trees
along its front." It was a two-story frame house, the second story being
really a gable roof, with quite a wide front. It was occupied by Charles
Ellis until his death in 1840 and was torn down in the early eighties.
Here Thomas Ellis's recollections of Edgar Poe began, and his clear
statement in the *Richmond Standard* is better than any paraphrase:

> No boy ever had a greater influence over me than he had. He
> was, indeed, a leader among boys; but my admiration for him
> scarcely knew bounds; the consequence was, he led me to do
> many a forbidden thing, for which I was punished. The only
> whipping I ever knew Mr. Allan to give him was for carrying me
> out into the fields and woods beyond Belvidere, one Saturday,
> and keeping me there all day and until after dark, without any-
> body at home knowing where we were, and for shooting a lot of
> domestic fowls, belonging to the proprietor of Belvidere (who
> was at that time, I think, Judge Bushrod Washington). He taught
> me to shoot, to swim, and to skate, to play bandy, &c.; and I ought
> to mention that he once saved me from drowning—for having
> thrown me into the falls headlong, that I might strike out for
> myself, he presently found it necessary to come to my help, or it
> would have been too late.

At the end of the year, Mr. Allan took a long low cottage house on
Fifth Street, fronting west, between Marshall and Clay Streets, northwest of the Capitol, but still within its neighborhood.

Edgar had not been forgotten in London. In a letter from Dr. N.
Arnott to John Allan, May 15, 1821, there is a curious passage: "You
know that I have Master Edgar still inhabiting one of my rooms. Your
not asking for him with these other things makes me hope that you do
mean to come back again." [4] This must refer to a sketch or picture of
Edgar of some kind, but it shows the impression the boy had made on
a mature man.

Shortly after the return to Richmond, Poe was sent to the school of
Joseph H. Clarke, which had recently moved to a building on the
south side of Broad Street between Fifth and Sixth Streets, over "Dr.
Lemosy's Store." [5] Five bills for tuition cover the period. The first,
June 11 to September 11, 1821, is "To tuition of son Edgar Poe,"
$12.50, which again indicates the way in which he was regarded in
the town. The second bill is for a period from September 11, 1821, to

---

[4] Ellis-Allan Papers, L. of C., Vol. 230.
[5] Advertisement, *Virginia Patriot,* October 2, 1818.

March 11, 1822, for $26.75. While the first bill had been paid in advance, this second account is for two terms, and on it is written, "By a/c paid the 17th of Decr up to the 11th of that month, $14." This partial payment reflects Allan's growing financial difficulties. The next bill is of special interest, for it is one of the few accounts of Poe's schooling which tell us what he was studying:

Mr. John Allan, Dr.

To present quarter's tuition of Master Poe from
    June 11th to September 11, 1822   .   .   . $12.50
    1 Horace 3.50 Cicero de Offi. 62½ 4.12½
    1 copybook—paper, pens & ink 87½

                                            $17.50

These items indicate that for a boy of thirteen, Poe was well advanced in Latin. The bills continue until December 11, 1822.[6]

On this point, however, there is testimony from Clarke himself. In a letter written to E. L. Didier, April 16, 1876,[7] he states that "When I left Richmond . . . Edgar's class was reading Horace and Cicero's Orations in Latin and Homer in Greek." Clarke's memory for dates was not accurate, for he gives 1818 as the beginning of Poe's term at his school, but his picture of Poe's character seems to ring true:

As to Edgar's disposition and character as a boy, though playful as most boys, his general deportment differed in some respect. from others. He was remarkable for self-respect, without haughtiness, strictly just and correct in his demeanor with his fellow playmates, which rendered him a favorite even with those above his years. His natural and predominate passion seemed to me, to be an enthusiastic ardor in everything he undertook; in his difference of opinion with his fellow students, he was very tenacious, and would not yield till his judgment was convinced. As a scholar he was ambitious to excel, and tho' not conspicuously studious always acquitted himself well in his classes. His imaginative powers seemed to take precedence of all his other faculties, he gave proof of this, in his juvenile compositions addressed to his young female friends. He had a sensitive and tender heart, and would strain every nerve to oblige a friend.

When the annual cost of a little more than sixty dollars is compared with that at Stoke Newington, it is rather startling, but Clarke's school

   [6] These bills are in the Ellis-Allan Papers, L. of C., Poe Volume.
   [7] Autograph Ms., now in Harvard College Library.

was apparently as good a one as could be found at that time in Richmond. He was probably carrying on in the British tradition of languages and mathematics. Poe also seems to have received special instruction in elocution. T. H. Ellis tells us again: "Talent for declamation was one of his gifts. I well remember a public exhibition at the close of a course of instruction in elocution which he had attended (in the old frame building that stood high above the present grade of Governor street, at the southwest corner of Governor and Franklin streets,) and my delight when he bore off the prize in competition with Channing Moore, Cary Wickham, Andrew Johnston, Nat Howard, and others who were regarded as among the most promising of the Richmond boys." [8]

On April 1, 1823, John Allan entered Poe in the school of William Burke, paying $30 in advance.[9] The payments in this school are not recorded with such fullness, though the cash books of the firm charge Allan with $30 again for five months from April 1, 1824. But from testimony of classmates [10] he clearly remained a pupil until the plan to send him to the University of Virginia may have required more special preparation.

Poe at this time was in fine physical condition. The story has often been told of his swimming in the James River from Ludlam's Wharf six miles to Warwick in a hot June sun, against the tide. He was an able boxer and a swift runner, and was chosen to represent the school in competition with others. His keen mind, disciplined, perhaps, more strictly than his fellows, permitted him to lead his classmates in their studies with ease. The reminiscences from his schoolmates, collected at first hand, especially by Ingram and Harrison, speak eloquently of his ability to "cap" Latin verses with others beginning with the same letter, of his fondness for the odes of Horace, of his unusual knowledge of French. Yet it is also indicated by these accounts that he was not popular in the usual sense of that word. Colonel John T. L. Preston, in one of the most interesting accounts of this period, offers an explanation:

At the time of which I speak, Richmond was one of the most aristocratic cities on this side the Atlantic. I hasten to say that this is not so now. Aristocracy, like capping verses, has fallen into

---

[8] *Richmond Standard,* May 7, 1881.
[9] Ms. Note Book or Journal of John Allan, two fragments of which are in the William H. Koester Collection.
[10] See Harrison, *Life,* Vol. I, p. 27.

desuetude—perhaps for the same reason: times having changed, other things pay better. Richmond was certainly then very English, and very aristocratic. A school is, of its nature, democratic; but still boys will unconsciously bear about the odour of their fathers' notions, good or bad. Of Edgar Poe it was known that his parents had been players, and that he was dependent upon the bounty that is bestowed upon an adopted son. All this had the effect of making the boys decline his leadership; and on looking back on it since, I fancy it gave him a fierceness he would otherwise not have had.[11]

There can be little question that Poe's heritage in the theatre did ·him little good in his social relations. The prejudice against the people of the stage was quite as strong as it had been in the days when his father felt called upon to sharpen with personal violence his protest against the unfair criticism of a gallant actress. But the extended discussion, pro and con, that has raged among Poe's biographers concerning his treatment by his schoolmates seems quite unnecessary. There is hardly any cruelty so relentless, even at times so savage, as that of a crowd of adolescents for one among them who is markedly superior in mental attainments, and who at the same time is gifted with a power of satire. Poe must have stung many of his fellows by adroit references to their stupidity or laziness. Helpless to meet him on that ground, they would take the inevitable revenge of the tribe, and make him feel that he was an outsider.

To imagine that he was without warm friends, however, is absurd. The favor or disfavor of the tribe is constantly shifting, and there is sufficient evidence that with boys like Robert Stanard, or Preston himself, there was a close tie. Robert Sully, nephew of the painter Thomas Sully, was a natural friend, since his father, Matthew, had acted with Poe's mother in the Virginia Company. Robert may have heard from his father how Matthew Sully and Elizabeth Hopkins kept the *Highland Reel* from failure in Norfolk in 1803.[12] He could have brought Poe one of the few living memories of his mother's career.

One friend he certainly did make. Rob Stanard, who was younger than he, took Poe one day to see his mother, Jane Craig Stanard. There

---

[11] *Edgar Allan Poe, A Memorial Volume*, edited by Sara S. Rice (Baltimore, 1877), pp. 40-41.

[12] *Norfolk Herald*, April 14, 1803, quoted on page 13. Sully played Robin Roughhead to Mrs. Hopkins' Nancy in *Fortune's Frolic*, and they danced together as Shelty and Jenny in *The Fruitless Precaution*.

seems to have been born between them instantly a bond of sympathy, which produced a deep effect upon the boy. She spoke some gracious words of welcome, she was beautiful, and he was in a mood in which a woman's sympathy must have been needed. Poe wrote years later to Mrs. Whitman,[13] "The lines I had written, in my passionate boyhood, to the first, purely ideal love of my soul—to the Helen Stannard [sic] of whom I told you, flashed upon my recollection."

Poe refers here to the lyric "To Helen," which was published first in 1831, but which he insisted had been written earlier. Helen was always a favorite name with him, and there need be no explanation necessary of his change from Mrs. Stanard's own first name. How often he saw her has become a matter of dispute. Mrs. Whitman, who took a very natural interest in the matter, since she was the inspiration for the second "To Helen," of 1848, wrote to Mrs. Clemm more than once to find facts concerning this early friendship. In one of these letters, written March 10, 1859,[14] she quotes Poe as stating that he had only once seen Mrs. Stanard and that she died a few weeks after the meeting. Later, however, Mrs. Whitman in speaking of the interview, says:

"This lady afterwards became the confidant of all his boyish sorrows, and her's [sic] was the one redeeming influence that saved and guided him in the earlier days of his turbulent and passionate youth. After the visitation of strange and peculiar sorrows she died, and for months after her decease it was his habit to visit nightly the cemetery where the object of his boyish idolatry lay entombed."[15]

Unfortunately, we do not know the date of that first interview. Mrs. Stanard for some time before her death, on April 28, 1824, was mentally unbalanced, and Poe could not have seen her. It seems unlikely that so deep an impression could have been made at one meeting, and yet it is equally improbable, considering her illness, that the intercourse extended over many months. Mrs. Clemm probably gave a partially correct explanation concerning Mrs. Stanard's relation to Poe when she told Mrs. Whitman—"When Eddie was unhappy at home (which was often the case), he went to her for sympathy, and she always consoled and comforted him, you are mistaken when you say

[13] Sunday night, October 1, 1848. Original Autograph Ms., Lilly Collection.

[14] Original Autograph Ms., Pratt Library.

[15] *Edgar Poe and his Critics*, p. 49. The nightly visitations seem doubtful, but they are among the romantic traditions concerning Poe which can neither be proved nor disproved.

MRS. JANE STITH CRAIG STANARD

From the oil painting by James Worrell, formerly in the collection of J. H. Whitty and in his possession for over twenty-five years. Reproduced for the first time through the courtesy of Mr. William H. Koester of Baltimore.

that you believe he saw her but once in her home. He visited there
for years, he only saw her once while she was ill. Robert has often
told me, of his, and Eddie's visits to her grave." [16] Whatever encouragement this young matron gave Edgar Poe, he repaid in full measure.
"To Helen" remains one of the most exquisite tributes ever paid by
man to woman.

Poe did not write the poem at once, for he would certainly have
realized its worth and included it when he was preparing his volumes
of verse in 1827 and 1829, in which it does not appear. Indeed, the
many speculations concerning the inspiration at this time for its two
oft-quoted lines:

> "To the glory that was Greece
> And the grandeur that was Rome"

are made in ignorance perhaps that these magnificent phrases appear
first, in this form, in *The Saturday Museum* in 1843. But knowing Poe's
habit of constantly revising his verses, it is quite possible that he began
to shape the poem during these early years in Richmond. We know
he was writing verse, and that he showed it to those who he thought
would appreciate it.

Any conception of Poe, however, as an abstracted and moody young
poet would be quite incorrect. There is definite evidence that Poe was
a natural leader in those activities in which a normal boy takes pleasure. T. H. Ellis gives a brief first-hand account of two of these
interests:

> I knew also of his Thespian performances, when he and William
> F. Ritchie and James Greenhow and Creed Thomas and Richard
> Cary Ambler and other schoolmates appeared in dramatic char
> acter under a tent erected on a vacant lot one or two squares be
> yond what is now St. James' Church on Fifth Street—admittance
> fee, one cent! But never was I prouder of him than when, dressed
> in the uniform of the 'Junior Morgan Riflemen' (a volunteer com
> pany composed of boys, and which General Lafayette, in his
> memorable visit to Richmond, selected as his bodyguard), he
> walked up and down in front of the marquee erected on the Capi
> tol Square, under which the old general held a grand reception in
> October, 1824.[17]

[16] Mrs. Clemm to Mrs. Whitman, Alexandria, April 14, 1859. Original
Autograph Ms., Lilly Collection.
[17] Statement of Ellis incorporated in "New Glimpses of Poe" by J. A.
Harrison, *Independent*, September 6, 1900.

Having the theatre in his blood, it was natural that Poe should try to act, but unfortunately we do not know what plays this boyish troupe selected.

The visit of LaFayette in the fall of 1824 was made a great occasion in Richmond.[18] The city had not forgotten his leadership in the Virginia campaign during the Revolution, and Richmond outdid itself to prove its gratitude.

The Junior Volunteers became for a time, at least, an organization of some importance, and the young officer of fifteen was naturally proud to join in this petition:

John Lyle (Capt.), Edgar A. Poe (Lt.) to the Governor:

At the request of the members of the Richmond Junior Volunteers, we beg leave to solicit your permission for them to retain the arms which they lately were permitted to draw from the Armory. We are authorized to say that each individual will not only pledge himself to take proper care of them, but we ourselves will promise to attend strictly to the order in which they are kept by the Company.

We are, etc.

Nov. 17, 1824,
Richmond.[19]

There was, however, trouble brewing in the Allan household for Edgar Poe. Allan's business affairs came to a crisis in 1822 when he made a personal assignment with permission to retain his property. In 1824 the firm of Ellis and Allan was dissolved by mutual consent.[20]

In the meantime, the family had moved again, this time to "a house on the northwest corner of Fourteenth Street and Tobacco Alley, where a very tall and attenuated house now stands fronting the west side of the Exchange Hotel." [21] This property belonged to William

[18] See Mary N. Stanard, *Richmond, Its People and Its Story* (Philadelphia, 1923), Chap. XVI.

[19] Calendar of Virginia State Papers, January 1, 1808, to December 31, 1835, preserved in the Capitol, at Richmond, X (Richmond, 1892), 518.

[20] T. H. Ellis, *Richmond Standard*, May 7, 1881. On January 23, 1824, John Allan wrote in his "Note Book," "My uncle said he was establishing his business for all our interests, that I was so hobbled that I could not be known;—but that Wm. [Galt] should have a third—when James [Galt] became a citizen he should—when I was at liberty I should have his third." The elder William Galt was preparing for his death, which was soon to enrich John Allan.

[21] T. H. Ellis, Ms., Valentine Collection, 1875. This house was still standing in 1941, and according to the Land Books of Richmond, it was

Galt and seems to have been given to John Allan, perhaps to help him
in a time of stress. Amid the many strange documents that becloud
the relations of Poe and John Allan, a letter from Allan to Henry Poe
in Baltimore, dated November 1, 1824, is one of the most peculiar:

Dear Henry,
 I have just seen your letter of the 25th ult. to Edgar and am
much afflicted, that he has not written you. He has had little else
to do for me he does nothing & seems quite miserable, sulky &
ill-tempered to all the Family. How we have acted to produce this
is beyond my conception—why I have put up so long with his conduct is little less wonderful. The boy possesses not a Spark of
affection for us not a particle of gratitude for all my care and
kindness towards him. I have given a much superior Education
than ever I received myself. If Rosalie has to relie on any affection from him God in his mercy preserve her—I fear his associates have led him to adopt a line of thinking & acting very
contrary to what he possessed when in England. I feel proudly
the difference between your principles & his & have my desire to
Stand as I ought to do in your Estimation. Had I done my duty as
faithfully to my God as I have to Edgar, then had Death come
when he will had no terrors for me, but I must end this with a
devout wish that God may yet bless him & you & that Success
may crown all your endeavors & between you your poor Sister
Rosalie may not suffer.
 At least She is half your Sister & God forbid my dear Henry
that We should visit upon the living the Errors & frailties of the
dead. Beleive me Dear Henry we take an affectionate interest in
your destinies and our United Prayers will be that the God of
Heaven will bless & protect you. rely on him my Brave & excellent Boy who is willing & ready to save to the uttermost. May he
keep you in Danger preserve you always is the prayer of your
Friend & Servant.[22]

JOHN ALLAN

not until 1822 that the value placed on this and the adjoining lot with
improvements reached $9,000, which indicates that the houses were built
at that time. The first insurance policy on the corner house is dated April 5,
1825, when it is described by John Allan as a three-story dwelling, "occupied by myself." It was valued at $3,000. William Galt took out a policy
in 1825 on the adjoining house, farther north. Richard Jeffries was the
tenant, and there seems no evidence that John Allan ever lived in the
second house. See "Notes on Richmond Houses," by M. W. Scott, Valentine Museum.
 [22] Ellis-Allan Papers, L. of C., Poe Volume. The letter is, of course, a
copy, but is written and signed by John Allan.

In the light of the universal esteem in which Mrs. David Poe was held through her courageous struggle to support her children and, possibly, her dying husband, the implicit accusation merits no consideration. It reflects only upon the character of the man who made it. Allan's flattery of Henry, whose career, little known as it is, certainly provides no basis for Allan's praise, is only another false note in the letter. The echo of Wolsey's parting speech to Cromwell in *Henry VIII* shows that Allan's fondness for Shakespeare, or what he thought was Shakespeare, is a still more artificial quality in a message sent for some purpose not apparent on the surface. In the light of these insincerities, Allan's picture of Edgar Poe loses what validity it otherwise might possess.

Whether Henry Poe sent the letter to Edgar it is impossible now to find out, but he probably brought it with him in 1825 when he seems to have visited his brother. Neither is it possible for us to know whether by this time Mrs. Allan had become aware of her husband's infidelities. Rumor would certainly have dealt with them before 1824, and it is hard to see how Poe could have remained ignorant of them. Was it the natural indignation of a lad of fifteen at the treatment his foster-mother had received, that made him appear the "miserable, sulky and ill-tempered" boy that Allan describes? Was John Allan preparing a counter attack in case Edgar Poe should call him to account? Allan's letter is not like his usual epistles—there is a sanctimonious, hypocritical tone which, to do him justice, occurs infrequently in his letters, but shows most definitely in his will, and in the fragments of his Journal or Note Book.

Edgar Poe naturally was not perfect. He was on an insecure foundation in the Allan household, and probably was just beginning to realize it. There may have been another reason for the disturbance of Poe's serenity. Just when he fell in love with Elmira Royster is, of course, not known. In view of the romance that has grown up concerning Poe and the "Enchanted Garden," on Second Street,[23] it is best to let her speak for herself.

There is in the Valentine Collection a manuscript in the handwrit-

---

[23] Elmira Royster did not live in a house at or near Second and Main Streets, and no one named Royster is given in any Richmond Directory as living there. The house was built after Poe's day. Miss Mary W. Scott has traced the records of that piece of property. (See her *Notes on Old Richmond Houses*, Valentine Museum.) Of course Poe and Elmira may have visited the garden, with linden trees in front, which was the property of Charles Ellis, but they evidently met after Poe left the neighborhood.

ing of Edward V. Valentine [24] which records a conversation with Mrs. Sarah Elmira Royster Shelton in 1875, long after she had become a widow. Since it is at second hand, it has only partial validity, and she is not responsible for the style, for it was evidently a series of answers to questions by Mr. Valentine. But the conversation has a directness and an informality which bear a flavor of truth:

> He was a beautiful boy—Not very talkative. When he did talk though he was pleasant but his general manner was sad—He was devoted to the first Mrs. Allan and she to him. We lived opposite to Poe on 5th. I made his acquaintance so. Our acquaintance was kept up until he left to go to the University, and during the time he was at the University he wrote to me frequently, but my father intercepted the letters because we were too young—no other reason. He never addressed any poems to me. It distresses me to see anything written in a scurrulous manner in regard to him—don't believe one tenth part of what they say. A great part caused by jealousy and envy. I have the greatest respect for his memory. He was very generous. On Churchill [Church Hill] a female (acquaintance?) called to see [me?] and made a coarse remark and Poe said I am surprized you should associate with anyone who would make such a remark. He had strong prejudices. Hated anything coarse and unrefined. Never spoke of his parents. He was kind to his sister as far as in his power. He was as warm and zealous in any cause he was interested in, very enthusiastic and impulsive, I was about 15 or 16 when he first addressed me and I engaged myself to him, and I was not aware that he wrote to me until I was married to Mr. Shelton when I was 17.

If she is correct in her statement that she met Poe when he lived on Fifth Street, she may refer to the house on Fifth Street between Marshall and Clay Streets, and again the romance of "the enchanted garden" on Second Street, seems to disappear. Poe was not more than thirteen or fourteen when he left this house, but he seems not to have gone through the stage of boyhood in which so many men are shy and bashful in their approach to women. Perhaps it was the essential purity which shines through his poetry that attracted them, and made him unaware of any reason why their friendship might not be sought.

[24] It is entitled "Conversation with Mrs. Shelton at Mr. Smith's corner 8th and Leigh Streets, Nov. 19, 1875." I prefer this original form to later versions of the same conversation, sent by Valentine to Ingram, and referred to incorrectly by later biographers as "Mrs. Shelton's Letters." They are found first in *Appleton's Journal*, New Series, IV (1878), 428-429, and are used later in Ingram's *Life*.

THE HOME OF JOHN ALLAN AT FIFTH AND MAIN STREETS, RICHMOND

From a sketch made by Harry Fenn for the *Century Magazine.*

If, as seems probable, Elmira refers to the Allan's new home on the southeast corner of Main and Fifth Streets, the real romance was of short duration. This house had been built by David Meade Randolph, the United States Marshal, sold by him to Joseph Gallego, the rich flour merchant, and left by Mr. Gallego to the care of Peter J. Chevallie, his executor. When the death of Allan's uncle, William Galt, in March, 1825, made his nephew a rich man, he purchased this house for $14,950. He took, or resumed, that prominent place in Richmond social life which his own and Mrs. Allan's fondness for entertainment prompted. By 1825 the neighborhood of Fifth and Main Streets had become fully established as a fashionable quarter of town. The house, torn down in the nineties, had two lofty stories, with wide porches and high ceilings. When John Allan purchased the house, June 28, 1825, there were not many buildings in the neighborhood, and the lot was an ample one. Poe's room, on the second floor, northeast corner, therefore gave him a charming view of the river and the surrounding country. On the wide porch stood a telescope, brought from England by John Allan, from which Poe learned his first lessons in star-gazing.[25]

If Poe did enjoy the comparative luxury of his surroundings, it was only for a few months, for in February, 1826, he entered the University of Virginia.

One of the most significant sentences in Elmira Shelton's reminiscences is that in which she denies that Poe "addressed" any poems to her. Considering the claims of other women, made early or late in their lives, concerning the dedication by Poe of his verses to them, and knowing Poe's habit of writing the same poem to his different feminine inspirations, her modesty seems at least authentic. The absence of poetic tributes may argue indeed for a brief courtship, which certainly ended in an engagement to be married. Much speculation has been indulged in concerning the cause for her father's objection to Poe as her fiancé. Mrs. Shelton insists that their youth was the only reason. But since Poe had no profession as yet, and was just entering a course at the University, Mr. Royster may have had other and very natural objections. Since Elmira Royster married Shelton when she was seventeen, her heart was evidently not broken, and, in all probability, neither was Edgar Poe's. If such early poems as

"I saw thee on thy bridal day,
    When a burning blush came o'er thee"

were inspired by this early disappointment, it was probably a dramatized sorrow. Yet Elmira revealed in her letter to Mrs. Clemm, of September 22, 1849, how strong her feelings had been when she saw Poe and Virginia together, soon after their marriage.[26]

Poe apparently had a visit from his brother, Henry, in 1825, and learned of the latter's ambitions and dreams of foreign adventure. Henry is a rather shadowy figure who was never of any real help to his brother, but was the cause of at least one calamity. Rosalie, who followed Edgar around Richmond more than he seemed to desire, was also a handicap. She was always a pathetic figure, and failed to develop mentally after she was about twelve years of age.

Poe was almost eighteen when his second Richmond period was over. He was educated not only by regular schooling, and by reading, but also by intercourse with the guests and friends of John and Frances Allan. In a glowing tribute to Ann Valentine, Thomas Ellis

[25] T. H. Ellis's description of the house, written for Woodberry (see his *Life*, II, 361-364), has been followed by all later biographers.

[26] See Chap. XIX. This sentence is omitted as the letter is usually printed.

speaks of her being a member of "that prominent and well esteemed old merchant set, to which Richmond owes so much of her present name and character.[27] He then gives a list of forty-six families, headed by William Galt, John Allan, and Charles Ellis. He speaks, also, of the family physicians, among them Dr. Foushee and Dr. Cabell; the judiciary, with Chief Justice Marshall at their head; and the bar, including John Wickham, James Innes, and Edmund Randolph, a total of about seventy leaders of public and social life. Although this testimony concerning the circle in which the Allans moved is discounted somewhat by T. H. Ellis's placing of his own family at its head, there can be no doubt that Poe had an opportunity to meet at his home men and women of breeding, whose professional and personal character was high. There can be little question concerning the effect this upbringing had upon him. He was never a democrat in any sense. His reference in *Tamerlane* to "the rabble-men" is characteristic. In "Some Words with a Mummy" Poe made his opinion of democracy even clearer. The Egyptian Mummy has been revived in Poe's day and is being questioned by the group of scientists who have brought him to life, concerning his opinion of modern ideas:

> We then spoke of the great beauty and importance of Democracy, and were at much trouble in impressing the Count with a due sense of the advantages we enjoyed in living where there was suffrage *ad libitum,* and no king.
> He listened with marked interest, and in fact seemed not a little amused. When we had done, he said that, a great while ago, there had occurred something of a very similar sort. Thirteen Egyptian provinces determined all at once to be free, and so set a magnificent example to the rest of mankind. They assembled their wise men, and concocted the most ingenious constitution it is possible to conceive. For a while they managed remarkably well; only their habit of bragging was prodigious. The thing ended, however, in the consolidation of the thirteen states, with some fifteen or twenty others, in the most odious and insupportable despotism that ever was heard of upon the face of the Earth.
> I asked what was the name of the usurping tyrant.
> As well as the Count could recollect, it was *Mob.*

Poe's own natural tendency toward that reserve which holds others at a certain distance was already in these boyhood days being fed by the surroundings of a Southern city. Virginia was a State which cher-

[27] T. H. Ellis Manuscript, Valentine Collection, writing in 1875.

ished the traditions of established caste inherited from England, and
which had, in comparatively recent times, given up the system of
primo-geniture. It must be remembered, however, that Virginia developed two forms of thinking—that based on the planter's ownership
of land, which could not disappear, and the possession of which carried with it the sense of responsibility for human life, including slaves,
which was dependent upon that land. There was another South, which
rested upon financial success in dealing in the products of the land,
such as tobacco, but which did not associate its wealth, as the planter
did, with the human beings who had produced it. This form of wealth
might vanish at any time, as Poe had seen John Allan's vanish. In between, linking these two societies, were the professional men, the law-
yers, doctors, and clergymen. While there was intermingling of all
groups, Poe saw less of the planter group than of the others. The old
Cavalier tradition of "the King and the Commons against the rest,"
which, though it may have been overstressed, was powerful in the
early South, and had not expired, seems not to have been the dominant
force in Richmond. The other tradition, which represented financial
solidity and commercial integrity, the rights of property rather than
broad humanity, apparently set the tone of the city. In other words,
it was the South of John Marshall rather than of Thomas Jefferson,
that shaped Poe's boyhood's thinking, and his later adoption of the
Whig party may not have been as accidental as it has appeared to be.
Though he went to the University founded by Thomas Jefferson, he
mentions him only once in his writings.

Poe never loved money for its own sake, but except in those desperate days at the University of Virginia, he was not extravagant. The
scrupulous sense of financial honesty, of which George Graham spoke
after Poe's death, may have come from his rearing in a house where
John Allan recorded even the few cents for postage that Edgar and
Rosalie cost him. On the other hand, Poe had seen John Allan prosper,
become bankrupt, and rise again to wealth. While there could hardly
have been a temptation for Edgar Poe at any time to enter John
Allan's business house, his determination to pursue his own course as
a creative artist may well have justified itself to him by his memory of
the disturbed days between 1822 and 1825, when the Allan household
must have been a good illustration of the transitory nature of the
dollar.

If he had really been John Allan's son, he would probably have proceeded to the study of law or to some other orderly profession. But he

knew by this time that his position was not secure in the Allan household, and the pride which was certainly one of Poe's most active traits grew with the very circumstances that threatened his tenure. There can only be sympathy for the boy who in this unsettled state of mind and heart was sent to a new environment whose very foundation was independence from guidance and restraint.

CHAPTER V

The University of Virginia

When Edgar Poe entered the University of Virginia on February 14, 1826, the University had had only one year of actual life. It was the culmination of Jefferson's deep interest in education, and was founded by him, among other aims, "to develop the reasoning faculties of our youth, enlarge their minds, cultivate their morals, and instil into them the precepts of virtue and order—and generally, to form them to habits of reflection and correct action, rendering them examples of virtue to others, and of happiness within themselves." [1]

It had been only after the most stubborn opposition that Jefferson succeeded in founding his University. Some of this adverse influence proceeded from William and Mary College, his own alma mater, but most of it arose from the nature of Jefferson's educational ideals. He was acquainted with the methods of English and Continental universities, and he endeavored to build upon the foundations of Central College in Albemarle County, Virginia, a type of university new to American education. In 1818, when he sent his proposals to the Legislature of Virginia, the colleges in the United States, with the exception of Pennsylvania and Columbia, were still largely under denominational influence. Jefferson's proposal that the University of Virginia be completely non-sectarian was a red rag to the conservative Church of England and Presbyterian elements of the State. But since the very essence of Jefferson's ideal was freedom, from the choice of professors to the selection by the students of their courses of study, he persisted and ultimately won his fight.

He chose for the site of his University, Charlottesville, lying in the valley between the Southwest Mountains on one side and the Blue Ridge on the other. Toward the south the Ragged Mountains rose, and on the north the land rolled away as far as the eye could reach.

---

[1] For Jefferson's complete list of the objects of higher education, see Herbert B. Adams, *Thomas Jefferson and the University of Virginia* (Washington, 1888), p. 89.

Through the valley the Rivanna River tumbled, with its tributary streams forcing their way through rocky ridges that disputed their free passage. Who can doubt that Poe remembered the view that must have rewarded his climb to one of the nearby hills, when in "Tamerlane" he placed his hero

> "on the crown
> Of a high mountain which looked down
> Afar from its proud natural towers
> Of rock and forest, on the hills—
> The dwindled hills: begirt with bowers."

Within this basin of natural beauty, Jefferson built the University. It began in 1817 when the corner stone for one of the pavilions, the modern Colonnade Club, was laid. While the building was slowly proceeding, Central College became the University of Virginia. Jefferson had the advice of practical architects, but the main conception was his. To him is due the lofty Rotunda, modelled on the Pantheon at Rome, and looking down on the West and East Ranges, each with its mingled Ionic, Doric, and Corinthian Pavilions. It still remains one of the most impressive examples of classic architecture on any American college campus, and to a lover of beauty like Poe, it must have been an inspiration.

While the University was being built, Jefferson had been selecting the Faculty. He sought both by correspondence and by sending an emissary to England, Francis W. Gilmer, to secure the foremost men available. The first Faculty certainly contained a number of fine scholars. George Long (1800-1879), a Fellow of Trinity College, Cambridge, although young when he accepted the Chair of Ancient Languages, established standards of scholarship during his brief stay from 1825 to 1828 which have become a tradition at Virginia. Receiving a call to the University of London, he returned to his native country. In his senior class, which Poe attended, he required during each period one hundred lines from Virgil or Thucydides to be read, followed by translations from Horace or some other author, Greek or Latin. At times he varied this program by written tests in Greek or Latin grammar. The grammatical constructions were illustrated by copious references to classical authors, and the class was instructed to follow up each reference and become familiar with the general texts of the authors used. Gessner Harrison, Long's foremost pupil and his successor in the Chair of Ancient Languages, has testified to the close

The University of Virginia in Poe's Day

attention and hard labor that was necessary. Long seems to have taught Latin and Greek with an understanding of history and geography that made them more alive than was usual in those days.[2]

George Blaettermann, the Professor of Modern Languages, was a native of Germany, but living in London, when on the recommendation of George Ticknor, of Harvard, he was appointed to that chair. He was an irascible person, who went so far as to cowhide his wife on the street, and he was dismissed in 1838 at the request of the undergraduate body. But he seems to have been a competent linguist. Poe, according to the testimony of William Wertenbaker, took French, Spanish, and Italian. On one occasion, Professor Blaettermann gave as a voluntary exercise a verse translation from Tasso.[3] Poe was the only student who responded, and his verse was highly praised by the none too genial teacher. That Poe was more interested in his modern language study than in his work in ancient languages may be indicated by the fact that his library cards were signed by Blaettermann, although, of course, this may have been accidental.

The reputation of the University spread rapidly. Among Jefferson's loyal supporters in the enterprise was General John H. Cocke, a public-spirited citizen. General Cocke was a friend of John Allan and it seems probable that Edgar was sent to the University at his suggestion.

The second session of the University began on February 1, 1826, and Poe was number 136 out of a total enrollment of 177 when he matriculated on February 14th. The following entry appeared in the Matriculation Books:

[2] See Philip A. Bruce, *History of the University of Virginia*, 5 vols. (New York, 1920), especially Vols. 1, 2, and 3; the monograph of Adams, already mentioned, and Harrison's *Life* for accounts of the University of Virginia in Poe's day. I have had the privilege of examining the manuscript Faculty Minutes for 1826. All biographers make use of the testimony of William Wertenbaker, who shared some of Poe's classes and was later Librarian. Wertenbaker prepared a statement in 1860 and later a more detailed sketch of Poe's career at Virginia, January 19, 1869, which he duplicated to answer many inquiries, and which was published in the *University of Virginia Magazine*, XIX, 45, and reprinted in Harrison's *Life*. Some of his statements are, however, incorrect. The publication of the Valentine Letters and the consequent comment by James Southall Wilson in "The Young Man Poe," *Virginia Quarterly*, II (1926), 238-253, as well as other articles by Dr. Wilson (see later references) correct the earlier accounts.

[3] Copy of Wertenbaker's statement, University of Virginia, signed May 12, 1860. He refers to Poe's card playing—but denies that he drank excessively.

Name	Date of Birth	Parent or Guardian	Place of Residence	Professors Attended	
				Long	Blätter
Edgar A. Poe	19 Jan. 1809	John Allen [sic]	Richmond	1	1

This entry is not in his own handwriting, or it would be of greater use in establishing his date of birth. But it shows that he registered for the Schools of Ancient and Modern Languages, of which Long and Blaettermann were the directors. Apparently the students were permitted to choose not only their studies, but also the subjects of their final examination. At the Faculty meeting on December 15, 1826, the names of the students who excelled were presented by their professors and approved. In Latin they are recorded as follows:

Senior Latin Class

Gessner Harrison

Albert S. Holladay
Berthier Jones
Edgar A. Poe
William Selden
William E. Taylor
Henry Tutweiler
H. H. Worthington

Two other groups follow, of seven and four respectively.[4] The line drawn after Harrison's name indicates that he was in a class by himself.[5] Poe was one of the second group of seven, arranged alphabetically, and since there were two other groups, all excellent, his rank was high.

The Faculty records also give the names of the excellent students in the

[4] Original Faculty Minutes, University of Virginia, Registrar's Office.

[5] Through the accident that Harrison is in alphabetical order with Holladay, Poe has usually been stated by his biographers to have been in the first rank in Latin. But the manuscript records show that Long intended to differentiate between Gessner Harrison, who became his successor, and the rest of the class.

Senior French Class

Philip Ambler
John Cary
Gessner Harrison
Wm. Michie
Conway Nutt
Edgar A. Poe
Wm. Selden
Henry Tutweiler

Here Poe is in the first and only group of distinguished students. Military drill was optional, and he may or may not have taken part in it.

The term ended December 15, 1826. He had then less than ten months of college (he says eight), and his schedule called for two hours daily, six days of the week. In 1826 the first class, to which Poe belonged, began its labors at seven o'clock, had a recess for half an hour to eat breakfast, and then reassembled for another hour.[6] Poe would then have had the day, after nine-thirty, for study, reading, recreation, or those other social activities, which, although intangible, mean so much to the university man of today. We can only speculate on this last phase. Poe says nothing in his two letters, written while at the University, concerning his intercourse with Professor Long or Professor Blaettermann, and does not mention meeting any of the other members of the Faculty. In 1875 when Ingram asked Long for his recollections of Poe, Long replied very frankly: "If Poe was at the University of Virginia in 1826, he was probably in my class which was the largest.... The beginning of the University of Virginia was very bad. There were some excellent young men, and some of the worst that ever I knew. I remember well the names of both, and I think that I remember the name of Poe, but the remembrance is very feeble; and if he was in my class, he could not be among the worst, and perhaps not among the best or I should certainly remember him."[7]

---

[6] According to Bruce, *History of the University of Virginia*, II, 131. This may not be exact. The Faculty on February 3, 1827, made "alterations" to this effect.

[7] See "Poe at the University of Virginia" by James Southall Wilson, *Alumni Bulletin, University of Virginia*, XVI (April, 1933), 163-168. Dr. Wilson printed here unpublished letters by George Long, J. Hewitt Key, and Miles George. In the same issue, of which he was editor, he reprinted "Edgar A. Poe and his College Contemporaries" by William M. Burwell, which had first appeared in the *Times-Democrat*, May 18, 1884.

He would probably have gained most from intercourse with George Tucker, the Professor of Ethics, a creative writer. His *Voyage to the Moon*, published in 1827 after Poe's term, seems, however, to have had no influence on Poe's "Hans Pfaall." The four English professors apparently kept to themselves. Jefferson made a point of inviting the students to dinner in rotation on Sundays, and Poe probably met him on other occasions, but again there is no record of any impression being made upon the young undergraduate by the founder.

Poe mentions in his letter of September 21st to John Allan that the Rotunda is nearly finished. "The pillars of the Portico are completed and it greatly improves the appearance of the whole—The books are removed into the library—and we have a very fine collection." [8]

The library reflected Jefferson's interests, and in 1826 the four hundred and nine titles touching the classics comprehended the largest number of volumes in any department. In English literature, as might have been expected, the older writers were much better represented than those of the newer romantic school. In "President Jefferson's Catalogue of Books for the University of Virginia Library," drawn up in 1825, Shakespeare, Dryden, Addison, Farquhar, Vanbrugh, Congreve, and Wycherly found places, but not Byron, or Scott. Jefferson's conception of the library was that of a storehouse for reference, and the books were to be solid and not for entertainment. The library really began to function only in April, 1826, and was not properly catalogued until after Poe left college. The regulations governing its use were forbidding in the extreme. No student could take out a volume unless his request was certified by a member of the Faculty, and he could not take more than three books. At first the librarian was required to be at his post only once a week for an hour, and only after October 17, 1826, was the library open every day. [9] As Bruce describes the process, "In February 1826, a box was placed outside of the library door, in which the petitions for books were to be dropped the day before the library opened; and on the latter day, the volumes were handed out like loaves of charity through the iron bars of a monastery." [10] Even for reference work, no student was permitted to enter the room unless he had asked permission in writing the day before. He was then given a ticket, but only twenty such tickets were issued in one day. Even after he had gained access to the room, he could not

[8] Valentine Letters, p. 48.
[9] Minutes of the Faculty.
[10] *History of the University of Virginia*, II, 202.

take a reference book from the shelves without the permission of the librarian, in writing.

The original record book of the library is, fortunately, available, and there are six entries charged to Edgar Poe:

June 13, 1826. 1st, 3d, 4th vols. Rollin's A. Hist.
    Aug. 8. 33d, 34th vols. Rollin (hist. Romaine)
    Aug. 15. 1st & 2d vols. Robertson's America
    Aug. 29. 1st and 2d vols. Marshall's Washington.
    Sept. 12. 9. 10. Voltaire.
    Nov. 4. 1st and 2d Dufief's Nature displayd.

There are some interesting connotations, given only in these original records. Poe evidently drew no books until he had been at the University four months, and the library was still open for this purpose only once a week. What effect Poe's reading had upon his future writing must remain only a speculation. He read Charles Rollin's *Oeuvres Complètes,* in the sixty-volume edition of Paris, 1807-1810, still preserved. That he read it in French may have been due to his competence in that language, but in any event he had no option. His references in his poems to the "Babylon like walls," to the "twins of Leda," to the Island of Zante, may have been inspired by their description in Rollin's *Histoire Ancienne.* While he began with Volume I of this work, he skipped to the seventeenth and eighteenth volumes of Rollin's *Histoire Romaine,*[11] which deal with Pompey and Julius Cæsar. "To Helen" and "The Coliseum" show how deep an impression the civilizations of Greece and Rome made upon him, but Byron's influence may account for the Coliseum, and the use of the two volumes among so many indicates a special task.

Robertson's *History of America,* which deals largely with the Spanish discoveries and settlements, had no marked influence upon Poe's writing, although in one of his earliest reviews, that of Theodore Irving's *Conquest of Florida,*[12] he speaks of "the romance in the details of the Spanish conquests in America." Nor was the legalistic style of Marshall's *Washington,* in all probability, attractive to Poe.

Nicholas Gouin Dufief's *Nature Displayed in her Mode of Teaching Language to Man* [13] was a popular textbook which had already run

[11] These are the thirty-fourth and thirty-fifth volumes in the complete set of sixty volumes.
[12] *Southern Literary Messenger,* July, 1835.
[13] Since this book has been quoted by recent biographers as a work in "Natural Science," the full title is given: *Nature Displayed in her Mode of*

through several editions. It provided Poe with drill in French nouns,
phrases, and conversations, besides giving him short pieces of French
literature to read. The Voltaire item has not been identified. When
Wertenbaker gave his account of Poe in 1869, he listed Voltaire's *Histoire Particulière* as the book Poe drew out. This does not correspond
to any title of Voltaire I have been able to discover.[14]

Considering the restrictions of the library, any picture of Poe spending many hours there may be dismissed. His general reading must
have depended upon the booksellers in the neighborhood. Their ledger
accounts show that Byron was the most popular writer among the
students, five of his books being sold for one by any other author.
The influence of Byron on Poe's early verse is apparent, and the Byronic pose was appealing to him as to many other youths in those
days. Thomas Campbell was next in popularity, and Poe showed the
influence of his crisp, almost staccato rhythm in "To One in Paradise"—

> "No more—no more—no more
> (Such language holds the solemn sea
> To the sands upon the shore)
> Shall bloom the thunderblasted tree,
> Or the stricken eagle soar!"

Poe joined the Jefferson Debating Society, and held office in it. But
judging from his letters, his attention was drawn most definitely by
other phases of undergraduate activity. His first letter to Allan in May,
1826, is taken up largely with an account of a disturbance in consequence of the indictment for gambling of a number of the "hotel
keepers" by the Grand Jury in the spring of 1826:

---

*Teaching Language to Man; or, A New and Infallible Method of Acquiring
a Language in the Shortest Time Possible Deduced from the Analysis of the
Human Mind and Consequently suited to every Capacity. Adapted to the
French by N. G. Dufief.*

[14] According to Mr. J. C. Wyllie, Custodian of the rare-book collection
at the University of Virginia, the editions of Voltaire's works (Paris, 1817,
25 vols.), or a collection of his letters (Paris, 1785, 12 vols.), both recorded
in 1828 in the first printed catalogue, were burned in 1895. Dr. Mabbott
suggests that since of several editions of the works published in 1817 none
is in 25 volumes (according to Bengesco (2145-2148), the Virginia set was
probably incomplete, or bound up in 25 volumes, hence its loss prevents
verification, from other copies. Wertenbaker's phrase suggests the *Essai sur
les moeurs*, the *Charles XII*, or some other of the "individual historical
works" was what he found, consulting the original set.

I this morning received the clothes you sent me, viz an uniform coat, six yards of striped cloth for pantaloons & four pair of socks— The coat is a beautiful one & fits me exactly—I thought it best not to write 'till I received the clothes—or I should have written before this. You have heard no doubt of the disturbances in College— Soon after you left here the Grand Jury met and put the Students in a terrible fright—so much so that the lectures were unattended —and those whose names were upon the Sheriff's list—travelled off into the woods & mountains—taking their beds & provisions along with them—there were about 50 on the list—so you may suppose the College was very well thinn'd—this was the first day of the fright—the second day, "A proclamation" was issued by the faculty forbidding "any student under pain of a major punishment to leave his dormitory between the hours of 8 & 10 A M— (at which time the Sheriffs would be about) or in any way to resist the lawful authority of the Sheriffs"—This order however was very little attended to—as the fear of the Faculty could not counterbalance that of the Grand Jury—most of the "indicted" ran off a second time into the woods—and upon an examination the next morning by the Faculty—Some were reprimanded—some suspended—and one expelled—James Albert Clarke from Manchester (I went to school with him at Burke's) was suspended for two months. Armstead Carter from this neighbourhood, for the remainder of the session—And Thomas Barclay for ever— [15]

In September Poe's second letter, after dwelling on the coming examinations, gives details of a still more brutal nature:

We have had a great many fights up here lately—The faculty expelled Wickliffe last night for general bad conduct—but more especially for biting one of the student's arms with whom he was fighting—I saw the whole affair—it took place before my door— Wickliffe was much the stronger but not content with that—after getting the other completely in his power, he began to bite—I saw the arm afterwards—and it was really a serious matter—It was bitten from the shoulder to the elbow—and it is likely that pieces of flesh as large as my hand will be obliged to be cut out—He is from Kentucky—the same one that was in suspension when you

[15] Valentine Letters, pp. 41-42. Poe's account is quite accurate, when checked with the Minutes of the Faculty for May 9th. Barclay's attitude reveals the difficulties under which discipline was administered. He told the Faculty members "they might do as they pleased."

were up here some time ago—Give my love to Ma and Miss Nancy —I remain, Yours affectionately.

Jefferson had hoped that student self-government would be a sufficient check upon disorder, but he was mistaken. The conditions became so bad by the end of the first year that the Faculty were given charge of discipline and naturally there was at first a reaction of stringent rules, which in their turn brought about student resentment and disorder. The undergraduates were recruited from the best families in the State, but their way of life had made them impatient of control. The students' self-government had broken down partly because their sense of honor forbade them reporting their friends. Some of the trouble could have been averted if there had been an able president in charge, but again Jefferson's plan made no provision for an executive head.

The responsibility for preservation of order was placed next upon the "hotel keepers." These officials were primarily providers of food for sections of the dormitory system, but it was hoped by Jefferson that they would also act as guides, philosophers, and friends to the students for whom they catered. They were selected from among some of the leading Virginia families, which at that time found themselves in straitened circumstances. One hotel keeper, G. W. Spotswood, was a distant cousin of Washington, and yet he seems to have been a constant source of irritation to the undergraduates, and was probably a participator in gambling, or at least a sympathizer with the gambling element.

It is obvious that the functions of discipline and catering were incompatible. The hotel keepers declined to report the students upon whom their living depended. Card playing was forbidden, but was frequent. In one of the dormitories Sterling Edmunds lost two hundred and forty dollars at a single sitting, and horsewhipped another student, Peyton, who, he believed, had cheated him.[16] This happened during Poe's year at college, and it may well be that he was present at similar episodes, as his card playing is established by his own statements.

Though it seems not to have been noticed by his biographers, there can be little doubt that in "William Wilson" Poe drew a picture of the gambling and other dissipation at the University. He lays the

[16] Faculty Minutes, May 24 and 27, 1826. Peyton was expelled and Edmunds was suspended until July 1st, being excused somewhat on account of "the weakness of his understanding."

scene, it is true, at Eton and Oxford, of which he knew nothing, but this transfer of locale is obviously necessary. It was safe to speak of Oxford as "the most dissolute university of Europe." It would hardly have been so safe to speak of the University of Virginia as the most dissipated college in the United States, and yet it would have been true in 1826. The scene in which William Wilson is detected cheating at cards is laid in "the chambers of a fellow-commoner (Mr. Preston)." [17] John Preston, Poe's friend, was a student at that time, and the use of his name shows clearly that Poe had his alma mater in mind when he drew the pictures of the drinking and gambling that wrecked the life of William Wilson. At first reading, it seems that Poe exaggerated the vices of his hero and his friends, but when we find that in 1826 a drunken student, driving from Charlottesville, publicly reviled one of the Faculty in the vilest language, although the professor was accompanied by his family,[18] it seems that the drinking as well as the gambling may not have been overstressed. Duelling, too, was in fashion, and although the ownership of pistols was forbidden, the law was violated. The riots which punctuated the sessions were made more dangerous, of course, and the culmination of disorder came in 1840 with the murder of Professor J. A. G. Davis while he was attempting to quell a disturbance.

It was in this environment that Poe met his first test of self-guidance, and that it was unfortunate for him can hardly be doubted. The testimony that has been gathered from his companions during this one year is, of course, contradictory in some respects, but in general agreement in others. As usual, one of the most frequently repeated stories, that of his fight with his room-mate, Miles George, and his change of dormitory, proves to be incorrect. George's letter to E. V. Valentine, sent May 18, 1880,[19] deals clearly and directly with a number of points about which there has been dispute:

> Poe and myself were at no time room mates, therefore he did not leave me, or I him.—Poe roomed on the west side of the Lawn, I on the East, he afterwards moved to the western range—I was often in both rooms, & recall the many happy hours spent therein —Of the pugilistic combat so minutely described, I have some

[17] *Tales of the Grotesque and Arabesque,* I, 47.
[18] Faculty Minutes, February 14, 1826.
[19] The original letter of Miles George is in the E. V. Valentine Collection in Richmond, and is here reproduced in part. On the Ms. is the following notation: "This letter was given me by Dr. Miles George May 18th 1880 E.V.V."

recollection: it was a boyish freak or frolic, & both fight & the
feeling in which it originated were by consent buried in oblivion
never again to be revived—Poe, as has been said, was fond of
quoting poetic authors and reading poetic productions of his own,
with which his friends were delighted & entertained, then suddenly a change would come over him & he would with a piece
of charcoal evince his versatile genius by sketching upon the
walls of his dormitory, whimsical, fanciful, & grotesque figures,
with so much artistic skill, as to leave us in doubt whether Poe in
future life would be Painter or Poet; He was very excitable &
restless, at times wayward, melancholic & morose, but again—in
his better moods frolicksome, full of fun & a most attractive &
agreeable companion. To calm & quiet the excessive nervous
excitability under which he labored, he would too often put himself under the influence of that "Invisible Spirit of Wine" which
the great Dramatist has said "If known by no other name should
be called Devil"—

My impressions of Poe do not agree with the idea that he was
"short of stature, thick & somewhat compactly set," on the contrary he was of rather a delicate & slender mould. His legs not
bowed, or so slightly so as to escape notice, and did not detract
either from the symmetry of his person or the ease & grace of his
carriage—To be practical & unpoetical I think his weight was between 130 & 140 pounds.

Poe's room, number 13, West Range, now set apart and dedicated
to his memory, had nothing to distinguish it from other college rooms
then and now. Miles George's recollections, combined with those of
other students, give us in their composite testimony a picture of a boy
whom many knew, but with whom few were intimate. Another friend,
William M. Burwell, remarks that Poe "was a very attractive companion, genial in his nature and familiar, by the varied life he had
already led, with persons and scenes new to the unsophisticated pro-
vincials among whom he was thrown." This superior knowledge of the
world might have made him a leader, or it may, on the other hand,
have been resented. It all depends upon how Poe made use of it.
Burwell also corroborates Poe's own statement in his later letter to
Allan that his reckless card playing "led to a loss of caste among his
high spirited and exclusive associates." [20] His drinking, especially of
"peach and honey," was for the effect and not because of any great
liking for the liquor itself. If he took part in disorders, there is no

[20] *Alumni Bulletin,* University of Virginia, XVI, pp. 168-169.

record on the books of the University of any disciplinary action concerning him. He was summoned as a witness in an investigation by the Faculty of charges that certain hotel keepers were in the habit of playing at games of chance with the students. Poe's name had been given by the chairman as one "who he supposed possessed some knowledge of the facts." While nearly all the witnesses were examined at length, the record of his examination is very brief. "Edgar Poe never heard until now of any Hotel-Keepers playing cards or drinking with students." [21]

Notwithstanding Poe's excellent scholastic record, John Allan refused to permit him to return. There were debts also which he declined to pay. These, largely on the testimony of Thomas H. Ellis, have been set at $2,500. Before accepting this evidence, however, Ellis's statement, made first in his manuscript account in 1875 and amplified in his article printed in the *Richmond Standard,* May 7, 1881, must be scrutinized carefully: "Mr. Allan went up to Charlottesville, inquired into his ways, paid every debt that he thought ought to be paid, and refusing to pay some gambling debts (which Mr. James Galt told me, in his lifetime, amounted to about $2,500) brought Edgar away in the month of December following, and for a time kept him in Ellis & Allan's countingroom (where they were engaged in winding up their old business)—thus attempting to give him some knowledge of book-keeping, accounts, and commercial correspondence."

The amount of the gambling debts rests, then, on James Galt's statement. As will be seen from Poe's letter to John Allan from West Point in 1831, he had applied to James Galt for help to pay his regular expenses, which had been refused. James Galt was to become an executor and contingent beneficiary of John Allan's will, and was probably not an entirely disinterested party. He may consequently have magnified the amount in order to give himself or others an excuse for having refused Poe's request for aid. Wertenbaker, quoting Poe himself, from a memory of forty-four years, placed the debts at $2,000, and probably no one knew their exact amount. In any event, the evidence from James Galt is at second hand, and is prefaced and followed by statements that will be seen to be incorrect. Before discussing them, however, it is necessary to let Poe speak for himself. In January, 1831, when he desired to leave West Point, he wrote to Allan, defending himself against charges made by Allan in a letter that has

[21] Faculty Minutes, December 20, 1826.

disappeared. These will be taken up later, but the description of the reasons for some of Poe's difficulties belongs here: [22]

You may probably urge that you have given me a liberal education. I will leave the decision of that question to those who know how far liberal educations can be obtained in 8 months at the University of Va. Here you will say that it was my own fault that I did not return—You would not let me return because bills were presented you for payment which I never wished nor desired you to pay. Had you let me return, my reformation had been sure—as my conduct the last 3 months gave every reason to believe—and you would never have heard more of my extravagances. But I am not about to proclaim myself guilty of all that has been alledged against me, and which I have hitherto endured, simply because I was too proud to reply. I will boldly say that it was wholly and entirely your own mistaken parsimony that caused all the difficulties in which I was involved while at Charlottesville. The expenses of the institution at the lowest estimate were $350 per annum. You sent me there with $110. Of this $50 were to be paid immediately for board—$60 for attendance upon 2 professors—and you even then did not miss the opportunity of abusing me because I did not attend 3. Then $15 more were to be paid for room-rent—remember that all this was to be paid in *advance,* with $110.—$12 more for a bed—and $12 more for room furniture. I had, of course, the mortification of running in debt for public property—against the known rules of the institution, and was immediately regarded in the light of a beggar. You will remember that in a week after my arrival, I wrote to you for some more money, and for books—You replied in terms of the utmost abuse—if I had been the vilest wretch on earth you could not have been more abusive than you were because I could not contrive to pay $150 with $110. I had enclosed to you in my letter (according to your express commands) an account of the expences incured amounting to $149—the balance to be paid was $39—you enclosed me $40, leaving me one dollar in pocket. In a short time afterwards I received a packet of books consisting of Gil Blas, and the Cambridge Mathematics in 2 vols: books for which I had no earthly use since I had no means of attending the mathematical lectures.

[22] Valentine Letters, pp. 259-262. The letter is dated "Jany 3, 1830," evidently an error for 1831, as Poe did not enter West Point until June, 1830.

But books must be had, If I intended to remain at the institution —and they were bought accordingly *upon credit*. In this manner debts were accumulated, and money borrowed of Jews in Charlottesville at extravagant interest—for I was obliged to hire a servant, to pay for wood, for washing, and a thousand other necessaries. It was then that I became dissolute, for how could it be otherwise? I could associate with no students, except those who were in a similar situation with myself—altho' from different causes—They from drunkenness, and extravagance—I, because it was my crime to have no one on Earth who cared for me, or loved me. I call God to witness that I have never loved dissipation —Those who know me know that my pursuits and habits are very far from anything of the kind. But I was drawn into it by my companions. Even their professions of friendship—hollow as they were—were a relief. Towards the close of the session you sent me $100—but it was too late—to be of any service in extricating me from my difficulties—I kept it for some time—thinking that if I could obtain more I could yet retrieve my character—I applied to James Galt—but he, I believe, from the best of motives refused to lend me any—I then became desperate and gambled—until I finally involved myself irretrievably. If I have been to blame in all this—place yourself in my situation, and tell me if you would not have been equally so. But these circumstances were all unknown to my friends when I returned home—They knew that I had been extravagant—but that was all—I had no hope of returning to Charlottesville, and I waited in vain in expectation that you would, at least, obtain me some employment.

Poe's statements concerning the charges of the University are correctly given, and indeed are understated.[23] During the first four years, 1825-1829, one hundred and fifty dollars was always expected from the student for his board. This covered the servants' attendance, which evidently Poe was unable to pay. For after Poe had ceased to attend the University, two letters [24] from George W. Spotswood were received by Allan, of which the second will be sufficient, since it repeats the request of the first:

1st May, 1827.

Dear Sir,

I presume when you sent Mr. Poe to the University of Virginia you felt yourself bound to pay all his necessary expenses—one is

[23] See Bruce, II, 78-79 for detailed account of the customary expenses.
[24] Ellis-Allan Papers, L. of C., Poe Volume.

that each young man is expected to have a servant to attend his room   Mr. Poe did not board with me but as I had hired a first rate servant who cost me a high price—I consider him under greater obligations to pay me for the service of my servant. I have written you two letters & have never recd. an answer to eather [sic] I beg again Sir that you will send me the small amt. due. I am distressed for money—& I am informed you are Rich both in purse & Honour.

Very respectfully

GEO. W. SPOTSWOOD

How galling it must have been for Poe to be in debt for such a small sum, it is not necessary to emphasize. That Allan's refusal to pay Poe's debts was not limited to the results of gambling is proved also by a bill from a merchant of Charlottesville, who was at times an agent of Ellis and Allan:

Mr. Edgar A. Powe

In Acct. With Samuel Leitch, Jr., Dr.

Dec. 4 To 3 yds Super Blue Cloth $13.00	$39.00	
" 3 " Linin 3/ 2 yds Cotten 1/6	$2.00	
" 2 3/4 " Blk Bombazette 3/ Padding 3/	1.88	
" Staying 3/ 1 set Best Gilt Buttons 7/6	1.75	
" 1 doz. Buttonmoulds 9d. 1 Cut Velvet Vest 30/	5.13	
" 3/4 yd. Blk Cassinette 27/	3.38	
" 1 " Staying 2/ 16 Hanks Silk, 6d	1.63	
" Hanks Thread at 3c 1 Spool Cotten 1/	.44	
" 1 Peace Tape 9d 1 1/2 doz. Buttons 6d	.25	$55.46
" 1 pr. Drab Pantaloones and Trimmings $13.00	13.00	
		$68.46 [25]

The date of this bill is not given, but it evidently belongs to 1826, as Leitch was still trying to collect it from John Allan in June, 1828.[26] These letters disprove Ellis's statement that Mr. Allan paid all Poe's legitimate debts. Students were expected to deposit with the "patron,"

[25] Ellis-Allan Papers, L. of C., Poe Volume.
[26] In a letter from Samuel Leitch to Mr. Charles Allis [Ellis], June 28, 1828, the former says: "Please let me know if Mr. Allen [sic] done anything with my account agains [t] Mr. Pow [sic]." Ellis-Allan Papers, L. of C., Vol. 261.

a financial officer, one hundred and fourteen dollars for clothes and pocket money. Allan evidently saved this sum by sending the uniform required by the University,[27] but failed to send any pocket money at all. To a college where the proctor estimated that the great majority of the young men spent at least five hundred dollars in one session,[28] Poe was sent by John Allan deliberately, without a decent allowance, or even the minimum charges of the institution. There is no possible escape from this conclusion. Allan was in easy circumstances, and yet he refused to contribute for a year's expenses less than a third of the amount he had paid in England when he was not by any means so well off.

There seems to have been an almost incredible meanness in one of the actions to which Poe refers, the abusing of the boy because he did not take three courses instead of two. There was a provision of the University requiring a student in the academic schools to register in three of them unless the parents requested permission for him to take a smaller number. If the rule was enforced, Allan had it called to his attention, and he must either have given his consent, or else he demanded that Poe register for another school, knowing that he did not have the necessary funds.

Some decided change had come over his relations with Poe. The natural inference is that he wished to have Edgar Poe out of Richmond as cheaply as possible, for fear of his finding out or disclosing certain actions of John Allan that have already been discussed. Of course, the bitterness of Poe's letter of 1831 must be discounted somewhat, especially in view of the affectionate tone of the two letters of 1826. But the main facts as Poe gave them are indisputable. Perhaps Mrs. Allan sent him some money secretly.

Certainly Poe seems to have enjoyed some phases of his University career. He took long walks in the neighborhood, which are reflected in "A Tale of the Ragged Mountains." This story begins, "During the fall of the year, 1827, while residing near Charlottesville, Virginia." The main plot of the story has no connection with the University, but Poe's own wandering inspired the description of the hero, Bedloe, "setting forth alone, or attended only by a dog, upon a long ramble among the chain of wild and dreary hills that lie westward and southward of Charlottesville, and are there dignified by the title of the Ragged Mountains." The story was not published until 1844, but the description of the scenery with its "delicious aspect of dreary desola-

[27] See Poe's letter of May, 1826.
[28] Bruce, II, 79.

tion," and the haze of Indian summer, which prepare Bedloe for his curious dream, probably was based on memories too deeply impressed on a young imaginative mind to be forgotten.

Jefferson's strong interest in landscape gardening had already in 1826 revealed itself in planning more conscious adornment of the campus by the planting of trees and shrubs. "The Landscape Garden" may rest upon the memory of a boy who was watching the efforts of the proctor in this direction. Ellison, the lover of artificial beauty who animates this story, has in him some decided Poe traits, and his very name may be a link with a past in which the name of Ellis is so closely associated.

With the close of Poe's term at the University of Virginia, his regular education was over. It has not been observed that this training both in school and college was limited largely to those subjects, the ancient and modern languages, whose main purpose, for an American at least, has been the development of the power of expression. This limitation was on the whole not altogether unfortunate for an artist who was to become one of the greatest creators of phrases the world has known. The training was probably thorough, and is distinctly a form of education which makes for power and skill in the choice of words. A broader curriculum might have given Poe wider interests, and more specific information, in history and science. The former he apparently sought in his reading, to judge from the books he drew from the library. But information obtained in college soon vanishes, if not immediately applied—power, particularly linguistic power, lasts longer, especially if, as in Poe's case, he was already beginning to write verses.

The conditions of Poe's life from his return from the University of Virginia in December, 1826, until he left Richmond for Boston in March, 1827, are not very clear. As usual, contradictions are plentiful. T. H. Ellis insists [29] that John Allan placed him in his counting house, where the firm of Ellis and Allan were closing out their business. But Poe's letter of "Monday," probably March 19, 1827, denies this. This letter has signal importance. After expressing his determination to leave Allan's house and his regret at his frustrated college ambitions, he continues: [30]

... but in a moment of caprice you have blasted my hope—because forsooth I disagreed with you in an opinion, which opinion I was forced to express—

[29] *Richmond Standard,* May 7, 1881.
[30] Valentine Letters, pp. 60-61.

Again, I have heard you say (when you little thought I was listening and therefore must have said it in earnest) that you had
no affection for me—
You have moreover ordered me to quit your house, and are continually upbraiding me with eating the bread of idleness, when
you yourself were the only person to remedy the evil by placing
me to some business—
You take delight in exposing me before those whom you think
likely to advance my interest in this world—
You suffer me to be subjected to the whims & caprice, not only of
your white family, but the complete authority of the blacks—these
grievances I could not submit to; and I am gone—

Poe, it is to be noticed, here attributes the failure of Allan to permit
him to return to Virginia not to the unpaid bills, but to "an opinion I
was forced to express." This expression points to his criticism of
Allan's conduct, which, it must also be noted, he never makes definite
in any of the published letters.

Allan replied at once, but the copy of his letter makes no explanation of Poe's charges—except that "the charge of eating the Bread of
Idleness, was to urge you to perseverance and industry in receiving the
classics, in perfecting yourself in the mathematics, etc." This can
hardly refer to the period after Poe's return to Richmond, and the
general tone of the letter is vague.[31] Before Poe received this note, he
had written again on Tuesday (March 20) requesting "the expence
of my passage to Boston ($12) and a little to support me there until I
shall be enabled to engage in some business. I sail on Saturday."

None of these letters is dated, but another letter dated March 25,
1827, from a friend of Poe, enables us to place them correctly: [32]

Dinwiddie County, March 25th, 1827

Dear Sir,
     When I saw you in Richmond a few days ago I should have
mentioned the difference between us if there had not been so
many persons present I must of course, as you did not mention
it to me enquire of you if you ever intend to pay it If you have
not the money write me word that you have not but do not be
perfectly silent I should be glad if you would write to me even
as a friend. there can certainly be no harm in your avowing candidly that you have no money if you have none but you can say

[31] Letter Number Five—Valentine Letters.
[32] Ellis-Allan Papers, L. of C., Poe Volume.

when you can pay me if you cannot now. I heard when I was in Richmond that Mr. Allen [sic] would probably discharge all your debts If mine was a gambling debt I should not think much of it But under the present circumstances I think very strangely of it Write to me upon the receipt of this letter and tell me candidly what is the matter.

Your friend EDWARD G. CRUMP.

Fortunately, Allan endorsed this letter "Edw G. Crump Mar. 25, 1827 to E. A. Poe, alias Henri Le Rennet." Crump's letter, which evidently never reached Poe, proves that he was still in Richmond "a few days" before March 25th. It also indicates that Poe had borrowed money for some purpose other than gambling. On March 27th Allan wrote a long letter to his sister, concerning the estate of William Galt, at the end of which he said: "I'm thinking Edgar has gone to sea to seek his own fortunes." [33]

These two letters of Poe, judging from the original scripts, were evidently written by one in great emotional disturbance. The handwriting is irregular and the pages are blotted. Perhaps the sentence which concludes the letter of March 20, "I have not one cent to provide any food," may explain their appearance. They are pitiful, in any event, in their desperate and defiant tone, and one might be tempted to disbelieve that Allan had deliberately cast him adrift had not Poe definitely repeated the statement in 1831 when he wrote, "I had no hope of returning to Charlottesville, and I waited in vain in expectation that you would, at least, obtain me some employment. I saw no prospect of this—and I could endure it no longer. Everyday threatened with a warrant." [34]

There was, of course, another reason for Poe's disturbed state of mind. When he returned from the University he found that his romance with Elmira Royster was over. While his sorrow was in all probability dramatized, yet the pride of a young lover had been hurt, and it is always difficult for an imaginative youngster to distinguish between a grievance and a grief.

Edgar Poe left Richmond, in all probability, on Saturday March 24, 1827. How he obtained the funds we do not know. John Allan evidently did not provide them. Perhaps Mrs. Allan did. He was leaving a home in which he had for many years been treated as a son, and in which at least one woman saw him leave with deep regret. Notwith-

[33] Ellis-Allan Papers, L. of C., Poe Volume.
[34] Letter Number Twenty-four, Valentine Letters, p. 261.

standing her nervous temperament, there is plenty of evidence, both in Poe's letters and in the writing of others, that Mrs. Allan loved him and that he loved her. Of Miss Valentine's attitude, we really know nothing. Although some biographers have built up a picture of "Aunt Nancy" as a good friend to him, it is all imaginary. According to Thomas Ellis's account of her in his manuscript, she was little short of an angel. Letters from her own younger relatives speak of her as "Aunt Nancy," and she seems to have been one of those women who was everybody's aunt. Yet in no one of Poe's letters does he refer to her in this way. When he asks to be remembered to her, which he does in about half the letters to Allan, he always speaks of "Miss Nancy" or "Miss Valentine." The matter is perhaps not of great importance, yet coupled with the fact that after her sister's death she remained in John Allan's household, it may indicate either that she did not altogether approve of Edgar's behavior, or that she was an unimportant element in his life.

Other romantic stories which were at one time believed, disappear also. The mythical trip to Europe, the joining of the Grecian Revolution, must be dismissed. There was no time for them.

CHAPTER VI

Tamerlane and the Army

Edgar Poe arrived at the city of his birth in April, 1827.[1] It was his first independent venture, taken on impulse, and probably prompted by Boston's reputation as a literary and publishing center. How he lived during the next two months is uncertain. T. H. Ellis, in his manuscript,[2] says, "The story of his going to St. Petersburg, etc., was all an invention. The occasional letters which he wrote home are dated 'St. Petersburg,' but were written while he was on the stage in Boston, or an enlisted soldier in the army." It would be a delightful task to speculate on Edgar Poe's theatrical career, but, of course, Ellis's testimony, unchecked, cannot be taken as sufficient evidence. However, since he was right in his statement concerning the Army, he may have been correct concerning Poe's attempt to go upon the stage. With the record of his parents' career, and his own amateur efforts in Richmond, it would have been a likely thing for Poe to attempt. Unfortunately, a careful scrutiny of the newspapers of Boston for the period reveals only one possible bit of evidence. On April 24, 1827, appeared the advertisement of the *Foundling of the Forest*, "the part of Bertrand by a young gentleman of Boston, his first appearance on any stage, who

---

[1] Mrs. Stanard in the Valentine Letters, p. 52, quotes a correspondent to the effect that "the only vessel directly from Richmond which reached Boston during this period was the Carrier, Captain Gill. The Carrier cast anchor April 7." My search of files of the *Boston Commercial Gazette* and the *Boston Centinel* reveals no such boat arriving in Boston, and as Dr. Mabbott has shown, the *Carrier* cleared *for* Richmond on April 7th, from Boston. The *Richmond Enquirer* and the *Constitutional Whig*, of Richmond, make no mention of this or any other boat leaving Richmond for Boston at this time. The Boston papers record the arrival, however, of the *Only Son*, Captain Hicks, on April 3rd, and the *President*, Captain Ames, both from Richmond. Poe may have come on either, but in the absence of passenger lists, the whole matter is one of conjecture. Poe may have stopped in Baltimore, en route. See T. O. Mabbott, Introduction to his edition of *Tamerlane* (New York, 1941).

[2] Valentine Collection.

has politely proffered his services on the occasion."[3] The fact that it was "a young gentleman of Boston" would dismiss the matter from consideration if we did not remember that Poe was to publish his first book shortly as "By a Bostonian," and was evidently, at that time, making the most of his fragile connections with his birthplace. Unfortunately, playbills of that date for Boston are exceedingly rare, and those examined give no evidence.

If Poe did make this attempt to follow his parents' stage career, it was not a success. It must have been an unhappy boy who enlisted in the United States Army as a private soldier on May 26, 1827. That he was not entering upon this career from any liking for a soldier's life is clear from the fact that he gave his name as Edgar A. Perry, born in Boston, and his age as twenty-two.[4] Since this last statement was a gratuitous misrepresentation, for minors were at that time accepted, it is evident that Poe intended to disappear.[5] Poe gave his occupation as a clerk, and he may indeed have secured such employment for a time.[6] He was assigned to Battery H of the First Artillery in Fort Independence, Boston Harbor.

The enlistment was an interruption to Poe's career, but shortly after came the beginning of the great business of his life, in the publication of his first volume of poems. *Tamerlane and Other Poems, By a Bostonian* was published, probably in the early summer of 1827, by a printer, Calvin F. S. Thomas, at 70 Washington Street. Little is known of the circumstances of the publication, and while Thomas had, later,

[3] *Boston Courier*, April 24, 1827, advertising the play for April 25th.

[4] The exact statement of the War Department Records as given to me, December 15, 1939, reads: "At the date of enlistment Perry gave his age as twenty-two years; birthplace, Boston, Massachusetts; occupation, clerk; height, five feet, eight inches; eyes, grey; hair, brown; and complexion, fair."

[5] Information concerning Poe's career in the Army has heretofore been based on the search of the records of the War Department made by Adjutant General Drum, for George E. Woodberry, who published the results in the *Atlantic Monthly*, December, 1884, and later in his *Edgar Allan Poe* (1885). His information was correctly given, so far as it went. Through the courtesy of Major General E. S. Adams, Adjutant General, a complete copy of Poe's army record has been furnished to me, and is given in the Appendix or in its appropriate places.

[6] There is an account of Poe's supposed meetings at Virginia, in Boston, and elsewhere with a certain Peter Pindar Pease, published by Theodore Pease Stearns in *The Outlook*, September 1, 1920, under the title, "A Prohibitionist Shakes Dice with Poe." It is at third hand, and seems to me untrustworthy as evidence. It does, however, support Poe's own statement that he was a clerk in Boston.

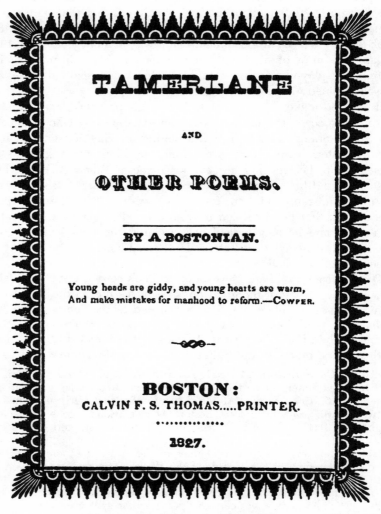

TAMERLANE

AND

OTHER POEMS.

BY A BOSTONIAN.

Young heads are giddy, and young hearts are warm,
And make mistakes for manhood to reform.—COWPER.

BOSTON:
CALVIN F. S. THOMAS.....PRINTER.

1827.

FRONT COVER AND TITLE PAGE OF *Tamerlane*
Reproduced from the original through the

TAMERLANE

AND

OTHER POEMS.

BY A BOSTONIAN.

Young heads are giddy, and young hearts are warm,
And make mistakes for manhood to reform.　　COWPER

—∞—

BOSTON:
CALVIN F. S. THOMAS.....PRINTER.
....
1827.

and Other Poems, POE'S FIRST BOOK
courtesy of the Huntington Library.

quite a career as a printer and editor,[7] he seems not to have made any
mention of Poe.

"Tamerlane," the title poem, in its first form contained four hundred
and six lines. In the edition of 1845, which represents Poe's final revision, it included only two hundred and thirty-four. The most striking
differences, however, occur between this first edition of 1827 and the
second, published in 1829. The latter is almost identical with the final
version, since the additions and deletions in the 1831 edition were
practically all discarded, and Poe returned to the 1829 version in his
final revision. In addition to these published versions there is a manuscript in the Pierpont Morgan Library which seems to be a form intermediate between those of 1827 and 1829. It is in an immature hand,
and is marked by scribbled suggestions for revision.[8]

"Tamerlane" in all three forms is, therefore, distinctly a poem of
Poe's youth, and they must be considered critically together. The
poem already represents several of his poetic principles, and many of
his metrical methods. Since the version of 1829 is markedly superior
to that of 1827, it reveals early in his career that capacity for self-
criticism and the striving for perfection which are two of the traits
that have won him the esteem of all competent judges of poetry.

The note first struck in "Tamerlane" is that of independence. The
"holy friar," who is simply a device through which Poe can express his
hero's emotions, is at once repudiated as an inspiration of hope. Hope
is not a gift which one soul can give to another. "It falls from an
eternal shrine," a rather effective line, amplified in 1829.

The next theme, that of pride, strikes at once a note of conflict with
earlier happiness and is coupled with regret. In his Introduction, Poe
states that "in Tamerlane, he has endeavored to expose the folly of
even *risking* the best feelings of the heart at the shrine of ambition."
Yet even in such stanzas as the third, beginning with its obvious influence of Byron,

> "I have not always been as now,"

[7] He was born in New York City, August 5, 1808. About 1830 he left
Boston for New York City, and from 1835 to 1868 he lived in Buffalo,
where he published the *Western Literary Messenger* and the *Buffalo Medical Journal*. He died in Buffalo September 19, 1876. For an extended account of Thomas, see Oscar Wegelin, *Bulletin New York Historical Society*,
January, 1940, and Mabbott's Introduction to *Tamerlane*.

[8] Certain corrections of obvious mistakes indicate that the manuscript is
later than the 1827 version. Cf. line 75 in "Tamerlane" (1827): "My soul in
mystery to sleep," with the Ms., "My soul in mystery to steep"; or in line
90, "Tamerlane," "lovliness" which becomes "loveliness" in the Ms.

there is a distinction between the worldly ambition that destroys happiness and the

> "heritage of a kingly mind
> And a proud spirit which hath striven
> Triumphantly with human kind."

The struggle to preserve spiritual integrity, which we shall have constantly to study in Poe's poetry and prose, is a consequence of a proper pride, and is here emphasized in his first poem of importance.

The themes of beauty and of love are naturally introduced together, in verses whose harmony clothes a figure of speech veracious and striking:

> "I have no words—alas!—to tell
> The loveliness of loving well!
> Nor would I now attempt to trace
> The more than beauty of a face
> Whose lineaments, upon my mind,
> Are—shadows on th' unstable wind:
> Thus I remember having dwelt
>   Some page of early lore upon,
> With loitering eye, till I have felt
> The letters—with their meaning—melt
>   To fantasies—with none."

The love that has come to him

> "was such as angel minds above might envy."

It is interesting that in "Annabel Lee" they loved

> "With a love that the winged seraphs of Heaven
> Coveted her and me."

Thus in his first and in his last poem he thought in terms of a spiritual passion that transcended human limits.

Any criticism of "Tamerlane" from the point of view of historical accuracy would be futile. Poe describes Tamerlane as

> "A cottager, I marked a throne
> Of half the world as all my own
> And murmured at such lowly lot."

The real Tamerlane was the son of Teragai, head of his tribe, and was descended from the chief minister of the son of Jenghiz Khan. Poe knew of his relation to Jenghiz Khan, as his notes prove, but he

probably felt that the rise of his hero was more dramatic if he was
"the son of a shepherd." It was from no love of democracy, however,
that Poe thus altered facts. Tamerlane is the symbol of the innate
patrician. He believes that

> "Among the rabble-men
> Lion ambition is chain'd down
> And crouches to a keeper's hand—
> Not so in deserts where the grand
> The wild—the terrible conspire
> With their own breath to fan his fire."

This attitude is, of course, not to be taken too seriously. Perhaps
the line from Byron's "Giaour"

> "In crowds a slave, in deserts free"

lingered in Poe's memory. Perhaps it was the dramatized loneliness of
boyhood. It was in Poe's case sincere, but it partook of that artificial
appreciation of the "wide open spaces" that is so often the characteristic of those who have grown up in cities.

With geography, as well as history, Poe took the license of a poet.
If there were any real inspiration for the scenery of "Tamerlane," it
probably lay in the hills around Charlottesville. But already Poe was
avoiding the concrete in his poetry. In the version of 1827 Tamerlane
speaks of himself as "Alexis" and of his love as "Ada." But in the 1829
version and, indeed, already in the manuscript (if it *is* an intermediate
stage), these proper names and a long account of his actual desertion
are omitted; to the great improvement of the poem. "Ada" is restored,
temporarily, in 1831.

The final theme, death, approaches as the conqueror of love, of
beauty, and of pride. Tamerlane has returned to find his love dead,
and the ending in the earliest version, with its lines, imitative of
Childe Harold,

> "The sound of revelry by night
> Comes o'er me"

gives place to a vastly superior climax in 1829:

> "Father, I firmly do believe—
> I *know*—for Death who comes for me
> From regions of the blest afar,
> Where there is nothing to deceive,
> Hath left his iron gate ajar,

And rays of truth you cannot see
Are flashing thro' Eternity—
I do believe that Eblis hath
A snare in ev'ry human path—
Else how, when in the holy grove
I wandered of the idol, Love,
Who daily scents his snowy wings
With incense of burnt offerings
From the most unpolluted things,
Whose pleasant bowers are yet so riven
Above with trelliced rays from Heaven
No mote may shun—no tiniest fly—
The light'ning of his eagle eye—
How was it that Ambition crept,
        Unseen, amid the revels there,
Till growing bold, he laughed and leapt
        In the tangles of Love's very hair?"

Throughout his career, Poe was to develop in many forms the four themes of pride, love, beauty, and death. They are all in his first poem,[9] and to any student of his life, they are natural selections. He was a worshipper of beauty, his capacity for love was unusual, his pride, as we will see, was intense, and his preoccupation with death was constant. It is easy to point to similarities both verbal and in conception of character and incident with Byron, especially with "Manfred." But in reality Poe read Byron because his own feeling was attuned to that form of romanticism of which Byron and Moore were the British representatives. Poe may have received the suggestion of his hero from Marlowe's *Tamburlaine,* from Rowe's *Tamerlane,* or "Monk" Lewis's play, but there is no evidence of any definite influence. In one of the prose interludes in Thomas Moore's *Lalla Rookh,* Fadladeen speaks of Aurungszebe as "the wisest and best of the descendants of Timur." That Poe was reading Moore at this period, or earlier, is clear, but any influence upon "Tamerlane" is of the most general kind.

While Poe was to advance just as steadily in his rhythmical skill as in his creative power, he showed in "Tamerlane" some of the traits

[9] "Lines to Louisa," attributed to Poe as an earlier poem than "Tamerlane," came from a novel, *George Barnwell* (1798) by Thomas Skinner Surr. See Sylvia T. Warner, *New Statesman and Nation,* N. S. VIII (November 17, 1934), 730. T. O. Mabbott in his Introduction to *Tamerlane* (1941) pp. xlix–lii, gives a synopsis of our shadowy information about Poe's possible writings before *Tamerlane.*

which mark him out from the majority of metrical artists. His verse form in "Tamerlane" is his favorite four-stress measure. He did not know, of course, of Dr. Holmes' later experiments,[10] which proved that the four-stress line coincides in time interval with human breathing, and that since there are four heart beats to each breath, it is the natural line. But Poe unerringly selected it for the effects he wished to produce. The unity of the line being secured by its fundamental physiological nature, Poe developed variety by subtle modifications of the preconceived verse scheme. In immediate succession appear lines like

> "You call it hope—that fire of fire!
> It is but agony of desire."

In the first line the accented syllables have almost exactly the same amount of stress, and they occur at almost exactly the same time interval. In other words, the feet are equivalent. In the second line, the accented syllables have different amounts of stress, and no time interval between them is the same. The contrast is immediate and effective. Another striking passage introduces a planet he was often to use:

> "What tho' the moon—the white moon—
> Shed all the splendor of her noon,
> *Her* smile is chilly—and *her* beam,
> In that time of dreariness, will seem
> (So like you gather in your breath)
> A portrait taken after death."

The same element of variety is secured, for no one of the verses is exactly like the others in metrical structure. Another element of variety is secured in the first line by an apparent violation of the old-fashioned metrical rules, which were still believed in during Poe's day. In the 1827 form, the line reads:

> "What though the moon—the silvery moon."

The substitution of "white" for "silvery" brings an additional stress on "white" and a consequent pause which aids in the emphasis.

In other words, Poe was following a basic law of English versification, which poets have always followed, while writers on versification have cluttered up the subject with academic rules, to which the poets have paid no attention. This basic law bids poets make their metrical form a servant to their thought, and never permit their metrical

---

[10] See O. W. Holmes, "The Physiology of Versification."

scheme to limit the free play of their ideas. Poe rejected, also, the limitation that springs from uniformity of end rime or of stanzaic structure. He rimes as the thought demands, in couplet, or quatrain form, in alternate or enclosed rimes. There are really no stanzas; the sections of the poem are uneven in length, and end simply when the thought is completed. In the early versions the sections are numbered, but even this indication of stanzaic structure is abandoned in the revision of 1845.

Of the remaining poems published with "Tamerlane" in 1827, "To ———," beginning with

> "I saw thee on thy bridal day;
>   When a burning blush came o'er thee"

may be based on Poe's broken engagement to Elmira Royster, but it has the usual lack of merit which self-pity gives to verse.

In "Visit of the Dead," there is a powerful conception of the relation of the soul, lonely so far as earthly ties are concerned, but not lonely in the larger reality of death, for

> "The spirits of the dead, who stood
>   In life before thee, are again
>   In death around thee, and their will
>   Shall then o'ershadow thee—be still."

"The Lake" is an early picture of pleasure in loneliness and the terror that

> "was not fright
>   But a tremulous delight."

While these poems must be credited definitely to this early period, "Imitation" belongs because of its many changes to a later period when it became "A Dream Within A Dream." Poe did not reprint "Evening Star," which is only of interest because it is the first appearance of the contrast between Astarté and the Moon, to culminate in "Ulalume." He also discarded those untitled verses which conclude with the striking lines,

> "That high tone of the spirit which hath striv'n,
>   Tho' not with Faith—with godliness—whose throne
>   With desp'rate energy 't hath beaten down;
>   Wearing its own deep feeling as a crown."

It seems strange that he did not recognize how well these words applied to himself—as did that other vivid flash in "Dreams,"

"to him whose heart must be
And hath been still, upon the lovely earth,
A chaos of deep passion, from his birth." [11]

In this first volume the love of dreaming is noteworthy, partly day dreaming, as in "Dreams" partly the mystical union of life and death. The perfection which marked Poe's greatest lyrics was, of course, not yet present. But the promise was there.

Tamerlane and Other Poems made practically no impression upon the critical or popular reader. It was noticed by two magazines, but without critical comment.[12] In a three-volume anthology, *Specimens of American Poetry*, edited by Samuel Kettell in 1829, it is listed,[13] but no selections were made from it. That it was listed at all was due probably to the fact that the publisher, S. G. Goodrich, was also "A Bostonian." It is not surprising that *Tamerlane* failed to challenge Kettell's approval. His anthology was a praiseworthy attempt to call attention to native poets, but an examination of the selections will reveal no poetry of the type Poe had written. They are mainly of the reflective or narrative varieties, and even those writers like Fitz-Greene Halleck, or John Neal, who also reflected the influence of Byron, did so in a different way.

While we may not believe that Poe was truthful in claiming, as he

[11] "Dreams" and "The Happiest Day, the Happiest Hour" were not reprinted by Poe in any of his volumes of verse. They appeared, however, in *The North American*, a weekly paper of Baltimore in 1827, over the signature of "W. H. P.," probably the initials of William Henry Poe. There are slight changes in "Dreams," usually improvements, and the two final stanzas of "The Happiest Day" have been omitted, while a new one of distinctly lower quality has been added. Whether Poe was a party to this reprinting is an open question, but the fact that he had published *Tamerlane* without revealing his own identity makes it at least possible. His omission of the poems from his later volumes indicates that he placed little value upon them. They could hardly have been dropped because of any joint authorship between Edgar and Henry Poe, for the other examples of the latter's writing have none of his brother's quality. They are to be found in a file of the *North American*, in the New York Public Library, or perhaps more conveniently in *Poe's Brother*, by Hervey Allen and Thomas Ollive Mabbott (New York, 1926).

[12] *The United States Review and Literary Gazette*, II (August, 1827), 399, and *The North American Review*, XXV (October, 1827), 47.

[13] Vol. III, p. 405.

does in his introduction to *Tamerlane,* that he had written the poems when he was only in his fourteenth year, the publication was still strikingly early for those days. Bryant was the only one of the American poets of first rank who had issued a volume. Emerson, who was Poe's senior by six years, did not publish a volume of verse until 1841; Whittier, who was two years older than Poe, waited until 1831; Longfellow, born in 1807, who had published verse as early as 1820, issued *Voices of the Night,* his first volume, in 1839; and Holmes, who was born during the same year as Poe, sent forth his first collection of poems, nine years later, in 1836. The early appearance of *Tamerlane* is only one illustration of Poe's quiet confidence that he had something original and authentic to offer. That he was right is now apparent. Of the eighteen other volumes of verse recorded by Kettell as being published in 1827, only one, Halleck's *Alnwick Castle,* is read even by the special student. But in *Tamerlane and Other Poems* there was a lyric fervor that had not appeared before in American poetry. By a grim and ironic justice, the book, which sold for twelve and one-half cents, is now one of the most sought and the most valuable of rare Americana.

Poe's battery of artillery was ordered to Fort Moultrie, on Sullivan's Island, Charleston Harbor, on October 31, 1827. He did not embark, however, until November 8th, on the brig *Waltham,* and he arrived November 18th. Here he remained until December 11, 1828, when his battery set sail on the ship *Harriet* for Fortress Monroe in Virginia,[14] where they landed on December 15, 1828. While he is not mentioned, the names of the officers identify the battery.

As a private or non-commissioned officer, Poe's social life in Charleston would have been limited. According to family tradition, however, he made warm friends with Colonel William Drayton, to whom he dedicated later the *Tales of the Grotesque and Arabesque* and with whom he continued a friendship when Colonel Drayton moved to Philadelphia.[15]

If he made any effort to trace his parents' theatrical history in these cities, we do not know it. The region, however, surrounding Charleston made a lasting impression upon Poe. Most definite, of course, was

[14] Dates given by the War Department are those on which the official orders were issued. The actual dates of sailing and arrival have been ascertained from the *Charleston Courier* and the *City Gazette and Commercial Daily Advertiser* by Dr. William S. Hoole. See "Poe in Charleston," *American Literature,* VI (March, 1934), 78-80.

[15] Letter of Dr. William Drayton, Jr. to the writer, October 29, 1940.

the inspiration which led later to the writing of "The Gold Bug." As usual, Poe made use of certain local characteristics, but changed scenery and other elements to suit his story. The description of Sullivan's Island with which "The Gold Bug" opens is on the whole correct. The picturesque ruins of Fort Moultrie, as it stood in Poe's day, remain, but the new fort and the many houses clustering around it present quite a different picture from that which he knew. The myrtles, especially on the eastern end, are still there, but they never were the European variety which Poe describes, but only a local plant. To his hero, Legrand, Poe attributes, as usual, some of his own traits and habits. Legrand saunters "along the beach and through the myrtles in quest of shells or entomological specimens." Poe's acceptance in 1839 of the task of rewriting Wyatt's textbook on conchology shows his interest in shells, which may date from this period. In 1826 there lived on Sullivan's Island Dr. Edmund Ravenel, a conchologist of distinction, and it seems most probable that Poe talked with him, and may have received from him his inspiration.

The story stems from the discovery of the gold bug by Legrand, and the mistake by which the teller of the tale returns to Legrand not the side of the parchment on which the bug has been sketched, but the cryptogram which tells the location of the treasure, is a clever device. The conversation of Jupiter, the colored servant of Legrand, leads up skilfully to the description of the bug.

The gold bug itself is at first glance entirely imaginary, for no such beetle exists. But it has been suggested [16] that Poe combined the characteristics of two beetles existing in the locality to make a new one suitable to his purpose. The *Callichroma splendidum* has a head of gleaming gold color, its wings are satiny green, and its abdomen is dull gold. This beetle is an inch and a half long by about one-half inch wide, and the antennæ are three inches long. The jaws are powerful and can inflict a real pinch. Jupiter's objection to it and his description of the beetle, "de bug is a goole bug, solid inside and all, sep him wing," are realistic. But this beetle has no black spots and its shape is wrong. There is, however, a fairly common insect known as the "Click Beetle," the *Alaus oculatus,* which has a ground color of black thickly spotted with white. On its large and prominent prothorax are two large, rounded, black eyelike spots, edged with white, giving, according to Professor Smyth, the appearance of a death's head. There is,

[16] Ellison A. Smyth, Jr., "Poe's Gold Bug from the Standpoint of an Entomologist." *Sewanee Review.* XVIII (January, 1910), 67-72.

however, no long black mark at the bottom, which Poe inserted to make the resemblance to the death's head more striking.[17] The fact that the *Callichroma splendidum* is not a "Scarabæus," but belongs to the family *Cerambycidae,* did not bother Poe, nor does it disturb any one else. There were common varieties of beetle in the neighborhood which did belong to this family, and the name Scarabæus is familiar to most readers. Indeed, this synthetic bug is probably, through the story, the best known of all beetles, even if, like the "sea coast of Bohemia," it never existed. Poe at times had almost an impish delight in the inaccuracy of unessentials. The parchment cryptogram is signed with the figure of a "kid"—though Captain Kidd did not enter Charleston harbor. There were many pirates who did, however, and "Blackbeard" and Bonnet would have provided possibilities for less obvious puns.

But Poe knew that the main interest in "The Gold Bug" lies in Legrand's solution of the pirate's cryptogram by which the treasure is discovered. He therefore takes liberties with the real country through which Legrand had searched for the "Bishop's Castle" from which he was to see the death's head on the tree under whose dead limb they were to dig. The low alluvial soil of the Isle of Palms, then known as Long Island, which they would have crossed before they reached the mainland, becomes the "country excessively wild and desolate" where "no trace of a human footstep was to be seen." The mainland, too, is low and marshy in places. But Poe had to find a lofty seat from which Legrand was to see the tall tulip tree on which the skull had been nailed. So he naturally invented the "narrow ledge" on the eastern face of the rock.[18] To one unfamiliar with the mainland north of Sullivan's Island it would seem incredible that a skull would have remained visible after the years that had elapsed since the pirate deposited the treasure there. But the few tulip trees that still remain after another lapse of time reveal, through their scanty foliage on many of their limbs, that Poe was not straying beyond the limits of

[17] Carroll Laverty suggests that Poe, who describes a "death's head moth" in his story of "The Sphinx" (1846), may have seen one in the *Saturday Magazine* of August 25, 1832, where a picture of the moth is given. It is possible. See "The Death's Head on the Gold Bug," *American Literature,* XII (March, 1940), 88-91.

[18] Miss Laura Bragg, former Director of the Charleston Museum, has called my attention to a lime kiln on the eastern side of the Isle of Palms, which might have suggested to Poe the "rocky seat." These lime kilns have been in the locality for many years, and the supposition is at least an interesting one.

possibility. And it is to be remembered, also, that it was a "dead limb" on which the skull was found.

It must be remembered, too, that while Poe invented rocks and cliffs where they have never been, the region through which Legrand and his companions made their way does partake even yet of a certain desolate quality. Houses are few today, and they must have been much fewer in 1828. The forests of the mainland and the barren sands of Sullivan's Island may well have seemed desolate to a young poet who was sick of soldiering. According to Colonel Gage, the genial commandant of Fort Moultrie when I first saw it, Poe would have had sufficient leisure in the "old army" days to take long walks on the mainland. The filmy drapery of "Spanish moss" falling over the thick growth of oaks, pines, and cypress—who can doubt that the moon "more filmy than the rest" whose "wide circumference"

> "In easy drapery falls
>
> . . . .
>
> O'er the strange woods—o'er the sea"

passed from the forests of South Carolina into "Fairyland," first printed in the volume of 1829. Even today when one comes upon the two columns of stately oaks lining the approach to the estate of "Oakland" in Christ Church Parish, the fine climax of Poe's first published story, "Metzengerstein," flashes at once into remembrance. "Up the long avenue of aged oaks which led from the forest to the main entrance of the Palace Metzengerstein, a steed, bearing an unbonneted and disordered rider, was seen leaping with an impetuosity which outstripped the very Demon of the Tempest." Here Poe was, as usual, combining a memory of a native background with the romantic convention that placed the scene in a distant land.

Sullivan's Island remained a vivid memory in Poe's mind. The travellers across the ocean in "The Balloon-Hoax" land on the beach "(The tide being out and the sand hard, smooth, and admirably adapted for a descent)." In "The Oblong Box" Charleston is simply a place from which to depart. But it was not the city of Charleston, it was rather the surroundings of Fort Moultrie and the shadows of the dense woods of South Carolina that stamped their impress upon Poe.

Poe had already decided that he was wasting his time in the Army. On December 1st, while they were under orders to sail from Fort Moultrie, he wrote to John Allan in the tone of a repentant son, asking his consent to withdrawing from the service. Evidently there had been previous correspondence, and Poe could hardly have been more solicitous for Mr. Allan's recovery from an "indisposition," if there had never been a dispute between them. His experience in the service had not made him less confident of success, and one sentence, "The period of an Enlistment is five years—the prime of my life would be wasted— I shall be driven to more decided measures, if you refuse to assist me," reveals Poe in his combination of appeal for help and vague threats if the help is not given, which forms one of his least attractive moods. He sends his "dearest love to Ma," and hopes "she will not let my wayward disposition wear away the love she used to have for me." [19]

Allan did not answer this letter, and shortly after Poe's arrival at Fortress Monroe he wrote again, recapitulating his earlier letter, addressing Allan as his "father," and signing himself, "Your affectionate son." [20] This also remained unanswered. Poe had served as an artificer from May 1, 1828, until January 1, 1829, when he was promoted to the rank of Sergeant Major, the highest non-commissioned grade in the Army, a promotion which establishes the ability with which he had conducted his duties. On February 4th he humbled his pride to ask Mr. Allan to use his interest in obtaining for him an appointment as a cadet to West Point. He refers to his "infamous conduct" at the University of Virginia, but excuses himself on the ground of youth.[21]

In this letter he sends his love to his foster-mother for the last time. On February 28, 1829, Frances Allan died, and since Poe arrived at Richmond, on leave, the day after the funeral, John Allan must have relented sufficiently to send him some money and join in his request for a furlough. The death of the woman who was the chief bond between them must have resulted in some form of reconciliation, for Allan gave him the following order:

Mr. Ellis,
   Please to furnish Edgar A. Poe with a suit of black clothes—3 pair socks or Half Hose—Mc Cr [erey?] will make them—also a pr. suspenders and Hat & Knife, pair of Gloves.

JOHN ALLAN
Mar. 4, 1828.[22]

Poe's letter, existing only in a fragment, which he wrote to Allan on

[19] Valentine Letters, pp. 80-82.
[20] Valentine Letters, p. 94.
[21] Valentine Letters, pp. 103-106.
[22] Ellis-Allan Papers, L. of C., Poe Volume. I believe this date an error for March 4, 1829, since Killis Campbell found a similar entry in the "Office Books" of Ellis and Allan dated March 3, 1829.

March 10, 1829, from Fortress Monroe [23] begins, "My dear Pa," and concludes, "Yours affectionately." The tone once more is that of the early letters from the University of Virginia, that of a confiding son to his father who is preparing to help him obtain a discharge from the service and an appointment to West Point. Two sentences are especially interesting: "If it were not for the late occurrences, should feel much happier than I have for a long time, I have had a fearful warning & have hardly ever known before what distress was." These words can refer only to the death of Mrs. Allan, and while the Army records show that he was present at Fortress Monroe on the day of her death, and could, therefore, not have seen her, perhaps some last message stung him with remorse. Whatever John Allan's treatment of him may have been, a sensitive and impressionable young man like Poe would naturally accuse himself of neglect of his foster-mother during the two years of his Army service. How often he may have written we do not know, but there is no mention of letters from him to Mrs. Allan in his correspondence with Allan.

With Allan's consent the proceedings necessary to a discharge proceeded normally. The letter of Poe's colonel is of interest because the jumble of fact and fiction represents information given to him both by Poe and by John Allan:

Fortress Monroe, March 30, '29.

GENERAL,—I request your permission to discharge from the service Edgar A. Perry, at present the Sergeant-Major of the 1st Reg't of Artillery, on his procuring a substitute.

The said Perry is one of a family of orphans whose unfortunate parents were the victims of the conflagration of the Richmond theatre, in 1809. The subject of this letter was taken under the protection of a Mr. Allen, [sic] a gentleman of wealth and respectability, of that city, who, as I understand, adopted his protégé as his son and heir;—with the intention of giving him a liberal education, he had placed him at the University of Virginia from which, after considerable progress in his studies, in a moment of youthful indiscretion he absconded,—and was not heard from by his Patron for several years; in the mean time, he became reduced to the necessity of enlisting into the service, and accordingly entered as a soldier in my Regiment, at Fort Independence, in 1827.—Since the arrival of his company at this place, he has made his situation known to his Patron, at whose request, the young man has been permitted to visit him; the result is, an entire reconciliation on the part of Mr. Allen, who reinstates him into his family and favor,—

[23] Valentine Letters, pp. 116-117.

and who in a letter I have received from him requests that his son may be discharged on procuring a substitute;—an experienced soldier and approved sergeant, is ready to take the place of Perry so soon as his discharge can be obtained. The good of the service, therefore, cannot be materially injured by the exchange.[24]

> I have the honor to be,
> With great respect, your obedient servant,
> JAS. HOUSE, Col. 1st Art'y.
> To the General Commanding the E. Dept. U. S. A. New York.

Under a Special Order No. 28, dated April 4, 1829, Sergeant Major "Edgar A. Perry" was discharged on April 15th. According to the records of the War Department, Sergeant Samuel Graves of Company H is shown to have enlisted April 17, 1829, and to have "re-enlisted substitute for Sgt. Major Perry." [25] Poe's usual bad luck followed him in this substitution. Poe explained to John Allan later, when his conduct had been called in question, that the officer commanding a company could, if he desired, enlist the first recruit who offered, and muster him in as a substitute for a retiring soldier, paying only the normal bounty of $12. But as Colonel House and Lieutenant Howard were both absent, this arrangement could not be carried out. Then Poe made one of those mistakes which are best described in his own words: "As I had told you it would only cost me $12—I did not wish to make you think me imposing upon you—so upon a substitute offering for $75—I gave him $25—& gave him my note of hand for the balance —when you remitted me $100—thinking I had more than I should want, I thought it my best opportunity of taking up my note—which I did." [26]

To a man like Allan, so exact in his accounts that he kept every scrap of paper connected with his business, this concealment amounted almost to a crime. But he apparently knew nothing of it when Poe arrived at Richmond, which he still looked upon as his home.

Before he left the post, Poe collected the following testimonials from his officers, to use in connection with his application to West Point:

> Fortress Monroe, Va., 20th Apl. 1829
> Edgar Poe late Serg't-Major in the 1st Art'y served under my command in H. company 1st Reg't of Artillery, from June, 1827,

[24] War Department Records.

[25] Letter from Adjutant General Adams, December 15, 1939. See Appendix.

[26] Valentine Letters of June 25 and July 26, 1829, pp. 151 and 163.

to January, 1829, during which time his conduct was unexceptionable.—He at once performed the duties of company clerk and assistant in the Subsistent Department, both of which duties were promptly and faithfully done. His habits are good and intirely [sic] free from drinking.

J. HOWARD,
Lieut. 1st Artillery.

In addition to the above, I have to say that Edgar Poe was appointed Sergeant-Major of the 1st Art'y: on the 1st of Jan'y, 1829, and up to this date, has been exemplary in his deportment, prompt and faithful in the discharge of his duties—and is highly worthy of confidence.

H. W. GRISWOLD,
Bt. Capt. and Adjt. 1st Art'y.

I have known and had an opportunity of observing the conduct of the above-mentioned Serg't-Majr. Poe some three months, during which his deportment has been highly praiseworthy and deserving of confidence. His education is of a very high order and he appears to be free from bad habits, in fact the testimony of Lt. Howard and Adjt. Griswold is full to that point. Understanding he is, thro' his friends, an applicant for cadet's warrant, I unhesitatingly recommend him as promising to aquit himself of the obligations of that station studiously and faithfully.

W. J. WORTH,
Lt. Col. Comd'g Fortress Monroe.

These credentials Poe took with him to Washington early in May to present to Major John Eaton, the Secretary of War. John Allan also wrote a letter of introduction, and the coldness of his tone is in marked contrast to that of Poe's officers:

Richmond, May 6, 1829

Dr. Sir,—The youth who presents this, is the same alluded to by Lt. Howard, Capt. Griswold, Colo. Worth, our representative and the speaker, the Hon'ble Andrew Stevenson, and my friend Major Jno. Campbell.

He left me in consequence of some gambling at the University at Charlottesville, because (I presume) I refused to sanction a rule that the shopkeepers and others had adopted there, making Debts of Honour of all indiscretions. I have much pleasure in asserting that he stood his examination at the close of the year with great credit to himself. His history is short. He is the grandson of Quartermaster-General Poe, of Maryland, whose widow as

I understand still receives a pension for the services or disabilities of her husband. Frankly, Sir, do I declare that he is no relation to me whatever; that I have many [in] whom I have taken an active interest to promote theirs; with no other feeling than that, every man is my care, if he be in distress. For myself I ask nothing, but I do request your kindness to aid this youth in the promotion of his future prospects. And it will afford me great pleasure to reciprocate any kindness you can show him. Pardon my frankness; but I address a soldier.

Your ob'd't se'v't,

JOHN ALLAN.

The Hon'ble John H. Eaton,
  Sec'y of War, Washington City.

It was also quite different from the strong letter from James P. Preston, who represented Allan's district in the House of Representatives, and who was the father of Poe's schoolmate. He and other friends wrote directly to the Secretary of War. Allan's letter of May 18th [27] to Poe, advising him how to proceed, is not uncordial, and it reveals, incidentally, how Poe was remembered by those who had seen him as a child. The Hon. John T. Barber, for example, who had not met Edgar Poe since they were both at "the Springs in 1812," did what he could to forward his application. John Allan, to do him justice, gave Poe fifty dollars, sent him one hundred more, and honored his draft for an additional fifty.[28] Perhaps it was the price he was willing to pay to have Poe out of Richmond.

[27] Valentine Letters, p. 123.
[28] Valentine Letters, p. 126.

CHAPTER VII

Hope Deferred—*Al Aaraaf*

While Poe waited in Baltimore the results of his application, he looked up his relatives, of whom there were already quite a few, and made other contacts. According to Poe's letter of May 20, 1829, to Allan from Baltimore, he was well received by men who had known his grandfather. He renewed his acquaintance with William Wirt, who had been offered the presidency and professorship of law at the University of Virginia during the year of Poe's residence there. Wirt had just returned to Baltimore after his distinguished career as Attorney General of the United States, but it was probably his fame as the biographer of Patrick Henry that led Poe to confide his own literary aspirations to the older man. Wirt treated him with great courtesy, read "Al Aaraaf" at one sitting, and advised Poe to consult Robert Walsh, the Editor of the *American Quarterly Review,* and Judge Joseph Hopkinson, who were leaders of literary opinion in Philadelphia. Wirt was naturally puzzled by "Al Aaraaf," but generously attributed the difficulty to his own supposed deficiency as a critic of poetry and prophesied that it would "please modern readers." [1]

Poe took his manuscript to Philadelphia, and submitted it to Isaac Lea, of Carey, Lea and Carey, one of the foremost publishers of that day. The letter accompanying the manuscript is of singular interest, and has never been published. It is undated, but it was answered on May 27, 1829. It is the earliest known letter by Poe outside of the Valentine Letters. [2]

Dear Sir,

I should have presumed upon the politeness of Mr. R. Walsh for a personal introduction to yourself, but was prevented by his leaving town the morning after my arrival—You will be so kind

---

[1] Valentine Letters, p. 131.

[2] I am indebted to the courtesy of Dr. Marie H. Law, Librarian of the Drexel Institute of Philadelphia, and to the President and Trustees, for permission to publish this letter.

POE'S LETTER TO ISAAC LEA, OF CAREY AND LEA, PUBLISHERS, IN PHILADELPHIA, EXPLAINING "AL AARAAF"

Poe's first extant letter outside of the correspondence with John Allan. Reproduced from the original for the first time through the courtesy of the Library of the Drexel Institute.

POE'S LETTER TO ISAAC LEA, CONTINUED

This shows that we do not have all of "Al Aaraaf."

POE'S LETTER TO ISAAC LEA, CONCLUDED

Here is his own statement that he is "irrecoverably a poet." Poe did not date his letter but some one at the publishers fortunately put the date of their reply on the first page.

as to consider this as a *literary* introduction until his return from N. Y. I send you, for your tenderest consideration, a poem—

"Some sins do bear their privilege on earth."

You will oblige me by placing this among the number.

> It was my choice or chance or curse
> To adopt the cause for better or worse
> And with my worldly goods & wit
> And soul & body worship it.

But not to detain you with my nonsense it were as well to speak of "the poem."

Its title is "Al Aaraaf" from the Al Aaraaf of the Arabians, a medium between Heaven and Hell where men suffer no punishment, but yet do not attain that tranquil & even happiness which they suppose to be the characteristic of heavenly enjoyment

> Un no rompido sueno
> Un dia puro, allegre, libre
> Quiera—
> Libre de amor, de zelo
> De odio, de esperanza, de rezelo—

I have placed this "Al Aaraaf" in the celebrated star discovered by Tycho Brahe which appeared & dissapeared [sic] so suddenly—It is represented as a messenger star of the Deity, &, at the time of its discovery by Tycho, as on an embassy to our world. One of the peculiarities of Al Aaraaf is that, even after death, those who make choice of the star as their residence do not enjoy immortality—but, after a second life of high excitement, sink into forgetfulness & death—This idea is taken from Job—"I would not live always—let me alone." I have imagined that some would not be pleased (excuse the bull) with an immortality even of bliss. The poem commences with a sonnet (illegitimate) a la mode de Byron in his prisoner of Chillon. But this is a digression—I have imagined some well known characters of the age of the star's appearance, as transferred to Al Aaraaf—viz Michael Angelo— and others—of these Michael Angelo as yet, alone appears. I send you parts 1st 2nd & 3d. I have reasons for wishing not to publish the 4th at present—for its character depends in a measure upon the success or failure of the others—

As these 3 parts will be insufficient for a volume—I have wished to publish some minor poems with Al Aaraaf—But as the work would depend for character upon the principal poem it is needless, at present to speak of the rest.

If the poem is published, succeed or not, I am "irrecoverably a poet." But to your opinion I leave it, and as I should be proud of the honor of your press, failing in that I will make no other application.

I should add a circumstance which, tho' no justification of a failure, is yet a boast in success. The poem is by a minor & truly written under extraordinary disadvantages.

With great respect

Your obt. sevt.

EDGAR A. POE

I am staying at

Heiskell's.

I cannot refrain from adding that Mr. Wirt's voice is in my favor.

Poe was staying at Heiskill's Indian Queen Hotel, 15 South Fourth Street, which stood until about ten years ago. How long he remained in Philadelphia is not known. Judging from his expression "my nonsense," the quatrain may be his own composition, but it certainly adds nothing to his fame.

The Spanish quotation is from "Vida Retirada" by the greatest mystical poet of Spain, Fray Luis de León. A literal translation is,

> "An unbroken sleep
> A day pure, joyful, free
> I wish—
> Free from love, from jealousy
> From hatred, from hopes, from suspicion." [3]

Poe compressed into his quotation two stanzas of the original, the sixth and the eighth, yet produced in their union a connected idea.

[3] Poe quotes this passage in his notes to "Al Aaraaf," attributing it correctly to Luis Ponce de León.

This indicates that he had a fairly accurate knowledge of Spanish.[4]

Of great interest are the statements concerning the origin of "Al Aaraaf" and its meaning, which, to save repetition, I shall discuss in my later analysis of the poem. But even more important is the fact that Poe sends only parts first, second, and third, although he has part fourth written. Evidently we do not have all of "Al Aaraaf." The boy of twenty was still confident, notwithstanding all his experiences. "Succeed or not, I am 'irrecoverably a poet.'" Though others doubted, *he* knew.

Poe's letter of May 29, 1829, to Allan, tells of his hopes:

> From such a man as Mr. Wirt—the flattering character he has given of the work, will surely be to you a recommendation in its favor.
>
> In the conclusion of the letter you will see that he advises me to "get a personal introduction to Mr. Walsh" the editor of the American Quaterly [sic] Review & get his interest in my favor— that interest, and his highest encomiums on the poem are already obtained—as Editor of the Review he promises to notice it,[5] which will assure it, if not of popularity, of success—
>
> Under these circumstances I have thought it my duty to write to you on the subject—Believing you to be free from prejudice, I

---

[4] The two stanzas he combined are:

> "Un no rompido sueño,
> un dia puro, alegre, libre quiero;
> no quiero ver el ceño
> vanamente severo
> de quien la sangre ensalza o el dinero. . . .
>
> Vivir quiero conmigo,
> gozar quiero del bien que debo al cielo,
> a solas sin testigo,
> libre de amor, de celo,
> de odio, de esperanzas, de recelo."

My colleague, Dr. M. Romera-Navarro, to whom I owe the information concerning Fray Luis de León, calls attention to the misspelling of "alegre." "Zelo" for "celo" is a possible sixteenth-century spelling. For further discussion of Fray Luis de León, see M. Romera-Navarro, *Historia de la Literatura Española* (New York, 1928), pp. 147-153.

[5] I have not been able to find any notice in the *American Quarterly Review* for 1829 or 1830. Mr. Walsh had an opportunity to say a word for Poe in his review of Kettell's *Specimens of American Poetry* in the *Review* for September, 1829, for the article is a general discussion of American poetry. But he did not say it.

think you will aid me, if you see cause; At my time of life there
is much in being *before the eye of the world*—if once noticed I
can easily cut out a path to reputation. It can certainly be of no
disadvantage as it will not, even for a moment, interfere with
other objects which I have in view.

I am aware of the difficulty of getting a poem published in
this country—Mr. Wirt & Mr. Walsh have advised me of that—
but the *difficulty* should be no object, with a proper aim in view.

If Messrs. Carey, Lea, & Carey, should decline publishing (as
I have no reason to think they will not—they having invariably
declined it with all our American poets) that is upon their *own
risk* the request I have to make is this—that you will give me a
letter to Messrs. Carey, Lea, & Carey saying that if in publishing
the poem "Al Aaraaf" they shall incur any *loss*—you will make it
good to them.

The cost of publishing the work, in a style equal to any of our
American publications, will at the extent be $100—This then, of
course, must be the limit of any loss supposing not a single copy
of the work to be sold—It is more than probable that the work
will be profitable & that I may gain instead of lose, even in a
pecuniary way.

I would remark, in conclusion that I have long given up *Byron*
as a model—for which, I think, I deserve some credit—If you will
help me in this matter I will be always grateful for your kindness.

If you conclude upon giving me a *trial* please enclose me the
letter to Messrs. Carey, Lea, & Carey—I shall wait anxiously for
your answer—.[6]

On this letter Allan has endorsed, "replied to Monday, 8th June
1829 strongly censuring his conduct—and refusing any aid." The manuscript was at least received by the publishers, probably due to Poe's
reference in the opening paragraph to Mr. Walsh's willingness to introduce him to the firm. When Poe writes to Allan on June 25th, the
firm still has the poem. The same note reveals another piece of bad
luck, which Poe tells Allan evidently because his foster-father had
objected to his request for further funds:

I will explain the matter clearly — ——— ——— ——— robbed me
at Beltzhoover's Hotel while I was asleep in the same room with
him of all the money I had with me (about 46$) of which I re-

[6] Valentine Letters, pp. 137-139.

covered $10—by searching his pockets the ensuing night, when he acknowledged the theft—I have been endeavouring in vain to obtain the balance from him—he says he has not got it & begs me not to expose him—& for his wife's sake I will not. I have a letter from him referring to the subject, which I will show you on arriving in Richmond.

I have been moderate in my expences & $50 of the money which you sent me I applied in paying a debt contracted at Old Point for my substitute, for which I gave my note.[7]

The robber was his second cousin, James Mosher Poe,[8] son of Jacob Poe. Poe was evidently not living with his relatives as yet. In his letter of July 15th he states definitely: "I am very anxious to return home thro' Washington when I have every hope of being appointed for Sepr. & besides by being detained at Baltimore I am incurring unnecessary expense as Grandmother is not in a situation to give me any accomodation."[9]

We can judge the nature of Allan's letters, from Poe's reply on July 26th, which throws light on Allan's growing coldness:

Baltimore
July 26—1829

Dear Pa,

I received yours of the 19th on the 22d ulto & am truly thankful for the money which you sent me, notwithstanding the taunt with which it was given "that men of genius ought not to apply to your aid"—It is too often their necessity to want that little timely assistance which would prevent such applications—

I did not answer your letter by return of mail on account of my departure for Washington the next morning—but before I proceed to tell the event of my application I think it my duty to say something concerning the accusations & suspicions which are contained in your letter—

After giving his explanation of the matter of the substitute, already quoted, Poe continues:

[7] Valentine Letters, pp. 150-151.

[8] While the name is rubbed out in the letter of June 25th, Poe speaks of "Mosher" in the letter of July 26th. See the facsimile of the original letter in the Valentine Letters, p. 164. In the printed version of the July letter, p. 158, curiously enough, the name is still omitted.

[9] Valentine Letters, p. 155.

If you will take into consideration the length of time I have been from home, which was occasioned by my not hearing from you (& I was unwilling to leave the city without your answer, expecting it every day) & other expenses, you will find that it has been impossible for me to enter into any extravagancies or improper expense—even supposing I had not lost the $46—the time which intervened between my letter & your answer in the first instance was 22 days—in the latter one month & 4 days—as I had no reason to suppose you would not reply to my letter as I was unconscious of having offended, it would have been imprudent to leave without your answer—this expense was unavoidable—As regards the money which was stolen I have sent you the only proof in my possession a letter from Mosher—in which there is an acknowledgement of the theft—I have no other. On receiving your last letter, I went immediately to Washington, on foot, & have returned the same way, having paid away $40 for my bill & being unwilling to spend the balance when I might avoid it, until I could see what prospects were in view—[10]

Poe can certainly not be accused of extravagance, and the walk to Washington may be put to the credit of his determination to obtain the appointment. After a detailed account of his interview with Secretary Eaton, who told him there were still ten names ahead of him on the roll, Poe concludes:

Having now explained every circumstance that seemed to require an explanation & shown that I have spared no exertions in the pursuit of my object, I write to you for information as to what course I must pursue—I would have returned home immediately but for the words in your letter "I am not particularly anxious to see you"—I know not how to interpret them

I could not help thinking that they amounted to a prohibition to return—if I had any means of support until I could obtain the appointment, I would not trouble you again—I am conscious of having offended you formerly—greatly—but I thought *that had been forgiven.* at least you told me so—I know that I have done nothing since to deserve your displeasure—

As regards the poem, I have offended only in asking your approbation—I can publish it upon the terms you mentioned—but will have no more to do with it without your entire approbation—I

[10] Valentine Letters, pp. 163-164.

will wait with great anxiety for your answer. You must be aware how important it is that I should hear from you soon—as I do not know how to act.[11]

Poe still thought of the Allan residence as "home," and he was puzzled because Allan evidently was not anxious to have him return. If John Allan's own statements in his will are to be credited, there were probably reasons, to be discussed later, why Allan was quite willing to have Poe out of Richmond. In the meantime, Poe was active in securing the publication of his new volume of poems, as the following letter indicates:

> Baltimore, July 28, 1829.
> [Received July 30, answered August 3]
> Messrs. Carey, Lea and Carey
> Having made a better disposition of my poems, than I had any right to expect (inducing me to decline publication on my own account) I would thank you to return me the Mss. ~~by a gentleman who will hand you this~~ by mail.
> I should have been proud of having your firm for my publishers and would have preferred publishing with your name even at a disadvantage, had my circumstances admitted of so doing.
> ... Mr. Lea, during our short interview at your store, mentioned "The Atlantic Souvenir" and spoke of my attempting something for that work.
> I know nothing which could give me greater pleasure than to see any of my productions in so becoming a dress ... notwithstanding the assertions of Mr. Jno. Neal to the contrary, who now and then hitting, thro' sheer impudence upon a correct judgment in matters of authorship, is most unenviably ridiculous whenever he touches the fine arts. As I am unacquainted with the method of proceeding in offering any piece for acceptance (having been some time absent from this country) would you, Gentlemen, have the kindness to set me in the right way?
> Nothing could give me greater pleasure than any communication from Messrs. Carey, Lea and Carey. With the greatest respect and best wishes, I am, Gentlemen, your most obedient servant,
>
> EDGAR A. POE [12]

---

[11] Valentine Letters, pp. 165-166.
[12] Original Autograph Ms., Young Collection, New York Public Library.

The statement concerning his recent absence from the country is one of those deliberate attempts to conceal his term of service in the Army, which must always be considered in judging Poe's credibility when he speaks of his own career. He did his best to conceal the Army period, because he was ashamed of it, and naturally he had to invent other episodes like the European trip to fill in the gap. The dates of the Valentine Letters and the letter to Mr. Lea prove, of course, that he had not recently been out of the United States.

Allan did not reply to Poe's letter of July 26th, so Poe wrote again and evidently received some help. His acknowledgment of August 10th contains an interesting picture of his family relations:

> Baltimore
> August 10th 1829

Dear Pa,

I received yours this morning which relieved me from more trouble than you can well imagine—I was afraid that you were offended & although I knew that I had done nothing to deserve your anger, I was in a most uncomfortable situation—without one cent of money—in a strange place & so quickly engaged in difficulties after the serious misfortunes which I have just escaped—My grandmother is extremely poor & ill (paralytic) My aunt Maria if possible still worse & Henry entirely given up to drink & unable to help himself, much less me—

I am unwilling to appear obstinate as regards the substitute so will say nothing more concerning it—only remarking that they will no longer enlist men for the *residue* of another's enlistment as formerly, consequently my substitute was enlisted for 5 years not 3—

I stated in my last letter (to which I refer you) that Mr. Eaton gave me strong hopes for Sepr. at any rate that the appt. could be obtained for June next—I can obtain decent board lodging & washing with other expenses of mending &c for 5 & perhaps even for 4 1/2$ per week—

If I obtain the appt. by the last of Sepr. the amt of expense would be at most $30—If I should be unfortunate & not obtain it until June I will not desire you to allow as much as that per week because by engaging for a longer period at a cheap boarding house I can do with much less—say even 10 even 8$ pr month—anything with which you think it possible to exist—I am not so anxious of obtaining money from your good nature as of preserving your good will—

I am extremely anxious that you should believe that I have not attempted to impose upon you—I will in the meantime (if you wish it) write you often, but pledge myself to apply for no other assistance than what you shall think proper to allow—

I left behind me in Richmond a small trunk containing books & some letters—will you forward it on to Baltimore to the care of *H. W. Bool Jr.* & if you think I may ask so much perhaps you will put in it for me some few clothes as I am nearly without—

Give my love to Miss Valentine—

I remain

Dear Pa

Yours affectionately

EDGAR A. POE.[13]

There is something pitiful in the details of the plan by which Poe hopes to keep down his expenses. More important, however, is the picture of the family. Mrs. David Poe had a very small pension of $240 a year from the State of Maryland, which was making a belated return for the money her husband had paid for the privilege of serving his adopted country. Henry Poe was, as usual, a liability. Mrs. Clemm, who was to play such a large part in his life, is also mentioned as not being of any assistance to him.

Maria Clemm, about whom there are almost as many varying opinions as there are about Poe, was the daughter of David Poe, Senior. She was born March 17, 1790.[14] She had married on July 12, 1817 [15] William Clemm, Jr., whose first wife, Harriet Poe, was the daughter of George Poe, and therefore her first cousin. There was, apparently, an objection on the part of the Clemm family to this marriage of William and Maria, but in any event she received no help from her husband's people. It is not clear how she maintained her children after her husband's death in 1826. Henry had been born in 1818; Virginia Maria, who was born August 22, 1820, had died and was buried November 5, 1822; Virginia Eliza, born August 15, 1822, and baptized November 5th, was to marry Edgar Poe.[16]

---

[13] Valentine Letters, pp. 185-187.

[14] Records of the First Presbyterian Church of Baltimore.

[15] Records of St. Paul's Protestant Episcopal Church of Baltimore.

[16] These dates are from copies of the Records of St. Paul's Church, Baltimore, sent me by the courtesy of Mr. Louis H. Dielman, Executive Secretary of the Peabody Institute. A custom, not unusual in those days, of naming a child after one who had just died, accounts for the two Virginias. The first Virginia, incidentally, is called Virginia Maria when she is bap-

Mrs. Clemm is listed in Matchett's Baltimore Directory for 1827 as the "preceptoress of school, Stiles Street, North Side near Foot Bridge." She does not appear in the 1829 Directory, which, incidentally, contains no one of the name of Poe. There is no certain evidence that Poe was living with her in 1829; the reference on August 10th implies that he was not.[17] Allan sent him fifty dollars on August 19th, but that was the last help Poe received from him until November 18th, when Allan sent him eighty dollars. The letter which drew this amount from his foster-father is indeed pitiful:

Balto. Nov: 12th 1829

Dear Pa,

I wrote you about a fortnight ago and as I have not heard from you, I was afraid you had forgotten me—

I would not trouble you so often if I was not extremely pinched —I am almost without clothes—and, as I board by the month, the lady with whom I board is anxious for her money—I have not had any (you know) since the middle of August—

I hope the letter I wrote last was received in which you will see that I have cleared myself from any censure of neglect as regards W. P.—

Hoping that you will not forget to write as soon as you receive this

I am   Dear Pa
Yours affectionately

EDGAR A. POE.[18]

Poe was evidently boarding and was not yet with Mrs. Clemm, although the letter of November 18th shows that she was helping him with his wardrobe. He acted as her agent on December 10th in the assignment of a slave, named Edwin, to Henry Ridgway, for a term of nine years. Mrs. Clemm received forty dollars for the services of the slave.[19] How she obtained him is not explained in the legal document, recently discovered in the courthouse at Baltimore.

---

tized, and Virginia Sarah when she is buried. Note that she is buried on the same day as Virginia Eliza was baptized.

[17] In the statements of Mrs. Maria Clemm taken in shorthand by E. L. Didier, and now in the Harvard College Library, Mrs. Clemm makes no mention of Poe's living with her until after he left West Point. This statement, like all those made by her, cannot be accepted as final evidence, but the omission may be significant.

[18] Valentine Letters, p. 205.

[19] May G. Evans, "When Edgar Allan Poe Sold a Slave," Baltimore *Evening Sun,* April 6, 1940.

Poe's letter of November 18th, in addition to the evidence that Mr. Allan had resumed his financial help, contained the important announcement:

"The Poems will be printed by Hatch & Dunning of this city upon terms advantageous to me they printing it & giving me 250 copies of the book:—I will send it on by Mr. Dunning who is going immediately to Richmond—" [20]

There is no evidence in the correspondence that Allan contributed to the publication of the poems. Yet Poe's very mention of them indicates that he had cause to believe that Allan had changed his mind since his earlier censure. Perhaps Allan's own abortive literary aspirations may have made him kinder, or the notice which John Neal printed in the September number of his magazine, *The Yankee and Boston Literary Gazette,* may have made some impression upon him. John Neal had lived in Baltimore from 1815 to 1823, while he was writing his Byronic poems and novels. He had belonged to the Delphians, a literary coterie of Baltimore, and had edited their periodical, *The Portico,* for a brief period. By his invasion of England from 1823 to 1827 he had won some reputation, and his word as a critic was important. The first published criticism of a poet's verses makes an impression upon him unlike any other that afterwards comes to him, and Neal's comment was not unfriendly: "If E. A. P. of Baltimore— whose lines about 'Heaven,' though he professes to regard them as altogether superior to anything in the whole range of American poetry, save two or three trifles referred to, are, though nonsense, rather exquisite nonsense—would but do himself justice [he] might make a beautiful and perhaps a magnificent poem. There is a good deal here to justify such a hope." [21] Neal then quoted from "Fairyland" which Poe had evidently called "Heaven" in sending the verses to Neal, and concluded: "He should have signed it Bah! We have no room for others."

Apparently this was not Poe's first connection with Neal. In a letter from the latter to Mary S. Gove, November 30, 1846,[22] Neal states that Poe would have dedicated his first volume of poems to Neal if he had

---

[20] Valentine Letters, p. 215.

[21] *The Yankee,* New Series, No. 3 (September, 1829), 168. Passages from "Al Aaraaf" had appeared in the *Baltimore Gazette,* of May 18, 1829, in the advertising columns, headed "Extract from Al Aaraaf, an unpublished Poem," and signed "Marlow." See Kenneth Rede, *American Literature,* V (March, 1933), 52-53.

[22] Griswold Collection, Boston Public Library.

not assured the young poet that "such a dedication would be a positive injury to him and his book." It is possible that Neal is referring to *Tamerlane* of 1827, since he returned to this country in the summer of 1827. In the original edition of 1827, there is no dedication to Neal, but in the 1829 edition the reprint of "Tamerlane" is "respectfully dedicated" to him. Neal may, of course, have been ignorant of the 1827 volume. To him, Poe's "first volume" may have meant *Al Aaraaf*, and the dedication of "Tamerlane" may have been without Neal's consent.

Poe evidently sent advance sheets of the new volume to editors, and Neal responded by printing Poe's letter, which contains his poetical creed and some specific interpretation of "Al Aaraaf." Under the heading of "Unpublished Poetry" Neal prefaced this letter with some good advice:

> The following passages are from the manuscript—works of a young author, about to be published in Baltimore. He is entirely a stranger to us, but with all their faults, if the remainder of "Al Aaraaf" and "Tamerlane" are as good as the body of the extracts here given—to say nothing of the more extraordinary parts, he will deserve to stand high—very high—in the estimation of the shining brotherhood. Whether he *will* do so, however, must depend, not so much upon his worth now in mere poetry, as upon his worth hereafter in something yet loftier and more generous—we allude to the stronger properties of the mind, to the magnanimous determination that enables a youth to endure the present, whatever the present may be, in the hope, or rather in the belief, the fixed, unwavering belief, that in the future he will find his reward. "I am young" he says in a letter to one who has laid it on our table for a good purpose, "I am young—not yet twenty—*am* a poet—if deep worship of all beauty can make me one—and wish to be so in the more common meaning of the word. I would give the world to embody one half the ideas afloat in my imagination. (By the way, do you remember—or did you ever read the exclamation of Shelley about Shakespeare?—'What a number of ideas must have been afloat before such an author could arise!') I appeal to you as a man that loves the same beauty which I adore—the beauty of the natural blue sky and the sunshiny earth—there can be no tie more strong than that of brother for brother—it is not so much that they love one another, as that they both love the same parent—their affections are always running in the same direction—the same channel—and cannot help mingling.
>
> "I am and have been, from my childhood, an idler. It cannot therefore be said that

> "'I left a calling for this idle trade,
>   A duty broke—a father disobeyed'—

for I have no father—nor mother.

"I am about to publish a volume of 'Poems,' the greater part written before I was fifteen. Speaking about 'Heaven,' the editor of the 'Yankee' says, 'He might write a beautiful, if not a magnificent poem'—(the very first words of encouragement I ever remember to have heard.) I am very certain that as yet I have not written *either*—but that I *can,* I will take oath—if they will give me time.

"The poems to be published are 'Al Aaraaf'—'Tamerlane'—one about four, and the other about three hundred lines, with smaller pieces. 'Al Aaraaf' has some good poetry, and much extravagance, which I have not had time to throw away.

"'Al Aaraaf' is a tale of another world—the star discovered by Tycho Brahe, which appeared and disappeared so suddenly—or rather, it is no tale at all. I will insert an extract about the palace of its presiding Deity, in which you will see that I have supposed many of the lost sculptures of our world to have flown (in spirit) to the star 'Al Aaraaf'—a delicate place, more suited to their divinity.

> "'Uprear'd upon such height arose a pile
>   Of gorgeous columns on th'unburthened air—
>   Flashing, from Parian marble, that twin-smile
>   Far down upon the wave that sparkled there.'"

Poe then quoted two passages from "Al Aaraaf," totalling forty-one lines, two passages from "Tamerlane," one of forty-three, and the final passage of twenty-two lines; and fourteen lines from "To —— ——," now called "A Dream Within A Dream." Neal concluded:

"Having allowed our youthful writer to be heard in his own behalf, —what more can we do for the lovers of genuine poetry? Nothing. They who are judges will not need more; and they who are not—why waste words upon them? We shall not." [23]

Among the editors to whom Poe had sent "Fairyland," Nathaniel Parker Willis included in his "Editor's Table" a rather contemptuous

[23] *The Yankee,* New Series, No. 6 (December, 1829), 295-298. Neal reprinted in *The Portland Advertiser* of April 26, 1850, a letter from Poe to him, of December 29, 1829, in which the latter said, "You will notice that I have made the alterations you suggest—'ventured out' in place of 'peer-ed.'" The original Ms. of this letter is (in part) in the Koester Collection.

AL AARAAF,

TAMERLANE,

AND

MINOR POEMS.

BY EDGAR A. POE.

BALTIMORE:

HATCH & DUNNING.

1829.

Title Page of *Al Aaraaf, Tamerlane, and Minor Poems*

Reproduced from the original through the courtesy of the
New York Public Library.

treatment of the verses beginning, "They use that moon no more." [24] One sentence especially must have galled Poe: "The flame creeps steadily along the edge of the first leaf, taking in its way a compliment to some bygone nonsense verses of our own, inserted in brackets by the author to conciliate our good will." But Willis was to make up for this unsympathetic greeting in the years to come.

Al Aaraaf, Tamerlane and Minor Poems was published in December, 1829. It is an octavo of seventy-two pages, and is a more attractive volume than *Tamerlane and Other Poems.* The title poem has usually been avoided by critics of Poe as unintelligible, but while it requires more than one reading, it possesses qualities which make it important in the development of Poe's poetic power. It was prompted, as Poe says, by the star discovered in Cassiopeia in 1572, by the Swedish astronomer, Tycho Brahe, who foretold disaster in consequence. Outside of the general tone of punishment for the breaking of God's laws, there is little carried over to the poem from this origin. Poe probably was acquainted with the Koran, although he changes the spelling of the star from Al Orf, or in the plural, Al Arâf, to Al Aaraaf. Al Arâf is derived from the word *arafa*, "to distinguish between things, or to part them." [25] There are differences of opinion among Mohammedan writers concerning the beings who inhabit Al Arâf, into which we fortunately do not have to go. In Poe's own words [26] it is "a medium between Heaven and Hell where men suffer no punishment, but yet do not attain that tranquil or even happiness which they suppose to be characteristic of heavenly enjoyment." In other words, it was similar to the conception of Purgatory. He locates this place not in a region, however, but in a Star.

The note struck at once in the poem is the preëminence of beauty. Nothing earthly is found on the star but that which is reflected from flowers, gems, or music, the handmaidens of beauty. Just so far as the dross of earth is shaken off may beauty be approached. Nesace, the Spirit of Beauty, is also the messenger of God. With that dextrous use of phrases that translate color into sound, Poe painted the beauty that is only visible as a cloud which does not impede the view of other beauties:

> "Now happiest, loveliest in yon lovely Earth,
> Whence sprang the 'Idea of Beauty' into birth

[24] *American Monthly Magazine,* I (November, 1829), 587.
[25] George Sale, *Preliminary Discourse on the Koran,* Section IV.
[26] Letter to Isaac Lea, May 27, 1829.

(Falling in wreaths thro' many a startled star,
Like woman's hair 'mid pearls, until, afar,
It lit on hills Achaian,[27] and there dwelt),
She look'd into Infinity—and knelt.
Rich clouds, for canopies, about her curled—
Fit emblems of the model of her world—
Seen but in beauty—not impeding sight
Of other beauty glittering thro' the light—
A wreath that twined each starry form around,
And all the opal'd air in color bound."

Nesace kneels amid the loveliness of flowers whose scent at times brings on the madness of ecstasy, and her song "is borne in odors up to Heaven." Her prayer is pure lyric:

"Spirit! that dwellest where,
    In the deep sky,
The terrible and fair,
    In beauty vie!
Beyond the line of blue—
    The boundary of the star
Which turneth at the view
    Of thy barrier and thy bar—
Of the barrier overgone
    By the comets who were cast
From their pride, and from their throne
    To be drudges till the last—
To be carriers of fire
    (The red fire of their heart)
With speed that may not tire
    And with pain that shall not part—
Who livest—that we know—
    In Eternity—we feel—
But the shadow of whose brow
    What spirit shall reveal?
Tho' the beings whom thy Nesace,
    Thy messenger hath known,
Have dream'd for thy Infinity
    A model of their own—

[27] Poe used Archaian for Achaian in 1829. It may be a misprint, but it is twice so spelled.

Thy will is done, oh, God!
　The star hath ridden high
Thro' many a tempest, but she rode
　Beneath thy burning eye;
And here, in thought, to thee—
　In thought that can alone
Ascend thy empire and so be
　A partner of thy throne—
By winged Fantasy,
　My embassy is given,
Till secrecy shall knowledge be
　In the environs of Heaven."

The symbolism here deals with the pride of the fallen angels, "comets" they are called, who have dared the unforgivable sin of creating a God in their own likeness, "a model of their own." Here Poe may have in mind the command of the Koran, "not to associate with God that concerning which he hath sent you down no authority, or to speak of God that which you know not." [28]

Perhaps, too, the answer to Nesace's prayer

"When thus in realms on high,
The eternal voice of God is passing by
And the red winds are withering in the sky,"

reflects the final stage cf the Mohammedan day of judgment—"a wind which shall sweep away the souls of all who have but a grain of faith in their hearts." [29] In any event, Nesace is sent to

"Worlds which sightless cycles run,
Link'd to a little system and one sun—"

with its suggestion of *Eureka*, long after. The mission of Nesace is to prevent the other stars from harboring the guilt of man. This may mean that as we love the sense of Beauty, we sin by losing the sense of Truth at the same time.

In the second part of the poem, Nesace returns from her mission to the palace on Al Aaraaf, amid the gorgeous sculptures which Poe men-

---

[28] Section VII of the Koran dealing with "Al Arâf." Poe, however, in his "Notes" to "Al Aaraaf" gives a lengthy discussion of the doctrine that God was supposed by certain heresies to have a human form, quoting commentaries on Milton, and Milton himself.

[29] Sale, *Preliminary Discourse*, IV, "The 17th sign."

tioned in his letter to Neal as having "flown (in spirit)" to the star. She wakes the attendant spirits with her charm:

> "'Neath blue-bell or streamer—
>   Or tufted wild spray
> That keeps, from the dreamer
>   The moonbeam away—
> Bright beings! that ponder,
>   With half closing eyes,
> On the stars which your wonder
>   Hath drawn from the skies,
> Till they glance thro' the shade, and
>   Come down to your brow
> Like—eyes of the maiden
>   Who calls on you now—
> Arise! from your dreaming
>   In violet bowers,
> To duty beseeming
>   These star-litten hours—
> And shake from your tresses
>   Encumber'd with dew
> The breath of those kisses
>   That cumber them too—
> (O, how, without you, Love
>   Could angels be blest?)
> Those kisses of true love
>   That lull'd ye to rest!
> Up!—shake from your wing
>   Each hindering thing:
> The dew of the night—
>   It would weigh down your flight;
> And true love caresses—
>   O! leave them apart:
> They are light on the tresses,
>   But hang on the heart."

A thousand seraphs obey this summons, but two lovers, Ianthe, the maiden angel, and Angelo,[30] her seraph-lover, prefer to continue their

---

[30] Angelo was drawn from Michael Angelo, and Poe evidently expected to transfer "other well known characters" to "Al Aaraaf." See his letter to Isaac Lea, p. 140.

love. Angelo tells of his last night on Earth, which was "hurled into chaos." He and Ianthe, who had always lived on Al Aaraaf, make a choice which is given clearly enough in Poe's own note: "Sorrow is not excluded from 'Al Aaraaf,' but it is that sorrow which the living love to cherish for the dead, and which, in some minds, resembles the delirium of opium. The passionate excitement of Love and the buoyancy of spirit attendant upon intoxication are its less holy pleasures—the price of which, to those souls who make choice of 'Al Aaraaf' as their residence after life, is final death and annihilation." It will be remembered that in his letter to Isaac Lea, he attributed the origin of this idea to Job.

It is an easy matter to see the general resemblances between "Al Aaraaf" and Moore's *Lalla Rookh,* and his *Loves of the Angels.* Poe was attracted to the oriental imagery of the former and the idea of union between mortals and immortals in the latter. In the story of the First Angel, the earth maiden is transported to a star instead of her angel lover, who has lost his power to return to Heaven because of his love for her. In the Third Angel's story, the seraph is nearest the throne because of his intense love for "Alla"—"so much doth love transcend all knowledge, ev'n in heaven!" This idea of the superiority of Love to Knowledge is carried over to "Al Aaraaf." [31] The influence of *Paradise Lost* also appears in the use of proper names and most definitely at the beginning of Part II.[31] The metrical form of the Songs resembles that of the song of the Fourth Spirit in Byron's *Manfred* and the Songs in the *Deformed Transformed.*

But as usual with Poe, after all the similarities are noted, it must be recognized that he took his models only as a starting point. The poetry of exalted passion was not the exclusive possession of Tom Moore, and it came naturally from Edgar Poe. The difficulty with "Al Aaraaf" lies in the fact that, to use his own words, written much later, there is a difference between the expression of obscurity and the obscurity of expression. It is the long passages whose links are not at once apparent, the too-abrupt transitions that puzzle readers still. Here Poe, if we are to judge him by his failure to present clear and connected images, is at fault. But that is not what Poe is trying to do in "Al Aaraaf."

[31] For specific passages in which these influences are reflected, see most conveniently the notes to Killis Campbell's edition of Poe's poems. The astronomical "machinery" of the poem is briefly discussed in T. O. Mabbott's *Select Poems of Poe* (1928), p. 125. My quotations are from his facsimile reprint of the 1829 edition of the poem (1933).

The poem is an experiment in the translation of feeling into the harmony of sound. The words have a definite meaning. They are not merely words, however; they become symbols of that fusing of thought and feeling which a musical symphony produces. Just as great music creates in the listeners emotions that are often inarticulate, but which struggle for expression, so poetry like the songs of Nesace, is intended to invert the process. The reader who sees the words but does not hear the music can, if he knows what poetry really is, read the songs so that the phrases create an effect that is neither words nor music alone, but a blending of both, by which something new is created. That it remains inarticulate is not Poe's fault. Just as there are sounds with so many or so few vibrations that the average human ear can not hear them, so there are overtones of verbal harmony that are beyond the immediate grasp of the mind, even if the emotions are profoundly stirred. Such poetry, it is true, does not meet the definition given by William Watson, in speaking of the poetry of Burns,

> "Right from the heart, right to the
> heart it sprang."

But if the exquisite lyrics of Nesace are not poetry, there is no such thing as poetry.

In any discussion of "Al Aaraaf," however, it must be remembered that it is not complete. Poe definitely states [32] that he is sending only three parts out of four to Carey, Lea and Carey, and in the letter to John Neal, he speaks of "Al Aaraaf" as being about four hundred lines. In the edition of 1829 it includes four hundred and twenty-two lines, and is divided into two parts, not three. At least the fourth part and possibly the third, are therefore missing. In view of what he said of other characters yet to be transferred to Al Aaraaf, it is reasonable to suppose that there would have been other episodes, as in the *Lives of the Angels*. The criticisms of "Al Aaraaf" as being inconclusive, while justified so far as the present form is concerned, must be modified in the light of Poe's intentions.

"Al Aaraaf" was the last effort of Poe at a poem of any length. His later and well known theory of poetry, while it ruled out of consideration anything but a brief poem, probably grew out of his realization that the pure lyrics of "Al Aaraaf" are clearly the outstanding portions of the poem. As a preface to "Al Aaraaf," Poe published his first sonnet, without a title. It is an attack upon Science:

[32] Letter to Isaac Lea, p. 140.

"Science! true daughter of Old Time thou art!
    Who alterest all things with thy peering eyes.
Why preyest thou thus upon the poet's heart,
    Vulture, whose wings are dull realities?
How should he love thee? or how deem thee wise,
    Who wouldst not leave him in his wandering
To seek for treasure in the jewelled skies,
    Albeit he soared with an undaunted wing?
Hast thou not dragged Diana from her car?
    And driven the Hamadryad from the wood
To seek a shelter in some happier star?
    Hast thou not torn the Naiad from her flood,
The Elfin from the green grass, and from me
    The summer dream beneath the tamarind tree?" [33]

Here again the later poetic credo of Poe is anticipated.

Poe thus early takes his place among the many men of letters of the Nineteenth and Twentieth Centuries who were or are impatient of the dogmatism of Science, and vary from Emerson's calm criticism, through Mark Twain's delightful parody of the methods of geology in *Life on the Mississippi*, to O'Neill's satiric comment in *Strange Interlude*. It is a different attitude from that taken by Keats, whose *Lamia* contains, in its first lines, an undoubted suggestion to Poe. Poe already was a reader of scientific works, and was to show all his life a keen interest in them. But in this early sonnet he carried the war into Africa. Science, he believes, does not reveal things as they really are. Science "alters" all things, and the true reality lies in the poet's heart. He sees man and Nature as a whole, not in isolated sections. Or to put it as O'Neill did when Nina speaks of the physician—"He believes if you pick a lie to pieces, the pieces are the truth." With Keats it was one form of romance, "the Faery Broods," who had driven out another, the Dryads and the Fauns. But Poe's attack looked forward rather than backward, and as usual, the important element in the poem was his own. This first sonnet was written in the English form rather than the Italian, but it has the rise to the climax at the end of the octave. [34]

Of the other poems in this volume, "Tamerlane" in its revised form

[33] Text is that of 1845.

[34] Poe referred to it as "illegitimate" in his letter to Lea, "a la mode de Byron in his prisoner of Chillon." This remark of Poe reveals his habit of making references without care, for Byron's "Sonnet on Chillon" is in the strict Italian form!

has already been treated. "To —— ——" ("I saw thee on thy bridal day"), "A Dream," "The Lake," were reprinted with minor alterations. "Visit of the Dead" became "Spirits of the Dead," greatly improved at the end by the lines

> 'The breeze—the breath of God—is still—
> And the mist upon the hill
> Shadowy—shadowy—yet unbroken,
> Is a symbol and a token—
> How it hangs upon the trees,
> A mystery of mysteries!"

"To —— ——" ("A Dream Within A Dream") is still far from its final form.

Of the new poems, "To —— ——" ("The bowers whereat in dreams, I see"), has one good stanza, the second, but neither this poem, nor the others, "To the River," and "To M——" ("I heed not that my earthly lot") need detain us. But it is far otherwise with "Romance" and "Fairyland."

"Romance," simply called "Preface" in 1829, contains another element of Poe's poetical creed. After expressing his devotion to Romance, and speaking of the "cares" that have kept him from poetry, he concludes:

> "And when an hour with calmer wings,
> Its down upon my spirit flings—
> That little tune with lyre and rhyme
> To while away—forbidden things!
> My heart would feel to be a crime
> Did it not tremble with the strings!"

Here Poe repudiates the Wordsworthian poetic ideal, of "emotion recollected in tranquillity," and gives his first expression of his belief that the poet must be in the grip of strong emotion. This belief becomes the keynote of "Israfel." Poe added a number of lines to "Romance" in the 1831 volume, but it is significant that he returned to the 1829 form in his final revision.

"Fairyland" is a strange mixture of fancy and imagination. In 1829 it begins without preamble:

> "Dim vales—and shadowy floods—
> And cloudy-looking woods,
> Whose forms we can't discover
> For the tears that drip all over—

Huge moons there wax and wane—
Again—again—again—
Every moment of the night—
Forever changing places—
And they put out the star-light
With the breath from their pale faces."

The weird sense of eternal restlessness, of the moons, breaking all natural laws, of the descent of the one moon upon the mountain top,

"While its wide circumference
In easy drapery falls
Over hamlets and rich halls,
Wherever they may be—
O'er the strange woods—o'er the sea—
Over spirits on the wing—
Over every drowsy thing—
And buries them up quite
In a labyrinth of light—
And then, how deep!—O, deep,
Is the passion of their sleep!"

This is imagination, and this is what attracted John Neal. The remainder of the poem is an almost impish fancy of Poe's, pretending to criticize the very imaginative conception he has just established. He solemnly calls attention to the "moony covering" which

"Is soaring in the skies,
With the tempests as they toss,
Like—almost anything—
Or a yellow Albatross."

as a "Plagiarism—see the works of Thomas Moore—passim." He may refer to a passage in the *Fire Worshippers* in which the albatross is represented as sleeping in the air, but the connection is so remote that I suspect Poe sought, by acknowledging here a faint resemblance to Moore, to cover more definite borrowings. As with "Tamerlane" and "Romance" Poe returned to the 1829 form of "Fairyland" after prefacing it by forty lines in 1831. The 1831 version introduces a maiden Isabel, who disappears again in later versions, very much to the advantage of the poem. For in such a scene as "Fairyland," a human being is an impertinence.

Al Aaraaf did not excite much comment. Mrs. Sarah Josepha Hale,

editor of the *Ladies Magazine,* briefly reviewed it in January, 1830: [35]
"It is very difficult to speak of these poems as they deserve. A part are
exceedingly boyish, feeble, and altogether deficient in the common
characteristics of poetry; but then we have parts too of considerable
length, which remind us of no less a poet than Shelly [sic]. The
author, who appears to be very young, is evidently a fine genius, but
he wants judgment, experience, tact." Poe, if he saw this review, must
have been consoled by the reference to Shelley!

John H. Hewitt, who was editing *Minerva,* a weekly paper in Baltimore, with Rufus Dawes, published a long and so far as "Al Aaraaf"
is concerned, a contemptuous review, in which the measure of the
poem is described as a "pile of brick bats." Hewitt was more appreciative of "Tamerlane." "Its faults are so few and so trifling," he said,
"that they may easily be passed over." He quoted extensively from
the minor poems, but his comments are not valuable, since he did
not take any of the poems seriously. The review,[36] which Poe believed
to be by Dawes, accounts probably for his later attacks on that poet.

The publication of *Al Aaraaf* had, however, improved Poe's standing with his relatives in Baltimore. Neilson Poe in a letter to his cousin
Josephine Clemm, whom he afterwards married, wrote on January 26,
1830, "Edgar Poe has published a volume of Poems one of which is
dedicated to John Neal the great autocrat of critics—Neal has accordingly published Edgar as a Poet of great genius etc.—*Our* name will
be a great one *yet.*" [37]

[35] Vol. III, No. 1, p. 47. Under "Literary Notices."
[36] The review is quoted by Hewitt in a long article on Poe, contributed
in June, 1885, to an unnamed paper. I read it in a manuscript found in the
William H. Koester Collection. Hewitt does not furnish the date of the
review in *Minerva.* He gives a rambling account of a fight with Poe on the
streets in Baltimore after the award of the *Visiter* in 1833, and other gossip,
which is not worth verification.
[37] Ms. copy in the handwriting of Amelia F. Poe, Pratt Library, Baltimore.

CHAPTER VIII

West Point and the *Poems* of 1831

Poe's residence from December, 1829, until May, 1830, is not fully established. He was certainly at home in Richmond for a part of the time,[1] waiting for the appointment to West Point, which came in March, 1830, through the influence of Powhatan Ellis, Senator from Mississippi, and the brother of T. H. Ellis. John Allan gave his formal permission on March 31st. Poe's letters to John Allan cease for a while. Again there seems to have been a temporary reconciliation, and Poe may have enjoyed his "home" for the last time. In a letter to an army comrade, "Bully Graves," written from Richmond May 3, 1830,[2] Poe says that he has not been in Washington "for some time." This letter, which was one of the most unfortunate Poe ever wrote, was evidently in response to a request for the repayment of money. It was from his army "substitute," as the second Mrs. Allan later stated.[3] Unfortunately, Graves' letter to Poe has disappeared. But he evidently reproached Poe with sending money to others, and quoted Allan to support his statement. Poe replied: "Mr. Allan is not very often sober—which accounts for it." The bad taste of this statement is as obvious as Poe's indiscretion in making it. Graves sent the letter to John Allan some months later, after Poe had gone to West Point, for the letter of Poe, written on January 3, 1831, is evidently in reply to recriminations by Allan based on the receipt of "Bully's" damaging communication. Poe then offered a defence that was at the same time an attack:

"As regards Sergt. Graves—I *did* write him that letter. As to the truth of its contents, I leave it to God, and your own conscience.—The time in which I wrote it was within a half hour after you had embittered every feeling of my heart against you by your abuse of my

---

[1] The Ellis-Allan "Daybook" for 1829-1832 contains the following entries: "Item, Jan. 8, 1830. John Allan for E. Poe 1 pr. Gloves 1.38./Jan. 30, 1830 John Allan for Mr. Poe. to ½ doz. Ret. L. Wool Hose. 4.50/May 13, 1830. John Allan for E. Poe. 4 blankets, 5.34. 7 (?) Hokfs. 4.63."

[2] Valentine Letters, pp. 225-227.

[3] See pp. 206-207 and Appendix VI.

family, and myself, under your own roof—and at a time when you knew that my heart was almost breaking." [4]

If there was a quarrel on May 3, 1830, as this letter states, it did not prevent Allan's furnishing Poe with some equipment on May 13th. [5]

The relations of Poe and his substitute have naturally been discussed at length on account of the charge made by Mrs. Louisa Allan that Poe spent for other purposes the money that John Allan sent him for the necessary payment for the substitute. [6] In an attempt to refute this charge Mrs. Stanard claimed that the now famous letter to "Bully Graves" of May 3, 1830 [7] did not refer to money owing to a substitute but to sums borrowed from a friend. Her plausible explanation has been adopted by later biographers. When the report of the War Department Records in December, 1939, showed that Sergeant Graves *was* Poe's substitute, I sent to General Adams a copy of Poe's statement to Allan asking if it could be checked, and received this reply:

War Department
The Adjutant General's Office
Washington

A. G. 201
In Reply   Perry, Edgar A.
Refer to   (12-22-39) OR   January 4, 1940.

Dear Sir:

Receipt is acknowledged of your letter of December 22, 1939 in further reference to the record of Edgar Allan Poe, known also as Edgar A. Perry, particularly concerning a quoted statement he is believed to have made to his foster father, John Allan.

A search has resulted in failure to find any record of the statement quoted. No record has been found of any financial arrangement which was made for a substitute for Edgar A. Perry. As previously stated, if such a financial transaction was made it was no doubt a private affair of which no record would be kept by the military authorities.

Very truly yours,

E. S. ADAMS
Major General,
The Adjutant General.

[4] Valentine Letters, p. 261.

[5] Cash Book, Ellis-Allan Papers, L. of C. The date of the entry, of course, may not have been the date on which Allan gave Poe the equipment.

[6] See pp. 206-207.

[7] Valentine Letters, p. 219.

In view of Graves' demand for money, what is to be made of Poe's statement in the letters of June 25 and July 26, 1829, that he had taken up the note for $50.00, cancelling the debt to Graves, and his later acknowledgment, in reply to Graves' demand, that he still owed him money? The only explanation which would save Poe's reputation for honesty is that he paid Graves for acting as his substitute, but that he still owed him for money borrowed for other reasons. Poe wrote to Graves, "I have never had it in my power as yet to pay either you or St. Griffith"—implying that the debts he owed to both of them were of the same nature. He says nothing of the substitution. It is, I am afraid, not a thoroughly satisfactory explanation.

Poe left Richmond before May 21st, and after stopping in Baltimore, went on to West Point. He was there on June 25th, for his letter of June 28th [8] acknowledged one from Allan, dated May 21st, and containing twenty dollars. John Allan had evidently seen Poe off on his way, for in the letter of January 3, 1831, Poe, looking back on the parting remarked "When I parted from you—at the steamboat, I knew that I should never see you again." [9]

In any final judgment on the relations of John Allan and Edgar Poe, the apparent ebb and flow of the affection between them must be taken into account. Either there was some remnant of regard left at this time, or else both were to a certain degree, hypocrites. There are definite facts, however, which may explain John Allan's willingness to speed the parting cadet. In Allan's will, the following significant paragraphs occur:

> I desire that my executors shall out out [sic] of my estate provide give to ——— a good english education for two boys sons of Mrs. Elizabeth Wills which she says are mine, I do not know their names—but the remaining fifth, four parts of which I have disposed off [sic] must go in equal shares to them of [or] the survivor of them but should they be dead before they attain the age of 21 years then their share to go to my sisters Fowlds children in equal proportions with the exception of three thousand dollars, which must go to Mrs. Wills and her daughter in perpetuity.
>
> JOHN ALLAN
> Dec. 31, 1832.

Then follows:

> This Memo in my own handwriting is to be taken as a Codicil and can be easily proven by any of my friends. . . . The twins were

[8] Valentine Letters, p. 237.
[9] Valentine Letters, p. 261.

born sometime about the the 1st of July 1830. I was married the 5th October 1830, in New York, my fault therefore happened before I ever saw my present wife and I did not hide it from her. . . .

Mar. 15 1833. I understand one [of] Mrs. Wills' twin sons died some weeks ago, there is therefore only one to provide for.[10]

The reference to the daughter indicates that this affair had been progressing even during the life of Frances Allan. The birth of the twins in July, 1830, was not in all probability disturbing the serenity of John Allan. He was courting Miss Louisa Gabriella Patterson, of Elizabethtown, New Jersey, a woman whose family was well established in and near New York City.[11]

Poe evidently took the examination for entrance to West Point during the last week in June, 1830, as required by the regulations. It consisted merely of a test in reading and writing and "the four ground rules of arithmetic." [12] During July and August he took his part in the encampment required, in which the instruction was entirely military, and in September he began his academic studies. For the fourth, or lowest class, these were principally in Mathematics and French, in both of which he was probably going over ground familiar to him.

The daily schedule was, however, quite strenuous. Cadet Edgar Poe began at sunrise with his classes, breakfasted at seven, attended classes again from eight until one, and from two to four. For variety, there were military exercises until sunset, and after supper classes again until half past nine. At the ten o'clock signal, he put out his lights, or was supposed to do so.

The Regulations, of which there were three hundred and four, mainly concerned with discipline, prescribed the actions of the Cadets for every moment of their lives. Drinking and smoking and card playing, as might have been expected, were proscribed, but Regulation No. 173, "No Cadet shall keep in his room any novel, poem or other book, not relating to his studies, without permission from the superintendent," or No. 176, which forbade such games as chess or backgammon, are two examples among many of rules which must have

[10] John Allan's Will is copied in Will Book No. 2. Chancery Court of Richmond, pp. 457-462.

[11] T. H. Ellis in his article, *Richmond Standard*, May 7, 1881, gives an extensive account of Mrs. Allan's ancestry and later social career in Richmond. They do not, however, concern this narrative.

[12] Statements concerning the curriculum and discipline are based on *Regulations of the U. S. Military Academy at West Point* (New York, 1832).

annoyed a young man of twenty-one, and which he probably disobeyed.

Although Allan's second marriage, on October 5, 1830, had its share in determining Poe to leave West Point, its effect was not immediate. His letter of November 6th, after expressing his disappointment at Allan's failure to visit him while he was in New York, speaks of his own "excellent standing in my class" and continues: "I have spent my time very pleasantly hitherto—but the study requisite is incessant, and the discipline exceedingly rigid.—I have seen Gen¹ Scott here since I came, and he was very polite and attentive. I am very much pleased with Colonel Thayer, and indeed with everything at the institution."

Poe also speaks of his having no deposit to cover books and other expenses, and it is evident that Allan had been as economical in providing the cadet as he had been in supplying the student at Virginia.

Poe also refers to the beauty of the river, and at least while at camp he would have had full opportunity to appreciate his picturesque and romantic surroundings. The scenery on the Hudson has been so long well known, that it is unnecessary to describe it here. But to Poe it must have seemed that the river, sweeping around Constitution Island on its way south, deliberately halted in its progress in order that the residents of West Point could see it constantly in one of the loveliest of its settings.[13]

Edgar Poe lodged in 28 South Barracks, a building demolished in 1849. Three cadets roomed together, and Room 28 was shared by Thomas W. Gibson and Timothy Pickering Jones. Both have recorded their memories of Poe, Gibson in 1867, and Jones in 1903 and 1904.[14] They are a mixture of fact and fancy, contradictory of each other in places, and also of the account of another classmate, General Allan B. Magruder.[15] They agree that Poe was liked by his friends, who admired his attainments, especially his ability at lampooning the officers,

---

[13] For an account of West Point nearly contemporary with Poe's term, see Roswell Park, *A Sketch of the History and Topography of West Point* (Philadelphia, 1840). For a very effective drawing of the Point and surroundings, especially that of Major L'Enfant, in 1780, the plan of Major Villefranche, and the photographs of South Barracks, in which Poe lived, and other buildings of his day, see *History of West Point,* by Captain Edward C. Boynton (New York, 1863).

[14] For Gibson's account, see *Harper's Magazine* (November 1867), pp. 754-756, reprinted in Ingram I, 82-87 and Harrison's *Life,* pp. 85-94; for Jones' "interview," recorded in the *New York Sun,* May 10, 1903, supplemented by a later "interview," May 29, 1904, see Woodberry, I, 369-372.

[15] See Woodberry, I, 70.

and that he seemed careworn, and reserved, except to his intimates, chiefly Virginians.

They disagree as to his ability in class, but the official records here show that he stood third in French and seventeenth in Mathematics in a class of eighty-seven. His roommates dwell on his fondness for drinking, and retail highly colored accounts of expeditions after "lights out" to "Benny's," a place where liquor could be surreptitiously obtained. Any one familiar with the conversation of classmates after a lapse of years knows that they discuss chiefly their escapades and violations of discipline, so that the accounts of Poe's dissipation may be discounted. But neither Gibson nor Pickering Jones, who was probably the "Old P——" of Gibson's story, could have invented completely the unrest and dissatisfaction of Poe. He was probably drinking again, although this offence was not one of the charges brought against him in his courtmartial.[16] Perhaps the most interesting contribution is Gibson's testimony that Poe was already criticizing the poet Campbell for plagiarism. In view of the influence of Campbell upon Poe's own early verse, this has an ironic flavor.

The only contemporary description of Poe by a West Point colleague occurs in a letter from David E. Hale, a cadet whose mother had noticed *Al Aaraaf* in her magazine. Writing to her on February 10, 1831, Hale says of Poe, "I have communicated what you wrote to Mr. Poe, of whom perhaps you would like to know something. He ran away from his adopted father in Virginia who was very rich, has been in S. America, England and has graduated at one of the Colleges there. He returned to America again and enlisted as a private soldier but feeling, perhaps a soldier's pride, he obtained a cadet's appointment and entered this Academy last June. He is thought a fellow of talent here but he is too mad a poet to like Mathematics." [17]

As Hale must have received his information from Poe, his letter indicates how unreliable were Poe's accounts of his life, and also that at this period he was not desirous of concealing his army record.

Poe's dislike of the Academy routine was probably growing during the early winter. His pride must have revolted at the drill which a former "top sergeant" knew by heart, and his plan of completing the whole course in six months went down before the rigidity of the curriculum. Yet it was not until January 3rd, the very day on which

[16] The books and records of the Adjutant's Office, containing the history of the Academy, were consumed by fire in 1838. Records of Poe's daily standing and conduct may have been included.

[17] Quoted in Sales Catalogue, Anderson Galleries, January 25, 1917.

the mid-term examinations began in 1831, that he wrote to John Allan his intention to leave West Point. This letter, portions of which have already been quoted in their appropriate places, for it is a summary of Poe's entire relations with his foster-father, was written in response to what must have been a bitter letter from Allan. John Allan had heard finally from "Bully Graves" and the opening sentence indicates a definite warning of a complete break:

West Point, Jany 3d 1830 [Error for 1831]

Sir,

I suppose, (altho' you desire no further communication with yourself, on my part,) that your restriction does not extend to my answering your final letter.

Did I, when an infant, sollicit [sic] your charity and protection, or was it of your own free will, that you volunteered your services in my behalf? It is well known to respectable individuals in Baltimore, and elsewhere, that my Grandfather (my natural protector at the time you interposed) was wealthy, and that I was his favourite grand-child—But the promises of adoption, and liberal education which you held forth to him in a letter which is now in possession of my family, induced him to resign all care of me into your hands.[18]

After the account of his career at the University of Virginia,[19] Poe proceeds:

You sent me to W. Point like a beggar. The same difficulties are threatening me as before at Charlottesville—and I must resign. ...I have no more to say—except that my future life (which thank God will not endure long) must be passed in indigence and sickness—I have no energy left, nor health, If it was possible to put up with the fatigues of this place, and the inconveniences which my absolute want of necessaries subject me to, and as I mentioned before it is my intention to resign—For this end it will be necessary that you (as my nominal guardian) enclose me your written permission. It will be useless to refuse me this last request —for I can leave the place without any permission—your refusal would only deprive me of the little pay which is now due as mileage.

From the time of writing this I shall neglect my studies and

[18] Valentine Letters, p. 259.
[19] See pp. 110-111.

duties at the institution—if I do not receive your answer in 10 days —I will leave the point without—for otherwise I should subject myself to dismission.[20]

John Allan endorsed this letter: "I recd this on the 10th & did not from its conclusion deem it necessary to reply. I make this note on the 13th & can see no good Reason to alter my opinion. I do not think the Boy has one good quality. He may do or act as he pleases, tho' I wd have saved him but on his own terms & conditions since I cannot believe a word he writes. His letter is the most barefaced one sided statement."

How much Poe really believed of his statement concerning his grandfather's "wealth," and whether his illness was physical or due to self-pity, it is impossible now to judge. Equally exaggerated is Allan's endorsement that Poe "had not one good trait"—but in any event, the letter proves the impossibility of any real understanding between the two men.

His statement that John Allan had sent him to West Point "like a beggar" is again a half truth. During Poe's period at West Point, he was paid monthly sixteen dollars, plus two rations a day, which were valued altogether at twenty-eight dollars. From this sum clothing and uniforms and all supplies were to be purchased, and four dollars were deducted for books.[21] It seems to have been the custom for cadets to have an allowance from home, which apparently Poe did not receive. He is correct in his statement concerning the necessity for John Allan's written consent to his resignation.[22]

This time he carried out his threat. A general courtmartial had been convened, to meet on January 5, 1831, and met, pursuant to adjournment on January 28th. On that day Cadet E. A. Poe was tried on the following charges:

First, "Gross neglect of Duty," which under "Specification 1st" included absenting himself from parades and roll calls, between January 7th, and January 27th, 1831, and under "Specification 2nd" absenting himself from "all his academical duties between the 15th and 27th of January 1831."

The second charge was "Disobedience of Orders." The first specification read "in this that he the said Cadet Poe, after having been directed by the officer of the day to attend church on the 23rd of

[20] Valentine Letters, pp. 261-262.
[21] *History of West Point*, p. 245.
[22] Regulation No. 148. Edition of 1832.

January, 1831, did fail to obey such order." The second specification referred to a direct defiance of orders on January 25th, by which he was absent from the Academy.

Poe pleaded "not guilty" to the first specification of the first charge, and "guilty" to the remaining charges. The court found him guilty on all charges and adjudged that he be dismissed from the service of the United States. The proceedings of the General Courtmartial were approved by the Secretary of War on February 8, 1831, but only to take effect after March 6, 1831.[23]

It is evident that Poe in pleading "not guilty" to detailed charges that could be easily proved, was deliberately putting himself in a position where he must be dismissed, especially as he declined to make a defence. It is also to be noted that there was no charge that reflected upon his moral character.

Poe's stay at West Point must be looked upon as an interruption of his real career. He was not aided by such education as he consented to receive, and he simply declined to continue, under circumstances which hampered his creative work. In endeavoring to understand his desire to enter the service, which seems to demand some explanation, one reason may be suggested. Poe had suffered for years from a social code which looked askance at the son of an actor and an actress. In Virginia, which held the only code Poe respected, a commission in the Army or Navy carried with it a definite status as "an officer and a gentleman." But he knew, as he said later in his curious "Autobiography" that the Army was "no place for a poor man." He must have anticipated more leisure to write at the Academy than he found there, and when his hope, still cherished, that John Allan would help him, vanished, no course was open but to resign.

The only concrete result of his stay at the Academy was a subscription list, circulated among his fellow students, which persuaded a New York publisher, Elam Bliss, to issue the new volume of poems. It is hard to see how Poe had much time to write poetry at West Point, and the new poems must have been conceived during the months in which he was waiting for the appointment.

Poe did not wait at West Point for March 6th, the date fixed by the Courtmartial as that of his dismissal. From the pitiful letter to John Allan, sent from New York on February 21st, we know that he left West Point on February 19, 1831. Poe was evidently ill with severe ear trouble, and the letter, upbraiding Allan for not giving his ap-

[23] The certified copy of the trial and the findings of the War Department are given in detail in the Appendix.

proval of Poe's resignation, and at the same time begging for money to help him out of his difficulties, is incoherent both in its tone and its physical appearance. How Poe lived in New York is a mystery, for the subscription of seventy-five cents a volume, which had been paid by many of the cadets, could hardly have netted Poe much, after the expenses had been paid. He was still in New York on March 10th, when he wrote to Superintendent Thayer, asking for a certificate of "standing" in order that he might volunteer in the Polish Army.[24]

This wild scheme coming to nothing, he may have obtained some employment in New York, for there is no evidence that he received any reply from Allan. The latter contented himself with an endorsement, written two years later, in which Poe is described as "the blackest heart and deepest ingratitude," a mixture of concrete and abstract terms which indicated Allan's state of mind in April, 1833.

It is not certain when the *Poems by Edgar A. Poe, Second Edition,* appeared, but it was probably in April, 1831, since it was reviewed in the *New York Mirror* on May 7th. The review, which may have been by Willis, or George P. Morris, is not unfriendly, but contains no real appreciation of the significance of the volume. It is a smaller book than *Al Aaraaf,* of one hundred and twenty-four pages, and is dedicated to "The U. S. Corps of Cadets."

Prefixed to the *Poems* of 1831 is an introduction by Poe in the form of a "Letter to Mr. —— ——" dated "West Point—1831," and beginning "Dear B——." who may have been Mr. Bliss, the publisher of the Volume. It has a definite interest as being probably the earliest of Poe's critical prose expressions to be printed. He states his belief that a poet makes the best critic, suggests that Milton preferred "Comus" to "Paradise Lost," and then attacks Wordsworth as a metaphysical poet. Poetry, to Poe, "is a beautiful painting whose tints, to minute inspection, are confusion worse confounded, but start boldly out to the cursory glance of the connoisseur." This foreshadowing of the doctrine of impressionism is worth remembering.

Poe pays a tribute to the genius of Coleridge and then adopts the first element of Coleridge's definition of a poem.[25] As Poe expressed it, "a poem, in my opinion, is opposed to a work of science by having, for its *immediate* object pleasure, not truth." Instead of proceeding, as Coleridge did, to speak of the relation of the part to the whole—Poe continues his sentence by saying that a poem is opposed "to romance, by having for its object an *indefinite* instead of a *definite* pleasure;

---

[24] The original autograph letter is preserved in the library at West Point.
[25] See Coleridge, *Biographia Literaria,* Chapter XIV.

POEMS

BY

EDGAR A. POE.

TOUT LE MONDE A RAISON.—ROCHEFOUCAULT.

SECOND EDITION.

New York:
PUBLISHED BY ELAM BLISS.
1831.

TITLE PAGE OF THE *Poems* OF 1831

Reproduced from the original through the courtesy of the
Library of the University of Pennsylvania.

romance presenting perceptible images with definite, poetry with indefinite sensations, to which end music is an essential, since the comprehension of sweet sound is our most indefinite conception."

Poe returned to this theory of poetry in later criticism, but it is
seldom that a poet of twenty-two knew so well his own special field
of creative art, and was able to express his fundamental conception in
such definite words. That he adopted the definition of Coleridge in
part is in accord with his later practise to start with an idea from
an earlier writer and develop it in his own way.

This theory of Poe's gains its importance from its relation to the
new poems in the edition of 1831. "To Helen," one of the lyrics which
approach perfection, illustrates not only Poe's standards, but also
certain general laws of versification:

"Helen, thy beauty is to me
　Like those Nicéan barks of yore,
That gently, o'er a perfumed sea,
　The weary, way-worn wanderer bore
　To his own native shore.

On desperate seas long wont to roam,
　Thy hyacinth hair, thy classic face,
Thy Naiad airs have brought me home
　To the glory that was Greece,
　And the grandeur that was Rome.

Lo! in yon brilliant window-niche
　How statue-like I see thee stand,
The agate lamp within thy hand!
　Ah, Psyche, from the regions which
　Are Holy-Land!"

I print it as it was perfected, through Poe's various alterations, in the
Philadelphia *Saturday Museum* in 1843, but these changes while very
important, lie in individual lines and not in the general conception of
the poem. Many and various have been the interpretations of the
meaning of "To Helen." Poe himself told Mrs. Whitman that he wrote
it in honor of Mrs. Stanard, and her beauty was probably his initial
inspiration. That he changed her own name "Jane" to Helen was
natural. "Helen" has become symbolic of beauty, of the Greek type.
That he wrote the poem as he claimed, in his "earliest boyhood" seems

incredible,[26] for he would surely have included it in the earlier volumes. Indeed, the woman becomes almost instantly symbolic of the poet's own emotional or creative state. This leads him back after years of spiritual wandering, to an earlier inspiration. The return may be to the definite civilizations of Greece and Rome, or they may be symbolical of beauty in its more general aspects. In the third stanza, it is clear from the invocation that Psyche, or the soul, is another name for Helen, and that the love is an ideal one. It is not hard to imagine that Poe, who was studying Horace, Cicero, and Homer about the time he met Mrs. Stanard, should associate his "native shore" with a culture in which his choice of later study at Virginia showed him to be interested. Indeed, the changes he made in the second stanza prove that this interest was not lessened by 1841. In the substitution of the magnificent phrases that have become an ornament to the language:

> "To the glory that was Greece
> And the grandeur that was Rome,[27]

for the earlier

> "To the beauty of fair Greece
> And the grandeur of old Rome"

Poe revealed once more that he wrote best when he wrote in phrases rather than words. The new lines are great ones not simply because of the alliteration, but because no two words in English could better epitomize the contrast between the civilizations of Greece and of Rome than "glory" and "grandeur." Invert them and the contrast is lost. "Glory" calls up the younger, brighter, more concrete culture which, through its drama and its sculpture, speaks to us with the voices of its undying art. "Grandeur" describes that more sophisticated, more abstract civilization, articulate through its laws and its power, through which we hear the tramp of the Roman legions, on their way to the conquest of the world. The substitution of the inevitable phrases, "that was Greece" for the obvious "of fair Greece" and "that was Rome" for "of old Rome," creates that atmosphere of finality, of a greatness that was but is no more, which adds immeasurably to the effect.

With this insight of Poe into the classic cultures, it is perhaps unnecessary to seek for further symbolism. The "regions which are Holy

---

[26] Preface to the 1845 edition of his poems.

[27] First printed in *Graham's Magazine*, XIX (September, 1841), 123, where, however, the second line read "To the grandeur that was Rome."

Land" may refer to Greece and Rome, or to the surroundings of Mrs. Stanard, who was to him a sacred presence. The fourteenth line in the 1831 form,

> "A Psyche from the regions which"

was changed to

> "Ah, Psyche, from the regions which."

This change seems to make the invocation more personal, but the earlier form may be merely a misprint.

Much discussion has raged, also, over the meaning of the word "Nicéan." [28] I prefer the explanation given to me thirty years ago by my colleague, John C. Rolfe, who identified the adjective with Nicaea, a city founded by Alexander the Great on the banks of the Hydaspes, or Jelum River in India, where a fleet was built to convey a portion of the army through the Red Sea homeward. I see, however, no great light shed upon the poem by any of these interpretations of "Nicaea." For true to Poe's conception of poetry, the effect of "To Helen" is pure pleasure in the exquisite harmony of the phrases, creating that unity in variety which makes for great art. The poem is through its meaning a unit, the recording of a soul reawakened to eternal beauty. Through its rhythmical form, it has variety of an unusual quality. Not only do the lines vary in number and intensities of stress, but the stanzas, each of five verses, vary in their rime schemes. If Poe had obeyed a metrical rule, introduced in Middle English from Romance sources, which required each stanza to conform to the succession of rimes established by the first, the immortal phrases of the second stanza could not have been written. In other words, Poe proved that this uniformity is not a *law* but only a *rule* which may be broken by a poet to whom the meaning always governs the expression. That this poet was master of the resources of expression makes this deliberate violation of an exotic rule more striking. That it is not a *law,* can easily be proved by asking anyone who reads the poem intelligently whether he has noticed the differences among the rime schemes of the three stanzas. The reply will always be in the negative.

Next came "Israfel," not so perfect in form but of singular interest in its revelation of Poe's own nature and his theory of poetry. The title is explained in the 1831 form by a footnote: "And the angel Israfel, who has the sweetest voice of all God's creatures—Koran."

---

[28] See Killis Campbell, *The Poems of Edgar Allan Poe,* p. 201, for several theories.

Poe may have derived this information from George Sale's *Preliminary Discourse on the Koran*,[29] where Israfel is also identified as the angel whose office it will be to sound the trumpet at the resurrection.[30]

If, as I have suggested below, Poe derived from Moore his central idea, that of the rivalry of a human voice to that of the angel Israfel, and the supernatural quality of the singer's lute, he made it in characteristic fashion, his own. The true lyric fervor resounds with the opening stanzas:

> "In Heaven a spirit doth dwell
>   'Whose heart-strings are a lute';
> None sing so wildly well
> As the angel Israfel,
> And the giddy stars (so legends tell)

[29] Section IV, paragraph 76. "Israfil" is the spelling used here, as in Moore's "Fire Worshippers," where a note explains a line, "Sweet as the Angel Israfil's" by "The Angel Israfil, who has the most melodious voice of all God's creatures." Poe might have taken the quotation from Moore without looking up the Koran, but "Al Aaraaf" indicates that he was at least acquainted with the Koran. Killis Campbell suggests that the line "whose heart strings are a lute" comes from two lines in Béranger's *Le Refus:*

> "Son coeur est un luth suspendu
>   Sitôt qu'on touche, il résonne."

which Poe used as a motto for his story "The Fall of the House of Usher" in 1845. This is quite possible. But both Campbell and Woodberry, who stated (I, 180 n.) that "the idea on which his poem is founded . . . is neither in Moore, Sale, or the Koran" apparently overlooked a passage in Moore's "The Light of the Haram":

> The Georgian's song was scarcely mute,
>   When the same measure, sound for sound,
> Was caught up by another lute,
>   And so divinely breathed around,
> That all stood hushed and wondering,
>   And turned and looked into the air,
> As if they thought to see the wing
>   Of Israfil, the Angel, there;—
> So powerfully on every soul
> That new, enchanted measure stole.
> While now a voice, sweet as the note
> Of the charmed lute, was heard to float
> Along its chords, and so entwine
>   Its sounds with theirs, that none knew whether
> The voice or lute was most divine,
>   So wondrously they went together:—

[30] *Preliminary Discourse*, Section IV, par. 8.

> Ceasing their hymns, attend the spell
>   Of his voice, all mute.
>
> . . . .
>
> And they say (the starry choir
>   And the other listening things)
> That Israfeli's fire
> Is owing to that lyre
>   By which he sits and sings—
>   The trembling living wire
>   Of those unusual strings." [31]

It is in the fifth stanza that Poe expresses his poetic creed:

> "Therefore, thou art not wrong,
>   Israfeli, who despisest
> An unimpassioned song;
> To thee the laurels belong,
>   Best bard, because the wisest!
> Merrily live, and long!"

As in "Romance," Poe limits poetry to the "impassioned song" wrung out of the heartstrings of the poet, by a great urge that will not be denied. In the seventh stanza, Poe indicates the supernatural as delicately and as effectively as he ever did:

> "Yes, Heaven is thine; but this
>   Is a world of sweets and sours;
>   Our flowers are merely—flowers,
> And the shadow of thy perfect bliss
>   Is the sunshine of ours."

Finally the challenge rang out:

> "If I could dwell
> Where Israfel
> Hath dwelt, and he where I,

[31] As before, I quote the best form, that of the Lorimer Graham copy of the 1845 edition. Important revisions were made in 1841, when the poem appeared in *Graham's Magazine,* and in 1843 in the *Saturday Museum.* The first stanza in 1831 read:

> "In Heaven a spirit doth dwell
>   Whose heartstrings are a lute—
>   None sing so wild—so well
> As the angel Israfel
> And the giddy stars are mute.

> He might not sing so wildly well
>   A mortal melody,
> While a bolder note than this might swell
>   From my lyre within the sky."

It is the utterance of a proud spirit, unawed even by the lyre of Israfel, willing to match his own voice with the angelic choir. For Poe was listening to an inner harmony, which the pain and sorrow of his outer life might disturb but could not weaken.

In "Israfel" no attempt is made at uniformity in the stanzas, and no loss is suffered. For the poem is a succession of outpourings of the spirit and in each stanza the mood, as is proper, dictates the metrical expression. The calm serenity of the seventh stanza is a prelude to the outburst of the last.

"The Doomed City," which became "The City of Sin" and finally "The City in the Sea," is a picture of the death of the soul, brought on by sin. Poe was constantly concerned in his poetry and prose with the effect of sin, rather than with sin itself. Just as something inherently pure in his nature kept Poe's great rival, Hawthorne, from describing the details of the adultery of Hester Prynne, so Poe, equally aware of the artistic value of reticence, leaves the sins for which the doomed city is punished to the imagination. Poe has so often been described as unmoral by those who fail to understand his work, that it will be necessary to call attention more than once to his realization of the dramatic values of the conflicts between Divine law and the idols wrought either by the strength or the weakness of mankind. Perhaps his own definition of a poem, quoted above, has led to this critical error. But although he speaks of a poem as having, for its *immediate* object, pleasure, not truth, he, like Coleridge, italicizes "immediate." The ultimate object may be the stirring of the reader's soul to its very depths, as in the "Raven," or "Ulalume."

"The City in the Sea" was foreshadowed in "Al Aaraaf." When the lovers are on the high mountain,

> "Rays from God shot down that meteor chain
> And hallowed all the beauty twice again,"

but for cities like Gomorrah, the wave is upon them, and their destruction is foreshadowed in four lines printed in *The Yankee* but later omitted,

> "Far down within the crystal of the lake
> Thy swollen pillars tremble—and so quake
> The hearts of many wanderers who look in
> Thy luridness of beauty—and of sin." [32]

"The City in the Sea" opens with a direct and challenging figure:

> "Lo! Death has reared himself a throne
> In a strange city lying alone
> Far down within the dim West,
> Where the good and the bad and the worst and
>   the best
> Have gone to their eternal rest.
> There shrines and palaces and towers
> (Time-eaten towers that tremble not!)
> Resemble nothing that is ours.
> Around, by lifting winds forgot,
> Resignedly beneath the sky
> The melancholy waters lie."

There is a temptation to forget that this is a biography and not a technical essay on versification. For where in our history has a boy of twenty-two showed such a mastery of nearly every form of temporal, accentual and tonal variety the English language affords? There are two poor lines in the 1831 form of "The City in the Sea," which I have omitted, but nearly all the great lines are there.

In contrast with "Al Aaraaf,"

> "No rays from the holy heaven come down
> On the long night-time of that town,"

it is only the light from the lurid sea that streams up the walls and turrets of the city.

Poe secures his effects here and elsewhere by a masterly use of negations. The towers "resemble nothing" that is ours; and later,

> "For no ripples curl, alas!
> Along that wilderness of glass—
> No swellings tell that winds may be
> Upon some far-off happier sea—
> No heavings hint that winds have been
> On seas less hideously serene."

[32] The Yankee, N. S., No. 6 (December, 1829), 296.

This complete absence of life and of motion, aids in preserving the unity of tone, wrought out of the harmony of the very elements of variety. If, as is possible, Poe remembered the picture of desolation in Byron's "Darkness," he has surpassed his former master in the remarkable economy of the strokes and in the handling of the climax.

"The Valley Nis" is a variant on the theme of "The City in the Sea." At the end of the introductory lines of 1831, which were happily omitted later, Poe explained,

> "But the 'Valley Nis' at best
> Means 'the valley of unrest,'"

and the poem is now known by that title. Some amusement may be gained by reading the elaborate efforts of at least one recent biographer to derive the title from the "Nisses" of Celtic fairy lore! Of course "Nis" is "Sin," inverted. The eternal restlessness is a punishment for an unknown sin. The effective method of negation is again used:

> "Nothing there is motionless."

There is one exception. In the revision, Poe changed the next two lines,

> "Helen, like thy human eye
> There th' uneasy violets lie"

to

> "Nothing save the airs that brood
> Over the magic solitude."

The omission of "Helen" marked the usual change to a less personal note. It may, of course, have referred to Mrs. Stanard. It was a great improvement to make the air, normally the most active element, the only exception to the eternal motion. In its final revision, the poem is almost perfect in its maintenance of tone.

"Irene" experienced many verbal changes before it emerged as "The Sleeper," in 1842. The lament for the death of a beautiful woman remains, however, the theme. Poe at one time preferred "The Sleeper" to "The Raven." [33] Few will agree with him, but in "The Sleeper" there is an uncanny association between the dead woman and

> "The bodiless airs, a wizard rout,"

which

> "Flit through thy chamber in and out."

[33] See Chapter XVI, Letter of Poe to Eveleth, December 15, 1846.

The old superstition that the night air was filled with evil spirits lasted long, and in 1831 few people slept with their windows open! Poe was developing his faculty of using words and phrases that were active and colorful.

"The ruin moulders into rest"

is an example of the progress from the obvious to the inevitable. If only he had omitted the line,

"Soft may the worms about her creep"

for which no defence can be made!

"A Pæan" with its short, almost jerky lines, and its frequent lapses into banality, is so far distant from "Lenore" of later days that it would misrepresent Poe's achievement in 1831 to speak of it here in that later and more familiar form. Yet the most truly poetical conception in "Lenore" is already in "A Pæan."

The revisions of "Tamerlane," "Al Aaraaf" and "Fairyland" have already been discussed; they were wisely abandoned and Poe returned to the earlier versions in his later publications. Their very existence proves that Poe had not yet completely established his standards of taste. But if the volume of 1829 contained poetry unlike any that had as yet appeared in the United States, the volume of 1831 gave us in "To Helen," "Israfel," "The Doomed City," "The Valley Nis" and "Irene," poetry of a kind that had not yet been written in the English language.

CHAPTER IX

Baltimore — The Early Fiction

Edgar Poe left New York early in 1831 and sought a refuge in the only home open to him, that of Mrs. Clemm in Mechanics Row, Wilks Street, in Baltimore. His grandmother and his brother, William Henry, were still alive, and Virginia, his future wife, was a little girl of eight years of age. These, together with Henry Clemm, a son of Mrs. Clemm, made up the family. From Poe's description of this household in August, 1829, they were probably in no condition to help him in 1831. Yet in the mysterious manner in which individuals who can not take care of themselves, if alone, manage to survive when joined in a group, they lived in a precarious way. Mrs. David Poe still had her pension, and Mrs. Clemm was managing the budget. Edgar Poe tried to find employment, for a letter dated May 6, 1831, to William Gwynn, an editor in Baltimore, asks for a position and continues: "I am very anxious to remain and settle myself in Baltimore, as Mr. Allan has married again and I no longer look upon Richmond as my place of residence."[1] Nothing came of this request or of another application for the position of teacher in a school.

Poe may have been attracted to Baltimore by its activity in various fields. Incorporated a city by the Legislature of Maryland, December 31, 1796, it had grown to be the third largest town in the United States. Two lines of steamboats, on one of which Poe was to take his last journey to Baltimore in 1849, had been established in 1827. The first railroad in the United States, the Baltimore and Ohio, had been opened for business on May 24, 1830, a picturesque touch being added by the presence in the car of Charles Carroll of Carrollton, the last surviving signer of the Declaration of Independence. Even if horses drew the first cars to Washington, steam soon took their places. With the advent of the railroad, Baltimore became one of the leaders in that spirit of expansion and speculation characteristic of the thirties. Political activity was rife, also, and shortly after Poe's arrival, his old friend, William Wirt, was nominated in Baltimore for President on the

[1] Original Autograph Ms., Dreer Collection, Historical Society of Pennsylvania.

Anti-Masonic ticket. But even the high position Wirt held in Baltimore did not sway his city to vote for him in 1832, for he carried, curiously enough, only the state of Vermont. Indeed, both Andrew Jackson and Henry Clay, the chief rivals for the Presidency in 1832, were nominated in Baltimore. Its central position probably accounted for the frequency with which conventions of all kinds met there. Its qualities as a port of entry made it the avenue of foreign trade in comparatively large quantities for a city of 80,000 inhabitants.

Poe may have been attracted, too, by the frequency with which journals were projected in Baltimore. Between 1815 and 1833, seventy-two new periodicals were announced for publication,[2] and although they did not by any means all survive, their inception is an indication of some intellectual interest. Two new theatres were established, one, the "New Theatre" in 1829, and the "Baltimore Museum" in 1830. How much Poe availed himself of these, or of the fairly good library, we can only surmise.

He escaped the cholera plague which raged in Baltimore in 1831, and it is possible that some of the details of the plague in his stories of "King Pest" or "The Masque of the Red Death" may be derived from Poe's observation in Baltimore, even though he lays the scene in London, or in no man's land. "King Pest" occurs in October, and the height of the cholera epidemic came in September.[3] Even more probable as a local source, this time for his story "Eiros and Charmion," was the rain of meteors visible in Baltimore in the early morning of November 13, 1833. The intense light which gave the sky the appearance of sunrise, the dread on the part of some of the beholders that the end of the world was at hand, the calmness of others, might easily have suggested to Poe the description by Eiros of the comet which brings destruction to the world.[4] There are no verbal similarities between the contemporary accounts and Poe's story. As usual, the essential part of the story, the growing sense of awe and terror, the intensification of all life, human and animal, are of Poe's creation. It is probable, also, that the "aspect of ill" in the heavens and the terror of the skies in "Shadow" may come from Poe's observation of Baltimore's reaction to celestial wonders.

One liability the household soon lost. Henry Poe, who had been in

[2] See John C. French, "Poe's Literary Baltimore," *Maryland Historical Magazine*, XXXII (June, 1937), 101-112.

[3] Scharf, *Chronicles of Baltimore*, pp. 460-461.

[4] See the vivid account from the newspapers of November 13th in Scharf, pp. 465-466.

poor health, probably brought on by too much liquor, died on August 1, 1831, at the age of twenty-four, and was buried on August 2nd in the Churchyard belonging to the First Presbyterian Church.[5] The funeral took place from Mrs. Clemm's home in Wilks [6] Street in the older part of the city, between Exeter and High Streets, not far from the spot where Edgar Poe was to be found in a dying condition in 1849. *The Baltimore American and Commercial Daily Advertiser* for August 2nd [7] contained the notice: "Died last evening W. H. Poe, aged 24 years. His friends and acquaintances are invited to attend his funeral this morning at 9, from the dwelling of Mrs. Clemm, in Wilkes Street." That he was not very well known may be judged from the fact that the *Baltimore Gazette* announced his death as that of "W. H. Pope," and made no correction in subsequent issues.

On October 16, 1831, Poe wrote to John Allan a letter singularly different in tone from his earlier or later appeals. In justice to John Allan, it must be given in part:

Baltimore
Octo: 16th 1831.

Dear Sir,

It is a long time since I have written to you unless with an application for money or assistance. I am sorry that it is so seldom that I hear from you or even *of* you—for all communication seems to be at an end; and when I think of the long twenty one years that I have called you father, and you have called me son, I could cry like a child to think that it should all end in this. You know me too well to think me interested—if so: why have I rejected your thousand offers of love and kindness? It is true that when I have been in great extremity, I have always applied to you

[5] Records of First Presbyterian Church.
[6] The spelling of the name of the street varies. But the following memorandum, sent me by Mr. R. H. Hart of the Pratt Library, in Baltimore, gives authentic information: "The spelling of the name is from a Baltimore City map of 1823 and has been checked in several other sources, so you can feel quite certain that this is correct. This 'Plan of the city of Baltimore laid out under the direction of the commissioners . . .' drawn by T. H. Poppleton, published in 1823, shows quite clearly the block, Mechanics Row, Wilks Street lying between Exeter and High Streets. The block of buildings was L shaped with the longer arm on Exeter Street. Wilks Street is now Eastern Avenue and this area is occupied by a large modern garage. The names of Exeter and High Streets are unchanged. The site of the Poe home is now in the four hundred block, probably 408-410 Eastern Avenue."
[7] Page 2, col. 4.

—for I had no other friend, but it is only at such a time as the present when I can write to you with the consciousness of making no application for assistance, that I dare to open my heart, or speak one word of old affection. When I look back upon the past and think of every thing—of how much you tried to do for me—of your forbearance and your generosity, in spite of the most flagrant ingratitude on my part, I can not help thinking myself the greatest fool in existence,—I am ready to curse the day when I was born.

But I am fully—truly conscious that all these better feelings have *come too late*— ...

I have nothing more to say—and *this time,* no favour to ask— Altho I am wretchedly poor, I have managed to get clear of the difficulty I spoke of in my last, and am *out of debt,* at any rate.

May God bless you—
E A P.

Will you not write one word to me? [8]

Unless Poe was an arrant hypocrite this letter proves that Allan and he had at one time really cared deeply for one another. It also disproves the theory that Allan was making him a regular allowance, or that Poe had visited Richmond in the summer of 1831 and had an altercation with his foster-father or with Mrs. Allan.[9]

If there had been any such quarrel, Poe would not only have felt differently about Allan, but he would not have turned to him when serious trouble came. On November 18, 1831, he wrote to Allan:

Balt:
Novr: 18. 1831,

My dear Pa,

I am in the greatest distress and have no other friend on earth to apply to except yourself if you refuse to help me I know not what I shall do. I was arrested eleven days ago for a debt which I never expected to have to pay, and which was incurred as much on Hy's. [Henry's] account as on my own about two years ago.

I would rather have done any thing on earth than apply to you

---

[8] Valentine Letters, pp. 283-284.

[9] Harrison gives an account (*Life of Poe,* p. 112) of such a visit, based upon a statement by Mrs. Allan's niece. She places it three weeks after the birth of Mrs. Allan's eldest son, which would bring it about the middle of September, 1831. Woodberry accepts this account but the Valentine Letters make it impossible.

again after your late kindness—but indeed I have no other resource, and I am in bad health, and unable to undergo as much
hardships as formerly or I never would have asked you to give me
another cent.

   If you will only send me this one time $80, by Wednesday next,
I will never forget your kindness & generosity.—if you refuse God
only knows what I shall do, & all my hopes & prospects are ruined
forever—

Yours affectionately

E A Poe

I have made every exertion but in vain.[10]

The debt was for $80. That Poe was actually arrested is improb-
able, and that he was not placed in jail has been established. Mr.
Louis H. Dielman and Dr. J. Hall Pleasants, well known historical
authorities of Baltimore, searched the jail records and Mr. Dielman
has written me as follows: "In regard to the jail records, Dr. J. Hall
Pleasants and myself examined the official docket for a period of six
months, extending three months each way from the alleged date of
his arrest. There was no result. Assuming that it was possible that
Poe was sentenced under an assumed name, the charges under which
prisoners were sentenced, and the amounts of the debts, for which
prisoners for debt were held, were carefully examined and no approxi-
mate amount, nor any misdemeanor that appeared to fit the case, were
found."

   That Poe had reason to fear arrest is unquestionable. In 1832 more
than half the prisoners in the Baltimore jail were insolvent debtors.[11]
No reply coming from Allan, Mrs. Clemm wrote to him on December
5th, and Poe appealed again on December 15th:

Balt. Dec. 15th, 1831.

Dear Pa,

   I am sure you could not refuse to assist me if you were well
aware of the distress I am in. How often have you relieved the
distress of a perfect stranger in circumstances less urgent than
mine. and yet when I beg and intreat you in the name of God to
send me succour you will still refuse to aid me. I know that I
have offended you past all forgiveness, and I know that I have

---

[10] Valentine Letters, p. 293.
[11] Lawrence C. Wroth, "Poe's Baltimore," *Johns Hopkins Alumni Magazine*, XVII (June, 1929), 4.

no longer any hopes of being again received into your favour, but for the sake of Christ. do not let me perish for a sum of money which you would never miss, and which would relieve me from the greatest earthly misery....[12]

The remainder of the letter is the most abject plea to forget past offenses—and it is signed "Yours affect'y."

The endorsement by John Allan is of especial interest: "Wrote on the 7th Decr. 1831 to John Walsh to procure his liberation & to give him $20 besides to keep him out of further difficulties & value on me for such amt as might be required—neglected sending it on till the 12th Jany 1832   Then put in the office myself."[13]

In the meantime, not hearing from Allan, Poe wrote again on December 29th, concluding:

> I know that I have no claim upon your generosity—and that what little share I had of your affection is long since forfeited, but, for the sake of what once was dear to you, for the sake of the love you bore me when I sat upon your knee and called you father do not forsake me this only time—and god will remember you accordingly—
>
> E A POE [14]

Perhaps this appeal made Allan hunt up the letter he had failed to mail. We would like to think so.

The year 1831 marks not only the publication of Poe's volume of poems with their distinct advance upon his earlier efforts, but it also records the creation of his first short stories. Despite all his troubles he was working hard in the second field in which he was to win international distinction. On June 4, 1831, *The Philadelphia Saturday Courier* announced a prize contest offering one hundred dollars for the best short story, and in succeeding issues printed further rules.[15] The stories had to be submitted by December 1, 1831, and the announcement of the prize, which was awarded to Delia S. Bacon, for her tale, "Love's Martyr," was made in the weekly issue of December 31st.

[12] Valentine Letters, pp. 303-304.
[13] Valentine Letters, p. 304.
[14] Valentine Letters, p. 307
[15] The discovery of the existence of these first stories of Poe was made by Killis Campbell, see the *Dial*, LX (February 17, 1916), 146. For details concerning the announcements, and facsimile reprints of the stories, see J. G. Varner, *Edgar Allan Poe and the Philadelphia Saturday Courier* (Charlottesville, 1933).

The judges, David Paul Brown and Richard Penn Smith, playwrights, William M. Meredith, Morton McMichael, John Musgrave, and Charles Alexander, evidently preferred the story of sentiment to any of the five tales which Poe submitted for the contest. The editors, however, saw some merit in them for they published them all in the *Courier*. "Metzengerstein" appeared on January 14, 1832, "The Duke de L'Omelette" on March 3rd, "A Tale of Jerusalem" on June 9th, "A Decided Loss" on November 10th, and "The Bargain Lost" on December 1st.

Whether Poe received any compensation for these stories is uncertain but doubtful. There is nothing in the various announcements of the prize contest concerning payment for the stories that did not win the prize, nor is there any statement that the tales would become the property of the paper. They appeared anonymously, as was usually the case with stories at this time, and it is hard to see what advantage there was to Poe in their publication, except the pleasure that comes to any writer in seeing his first stories in print. But since they are his earliest known publications in fiction, they are of unusual interest to any student of Poe. "Metzengerstein" stands out in contrast to the others in the group, not only in its excellence but also in its general tone. While it is true that on its republication in the *Southern Literary Messenger* in 1836, it has as subtitle "In Imitation of the German," this is omitted in the *Tales of the Grotesque and Arabesque* in 1840, and was probably inserted in 1836 to catch the popular interest in German horror tales. "Metzengerstein," however, is no mere burlesque. It is a powerful story of evil passions in a young man's soul, born of hereditary family hate, and nurtured by his own headstrong nature. These are made concrete by his mysterious association with a horse which steps out of an old tapestry in which is portrayed an ancestor of Metzengerstein murdering one of his hated rivals.[16]

Already in this first story the unity of construction and of tone, the masterly suggestion of the supernatural, the preservation of suspense, and the handling of the climax—many of the great Poe qualities—these are in "Metzengerstein." Where before had a boy of twenty-two showed his ability in marshalling the resources of the English language to depict such a scene of terror as closes the career of Baron Metzengerstein?

[16] The figure of a horse in the tapestry of the Prince Little Lilliput in Disraeli's *Vivian Grey* has been suggested as the origin of the horse in "Metzengerstein." Poe read *Vivian Grey*, but the horse is mentioned only once, and Poe's use of the animal is entirely his own.

The career of the horseman was, indisputably on his own part, uncontrollable. The agony of his countenance, the convulsive struggling of his frame gave evidence of superhuman exertion; but no sound, save a solitary shriek, escaped from his lacerated lips, which were bitten through and through, in the intensity of terror. One instant, and the clattering of hoofs resounded sharply, and shrilly, above the roaring of the flames, and the shrieking of the winds—another, and clearing, at a single plunge, the gateway, and the moat, the animal bounded, with its rider, far up the tottering staircase of the palace, and was lost in the whirlwind of hissing, and chaotic fire.

"Metzengerstein" may be an allegory and the lesson that evil may become so powerful that the human soul who has given way to it has lost the power to resist, may be drawn from the hapless rider chained to the wild steed. But Poe does not suggest this moral. Poe made several changes in "Metzengerstein" in its various republications. Baron Frederick is fifteen in the *Courier,* eighteen in the *Messenger,* fifteen once more in the *Tales of the Grotesque and Arabesque,* and finally eighteen. The passage describing Lady Mary's death from consumption, including the sentences "It is a path I have prayed to follow. I would wish all I love to perish of that gentle disease" was preserved as far as the edition of 1840, and afterwards omitted. But the important qualities were all present in 1831. The best way to appreciate them is to compare Poe's use of the Gothic material with Walpole's absurd treatment in the *Castle of Otranto,* which has been suggested as its source.

In his fiction, as well as in his poetry, Poe published early. Nearly five years his senior, Hawthorne, after suppressing his novel, *Fanshawe,* had found a place for his first published short story about a year before "Metzengerstein" appeared. "The Hollow of the Three Hills" [17] has also the combination of the supernatural and the study of the effect of sin upon the soul.

Poe's other stories published in the *Courier* have a distinct flavor, not only of irony, but even of burlesque. Compared with "Metzengerstein," "The Duke de L'Omelette" and "A Tale of Jerusalem" are trifles, deliberate imitations of the style of popular stories or novels. "A Tale of Jerusalem" is a burlesque of one episode in Horace Smith's *Zillah, A Tale of the Holy City.* [18] "A Decided Loss" has some more

[17] *Salem Gazette,* November 12, 1830.

[18] See James S. Wilson, "The Devil Was In It," *American Mercury,* XXIV (1931), 219.

interest on account of Poe's references to contemporary literature. The narrator who has "lost his breath" in vilifying his wife finds that he can be heard if he limits himself to guttural sounds, and he memorizes the "tragedies of *Metamora* and *Miantonimoh*" since the hero of each speaks in a monotonous, low tone. Poe could not have studied the plays, since neither was published, but his comments show that he had seen them, which indicates his early interest in the stage.[19] He speaks sarcastically of John H. Hewitt, soon to be his rival in the *Visiter* contest, who had reviewed *Al Aaraaf* in no very complimentary terms. When the story reappeared as "Loss of Breath" in the *Messenger,* Poe added a long description of the sensations of a man being hanged, which is not badly done, and he peppered the story with literary references.

"The Bargain Lost," like "The Duke de L'Omelette" introduces a contest between the devil and the hero, Pedro Garcia, a restaurant keeper and a metaphysician of Venice, who in the later version, "Bon-Bon," became Pierre, the proprietor of a café in Rouen. Here, too, Poe showers the conversation with references to Greek and Latin authors, probably as a satire on the pretence of scholarship, though perhaps also with some parade of his own. In view of the uncertainty of the reference to Voltaire in the record of Poe's reading at the University of Virginia,[20] it is interesting to see that the climax of the story occurs when the devil exhibits the receipt for the soul of "François Marie Arouet," Voltaire's real name. At the beginning of his work in fiction, therefore, Poe produced examples of two classes of his stories. "Metzengerstein" is an arabesque, the others are grotesques.

How Poe supported himself during the year 1832 is still an unsolved problem, and his personal life has been clouded by testimony which is extremely dubious. He still had his home with Mrs. Clemm, on Wilks Street. The letters to John Allan cease from December, 1831 until April, 1833. The one certain fact lies in an editorial in the Baltimore *Saturday Visiter* on August 4, 1832:

> Mr. Edgar A. Poe, has favoured us with the perusal of some manuscript tales written by him. If we were merely to say that we had *read* them, it would be a compliment, for manuscripts of

[19] Stone's *Metamora* was produced first at the Park Theatre in New York, December 15, 1829, and Forrest toured the principal cities with it. There were two *Miantonimohs;* put on in New York in November, 1830, and in Philadelphia, May 23, 1831.

[20] See p. 104, text and Note 14, for a discussion of the work of Voltaire, read by Poe at the University of Virginia.

this kind are very seldom read by any one but the author. But we may further say that we have read these tales every syllable, with the greatest pleasure, and for originality, richness of imagery and purity of the style, few American authors in our opinion have produced any thing superior. With Mr. Poe's permission we may hereafter lay one or two of the tales before our readers.[21]

This notice, which may be the earliest published critical comment on Poe's tales, was probably written by Lambert A. Wilmer, literary editor of the *Visiter*, who was a friend of Poe. It indicates that Poe was working steadily at short-story writing, and it seems to prove that he was in Baltimore in the summer of 1832.

There is a persistent tradition that Poe visited his former home in Richmond in 1831 or 1832. As we have seen, the Valentine Letters make the first date improbable. It is not impossible that he went down in 1832, but there is no satisfactory evidence to that effect.[22] What there is, points the other way. T. H. Ellis [23] states that Mrs. Allan's first meeting with Poe was in March, 1834. Poe's own letter of April 12, 1833, which is a cry from the depths, seems to disprove any recent meeting:

Baltimore April 12th 1833

It has now been more than two years since you have assisted me, and more than three since you have spoken to me. I feel little hope that you will pay any regard to this letter, but still I cannot refrain from making one more attempt to interest you in my behalf. If you will only consider in what a situation I am placed you will surely pity me—without friends, without any means, consequently of obtaining employment, I am perishing—absolutely perishing for want of aid. And yet I am not idle—nor addicted to any vice—nor have I committed any offence against society which would render me deserving of so hard a fate. For God's sake pity me, and save me from destruction.

E A POE [24]

[21] Vol. II, No. 27, p. 3 of the file in the Maryland Historical Society.
[22] The 1832 visit seems to depend on Mr. J. H. Whitty's statement in his "Memoir" in 1911, and is based on the testimony of "an old printer." It assumes that Poe was in constant touch with friends in Richmond and hearing of Mr. Allan's will, went to Richmond in consequence. Poe's letter of October 16, 1831, contradicts this assumption of close acquaintance with events in Richmond: "I am sorry that it is so seldom that I hear from you or even *of* you—for all communication seems to be at an end."
[23] *Richmond Standard*, May 7, 1881.
[24] Valentine Letters, p. 315.

If there was no such meeting in 1832, all the stories about Poe's forcing his way into Mrs. Allan's bedchamber disappear. Another series of stories, concerning Poe's love affairs during his Baltimore period, rest upon evidence that bears contradiction upon its face. The long account of Poe's courtship of "Mary Devereaux" could be dismissed entirely if it had not been treated so seriously and extensively by some of his biographers,[25] and if it did not suggest a necessary discussion of the principles that should guide the selection of evidence concerning Edgar Poe. The romantic story of "Poe's Mary" rests upon a magazine article [26] purporting to give the reminiscences of a woman of seventy-one, who claimed that Poe was passionately in love with her, tried to force his way into her room, and cowhided her uncle who objected to the match. There are many other details, too silly for repetition. This evidence is secondary, dressed up to sell to a magazine, and published without the lady's name being given.[27] If there is any form of evidence that is fundamentally unreliable, it is that of an elderly woman concerning her youthful love affair with a man who has since become famous. She dramatizes and magnifies their relations unconsciously, and every desperate act of her lover becomes a tribute to her attractions. "Mary ———" probably did know Poe, and he probably flirted with her, but that he behaved as she said he did is inconceivable. Her evident exaggerations, "He visited me every evening for a year," her statement that "Eddie told me that Mr. Allan's second wife had been his housekeeper. She said she could not take care of him unless she was his wife," should have relegated this account to the trash-basket long ago. But it may have served some purpose if it helps to establish a fundamental test in biography. If one account differs in the vital essentials of the hero's character, which are based on the known and proved facts of his life, the burden of proof lies heavily upon it. Poe did many things which his biographers must acknowledge with regret. But when "Mary" says "He didn't value the laws of God or man. He was an atheist. He would just as lief have

<hr />

[25] Mary E. Phillips, *Poe the Man,* pp. 340-347, Hervey Allen, *Israfel,* pp. 331-336.

[26] Augustus Van Cleef, "Poe's Mary," *Harper's Magazine,* LXXVIII (March, 1889), 634-640.

[27] In *Israfel,* p. 355, her name is printed as appearing in the original article, but she is referred to there simply as Miss ———. The name has been given on the authority of J. H. Whitty's "Memoir," p. xxxiv—and is itself incorrect. Since my text was in type, I learn that a friend met Mary's granddaughter in 1936, and that she is not yet willing to have the last name published.

lived with a woman without being married to her as not," she laughs herself out of court. Among all the women who knew him, she alone has spoken of him in this way.

But enough of "Poe's Mary." It is not helpful in establishing the true record of his life to fill up the vacant months with this kind of gossip. He had some social life, of course. He visited his cousin, Elizabeth Herring, daughter of his Aunt Eliza who had written to John Allan when he was a child. Elizabeth Herring was fond of him, and Poe wrote poems to her, probably during this Baltimore period. One of these, "Elizabeth," starts in the sonnet form, but since he desired to begin each line with an initial of her name, Elizabeth Rebecca, it finally became sixteen lines in length. Poe never published this poem.[28] Elizabeth married some one else and so did "Mary."

That he made any deep impression upon the literary groups in Baltimore up to the time of the *Visiter* contest is unlikely. Certainly John P. Kennedy did not know of him when he won the prize award in 1833. Poe had friends like Lambert Wilmer and acquaintances like John H. Hewitt, both newspaper men. Wilmer took long walks with him and discussed "a variety of subjects" but unfortunately does not tell us what they were. He does deny categorically the stories concerning Poe's drinking, and since Wilmer spoke of Poe's intemperance later, in Philadelphia, his testimony as to his friend's sobriety at this period has some significance. His tribute to Poe's industry rings true: "He appeared to me to be one of the most hardworking men in the world. I called to see him at all hours, and always found him employed."

His description of Poe's appearance at this time helps, too, in its implications: "I never saw him in any dress which was not fashionably neat, with some approximation to elegance. Indeed I often wondered how he could contrive to equip himself so handsomely, considering that his pecuniary resources were generally scanty and precarious enough."

Wilmer's long account is evidently at times unreliable, but his description of Poe's relations with Virginia cannot have been entirely imaginary:

> I could mention several striking examples of Poe's sensibility if my limits would permit. He was unquestionably of an affec-

---

[28] Its authorship has been the subject of dispute, but the verses are clearly by Poe. An original autograph manuscript is in the collection of Mr. Henry Bradley Martin.

tionate disposition; of which he gave the best kind of proof when he labored cheerfully for the maintenance of his aunt and cousin, before his marriage with the latter. While he was editor of the *Southern Literary Messenger* he devoted a large part of his salary to Virginia's education, and she was instructed in every elegant accomplishment at his expense. He himself became her tutor at another time, when his income was not sufficient to provide for a more regular course of instruction. I remember once finding him engaged, on a certain Sunday, in giving Virginia lessons in Algebra.

One of his severe chroniclers says: "It is believed by some that he really loved his wife; if he did, he had a strange way of showing his affection." Now it appears to me that he showed his affection in the right way, by endeavoring to make his companion happy. According to the opportunities he possessed, he supplied her with the comforts and luxuries of life. He kept a piano to gratify her taste for music, at a time when his income could scarcely afford such an indulgence. I never knew him to give her an unkind word, and doubt if they ever had any disagreement. That Virginia loved him, I am quite certain, for she was by far too artless to assume the appearance of an affection which she did not feel.[29]

Moreover, since Wilmer's stay in Baltimore lasted only from January to October, 1832, his testimony is useful in establishing Poe's whereabouts in this year. "Every elegant accomplishment" is an exaggerated statement, of course, but there is a reality about the algebra lessons which helps to establish Virginia's mental growth.

Poe's own letter to Allan in April, 1833, supported by Wilmer's testimony, is worth a dozen feminine reminiscences in giving us an insight into his thoughts and feelings at this time. Far from being the philandering young poet, wasting his time in harrowing up the emotions of young women, he was a hard-working writer of fiction, probably also of unidentified hack work for newspapers, and was self-respecting in habits and appearance. He was living quietly with Mrs. Clemm,

[29] Wilmer's "Recollections of Edgar A. Poe" were published first in the Baltimore *Daily Commercial*, May 23, 1866. Woodberry reprinted the article in part, but it has been reprinted completely for the first time by Thomas O. Mabbott, in his edition of Wilmer's dramatic poem *Merlin*, for the Scholars' Facsimiles and Reprints (New York, 1941). Dr. Mabbott's introduction gives interesting facts concerning *Merlin*, which reflects Poe's own love affair with Elmira Royster. He also reprints Wilmer's defence of Poe in *Our Press Gang*, 1860.

depending for the sympathy, without which he was never able to live, upon a few friends, and cut off by his poverty from any wide acquaintance with social life or literary coteries in Baltimore. That he was desperately unhappy, his letter shows, and that he resented his fate is equally clear. It is the appeal of a normal young man who wishes to work and can find no one to employ him. However, he was not sitting idle in despair. In the *Visiter* for April 20, 1833, appeared a poem "Serenade, by E. A. Poe." Although Poe did not reprint this poem in his collected edition of 1845, it has considerable merit. Perhaps he recognized that it was reminiscent of other poems of his early period dealing with the relations of sleep and dreams. It was addressed to "Adeline." [30]

Fortunately, some slight measure of good fortune was in store for Poe. He was industriously writing short stories and endeavoring to have them published. One of his letters has especial interest in its description of his projected volume. It was sent with the manuscript of "Epimanes" to the editors of the *New England Magazine:*

Baltimore May 4th 1833

Gentlemen,

I send you an original tale in hope of your accepting it for the N. E. Magazine. It is one of a number of similar pieces which I have contemplated publishing under the title of "Eleven Tales of the Arabesque." They are supposed to be read at table by the eleven members of a literary club, and are followed by the remarks of the company upon each. These remarks are intended as a burlesque upon criticism. In the whole, originality more than any thing else has been attempted. I have said this much with a view of offering you the entire M.S. If you like the specimen which I have sent I will forward the rest at your suggestion—but if you decide upon publishing all the tales, it would not be proper to print the one I now send until it can be printed in its place with the others. It is however optional with you either to accept them

---

[30] This poem was first discovered by Dr. John C. French, who found also two poems signed "Tamerlane" which may be by Poe. See "Poe and the *Baltimore Saturday Visiter*," *Mod. Lang. Notes*, XXXIII (May, 1918), 257-267. The first authentic account of the *Visiter* contest was also given by Dr. French in this article, after his discovery of a file of the magazine, supposed to be completely lost. This file, containing issues from February 2, 1833 to January 25, 1834, is now in the collection of Mr. William Koester of Baltimore. A file (incomplete) is in the Maryland Historical Society.

Baltimore May 4th 1933

EPIMANES

Chacun a ses vertus ———
Crébillon's *Xerxes*

AUTOGRAPH LETTER FROM POE TO THE EDITORS OF THE *New England Magazine*, OFFERING HIS "TALES OF THE ARABESQUE"

Reproduced from the facsimile of the original by the courtesy of the late George Blumenthal, and by permission of the present owner, Mr. Henry Bradley Martin.

all, or publish "Epimanes" and reject the rest—if indeed you do not reject them altogether.

Very resp^y.

Yr. Obt. St.

EDGAR ALLAN POE

Messrs. Buckingham.

Please reply by letter as I have few opportunities of seeing your Magazine.[31]

P. S. I am poor

Poe had evidently written, by this date, eleven of the group of stories later to be known as the *Tales of the Folio Club*. He conceived of them as a unit in their tone, and as being original. While the magazines declined to publish the stories, Poe at last found an outlet. In the issue of June 15, 1833, the *Baltimore Saturday Visiter* printed the following:

Premiums

The proprietors of the *Baltimore Saturday Visiter* feeling desirous of encouraging literature, and at the same time serving their readers with the best that lies within their reach, offer a premium of 50 dollars for the best Tale and 25 dollars for the best Poem, not exceeding one hundred lines, that shall be offered them between the present period and the first of October next.

The following gentlemen have been chosen to decide on the merits of the productions:

John P. Kennedy, Esq.
John H. B. Latrobe, Esq.
Doctor James H. Miller

Those writers throughout the country who are desirous of entering the lists, will please forward their productions to *Cloud and Pouder*, Baltimore, before the first of October (postpaid) enclosed in an envelope bearing the name of the writer. If secrecy is preferred, the name may be enclosed in a separate envelope, which will not be opened, except in the case of the successful author. We wish those who may write for either of the premiums to understand that all manuscripts submitted will become the property of the Publishers.

[31] The original manuscript of "Epimanes" with this letter, written on the top of the first sheet, is in the Henry Bradley Martin Collection. The story is in his clear printlike characters—the letter in his own handwriting but of a less formal character. "I am poor" is on the covering page.

Silver medals to the amount of the above rewards will be given in lieu of cash, if required.

For these prizes Poe submitted his poem "The Coliseum," and six stories, under the general title of *Tales of the Folio Club*. They were "Epimanes," "The Manuscript Found in a Bottle," "Lionizing," "The Visionary," "Siope," and, possibly, "A Descent into the Maelstrom." [32]

In the issue of October 12, 1833, the judges' decision was announced:

The Premiums

It will be seen by the following letter that the Committee have decided on the merits of the various productions sent for the premiums offered by us. The "Manuscript found in a bottle" is the production of Edgar A. Poe, of Baltimore.

The poem entitled "The Song of the Winds" by Henry Wilton, of Baltimore.

The prize pieces shall be published next week.

Messer. Cloud and Pouder—

Gentlemen:—We have received two pacquets containing the Poems and Tales submitted as competitors for the prizes offered by you in July last, and in accordance with your request have carefully perused them with a view to the award of the premiums.

Amongst the poems we have selected a short one, entitled "Song of the Winds," as the most finished production offered. There were several others of such a degree of merit as greatly to perplex our choice and cause some hesitation in the award we have made.

Of the tales submitted there were many of various and distinguished excellence; but the singular force and beauty of those offered by "The Tales of the Folio Club," it may be said without disparagement to the high merit of others presented in the competition, left us no ground for doubt in making choice of one from that collection. We have accordingly, awarded the prize in this department to the tale bearing the title of "A MS Found in a Bottle." It would scarcely be doing justice to the author of this collection to say the tale we have chosen is the best of the six offered by him. We have read them all with unusual interest, and can not refrain from the expression of the opinion that the writer owes it to his own reputation, as well as to the gratification

[32] See Appendix for discussion of the stories belonging to the *Tales of the Folio Club*.

of the community to publish the whole volume. These tales are eminently distinguished by a wild, vigorous and poetical imagination, a rich style, a fertile invention, and varied and curious learning. Our selection of "A MS Found in a bottle" was rather dictated by the originality of its conception and its length, than by any superior merit in its execution over the others by the same author.

The general excellence of the whole of the compositions offered for the prizes is very creditable to the rising literature of our country.

Very Respectfully Gentl'n

John P. Kennedy

Jno. H. B. Latrobe

J. H. Miller

The prize for the poem was won by John H. Hewitt, who was the editor of the *Visiter* and who had competed under an assumed name. Poe insisted [33] that both Kennedy and Latrobe told him his poem would have received the prize also had he not been the winner of the contest for the short story. Latrobe's reminiscences of the occasion give some support to this claim.

The "Song of the Winds" and the "Manuscript Found in a Bottle" were published in the next issue, October 19th.[34] We can imagine Poe's feelings when he read his story, which begins after the poem, in the first column of the first page and covers four columns of fine print. For the first time his name was associated with success.[35]

"The Coliseum" appeared in the next issue of the *Visiter,* that of October 26th, with an opening line,

"Lone amphitheatre! Grey Coliseum!"

afterwards abandoned. A notice in the same issue of an edition of Poe's *Tales of the Folio Club* to be published by subscription, at the cost of one dollar a volume, proved premature, for Poe had decided to offer them to Carey and Lea. But the editorial notice was friendly.

One of the judges, Latrobe, gave a picturesque, if at times inaccurate account of their meeting, in his address at the Poe Memorial

---

[33] Letter to T. W. White, July 20, 1835.

[34] Vol. III, No. 38, p. 1.

[35] The text does not vary greatly from later versions. The exact title is "Prize Tale / by Edgar A. Poe / Ms. Found in a Bottle / A Wet Sheet and a flowing Sea / Cunningham." This quotation was repeated in the *Messenger,* and the *Gift,* omitted in the *Tales of the Grotesque and Arabesque* and a new one substituted later.

Exercises in Baltimore in 1877. His picture of Poe, who called to thank him, is singularly vivid after a lapse of years:

> His figure was remarkably good, and he carried himself erect and well, as one who had been trained to it. He was dressed in black, and his frockcoat was buttoned to the throat, where it met the black stock, then almost universally worn. Not a particle of white was visible. Coat, hat, boots, and gloves had very evidently seen their best days, but so far as mending and brushing go, everything had been done, apparently, to make them presentable. On most men his clothes would have looked shabby and seedy, but there was something about this man that prevented one from criticising his garments, and the details I have mentioned were only recalled afterwards. The impression made, however, was that the award in Mr. Poe's favor was not inopportune.

The most important result of the contest was the friendship with John Pendleton Kennedy. Kennedy, then thirty-eight years of age, was one of the most respected men in Baltimore, and a prominent member of the bar. He had published his first novel, *Swallow Barn,* in 1832, and was to write in 1835 *Horse-Shoe Robinson,* a novel of the Revolution which still divides the honors with *The Spy* and *Hugh Wynne.* It was not only in his material help, but more particularly in the sympathy and understanding which only one writer can give to another, that Kennedy helped Poe. This came in its most helpful aspects only a little later. The publication of "The Visionary," later "The Assignation" in Godey's *Lady's Book* in January, 1834, may have been due to Mrs. Hale's knowledge of Poe through her son, but Kennedy may have said a good word also. It was certainly at his suggestion that Poe sent his *Tales of the Folio Club* to Carey and Lea,[36] and Kennedy did his best with that firm, who, of course, had known of Poe as a poet as early as 1829. Kennedy further advised him to sell the stories first for periodical publication and remitted him fifteen dollars which he said Carey had obtained from Miss Leslie, the editress of the *Atlantic Souvenir.* No story appeared in that annual, however, and Carey and Lea ultimately declined to publish the volume.[37]

[36] Kennedy's note on the third leaf of Poe's letter to him in November, 1834.

[37] The *Souvenir* had already been merged in *The Token* in 1832, and no story by Poe appeared in that annual either. Dr. Ralph Thompson, whose *American Literary Annuals and Giftbooks* (New York, 1936), is the best treatment of that subject, suggests in response to my inquiry, that

Shortly after Poe had written his last despairing letter to John Allan, he moved with Mrs. Clemm to No. 3 Amity Street, between Saratoga and Lexington Streets, in the western part of the town, now 203 Amity Street. It is a very modest two-story dwelling, still standing, and now occupied by Negroes. There is a fair-sized living room, a dining room and a kitchen, with two bedrooms on the second floor, which had no back building. Since Mrs. David Poe was still living when the family moved there, the accommodations must have been insufficient. By one of those ironic touches so common in the associations of Poe, the neighborhood has been the site recently of a "slum clearance project" for the Works Progress Administration. Visitors to the district see two large placards announcing "Edgar Allan Poe Homes" to prospective settlers.[38]

If Poe made one last effort to see his foster-father, it was early in 1834. John Allan was nearing his end and knew it. On December 16, 1833, he wrote to his former partner, Charles Ellis, urging a final settlement of the affairs of their old firm. "My health," he said, "is perhaps as good now as it ever will be. While therefore I can attend to these matters it were wise to do it."[39] T. H. Ellis's account of Poe's visit runs as follows:

> She [Mrs. Louisa Allan] never saw Edgar Poe but twice in her life. The account I have heard of her first meeting him was this:
> A short time previous to Mr. Allan's death, on the 27th of March, 1834, he was greatly distressed by dropsy, was unable to lie down, and sat in an arm-chair night and day; several times a day, by the advice of his physician, he walked across the room for exercise, leaning on his cane, and assisted by his wife and a man-servant. During this illness of her husband, Mrs. Allan was on an occasion passing through the hall of this house, when hearing the front door bell ring, she opened the door herself. A man of remarkable appearance stood there, and without giving his name asked if he could see Mr. Allan. She replied that Mr. Allan's condition was such that his physicians had prohibited any person from seeing him except his nurses. The man was Edgar A.

E. L. Carey had not yet decided on a name for his new Annual, which was to become *The Gift*. In its first number for 1836, Poe's "Ms. Found in a Bottle" was reprinted.

[38] Miss Mary G. Evans established finally by search of land records, maps, directories, and ordinances that this house was the Poe home. It has been preserved by the city as a branch health centre, and a tablet has been placed on it by the Poe Society of Baltimore.

[39] Ellis-Allan Papers, L. of C., Vol. 291.

Poe, who was, of course, perfectly familiar with the house. Thrusting her aside, and without noticing her reply, he passed rapidly up stairs to Mr. Allan's chamber, followed by Mrs. Allan. As soon as he entered the chamber, Mr. Allan raised his cane, and threatening to strike him if he came within his reach, ordered him out; upon which Poe withdrew; and that was the last time they ever met.

I have forgotten the particulars of the other occasion on which she saw him, but my impression is that it was after Mr. Allan's death; that she was sitting at one of the front windows of her chamber, and seeing him enter the gate and walk towards the door, she sent her chambermaid down to say that she begged to be excused from receiving him.[40]

The testimony of Thomas Ellis is one of the most difficult of all contemporary accounts of Poe to evaluate. In matters of which he knew at first hand and which he is relating without prejudice, he is a useful witness. But the long letter just quoted is written definitely to defend Mrs. Louisa Allan "in order that I may perform an act of justice to one of the most admirable ladies I have ever known." The account, it will be noticed, is one he had "heard" and he follows it with the account of another visit, which is very vague. He then proceeds to quote from a letter written to him by Mrs. Allan at his request:

As regards Edgar Poe, of my own knowledge I know nothing; I only saw him twice; but all I heard of him, from those who had lived with him, was a tissue of ingratitude, fraud, and deceit. Mr. Poe had not lived under Mr. Allan's roof for two years before my marriage; and no one knew his whereabouts; his letters, which were very scarce, were dated from St. Petersburg, Russia, although he had enlisted in the army at Boston. After he became tired of army life, he wrote to his benefactor, expressing a desire to have a substitute if the money could be sent to him; Mr. Allan sent it, Poe spent it; and after the substitute was tired out, waiting, and getting letters and excuses, he (the substitute) enclosed one of Poe's letters to Mr. Allan which was too black to be credited if it had not contained the author's signature. Mr. Allan sent the money to the man, and banished Poe from his affections; and he never lived here again. I must say, in justice, I never influenced Mr. Allan against him in the slightest degree; indeed, I would not have presumed to have interfered or advised concerning him. Poe was never spoken of between us.

[40] *Richmond Standard,* May 7, 1881.

THE HOME OF POE AND MRS. CLEMM

Still standing in Amity Street in Baltimore. Courtesy of the Pratt Library.

As many of the unfavorable rumors concerning Edgar Poe come from the Ellis-Allan tradition, it is noteworthy that the tone of Mrs. Allan's statement is distinctly prejudiced, and the evidence secondary and contradictory. Poe had left the army eighteen months before she married Allan, so the account of the substitute must have come from him. How did she know that John Allan had banished Poe from his affections, if "Poe was never spoken of between us"?

Evidently if this account is correct, there was no meeting between Mrs. Allan and Poe in 1832. If there was such a meeting, Ellis is wrong in this later statement, for Mrs. Allan would have known Poe in 1834. In any event, this supposed visit, which has formed the basis for so much dramatized romance, rests upon very insecure foundations.

Thomas Ellis is right in one particular, however. John Allan did die on March 27, 1834. We may be sure that his strange will, made originally on April 17, 1832, with its still stranger codicils of December 31, 1832, and March 15, 1833,[41] made a stir in Richmond. While he tried to make provision for his illegitimate children, both those of whose claims upon him he was certain and those of which he was doubtful, he made no mention of his foster-son. And yet except for him, John Allan would now be forgotten. Mrs. Allan promptly repudiated the will.[42]

We know almost as little concerning Poe's personal life during 1834 as in 1832. On March 15, 1835, he asked Kennedy's help in obtaining a position as teacher in a public school, but he did not secure the post. Kennedy's reply was an immediate invitation to dinner, which drew the letter that revealed to what depths Poe must have been reduced:

> Dr. Sir,—Your kind invitation to dinner today has wounded me to the quick. I cannot come—and for reasons of the most humiliating nature in my personal appearance. You may conceive my deep mortification in making this disclosure to you—but it was necessary. If you will be my friend so far as to loan me $20, I will call on you to-morrow—otherwise it will be impossible, and I must submit to my fate.
>
> Sincerely yours,
>
> Sunday, 15th [1835].[43]   E. A. POE.

[41] See details on pp. 168-169 of this biography. A copy of the will was filed in the Chancery Court of the City of Richmond, July 10, 1881, and is recorded in Will Book, No. 2, pp. 457-462. The location of the original is not known.

[42] There were three sons by John Allan's second marriage, see p. 30.

[43] Original Autograph Ms., Peabody Institute, Baltimore.

That Kennedy at once took practical steps to assist Poe is shown by an entry in the former's journal, written after Poe's death in 1849:

It is many years ago, I think perhaps as early as 1833 or '34, that I found him in Baltimore in a state of starvation. I gave him clothing, free access to my table and the use of a horse for exercise whenever he chose; in fact brought him up from the very verge of despair. I then got him employment with Mr. White, in one department of the editorship of the *Southern Literary* newspaper at Richmond. His talents made that periodical quite brilliant while he was connected with it. But he was irregular, eccentric, and querulous, and soon gave up his place for other employments of the same character in Philadelphia and New York. His destiny in these places was as sad and fickle as in Richmond. He always remembered my kindness with gratitude, as his many letters to me testify. He is gone—a bright but unsteady light has been awfully quenched.[44]

Although Kennedy is mistaken in the year, his memory is otherwise correct. He secured publication of Poe's stories in *The Southern Literary Messenger* of Richmond, "Berenice" appearing in March, 1835, "Morella" in April, "Lionizing" in May, and "Hans Phaall, a Tale" in June.

The Messenger was established by Thomas Willis White, a printer of Richmond, the first number appearing in August, 1834. He was strong in his hope of lifting Southern letters to a more lofty plane, and more especially of inducing Southerners to support their own periodicals. The first editor was James E. Heath, who, in addition to filling various political offices, wrote the clever play, *Whigs and Democrats,* anonymously printed by White in 1839 and produced at the Arch Street Theatre in Philadelphia, October 31, 1844. Heath acted as editor without compensation until April, 1835, when Edward V. Sparhawk took charge for three months.[45] The letters from Poe to White during May and June prove that Poe was contributing critical articles as well as short stories. It is pathetic to see the gratitude Poe evinces for the trifling sums of $5.00 and $4.94, which White sent him through Kennedy. We can only hope these sums were paid for Poe's reviews of Robert Montgomery Bird's *Calavar* and Kennedy's *Horse-*

[44] Henry T. Tuckerman, *The Life of John Pendleton Kennedy* (New York, 1871), pp. 376-377.
[45] David K. Jackson, *Poe and the Southern Literary Messenger* (Richmond, 1934).

Shoe Robinson and not for the short stories. Poe was "too unwell to go abroad" in May,[46] and did not do justice to Kennedy's novel in consequence, as he recognized himself. Poe's letters also reveal his acquaintance with the editors of the *Baltimore American* and the *Republican* and his ability to secure notices of the *Messenger* in their columns. This supports the belief that he had been making at least small sums by writing for the newspapers and it may well be that some of his earliest work is hidden anonymously in their columns. Poe even in his poverty was self-respecting, for he declined being paid by White for securing the publication of these friendly notices.[47] It is no wonder that White soon made overtures to Poe to help him with the *Messenger*. Poe's letter of June 22nd shows his knowledge of journalism:

Balt: June 22d 1835.

My dear Sir,—I rec⁴ your letter of the 18th yesterday, and this morning your reprint of the Messenger No. 3. While I entirely agree with you, and with many of your correspondents, in your opinion of this number (it being in fact one of the very best issued), I cannot help entertaining a doubt whether it would be of any advantage to you to have the public attention called to this its second appearance by any detailed notice in the papers. There would be an air of irregularity about it—as the first edition was issued so long ago—which might even have a prejudicial effect. For indeed the veriest trifles—the mere semblance of anything unusual or *outré*—will frequently have a pernicious influence in cases similar to this; and you must be aware that of all the delicate things in the world the character of a young Periodical is the most easily injured. Besides, it is undeniable that the public will not think of judging you by the appearance, or the merit of your Magazine in November. Its *present* character, whether that be good or bad, is all that will influence them. I would therefore look zealously to the future, letting the past take care of itself. Adopting this view of the case, I thought it best to delay doing anything until I should hear further from you—being fully assured that a little reflection will enable you to see the matter in the same light as myself. One important objection to what you proposed is the insuperable dislike entertained by the Daily Editors to notice

[46] Letter to White, May 30, 1835. Original Autograph Ms., Griswold Collection, Boston Public Library.

[47] Original Autograph Ms., Poe to White, Baltimore, June 12, 1835, Griswold Collection, Boston Public Library.

any but the most recent publications. And although I dare say
that I could, if you insist upon it, overcome this aversion in the
present case, still it would be trifling to no purpose with your
interest in that quarter. If however you disagree with me in
these opinions I will undoubtedly (upon hearing from you) do as
you desire. Of course the remarks I now make will equally apply
to any other of the back numbers. . . .

You ask me if I would be willing to come on to Richmond if
you should have occasion for my services during the coming
winter. I reply that nothing would give me greater pleasure. I
have been desirous, for some time past, of paying a visit to Richmond, and would be glad of any reasonable excuse for so doing.
Indeed I am anxious to settle myself in that city, and if, by any
chance, you hear of a situation likely to suit me, I would gladly
accept it, were the salary even the merest trifle. I should indeed
feel myself greatly indebted to you, if th[r]ough your means, I could
accomplish this object. What you say in the conclusion of your
letter, in relation to the supervision of proof-sheets, gives me reason to hope that possibly you might find something for me to do
in your office. If so I should be very glad—for at present a very small
portion of my time is employed.[48]

It is one of the usual commonplaces of criticism to speak of Poe
as outside the current of the literature of his time. Fortunately, we
have the refutation of this error, so far as his fiction is concerned, from
his own pen. In a letter to White, written on April 30, 1835, he describes the kind of stories most in demand by the periodicals of that
time, and provides scholars of today with information as to possible
sources for his own tales.

A word or two in relation to Berenice. Your opinion of it is
very just. The subject is by far too horrible, and I confess that I
hesitated in sending it you especially as a specimen of my capa-
bility. The Tale originated in a bet that I could produce nothing
effective on a subject so singular, provided I treated it seriously.
But what I wish to say relates to the character of your Magazine
more than to any articles I may offer, and I beg you to believe
that I have no intention of giving you advice, being fully confident
that, upon consideration, you will agree with me. The history of
all Magazines shows plainly that those which have attained celeb-

<hr />

[48] Original Autograph Ms., Griswold Collection, Boston Public Library.

rity were indebted for it to articles *similar in nature to Berenice*—
although, I grant you, far superior in style and execution. I say
similar in *nature*. You ask me in what does this nature consist?
In the ludicrous heightened into the grotesque: the fearful col-
oured into the horrible: the witty exaggerated into the burlesque:
the singular wrought out into the strange and mystical. You may
say all this is bad taste. I have my doubts about it. Nobody is
more aware than I am that simplicity is the cant of the day—but
take my word for it no one cares any thing about simplicity in
their hearts. Believe me also, in spite of what people say to the
contrary, that there is nothing easier in the world than to be
extremely simple. But whether the articles of which I speak are,
or are not in bad taste is little to the purpose. To be appreciated
you must be *read,* and these things are invariably sought after
with avidity. They are, if you will take notice, the articles which
find their way into other periodicals, and into the papers, and in
this manner, taking hold upon the public mind they augment the
reputation of the source where they originated. Such articles are
the "M.S. found in a Madhouse" and the "Monos and Daimonos"
of the London New Monthly—the "Confessions of an Opium-
Eater" and the "Man in the Bell" of Blackwood. The two first
were written by no less a man than Bulwer—the *Confessions*
[were?] [49] universally attributed to Coleridge—although unjustly.
Thus the first men in [Europe?] have not thought writings of this
nature unworthy of their talents, and I have good reason to believe that some very high names valued themselves *principally*
upon this species of literature. To be sure originality is an essential in these things—great attention must be paid to style, and
much labour spent in their composition, or they will degenerate
into the turgid or the absurd. If I am not mistaken you will find
Mr. Kennedy, whose writings you admire, and whose Swallow-
Barn is unrivalled for purity of style and thought[,] of my opinion
in this matter. It is unnecessary for you to pay much attention to
the many who will no doubt favour you with their critiques. In
respect to Berenice individually I allow that it approaches the
very verge of bad taste—but I will not sin quite so egregiously
again. I propose to furnish you every month with a Tale of the
nature which I have alluded to. The effect—if any—will be estimated better by the circulation of the Magazine than bv any

[49] Ms. blurred.

comments upon its contents. This much, however, it is necessary to premise, that no two of these Tales will have the slightest resemblance one to the other either in matter or manner—still however preserving the character which I speak of.[50]

Poe did not by any means exhaust the forms of short story then popular, but he was evidently studying the magazines and not writing simply to suit himself in defiance of editorial tastes.

By the time Poe left Baltimore to join the staff of the *Messenger* in the summer of 1835, he had published eleven stories, and had written at least sixteen. These early stories have been referred to as *The Tales of the Folio Club*. No such volume was ever published, however, and the number varied at different times.[51] When Poe submitted his stories to the *New England Magazine* in 1833, he had eleven in mind, and he then spoke of them as *Eleven Tales of the Arabesque*. His conception of the Folio Club was that of a group of eleven "Dunderheads" who held monthly meetings, at which each of the members read a story. The ensuing criticism was in burlesque of some well known style of writing of the time.[52] The most significant fact concerning the early stories lies in Poe's progress from the merely grotesque to the arabesques, or the stories which were the product of imaginative power. He had begun with an arabesque, "Metzengerstein," but he had followed this tale with four grotesques. In "The Manuscript Found in a Bottle" he returned to that mingling of the natural and the supernatural of which he is one of the great exponents. The title itself is a foreshadowing of death, and the description of the "Simoom" is a good example of controlled exaggeration, in which also Poe was a master. The ancient ship, of deep black, hovering upon the summit of a wave of more than a hundred times her own altitude, pausing for a moment of intense terror, then trembling, tottering and coming down upon the wreck from which the narrator is momentarily ex-

[50] Original Autograph Ms. Fragment, Huntington Library. The date is endorsed, in a hand which may be that of White. The fragment is signed, "Edgar A. Poe." I have not quoted the last paragraph, which is not important.

[51] In a letter to Harrison Hall, a publisher in Philadelphia, on September 2, 1836, Poe speaks of them as being seventeen in number. See T. O. Mabbott, "On Poe's Tales of the Folio Club," *Sewanee Review*, XXXVI (1928), 171-176.

[52] See Appendix for a list of the members of the Folio Club and a discussion concerning the tales to be included. The complete list is not agreed upon, and it is of value chiefly as showing which stories were written considerably in advance of their dates of publication.

pecting to be hurled, is a fine example of suspense. The supernatural quality of the ghostly Spanish ship is established by that unobtrusive denial of the natural which Poe had employed in his poetry. An especially good touch is the way in which the crew *refuse* to see him. The final plunge into the whirlpool suggests that this story ends, in a way, where "The Descent into the Maelström" begins. Latrobe said that the latter story was also among the six submitted for the *Visiter* prize, but its date of publication, 1841, has led to the assumption of a mistake on his part.

Two of the stories, "Berenice" and "Morella," at once challenge attention, not only because they both deal with a death of a woman, who has loved the narrator without his returning her love, but because they are both concerned with a more profound theme. The preservation of physical life has always been the most universal concern of human beings, but Poe went far beyond this topic to incarnate characters who represent the struggle to preserve or to destroy the integrity of spiritual identity. He was to rise to much greater heights in treating this theme, but "Berenice" and "Morella" are preliminary studies. In "Berenice" the woman is the cousin of the narrator and is to marry him, but his passions have never been of the heart but always of the mind. Consequently, he is marrying her out of pity, notwithstanding her moral disease. He is a self-hypnotist and dims the outer shell of his mental integrity by long days of contemplation of unimportant things. Poe's analysis of the ordinary day dream is quite accurate. It is speculative and wanders from the original idea, but his hero's dreams are of another quality. This prepares the way for the obsession which the teeth of Berenice kindle within him, and which in the later versions of the story hold out to him a promise of cure for his own disease. The premature burial of Berenice and the revelation that he has torn from her living body the teeth which he desires, are described cleverly enough, but the sentiment awakened is that of horror rather than terror, and the tale fails for that reason. One long passage in which the hero pays a visit to the death chamber of Bernice is mercifully cut out of the later versions, beginning with the *Broadway Journal*, though it still persisted in 1840 in the *Tales of the Grotesque and Arabesque*.

"Morella" is on a higher plane, and is a preliminary study for "Ligeia," probably his greatest story. Again the passions are of the mind, but Morella, instead of being a moral leper, is a profound student. To the narrator "the notion of that identity which at death is or is not lost forever, was...at all times a consideration of intense interest" and Morella shared it. Morella dies, however, and leaves him a daughter, who remains nameless, and whom he loves devotedly. But here Poe introduces the idea that identity can be *too* perfect, and the father cannot bear to hear the tones and see the bewildering glances of Morella re-incarnated. Poe handles the climax skilfully enough. When, for the first time at her baptism, her father speaks Morella's name, the dead woman responds, "I am here," and when upon the daughter's death and entombment he finds no body of his wife, the reader is prepared to accept the triumph of one human being's desire to live again. But the touch is not yet sure, as it became later. In a manuscript version of "Morella," the story ends with the death of the older woman.[53]

"The Visionary," later "The Assignation," is sheer melodrama, in which Poe took the situation from E. T. A. Hoffmann's "Doge und Dogaressa." [54] It contains within it one of Poe's most melodious poems, now called "To One in Paradise."

"Lionizing" is amusing on account of its satire of the methods of puffery then rampant, and of the assumption of scholarship in the many references to classical authors. Poe added, subtracted and modified these references during his constant revisions of the story. In its lack of appeal today, however, it illustrates the penalty paid by any writer who deals with the contemporary in the satirical spirit.

"King Pest" is on the border line between the grotesque and the arabesque, there being a certain power in the description of the pestilence. The main situation, that of two sailors forcing their way into the shop of an undertaker where six strange beings are drinking out of skulls, is based upon the "Palace of the Wines," Chapter I, Book VI of Disraeli's *Vivian Grey*. Poe's story is a burlesque of a romantic satire, in which Disraeli departed for a brief interlude from the political and social satire of *Vivian Grey*. The success of such a burlesque depends upon its original being familiar, and Poe assumed that *Vivian Grey* was widely known. The novel is therefore not a source but a point of attack. Poe's debt to Disraeli lies not so much in his situations as in the ironic tone in which the future Lord Beaconsfield treated pretence in high places, and artificiality anywhere.

[53] Now in the Huntington Library. This undated manuscript is in the clear, print-like characters Poe often employed. It is written on both sides of a large sheet, and there is plenty of room on the second page, if Poe had intended to continue at that time.

[54] See Palmer Cobb, *The Influence of E. T. A. Hoffmann on the Tales of Edgar Allan Poe* (Chapel Hill, 1908).

To solemnly discuss Poe's "sources" in his grotesques is to misunderstand his purpose in writing them.[55]

"Epimanes" ("Four Beasts in One") is a satire upon the adulation of a King of Syria by the mob, whose real nature is revealed when he dresses like a cameleopard and the beasts chase him. Poe had here his usual dislike of the mob as an incentive to satire. "Von Jung" ("Mystification") has its relation to the time, in its satire upon duelling, under attack both by novelists and playwrights during the first half of the century.[56] These stories are, however, among his weakest.

"Hans Phaall," as it was first spelled, was written by Poe as a hoax and a burlesque upon romantic, scientific tales of journeys to the moon. Yet within the framework of burlesque he creates such a plausible and, at times, imaginative account of Hans Phaall's voyage, that it passes from the grotesque into the arabesque group. The plea for intuition in scientific investigation, his arguments concerning the limits of our atmosphere, are foreshadowings of his later and more serious scientific creations. Fortunately, Poe could not content himself with mere burlesque. It was his passion for accuracy which made him depict details in the voyage that build up an illusion of reality.

It was also his passion for perfection that makes "Siope" ("Silence") a work of art. It has as a subtitle "In the Manner of the Psychological Autobiographists" and at first glance it would seem to be a burlesque, probably of Bulwer's "Monos and Daimonos." [57] But Bulwer's tale is a rambling narrative of a man who loved solitude and sat on a rock. If "Siope" began as a burlesque, it became a piece of imaginative prose. That Poe meant it for this is shown in the use he makes of phrases which he had already used in his poem, "The Valley Nis," in 1831, and which he was to republish, much improved, as "The Valley of Unrest" in 1836. Poe would not have treated his own poetry so scornfully. "Siope" belongs with "Shadow," Poe's supreme prose expression of this period. Perfectly unified in tone, with an economy of style that makes each phrase a thing of beauty, "Shadow" derived from Poe's

[55] Woodberry, in the *Works of Poe*, IV, 295-297, called attention to the influence of Disraeli, in "King Pest." For a discussion of Poe's relation to his models, see J. S. Wilson, "The Devil Was in It," *American Mercury*, XXIV (1931), 214-220. See also R. L. Hudson, "Poe and Disraeli," *American Literature*, VIII (January, 1937), 402-416.

[56] See among others, J. B. White's *Modern Honour* (1812) and T. S. Fay's *Hoboken* (1843).

[57] "Monos and Daimonos" had been published in the *New Monthly Magazine* and *Literary Journal*, XXVII (1830), 387-392. Poe refers to it in his letter of April 30, 1835, to White.

own experience of the cholera "the terror for which there is no name upon the earth." Again, from the fear that had fallen on Baltimore at the approach of the comet came, perhaps, the warning from the skies "which made itself manifest not only in the physical orb of the earth, but in the souls, imaginations and meditations of mankind." With this brief inspiration from experience, Poe painted the picture of the seven friends sitting around the dead body of their comrade, distorted from the plague. But no paraphase should disturb that climax:

And lo! from among those sable draperies where the sounds of the song departed, there came forth a dark and undefined shadow —a shadow such as the moon, when low in heaven, might fashion from the figure of a man: but it was the shadow neither of man, nor of God, nor of any familiar thing. And, quivering awhile among the draperies of the room, it at length rested in full view upon the surface of the door of brass. But the shadow was vague, and formless, and indefinite, and was the shadow neither of man, nor of God—neither God of Greece, nor God of Chaldæa, nor any Egyptian God. And the shadow rested upon the brazen doorway, and under the arch of the entablature of the door, and moved not, nor spoke any word, but there became stationary and remained. And the door whereupon the shadow rested was, if I remember aright, over against the feet of the young Zoilus enshrouded. But we, the seven there assembled, having seen the shadow as it came out from among the draperies, dared not steadily behold it, but cast down our eyes, and gazed continually into the depths of the mirror of ebony. And at length I, Oinos, speaking some low words, demanded of the shadow its dwelling and its appellation. And the shadow answered, "I am SHADOW, and my dwelling is near to the Catacombs of Ptolemais, and hard by those dim plains of Helusion which border upon the foul Charonian canal." And .then did we, the seven, start from our seats in horror, and stand trembling, and shuddering, and aghast: for the tones in the voice of the shadow were not the tones of any one being, but of a multitude of beings, and, varying in their cadences from syllable to syllable, fell duskily upon our ears in the well remembered and familiar accents of many thousand departed friends.

The inevitability of the phrases reminds us of the prose of the Bible, and it is not surprising that Poe added in his revision of the story, as a motto, "Yea, though I walk through the Valley of the Shadow," *Psalm of David*.[58]

[58] The motto first appears in the *Phantasy Pieces*, the Ms. revision of the *Tales of the Grotesque and Arabesque*, now in the library of Mr. Henry Bradley Martin.

This Baltimore period was productive of three fine poems. Of these, "The Coliseum" will be spoken of later. "To One in Paradise," printed originally without title in "The Visionary" is one of the most melodious of his poems. The refrain "No more—no more—no more" is significant in view of its later use. And the last stanza is sheer harmony:

"And all my days are trances
And all my nightly dreams
Are where thy dark eye glances
And where thy footstep gleams—
In what ethereal dances
By what eternal streams."

The "Hymn," originally included in "Morella," reveals Poe's desperate state in these days. That he should turn to the "Mother of God"

"Now, when storms of Fate o'ercast
Darkly my Present and my Past"

is an indication of a devotional feeling not otherwise to be found in his work. The "Hymn" seems to demand musical accompaniment. "To Mary," which was published in the *Messenger* in July, 1835, is hardly up to the standard of these three, although there are fine lines in it. It was transferred later to Mrs. Osgood.

In these years in Baltimore, dubious in their personal details, Poe had made progress, after all, in the great purpose of his life. When he came back in 1831, he had proved that he could write poetry. During these four years he had learned how to write fiction. If he had spent too much time in heightening the ludicrous into the grotesque, or exaggerating the witty into the burlesque, he had written at least six of the stories which will remain. In these days when Americans were pioneering in all directions, Poe, like his chief rival, Hawthorne, was exploring the inmost recesses and the outermost limits of the human soul. He was experimenting, too, in his critical judgments upon the work of others. For this field there was needed a literary magazine, and since no opening presented itself in Baltimore, he turned, naturally, to Richmond, where such a career seemed to await him.

CHAPTER X

The Editor of the *Messenger*

It was in the heat of a Richmond summer that Poe returned to his early surroundings.[1] His engagements with the *Southern Literary Messenger* were tentative. White wrote to his friend, Lucian Minor, on August 18, 1835: "Mr. Poe is here also—He tarries one month—and will aid me all that lies in his power." [2] White did not at once give to Poe the title of editor, and it is evident from his correspondence that he intended to keep personal control of the *Messenger*.

It needs little power of imagination to understand why Poe was at this time desperately unhappy. There were before him in Richmond at every turn scenes which called up memories of happiness, and of sorrows which only childhood can suffer and only youth can remember in their bitter intensity. Above all, he was lonely and he missed the womanly sympathy without which he could never be quite a man. His thoughts turned naturally back to Baltimore where that sympathy was always at his command. His grandmother, Mrs. David Poe, had died on July 7, 1835, in the seventy-ninth year of her age.[3] As he had followed her to her grave from the Amity Street house, accompanied by Mrs. Clemm and Virginia, perhaps the uppermost thought in the minds of his aunt and himself was the question of their future. Mrs. Poe's annual pension of two hundred and forty dollars [4] died with her, and Poe would have been more than callous if he had not felt anxious

[1] Poe's letter to White from Baltimore, July 20th, and T. W. White's letter to Lucian Minor of August 18th, from Richmond, show that Poe went to Richmond between those dates. Poe's letter to William Poe, August 20, 1835, is written from Richmond.

[2] For White's correspondence with his friends and advisers, Lucian Minor, Beverley Tucker, and John M. Speed, see David K. Jackson, *Poe and the Southern Literary Messenger* (Richmond, 1934).

[3] "Died yesterday morning, July 7th in the 79th year of her age, Mrs. Elizabeth Poe, relict of General Poe of this city. Her friends are requested to attend her funeral without further invitation, from the residence of her daughter Mrs. William Clemm, in Amity Street, at 9 o'clock this morning." *Baltimore American* (July 8, 1835), p. 2.

[4] See Poe's letter to J. H. Causten, June 3, 1836, pp. 256-257.

concerning their well being. He was in constant correspondence with Mrs. Clemm, and sent her money, all he could spare. Then he received a letter from Mrs. Clemm in which she asked his advice concerning the offer of Neilson Poe to provide for Virginia's education and support. Virginia was just thirteen, having been born August 15, 1822, and Neilson Poe, who had married her half-sister, Josephine Clemm, and was her own second cousin,[5] might well have felt that she was too young to marry Edgar. Evidently the marriage had been discussed among the growing Poe connections. It has usually been supposed that Mrs. Clemm arranged the marriage between Edgar and Virginia in order to keep the little family together. But a letter from Poe to Mrs. Clemm, written on August 29, 1835, which appears for the first time in a biography, makes clear that Edgar Poe loved his little cousin not only with the affection of a brother, but also with the passionate devotion of a lover and a prospective husband. The letter reveals Poe's situation so completely that it becomes one of the most important documents in his biography:

Aug: 29th

My dearest Aunty,

I am blinded with tears while writing this letter—I have no wish to live another hour. Amid sorrow, and the deepest anxiety your letter reached [me]—and you well know how little I am able to bear up under the pressure of grief—My bitterest enemy would pity me could he now read my heart—My last my last my only hold on life is cruelly torn away—I have no desire to live and *will not*. But let my duty be done. I love, *you know* I love Virginia passionately devotedly. I cannot express in words the fervent devotion I feel towards my dear little cousin—my own darling. But what can [I] say. Oh think for me for I am incapable of thinking. All [my] thoughts are occupied with the supposition that both you & she will prefer to go with N. Poe; I do sincerely believe that your *comforts* will for the present be secured —I cannot speak as regards your peace—your happiness. You have both tender hearts—and you will always have the reflection that my agony is more than I can bear—that you have driven me to the grave—for love like mine can never be gotten over. It is useless to disguise the truth that when Virginia goes with N. P. that I shall never behold her again—that is absolutely sure. Pity me, my dear Aunty, pity me. I have no one now to fly to—I am

[5] See Appendix II.

Aug: 29th

My dearest Aunty,

I am blinded with tears while writing this letter - I have no wish to live another hour. Amid sorrow, and the deepest anxiety your letter reached - and you well know how little I am able to bear up under the pressure of grief. My bitterest enemy would pity me could he now read my heart - alas last my last my only hold on life is cruelly torn away - I have no desire to live and will not. But let my duty be done. I love, you know I love Virginia passionately devotedly. I cannot express in words the fervent devotion I feel towards my dear little cousin - my own darling. But what can say! Oh think for me for I am incapable of thinking. All [my] thoughts are occupied with the supposition that both you & she will prefer to go with Mr Poe; I do sincerely believe that your comforts will for the present be secured - I cannot speak as regards your peace - your happiness. You have both tender hearts - and you will always have the reflection that my agony is more than I can bear - that you have driven me to the grave - for love like mine can never be gotten over. It is useless to disguise the truth that when Virginia goes with N. P. that I shall never behold her again - that is absolutely sure. Pity me, my dear Aunty, pity me. I have no one now to fly to. I am among strangers, and my wretchedness is more than I can bear. It is useless to expect advice from me - what can I say! . Can I, in honour & in truth say - Virginia! do not go! - do not go where you can be comfortable & perhaps happy - and on the other hand can I calmly resign my - life itself. If she had truly loved me would she not have rejected the offer with scorn? Oh God have mercy on me!

POE'S PLEA TO MRS. CLEMM NOT TO POSTPONE HIS MARRIAGE WITH VIRGINIA

Reproduced from the original autograph manuscript through the courtesy of the Enoch Pratt Library.

If she goes with N. P. what are you to do, my own Aunty,?

I had procured a sweet little house in a retired situation on Church hill — newly done up and with a large garden and oy convenience — at only $5 per month. I have been dreaming every day & night since of the rapture I should feel in having my only friends — all I love on Earth with me there; the pride I would take in making you both comfor —— & in calling, her my wife. But this dream is over God have mercy on me. What have I *to live for*? Among Strangers with *not one soul to love me*.

The situation has this morning been conferred upon another. Browns I. Saunders. but White has engaged to make my salary $60 a month, and we could live in comparative comfort & happiness — even this $4 a week that I am now paying for board would support us all — but I shall have $15. a week. & what need would we have of more? I had thought to send you on a little money every week until you could either hear from Hall or Wm. Poe. and then we could get our furniture for a start — for White will not be able [to] advance any. After that all would go well — or I would make a desperate exertion & try to borrow enough for that purpose. There is little danger of the house being taken immediately. I would send you on $5 now — for White paid me the $8 2 days since — but you appear not to have received my last letter and I am afraid to trust it to the mail, as the letters are continually robbed. I have it for you & will keep it until I hear from you when I will send it & more if I get any in the meantime. I wrote you that Wm. Poe had written to me concerning you & has offered to assist you asking me questions concerning you which I answered. He will beyond doubt aid you shortly & with an effectual aid. Trust in God.

The tone of your letter wounds me to the soul — Oh Aunty, Aunty you loved me once — how can you be so cruel now? You speak of Virginia acquiring accomplishments, and entering into

THE SECOND PAGE OF POE'S LETTER TO MRS. CLEMM

society — you speak always in so worldly a tone. Are you sure she would be more happy: Do you think any one could love her more dearly than I.? She will have far — very far better opportunities of entering into society here than with N. P. Every one here receives me with open arms.

Adieu my dear aunty. I cannot advise you. Ask Virginia. Leave it to her. Let me have, under her own hand, a letter bidding me good bye — forever: and I may die — my heart will break — but I will say no more.

E A P.

Kiss her for me — a million times

To Virginia,

My love, my own sweetest Sissy, my darling little wify, think well before you break the heart of your cousin. Eddy.

1st I open this letter to inclose the 5$. I have just received another letter from you announcing the rec't. of mine. My heart bleeds for you. Dearest Aunty consider my happiness while you are thinking about your own. I am saving all I can. The only money I have yet spent is 50 cts for washing — I have now 2,25. left. & I will shortly send you more. Write immediately. I shall be all anxiety & dread until I hear from you. Try and convince my dear Virga how devotedly I love her. I wish you would get me the Republican wh. noticed the cheresage & send it on immediately by mail. God bless & protect you both.

POE'S POSTSCRIPT TO VIRGINIA, BEGGING HER NOT TO DESERT HIM

among strangers, and my wretchedness is more than I can bear. It is useless to expect advice from me—what can I say? Can I, in honour & in truth say—Virginia! do not go!—do not go where you can be comfortable & perhaps happy—and on the other hand can I calmly resign my—life itself. If she had truly loved me would she not have rejected the offer with scorn? Oh God have mercy on me! If she goes with N. P. what are you to do, my own Aunty?

I had procured a sweet little house in a retired situation on Church hill—newly done up and with a large garden and [ever]y convenience—at only $5 per month. I have been dreaming every day & night since of the rapture I should feel in [seeing] my only friends—all I love on Earth with me there; the pride I would take in making you both comfor [table] & in calling her my wife. But the dream is over [G]od have mercy on me. What have I *to live for?* Among strangers with *not one soul to love me.*

The situation has this morning been conferred upon another. Branch T. Saunders. but White has engaged to make my salary $60 a month, and we could live in comparative comfort & happiness—even the $4 a week I am now paying for board would support us all—but I shall have $15 a week & what need would we have of more? I had thought to send you on a little money every week until you could either hear from Hall or Wm. Poe, and then we could get [a little?] furniture for a start—for White will not be able [to] [a]dvance any. After that all would go well —or I would make a desperate exertion & try to borrow enough for that purpose. There is little danger of the house being taken immediately. I would send you on $5 now—for White paid me the $8 2 days since—but you appear not to have received my last letter and I am afraid to trust it to the mail, as the letters are continually robbed. I have it *for* you & will keep it until I hear from you when I will send it & more if I get any in the meantime. I wrote you that Wm. Poe had written to me concerning you & has offered to assist you asking me questions concerning you which I answered. He will beyond doubt aid you shortly & with an effectual aid. Trust in God.

The tone of your letter wounds me to the soul—Oh Aunty, Aunty you loved me once—how can you be so cruel now? You speak of Virginia acquiring accomplishments, and entering into society—you speak in so *worldly* a tone. Are you sure she would be more happy—Do you think any one could love her more dearly than I? She will have far—very far better opportunity of entering into society here than with N.P. Every one here receives me with open arms.

Adieu my dear Aunty. I *cannot advise you*. Ask Virginia. Leave it to her. Let me have, under her own hand, a letter, bidding me *good bye*—forever—and I may die—my heart will break—but I will say no more.

E A P.

Kiss her for me—a million times

For Virginia,

My love, my own sweetest Sissy, my darling little wifey, think well before you break the heart of your cousin Eddy.

[Illegible. Probably "Dear Aunty"] I open this letter to inclose the 5$—I have just received another letter from you announcing the rec't of mine. My heart bleeds for you. Dearest Aunty consider my happiness while you are thinking about your own. I am saving all I can. The only money I have yet spent is 50 cts for washing—I have now 2.25 left. I will shortly send you more. Write immediately. I shall be all anxiety & dread until I hear from you. Try and convince my dear Virg'a. how devotedly I love her. I wish you would get me the Republican wh: [ich] noticed the Messenger & send it on immediately by mail. God bless & protect you both.[6]

If it were not so necessary to correct the errors that have constantly been made with regard to Poe's feeling for Virginia, the publication of this letter might almost be deemed a violation of the privacy to which even a dead man is entitled. We seem to be looking into a naked soul, pouring out his passion, his craving for sympathy, his weakness of will, his willingness to sacrifice himself, his appeal that Mrs. Clemm will decide for him and for Virginia, the destiny of their lives. Poe's incoherency at times, even his self-contradiction in the matter of his reception at Richmond, might be attributed to drink, but his exact statements concerning his receipts from White and his plans for the house could not have been written by a drunken man, or a man addicted to the drug habit.

[6] This letter was first published in *Edgar Allan Poe Letters and Documents in the Enoch Pratt Library,* ed. by A. H. Quinn and R. H. Hart (New York, 1941). Permission to reprint it has been given by Dr. Joseph Wheeler, Librarian of the Pratt Library.

This nervous depression continued into September, and in his distress Poe turned to the man who had helped him most. On September 11, 1835, he wrote to Kennedy from Richmond:

Dear Sir,—I received a letter yesterday from Dr. Miller, in which he tells me you are in town. I hasten, therefore, to write you—and express by letter what I have always found it impossible to express orally—my deep sense of gratitude for your frequent and effectual assistance and kindness. Through your influence Mr. White has been induced to employ me in assisting him with the Editorial duties of his Magazine at a salary of $520 per annum. The situation is agreeable to me for many reasons—but alas! it appears to me that nothing can now give me pleasure—or the slightest gratification. Excuse me, my dear Sir, if in this letter you find much incoherency. My feelings at this moment are pitiable indeed. I am suffering under a depression of spirits such as I have never felt before. I have struggled in vain against the influence of this melancholy—*You will believe* me, when I say that I am still miserable in spite of the great improvement in my circumstances. I say you will believe me, and for this simple reason, that a man who is writing for *effect* does not write *thus*. My heart is open before you—if it be worth reading, read it. I am wretched, and know not why. Console me,—for you can. But let it be quickly—or it will be too late. Write me immediately. Convince me that it is worth one's while—that it is at all necessary to live, and you will prove yourself indeed my friend. Persuade me to do what is right. I do not mean this. I do not mean that you should consider what I now write you a jest—oh, pity me! for I feel that my words are incoherent—but I will recover myself. You will not fail to see that I am suffering under a depression of spirits which will (not fail to) ruin me should it be long continued. Write me then, and quickly. Urge me to do what is right. Your words will have more weight with me than the words of others—for you were my friend when no else was. Fail not—as you value your peace of mind hereafter.

E. A. Poe

Mr. White desires me to say that if you could send him any contribution for the "Messenger" it would serve him most effectually. I would consider it a personal favor if you could do so without incommoding yourself. I will write you more fully here-after.

John P. Kennedy, Esquire.

I see the "Gift" [Carey and Hart's *Annual* for 1836] is out. They have published "The Ms. found in a Bottle" (the prize tale you will remember), although I not only told Mr. Carey myself that it had been published, but wrote him to that effect after my re-turn to Baltimore, and sent him another tale in place of it ("Epimanes") ["Four Beasts in One"]. I cannot understand why they have published it—or why they have *not* published either "Siope" ["Silence"] or "Epimanes."

Mr. White is willing to publish my *Tales of the Folio Club*—that is, to *print* them. Would you oblige me by ascertaining from Carey & Lea whether they would, in that case, appear nominally as the publishers, the books, when printed, being sent on to them, as in the case of "H [orse] S [hoe] Robinson"? Have you seen the "Discoveries in the Moon"? Do you not think it altogether sug-gested by Hans Phaal? It is very singular, but when I first pur-posed writing a Tale concerning the Moon, the idea of *Telescopic* discoveries suggested itself to me—but I afterwards abandoned it. I had, however, spoken of it freely, and from many little incidents and apparently trivial remarks in those *Discoveries,* I am con-vinced that the idea was stolen from myself.

Yours most sincerely,[7]

EDGAR A. POE

In order to understand Poe, his duality, revealed by these two let-ters to Mrs. Clemm and to Kennedy, must always be remembered. With the surface of his mind he wrote of details of the publication of his stories. Within his inner and deeper consciousness he was fighting the most desperate conflict any man can face, the struggle for sanity. He tells Kennedy that he does not know the cause of his wretchedness. Evidently he must have had a satisfactory reply from Mrs. Clemm, or he could hardly have failed to find a reason for his depression. But the highly sensitive natures like Poe need no cause for their unhappi-ness, and he had reason enough for his. The recent death of his brother through mental and physical exhaustion, the reminder, through Rosalie's lack of mental growth, of the heritage that was his,

[7] Original Autograph Ms. in Peabody Institute, Baltimore. The words "(not fail to)" are crossed out in the Ms.

must have brought up over and over again the fear that one day he himself would pass over the line that divides the sane from the insane. Only those who have known such a fear or have been associated with those who have been subject to such a terror can understand how real a suffering Edgar Poe was experiencing in the drab surroundings of a cheap boarding house in Richmond. If he drank at times to relieve his cares, he did so for no love of liquor. He drank because he could forget for a short time who and where he was. His physical condition was weakened, too, by privation and anxiety and he could not throw off the dread that even he could have dismissed in earlier times. It must be remembered, too, that in those days sanity and insanity were final terms and the possibility of returning across that line into mental health had hardly begun to be understood.

Kennedy replied:

> Baltimore, September 19, 1835.
>
> My dear Poe,—I am sorry to see you in such plight as your letter shows you in.—It is strange that just at the time when every body is praising you and when Fortune has begun to smile upon your hitherto wretched circumstances you should be invaded by these villainous blue devils.—It belongs, however, to your age and temper to be thus buffeted,—but be assured it only wants a little resolution to master the adversary forever.—Rise early, live generously, and make cheerful acquaintances and I have no doubt you will send these misgivings of the heart all to the Devil.—You will doubtless do well henceforth in literature and add to your comforts as well as to your reputation which, it gives me great pleasure to tell you, is every where rising in popular esteem. Can't you write some farces after the manner of the French Vaudevilles? if you can—(and I think you can—) you may turn them to excellent account by selling them to the managers in New York.— I wish you would give your thoughts to this suggestion.[8]

Whether Poe was helped by this sane and friendly advice or not, he had returned to Baltimore by September 22, 1835, when a license was taken out for his marriage to Virginia. The rumors that a secret marriage took place at this time could be dismissed without discussion if the most widely circulated of the recent biographies of Poe did not assert their validity.[9] The only affirmative evidence is an unsupported statement made by Eugene L. Didier: "Before leaving Balti-

[8] Griswold Manuscripts, Boston Public Library.
[9] Hervey Allen, *Israfel*, I, 384. Mr. Allen repeats the statement in the revised edition of 1934, p. 309, and defends his position in his Preface, p. vii. He presents no new evidence.

more he [Poe] persuaded Mrs. Clemm to allow him to marry Virginia, and on the 2nd of September, 1835, they were married, at Old Christ Church, by the Rev. John Johns, D. D., afterward the Protestant Episcopal Bishop of Virginia. The next day he went to Richmond, and did not see his darling little wife for a year, when she and her mother joined him in that city." [10] Harrison proved in 1902 that there was no record of the marriage in the books of St. Paul's Church, where the records of old Christ Church would be kept, and that there was no supporting tradition in the family of the Rev. John Johns.[11] Woodberry, however, revived the rumor by repeating in 1909 his statement, made in 1885,[12] "It has been said, on the authority of Mrs. Clemm's conversation taken down in shorthand, that the ceremony was performed by the Rev. John Johns, at old Christ Church." Woodberry referred to "Didier, p. 58." But it will be noticed that Didier says nothing in this connection about a statement of Mrs. Clemm "taken down by him in shorthand." There is a shorthand record now in the Harvard College Library, of a conversation between Mrs. Clemm and Didier but in it Mrs. Clemm makes no mention of the marriage. The rumor rests, therefore, entirely upon the authority of Didier. Since every other item of his account, even the date, has been proved to be incorrect, and since Didier himself in his later memoir of Poe omits any reference to the "secret marriage," and mentions only the 1836 wedding,[13] it is obvious that the rumor may be dismissed.

Poe did not return immediately to Richmond, for on September 29th, T. W. White wrote him a fatherly letter which reveals Poe's earlier lapses from sobriety, and also shows clearly White's attitude toward his "assistant."

Richmond, Sept. 29, 1835.

Dear Edgar,

Would that it were in my power to unbosom myself to you, in language such as I could on the present occasion, wish myself master of. I cannot do it—and therefore must be content to speak to you in my plain way.

That you are sincere in all your promises, I firmly believe. But, Edgar, when you once again tread these streets, I have my fears that your resolve would fall through,—and that you would again

[10] E. L. Didier, *The Life and Poems of Edgar Allan Poe* (New York, 1877), p. 58.
[11] Virginia Edition, I, 114-115.
[12] *Life of Poe* (1885), p. 77; repeated in the edition of 1909, I, 143.
[13] Didier, *The Poe Cult* (New York, 1909), p. 24, also p. 127.

sip the juice, even till it stole away your senses. Rely on your own strength, and you are gone! Look to your Maker for help, and you are safe!

How much I regretted parting with you, is unknown to any one on this earth, except myself. I was attached to you—and am still, —and willingly would I say return, if I did not dread the hour of separation very shortly again.

If you could make yourself contented to take up your quarters in my family, or in any other private family where liquor is not used, I should think there was hopes of you.—But, if you go to a tavern, or to any other place where it is used at table, you are not safe. I speak from experience.

You have fine talents Edgar,—and you ought to have them respected, as well as yourself. Learn to respect yourself, and you will very soon find that you are respected. Separate yourself from the bottle, and bottle companions, for ever!

Tell me if you can and will do so—and let me hear that it is your fixed purpose never to yield to temptation.

If you should come to Richmond again, and again should be an assistant in my office, it must be especially understood by us that all engagements on my part would be dissolved, the moment you get drunk.

No man is safe who drinks before breakfast! No man can do so, and attend to business properly.

I have thought over the matter seriously about the Autograph article, and have come to the conclusion that it will be best to omit it in its present dress. I should not be at all surprised were I to send it out, to hear that Cooper had sued me for a libel.

The form containing it has been ready for press three days—and I have been just as many days deciding the question.

I am your true Friend,

T. W. WHITE.

E. A. Poe, Esq.[14]

What promise Poe gave, we do not know, but by October 20th he was once more assisting White.[15] He had brought Mrs. Clemm and

[14] Original Autograph Ms., Griswold Collection, Boston Public Library. When Griswold published this letter in his "Memoir," p. xiv, he altered several sentences, in order to distort the degree of Poe's intemperance. "Sip the juice, even till it stole away your senses" became "Drink till your senses are lost." After "return" (third paragraph) Griswold inserted "did not a knowledge of your past life make me dread a speedy renewal of our separation."

[15] White to Minor. October 20, 1835.

Virginia to Richmond early in October,[16] and soon all three were living at the boarding house of Mrs. James Yarrington, on the corner of Twelfth and Bank Streets fronting the Capitol Square. It must have been a fairly respectable but modest house, for the total cost of board for the week was nine dollars.[17] The companionship of Virginia and Mrs. Clemm restored Poe to a better frame of mind. He had for the first time, apparently, a definite employment of a character suited to his tastes, and his stories were being published in the *Messenger*. According to the policy of the *Messenger*, while "Shadow—A Fable" and "King Pest the First" which were new stories, were published anonymously in the September number, "Loss of Breath," which had appeared in the *Courier*, was announced as by Edgar A. Poe. "Lines written in an Album," beginning "Eliza, let thy generous heart" was also signed. "Eliza" may have been his cousin Elizabeth Herring, or Eliza White, the daughter of the proprietor, but since he dedicated the poem much later to Mrs. Osgood, it does not matter much. Poe also wrote all the critical and literary notices.[18] No wonder that White took him back!

That White hoped to keep Poe in a dependent position is shown in his letter to Minor on October 24th. "You may introduce Mr. Poe's name as amongst those engaged to contribute for its columns taking care not to say as editor." There were no issues of the *Messenger* for October and November, 1835, and in the December number, White ventured so far as to announce that the "intellectual department of the paper is now under the conduct of the proprietor assisted by a gentleman of distinguished literary talents." Then after expressing his assurance that the paper would succeed, when he (White) was "seconded" by this gentleman, he proceeded: "Some of the contributors, whose effusions have received the largest share of praise from critics, and (what is better still) have been read with most pleasure by that larger, unsophisticated class, whom Sterne loved for reading and being pleased 'they knew not why, and care not wherefore'—may be expected to continue their favors. Among these, we hope to be par-

---

[16] According to a letter from Mrs. Clemm to William Poe, dated October 7, 1835, they had arrived in Richmond "on Saturday evening last." "Saturday last" must have been October 3, 1835. In the Virginia Edition, XVII, 379, the letter is dated "1836," but a certified copy of the original autograph, sent me by the courtesy of Mr. H. T. Poe, Jr., gives the correct date.

[17] Poe to George Poe, January 12, 1836. Original Autograph Ms., Pratt Library.

[18] White to Minor, September 8, 1835.

RICHMOND IN POE'S DAY

Engraved by W. J. Bennett from a painting by G. Cooke, about 1834.
Courtesy of the Valentine Museum.

doned for singling out the name of Mr. Edgar A. Poe; not with design
to make any invidious distinction, but because such a mention of him
finds numberless precedents in the journals on every side, which have
rung the praises of his uniquely original vein of imagination, and of
humorous, delicate satire." From this time Poe did practically all
the editorial work but he was not given the recognition or even the
authority he deserved.

In the December, 1835, issue of the *Messenger*, Poe included three
"Scenes from an Unpublished Drama," and added two more in January, 1836. Since "Politian," as it was afterwards called, was Poe's only
attempt at drama and was based on actual occurrences in the United
States which were used frequently by other writers, it has unusual
importance. It was founded on the so-called "Kentucky Tragedy"
which took place in Frankfort, Kentucky, in 1825. Solomon P. Sharp,
a lawyer of some prominence, had seduced Anne Cooke, a few years
before the tragedy. After many refusals, she finally agreed to marry
Jereboam Beauchamp, but insisted that her husband revenge her
upon her betrayer. Beauchamp challenged Sharp, who refused to
meet him, and finally Beauchamp stabbed him fatally on November 7, 1825. Beauchamp and his wife were convicted of murder, and
both attempted suicide in prison. She was successful, but Beauchamp
was revived and executed July 7, 1826. The tragedy attracted wide
attention, and soon passed into drama and fiction. Thomas Holley
Chivers, later to become associated with Poe, wrote in 1834 his *Conrad
and Eudora; or, The Death of Alonzo*, a drama in five acts. It is in
verse, and is laid in Frankfort, but the characters really might live
anywhere or rather nowhere, for a more absurd production would be
hard to find. It had no influence upon Poe, in any event. Neither this
nor "Politian" saw the stage, but in 1837 Charlotte Barnes produced a
successful tragedy, *Octavia Bragaldi*, at the National Theatre, New
York, and later played it in London. Charles Fenno Hoffman's novel,
Greyslaer (1840) touched upon the theme, although the crime was
abduction, not seduction. William Gilmore Simms based his novel
Beauchampe in 1842 upon the actual deeds of the characters [19] and
used their real names.

When John Savage dramatized *Beauchampe* as *Sybil* in 1858 he

---

[19] Contrary to the usual statements, Simms wrote only one novel upon
the tragedy. The first edition of *Beauchampe* (1842) is in two volumes. The
first volume was revised and published in 1856 as *Charlemont*, and the
second volume became *Beauchampe, a Sequel to Charlemont*, also republished in 1856.

laid the scene in Kentucky. While the novelists did not hesitate to use real places and names, Poe changed the scene to Rome, and while the time is not indicated, a quotation from *Comus* places it not earlier than the Seventeenth Century. In thus changing the scene and century, Poe was simply following a literary convention of the time. Miss Barnes placed her *Octavia Bragaldi* in Milan in the Fifteenth Century. Payne's *Brutus,* Bird's *Gladiator* and *Broker of Bogota,* Willis's *Tortesa the Usurer,* successful tragedies of that day in America, all illustrate the belief that for the stage, it was best to remove the scene to a distance, so that liberties could be taken with the plot and the characters.

Poe published only five of the eleven scenes, but the entire drama has been edited from the original manuscript [20] by Dr. T. O. Mabbott. For his names and characters Poe used Italian history. Politian, the hero of the play, who corresponds to Colonel Beauchamp, was suggested by the Florentine scholar, Angelo Poliziano; Alessandra whom Castiglione is to marry, is the name of Alessandra Scala, a woman friend of Poliziano. Castiglione, the villain of the play, who represents Colonel Sharp, and Baldazzar, Politian's friend, are derived from Baldassare Castiglione, the author of the *Book of the Courtyer.* Lalage, the heroine, was probably suggested by Horace. Di Broglio is probably an Italianized form of De Broglie, a French name prominent in the early Nineteenth Century.[21]

Poe made several changes in the characters of the principal actors in the drama. Politian is an Englishman, the Earl of Leicester, on a visit to Rome, and instead of being acquainted with the heroine as in Kentucky, he is so attracted by her voice as she sings in another room of the castle, that he falls in love with her before he sees her. In the descriptions of Politian's nature by the other characters, there is evidently a reflection of the varying opinions concerning Poe himself of which he probably by that time was quite aware. The Count di Broglio has heard of Politian as "a man quite young in years but grey in fame." Alessandra knows of him

> "As of one who entered madly into life,
> Drinking the cup of pleasure to the dregs."

[20] *Politian, an Unfinished Tragedy, by Edgar A. Poe, edited from the Original Sources, including the Autograph Ms. in the Pierpont Morgan Library* by Thomas Ollive Mabbott (Richmond, 1923).

[21] For these identifications and other suggestions not quite so certain, we are indebted to Killis Campbell in the notes to his edition of the *Poems of Edgar A. Poe,* p. 229. See also Dr. Mabbott's notes to *Politian.*

Castiglione, who has actually known Politian, insists that he is "a dreamer, shut out from common passions." Castiglione is not quite as deep dyed a villain as Sharp has been represented by the other authors who have used the plot. His refusal to fight Politian is due to his remorse at his own treatment of Lalage, and is made quite dramatic by Poe. Lalage is, however, hopeless; her humility before even her maid servant and her constant weeping tend to remove her from sympathy.

Why did Poe omit the first, second, fifth, eighth, tenth, and eleventh scenes? The last, which is made up almost entirely of the verses known as "The Coliseum," he probably felt was a repetition since he had already published that poem twice. The others are low comedy, often ironic, and introduce servants and another patrician character, San Ozzo, who have little to do with the action. Poe's constant desire to preserve unity, and his realization that these scenes are not poetry, probably caused him to omit them. From the theatrical point of view, they would probably act quite well. We do not know whether Poe, like so many other writers of that time, hoped to see his drama presented on the stage, for he makes no mention of such a desire in his letters. Probably he considered it simply as a poem. It waited for stage production until 1933 when it was produced, apparently with success, by the Virginia Players at the University of Virginia.

"Politian" is not one of Poe's great poems, and he did not return to the dramatic form. That he was wise is proved by the way in which the descriptive lyric, "The Coliseum" at once takes its place in a different order of poetry. It was injected into the drama and Poe wisely withdrew it. Viewed as an invocation to a great symbol of the past, it has a majesty and a powerful rhythmical sweep which reveal Poe's mastery over blank verse, not often his chosen medium. It is not merely the description of an ancient building, it is the revelation of an imaginative soul, inspired by the ruins of a great race to the recreation of a picture of that race in the time of its glory. Poe undoubtedly knew Byron's description of the Coliseum in *Childe Harold,* but the verbal resemblances are few and faint. Indeed the reactions of the two poets are quite opposite—Byron sums up with

"Rome and her Ruin past Redemption's skill,
The World, the same wide den—of thieves, or
what ye will" [22]

[22] *Childe Harold,* Book IV, Stanza CXLV.

Poe puts the question to himself whether these stones are all that is left—and his reply has a loftier tone than Byron:

.Not all"—the Echoes answer me—"not all!
Prophetic sounds and loud, arise forever
From us, and from all Ruin, unto the wise,
As melody from Memnon to the Sun.
We rule the hearts of mightiest men—we rule
With a despotic sway all giant minds.
We are not impotent—we pallid stones.
Not all our power is gone—not all our fame—
Not all the magic of our high renown—
Not all the wonder that encircles us—
Not all the mysteries that in us lie—
Not all the memories that hang upon
And cling around about us as a garment,
Clothing us in a robe of more than glory."

Poe continued to print or reprint his short stories, which had been written before he left Baltimore, if we are to believe his own statement to Kennedy. They have been discussed and no new fiction appeared during 1836. Several of the poems were also reprinted with alterations. "A Pæan" was changed to include a reference to "Helen" which later was withdrawn again. "Irene" was rewritten, with some decided improvements, most of which were preserved when it became "The Sleeper."

While his connection with the *Messenger* was still in a tentative state, Poe entered into correspondence with other authors, discussing principles of composition which reveal his constant preoccupation with methods of writing. One of the most interesting of these correspondences was initiated by Nathaniel Beverley Tucker, Professor of Law at William and Mary College, and author of *George Balcombe* and *The Partisan Leader*. Tucker wrote first to White:

Williamsburg, November 29, 1835.
My dear Sir,—... I am much flattered by Mr. Poe's opinion of my lines. Original thoughts come to me "like angels' visits few and far between." To Mr. P. they come thronging unbidden, crowding themselves upon him in such numbers as to require the black rod of that master of ceremonies, Criticism, to keep them in order. I hope he will take this and other suggestions of mine kindly. I am interested in him, and am glad he has found a

position in which his pursuit of fame may be neither retarded, nor, what is worse, hurried by necessity. His history, as I have heard it, reminds me of Coleridge's,—With the example of Coleridge's virtues and success before him, he can need n͡ other guide. Yet a companion by the way to hint that "more haste makes less speed" may not be amiss. Will he admit me to this office? Without the tithe of his genius, I am old enough to be his father (if I do not mistake his filiation, I remember his beautiful mother when a girl), and I presume I have had advantages the want of which he feels.... He may perhaps demur to what I have said of the metre of his drama, and quote some of Shakspear's [sic] rough lines in vindication of his. But a man of genius should imitate no one, especially in his faults....

Now one word more. If Mr. P. takes well what I have said, he shall have as much more of it whenever occasion calls for it. If not, his silence alone will effectually rebuke my impertinence.

Yours truly,

B. T.[23]

Poe's reply may now be fitted into its proper place:

Richmond
Dec: 1. 35.

Dear Sir,

Mr. White was so kind as to read me some portions of your letter to himself, dated Nov. 29, and I feel impelled, as much by gratitude for your many friendly expressions of interest in my behalf, as by a desire to make some little explanations, to answer, personally, the passages alluded to.

And firstly—in relation to your own verses. That they *are not poetry* I will not allow, even when judging them by your own rules. A very cursory perusal enabled me, when I first saw them, to point out many instances of the ποίησις you mention. Had I the lines before me now I would particularize them. But is there not a more lofty species of originality than originality of individual thoughts or individual passages? I doubt very much whether a composition may not even be full of original things, and still be pure imitation as a whole. On the other hand I have seen writings, devoid of any new thought, and frequently destitute of any new expression—writings which I could not help considering as full of creative power. But I have no wish to refine, and I dare say that you have little desire that I should do so. What *is*, or

[23] Original Autograph Ms., Boston Public Library.

is not, poetry must not be told in a mere epistle. I sincerely think your lines excellent. . . .

Your opinion of "The MS. found in a Bottle" is just. The Tale was written some years ago, and was one among the first I ever wrote. I have met with no one, with the exception of yourself & P. P. Cooke of Winchester, whose judgment concerning these Tales I place any value upon. Generally, people praise extravagantly those of which I am ashamed, and pass in silence what I fancy to be praise worthy. The last tale I wrote was Morella and it was my best. When I write again it will be something better than Morella. At present, having no time upon my hands, from my editorial duties, I can write nothing worth reading. What articles I have published *since Morella* were all written some time ago. I mention this to account for the "mere physique" of the horrible which prevails in the "MS. found in a Bottle." I do not think I would be guilty of a similar absurdity *now*. One or two words more of Egotism.

I do not entirely acquiesce in your strictures on the versification of my Drama. I find that versification is a point on which, very frequently, persons who agree in all important particulars, differ very essentially. I do not remember to have known any two persons agree, thoroughly, about metre. I have been puzzled to assign a reason for this—but can find none more satisfactory than that music is a most indefinite conception. I have made prosody, in all languages which I have studied, a particular subject of inquiry. I have written many verses, and read more than you would be inclined to imagine. In short—I especially pride myself upon the accuracy of my ear—and have established the fact of its accuracy—to my own satisfaction at least, by some odd chromatic experiments. I was therefore astonished to find you objecting to the *melody* of my lines. Had I time just now, and were I not afraid of tiring you, I would like to discuss this point more fully. There is much room for speculation here. Your own verses (I remarked this, upon first reading them, to Mr. White) are absolutely faultless, if considered as "pure harmony"—I mean to speak technically—"without the intervention of any discords." I was formerly accustomed to write thus, and it would be an easy thing to convince you of the accuracy of my ear by writing such at present—but imperceptibly the *love of these discords* grew upon me as my love of music grew stronger, and I at length came to feel all the melody of Pope's later versification, and that of the present T. Moore. I should like to hear from you on this subject. *The Dream* was admitted solely thro' necessity. I know not the author.

In speaking of my mother you have touched a string to which my heart fully responds. To have known her is to be an object of great interest in my eyes. I myself never knew her—and never knew the affection of a father. Both died (as you may remember) within a few weeks of each other. I have many occasional dealings with Adversity—but the want of parental affection has been the heaviest of my trials.

I would be proud if you would honor me frequently with your criticism. Believe me when I say that I *value it*. I would be gratified, also, if you write me in reply to this letter. It will assure me that you have excused my impertinence in addressing you without a previous acquaintance.

Very respy. & sincerely
Y. ob. st.

EDGAR A. POE

Judge Beverly Tucker.[24]

Poe's reference to his study of versification shows that he was only partially aware of the principles upon which English verse was established. What he speaks of as "discords" were his variations from a preconceived metrical pattern which are responsible for some of his finest effects, and which are, of course, in accord with the accentual nature of English verse. His statement that he never knew his mother is important and his repetition of his belief that his parents died within a few weeks of each other is equally significant. Here he is not writing for publication but to a gentleman who could have known the facts and whom he would have had no purpose in deceiving.

Tucker replied in a long letter [25] on December 5th, dealing largely with questions of versification. Tucker believed that the time element in English verse was all important, and made the same errors as Sidney Lanier did later. Tucker's estimate of Poe's criticism is valuable because, as is shown in a letter to White on January 26, 1836,[26] he makes clear that he does not admire all of Poe's writing. Yet in the

[24] See James Southall Wilson, "Unpublished Letters of Edgar Allan Poe," *Century Magazine,* LXXXV (March, 1924), 652-656.

[25] Original Autograph Ms., Griswold Collection, Boston Public Library. The letter is given complete in the Virginia Edition, XVII, 21-24.

[26] Original Autograph Ms., Griswold Collection, Boston Public Library.

same letter he speaks of his lack of admiration of "Mrs. Sigourney & Co." and adds, "I only mention this to say that Mr. P's review of the writings of a leash of these ladies, in your last number, is a specimen of criticism, which for niceness of discrimination, delicacy of expression, and all that shows familiarity with the art, may well compare with any I have seen." Tucker refers to Poe's review of volumes of poems by Mrs. Sigourney, Mrs. H. F. Gould and Mrs. E. F. Ellet, in the January, 1835, number of the *Messenger*. Mrs. Ellet was to give him trouble in later years.

A letter to Mrs. Sigourney, who had evidently objected to Poe's review of her poems in the January number, indicates his tact in dealing with a delicate question, for his strictures had been a bit severe, though not unfair:

Richmond, Va.
April 12th, 1836.

Mrs. L. H. Sigourney,
    Madam,

At the request of Mr. T. W. White, I take the liberty of replying to your letter of the 6th ult.

I am vexed to hear that you have not received the Messenger regularly, and am confident that upon reception of the January number (now again forwarded to your address) you will be fully convinced that your friends, in their zeal for your literary reputation, have misconceived the spirit of the criticism to which you have alluded. To yourself, personally, we commit our review, with a perfect certainty of being understood. That we have evinced any "severity amounting to unkindness" is an accusation of which you will, I sincerely hope, unhesitatingly acquit us. We refer you, especially, to the concluding sentences of the critique.

Mr. White desires me to express his regret at the mistake in relation to your package of books. He would have placed them immediately in the hands of some bookseller here, but was not sure that your views would be met in so doing. They are now properly disposed of.

You will, I hope, allow us still to send you the Messenger. We are grieved, and mortified to hear that you cannot again contribute to its pages, but your objection in respect to receiving a copy without equivalent is untenable—any one of your pieces already published in our Journal being more than an equivalent to a subscription *in perpetuo*. This we say as publishers, without any intention to flatter, and having reference merely to the sum usually paid, to writers of far less reputation, for articles immeasurably inferior.

In respect to your question touching the Editor of the Messenger, I have to reply that, for the last six months, the Editorial duties have been undertaken by myself. Of course, therefore, I plead guilty to all the criticisms of the Journal during the period mentioned. In addition to what evidence of misconception on the part of your friends you will assuredly find in the January number, I have now only to say that sincere admiration of the book reviewed was the predominant feeling in my bosom while penning the review.

It would afford me the highest gratification should I find that you acquit me of this "foul charge." I will look with great anxiety for your reply.

Very respy. & truly

Yr. Ob. St.

EDGAR A. POE [27]

This letter is proof, if we needed it, that Poe had been writing all the reviews since the magazine resumed publication in December, 1835. Mrs. Sigourney's reply,[28] on April 23rd, reveals a mollified poetess, who respects Poe's judgments.

Poe's letters to Kennedy continue and contain both personal and literary matters of interest:

Richmond, Jan. 22, 1836.

Dear Sir,—Although I have never yet acknowledged the receipt of your kind of letter of advice some months ago, it was not without great influence upon me. I have, since then, fought the enemy manfully, and am now, in every respect, comfortable and happy. I know you will be pleased to hear this. My health is better than for years past, my mind is fully occupied, my pecuniary difficulties have vanished, I have a fair prospect of future success—in a word all is right. I shall never forget to whom all this happiness is in great degree to be attributed. I know without your timely aid I should have sunk under my trials. Mr. White is very liberal, and besides my salary of 520$ pays me liberally for extra work, so that I receive nearly $800. Next year, that is at the

---

[27] Original Autograph Ms., W. H. Koester Collection. Published here for the first time.

[28] Virginia Edition, XVII. 33-35.

commencement of the second volume, I am to get $1000. Besides this I receive, from Publishers, nearly all new publications. My friends in Richmond have received me with open arms, and my reputation is extending—especially in the South. Contrast all this with those circumstances of absolute despair in which you found me, and you will see how great reason I have to be grateful to God—and to yourself.

Some matters in relation to the death of Mrs. Catherine Clemm, who resided at Mount Prospect, four miles from Baltimore, render it necessary for me to apply to an attorney, and I have thought it probable you would be kind enough to advise me... [the omitted passage refers to family history.] Mrs. Clemm, the widow of William Clemm, Jr., is now residing under my protection at Richmond. She has two children who have an interest in this one fifth [of the Clemm Estate]—one of them, Virginia, is living with her here—the other, Henry, is absent (at sea).... Mrs. Clemm wishes me (if possible) to be appointed the guardian of her two children. Henry is seventeen and Virginia fifteen.... I should be glad to have your opinion in regard to my Editorial course in the "Messenger." How do you like my Critical Notices? I have understood (from the Preface to your 3d Edition of "Horseshoe") that you are engaged in another work. If so, can you not send me on a copy in advance of the publication. Remember me to your family, and believe me with the highest respect and esteem,

Yours very truly,

EDGAR A. POE.[29]

John P. Kennedy, Esq[re]

Kennedy's reply on February 9, 1836, indicates the impression Poe's grotesque stories made upon another writer: "You are strong enough now to be criticised. Your fault is your love of the extravagant. Pray beware of it. You find a hundred intense writers for one *natural* one. Some of your *bizarreries* have been mistaken for satire—and admired too in that character. *They* deserved it, but *you* did not, for you did not intend them so. I like your grotesque—it is of the very best stamp;

---

[29] Original Autograph Ms., Peabody Institute, Baltimore. Catherine Clemm was the widow of William Clemm, Sr. His son William, Jr. had married Maria Poe, and Mrs. Clemm was evidently claiming a share of her husband's interest in the estate. The omitted portions of the letter give in detail the family history.

and I am sure you will do wonders for yourself in the comic—I mean the *serio-tragicomic*." Then he concludes with a repetition of some good advice as to Poe's habits.[30]

Poe only partially agreed with Kennedy as to the artistic purpose of his grotesques. In a letter of February 11, 1836, he says:

> You are nearly, but not altogether right in relation to the satire of some of my Tales. Most of them were *intended* for half banter, half satire—although I might not have fully acknowledged this to be their aim even to myself. "Lionizing" and "Loss of Breath" were satires properly speaking—at least so meant—the one of the rage for Lions, and the facility of becoming one—the other of the extravagancies of Blackwood. I find no difficulty in keeping pace with the demands of the Magazine. In the February number, which is now in the binder's hands, are no less than 40 *pages* of Editorial—perhaps this is a little *de trop*
>
> There was *no* November number issued—Mr. W. having got so far behind hand in regard to time, as to render it expedient to date the number which *should have* been the November number December.
>
> I am rejoiced that you will attend to the matters I spoke of in my last. Mr. W. has increased my salary, since I wrote, 104$., for the present year—This is being liberal beyond my expectations. He is exceedingly kind in every respect. You did not reply to my query touching the 'new work.' But I do not mean to be inquisitive.
>
> Most sincerely yours,
>
> EDGAR A. POE.[31]

While the readers of the *Messenger* were having an opportunity to read his stories and poems, it was as a critic that Poe made his definite impression upon a public as yet not quite aware of him. Historians of our criticism have usually credited Poe with being the first American critic in time as well as in merit. This statement is by no means accurate,[32] and Poe's achievement will not suffer if we are acquainted with the real characteristics of American criticism before

---

[30] Original Autograph Ms., Peabody Institute.

[31] Original Autograph Ms., Peabody Institute. The letter begins with a long account of Poe's efforts to obtain a picture for Kennedy, of no interest to this narrative.

[32] For a scholarly discussion of American criticism before Poe, see William Charvat, *American Critical Thought, 1810-1835* (Philadelphia, 1936).

his day. To a certain degree he continued the critical methods of his predecessors, and in other respects he differed from them.

Literary criticism takes four general forms, descriptive, destructive, analytic, and constructive. The vast mass of criticism is descriptive; it merely tells about the book in question, gives the critic's personal praise or blame, and is seldom of value. Destructive criticism is easily written by a clever phrase maker and Poe, who could succeed brilliantly in this form, yielded too often to the temptation. Analytic criticism, which seeks really to understand what the author has been trying to accomplish, then goes to the heart of the work in question, refusing to deal with nonessentials, and presents to the reader a clear picture of the accomplishment of the writer, is much rarer than the two first forms. Poe shone here.

Constructive criticism is extremely rare. In order to write it, a critic must be widely read, he must have a keen sense of comparative values, an innate knowledge of the capacity and limitations of a literary form. Just as a literary historian must be a critic if he is to make any real contribution, so a constructive critic must have the historian's perspective even if he does not write history. He can then establish general principles of criticism, as Poe did in his definition of the short story, which will become permanent contributions, and by whose standard other critics will be judged.

Before and during Poe's day criticism in America was institutional rather than personal. Little criticism was signed; the weight it carried was that of the periodical in which it appeared and back of the periodical was the class in the community which it represented. Dr. Charvat has called attention to the fact that out of forty important critics of the period 1810 to 1835, eight of the ten most significant, George Bancroft, W. C. Bryant, E. T. Channing, W. E. Channing, R. H. Dana, Senior, Joseph Dennie, A. H. Everett, W. H. Prescott, Robert Sands, and Robert Walsh, were trained for the law. Naturally, they would be judicial, and defenders of social law. They were guides of morals as well of taste; the social implications of literature rather than the ideals of art, were their concern. They usually disliked the mob, and here Poe was akin to them. They distrusted the mystical and here he differed from them. Scottish philosophy, beginning with Kames and affecting *Blackwood's Edinburgh Review,* had a great influence upon American thinking in this period, and with *Blackwood's* Poe was well acquainted. In 1817, the year of the foundation of *Blackwood's,* Dennie's *Portfolio* printed extracts from the works of A. W. Schlegel and in 1818 a translation of Friedrich Schlegel's *Lectures* was published in Philadelphia.

Since critics like Prescott knew and assimilated the principles of the Schlegels and yet did not slavishly follow them, his essays in the *North American Review* may well have given Poe direction, if not inspiration. Prescott's analysis and history of the essay in the *North American Review*[33] could have shown Poe the way to his famous essay on the short story, twenty years later.

In their liberal views upon the structure of verse, Bryant and the elder Dana prepared the way for Poe.[34] Critics generally, especially in the South, favored the general and abstract term, as opposed to the specific and concrete. Perhaps this attitude accounted for Poe's use of abstract terms in his poetry and his deliberate dropping of names from his verse in his revisions of "Tamerlane" and other early poems.

Poe was independent, but was not our first independent critic. The magazines of this early period did not contain advertisements of books, and on the whole the criticism of the *American Quarterly,* of the *Portfolio,* of the *North American Review,* was honest. If it was too dependent, it was dependent upon a self-imposed standard rather than upon personal likes or dislikes. Poe's independence, as we shall see, lay rather in his refusal to accord with earlier standards, unless he agreed with them. He was prompt to see merit in new writers, in fact he overpraised some that have hardly justified his encomiums.

Poe had contributed a number of criticisms beginning with the February, 1835, number of the *Messenger,* in which he reviewed *Calavar,* Robert Montgomery Bird's stirring novel of the conquest of Mexico. Poe began his review with an answer to Sydney Smith's taunt, "Who reads an American book?" and thus identified himself at once with those who refused to apologize, even implicitly, for American literature. In this review, as also in his notice of Bird's sequel to *Calavar, The Infidel,* Poe showed his discrimination in praising judiciously the early work of a writer who is only recently beginning to be appreciated. In the December, 1835, issue, when he really became editor, he increased greatly the number of his reviews. His savage attack on *Norman Leslie,* a novel by Theodore S. Fay, while it was, in one sense, justified by the absurd conversation and melodramatic incident of the book, is an example of Poe's destructive criticism which

[33] Vol. XIV (1822), pp. 319-350.
[34] See Bryant's *Lectures on Poetry,* delivered in New York in 1825, or Dana's review of Pollok's *Course of Time, Spirit of the Pilgrims,* I (1828), 523, quoted in Charvat, p. 96.

does him little credit. Fay was one of the Editors of the *New York Mirror*, and the journalistic group of which he was one of the most prominent, remembered the attack and revenged him upon Poe when the latter went to New York. If Poe's critique had been a dignified but stinging protest against the kind of puffery and log-rolling which, he claimed, had preceded the publication of *Norman Leslie*, we could only admire his courage in attacking one of the most powerful literary cliques in America. But to spend nearly four thousand words to prove that *Norman Leslie* was not worth reading, and that Fay was ignorant of the rules of grammar, was unworthy of Poe. He descended to the level of those who worship mere smartness and he won the easy distinction of unsuitable language. Worst of all, the superficial cleverness of the review attracted attention and Poe learned how easy it was to win notoriety by such means. Again and again through his career he made enemies and alienated friends by the viciousness of his attacks, often unfair, and apparently made to satisfy some bitterness of spirit which demanded expression.

Even more unfortunate was his descent into personalities. In his review of William Gilmore Simms' *The Partisan*, in January, 1836, he began with a totally unnecessary burlesque of Simms' modest dedication to Richard Yeadon. Then, imagining a sycophantic visit by Simms to Yeadon, he concluded with the sentence, "Mr. Y. feels it his duty to kick the author of *The Yemassee* downstairs." Insufferably bad taste like this is hard to overlook, and it discounts some excellent analysis of *The Partisan* such as that which pronounced Porgy, the comic character, as "an insufferable bore." What Poe needed was a friendly critic like Sophia Hawthorne, some good angel like Olivia Clemens, to advise him. But much as Virginia or Mrs. Clemm adored him, they were no check at this time, upon his besetting sin.

It is pleasant to turn from this destructive criticism to those analyses in which Poe continued to discuss the nature of poetry. In January, 1836, he chose the occasion of his review of several volumes of recent verse to question the effect of a long poem upon the reader, and to continue: "But in pieces of less extent—the pleasure is unique, in the proper acceptation of that term—the understanding is employed, without difficulty, in the contemplation of the picture as a whole—and thus its effect will depend in a very great degree, upon the perfection of its finish, upon the nice adaptation of its constituent parts, and especially upon what is rightly termed by Schlegel, the *unity or totality of interest*." It is one of his earliest statements of the principle of unity which became a cardinal doctrine of his critical theory.

In April, 1836, Poe wrote the best of his early critical analyses in his review of Joseph Rodman Drake's *The Culprit Fay; and Other Poems,* and Fitz-Greene Halleck's *Alnwick Castle with Other Poems.* He began with a comparison of the earlier state of American criticism with its "subserviency" to English opinion, and the "boisterous and arrogant" tone of the newer criticism which likes "a stupid book the better because sure enough, its stupidity is American." These statements are generalities, of course, and are, as we have already seen, only half true. But the extent of Poe's influence is manifest in the fact that nearly every historian of our literature has accepted them as gospel, simply because he said them. Poe insists that it has been his constant endeavor "to stem a current so disastrously undermining the health and prosperity of our literature."

He quotes in order to combat them, attacks upon his own criticisms, from New York and Philadelphia journals,[35] in which the weaknesses of his destructive criticisms are fairly pointed out. Today this discussion is of value mainly as showing the extent of his influence. Returning to the matter in hand, Poe created one of the most eloquent of his definitions of poetry.

Poetry has never been defined to the satisfaction of all parties. Perhaps, in the present condition of language it never will be. Words cannot hem it in. Its intangible and purely spiritual nature refuses to be bound down within the widest horizon of mere sounds. But it is not, therefore, misunderstood—at least, not by all men is it misunderstood. Very far from it. If, indeed, there be any one circle of thought distinctly and palpably marked out from amid the jarring and tumultuous chaos of human intelligence, it is that evergreen and radiant Paradise which the true poet knows, and knows alone, as the limited realm of his authority—as the circumscribed Eden of his dreams. But a definition is a thing of words—a conception of ideas. And thus while we readily believe that Poesy, the term, it will be troublesome, if not impossible to define—still, with its image vividly existing in the world, we apprehend no difficulty in so describing Poesy, the Sentiment, as to imbue even the most obtuse intellect with a comprehension of it sufficiently distinct for all the purposes of practical analysis.

[35] *The New York Commercial Advertiser,* quoting and agreeing with the *Philadelphia Gazette;* also from *The New York Mirror. The Philadelphia Gazette* was edited by Willis Gaylord Clark, and this may be the beginning of the feud between Poe and Lewis Gaylord Clark, twin brother of Willis.

Poe speaks of Veneration and Ideality as two of the most potent Faculties creating poetry.

Poesy [he continues], is the sentiment of Intellectual Happiness here, and the Hope of a higher Intellectual Happiness hereafter.

Imagination is its soul. With the *passions* of mankind—although it may modify them greatly—although it may exalt, or inflame, or purify, or control them—it would require little ingenuity to prove that it has no inevitable, and indeed no necessary co-existence.

After a tribute to Coleridge, who owes his preeminence "rather to metaphysical than poetical powers," Poe made his criticism of Drake's poetry an occasion to discuss the difference between Imagination and Fancy. "The Culprit Fay" had been given additional interest by Drake's early death. Poe quotes copiously to prove his first point, that Drake's lines, charming as the description of the fairy world may be, are the result of a talent for comparison, not of an imaginative power, springing "from the brain of the poet, enveloped in the moral sentiments of grace, of color, of motion—of the mystical, of the august— in short of the ideal." In order to prove what he means by this abstract conception, he names some of the great poems of the world, which do spring from imaginative power, including the *Inferno, Comus, Christabel,* and *Queen Mab.* That this contrast is hardly fair to Drake did not seem to occur to Poe. Nor is it fair to demand a close adherence to human relations in what is intended by the poet as a departure from them. The detailed criticism of Drake's lines is not, however, the important element in the review. It is Poe's recognition that great poetry springs not from mere comparison, which leaves the objects compared still separate and distinct, but in that imaginative process which fuses their qualities into some new creation, springing from their union in the poet's mind. He does not say this in so many words, but his definition of Ideality means it implicitly, and he could have derived it from Coleridge's *Biographia Literaria* [36] which he had undoubtedly read.

It would be a brave critic, however, who would attempt to give the exact source of any particular passage in Poe's critical writing. He read Coleridge surely and he refers to Schlegel, meaning probably A. W. Schlegel, but in view of Poe's well known habit of referring to a primary source an idea he has taken from a secondary one, it is dangerous to assume that he has read a book or known an author

[36] Chapter XIV.

because he quotes from them. Moreover, he was a constant reader of magazines, and the English and American journals frequently discussed both A. W. and Friedrich Schlegel. Friedrich Schlegel's *Lectures on the History of Literature Ancient and Modern* was published in translation in Philadelphia in 1818, and while the translation of A. W. Schlegel's *Lectures on Dramatic Art and Literature,* published in Philadelphia in 1833, seems to be the first American edition, James Black's English translation in 1815 must have been easy of access to American critics, judging from the references to the Schlegels in magazines after 1817. To attribute, therefore, Poe's theory that a long poem is a contradiction in terms to A. W. Schlegel, simply because Poe refers to him, is hardly judicious, to say the least. Moreover, when we remember that before Poe, Bryant expressed the opinion that there is no such thing as a long poem, that it is as impossible as long ecstasy,[37] and think of the occasions on which Bryant might have expressed this opinion anonymously in his own journal or elsewhere, it becomes apparent that Poe's sources as a critic must be identified only in the most general terms. Woodberry is unfair, therefore, in speaking of Poe's "constant parroting of Coleridge." [38] Poe was an assimilative critic. He took what he pleased, where he pleased, and his use of the material was by no means consistent. At times, he made a parade of learning he did not possess, but when he was dealing with a matter of vital concern to him, he thought things through and he enriched the suggestions of others by the insight and power of clear expression until the process became a creative one.

His taste in selecting from the work of another poet the verses most worthy of praise is shown well in the review of Halleck's *Alnwick Castle with Other Poems.* He chooses the "Lines on the Death of Joseph Rodman Drake," one of the most simple and heartfelt elegies in our language, as Halleck's best poem, and selects unerringly that stanza of "Marco Bozzaris," the sixth, in which Halleck rises momentarily from rhetoric to poetry. Yet his objection to Halleck's lines in "Alnwick Castle" such as

"True as the steel of their tried blades"

because "the proper course of the rhythm would demand an accent upon syllables too unimportant to sustain it," shows that Poe still did not understand the true basis of English versification, although he

---

[37] Parke Godwin, *A Biography of William Cullen Bryant,* I, 186.
[38] *Life of Poe,* I, 177.

had already in his own verse, disregarded mere syllable counting and preconceived metrical schemes.

Poe's critical discrimination was also shown in his appreciation of Longstreet's *Georgia Scenes,* and in his early recognition of Dickens' *Watkins Tottle and Other Sketches. By Boz.* In this latter review, he expressed his preference for the "brief article" as opposed to the novel, because of the unity possible in the shorter form. His favorable review of Dr. Bird's *Sheppard Lee,* published anonymously, gave him an opportunity for some interesting speculations upon the transmigration of souls, although his usual penetration was not present, for he failed to recognize that the novel was written by Dr. Bird, with whose work he was familiar.

In the April issue of the *Messenger,* Poe analyzed the famous chess player, supposed to be a purely mechanical device, which had been invented by Baron Wolfgang von Kempelen in 1769 and sold to a Bavarian mechanic, J. N. Maelzel, who exhibited the Turkish figure throughout various cities in the United States. It was finally purchased by Dr. John K. Mitchell of Philadelphia, and stood in the Chinese Museum at Ninth and Sansom Streets until it was destroyed by fire in 1854. When Maelzel first exhibited it in Baltimore in 1827, two boys, secreted on a roof, saw the human figure of Maelzel's assistant come out of the machine. An article, "The Chess-Player Discovered," appeared in the *Baltimore Gazette* on Friday, June 1, 1827, exposing the matter.[39] Whether Poe saw the article we cannot tell, but as he was in the army at Fort Independence, it is unlikely. Rumors of the exposure, however, may still have been extant in Baltimore when he returned. Many attempts had been made to solve the puzzle, especially by Sir David Brewster, in his *Letters on Natural Magic* in 1832, to which Poe refers in his own article. Poe's achievement lay in his ability to use material already in print and to prove by clear reasoning that the machine must be operated by human agency. He pursued his usual method of selecting the unusual elements in the problem, among others that the Turk always used his *left* hand.

Those who speak of Poe as a stranger in a land where he was an accident, have evidently never read his criticisms in the *Messenger* upon books dealing with public affairs. In his review of Lucian

[39] For an interesting account of the chess player, and Bibliography of the attempted solutions, see Henry R. Evans, *Edgar Allan Poe and Baron von Kempelen's Chess-Playing Automaton* (Kenton, Ohio, 1939). Also W. K. Wimsatt, Jr., "Poe and the Chess Automaton," *American Literature,* XI (May, 1939), 138-151.

Minor's *Address on Education*,[40] he did not hesitate to call attention to the lack of free public education in Virginia. "Her once great name is becoming, in the North, a bye-word for imbecility" was strong language to say the least. He was equally willing, however, to defend a Southern institution like Slavery. In his review of Paulding's *Slavery in the United States* and an anonymous work, *The South Vindicated from the Treason and Fanaticism of the Northern Abolitionists*,[41] he drew a parallel between the anti-slavery agitation, which about 1835 was renewing its efforts, and the revolutions of Cromwell and the French Revolution, all being an attack upon property; and all being prompted, he says, by a desire to free those who have been enslaved. "Recent events in the West Indies and the parallel movement here, give an awful importance to these thoughts in our minds." The possibility of a slave insurrection was, of course, fresh in the minds of Southerners. Poe defends slavery mainly on the ground of the loyalty of the slave, and the reciprocal sense of responsibility on the master's part. He relates some affecting incidents illustrating these sentiments. Poe's article, for it is rather his own defence of slavery than a review, is calmly and sanely written from the point of view of a Southerner who had grown up in a family which owned slaves and who had sold a slave himself. It shows also that Poe had been thinking a good deal about the matter, and his knowledge of the actual conditions was much more accurate than that of Emerson or Whittier. Throughout his editorship of the *Messenger* he continually made reference to affairs of the day.

In the August number of the *Messenger,* Poe published a collection of paragraphs containing miscellaneous information, usually dealing with ancient history, which he called "Pinakidia or Tablets." In the introductory paragraphs, as Woodberry has shown,[42] he unfortunately, through a misprint, was led to say that most of the matter was "original" when he meant "not original," for Poe adds: "Some portions of it may have been written down in the words, or nearly in the words, of the primitive authorities." But Woodberry also showed that the authorities of which Poe speaks as providing similar collectors with material, are examples of his quoting from secondary sources as though they were primary. The most amusing is his reference to the " 'Melanges Literaires' [sic] of Suard and André" where he copied an incorrect reference from the translation of Schlegel's *Lectures on Dra-*

---

[40] *Southern Literary Messenger*, II (December, 1835), 50-51.
[41] *Southern Literary Messenger*, II (April, 1836), 336-339.
[42] *Life of Poe*, I, 179. For Introduction, see *Messenger,* II, 573-574.

matic Art and Literature, the original reference being to "Suard und andere." This slip incidentally is illuminating in its revelation of how much, or rather how little, German, Poe knew. Recent investigation has revealed the sources of much of the "Pinakidia," which are drawn largely from Isaac Disraeli's *Curiosities of Literature,* Baron Bielfeld's *Elements of Universal Erudition,* Jacob Bryant's *Mythology,* James Montgomery's *Lectures on Poetry and General Literature,* and J. F. Cooper's *Excursions in Switzerland.*[43] Eighty of the one hundred and seventy-two items have been identified. Poe may have intended them originally for "fillers" or short paragraphs used to complete pages of the magazine, in which custom he would have followed the earlier editors of the *Messenger.*

Poe naturally took advantage of his widening reputation as a critic in his attempts to secure a publisher for a volume of his short stories, Carey and Lea having declined to assume the risk. Through White he secured the good offices of James K. Paulding with Harper and Brothers, but Paulding wrote White in March that the firm had decided against the project. Paulding took occasion to suggest to Poe that "he apply his fine humor, and his extensive acquirements to more familiar subjects of satire; to the faults and foibles of our own people and above all to the ridiculous affectations and extravagancies of the fashionable English Literature of the day." Paulding also gave him the good advice that satire, if it is to be relished, should be levelled at something familiar to American readers. Harpers finally returned the manuscript with a letter which has some importance in the history of American publishing, and shows the respect with which Poe's reviews were received:

New York, June, 1836.

Edgar A. Poe, Esq.
    Richmond, Va.
        Dr. Sir,

We have the honour to acknowledge the receipt of yours dated the 3d Inst. Since it was written, the MSS. to which you refer have reached you safely, as we learn from Mr. Paulding, who has been so informed we presume by Mr. White.

---

[43] For a thorough discussion, see Earl L. Griggs, "Five Sources of Edgar Allan Poe's 'Pinakidia,'" *American Literature,* I (May, 1929), 196-199; also David K. Jackson, "Poe Notes: 'Pinakidia' and 'Some Ancient Greek Authors,'" *American Literature,* V (November, 1933), 258-267. Dr. Mabbott writes he has also identified some of Schlegel's *Lectures* and an anonymous book called *Antediluvian Antiquities,* as well as Malone's notes in Boswell's *Johnson.*

The reasons why we declined publishing them were threefold. First, because the greater portion of them had already appeared in print—Secondly, because they consisted of detached tales and pieces; and our long experience has taught us that both these are very serious objections to the success of any publication. Readers in this country have a decided and strong preference for works (especially fiction) in which a single and connected story occupies the whole volume, or number of volumes, as the case may be; and we have always found that republications of magazine articles, known to be such, are the most unsaleable of all literary performances. The third objection was equally cogent. The papers are too learned and mystical. They would be understood and relished only by a very few—not by the multitude. The numbers of readers in this country capable of appreciating and enjoying such writings as those you submitted to us is very small indeed. We were therefore inclined to believe that it was for your own interest not to publish them. It is all important to an author that his *first* work should be popular. Nothing is more difficult, in regard to literary reputation, than to overcome the injurious effect of a first failure.

We are pleased with your criticisms generally—although we do not always agree with you in particulars, we like the bold, decided, energetic tone of your animadversions, and shall take pleasure in forwarding to you all the works we publish—or at least such of them as are worthy of your notice. We are obliged to publish works occasionally, which it would scarcely be expected of the Messenger to make the subject of comment.

The last number of the Messenger came to hand last evening, and in our opinion fully sustains the high character which it has acquired for itself. The notices of the Life of Washington, and Sallust we presume will prove highly pleasing to Mr. Paulding and Professor Anthon.

We are, very respectfully,
Your Obdt. Servant,
HARPER & BROTHERS.[44]

It was also through White that Edward Johnston, a writer in New York, interested Saunders and Otley, the English publishers. But though this firm was receptive, even to the extent of offering to send the manuscript to the home office, in London, nothing came of it.[45]

[44] Original Autograph Ms., Griswold Collection, Boston Public Library.
[45] Johnston to White, Autograph Ms. letter, October 4, 1836, Koester Collection. Johnston urges Poe to complete the writing of the tales in their finished form, which is a curious statement, considering Poe's scrupulous care in submitting manuscripts.

It must have been galling to Poe to realize that the door to recognition was shut in his face. During the same year, 1836, Hawthorne was having a similar discouraging reception in his efforts to have *Twice Told Tales* published. In consequence, he had been going through a nervous depression that made his friend, Horatio Bridges, caution him against suicide. But no biographer of Hawthorne has in consequence treated him as a pathological case! Bridges risked two hundred and fifty dollars to secure the issue of *Twice Told Tales* in 1837, and a little later Hawthorne's classmate, Longfellow, helped materially with his cordial critique in the *North American Review*. But Poe had no friend who would risk the money and no classmate to give the book a push. *Twice Told Tales* had only a moderate success at the time, but in view of the fact that probably no two volumes of short stories have ever had the large and steady sale of those of Poe and Hawthorne, it is at least open to question whether the fault lay in the material or in the lack of courage and skill in the firms that refused them. The irony of publishing is exemplified by the payment of thirty thousand francs by Harper and Brothers to Gustave Doré for his illustrations for "The Raven," which was published as an art book for the holiday season of 1883! [46]

Meanwhile Poe was endeavoring to aid Mrs. Clemm in her efforts, which were perennial, to obtain some help from her relatives. William Poe, of Augusta, Georgia, assisted her, and George Poe, Jr., who had declined to help David Poe, Jr., in 1809 and who was the cashier of a bank in Mobile, Alabama, was appealed to on January 12, 1836, for one hundred dollars, to assist Mrs. Clemm in establishing a boarding house. On this letter George Poe [47] endorsed the laconic statement: "Sent check—$100." But there seems to have been no boarding house in consequence.

On May 16, 1836, a marriage bond was filed in the office of the Clerk of the Hustings Court for the City of Richmond by Edgar A. Poe and Thomas W. Cleland, in connection with the marriage of Edgar Poe and Virginia Clemm. Mr. Cleland also made an affidavit that Virginia was "of the full age of twenty-one years," while, of course, she was not quite fourteen. The ceremony was performed in the evening of the same day [48] at Mrs. Yarrington's house by the

[46] J. Henry Harper, *The House of Harper* (New York, 1912), p. 514.
[47] Original Autograph Ms., Pratt Library, Baltimore.
[48] The *Richmond Enquirer* of Friday, May 20th, has under "Marriages": "Married, on Monday, May 16th, by the Reverend Mr. Converse, Mr. Edgar A. Poe to Miss Virginia Eliza Clemm."

KNOW ALL MEN BY THESE PRESENTS, That we *Edgar A Poe and Thomas W Cleland* ~~and acting as governor~~ are held and firmly bound unto *Wyndham Robertson, Lieutenant* Governor of the Commonwealth of Virginia, in the just and full sum of ONE HUNDRED AND FIFTY DOLLARS, to the payment whereof, well and truly to be made to the said Governor, or his successors, for the use of the said Commonwealth, we bind ourselves and each of us, our and each of our heirs, executors and administrators, jointly and severally, firmly by these presents. Sealed with our seals, and dated this *16th* day of *May* 183*6*.

THE CONDITION OF THE ABOVE OBLIGATION IS SUCH, That whereas a marriage is shortly intended to be had and solemnized between the above bound *Edgar A Poe* —————— and *Virginia E Clemm*. of the City of Richmond. Now if there is no lawful cause to obstruct said marriage, then the above obligation to be void, else to remain in full force and virtue.

Signed, sealed and delivered }
in the presence of }

Cho Howard

Edgar A Poe [SEAL.]

Tho. W. Cleland [SEAL.]

CITY OF RICHMOND, To wit :
    This day *Thomas W Cleland*   above named, made oath
before me, as *Deputy* Clerk of the Court of Hustings for the said City, that
Virginia E Clemm is of the full age of twenty-one years, and a
resident of the said City. Given under my hand, this *16* day of *May* 183*6*

Chs Howard

MARRIAGE BOND OF EDGAR POE AND VIRGINIA CLEMM
Reproduced from facsimile of the original bond in the Hustings Court of
Richmond, through the courtesy of the Poe Shrine.

Reverend Amasa Converse, a Presbyterian minister, who apparently asked no questions. Poe and his bride spent a brief honeymoon at Petersburg, Virginia. This ceremony seems to be the best evidence that no secret marriage took place in 1835. With this marriage, Poe's responsibility for Virginia and Mrs. Clemm passed from a voluntary assistance, to an obligation. The result was the revival of the plan for a boarding house and Poe turned for help to Kennedy:

Richmond, Va. June 7, 1836.

Dear Sir,

Having got into a little temporary difficulty I venture to ask you, once more, for aid, rather than apply to any of my new friends in Richmond.

Mr. White, having purchased a new house, at $10,000, made propositions to my aunt to rent it to her, and to board himself and family with her. This plan was highly advantageous to us, and, having accepted it, all arrangements were made, and I obtained credit for some furniture &c to the amount of $200, above what little money I had. But upon examination of the premises purchased, it appears that the house will barely be large enough for one family, and the scheme is laid aside—leaving me now in debt (to a small amount) without those means of discharging it upon which I had depended.

In this dilemma I would be greatly indebted to you for the loan of $100 for 6 months. This will enable me to meet a note for $100 due in 3 months—and allow me 3 months to return your money. I shall have no difficulty in doing this, as beyond this 100$, I owe nothing, and I am now receiving 15$ per week, and am to receive $20 after November. All Mr. White's disposable money has been required to make his first payment.

Have you heard anything further in relation to Mrs. Clemm's estate?

Our Messenger is thriving beyond all expectation, and I myself have every prospect of success.

It is our design to issue, as soon as possible, a number of the Magazine consisting entirely of articles from our most distinguished *literati*. To this end we have received and have been promised, a variety of aid from the highest source—Mrs. Sigourney, Miss Sedgwick, Paulding, Flint, Halleck, Cooper, Judge Hopkinson, Dow, Governor Cass—J. Q. Adams, and many others. Could you not do me so great a favor as to send a scrap, however small from your portfolio? Your name is of the greatest influence in that region where we direct our greatest efforts—in the South. Any little reminiscences, tale, jeu d'esprit, historical anecdote—anything, in short, *with your name*, will answer all our purposes.

I presume you have heard of my marriage.

With sincere respect and esteem

Yours truly

EDGAR A. POE.[49]

J. P. Kennedy

There is no record of Kennedy's reply, and Mrs. Weiss's [50] statement that "they lived in a cheap tenement on Seventh Street" must be received with that doubt that unfortunately is to be attached to any statement which that lady made at second hand. In any event, they could not have lived there long.

Since practically all the many speculations concerning the relations of Poe and his "child wife" have been written in ignorance of his letter of August 29, 1835, they can be disregarded. Poe loved her and she adored him. Being fourteen, she was naturally immature, but that she remained so or that she "very closely resembled Rosalie," as is stated so positively in a recent biography,[51] is unsupported by any good evidence. Poe's life-long devotion to Virginia is beyond question, and his own answer to the criticisms which his marriage created in Richmond and elsewhere is given in "Eleonora" and "Annabel Lee." It is, incidentally, the only answer a gentleman could make. "Eleonora" is, of course, an ideal picture, but its description of the passing of cousinship into passion has more verity than the testimony of feminine friends whose emphasis upon Virginia's mental immaturity was perhaps based upon a wish rather than a fact. Such evidence as there is can be taken up at a later time. But of one thing we can be sure. If Virginia was the prototype of Eleonora she was not the model for Morella or Berenice or Ligeia. They were of a different breed.

Poe was acting as the head of the family in more than one way. The following letter reveals his ability to express clearly a legal claim, even if, apparently, it came to nothing:

[49] Original Autograph Ms., Bradley Martin Collection. The letter in the Griswold Collection is a copy.

[50] *Home Life of Poe*, p. 85.

[51] Hervey Allen, *Israfel*, p. 387; 1934, Rev. Ed., p. 311.

Richmond, Va.
June 3, 1836.

Dr Sir,

Understanding that you have been engaged, at different times, in the prosecution of private claims against the Government of the U. S. I have taken the liberty of addressing you on a subject of this nature.

I believe you were personally acquainted with some branches of my family in Baltimore. I am the son of David Poe Jr. of that city. It appears to me (and to some others to whom I have mentioned the subject) that my aunt, Mrs. Maria Clemm (who now resides with me in Richmond, I having married her daughter) has a claim against the U. S. to a large amount which might be carried to a successful issue if properly managed. I will state, as briefly as possible, the nature of the claim, of which I pretend to give merely an outline, not vouching for particular dates or amounts.

During the war of the Revolution, Mrs. C's father, Gen: David Poe, was a quarter-master in what was then called the Maryland line. He, at various times, loaned money to the State of Maryland, and about seventeen years ago died, while engaged in making arrangements for the prosecution of his claim. His widow, Mrs. Elizabeth Poe, applied to the State Government, which, finding itself too impoverished to think of paying the whole amount (then nearly $40,000) passed a bill, for the immediate time, granting Mrs. Poe an annuity of $240—thus tacitly acknowledging the validity of the vouchers adduced. Mrs. Poe is now dead, and I am inclined to believe, from the successful prosecution of several claims of far less promise, but of a similar nature, that the whole claim might be substantiated before the General Government—which has provided for a liberal interpretation of all vouchers in such cases. Among these vouchers (now in proper form at Annapolis) are, I believe, letters from Washington, La Fayette, & many others speaking in high terms of the services and patriotism of Gen: Poe. I have never seen the bill granting the annuity to Mrs. Poe, but it may possibly contain a proviso against any future claim. This however, would be of little moment, if the matter were properly brought before Congress.

My object in addressing you is to inquire if you would be willing to investigate and conduct this claim—leaving the terms for your own consideration. Mrs. C. authorizes me to act for her in every respect. I would be glad to hear from you as soon as you can make it convenient.

Very resp^y.

Yr. Ob. S^t.

EDGAR A. POE [52]

James H. Causten Esq.

Nothing came of this application, for Henry Herring, who had married Elizabeth Poe, and was therefore a son-in-law of David Poe, Senior, submitted in 1837 a claim in behalf of all the heirs. That claim was not allowed, as Elizabeth Poe had died prior to the act of July 4, 1836, under which he had applied.[53]

In September, 1836, the issue of the *Messenger* was delayed, owing to "the illness of both Publisher and Editor." According to White, he notified Poe in September that the connection was dissolved.[54] We do not have Poe's version of the break, which was temporary. In October Poe was back at his post. In a letter to Mrs. Sarah J. Hale, Editor of the *Ladies' Book* in Boston, misdated October 20, 1837, but clearly referring to 1836, he shows his reluctance to compose hastily, and refers to his late illness:

Richmond

Oct 20 1837. [1836]

Dear Madam

    I was somewhat astonished to day at receiving a letter addressed to "W. G. Simms Esqr. Editor of the S. L. Messenger" and hesitated about my right to open it, until I reflected that, in forwarding it to Mr. S., I should place him in a similar dilemma. I therefore broke the seal—but the address, even within, was "W. G. Simms." I could arrive, therefore at no other conclusion than that, by some missapprehension, you have imagined Mr. S. to be actually Editor of the Messenger, altho' I wrote you, but lately, in that capacity myself.

[52] Original Autograph Ms., Koester Collection. The record to which Poe refers is as follows: "Poe, Captain, of Baltimore. Passed February 1822, No. 23, p. 176. Treas. Western Shore pay to Elizabeth Poe, of Baltimore, a sum of money equal to the halfpay of a captain of the Md. Line." Gaius M. Brumbaugh, *Maryland Records*, II, 382.

[53] Letter from Dr. P. M. Hamer, Chief, Division of Reference, National Archives.

[54] Letter of White to Tucker, December 27, 1836. See J. S. Wilson, as above.

Of course, under the circumstances, it is difficult to reply to one portion of your letter—that touching the prose article desired. If however, it was your wish *I* should furnish it, I am grieved to say that it will be impossible for me to make a definite promise just now, as I am unfortunately overwhelmed with business, having been sadly thrown back by late illness. I regret this the more sincerely as I would be proud to find my name in any publication you edit, and as you have been so kind as to aid the Messenger so effectually in a similar manner yourself. To send you a crude or hastily written article would be injurious to me, and an insult to yourself—and I fear that I could, at present, do little more.

As Editor of the Messenger I can however say that it will afford me sincere pleasure to do you any service in my power. I shall look anxiously for the "Ladies' Wreath."

I am surprised and grieved to learn that your son (with whom I had a slight acquaintance at W. Point) should have been vexed about the autographs. So mere nonsense it was hardly worth while to find fault with. Most assuredly as regards yourself, Madam, I had no intention of giving offence—in respect to the "Mirror" I am somewhat less scrupulous.

With the highest regard
I am
Yr obdt.
EDGAR A. POE [55]

Mrs. Sarah J. Hale

Poe wrote the critical notices for October and November. In his review of *Peter Snook,* he expressed his opinion of originality. "To originate" he said "is carefully patiently and understandingly to combine." But the break was inevitable. White's attitude toward Poe is revealed clearly not only in letters to Minor, but also in a hitherto unpublished correspondence with William Scott [56] the proprietor of the New York *Weekly Messenger.* On August 25, 1836, White wrote Scott concerning a proposed contribution: "Courtesy to Mr. Poe whom I employ to edit my paper makes it a matter of etiquette with me to

[55] The original manuscript in the Bradley Martin Collection is clearly dated "1837," but Poe had no connection with the *Messenger* at that time.

[56] Manuscripts are in the Abernethy Library of American Literature at Middlebury College. I am indebted to the courtesy of the Curator, Dr. Viola C. White, and the Library, for permission to print them.

submit all articles intended for the *Messenger* to his judgment and I abide by his dicta."

White's letters in November and December explain why there was no December issue. He complains that "we are all without money in Richmond," and laments his own illness and a printers' strike.[57] These disturbed conditions may well have been contributing causes for Poe's resignation.

White's letter to Tucker of December 27, 1836, already referred to, begins,

> Highly as I really think of Mr. Poe's talents, I shall be forced to give him notice in a week or so at farthest that I can no longer recognize him as editor of my Messenger. Three months ago I felt it my duty to give him a similar notice,—and was afterwards over-persuaded to restore him to his situation on certain conditions— which conditions he has again forfeited.[58]

> Added to all this, I am cramped by him in the exercise of my own judgment, as to what articles I shall or shall not admit into my work. It is true that I neither have his sagacity, nor his learning—but I do believe I know a handspike from a saw. Be that as it may, however,—and let me even be a jackass, as I dare say I am in his estimation, I will again throw myself on my own resources—and trust my little bark to the care of those friends who stood by me in my earlier, if not darker days. You, my friend, are my helmsman. And I again beg you to stand by the rudder.[59]

The second paragraph of this letter really explains the matter. White recognized Poe's ability, but refused to give him authority. Poe, too, was dissatisfied. In a letter to William Poe, at Augusta, Georgia, dated from Philadelphia, August 15, 1840, Poe, in speaking of his reasons for leaving the *Southern Literary Messenger,* said, "The drudgery was excessive, the salary was contemptible. In fact, I soon found that whatever reputation I might personally gain, this repu- tation would be all. I stood no chance of bettering my pecuniary condition, while my best energies were wasted in the service of an illiterate and vulgar, although well meaning man, who had neither the capacity to appreciate my labors, nor the will to reward them." [60]

[57] Ms. Letters, November 24 and December 15, 1836, Middlebury Col- lege Library.

[58] There can be no doubt that Poe drank at intervals during his Rich- mond residence. See his own frank statements to Snodgrass in his letter of April, 1841.

[59] J. S. Wilson, *Century,* LXXXV, 656.

[60] Original Autograph Ms., Huntington Library. P. O. stamp is Aug. 14.

The January number of the *Messenger* contained in very small type, Poe's "Valedictory:" [61] "Mr. Poe's attention being called in another direction, he will decline with the present number, the Editorial duties of the 'Messenger.' His critical notices for this month end with Professor Anthon's Cicero—what follows is from another hand. With the best wishes to the Magazine, and to its few foes as well as to its many friends, he is now desirous of bidding all parties a peaceable farewell." Poe ceased to be Editor on January 3, 1837, but he continued editorial services until late in the month. White's letter to Scott shows how he still depended on Poe's judgment:

Richmond, Jan. 23, '37.
(Private)

Previous to writing you I had submitted your manuscript to Mr. Poe, who handed it back to me as being suitable for the Messenger. After I had it put in type, I sent a corrected proof of it to him. He returned it as you will see, making several corrections—and amongst other things, striking out your first paragraph, or exordium. He also struck out your two concluding paragraphs, but I thought them worth preserving—and therefore took upon myself the responsibility of retaining them. I have no doubt whatever, that Mr. Poe done [!] what he has done for the best. Be that as it may, I assure you there was not the slightest intention on my part (nor do I believe there was on that of Mr. Poe) to mar your productions.... Mr. Poe retired from the editorship of my work on the 3d inst. I am once more at the head of affairs. Nevertheless I have private friends to whom I submit all articles —and I have consented to abide by their judgment. [62]

Notwithstanding the separation, the number for January, 1837, contained several important contributions from Poe. There were two new poems, "Ballad," later "Bridal Ballad," and "Zante." "Ballad" is a lament for a dead lover by a bride on her wedding day. It is not one of Poe's best poems, but it is unique in his poetry in that it is a lyric in which the speaker is a woman. "Zante" is a sonnet addressed to an island close to Greece. It is noteworthy for the repetition of "no more" which was becoming a favorite phrase with Poe. The initial installment of "Arthur Gordon Pym" introduced Poe's first attempt at a long story. He was taking Harpers' advice, in all probability, for that firm published the story in book form in 1838.

Poe wrote five critical reviews for the January number. His clear,

[61] Vol. III, p. 72.
[62] Ms., Middlebury College Library.

forcible analysis of Irving's *Astoria* is remarkable for the way in which he selects from that fascinating account of the struggle for the Northwest fur trade the right details to make a connected narrative, even if he paraphrased too often the very language of *Astoria*. Even more important, however, was his review of Bryant's *Poems*, one of his major critical documents. In this critique he again illustrated that combination of fine taste in the selection of those individual poems which seemed best to him, with that curious lapse in humor which permitted him to rewrite some of Bryant's lines in order to improve them. Poe took up the poems individually and first analyzed their metrical structure. This caused him to enunciate a principle of versification which he believed to be new. In suggesting the addition of a syllable in one of Bryant's lines, and defending Willis against a charge of "incorrectness," he proceeds:

> The excesses of measure are here employed (perhaps without any definite design on the part of the writer, who may have been guided solely by ear) with reference to the proper equalization, of *balancing*, if we may so term it, of time, *throughout an entire sentence*. This, we confess, is a novel idea, but, we think, perfectly tenable. Any musician will understand us. Efforts for the relief of monotone will necessarily produce fluctuations in the time of any metre, which fluctuations, if not subsequently counterbalanced, affect the ear like unresolved discords in music. The deviations then of which we have been speaking, from the strict rules of prosodial art, are but improvements upon the rigor of those rules, and are a merit, not a fault. It is the nicety of this species of equalization more than any other metrical merit, which elevates Pope as a versifier above the mere couplet-maker of his day; and, on the other hand, it is the extension of the principle to *sentences of greater length* which elevates Milton above Pope.

This is another striking instance of Poe's appreciating the subtle, harmonious effects of Pope while attributing them to the wrong cause. Pope's effects were secured not by deviating from rules, but by ignoring them, and following the fundamental laws of English verse. Poe was just then riding this theory of equalization hard. He attributes the "sonorous grandeur" of Goldsmith's line

"Luke's iron crown and Damien's bed of steel"

to the fact that there is an "extra" syllable in "Damien." Of course, the sonorous quality arises from the contrast of open and close vowel sounds, a contrast which Poe often employs in his own verse. The absurdity of this theory is shown at its worst in Poe's rewriting of the concluding verses of Bryant's "Forest Hymn":

> "And to the beautiful order of thy works,
> Learn to conform the order of our lives"

to read:

> "And to the perfect order of thy works
> Conform, if we can, the order of our lives"

in order to admit an "extra syllable" in the last verse!

The sonnets of Bryant led Poe to announce the qualities a sonnet should possess—"point, strength, unity, compression, and a species of completeness." He rightly praises "November" because "A single thought pervades and gives unity to the piece." That Poe chose to use the English form of sonnet deliberately is evidenced by the remark "Mr. Bryant has very wisely declined confining himself to the laws of the Italian poem." The wisdom of this choice is, of course, open to question, but Poe had good authority. It is a relief to turn from this meticulous and often misguided analysis of the metrical effects of Bryant's verse to the general appraisal of his poetry, in which Poe, while recognizing Bryant's limitations, still saw that "as far as he appreciates her [Nature's] loveliness or her augustness, no appreciation can be more ardent, more full of heart, more replete with the glowing soul of adoration."

There was a second installment of *Arthur Gordon Pym* in the February *Messenger,* carrying the story to the point when the crew are pinioned and thrown on their backs by the mutineers. But no more installments were published.

It is obvious from the letter of January 23, 1837, that White was relieved to be once more "at the head of affairs." That he gave up the services of one of the best editors then living in the United States, who had brought up the circulation of the paper from about five hundred to thirty-five hundred copies, and had made it nationally known, seems to prove that White was not a competent publisher. There were good reasons why Poe was willing to break the relation. His earlier gratitude to White for his meagre salary had given place to a restless feeling that he was not being fully repaid for his skill and industry. The disturbed conditions in Richmond, his longing for a wider sphere, the pressure of financial necessity, may have caused him to feel that the risk lay not in leaving but in staying as the Editor.

On April 5, 1837, White wrote to Scott: "Tell me when you write what Poe is driving at. . . . I have not heard from him since he left here." Perhaps he was already beginning to regret.

CHAPTER XI

Philadelphia—The *Tales of the Grotesque and Arabesque*

It was probably in February, 1837, that Poe took Mrs. Clemm and Virginia to New York. Although Poe's attempt to establish himself in New York was not successful, it was natural that he should seek that city. From Richmond with its 20,000 inhabitants to New York with nearly 300,000, an ambitious writer could easily justify his hope for a wider opportunity. He had some prospect of employment on the *New York Review*, but apart from one extensive criticism, that of J. L. Stephens' *Incidents of Travel in Egypt, Arabia and the Holy Land,* in which he depended on Professor Charles Anthon, of Columbia College, for rather minute textual criticism in Hebrew, he seems not to have printed anything in the *Review.*

During the first few months in New York, Poe may have decided to take Harpers' advice and write a long story. Much of the *Narrative of A. Gordon Pym* must have been written in Richmond, but he had discontinued its publication after two installments had appeared in the *Messenger.* It was copyrighted by Harpers in June, 1837, but was not published until July, 1838. The title page [1] indicates the hope of the author and publishers that horrors would sell. But the book was not generally popular even though it was reprinted in England in the same year and ran through more than one edition there.

[1] *The Narrative of Arthur Gordon Pym, of Nantucket;* comprising the Details of a Mutiny and Atrocious Butchery on board the American Brig Grampus, on her Way to the South Seas in the Month of June, 1827.—With an Account of the Recapture of the Vessel by the Survivors; their Shipwreck, and subsequent Horrible Sufferings from Famine; their Deliverance by means of the British Schooner Jane Guy; the brief Cruise of this latter Vessel in the Antarctic Ocean; her Capture, and the Massacre of her Crew among a Group of Islands in the 84th parallel of Southern latitude; together with the incredible Adventures and Discoveries still farther South, to which that distressing Calamity gave rise. New York: Harper & Brothers, 1838.

A very unfavorable review in Burton's *Gentleman's Magazine*[2] shows that the critic took the book to be an account of a real voyage, and solemnly critized the author for the improbability of his incidents. In England, too, the story was treated as a narrative of real events.

The Narrative of A. Gordon Pym was well told, but the story is weakest through the very quality that deceived some of the reviewers. This was Poe's scrupulous attempt to give to every detail the illusion of accuracy. The account of the stowaway grows tiresome even if the suspense of Pym in his hiding place is maintained with skill. The scientific details which Poe gives so generously in his description of the voyages in the South Seas finally clog the narrative. For his background he had drawn upon Benjamin Morell's *Narrative of Four Voyages to the South Seas and the Pacific, 1822-1831* (1832) and the address of Jeremiah N. Reynolds, delivered in the House of Representatives in 1836. Poe called attention to these two sources in his text, and they have been sufficiently analyzed.[3] But the really significant portions of the book are imaginary. Here, however, Poe showed, as he did later in "The Case of M. Valdemar," that he did not fully recognize the distinction between terror and horror as a motive in art. The butchery of the mutiny on the *Grampus* is kept within bounds and our sympathy with Pym is maintained skilfully by keeping him from killing anyone during the fight in which he and his companions regain the vessel. But the descriptions of the cannibal feast, in which Pym shares, and of the floating horror of the plague-stricken ship which bears down upon the survivors, lead from interest to disgust.

It is far otherwise with those scenes in which terror is the motive. The growing danger of the *Jane Guy*, on which Pym and his rescued companion make their voyage to the far South Seas, is a danger from human beings. The savages of the island are, therefore, described with a realistic power which is unhampered by Poe's dependence upon anyone but himself. There is a remarkable picture of the feeling of Pym when he has to descend the island precipice at whose foot lies safety. The passing from fear lest he fall to the longing to fall and have it over, is drawn with that insight into the springs of terror in which Poe was a master. But even finer and more original is the climax when the canoe on which Pym and Peters have escaped, taking Nu-Nu, the savage, with them, drifts with increasing velocity into the

[2] III (September, 1838), 210-211.
[3] See R. L. Rhea, "Some Observations on Poe's Origins," *University of Texas Bulletin*, V (1930), 135-145.

THE NARRATIVE

OF

ARTHUR GORDON PYM.

OF NANTUCKET.

COMPRISING THE DETAILS OF A MUTINY AND ATROCIOUS BUTCHERY
ON BOARD THE AMERICAN BRIG GRAMPUS, ON HER WAY TO
THE SOUTH SEAS, IN THE MONTH OF JUNE, 1827.

WITH AN ACCOUNT OF THE RECAPTURE OF THE VESSEL BY THE
SURVIVERS; THEIR SHIPWRECK AND SUBSEQUENT HORRIBLE
SUFFERINGS FROM FAMINE; THEIR DELIVERANCE BY
MEANS OF THE BRITISH SCHOONER JANE GUY; THE
BRIEF CRUISE OF THIS LATTER VESSEL IN THE
ANTARCTIC OCEAN; HER CAPTURE, AND THE
MASSACRE OF HER CREW AMONG A
GROUP OF ISLANDS IN THE

EIGHTY-FOURTH PARALLEL OF SOUTHERN LATITUDE;

TOGETHER WITH THE INCREDIBLE ADVENTURES AND
DISCOVERIES

STILL FARTHER SOUTH

TO WHICH THAT DISTRESSING CALAMITY GAVE RISE.

NEW-YORK:

HARPER & BROTHERS, 82 CLIFF-ST.

———

1838.

TITLE PAGE OF *Arthur Gordon Pym*

yawning chasm. The fear of the white birds has stunned Nu-Nu. Then the journal of Arthur Gordon Pym comes to an end:

> March 21. A sullen darkness now hovered above us—but from out the milky depths of the ocean a luminous glare arose, and stole up along the bulwarks of the boat. We were nearly overwhelmed by the white ashy shower which settled upon us and upon the canoe, but melted into the water as it fell. The summit of the cataract was utterly lost in the dimness and the distance. Yet we were evidently approaching it with a hideous velocity. At intervals there were visible in it wide, yawning, but momentary rents, and from out these rents, within which was a chaos of flitting and indistinct images, there came rushing and mighty, but soundless winds, tearing up the enkindled ocean in their course.

> March 22. The darkness had materially increased, relieved only by the glare of the water thrown back from the white curtain before us. Many gigantic and pallidly white birds flew continuously now from beyond the veil, and their scream was the eternal *Tekeli-li!* as they retreated from our vision. Hereupon Nu-Nu stirred in the bottom of the boat; but upon touching him, we found his spirit departed. And now we rushed into the embraces of the cataract, where a chasm threw itself open to receive us. But there arose in our pathway a shrouded human figure, very far larger in its proportions than any dweller among men. And the hue of the skin of the figure was of the perfect whiteness of the snow.

There have been critics who object to what they are pleased to call an inconclusive ending. But when the details of the voyages have long been forgotten, the picture of the mysterious figure remains, stimulating the imagination of those readers who do not have to have everything explained to them in words of one syllable.

The only short stories published during this stay in New York were "Von Jung, the Mystific" [4] and "Siope—A Fable" [5] ("Silence"), both included in the earlier *Tales of the Folio Club*. It may be that the editors in New York were taking revenge upon Poe for his earlier attack on *Norman Leslie*, or perhaps the general uncertainty caused by the panic of 1837 prevented his employment as a critic. In any event, he left New York. The small quantity of his work published

[4] *American Monthly Magazine*, June, 1837.

[5] *Baltimore Book* for 1838, which issued its first edition in the fall of 1837.

during these months is noteworthy. But in time of panic, literature becomes unsalable as quickly as any other form of luxury.

Of Poe's personal life little has come down from this New York sojourn. The family seem to have lived first at Sixth Avenue and Waverley Place, and later at 113½ Carmine Street. Mrs. Clemm was keeping a boarding house, and from one of her guests, William Gowans, a Scot who later became a prominent bookseller, there is evidence of Poe's sobriety and hard work. Gowans wrote, it is true, years afterwards, when he was incensed by an article he had read in *Fraser's Magazine*, but his tribute is apparently sincere:

> I therefore will also show you my opinion of this gifted but unfortunate genius. It may be estimated as worth little, but it has this merit; it comes from an eye and ear witness, and this, it must be remembered is the very highest of legal evidence. For eight months, or more, 'one house contained us, us one table fed.' During that time I saw much of him, and had an opportunity of conversing with him often, and I must say I never saw him the least affected with liquor, nor even descend to any known vice, while he was one of the most courteous, gentlemanly, and intelligent companions I have met with during my journeyings and haltings through divers divisions of the globe; besides, he had an extra inducement to be a good man as well as a good husband, for he had a wife of matchless beauty and loveliness, her eye could match that of any houri, and her face defy the genius of a Canova to imitate; a temper and disposition of surpassing sweetness; besides, she seemed as much devoted to him and his every interest as a young mother is to her first born. During this time he wrote his longest prose romance, entitled the *Adventures of Arthur Gordon Pym*. This was the most unsuccessful of all his writings, although published by the influential house of Harper & Brothers, who have the means of distributing a single edition of any book in one week, still it did not sell. Poe had a remarkably pleasing and prepossessing countenance, what the ladies would call decidedly handsome.[6]

Gowans' enthusiasm for Poe and Virginia was personal rather than professional, for an examination of his sale catalogues reveals the sad fact that in 1852 he sold a copy of the 1843 edition of Poe's *Prose Romances*, now one of the rarest of Poeana, for thirty-eight cents, while *Eureka* brought only half-a-dollar.

[6] Gowans, *Catalogue of American Books*, No. 28 (1870), p. 11. Further accounts of Gowans may be found in *The Old Booksellers of New York*, by William Loring Andrews (New York, 1895); in the *D.A.B.*, etc.

Sometime in the summer of 1838 Poe took his family to Philadelphia. While it had begun to lose its priority among the cities of the United States, it had still its proud traditions, among which it lived perhaps too contentedly. In the census of 1840 it had 220,000 inhabitants, and its seven municipalities were only beginning to fuse their identities. Even in the late thirties it had its distinct characteristics. Visitors who at first thought it was Sunday on account of its quiet, soon after became convinced that it was perpetual washing day, from the habit of scrubbing the pavements. It was only a few years since churches had been permitted to stretch chains across the streets on Sundays to prevent their congregations from being disturbed by noise of traffic. But this peace was broken rudely by the waves of intolerance that were sweeping over the country. Two months before the Poes arrived in Philadelphia, Whittier had stood in disguise to watch the pro-slavery mob burn down the office of his paper, the *Pennsylvania Freeman*. Historians are prone to dwell upon such disturbances or on the "Native American" riots which destroyed St. Philip's and St. Augustine's Churches just after Poe left the city in 1844. It was not all peace and quiet in the Philadelphia of that time.

But there was another Philadelphia that does not get into the histories. It is more pleasant to think of the city of which my grandmother told me, of the quiet unobtrusive kindness of the older families, often Quakers, who sent their children to be taught at the "Seminary" of a young widow from Dublin whose husband had just died in a strange land. It was the same flavor of humanity that Poe met from Dr. John Kearsley Mitchell, a native of Virginia, Professor of Medical Practice at Jefferson Medical College, who had lived in the Almshouse during an epidemic so that he could treat those who had no funds for private physicians. His son, Dr. S. Weir Mitchell, once met Poe in his father's office.

It was natural that Poe, after his disappointment in New York, should turn to a city that divided the honors with New York as a publishing center. Poe had published in Philadelphia his first short story, and his earlier relations with Carey and Lea, while not fruitful, were to lead to the publication of the first collected edition of his stories. The earlier magazines of a patrician and scholarly tone, like Joseph Dennie's *Portfolio* and Robert Walsh's *American Quarterly*, had died, it is true. Poe would probably have found them more in keeping with his own tastes, for they were willing to print the thorough and analytic reviews which he liked to write.

There were rising in Philadelphia the group of magazines which were planned to appeal to large audiences—*The Saturday Evening Post,* which Thomas Cottrell Clarke had revived in 1821, the *Lady's Book* of Louis A. Godey, which had merged with the *Ladies' Magazine* of Boston in 1837, and under the editorship of Mrs. Sarah Hale, whom Poe knew, was to become a great success of its kind. Mrs. Hale came to Philadelphia in 1841, but it is singular that Poe published very little in *Godey's* while he was in Philadelphia. Poe was to take his share in this development of Philadelphia magazines through his editorial connection with *Burton's Gentleman's Magazine* and *Graham's Magazine,* but his ideal for a magazine was not that of the *Post* or *Godey's.* They cost two or three dollars a year; his ideal journal was to cost five dollars and be of another class. This conflict between his own theories of magazine publishing and the tendency of the times to cater to a large, democratic public, must be understood when we analyze the causes of his constant failure to found and keep a journal of his own.

It was not, however, to the Philadelphia magazines that Poe contributed "Ligeia," one of his greatest short stories, and "The Haunted Palace," one of his finest poems. They appeared in a Baltimore journal, the *American Museum,* edited by his friends, Dr. N. C. Brooks, and Dr. J. E. Snodgrass. This short-lived magazine deserved a better fate, for it was well printed and edited. In a letter to Brooks on September 4, 1838, Poe acknowledged the receipt of ten dollars which may have been the payment for "Ligeia." [7] In the same note, Poe declined writing a general appraisement of Irving's work because he would not have time to make a thorough study of his writings.[8]

If the quantity of Poe's creative writing during 1837 and 1838 was small,[9] the quality was high. He took a poetic conception from "Al Aaraaf," Ligeia, the soul of beauty, and developed it in a prose story. In "Ligeia" the human will storms the gates of death and holds them open, even if only for a brief moment, at the command of a woman's love, not only for her husband, but also for life itself. In "Morella" which was a preliminary study for "Ligeia," the dead wife lives again in her daughter. But Ligeia returns in her own person and the conflict of contending human emotions can hardly have a more dramatic setting. For the soul of Ligeia takes possession of the body of her rival, Rowena, the second wife, shortly after the apprehension of the

[7] *American Museum,* I (September, 1838), 25-37.
[8] Ingram, *Life,* I, 154-155.
[9] See Appendix for a possible new Poe item.

latter's death has stiffened into certainty. The two women, therefore, meet for their struggle in the other world, and Ligeia's triumph over her rival is that of an immortal over an immortal. Skilfully Poe identified the emotions of the husband and watcher by Rowena's bedside with that struggle. He sees the efforts which Rowena is apparently making to revive; he tries to aid them, but all the time his thoughts are upon Ligeia, and it is as though his own deep passion for her were sending its aid across death's barrier to help her, unknowing, in her conquest. Even in the supremely imaginative climax, Poe did not forget how the realism of detail secures for a romantic conception the possibility of belief:

> Could it, indeed, be the *living* Rowena who confronted me? Could it indeed be Rowena at all—the fair-haired, the blue-eyed Lady Rowena Trevanion of Tremaine? Why, *why* should I doubt it? The bandage lay heavily about the mouth—but then might it not be the mouth of the breathing Lady of Tremaine? And the cheeks—there were the roses as in her noon of life—yes, these might indeed be the fair cheeks of the living Lady of Tremaine. And the chin, with its dimples, as in health, might it not be hers? —but *had she then grown taller since her malady?* What inexpressible madness seized me with that thought? One bound, and I had reached her feet! Shrinking from my touch, she let fall from her head, unloosened, the ghastly cerements which had confined it, and there streamed forth, into the rushing atmosphere of the chamber, huge masses of long and dishevelled hair. *It was blacker than the raven wings of midnight!* And now slowly opened the eyes of the figure which stood before me. "Here then, at least," I shrieked aloud, "can I never—can I never be mistaken—these are the full, and the black, and the wild eyes—of my lost love—of the Lady—of the Lady Ligeia."

The mouth, heavily bound, and the color of the cheeks might be doubtful evidence, but the height, the black hair, and finally the eyes, the queen of all the features—these are unmistakable. And Poe does not spoil the climax by one unnecessary word. He had prepared the reader at the opening of the story by his description, in the same order, of the charms of Ligeia, and he expected them to be remembered. The supernatural ending is prepared for, also, in the very first sentence of the story. "I cannot, for my soul, remember how, when, or even precisely where, I first became acquainted with the Lady Ligeia." In her beauty, in her knowledge, in her mental power, in the strength of her passion, she is superhuman. Poe a little later agreed with Philip

Pendleton Cooke,[10] the Southern poet, who had suggested that a gradual possession of Rowena's body would have been more artistic. But since Poe had already used this theme in "Morella," he preferred the more rapid change. He added: "I should have intimated that the will did not perfect its intention—there should have been a relapse— a final one—and Ligeia (who had only succeeded in so much as to convey an idea of the truth to the narrator) should be at length entombed as Rowena—the bodily alterations having gradually faded away." But I think we may be glad that Poe left "Ligeia" as it is.

While in "Eleonora" Poe paid a tribute to the natural love of the wife who took care of him with a devotion he returned in full measure, "Ligeia" depicts a marriage based on an intellectual kinship, which Virginia at sixteen, could not yet have given him. Later on he was to seek that comradeship from a number of women. But in 1838 he may have sought it in those day dreams in which he must have spent a considerable portion of his time.[11] His mental and emotional life, which were his real life, are more important for us than his quarrels and disputes with persons now forgotten. It was an intense life, and at this time it flowered in poetry as in fiction, into one of his greatest achievements. "The Haunted Palace" depicts, under the allegorical disguise of the ruin of a palace, the decay of a human soul. It was first published separately in the *Museum* for April, 1839, and later was incorporated in "The Fall of the House of Usher," a prose treatment of a similar theme. With such a family history as Poe's, even an exceptional writer might have avoided such a topic. But Poe seemed drawn with a fatal fascination to those problems of spiritual integrity which lead to tragedy. The contrast is masterly between the beginning,

> "In the greenest of our valleys
> By good angels tenanted,
> Once a fair and stately palace
> Radiant [12] palace—reared its head."

and the ending when:

---

[10] Poe to Cooke, September 16, 1839. Original Autograph Ms., Griswold Collection, Boston Public Library.

[11] In the copy of the *Broadway Journal* which he sent to Mrs. Whitman, and which is now in the Huntington Library, Poe wrote on the issue of September 27, 1845—"The poem [*To Helen*—of 1848] which I sent you contained all the events of a *dream* which occurred to me soon after I knew you. Ligeia was also suggested by a *dream*—observe the *eyes* in both tale and poem."

[12] "Snow white" in the *American Museum*.

"A hideous throng rush out forever
And laugh—but smile no more."

Poe makes just the right distinction between sanity and insanity.

It is not only the thought, however, but also the form of the poem which has given "The Haunted Palace" its secure position. In the second line, quoted above, Poe defied once more a metrical rule, which in this case forbids a weak syllable in a riming position, and he produced a harmony baffling to lesser poets who have observed all the rules. Poe's use of the subtler harmonies of tone color, such as the contrast of open and close vowels, his variations in the amount of stress and in the time intervals between the stresses, produced such matchless lines as:

"But evil things, in robes of sorrow,
    Assailed the monarch's high estate.
(Ah, let us mourn!—for never morrow
    Shall dawn upon him, desolate!)
And round about his home the glory
    That blushed and bloomed,
Is but a dim-remembered story,
    Of the old time entombed."

In November two stories, "The Psyche Zenobia" and "The Scythe of Time," [13] later to become "How to Write a Blackwood Article" and "A Predicament," appeared, and Poe also contributed "Literary Small Talk," mostly on classical subjects, to the January and February numbers. "How to Write a Blackwood Article" is interesting now mainly to those who seek Poe's sources. He speaks of stories called "The Dead Alive" [14] and the "Confessions of an Opium Eater," which should warn those who base their belief in Poe's use of opium on his references in "Ligeia" and elsewhere as to the effect of that drug. The instructions to Zenobia how to appear to know languages, and to be familiar with references of which the writer is ignorant, are given with a reality which unfortunately was not based entirely on Poe's reading of Blackwood's Magazine.

"The Scythe of Time" is a burlesque, probably of the type of story of which "The Man in the Bell" in Blackwood's in 1830 is an example. A man goes up into the belfry of a cathedral and is caught with his head in the clockface, until the hand of the clock cuts his head off.

[13] American Museum, I (November, 1838), 301-310, 310-317.
[14] Not in Blackwood's. In Fraser's Magazine, April, 1834.

In the letter to Brooks of September, 1838, already referred to, Poe remarked, "I am just leaving Arch Street for a small house." The family had apparently spent a short time in temporary quarters on Twelfth Street above Arch Street, or Mulberry Street, as it was still called by old settlers, and then at 127 Arch Street, near Fourth Street, where Lowell and his first wife were later to live. The "small house" was on Sixteenth, or as it was then called, "Schuylkill Seventh" Street, near Locust Street.[15] Philadelphia, lying between the Schuylkill and Delaware Rivers, began to number its streets from both streams, the numbers meeting at Broad or Fourteenth Street.

Virginia's health brought about their further move to Coates Street, near Fairmount Park. This house, later numbered 2502, was removed in consequence of the building of the Parkway. When the family moved to the Fairmount district is also uncertain. The date usually given, September, 1839, rests apparently upon Woodberry's statement,[16] but that, in turn, is based upon his mistake in dating Poe's letter to Brooks in September, 1839, and his assumption that "the small house" was the Coates Street home.

An unpublished letter of this period from Poe to H. Haines of Petersburg, Virginia,[17] while it does not settle the matter of their residence, gives by implication a picture of a household not unhappy:

Philadelphia
April 24, 1840

My dear Sir:

Having been absent from the city for a fortnight I have only just received your kind letter of March the 24th and hasten to thank you for the "Star" as well as for your offer of the fawn for Mrs. P. She desires me to thank you with all her heart—but unhappily, I cannot point out a mode of conveyance. What can be done? Perhaps some opportunity may offer itself hereafter—some friend from Petersburg may be about to pay us a visit. In the meantime accept our best acknowledgments, precisely as if the little fellow were already nibbling the grass before our windows in Philadelphia.

[15] John Sartain, *Reminiscences of a Very Old Man* (New York, 1900), p. 217, quoting Anne E. Clarke, daughter of Thomas Cottrell Clarke. Poe does not give the location of this house.

[16] *Life*, II, 35n.

[17] Original Autograph Ms., Poe Shrine. Courtesy of Mr. Granville Valentine.

I will immediately attend to what you say respecting exchanges. The "Star" has my best wishes, and if you really intend to push it with energy, there cannot be a doubt of its full success. If you can mention anything in the world that I can do here to promote its interests and your own, it will give me a true pleasure. It is not impossible that I may pay you a visit in Petersburg a month or two hence. Till then, believe me

Most sincerely,
Your friend,
EDGAR A. POE.

H. Haines, Esq.,
Office Gentleman's Magazine

Whether this house was on Sixteenth Street or Coates Street, it had a garden large enough to have held the fawn. Virginia undoubtedly had her flowers there, as we know she had later. It may be that the stay at Sixteenth Street was longer than is usually supposed. McElroy's Philadelphia Directory does not give Poe's name until 1843, when it reads, "Editor Coates n. F.M." In a letter to Thomas, May 25, 1842,[18] Poe says "I have moved from the old place." This must refer to the Sixteenth Street house, since in a later letter to Thomas, on September 12, 1842, he remarks "Since you were here I have moved out to the neighborhood of Fairmount." [19] While Anne Clarke's remembrances, as passed through the memory of John Sartain, cannot be considered authentic, her picture of Poe dropping in to her father's house at Twelfth and Walnut Streets on his way home to Sixteenth Street, indicates a residence there of some duration, as well as a comradeship with other writers.

According to one tradition, Poe was accustomed to attend meetings of artists, actors, and writers in the old Falstaff Hotel, on Sixth Street above Chestnut Street, Thomas Sully and John Sartain being members of the group. Thomas Sully painted Poe's portrait, draped in a cloak which, according to the same tradition, was chosen by Sully because it savored of Byron. This portrait, which differs from almost any other of Poe, represents him as Sartain afterwards described him —"Poe's face was handsome. Although his forehead when seen in profile showed a receding line from the brow up, viewed from the

---

[18] Virginia Edition, XVII, 110-111.
[19] Autograph Ms., Anthony Collection, New York Public Library.

front it presented a broad and noble expanse, very large at and above the temples. His lips were thin and very delicately molded." [20]

While Poe knew Sartain well and would naturally have known Sully through family associations, and while it would be easy to build up a picture of these meetings at the Falstaff Hotel, we really know little concerning them. Burton probably invited Poe to the dinner parties which he is reputed to have given at his home on North Ninth Street near Race Street. It would also be easy, considering Poe's relations with Burton during 1839-1840, to picture him as a constant attendant at the Walnut Street Theatre, to which Burton could have secured him admission. Yet Poe does not speak, in his correspondence, of his attendance at the theatre in Philadelphia, nor does he mention his amusements or social life. This omission, however, is no proof that he had none, for he retained the friendship of a man like Colonel William Drayton. After his boyish assurance to John Allan of his favorable reception by men of letters in Baltimore and Philadelphia, Poe rarely, if ever, speaks of his social engagements.

Poe was working during the winter of 1838-1839 on a piece of hack work which later subjected him to a charge of plagiarism. It was *The Conchologist's First Book: or, A System of Testaceous Malacology, Arranged expressly for the use of Schools*, etc., published by Haswell, Barrington and Haswell in Philadelphia early in 1839. Poe was accused of preparing his book by the simple process of reprinting *The Conchologist's Text Book* by Captain Thomas Brown, published in Glasgow, in 1833, and putting his own name on the title page. Poe's own statement [21] is only partially correct:

> In 1840 I published a book with the title—"The Conchologist's First Book—A System of Testaceous Malacology, arranged expressly for the use of Schools, in which the animals, *according to Cuvier*, are given with the shells, a great number of new species added, and the whole brought up, as accurately as possible, to the present condition of the science. By Edgar A. Poe. With illustrations of 215 shells, presenting a correct type of each genus." This, I presume, is the work referred to. I wrote it in conjunction with Professor Thomas Wyatt, and Professor McMurtrie, of

[20] John Sartain, *Reminiscences of a Very Old Man*, p. 215. The Falstaff Hotel tradition is based on a statement by Dr. I. W. Heysinger, who once owned the Sully portrait, in *The Life and Works of Thomas Sully*, by Edward Biddle and Mantle Fielding (Philadelphia, 1921), p. 249.

[21] Letter to G. W. Eveleth, February 16, 1847. Original Autograph Ms., Berg Collection, New York Public Library.

THE

CONCHOLOGIST'S FIRST BOOK:

OR,

A SYSTEM

OF

TESTACEOUS MALACOLOGY,

Arranged expressly for the use of Schools,

IN WHICH

THE ANIMALS, ACCORDING TO CUVIER, ARE GIVEN
WITH THE SHELLS,

A GREAT NUMBER OF NEW SPECIES ADDED,

AND THE WHOLE BROUGHT UP, AS ACCURATELY AS POSSIBLE, TO
THE PRESENT CONDITION OF THE SCIENCE.

———

BY EDGAR A. POE.

———

WITH ILLUSTRATIONS OF TWO HUNDRED AND FIFTEEN SHELLS,
PRESENTING A CORRECT TYPE OF EACH GENUS.

PHILADELPHIA:

PUBLISHED FOR THE AUTHOR, BY

HASWELL, BARRINGTON, AND HASWELL,

AND FOR SALE BY THE PRINCIPAL BOOKSELLERS IN THE
UNITED STATES.

1839.

TITLE PAGE OF *The Conchologist's First Book*

Ph[iladelphi]a—my name being put to the work, as best known and most likely to aid its circulation. I wrote the Preface and Introduction, and translated from Cuvier, the accounts of the animals, etc. *All* School-books are necessarily made in a similar way. The very title-page acknowledges that the animals are given "according to Cuvier."

This charge is infamous, and I shall prosecute for it, as soon as I settle my accounts with the "Mirror."

The curious may find a close parallel between Poe's Introduction and Brown's,[22] and the pictures of the shells are also copied. The "Explanation of the Parts of Shells" is verbatim from Brown. The bulk of the book is a paraphrase from Wyatt's *Conchology,* with Wyatt's consent. The best explanation was given by Woodberry.[23] Wyatt had published a Conchology with Harpers in the previous year which proved too expensive. Harpers declined to bring it out in a cheaper form, so Wyatt decided to have a book prepared which he could sell in connection with his lectures and Poe put his name on the title page for a consideration. He did, apparently, translate the description of the animals from Cuvier as he announced on the title-page. It was not entirely a piece of hack work, for Poe had had plenty of opportunity to talk with Dr. Edmund Ravenel, an eminent conchologist who lived during Poe's army service on Sullivan's Island. The book remains, however, out of the current of Poe's creative work. It is grimly ironic, however, that it is probably the only volume by Poe that went into a second edition in the United States during Poe's lifetime.

It was probably Poe's necessities which made him propose to William E. Burton, an English actor who had recently established the *Gentleman's Magazine,* that he share in Burton's editorial labors. Burton, who was thirty years old when he came to Philadelphia, was a comedian of real ability, who had always desired to be an editor, and had at that time written one successful play, *Ellen Wareham.* He founded the *Gentleman's Magazine* in July, 1837. Although printed in that infinitesimal type with which our ancestors tried their eyes, it was successful enough to survive the depression of that year. Burton wrote for it short stories, usually romantic, reminiscences of the theatre, and brief criticisms. In January, 1839, he added the sub-title of

[22] See J. W. Robertson's *Bibliography of Poe,* I, 44-45.
[23] *Life,* I, 197. From a manuscript letter by John G. Anthony, who had his information from Wyatt.

American Monthly Review. His letter to Poe, dated May 11, 1839,[24] indicates the basis on which Poe became associated with him:

> Edgar A. Poe, Esq.:
>
> My dear Sir,—I have given your proposal a fair consideration. I wish to form some such engagement as that which you have proposed, and know of no one more likely to suit my views than yourself. The expenses of the Magazine are already wofully heavy; more so than my circulation warrants. I am certain that my expenditure exceeds that of any publication now extant, including the monthlies which are double in price. Competition is high —new claimants are daily rising. I am therefore compelled to give expensive plates, thicker paper, and better printing than my antagonists, or allow them to win the goal. My contributors cost me something handsome, and the losses upon credit, exchange, etc., are becoming frequent and serious. I mention this list of difficulties as some slight reason why I do not close with your offer, which is indubitably liberal, without any delay.
>
> Shall we say ten dollars per week for the remaining portion of this year? Should we remain together, which I see no reason to negative, your proposition shall be in force for 1840. A month's notice to be given on either side previous to a separation.
>
> Two hours a day, except occasionally, will, I believe, be sufficent for all required, except in the production of any article of your own. At all events you could easily find time for any other light avocation—supposing that you did not exercise your talents in behalf of any publication interfering with the prospects of the G.M.
>
> I shall dine at home today at 3. If you will cut your mutton with me, good. If not, write or see me at your leisure.
>
> I am, my dear Sir, your obedt. Servt.,
>
> W. E. BURTON.

On the back wrappers of the magazine for June, 1839, Burton states that he has made arrangements with Edgar A. Poe, Esq., late Editor of the *Southern Literary Messenger,* to devote his abilities and experience to a portion of the editorial duties of the *Gentleman's Magazine.* Edgar A. Poe was always an assistant to Burton.

Amid the collapse of the Philadelphia theatres, Burton was looking forward to a theatre of his own. He therefore needed assistance in the

[24] The date on the original letter in the Griswold Manuscripts, Boston Public Library, is Saturday, May 11, 1839, changed to May 10th, under which it appears in the biographies. In 1839, Saturday could only have been May 11th.

conduct of his magazine. Poe had evidently asked a larger salary and must have replied with some counter-proposition which Burton did not care to consider, for he sent Poe a letter, dated clearly, May 30, 1839. It is of singular importance because, although frequently quoted,[25] it has never been published as it was written by Burton. In Griswold's "Memoir" of Poe, prefixed to the volume containing *The Literati*,[26] Griswold inserted a distorted version of the letter, representing it as "undated" but placing it "two or three months" before the final break in June, 1840. I am printing the two letters in parallel columns, italicizing Griswold's forged insertions. Minor differences in expression are not indicated:

Correct Letter

My dear Sir,

I am sorry that you thought necessary to send me such a letter as your last. The troubles of the world have given a morbid tone to your feelings which it is your duty to discourage. I cannot agree to entertain your proposition, either in justice to yourself or to my own interests. The worldly experience of which you speak has *not* taught me [to?] conciliate authors of whom I know nothing and from whom I can expect nothing. Such a supposition is but a poor comment upon my honesty of opinion, or the principles of expediency which you would insinuate as actuating my conduct. I have been as severely handled in the world as you can possibly have been, but my sufferings have not tinged my mind with a

Griswold's Version

I am sorry you have thought it necessary to send me such a letter. *Your troubles* have given a morbid tone to your feelings which it is your duty to discourage. I myself have been as severely handled by the world as you can possibly have been, but my sufferings have not tinged my mind with melancholy, nor jaundiced my views of society. You must rouse your energies, and if care assail you, conquer it. *I will gladly overlook the past. I hope you will as easily fulfil your pledges for the future.* We shall agree very well, *though I cannot permit the magazine to be made a vehicle for that sort of severity which you think is so "successful with the mob." I am truly much less anxious about making a monthly "sensation" than I am upon the*

---

[25] Woodberry, I, 240; Hervey Allen, Rev. Ed., p. 371; M. E. Phillips, p. 600.

[26] New York, 1850, p. xvi.

My dear Sir,

I am sorry that you thought necessary to send me such a letter as your last. The troubles of the world have given a morbid tone to your feelings which it is your duty to discourage. I cannot agree to entertain your proposition, either in justice to yourself or to my own interest. The worldly experience of which you speak has not taught me conciliate authors of whom I know nothing and from whom I can expect nothing. Such a supposition is but a poor comment upon my honesty of opinion, or the principles of expediency which you would insinuate as actuating my conduct. I have been as severely handled in the world as you can possibly have been, but my sufferings have not tinged my mind with a melancholy hue, nor do I allow my views of my fellow creatures to be jaundiced by the fogs of my own creation. You must rouse your energies, and conquer the insidious attacks of the foul fiend, care. We shall agree very well, but you must get rid of your avowed ill-feelings towards your brother authors — you see that I speak plainly — indeed, I cannot speak otherwise. Several of my friends, hearing of our connexion, have warned me of your uncalled for severity in criticism — and I confess that your article on Dawes is

not written with that spirit of fairness which, in a more healthy state of mind, you would undoubtedly have used. The independence of my book reviews has been noticed throughout the Union — my remarks upon my friend Bird's last novel evince my freedom from the trammels of expediency, but there is no necessity for undue severity. I wish particularly to deal leniently with the faults of genius, and feeling satisfied that Dawes possesses a portion of the true fire, I regretted the word-catching tone of your critique.

Let us meet as if we had not exchanged letters. Use more exercise, write only when the feelings prompt, and be assured of my friendly feelings. You will soon regain a wholesome activity of mind, and laugh at your past vagaries.

I am, my dear Sir,
Your obedient servant,
W E Burton

Phila. May 30, 1839.

THE AUTOGRAPH LETTER OF BURTON TO POE, IN WHICH GRISWOLD INSERTED HIS FORGED SENTENCES

Reproduced from the original through the courtesy of the Boston Public Library.

Correct Letter

melancholy hue, nor do I allow my views of my fellow creatures to be jaundiced by the fogs of my own creation. You must rouse your energies, and conquer the insidious attacks of the foul fiend, care. We shall agree very well, but you must get rid of your avowed ill-feelings towards your brother authors—you see that I speak plainly—indeed, I cannot speak otherwise. Several of my friends, hearing of our connexion, have warned me of your uncalled for severity in criticism—and I confess that your article on Dawes is not written with that spirit of fairness which, in a more healthy state of mind, you would undoubtedly have used. The independence of my book reviews has been noticed throughout the Union—my remarks upon my friend Bird's last novel evince my freedom from the trammels of expediency, but there is no necessity for undue severity. I wish particularly to deal leniently with the faults of genius, and feeling satisfied that Dawes possesses a portion of the true fire, I regretted the word-catching tone of your critique.

Let us meet as if we had not exchanged letters. Use more exercise, write only when the feelings prompt, and be assured of my friendship. You will soon regain a wholesome activity of

Griswold's Version

point of fairness. You must, my dear sir, get rid of your avowed ill-feelings toward your brother authors. You see I speak plainly: I cannot do otherwise upon such a subject. *You say the people love havoc. I think they love justice.* I think you yourself would not have written the article on Dawes, in a more healthy state of mind. I am not trammelled by any vulgar consideration of expediency; *I would rather lose money than by such undue severity wound the feelings of a kind-hearted and honorable man.* And I am satisfied that Dawes has something of the true fire in him. I regretted your word-catching spirit. But I wander from my design. *I accept your proposition to recommence your interrupted avocations upon the Maga.* Let us meet as if we had not exchanged letters. Use more exercise, write when feelings prompt, and be assured of my friendship. You will soon regain a healthy activity of mind, and laugh at your past vagaries.

Correct Letter

mind, and laugh at your past
vagaries.

I am, my dear Sir,
　　Your obedient Servant,
　　　　　W. E. BURTON
Phila. May 30, 1839.[27]

Resuming his "Memoir," Griswold says "This letter is kind and
judicious. It gives us a glimpse of Poe's theory of criticism and displays the temper and principles of the literary comedian in an honorable light."

It is to be noticed that several of the interpolated sentences, which
Burton did not write, contain forged quotations from an implied letter
from Poe, which he also did not write. To Poe has, in consequence,
been attributed a desire "to be successful with the mob," to "create a
monthly sensation" and to "play havoc" unjustly to gain popular applause. Moreover, he is made to say these things, which he never
did say, in an article published after he was dead. Notice also that
Burton in the real letter says nothing about Poe resuming "interrupted
avocations" upon the Magazine. This point is of especial importance, as
we shall see later.

Altogether, it is one of the most dastardly, as well as the cleverest
bits of literary dishonesty that Griswold perpetrated.[28] It deceived
even Woodberry, who quoted Griswold's version, called it "undated"
but placed it in 1840 and followed it with a letter from Poe which is
obviously, from its contents, *not* a reply to Burton's note.[29] The tenacity of a false quotation when once printed is illustrated by an account
of *Burton's* in an authoritative history of American magazines. Two

[27] Griswold Manuscripts, Boston Public Library. Personally examined
and photostat furnished through the courtesy of the Rare Book Division.
The reference to Dawes is puzzling, for neither the notice of Dawes'
Poems in *Burton's* in March, 1839, nor that of his story *Nix's Mate*, in
December, 1839, is anything but friendly. Perhaps Burton had received a
criticism of Dawes from Poe which he did not print. The reference to
Bird's novel may be concerned with the review of *The Adventures of Robin
Day*, which appeared in the June number, 1839, and which was, of course,
in type, at least, by May 20th.

[28] That it was deliberate is shown in the publication by W. M. Griswold
in the *Correspondence of Rufus W. Griswold*, pp. 90-91, a portion of the
original letter dated 30 May, 1839. While W. M. Griswold prints only
seven sentences, none of the forged sentences are included.

[29] See pp. 297-300.

of Griswold's interpolations and *only* those, are quoted as representing the relations of Burton and Poe![30]

The *Gentleman's Magazine* carried as Editors on the title page of Volume Five the names of William E. Burton and Edgar A. Poe. In this July number of 1839 Poe reprinted under the title of "To Ianthe in Heaven" his lyric originally included in his story, "The Visionary." He signed this poem, but reprinted "Spirits of the Dead" anonymously, and from the spacing it seems that he inserted it to fill in a vacant half page. He wrote all the reviews in the July number and all in the August and September numbers except the first three in each issue, Burton being responsible for them.[31] The leading review in July was on Cooper's new *History of the United States Navy,* and while Poe praised that book, his remarks upon the recent work of Cooper as "a flashy succession of ill-conceived and miserably executed literary productions, each more silly than its predecessor, . . . [which] had taught the public to suspect even a radical taint in the intellect, an absolute and irreparable mental leprosy"[32] must have given the author of "Homeward Bound" and "Home as Found" some reason to dislike Poe. It was Cooper's weakest period in fiction, but Poe's strictures were certainly not justified.

In August, Poe printed for the first time "The Man that was Used Up," a Grotesque that Poe apparently thought of highly, for he selected it to accompany "The Murders in the Rue Morgue" in 1843 in the first volume of that projected series of his tales. There may be some profound meaning in this satire upon a general who is made up of cork legs, false teeth, and other artificial limbs, but it escapes the present writer. "Fairyland" is also reprinted, but merely signed "P" and an attempt is made in a preliminary note to indicate it is by another hand. Poe's poem "To ———" has lost its attribution to "Eliza" and become temporarily addressed to a "Fair Maiden," later, however, to be attached to Mrs. Osgood. "To the River," like the others, is used clearly to fill a page, and Poe made no important changes in these poems.

In his review of *Tortesa, the Usurer,* reprinted in part from a criticism he had sold to the Pittsburgh *Literary Examiner,* and for

[30] F. L. Mott, *A History of American Magazines, 1741-1850* (New York, 1930), p. 675.

[31] Poe to Cooke, September 21, 1839. Woodberry, in *Century Magazine* XLVIII (September, 1894), 726-729, attributes it to the Griswold Mss., where it seems not to be at present.

[32] Vol. V (July), p. 56.

which the Editor of that short-lived paper had probably not paid him, Poe has given us an important contribution toward the understanding of his critical creed. Willis's play had been given at the Walnut Street Theatre, Philadelphia, on June 20, 1839, and had later been repeated, so Poe could have seen it. It is one of the finest plays of its time, and held the stage for years. But Poe apparently spoke of the printed drama alone. Of that he said: " 'Tortesa' is, we think, by far the best play from the pen of an American author. Its merits lie among the higher and most difficult dramatic qualities, and, although few in number, are extensive in their influence upon the whole work; pervading it, and fully redeeming it from the sin of its multitudinous minor defects. These merits are naturalness, truthfulness, and appropriateness, upon all occasions, of sentiment and language; a manly vigour and breadth in the conception of character; and a fine ideal elevation or exaggeration throughout—a matter forgotten or avoided by those who, with true Flemish perception of truth, wish to copy her peculiarities in disarray. Mr. Willis has not lost sight of the important consideration that the perfection of dramatic, as well as of plastic skill, is found not in the imitation of Nature, but in the artistical adjustment and amplification of her features."

It was the "ideal" toward which Poe was himself constantly striving, and even those who do not credit him with fidelity to reality must acknowledge that he could create ideal figures of extraordinary power.

In September, Poe presented *Burton's* with one of his very greatest stories, "The Fall of the House of Usher." It continues the treatment of the theme of identity, but this time the fear of Roderick Usher that the building will decay deepens his terror of the loss of identity into his apprehension of racial ruin. At the very outset of the story the atmosphere of tragedy is established with consummate art. Through the eyes of the narrator, that nameless person who is so much more real than he is usually credited with being, the house becomes alive with meaning. The very bareness and desolation are active forces calling up those unusual emotions which only in the hands of a master can spring from the contemplation of ordinary things. The effort of the visitor to rearrange his view of these forbidding objects and thus destroy this effect of desolation is shown to be fruitless. One of the most common errors in Poe criticism lies in the assumption of the absence of heart in his characters. But the narrator has come a long distance simply because the appeal of Roderick Usher has clutched at his friendship through that quality—"It was the apparent *heart* that went with his request." Roderick and he are bound with the tie that is next to love and family affection, the friendship that comes only in early youth, before distrust becomes a duty.

The relation between Roderick and Madeline, his twin sister, is once more an identity of a strange and baffling kind. Her disease threatens that identity; but her death restores it in another world. Poe's own knowledge of drawing creates an intriguing episode in the painting of the long tunnel, lighted by rays that admit of no explanation. Every sense, therefore, sight and hearing especially, are keyed above the normal, and lead to the poetic fantasy which had earlier been published as "The Haunted Palace," but which is here ascribed to Roderick and intensifies his mood of terror. Poe transferred to Roderick his own fear of impending mental decay which came at times during his life. The loss of spiritual identity is naturally the final human danger, and Roderick lives in its shadow. The approach to the climax of the story, through the entombment of Madeline, her rising from the coffin and her return to her brother just before her real death, is controlled by Poe with a skill of which his earlier stories of premature burial had given promise. The madness of Roderick, the flight of the visitor, and the rending of the house into ruin are portrayed with that economy of which Poe alone among writers of the short story was at that time possessed.

In October, 1839, Poe reprinted "William Wilson" from the *Gift*, for 1840, which like all the annuals or gift books, appeared early enough to secure the Christmas business. Carey and Hart published the *Gift* and its editor, Miss Eliza Leslie, had reprinted Poe's "Manuscript Found in a Bottle" in that annual for 1836. These literary annuals, or gift books, represent a very significant episode in American Literature. Through their wide popularity some American short-story writers, especially Hawthorne, were given opportunities that might otherwise not have occurred. They were usually well printed and the engravings, often by artists like John Sartain, are of interest today for they represent that perennial desire to look at pictures which is characteristic of Americans.

Poe had contributed "Siope" to the *Baltimore Book* for 1838, but his principal outlet was the *Gift*, in which there appeared "Eleonora" (1842), "The Pit and the Pendulum" (1843), and "The Purloined Letter" (1845). Poe was probably quite willing to contribute to others, for they paid usually better than magazines,[33] but if this list is com-

---

[33] The *Gift* paid on an average of two dollars a page, but the page was small. "Eleonora" probably netted Poe eighteen or twenty dollars.

pared with the twenty-seven stories clearly identified as by Hawthorne in the *Token,* C. S. Goodrich's Annual, it is seen to be small. In this, as in other matters, Poe was not as fortunate as his chief rival in the short story.

"William Wilson" is a study of the effects of conscience upon a man who is the descendant of a race whose imaginative powers have been abnormally developed. He is rather proud of his evil deeds because they are unusual. Such a theme was not new in literature, but Poe made it his own. He probably took a few hints from an article by Washington Irving in the *Gift* for 1836, on "An Unwritten Drama of Lord Byron," [34] in which Irving outlines a drama which Byron planned but never wrote.[35] The relation of Poe's own career to the story of "William Wilson" has already been discussed.[36] It is significant that in *Burton's* for October, 1839, William Wilson remarks "my namesake was born on the nineteenth of January, 1811—and this is precisely the day of my own nativity." In the *Tales of the Grotesque and Arabesque* this date has become "1809," in the *Phantasy Pieces* "1811" and in the *Broadway Journal* "1813." These changes reflect either Poe's uncertainty concerning his birthdate, or his deliberate attempt to alter it for reasons of his own.

"William Wilson" is a natural development in Poe's fiction. In "Ligeia" there had been a struggle to preserve physical and mental identity. In "William Wilson" the tragic consequences of a separation of moral and physical identity are portrayed. Every interposition of the second William Wilson, the conscience, is bitterly resented by the first. Poe's art is revealed through the gradual realization by Wilson that he and his double are the same. At first, it is but a dim feeling, going back to "a time when memory herself was yet unborn." Then comes

[34] *The Gift. A Christmas and New Year's Present for 1836,* edited by Miss Leslie, pp. 166-171.

[35] The hero was to have been a Spanish nobleman, Alfonso, who like William Wilson was spoiled by his parents, and who was followed by a masked figure who interfered with his vicious pursuits. At the very end, Alfonso drops his mask and cloak, just as Wilson does. But the story is only a bare outline, and the important elements of "William Wilson" are Poe's own. Irving states that the story was taken from a Spanish play, the *Embozado,* by Calderón, which he had been unable to find. Woodberry showed, I, 232n, that there was no such play, but that the character of Un Hombre Embozado occurs in *El Purgatorio de San Patricio,* a favorite of Shelley's. There is no evidence that Poe saw the Spanish play. He did not need to do so, for he undoubtedly read Irving's account, since it occurred in the number of the *Gift* in which a story of his own appeared.

[36] Chapter III, 74-76; Chapter VI, 106-107.

the visit of Wilson to his schoolfellow's room at night, when we are told only by implication of a likeness that sends Wilson away from those halls forever. The episodes grow in concreteness until the climax, when Wilson plunges his sword into the bosom of his namesake. This climax must be given in Poe's own words:

"Not a thread in all his raiment—not a line in all the marked and singular lineaments of his face which was not, even in the most absolute identity, *mine own.*

"It was Wilson: but he spoke no longer in a whisper, and I could have fancied that I myself was speaking while he said:

'*You have conquered, and I yield. Yet henceforward art thou also dead—dead to the World, to Heaven, and to Hope! In me didst thou exist—and in my death, see by this image, which is thine own, how utterly thou hast murdered thyself.'*"

The moral life has triumphed over the sensual life of Wilson, who has defied the principle of identity, which takes its own revenge.

During 1839 the only other new story in *Burton's* was "The Conversation of Eiros and Charmion" laid in the next world. While the destruction of this world, as described by Eiros, is limited as all such episodes must be, there is a certain reality due, perhaps, to Poe's observation of the feelings of the people in Baltimore in 1833 at the approach of a rain of meteors.[37] He also probably saw Halley's Comet in 1835.

When Poe reprinted "Morella" in November, 1839, he announced that it was "Extracted by permission of the publishers, Messrs. Lea and Blanchard, from forthcoming *Tales of the Grotesque and Arabesque.*" Poe had at last secured the publication of his volume of short stories. Lea and Blanchard's letter to him is hardly enthusiastic; the profit will be small and will be theirs. Poe is to have the copyright and "a few copies" for his friends:

Phila. Sept. 28/39

Dear Sir—

As your wish in having your Tales printed is not immediately pecuniary, we will at our own risque and expense print a Small Ed. say 1750 [38] copies. This sum if sold—will pay but a small profit which if realized is to be ours—The copyright will remain with

[37] See p. 187.

[38] All the biographies give 750 as the size of the Edition, depending upon Henry C. Lea's statement, "a reference to memoranda of that time shows that the Edition consisted of but 750 copies." (*The Nation,* XXXI, December 9, 1880, p. 408). I have personally examined this manuscript, in the Griswold Collection, Boston Public Library, and this letter is printed from

TALES

GROTESQUE AND ARABESQUE.

BY EDGAR A. POE.

Seltsamen tochter Jovis
Seinem schosskinde
Der *Phantasie.*

GOETHE.

IN TWO VOLUMES.

VOL. I.

PHILADELPHIA:

LEA AND BLANCHARD.

1840.

TITLE PAGE OF *Tales of the Grotesque and Arabesque*
Reproduced from the original through the courtesy of the Library of the
University of Pennsylvania.

you, and when ready a few copies for distribution among your friends will be at your Service.

If this is agreeable will you have them prepared & Mr. Haswell will be ready to go on, say by Tuesday—[39]

Very Resp't'
LEA & BLANCHARD

Edgar A. Poe Esq.

The st. make 2 vols. of a page like Isabel, 240 pages each.

The *Tales* included twenty-five stories, all that Poe had written up to that time. The only one that had not had previous magazine publication was the Grotesque, "Why the Little Frenchman Wears His Hand in a Sling." It is one of Poe's poorest and need not detain us. "The Devil in the Belfry" had been published in the *Philadelphia Saturday Chronicle* in May, 1839. This is an amusing satire, in the Irving manner, of the small-town mind, an institution which has been the subject of attack by literary artists at least since Chaucer.

In the Preface to the *Tales* Poe began with the statement, "The epithets 'Grotesque' and 'Arabesque' will be found to indicate with sufficient precision the prevalent tenor of the tales here published." He eluded a definition of the terms, which he had derived from an article by Walter Scott, "On the Supernatural in Fictitious Composition," [40] and he uses them differently at different times, but generally speaking, the Arabesques are the product of powerful imagination and the Grotesques have a burlesque or satirical quality. Poe also meets in this Preface, the charge that his stories were permeated by "Germanism and gloom." Germanism, he says, is in the vein for the time being, but "If in many of my productions terror has been the thesis, I maintain that terror is not of Germany but of the soul—"

The judgment of time has agreed with Poe. The attempt to derive his work from German sources has not been very successful. The apparent resemblances between "William Wilson" and E. T. A. Hoffman's "Elixiere des Teufels" can be derived more easily from Irving's account, already mentioned, and the victory of the monk over his insane double is quite different from the climax of "William Wilson."

Poe revised the tales extensively for this edition, although usually

the photostat, made by the courtesy of the Rare Book department. The original Ms. letter is at least as good evidence as the "memoranda" Lea found, forty years after.

[39] Tuesday in 1839 was October 1st. Considering the delays incident to publishing, the *Tales* could hardly have appeared before November.

[40] *Foreign Quarterly Review,* I (July, 1827), 60-98.

in matters of expression.[41] It was his bid for fame, and while the volumes were favorably reviewed, they did not sell rapidly. Yet they contained some of the greatest short stories in the literature of the world.

During Poe's connection with *Burton's*, he was constantly in correspondence with friends, usually professional, and in the absence of many trustworthy details concerning his personal or family life in 1838 or 1839, these letters help to build up a picture of his character. Poe was industrious, and evidently the two hours agreed upon was not the limit of his service at *Burton's*. His correspondence with Dr. J. E. Snodgrass of Baltimore, who had been one of the editors of the *Museum*, is especially interesting. On September 11, 1839, Poe asks Snodgrass to write a "rigidly just" notice of the September number of the *Gentleman's Magazine*, embodying in it a laudatory notice of Poe which had appeared in the *St. Louis Bulletin* and which Snodgrass had sent him: "The general tone and character of this work (the 'S. L. Messenger') impart lustre to our periodical literature; and we really congratulate its publisher upon the sound and steadfast popularity which it has acquired. Let it never be forgotten, however, that the first impetus to the favor of *literary* men which it received was given by the glowing pen of Edgar A. Poe, now assistant editor of 'Burton's Gentleman's Magazine,' and, although, since he has left it, has well maintained its claims to respectability, yet there are few writers in this country—take Neal, Irving, and Willis away and we would say *none*—who can compete successfully, in many respects, with Poe. With an acuteness of observation, a vigorous and effective style, and an independence that defies control, he unites a fervid fancy and a most beautiful enthusiasm. His is a high destiny." [42]

---

[41] Indeed, despite later revisions, the form of some of the stories, notably "Ligeia" and "William Wilson," is, I believe, to be preferred.

[42] Some of these letters to Snodgrass, which were once in the possession of the late William Hand Browne, of the Faculty of Johns Hopkins, passed to Edward Spencer of Baltimore, who published a portion of them in the *New York Herald*, March 27, 1881. Several of these letters (September 11, 1839, November 11 [1839], January 17, 1841, September 19, 1841) have been published in facsimile under the title of *"Some Edgar Allan Poe Letters. Printed from the originals in the Collection of W. K. Bixby.* St. Louis, Mo., MCMXV." Harrison states that he printed his summaries from the originals. Woodberry quotes usually from the copies made by W. H. Browne. There are discrepancies, and I have checked where possible with originals in the Huntington Library, the Morgan Library, or with copies by William Hand Browne, in the Library of the University of Virginia. The

Poe gives a list of the magazines that had praised "The House of Usher" and states that he has made a profitable engagement with *Blackwood's Magazine.* No concrete result has so far been discovered of this "engagement." It is quite possible that contributions by Poe were made to some English periodicals.[43] Poe had begun the letter with a record of his satisfaction that Snodgrass "has had no share in the feelings of ill will toward me which are somewhat prevalent (God only knows why) in Baltimore." Judging from a passage in his next letter to Snodgrass, October 7, 1839, he blamed this prejudice upon Neilson Poe, his cousin. This passage has been omitted by biographers generally, in the interest, I presume, of good taste. But since the object of this biography is to paint a picture of Poe as he really was, the letter is given as he wrote it:

Phila: Oct. 7, '39.

My dear Sir,

I rec^d your kind letter and now write a few hasty words in reply, merely to thank you for your exertions in my behalf, and to say that I send today, the Octo. No. We have been delayed with it, for various reasons.

I *felt* that N. Poe would not insert the article editorially. In your private ear, I believe him to be the bitterest enemy I have in the world. He is the more despicable in this, since he makes loud professions of friendship. Was it "relationship &c" which prevented him saying *anything at all* of the 2 or 3 last Nos. of the Gent's Mag? I can not account for his hostility except in being vain enough to imagine him jealous of the little literary reputation I have of late years obtained. But enough of the little dog.

I sincerely thank you for the interest you have taken in my well-doing. The friendship of a man of talent, who is at the same time a man of honorable feeling, is especially valuable in these days of double-dealing. I hope I shall always deserve your good opinion.

-----

letters have been collected in a convenient form, under title of "A Poe Correspondence Re-Edited," by J. W. Ostrom, in *Americana,* XXXIV (July, 1940), 1-38.

[43] "Why the Little Frenchman Wears his Hand in a Sling" was republished in *Bentley's Miscellany,* XLIII (July 1, 1840), 45-48, as "The Irish Gentleman and the Little Frenchman," but Poe hardly profited by such reprinting.

In the Octo. no: all the criticisms are mine—also the gymnastic article.

My book will be out in the beg^g. of Nov.

In haste, your most truly

EDGAR A. POE [44]

Dr. J. E. Snodgrass.

The "gymnastic article" or rather, the "Chapter on Field Sports and Manly Pastimes, by an Experienced Practitioner" [45] which Poe states in this letter is his, is of interest because it indicates that Poe may have been attending a gymnasium and endeavoring to keep himself in good physical condition. A picture is given of Barrett's gymnasium on Walnut Street, Philadelphia, and the articles, while, of course, hack work, are nevertheless clearly written.

Poe was one of those oversensitive persons to whom any unwillingness to help him was a sign of jealousy or envy. Of course, he did not expect the description of Neilson Poe to be published. In a letter of November 11, 1839 [46] to Snodgrass, Poe speaks of two letters from Irving, abounding in high praises, which his publishers desire to use. In one of these,[47] Irving speaks of "William Wilson" as superior to "The Fall of the House of Usher," on account of its greater simplicity. He also suggests "relieving the style of some of the epithets." It is, perhaps, fortunate that the founder of the American Short Story did not influence Poe as definitely as he did others, who could profit more. Snodgrass was evidently sending Poe his own essays in competition for premiums offered by Burton, and Poe makes it clear that *he* is not responsible for their offer. He also remarks on December 19th, that "we only put in poetry in the odds and ends of our pages—that is to fill out a vacancy left at the foot of a prose article." In a letter of January 20, 1840, Poe regrets that he cannot say anything about the *Baltimore Museum* in the *Gentleman's Magazine,* because "Burton is a warm friend of N. C. Brooks, *verb. sap. sat.*" [48] Brooks and Snodgrass evidently had a disagreement. In more than one way Poe was

[44] From copy made by William Hand Browne, Ingram Collection, University of Virginia.

[45] *Gentleman's Magazine,* V (September and October, 1839), 161-163, 221-226.

[46] Facsimile, Bixby Letters.

[47] Woodberry, I, 216, attributed by him to the "Griswold Mss," where it seems not to be at present.

[48] A curious error. The *Museum* had died in June, 1839.

made to feel that Burton, not he, controlled the magazine. With Volume VI, beginning in January, 1840, Burton began to feature his own name on the front wrappers with larger display type.[49] Yet Poe was acting as Editor during Burton's absences on the road. On December 9th he wrote to Carey and Hart asking for an advance chapter of Captain Marryat's new book for the January number, and his letter [50] is probably only one of many which he had to write.

Poe was undoubtedly cheered by the discriminating comment given by the Virginia poet, Philip Pendleton Cooke. In a letter of December 19, 1839,[51] Cooke, in speaking of Poe's stories said, "You do not make your sentences pictures—but you mould them into an artful excellence—bestow a care which is pleasantly perceptible and accomplish an effect which I can only characterize as the visible presentation of your ideas instead of the mere expression of them."

To judge from the increase in the number of pages Poe contributed to *Burton's* in 1840, he gave the publisher full value. In January he commenced his long narrative, "The Journal of Julius Rodman, being an Account of the First Passage across the Rocky Mountains of North America ever achieved by Civilized Man." It was annotated "Eds. G. M.," but it has been attributed to Poe on the basis of his statement [52] to Burton. Poe called attention early in the narrative to the expeditions of Lewis and Clarke and of Captain Bonneville, and his use of these sources has been made clear by comparative studies.[53] At the beginning, Poe evidently intended to build up a character in Julius Rodman, for he establishes Rodman's emotional, even at times rhapsodic, nature, but he did not carry out this intention. "Julius Rodman," was continued until the June number of 1840, then with Poe's departure from the magazine it ceased, unfinished, leaving the pioneers stranded on the banks of the Missouri River. There were fairly good descriptions of the defence against the attacks of the Sioux, and of the hope-

[49] See "Poeana," *American Book Collector,* II (December, 1932), 348-352, for discussion of the differences in the title pages of the Magazine.

[50] Original Autograph Ms., Berg Collection, New York Public Library.

[51] Autograph Ms., Griswold Collection, Boston Public Library.

[52] Poe to Burton, June 1, 1840.

[53] See articles by P. P. Crawford and H. A. Turner, *University of Texas Studies in English,* XII (1932), 158-170, and X (1930), 147-151. J. A. Robertson, *Bibliography of Poe,* II, 191, suggests that John K. Townsend's *Narrative of a Journey Across the Rocky Mountains to the Columbia River,* etc. (Philadelphia, 1839), was the account most closely followed by Poe. Poe probably saw the book, and the title may have led him to write one with a similar name. But I can see no influence of any significance exercised by Townsend's book on "Julius Rodman."

less struggle of the drowning bears, but there was nothing even approaching the final scenes of *Arthur Gordon Pym*. Poe and Burton probably thought the narrative would catch the interest in the West. But there is too much detail, and any analysis of it here is unnecessary. Poe never completed it or published it in book form. The only significant result of his experiments in the long story was to prove to him that his ability lay in the writing of shorter fiction.

Poe's only short story in *Burton's* for 1840, "Peter Pendulum, the Business Man" was an amusing if unimportant satire on methods of obtaining money on false pretences. In it, however, he expressed one fundamental principle, "In biography the truth is everything." It is as though he were sounding a warning to the many, including himself, who have written about his life without apparently being aware of this principle!

Poe contributed no new poems to *Burton's*, but reprinted his fine "Sonnet—Silence" in April, 1840. It had first appeared on January 4, 1840 in the Philadelphia *Saturday Courier:*

> "There are some qualities—some incorporate things,
>   That have a double life, which thus is made
> A type of that twin entity which springs
>   From matter and light, evinced in solid and shade.
> There is a two-fold *Silence*—sea and shore—
>   Body and soul. One dwells in lonely places,
>   Newly with grass o'ergrown; some solemn graces,
> Some human memories and tearful lore, .
> Render him terrorless: his name's "No More."
> He is the corporate Silence: dread him not!
>   No power hath he of evil in himself;
> But should some urgent fate (untimely lot!)
>   Bring thee to meet his shadow (nameless elf,
> That haunteth the lone regions where hath trod
> No foot of man,) commend thyself to God!"

It is not strictly a sonnet since it contains fifteen lines, but here again Poe showed his disregard of stanzaic structure. Poe had for some time been a student of the effect of silence upon human beings, his short story "Silence" dating in its inception as early as 1833. In the sonnet he draws a striking contrast between the merely passive silence that hovers over those resting places of human souls we have loved, and that shadow cast by silence upon the soul, which is an active breeder of terror. Poe suggests, rather than states, the nature of this terror—proceeding by negations as usual. Thus he leaves to the imaginative reader a frame into which he may fit any fear he desires. The harmless silence is called "no more"—but the evil silence is nameless.

This was the only poem published by Poe in 1840. He was, however, constantly publishing in *Burton's* verse by others, among them Dr. Thomas Dunn English, who had just graduated from the School of Medicine of the University of Pennsylvania, and who was at first Poe's friend and later his enemy. English at this time was only twenty, and it may have been Poe's desire to help a young poet that prompted him to publish English's galloping narrative verse.

Poe's reviews in *Burton's* were usually mere paragraphs of a perfunctory nature. In February, 1840, however, he wrote a more elaborate criticism of Longfellow's *Voices of the Night*. He had already shown his complete failure to understand Longfellow's prose romance *Hyperion,* and while he praised Longfellow's "Hymn to the Night" and "Beleaguered City," he insisted that Longfellow was lacking "in combining or binding force," and added, "He has absolutely nothing of unity." These are, of course, two of the qualities which Longfellow possessed in large measure, even if he had not yet attained to the serene unity of his later sonnets. Poe also attacked Longfellow for plagiarizing Tennyson in his "Midnight Mass for the Dying Year," which was as absurd as any of the many similar charges he levelled later at Longfellow.

Poe was using some earlier material even in his criticisms, for his account of Bryant in *Burton's* for May includes a portion of his review of Bryant's poems in the *Southern Literary Messenger.* He is quite frank, however, about this insertion. He certainly did not give the same care to his reviews as he had done in the *Messenger* days. To do him justice, however, he probably did most of the editing and there are unsigned articles which may perhaps be his. It is impossible to reconcile the articles he signed with his later statement to Burton of the number of pages he had contributed each month. A series of short paragraphs which appeared under the general title of "A Chapter on Science and Art," in March, April and May, 1840, are probably by Poe. They deal with balloons, steam engines, new methods in daguerreotyping, new steam frigates, the recommendations for the establishment of a scientific foundation in Washington on the basis of the Smithson bequest, and kindred topics. The style of these paragraphs resembles Poe somewhat, and since one issue is signed "Eds. G. M.," he probably had at least some share in them. If this supposition is correct, his interests were wide, and his comments apt. He may be the author, also, of "Omniana," a collection of paragraphs appearing in April, May, and June, on things in general. In this column for May appeared some verses under the general head of "Palindromes," which had first been published in the Philadelphia *Saturday Evening Post*, March 15, 1827. If these verses are by Poe, they are his earliest to be found in print, but they are of no especial merit.

If I have emphasized, perhaps unduly, Poe's minor contributions to *Burton's* during these later months, it was to show his continued and uninterrupted appearances in the *Magazine*. These do not agree with the persistent legend of his quarrel and reconciliation with Burton some months before the final break came. If there were an earlier quarrel, there arises, of course, the question whether Poe's habits were responsible. But this legend rests upon the so-called "undated" letter of Burton to Poe, which has proved to be dated May 30, 1839, only twenty days after Burton made his first offer to Poe. When the sentences, "I will gladly overlook the past. I hope you will as easily fulfil your pledges for the future" and later, "I accept your proposition to recommence your interrupted avocations upon the *Maga*," which have been shown to be forgeries of Griswold's, are eliminated, there is no good evidence to support the story of any cessation of Poe's work as editor of *Burton's* from July, 1839, to June, 1840. In the light of these forgeries, Griswold's account of the parting of Burton and Poe also disappears from consideration. The story of Mr. Rosenbach concerning Poe's neglect of his duties [54] and consequent discharge, is also apocryphal.

The testimony of Charles W. Alexander, who published the *Gentleman's Magazine* until Burton purchased it, when he still continued to print the journal, is convincing:

Philadelphia, Oct. 20th, 1850.
My dear Sir,—I very cheerfully reply to your request made in reference to our friend Edgar Allan Poe.

I well remember his connection with the "Gentleman's Maga-

---

[54] Quoted from *The American*, February 26, 1887, by Woodberry, *Life*, I, 242; and adopted by Allen, *Israfel*, Rev. Ed., p. 378. I am authorized by Dr. Abram S. W. Rosenbach, to state that this account is without foundation.

zine," of which Mr. Burton was editor, and myself the publisher, at the period referred to in connection with Mr. Poe.

The absence of the principal editor on professional duties left the matter frequently in the hands of Mr. Poe, whose unfortunate failing may have occasioned some disappointment in the preparation of a particular article expected from *him*, but never interfering with the regular publication of the "Gentleman's Magazine," as its monthly issue was never interrupted upon any occasion, either from Mr. Poe's deficiency, or from any other cause, during my publication of it, embracing the whole time of Mr. Poe's connection with it. That Mr. Poe had faults seriously detrimental to his own interests, none, of course, will deny. They were unfortunately, too well known in the literary circles of Philadelphia, were there any disposition to conceal them. But he alone was the sufferer, and not those who received the benefit of his pre-eminent talents, however irregular his habits or uncertain his contributions may occasionally have been.

I had long and familiar intercourse with him, and very cheerfully embrace the opportunity which you now offer of bearing testimony to the uniform *gentleness of disposition* and kindness of heart which distinguished Mr. Poe in all my intercourse with him. With all his faults, he was a gentleman; which is more than can be said of some who have undertaken the ungracious task of blacking the reputation which Mr. Poe, of all others, esteemed "the precious jewel of his soul."

Yours truly,

C. ALEXANDER.[55]

To Mr. T. C. Clarke.

Burton evidently wrote a letter to Poe on May 30, 1840, which has unfortunately disappeared. It must have had quite a different tone from that of May 30, 1839. In reply Poe sent the following:

Sir,—I find myself at leisure this Monday morning, June 1, to notice your very singular letter of Saturday, and you shall now hear what I have to say. In the first place, your attempts to bully me excite in my mind scarcely any other sentiment than mirth. When you address me again, preserve, if you can, the dignity of a gentleman. If by accident you have taken it into your head that I am to be insulted with impunity I can only assume that you are an ass. This one point being distinctly understood I shall feel myself more at liberty to be explicit. As for the rest, you do me

[55] Gill, *Life of Edgar Allan Poe*, pp. 96-97.

gross injustice; and you know it. As usual you have wrought yourself into a passion with me on account of some imaginary wrong; for no real injury, or attempt at injury, have you ever received at my hands. As I live, I am utterly unable to say why you are angry, or what true grounds of complaint you have against me. You are a man of impulses; have made yourself, in consequence, some enemies; have been in many respects ill treated by those whom you had looked upon as friends—and these things have rendered you suspicious. You once wrote in your magazine a sharp critique upon a book of mine—a very silly book —Pym. Had I written a similar critici[sm] upon a book of yours, you feel that you would have been my enemy for life, and you therefore imagine in my bosom a latent hostility towards yourself. This has been a mainspring in your whole conduct towards me since our first acquaintance. It has acted to prevent all cordiality. In a general view of human nature your idea is just—but you will find yourself puzzled in judging me by ordinary motives. Your criticism was essentially correct and therefore, although severe, it did not occasion in me one solitary emotion either of anger or dislike. But even while I write these words, I am sure you will not believe them. Did I not still think you, in spite of the exceeding bitterness of some of your hurried actions, a man of many honorable impulses, I should not now take the trouble to send you this letter. I cannot permit myself to suppose that you would say to me in cold blood what you said in your letter of yesterday. You are, of course, only mistaken, in asserting that I owe you a hundred dollars, and you will rectify the mistake at once when you come to look at your accounts. Soon after I joined you, you made me an offer of money, and I accepted $20. Upon another occasion, at my request, you sent me enclosed in a letter $30. Of this 30, I repaid 20 within the next fortnight (drawing no salary for that period.) I was thus still in your debt $30, when not long ago I again asked a loan of $30, which you promptly handed to me at your own house. Within the last 3 weeks, 3 $ each week have been retained from my salary, an indignity which I have felt deeply but did not resent. You state the sum retained as $8, but this I believe is through a mistake of Mr. Morrell. My postage bill at a guess, might be 9 or 10$—and I therefore am indebted to you, upon the whole, in the amount of about $60. More than this sum I shall not pay. You state that you can no longer afford to pay $50 per month for 2 or 3 pp. of M.S. Your error here can be shown by reference to the magazine. During my year with you I have written

July—	5	pp	
August	9		
Sept.	16		
Octo.	4		
Nov.	5		
Dec.	12		
Jan.	9		
Feb.	12		
Mar.	11		
April	17		
May	14	5 copied—Miss McMichael's M.S.	
June	9	3 " Chandlers	

132 [56]

Dividing this sum by 12 we have an average of 11 pp per month—not 2 or 3. And this estimate leaves out of question every thing in the way of extract or compilation. Nothing is counted but bonâ fiede composition. 11 pp at $3 per p. would be $33, at the usual Magazine prices. Deduct this from $50, my monthly salary, and we have left 17$ per month, or 4\frac{25}{100}$ per week, for the services of proof-reading; general superintendence at the printing-office; reading, alteration, & preparation of M.S.S., with compilation of various articles, such as Plate articles, Field Sports &c. Neither has anything been said of my name upon your title page, a small item you will say—but still something as you know. Snowden pays his editresses $2 per week each for their names *solely*. Upon the whole I am not willing to admit that you have greatly overpaid me. That I did not do 4 times as much as I did for the Magazine, was your own fault. At first I wrote long articles which you deemed inadmissable, [sic] & never did I suggest any to which you had not some immediate and decided objection. Of course I grew discouraged & could feel no interest in the Journal. I am at a loss to know why you call me selfish. If you mean that I borrowed money of you—you know that you offered it—and you know that I am poor. In what instance has any one ever found

[56] Really 131 pages.

me selfish? Was there selfishness in the affront I offered Benjamin (whom I respect, and who spoke well of me.) because I deemed it a duty not to receive from any one commendation at your expense? I had no hesitation in making him my enemy (which he now must be) through a sense of my obligations as your coadjutor. I have said that I could not tell why you were angry. Place yourself in my situation & see whether you would not have acted as I have done. You first "enforced," as you say, a deduction of salary: giving me to understand thereby that you thought of parting company—You next spoke disrespectfully of me behind my back—this as an habitual thing—to those whom you supposed your friends, and who punctually retailed me, as a matter of course, every ill-natured word which you uttered. Lastly, you advertised your magazine for sale without saying a word to me about it. I felt no anger at what you did—none in the world. Had I not firmly believed it your design to give up your journal, with a view of attending to [the] theatre, I should [never] have dreamed of attempting one of my own. The opportunity of doing something for myself seemed a good one—(I was about to be thrown out of business)—and I embraced it. Now I ask you, as a man of honor and as a man of sense—what is there wrong in all this? What have I done at which you have any right to take offense? I can give you no definitive answer (respecting the continuation [of] "Rodman's Journal") until I hear from you again. The charge of $100 I shall not admit for an instant. If you persist in it our intercourse is at an end, and we can each adopt our own measures.

In the meantime, I am,

Yr. Obt. St.,

EDGAR A. POE.

Wm. E. Burton, Esqr.[57]

---

[57] This letter is probably a rough draft and Poe may not have sent it in this exact form to Burton. Mrs. Richmond, however, wrote on May 27, 1877, to Ingram, "I enclose a copy of a letter I gave to a friend long ago, which I know is correct in every particular. I urged him to send you the original,—but he did not like to trust it out of his sight. I am sure it is a perfect copy, for he is most reliable and he assured me that every erasure was precisely like the original." Through the courtesy of Professor James S. Wilson and Mr. W. D. Hull of the University of Virginia, I am able to print the letter in the exact form of the copy sent to Ingram. Ingram printed it (I, 175-179) with omissions, not only of the lines Poe crossed out, but also of some he left untouched. On the other hand he inserted lines Poe had erased. It

This letter seems to ring true, although Poe's statement concerning his projected magazine is hardly correct. He had had that project in mind for a long time.

The break with Burton was, in fact, inevitable. Burton had been forced to suspend payments for contributions,[58] and was interested in his new theatrical project, the National Theatre on Chestnut Street, east of Ninth Street, which opened on August 31, 1840. Francis C. Wemyss, the manager of the Walnut Street Theatre, by whom Burton was engaged as a star during 1839, has given an interesting picture of his character. "As an actor, Mr. W. E. Burton has no superior on the American Stage—but as a manager, his faults are, first, want of nerve to fight a losing battle; in success he is a great general, but in any sudden reverse, his first thought is not to maintain his position, but to retreat." [59]

Poe, knowing his own ability, could hardly have been satisfied with the secondary position he occupied. His own statement to Snodgrass on June 17, 1840, concerning an essay of the latter that had disappeared, shows this clearly: "Were I in your place I would take some summary method of dealing with the scoundrel, whose infamous line of conduct in regard to this whole Premium scheme merits, and shall receive exposure. I am firmly convinced that it was never his intention to pay one dollar of the money offered; and indeed his plain intimations to that effect, made to me personally and directly were the immediate reason of my cutting the connexion so abruptly as I did."

Burton must have circulated rumors concerning Poe's drinking habits for in another letter to Snodgrass April 1, 1841, Poe wrote with apparent sincerity:

Philadelphia, April 1, 1841.

My dear Snodgrass—I fear you have been thinking it was not my design to answer your kind letter at all. It is now April Fool's Day, and yours is dated March 8th; but believe me, although, for good reason, I may occasionally postpone my reply to your favors, I am never in danger of forgetting them. . . .

---

seems best to print it as Poe wished Burton to see it, so far as this is now possible.

[58] Poe to Snodgrass, November 11, 1839.

[59] Wemyss, *Twenty-Six Years of the Life of an Actor and Manager* (New York, 1847), II, 334.

[Omitted portion refers to unimportant details connected with *Graham's Magazine,* which are out of place here.]

In regard to Burton, I feel indebted to you for the kind interest you express; but scarcely know how to reply. My situation is embarrassing. It is impossible, as you say, to notice a buffoon and a felon, as one gentleman would notice another. The law, then, is my only resource. Now, if the truth of a scandal could be admitted in justification—I mean of what the law terms a *scandal*—I would have matters all my own way. I would institute a suit, forthwith, for his personal defamation of myself. He would be unable to prove the truth of his allegations. I could prove their falsity and their malicious intent by witnesses who, seeing me at all hours of every day, would have the best right to speak—I mean Burton's own clerk, Morrell, and the compositors of the printing office. In fact, I could prove the scandal almost by acclamation. I should obtain damages. But, on the other hand, I have never been scrupulous in regard to what I have said of him. I have always told *him* to his face, and everybody else, that I looked upon him as a blackguard and a villain. This is notorious. He would meet me with a cross action. The truth of the allegation —which I could easily prove as he would find it difficult to prove the truth of his own respecting me—would not avail me. The law will not admit, as justification of my calling Billy Burton a scoundrel, that Billy Burton is really such. What then can I do? If I sue, he sues: you see how it is.

At the same time—as I may, after further reflection, be induced to sue, I would take it as an act of kindness—not to say *justice*—on your part, if you would see the gentleman of whom you spoke, and ascertain with accuracy all that may legally avail me; that is to say, what and when were the words used, and whether your friend would be willing for your sake, for my sake, and for the sake of truth, to give evidence if called upon. Will you do this for me?

So far for the matter inasmuch as it concerns Burton. I have now to thank you for your defence of myself, as stated. You are a physician, and I presume no physician can have difficulty in detecting the *drunkard* at a glance. You are, moreover, a literary man, well read in morals. You will never be brought to believe that I could write what I daily write, as I write it, were I as this villain would induce those who know me not, to believe. In fine, I pledge you, before God. the solemn word of a gentleman, that

I am temperate even to rigor. From the hour in which I first saw this basest of calumniators to the hour in which I retired from his office in uncontrollable disgust at his chicanery, arrogance, ignorance and brutality, *nothing stronger than water ever passed my lips.*

It is, however, due to candor that I inform you upon what foundation he has erected his slanders. At no period of my life was I ever what men call intemperate. I never was in the *habit* of intoxication. I never drunk drams, &c. But, for a brief period, while I resided in Richmond, and edited the *Messenger* I certainly did give way, at long intervals, to the temptation held out on all sides by the spirit of Southern conviviality. My sensitive temperament could not stand an excitement which was an everyday matter to my companions. In short, it sometimes happened that I was completely intoxicated. For some days after each excess I was invariably confined to bed. But it is now quite four years since I have abandoned every kind of alcoholic drink—four years, with the exception of a single deviation, which occurred shortly *after* my leaving Burton, and when I was induced to resort to the occasional use of *cider*, with the hope of relieving a nervous attack.

You will thus see, frankly stated, the whole amount of my sin. You will also see the blackness of that heart which could *revive* a slander of this nature. Neither can you fail to perceive how desperate the malignity of the slanderer must be—how resolute he must be to slander, and how slight the grounds upon which he would build up a defamation—since he can find nothing better with which to charge me than an accusation which can be disproved by each and every man with whom I am in habit of daily intercourse.

I have now only to repeat to you, in general, my solemn assurance that my habits are as far removed from intemperance as the day from the night. My sole drink is water.

Will you do me the kindness to repeat this assurance to such of your own friends as happen to speak of me in your hearing?

I feel that nothing more is requisite, and you will agree with me upon reflection.

Hoping soon to hear from you, I am,

Yours most cordially,
EDGAR A. POE.

Dr. J. E. Snodgrass.[60]

[60] This letter was published separately in the *Baltimore American* of

In any event, Poe's connection with the *Gentleman's Magazine* terminated with the June number for 1840. He had published in it one of the greatest of his short stories, but no new poetry. He had given a promise of development in a new direction, in his essay in May, 1840, on the "Philosophy of Furniture." Poe might have had a career as an interior decorator had there been such a profession then in the United States. On the whole, his association with Burton's had been an interruption to his creative work, made necessary by the earning of his living.

Of all the reasons for the break, the most potent, however, was his desire to have a magazine of his own.

April 4, 1881, with editorial comment. The editor states that it was furnished by the widow of Dr. J. E. Snodgrass, and had not yet been published. I have reproduced it from the account in the *American* from photostat sent by Mr. L. H. Dielman, of Baltimore.

CHAPTER XII

At the Summit — The Editor of *Graham's Magazine*

In the discussions which took place in the "small house" that held the little family in the summer of 1840, the project of the "Penn Magazine" must have been the leading topic. It certainly filled Poe's mind, and he probably welcomed the release from *Burton's* as an opportunity to proceed with his dream of owning, as well as editing, a magazine. The dream was, after all, not quite such an illusion as at first glance it appears to be. No American author of importance had yet proved his ability to make a living exclusively by creative work. Bryant had wisely bought a half share in the *Evening Post* when he became editor of it in 1829, and although he was so discouraged in 1837 that he thought seriously of selling his share and going West, Poe could hardly have known that fact. Longfellow had recently been called to Harvard as Smith Professor of Modern Languages and Belles Lettres; Whittier had been trying with no great success to edit antislavery journals in New York and Philadelphia; Hawthorne had been taken care of by his political friends and was in the Boston Custom House; Emerson had inherited enough money from the estate of his first wife's father to support him; Willis, the most popular of all, had made an effort to retire from active journalism to write the charming essays and the plays that still repay reading, but he had to come back to New York to make a living. Lowell was very soon to start his abortive effort with *The Pioneer*. Some occupation or independent means was necessary in order to give a writer the opportunity to spend such leisure hours as he had in the creation of literature.

The reasons why there was no substantial career as yet for an American writer lay, first, in a lack of international copyright. A publisher who could sell Dickens' novels without paying Dickens anything hesitated to encourage an American novelist who would, perhaps, be unreasonable enough to require some payment for his efforts. Poetry, naturally, was not to be paid for at all, and short stories were a bad risk. But even more hopeless, as we now look back on it, was the attitude of the publisher. To him the American author was a petitioner, suing for a favor. Even Lea and Blanchard had quickly regretted their momentary relapse into generosity in agreeing to publish the *Tales of the Grotesque and Arabesque,* without paying Poe anything.

But for Poe there was no money from Virginia's family, no father to send him abroad to study languages, in which he was singularly proficient, no political friends to get him an office. He had had two experiences of being a paid employee in the service of a publisher whom he could not recognize as his intellectual equal. It is no wonder that he made the effort to found a journal of his own.

The publication of the *Penn Magazine* was announced in the Philadelphia *Saturday Courier* as early as June 13, 1840, to appear on January 1, 1841.[1] Poe had a prospectus printed and frequently used the reverse side of these sheets for his correspondence:

PROSPECTUS

of

THE PENN MAGAZINE,

A MONTHLY LITERARY JOURNAL,

To be Edited and Published in the City of Philadelphia,

By Edgar A. Poe.

To the Public.—Since resigning the conduct of The Southern Literary Messenger, at the commencement of its third year, I have had always in view the establishment of a Magazine which should retain some of the chief features of that Journal, abandoning or greatly modifying the rest. Delay, however, has been occasioned by a variety of causes, and not until now have I found myself at liberty to attempt the execution of the design.

I will be pardoned for speaking more directly of The Messenger. Having in it no proprietary right, my objects too being at variance in many respects with those of its very worthy owner, I found difficulty in stamping upon its pages that *individuality* which I believe essential to the full success of all similar publications. In regard to their permanent influence, it appears to me that a continuous, definite character, and a marked certainty of purpose, are desiderata of vital importance, and only attainable where one mind alone has the general direction of the undertaking. Experience has rendered obvious, what might indeed

[1] Philadelphia *Saturday Courier,* X (June 13, 1840), No. 481, p. 2.

have been demonstrated *a priori;* that in founding a Magazine of my own lies my sole chance of carrying out to completion whatever peculiar intentions I may have entertained.

To those who remember the early days of the Southern periodical in question it will be scarcely necessary to say that its main feature was a somewhat overdone causticity in its department of Critical Notices of new books. The Penn Magazine will retain this trait of severity in so much only as the calmest yet sternest sense of justice will permit. Some years since elapsed may have mellowed down the petulance without interfering with the rigor of the critic. Most surely they have not yet taught him to read through the medium of a publisher's will, nor convinced him that the interests of letters are unallied with the interests of truth. It shall be the first and chief purpose of the Magazine now proposed to become known as one where may be found at all times, and upon all subjects, an honest and a fearless opinion. It shall be a leading object to assert in precept, and to maintain in practice the rights, while in effect it demonstrates the advantages, of an absolutely independent criticism—a criticism self-sustained; guiding itself only by the purest rules of Art; analyzing and urging these rules as it applies them; holding itself aloof from all personal bias; acknowledging no fear save that of outraging the right; yielding no point either to the vanity of the author, or to the assumptions of antique prejudice, or to the involute and anonymous cant of the Quarterlies, or to the arrogance of those organized *cliques* which, hanging like nightmares upon American literature, manufacture, at the nod of our principal booksellers, a pseudo-public-opinion by wholesale. These are objects of which no man need be ashamed. They are purposes, moreover, whose novelty at least will give them interest. For assurance that I will fulfil them in the best spirit and to the very letter, I appeal with confidence to the many thousands of my friends, and especially of my Southern friends, who sustained me in the Messenger, where I had but a very partial opportunity of completing my own plans.

In respect to the other features of the Penn Magazine, a few words here will suffice. It will endeavour to support the general interests of the republic of letters, without reference to particular regions; regarding the world at large as the true audience of the author. Beyond the precincts of literature, properly so called, it will leave in better hands the task of instruction upon all matters of *very* grave moment. Its aim chiefly shall be to *please;* and this through means of versatility, originality, and pungency. It may be as well here to observe that nothing said in this Prospectus should be construed into a design of sullying the Magazine with any tincture of the buffoonery, scurrillity, or profanity, which are the blemish of some of the most vigorous of the European prints. In all branches of the literary department, the best aid, from the highest and purest sources, is secured.

To the mechanical execution of the work the greatest attention will be given which such a matter can require. In this respect it is proposed to surpass, by very much, the ordinary Magazine style. The form will nearly resemble that of The Knickerbocker; the paper will be equal to that of The North American Review; the pictorial embellishments will be numerous, and by the leading artists of the country, but will be introduced only in the necessary illustration of the text.

The Penn Magazine will be published in Philadelphia, on the first of each month, and will form, half-yearly, a volume of about 500 pages. The price will be $5 per annum, payable in advance, or upon the receipt of the first number, which will be issued on the first of January, 1841. Letters addressed to the Editor and Proprietor,

EDGAR A. POE.[2]

Poe was also able to secure the publication of the prospectus, slightly modified, in the daily press.[3] It is worth noting that he began by referring to his editorship of the *Southern Literary Messenger,* without any mention of *Burton's.* On January 1, 1841, the publication was postponed until March 1st. Poe had been ill, as he wrote to his friend Snodgrass on January 17, 1841, but he was still confident concerning his prospects for the magazine. He was determined to have none but the "best pens" to write for it, and he had one or two articles of his own which he believed would make Snodgrass stare, on account of the oddity of their conception.[4]

[2] The Prospectus is reproduced, from the original in the Historical Society of Pennsylvania, as Poe revised it, sometime previous to August 20, 1840. It contains several sentences not in the June issue, notably the passage concerning the criticism of that day. In general the language is improved. The Prospectus fills page 1; page 2 is blank; page 3 bears a letter from Poe to Joseph B. Boyd, in Cincinnati, dated August 20, 1840, and page 4 the address. Poe asks Boyd for help in obtaining subscriptions. The only Joseph B. Boyd in the City Directory of Cincinnati for 1840 is a watch maker, an unlikely person for Poe to ask for help. Another original is in the Huntington Library with a letter to John Tomlin, September 16th, thanking him for subscriptions.

[3] The Philadelphia *Daily Chronicle,* I (Monday, October 12, 1840), 3. Collection of W. H. Koester, Baltimore.

[4] Original Autograph Ms., Berg Collection, New York Public Library.

Poe wrote to Kennedy on December 31, 1840, asking for contributions for the new magazine. That he was not ungrateful for Kennedy's earlier assistance is shown clearly: "Since you gave me my first start in the literary world, and since indeed I seriously say that without the timely kindness you once evinced towards me, I should not at this moment be among the living,—you will not feel surprised that I look anxiously to you for encouragement in this new enterprise." [5]

Among others whose support he solicited was Judge Joseph Hopkinson, of Philadelphia, who evidently remembered him from the days of *Al Aaraaf* and sagely warned him against distant subscribers who will cost him money.[6] The postal rates for magazines were indeed one of the handicaps under which Poe labored. The five dollar magazines paid from nine to seventeen cents for each number, depending on size and distance. It was not until 1845 that Congress abolished the distance provision.[7]

In a postscript to his letter to Snodgrass of April 1, 1841, Poe wrote his friend: "P. P. S.—The *Penn*, I hope, is only 'scotched, not killed.' It would have appeared under glorious auspices, and with capital at command, in March, as advertised, but for the unexpected bank suspensions. In the meantime, Mr. Graham has made me a liberal offer, which I had great pleasure in accepting. The *Penn* project will unquestionably be resumed hereafter."

When the plans for the *Penn Magazine* had to be postponed, Poe joined the editorial staff of *Graham's Magazine*. George Rex Graham was a young Philadelphian, who, although only twenty-seven years old, had supported himself as a cabinet maker, while he prepared himself for admission to the bar. He also became assistant editor of Atkinson's *Saturday Evening Post* and bought from Atkinson, the *Casket*, a monthly magazine of the sentimental type. When Burton offered to sell him the *Gentleman's Magazine* in November, 1840, he purchased it for $3,500, on the ground, apparently, that each subscriber was worth a dollar. Burton had thirty-five hundred subscribers, and the *Casket* had fifteen hundred, so that *Graham's Magazine*, as the combination was called, started with about five thousand. The number for December, 1840, contained Poe's story "The Man of the

---

[5] Original Autograph Ms., Peabody Institute.
[6] Original Autograph Ms., Joseph Hopkinson to Poe, January 25, 1841. Griswold Collection, Boston Public Library.
[7] Mott, *History of American Magazines*, pp. 517-518.

Crowd," although he did not actually join the staff until the issue for April, 1841, was being prepared.[8]

"The Man of the Crowd" is a powerful story of a human being, driven by the search for some lost companion, or by the memory of a crime, who walks through the crowded streets of London without cessation, dreading to be alone. The narrator, who has left his comfortable seat at the window of his Club to follow this old man in his wanderings, finally gives up the chase. Here the terror is of a man's own thoughts. The story made such an impression upon the critic of *Blackwood's Edinburgh Magazine* when he found it in the *Tales* of 1845, that he selected it for extended treatment.[9] As he very properly observed, such a story cannot be judged by its probability. Poe was portraying the power of a moral idea upon the human soul; the incidents are contributory to that idea, and are not of importance in themselves.

Several book reviews in *Graham's* have been tentatively assigned to Poe during the next three months, but purely on internal evidence. None of them is of importance. In April, however, appeared "The Murders in the Rue Morgue," the first of his stories of ratiocination, as he called them. While not the originator of this type of fiction, known popularly as "detective stories," Poe differed from Voltaire or others who had preceded him, whose cleverness consisted in apparently correct guessing, based on close observation. That the solution is built up from a fact already known to the author is, of course, obvious. Poe was not above this appeal to the reader by exciting his wonder at the mental alertness of his detective, but he did not stop there. He created the character of C. Auguste Dupin, a name which he borrowed from the heroine, Marie Dupin, of a story, "Marie Laurent," the first of a series of "Unpublished Passages in the Life of Vidocq, the French

---

.[8] An editorial in the *Saturday Evening Post* for February 20, 1841, says, "We have secured the services of Mr. Poe as one of the Editors of *Graham's* Magazine." On the second page of the cover of *Graham's* for April, 1841, the "Proprietor" announces that he has made arrangements with Poe "Commencing with the present number." The story that Burton in arranging for the sale told Graham, "I want you to take care of my young editor," rests on Graham's statement to the late Albert H. Smyth, a member of the Faculty of the Central High School of Philadelphia, and a good witness. See his *Philadelphia Magazines and Their Contributors* (Philadelphia, 1892), p. 217. Yet the relations between Burton and Poe make such a condition improbable, and Graham as an old man may have been a bit romantic in his memory.

[9] Vol. LXII (November, 1847), pp. 582-585.

Minister of Police." These appeared in *Burton's* from September to December, 1838, and are signed "J. M. B." [10] Poe must have read these because he refers to Vidocq in "The Murders in the Rue Morgue" as "a good guesser," but one who "impaired his vision by holding the object too close." They probably suggested to Poe that he attempt a story in which a crime is solved, but his method is quite different. There is no cleverness in the solution of a problem in these passages in M. Vidocq's life. Marie Dupin, for example, marries a worthless young farmer, Laurent, who abandons her and when, years later in Paris, he and his fellow criminals attempt to rob the house of her employer, Vidocq accidentally sees them enter and captures them. Vidocq, the narrator, remains usually outside the stories, which deal with murder or seduction.

Poe in the person of C. Auguste Dupin, proceeds not by guessing but by analysis. In the opening paragraph of the story, as it appeared in *Graham's*, he spoke of the possibility of there being a distinct organ devoted to analysis,[11] and he suggested that analysis might be one element of ideality. Later in the story he even places the analytic faculty higher than the constructive. While this is open to question, there can be little doubt of the analytic power displayed in the methods by which Poe secured his results, methods which are so clever that they seem to be intuitive.

Poe introduces the crime to the reader by the usual medium through which one becomes aware of crime, the newspaper account. He then proceeds with the witnesses at the inquest. He begins with the name of Pauline Dubourg, a recollection of the Misses Dubourg who kept the school in London he had attended as a boy. The reader becomes aware of the relations of the dead mother and daughter, Madame and Mademoiselle L'Espanaye, of their seclusion in this four-story house, and of their having a large sum of money, recently drawn from their bank. Here at once Poe's methods differ from those of his many imitators. They would have led the reader for a time into a belief that the bank clerk, M. Le Bon, who brought the gold to the address in the Rue Morgue, had murdered the women for their money. Nearly

[10] These may be based on the various *Mémoires* of Vidocq, one set of which had appeared in 1828. They are generally believed to be spurious, so far, at least, as the authorship of the real detective, François Eugène Vidocq (1775-1857), is concerned.

[11] This paragraph occurs in the original Ms. in the Drexel Institute, Philadelphia, and in the story as printed in the *Prose Romances* of 1843. It was omitted in the *Tales* of 1845, and this text has since been followed.

all detective stories consist of such attempts to throw dust in the eyes of their readers, while in reality the problem is not as complicated as he is made to believe. Poe never lets his reader believe in the guilt of M. Le Bon, the clerk, who has been arrested on suspicion. He simply uses Dupin's gratitude to Le Bon as a reason for his entrance into the case. With Poe there always is a problem, and he gradually leads the reader into an identification with the methods of solution until he almost credits himself with a part in it. Yet the reader never does reach the solution until Poe permits it. Poe proceeds on the assumption that the unusual elements in any problem are the means most likely to assist in its solution. Therefore, the testimony of the witnesses, each of whom heard two voices, one that of a Frenchman, the other the shrill or harsh voice of a foreigner who speaks in a language which the witness does not understand, convinces Dupin that it is not a human being who is speaking. Every other element in the problem is then taken apart in its turn until one or more of its elements aids in the solution, namely that the murder has been committed by an orang-outang, who has escaped from its owner. This owner, a sailor, has followed the animal until he sees through the window the brutal murder without being able to prevent it. He therefore keeps silent, hoping to escape notice.[12]

In May 1841, Poe contributed "A Descent into the Maelström." He called attention to a description of this whirlpool in the Encyclopædia Britannica, in order, apparently, to differ with that authority as to the causes of the phenomenon. He did not acknowledge, however, that his quotation from Jonas Ramus was also taken from the Encyclopædia, which in its turn had quoted without credit from Erich Pontoppidan's *Natural History of Norway*. Woodberry, who made this discovery, quotes also the amusing fact that in the ninth edition of

---

[12] It has been suggested by John K. Moore, in "Poe, Scott, and the 'Murders in the Rue Morgue,'" *American Literature*, VIII (March, 1936), 52-58, that Poe based his selection of the orang-outang upon Sylvan, the orang-outang in Scott's *Count Robert of Paris*. It is quite possible that the introduction of the animal in Scott's novel in Chapter XVI, "A strange, chuckling, hoarse voice, in a language totally unintelligible to Count Robert, was heard to respond," may have started Poe thinking of the use to which such a voice might be put. But this similarity of the voice of the orang-outang to a human voice is not made use of by Scott in solving the problem of the death of Agelastes, who is strangled by Sylvan. No attempt indeed is made to solve it, since it is deliberately concealed, for reasons of state, by those who saw it. It is simply another case of Poe taking a slight suggestion and inventing the most important element in the story.

the Encyclopædia, the author of the article on "Whirlpool" credits Poe with erudition taken from an earlier edition of the same Encyclopædia, which, in its turn, had stolen the learning from another source, and then quotes from Poe as facts portions he had invented! [13]

But in reality the source of the details is of slight importance. What makes the story impressive is the establishment of a mood of terror. The narrator, to whom the old seaman tells the tale, is himself aghast when he merely looks down at the sea from the heights of Helseggen. The terror arises from the fear of the forces of nature, so they are magnified by Poe's usual denials of limits: "Such a hurricane as then blew it is folly to attempt describing. The oldest seaman in Norway never experienced anything like it." That is a mere device. But the picture of the moon looking down at the black funnel of water in which the doomed boat goes round and round, this is no device. And the succession of moods; the decrease of terror when hope is abandoned—the interest taken in the race of the different objects toward the "horrible inner edge" of the Maelström; the "new hope that made the heart beat more heavily" all identify the reader's own feelings with the most universal of all emotions, the struggle for self-preservation. The seaman is saved, too, not by accident, but by his observation that all cylindrical forms go down more slowly and by his lashing himself to the cask which his brother had abandoned. "A Descent into the Maelström" is in Poe's best manner—notwithstanding his statement [14] that it was finished in a hurry. If this is true, Latrobe's mention of it as being among the *Tales of the Folio Club* is evidently an error.

As if to prove his versatility, Poe printed in the June number of *Graham's*, "The Island of the Fay," a prose poem, almost perfect in its tone. It is a study of natural beauty touched with the supernatural that results from the stimulation which loneliness brings to the poet: "In truth, the man who would behold aright the glory of God upon earth must in solitude behold that glory." Poe goes to extremes in this story—as he continues: "To me, at least, the presence—not of human life only, but of life in any other form than that of the green things

---

[13] Woodberry, *Works of Poe*, IV, 289-294. The quotation from Joseph Glanvill, as Woodberry also pointed out, is from *Essays on Several Important Subjects in Philosophy and Religion* (London, 1676), p. 15. Poe is, as often, not quite correct. The original reads: "The ways of God in Nature (as *in Providence*) are not as *ours* are: Nor are the Models that we frame any way commensurate to the vastness and profundity of his Works; which have a depth in them greater than the *Well of Democritus.*"

[14] Poe to Snodgrass, July 12, 1841.

which grow upon the soil and are voiceless—is a stain upon the landscape—is at war with the genius of the scene." Since the greatest of
his poems and stories deal with the conflict of human emotions, rather
than the background of inanimate nature, this sentence might be misunderstood were it not followed by: "I love, indeed, to regard the dark
valleys, and the grey rocks, and the waters that silently smile, and the
forests that sigh in uneasy slumbers,—and the proud watchful mountains that look down upon all—I love to regard these as themselves
but the colossal members of one vast animate and sentient whole—a
whole whose form (that of the sphere) is the most perfect and most
inclusive of all; whose path is among associate planets; whose meek
handmaiden is the moon; whose mediate sovereign is the sun; whose
life is eternity; whose thought is that of a God; whose enjoyment is
knowledge; whose destinies are lost in immensity." Here the magnificent phrases are marshalled into the service of that unity to which
Poe loved to pay tribute. This story might be looked upon as a companion piece to "The City in the Sea"; in fact two lines from that
poem, somewhat altered, are quoted:

> "So blended bank and shadow there
> That each seemed pendulous in air."

But there is no moral flavor in the constant passage of shadows of
the trees into the water, as there was in the collapse of the doomed
city. "I fancied," Poe continues, "that each shadow, as the sun descended lower and lower, separated itself sullenly from the trunk that
gave it birth and thus became absorbed by the stream; while other
shadows issued momently from the trees, taking the place of their
predecessors thus entombed."

Poe's concern with shadows was constant, and the passage of the
Fay from light to darkness has a symbolic meaning, which would require a quotation of the complete story to establish. It is prefaced by
the Sonnet "To Science," reprinted with changes which made the poem
conclude with a reference to the Fay—but Poe reverted to the earlier
form in his later revisions.

When Poe became definitely attached to *Graham's* he contributed
three criticisms in which his acute sense of literary values lifts his
work above the level of a mere review. In these he analyzed the work
of Bulwer, Dickens, and Macaulay. In April, 1841, he paid tribute to
Bulwer's plot structure in his novel, *Night and Morning*, and Poe's
definition of a plot as "that in which no part can be displaced without
ruin to the whole," has some interest. He shows that Bulwer sacrifices

nearly everything else to plot, and his general estimate of Bulwer is that of the best judgment today. When he treated *The Old Curiosity Shop* and *Master Humphrey's Clock* in May, however, he recognized in Dickens a kindred spirit. Dickens and Poe are both idealists, that is, their method is to proceed by accentuating the traits of their characters until they become ideal creations. Poe uses romantic material, of which the charm lies in its strange and unusual quality. Dickens usually, though not always, deals with familiar life. His material is classic, for that is the proper antithesis to "romantic" and not "realistic" which should refer to method of treatment and not to material. This similarity in method permitted Poe to understand the nature of Dickens' characters. "We have heard some of them called caricatures," Poe says, "but the charge is grossly ill-founded. No critical principle is more firmly based in reason than that a certain amount of exaggeration is essential in the proper depicting of truth itself. We do not paint an object to be true, but to appear true to the beholder."

Poe realized that the imagination of Dickens placed him upon a lofty plane and he then illustrated his capacity for a critical comparison by this passage:

> The art of Mr. Dickens, although elaborate and great, seems only a happy modification of Nature. In this respect he differs remarkably from the author of "Night and Morning." The latter, by excessive care and by patient reflection, aided by much rhetorical knowledge, and general information, has arrived at the capability of producing books which might be mistaken by ninety-nine readers out of a hundred for the genuine inspirations of genius. The former, by the promptings of the truest genius itself, has been brought to compose, and evidently without effort, works which have effected a long sought consummation—which have rendered him the idol of the people, while defying and enchanting the critics. Mr. Bulwer, through Art, has almost created a genius. Mr. Dickens, through genius, has perfected a standard from which Art itself will derive its essence, its rules.

This was written before Dickens had published *Bleak House, David Copperfield,* or *Great Expectations.* Poe's ability to see the weakness of a popular idol is illustrated by his critique of Macaulay's *Critical and Miscellaneous Essays,* in *Graham's* for June, 1841:

> Macaulay has obtained a reputation which, although deservedly great, is yet in a remarkable measure undeserved. The few who regard him merely as a terse, forcible, and logical writer, full of thought, and abounding in original views—often sagacious and

never otherwise than admirably expressed—appear to us precisely in the right. The many who look upon him as not only all this, but as a comprehensive and profound thinker, little prone to error, err essentially themselves. The source of the general mistake lies in a very singular consideration,—yet in one upon which we do not remember ever to have heard a word of comment. We allude to a tendency in the public mind towards logic for logic's sake—a liability to confound the vehicle with the conveyed—an aptitude to be so dazzled by the luminousness with which an idea is set forth as to mistake it for the luminousness of the idea itself. The error is one exactly analogous with that which leads the immature poet to think himself sublime wherever he is obscure, because obscurity is a source of the sublime—thus confounding obscurity of expression with the expression of obscurity. In the case of Macaulay—and we may say, *en passant*, of our own Channing—we assent to what he says, too often because we so very clearly understand what it is that he intends to say. Comprehending vividly the points and the sequence of his argument, we fancy that we are concurring in the argument itself.

If Edgar Poe were only here today, to penetrate with that critical vision which no popular acclaim could dim, the reputations which have been made by certain poets who are constantly "confounding obscurity of expression with the expression of obscurity!"

In the first volume of *Graham's* which closed in June, 1841, the contributors' names would hardly be known today; in fact, not all the contributions were signed with their real names. Poe evidently urged Graham to secure attractive names, and, more important, to pay the authors well. A letter to Longfellow illustrates one of Poe's functions as editor of *Graham's*:

Philadelphia, May 3, 1841.

Dear Sir,—Mr. George R. Graham, proprietor of Graham's Magazine, a monthly journal published in this city and edited by myself, desires me to beg of you the honor of your contribution to its pages. Upon the principle that we seldom obtain what we *very* anxiously covet, I confess that I have but little hope of inducing you to write for us,—and, to say truth, I fear that Mr. Graham would have opened the negotiation much better in his own person, for I have no reason to think myself favorably known to you; but the attempt was to be made, and I make it.

I should be overjoyed if we could get from you an article each month,—either poetry or prose,—length and subject *à discrétion.*

In respect to terms, we would gladly offer you *carte blanche;* and the periods of payment should also be made to suit yourself.

In conclusion, I cannot refrain from availing myself of this, the only opportunity I may ever have, to assure the author of the "Hymn to the Night," of the "Beleaguered City," and of the "Skeleton in Armor," of the fervent admiration with which his genius has inspired me; and yet I would scarcely hazard a declaration whose import might be so easily misconstrued, and which bears with it, at best, more or less of *niaiserie,* were I not convinced that Professor Longfellow, writing and thinking as he does, will be at no loss to feel and to appreciate the *honest sincerity* of what I say. With the highest respect,

Your obedient servant,
EDGAR A. POE [15]

Longfellow's reply indicates that he already appreciated Poe's merits:

May 19, 1841.

Your favor of the 3rd inst., with the two numbers of the Magazine, reached me only a day or two ago.

I am much obliged to you for your kind expressions of regard, and to Mr. Graham for his very generous offer, of which I should gladly avail myself under other circumstances. But I am so much occupied at present that I could not do it with any satisfaction either to you or to myself. I must therefore respectfully decline his proposition.

You are mistaken in supposing that you are not "favorably known to me." On the contrary, all that I have read from your pen has inspired me with a high idea of your power; and I think you are destined to stand among the first romance-writers of the country, if such be your aim.[16]

Poe's relation to *Graham's* was begun without any concealment of his continued desire for a magazine of his own. In fact, he believed that Graham might join him. In this project of publishing two magazines, one for a large audience and one for a more limited group at higher prices, he was only anticipating methods of magazine publish-

---

[15] *Final Memorials of Henry W. Longfellow,* Ed. by Samuel Longfellow (Boston, 1887), pp. 13-14.
[16] Samuel Longfellow, *Life of Henry Wadsworth Longfellow* (Boston, 1886), I, 376-377.

ing which have reached their peak of success today. Poe wrote to
Kennedy:

Philadelphia, June, 1841.

My dear Sir,—Mr. George R. Graham (of this city) and myself
desire to establish a Monthly Magazine upon certain conditions—
one of which is the procuring your assistance in the enterprise.
Will you permit me to send a few words on the subject?

I need not call your attention to the signs of the times in respect
to magazine literature. You will admit that the tendency of the
age lies in this way—so far at least as regards the lighter letters.
The brief, the terse, the condensed, and the readily circulated
will take place of the diffuse, the ponderous, and the inaccessible.
Even our reviews (*lucus a non lucendo*) are found too massive
for the taste of the day: I do not mean for the taste of the taste-
less, but also for that of the few. In the mean time the finest minds
of Europe are beginning to lend their spirit to magazines. In this
country, unhappily, we have not any journal of the class which
either can afford to offer pecuniary inducement to the highest
talent, or which would be, in all respects, a fitting vehicle for its
thoughts. In the supply of this deficiency there would be a point
gained.

Mr. Graham is a lawyer, but for some years past has been
occupied in publishing. His experience of the periodical business
is extensive. He is a gentleman of high social standing, and
possessed of ample pecuniary means. Together we would enter
the field with a full knowledge of the difficulties to be encountered, and with perfect assurance of being able to overcome them.

The work will be an octavo of 96 pages. The paper will be of
excellent quality—far superior to that of the "North American
Review." The type will be new (always new), clear, and bold,
with distinct face. The matter will be disposed in a single column.
The printing will be done upon a hand-press in the best manner.
There will be a broad margin. There will be no engravings, except occasional wood cuts (by Adams) when demanded in obvious illustration of the text; and, when so required, they will be
worked in with the type—not upon separate pages as in "Arcturus." The stitching will be done in the French style, permitting
the book to lie fully open. Upon the cover, and throughout, the
endeavour will be to preserve the greatest purity of taste consistent with decision and force. The price will be five dollars.

I believe I sent you, some time ago, a Prospectus of the "Penn

Magazine," the scheme of which was broken up by the breaking up of the banks. The name will be preserved—and the general intentions, of that journal. A vigorous independence shall be my watchword still—*truth*, not so much for truth's sake, as for the sake of the novelty of the thing.

The chief feature in the literary department will be that of contributions from the most distinguished pens (of America) exclusively: or if this plan cannot be wholly carried out, we propose, at least, to procure the aid of some five or six of the most distinguished—admitting no articles from other sources, none which are not of a high order of merit. We shall endeavor to engage the permanent service of yourself, Mr. Irving, Mr. Cooper, Mr. Paulding, Mr. Longfellow, Mr. Bryant, Mr. Halleck, Mr. Willis, and one or two others. In fact, our ability to make these arrangements is a condition without which the Magazine will not go into operation; and my object in writing you this letter is to ascertain how far I may look to yourself for aid.

It would be desirable that you should agree to furnish one paper each month—prose or poetry, absolute or serial,—and of such length as you might deem proper. Should illustrations be desired by you, these will be engraved at our expense, from designs at your own, superintended by yourself. We leave the matter of terms, as before, to your own decision. The sums agreed upon would be paid as you might suggest. It would be necessary that our agreement should be made for one year—during which period you should be pledged not to write for any other (American) Magazine. The journal will not be commenced until the first of January, 1842.

I look most anxiously for your answer, for it is of vital importance to me, personally. This you will see at once. Mr. Graham is to furnish all supplies, and will give me merely for editorial service and my list of subscribers to the old "Penn" a half interest in the proposed Magazine—but he will only engage in the enterprise on the conditions before stated—on condition that I can obtain as contributors the gentlemen above named—or at least the most of them—giving them carte blanche as to terms. Your name will enable me, I know, to get several of the others. You will not fail me at this crisis! If I get this Magazine fairly afloat, with money to back me as now, I will have everything my own way.

With this letter I despatch one of the same tenor to each of

the gentlemen before named. If you cannot consent to an unconditional reply, will you be kind enough to say whether you will
write for us upon condition that we succeed in our engagements
with the others—specifying what others.

Most truly yours,

EDGAR A. POE.

John P. Kennedy, Esq.

N. B.   If you have a novel on the tapis, you could not dispose of
it in any way so advantageously as by selling it to us. You would
get more for it than L. & B. would give. It would be printed in
finer style than they could afford to print it—and it would have a
far wider circulation in our Magazine than in book form. We will
commence with an edition of 3000.[17]

Poe wrote similar letters to Irving,[18] to Longfellow, to Fitz-Greene
Halleck, and to the others named. In a letter to Snodgrass in September, 1841, he still has hopes of Graham's coöperation, but the
inquiry concerning Baltimore reveals Poe's growing doubts on that
subject:

Philadelphia,—Sep. 19. 41.

My Dear Snodgrass,

I seize the first moment of leisure to say a few words in reply
to yours of Sep. 6.

Touching the "Reproof of a Bird," I hope you will give yourself no uneasiness about it. We don't mind the contretemps; and
as for Godey, it serves him right, as you say. The moment I saw
the article in the "Lady's Book," I saw at once how it all happened.

You are mistaken about "The Dial." I have no quarrel in the
world with that illustrious journal, nor it with me. I am not aware
that it ever mentioned my name, or alluded to me either directly
or indirectly. My slaps at it were only in "a general way." The
tale in question is a mere Extravaganza levelled at no one in
particular, but hitting right & left at things in general.

---

[17] Original Autograph Ms., Peabody Institute, Baltimore.
[18] See Stanley T. Williams, *The Life of Washington Irving* (New York,
1935), II, 358, where the letter to Irving is reprinted in part. See Woodberry, I, 277-280, for the letter to Longfellow. The letter to Halleck is in
Ms. at the Huntington Library. Rep. in Virginia Ed., XVII, 89. They differ
somewhat, but Kennedy's is most inclusive.

The "Knickerbocker" has been purchased by Otis Broaders & Co of Boston. I believe it is still edited by Clark the brother of W. Gaylord.

Thank you for attending to the Kennedy matter. We have no news here just yet—something may turn up by & bye. It is not impossible that Graham will join me in The "Penn." He has money. By the way, is it impossible to start a first-class Mag. in Baltimore? Is there no publisher or gentleman of moderate capital who would join me in the scheme?—publishing the work in the City of Monuments.

Do write me soon & tell me the news,
Yours most cordially
EDGAR A. POE.[19]

Poe's hopes and plans are made clear through his letters to Snodgrass or to Frederick W. Thomas, who, though born in Providence, Rhode Island, liked to think of himself as belonging to Charleston, South Carolina, where, indeed, he spent his childhood. He was a lawyer with literary leanings and side glances at politics, who had met Henry Poe in Baltimore before Edgar had joined the Clemm household. Coming East to the Baltimore Convention in May, 1840, he met Edgar Poe in Philadelphia afterwards, and their friendship remained constant.[20] Thomas had published in 1835 a novel of city life, *Clinton Bradshaw*, with quite realistic descriptions of its seamy side. Poe had reviewed the novel unfavorably in the *Southern Literary Messenger* in December, 1835, but after he knew Thomas, he praised it for "A frank, unscrupulous portraiture of men and things, in high life and low." [21] Incidentally, Poe was much more correct in his revised judgment, for *Clinton Bradshaw* is quite refreshing among the sentimental novels with a similar background.

In May, 1841, Thomas wrote to Poe, suggesting that his friend apply for an office under the Tyler administration. Thomas, who had secured a temporary clerkship in the Treasury Department, painted a glowing picture of the life of an office holder who left his desk at two o'clock, and if he had anything to do, "found it an agreeable relaxation

[19] Original Autograph Ms., Huntington Library. The tale in question was "Never Bet Your Head," which appeared in the September number of *Graham's*.

[20] His letter to Poe, August 3, 1841, in the Boston Public Library gives full details concerning his life. He was lame in consequence of a fall.

[21] "A Chapter on Autography," *Graham's Magazine*, December, 1841.

from the monotonous laziness of the day." Thomas also remarked that everything was in apple pie order on the desk, and "if you choose to lucubrate in a literary way, why you can lucubrate." [22] Poe replied on June 26th:

> I have just heard through Graham, who obtained his information from Ingraham, that you have stepped into an office at Washington—salary $1000. From the bottom of my heart I wish you joy. You can now lucubrate more at your ease & will infallibly do something worthy yourself.
>
> For my own part, notwithstanding Graham's unceasing civility and real kindness, I feel more & more disgusted with my situation. Would to God, I could do as you have done. Do you seriously think that an application on my part to Tyler would have a good result? My claims, to be sure, are few. I am a Virginian—at least I call myself one, for I have resided all my life, until within the last few years, in Richmond. My political principles have always been, as nearly as may be, with the existing administration, and I battled with right good-will for Harrison, when opportunity offered. With Mr. Tyler I have some slight personal acquaintance—although this is a matter which he has possibly forgotten. For the rest, I am a literary man—and I see a disposition in government to cherish letters. Have I any chance? I would be greatly indebted to you if you reply to this as soon as you can, and tell me if it would, in your opinion, be worth my while to make an effort—and, if so—put me upon the right track. This could not be better done than by detailing to me your own mode of proceeding. [23]

Thomas replied to Poe on July 1st, suggesting that Poe come down himself, and that Kennedy's influence be secured. He also acknowledged frankly that he had not seen Tyler himself, although he knew the President's sons. Poe wrote again on July 4, 1841:

> My Dear Thomas,
> I rec⁴ yours of the 1st this morning, and have again to thank you for the interest you take in my welfare. I wish to God I could visit Washington—but the old story, you know—I have no money—not even enough to take me there, saying nothing of

---

[22] Original Autograph Ms., Griswold Collection, Boston Public Library.
[23] Original Autograph Ms.. Anthony Collection, New York Public Library.

getting back. It is a hard thing to be poor—but as I am kept so by an honest motive I dare not complain.

Your suggestion about Mr. Kennedy is well-timed, and here, Thomas, you can do me a true service. Call upon Kennedy—you know him, I believe—if not, introduce yourself—he is a perfect gentleman and will give you cordial welcome. Speak to him of my wishes, and urge him to see the Secretary of War in my behalf—or one of the other Secretaries—or President Tyler. I mention in particular the Secretary of War, because I have been to W. Point, and this may stand me in some stead. I would be glad to get almost any appointment—even a $500 one—so that I have something independent of letters for a subsistence. To coin one's brain into silver, at the nod of a master, is to my thinking, the hardest task in the world. Mr. Kennedy has been, at all times, a true friend to me—he was the first true friend I ever had—I am indebted to him *for life itself*. He will be willing to help me now— but *needs urging*, for he is always head and ears in business. Thomas, may I depend upon you? By the way, I wrote to Mr. K. about ten days ago on the subject of a Magazine—a project of mine in conjunction with Graham—and have not yet heard from him. Ten to one I misdirected the letter, or sent it to Baltimore —for I am very thoughtless about such matters.[24]

Poe evidently was experiencing that dread of having written himself out which comes, at times, to every writer. Thomas wrote again on July 19th [25] telling Poe that though he had attended a formal dinner at the White House he had had no opportunity to speak to the President, and that he was to see Kennedy who was in the House of Representatives. The matter dragged on through the summer of 1841. Tyler was in difficulty owing to his inability to reconcile his natural feeling as a Southern Democrat with the policies of the Whig party, which had elected him. He was also resisting the clamor of Whig office seekers who were having their first opportunity at the public crib. The appointment of a man of letters to a clerkship was evidently not a matter of vital concern to him.

In this effort to obtain a government position, Poe met his customary hard luck. He was a Whig, and only twice during their history were

[24] Original Autograph Ms., Author's Club, New York. From photostat furnished by New York Public Library. The remainder of this long letter deals with cryptography.

[25] Original Autograph Ms., Griswold Collection, Boston Public Library.

the Whigs in power in Washington. Irving had succeeded in spite of his Federalist leanings in adapting himself to the Democratic party sufficiently to permit him to accept the diplomatic posts which his real ability deserved. Cooper and Hawthorne were Democrats and Hawthorne had the good fortune to possess influential friends like Bancroft and devoted college mates like Pierce, who provided him with offices from 1839 to 1841, from 1846 to 1849, and from 1853 to 1857. What would have happened to him without this help, may only be surmised. Yet from the point of view of his creative achievements, Poe's ill-fortune in political preferment was a distinct gain to us. Hawthorne published very little during his term of office in the Salem Custom House, and during his Consulate at Liverpool, nothing at all. Poe would have suffered fewer hardships had Tyler appointed him to office in July, 1841. But we might not have "Eleonora," "The Mask of the Red Death," "The Pit and the Pendulum," or "The Gold Bug."

Poe's personal relations with Graham were friendly. *Graham's* was growing in circulation, and Poe must have had his share in establishing the policy of paying good prices to those authors who had interesting stories, essays, or poems to contribute. Graham depended on him even more for his ability to discover new talent.

In the second volume of *Graham's*, which ran from July to December, 1841, Lowell contributed to the October number his "Ballad," a turgid and immature poem which he declined to reprint in his collected works. Poe spoke in high praise of it in his "Autography," but the judgment of time is with Lowell. If the names of the contributors still are comparatively unknown to modern readers, there were several popular favorites of that day.

There were poets like George P. Morris, the author of "Woodman, Spare that Tree," Henry B. Hirst, of Philadelphia, whose lyrics were not at all bad, Mrs. E. Clementine Stedman, whose more famous son was to write one of the best essays on Poe and edit a standard edition of his works. Romantic novelists like J. H. Ingraham, whose work was so popular that publishers, to his great annoyance, attributed other men's novels to him, were plowing the fields of history. Theodore S. Fay, whose *Norman Leslie* Poe had reviewed so unmercifully, was represented with three long papers on Shakespeare.

Against the background of these productions, Poe's own contributions to *Graham's* stand out in a quality which, unfortunately, received less recognition in 1841 than it does today. His short story, "The Colloquy of Monos and Una," is at once an interpretation of the after life and a criticism of the life from which these lovers have departed. Naturally, the latter is the easier task, and Poe relieved himself of his dislike of the Jacksonian era in one of those half truths which have expressed the philosophy of oligarchy through all ages: "He [man] grew infected with system, and with abstraction. He enwrapped himself in generalities. Among other odd ideas, that of universal equality gained ground; and in the face of analogy and of God —in despite of the loud warning voice of the laws of *gradation* so visibly pervading all things in Earth and Heaven—wild attempts at an omni-prevalent Democracy were made." The only cure was to be born again in a new life. Into the description of that new life, Poe carried his favorite theme, that of "identity." The senses lose their identity. "The taste and the smell were inextricably confounded, and became one sentiment, abnormal and intense." ... Sight was appreciated only as sound, sound sweet or discordant, as the matters presenting themselves were light or dark in shade. A sixth sense, that of duration, rose out of the ashes of the others, and gave Monos a wild delight. This sense "was the first obvious and certain step of the intemporal soul upon the threshold of the temporal Eternity." If "Monos and Una" is not meat for babes, it nevertheless avoids that absurdity into which nearly all descriptions of the after life have fallen. Poe does not carry over temporal limitations into eternity, with the consequent contradictions that arise. For sense of individual being departs and "the autocrats Place and Time" are dominant. "Monos and Una" was one of the preliminary steps to "Eureka."

Poe contributed quite a different story to the September number, "Never Bet Your Head, A Moral Tale." It is an amusing satire on things in general, the New England Transcendentalists in particular, and contains a defence by Poe against the charge that he had never written a moral tale. It may be a burlesque on some moralist of an earlier period.[26] In any event, it is a trifle. But in the same number, almost lost to view at the bottom of a page, Poe printed a revised version of "To Helen," in which for the first time the two lines

> "To the glory that was Greece
> To the grandeur that was Rome,"

contain the magnificent contrast of civilizations which has already been analyzed.[27]

[26] See James S. Wilson, "The Devil Was In It," *American Mercury*, XXIV (1931), 215-220.
[27] Pp. 177-179.

"Israfel" was printed in October, again improved by verbal changes extending to the insertion of new lines and omission of others. There is no such vital change, however, as there had been in "To Helen."

The only important criticism contributed by Poe to the second volume of *Graham's* was his review of his friend Wilmer's "Quacks of Helicon," a verse satire on the *literati* of that time. It gave Poe an opportunity to attack the literary and publishing cliques who vied with each other in overpraising their friends. It must have been some concrete and definite injury to Poe's own reputation which prompted him to say:

"And if, in one, or perhaps two, insulated cases, the spirit of severe truth, sustained by an unconquerable will, was not to be put down, then, forthwith, were private chicaneries set in motion; then was had resort, on the part of those who considered themselves injured by the severity of criticism (and who were so, if the just contempt of every ingenuous man is injury) resort to arts of the most virulent indignity, to untraceable slanders, to ruthless assassination in the dark."

It would be a mistake to dismiss this protest as a result of a mania of persecution on Poe's part. It was a time of ruthless warfare, political, religious, and economic, in which both Henry Clay and Martin van Buren lost the presidency by daring to publish a courageous statement of principle. It was not to be expected that a courageous literary critic would be exempt from reprisals. In this review Poe defined true criticism as "a reflection of the thing criticized upon the spirit of the critic." He also made a cutting attack on vulgarity.

Poe contributed during 1841 two series of articles to *Graham's* which were inspired by his sure instincts as a journalist. They were articles on cryptography and on autography. Poe was interested in the solution of cryptograms early in 1840, judging from his statement in July, 1841, in *Graham's* [28] that "in one of the weekly papers of this city, about eighteen months ago, the writer of this article ... ventured to assert that no cipher of the character above described could be sent to the address of the paper, which he would not be able to resolve." [29] According to his own statement, Poe received about one hundred

[28] "A Few Words on Secret Writing," *Graham's Magazine*, XIX (July, 1841), 33-38.

[29] *Alexander's Weekly Messenger*. Poe's article, "Enigmatical and Conundrum-ical," in the issue of December 18, 1839, includes the offer to solve cryptograms. Many solutions appeared, January 1 to April 29, 1840. The file for 1839 (in the Ohio State Hist. Soc.) was examined by Dr. Mabbott. While my book is in press an article will appear describing a file for 1840, now in the American Antiquarian Society.

cryptograms, all of which he solved but one, which he proved was impossible of solution.

In April, 1841, while reviewing R. M. Walsh's translation of *Sketches of Conspicuous Living Characters of France*,[30] Poe spoke of the difficulty of solving cryptograms in a foreign language, but issued a new challenge: "Anyone who will take the trouble, may address us a note, in the same manner as here proposed, and the key-phrase may be either in French, Italian, Spanish, German, Latin or Greek (or in any of the dialects of these languages), and we pledge ourselves for the solution of the riddle. The experiment may afford our readers some amusement—let them try it."

Poe announced in the July issue that he had received only one reply to this challenge, including two cryptograms, and he presented them with their solutions. Of these, he added that "the second proved to be exceedingly difficult, and it was only by calling every faculty into play that we could read it at all."

It has recently been stated upon good authority [31] that Poe's knowledge of cryptography was that of an amateur, that the difficulties of the specimens he solved existed largely in his own imagination, or were overemphasized. On the other hand, Poe was consulted by the Land Office of the United States, through Dr. Frailey, who sent him a writing in cipher for solution.[32] The late Colonel John M. Manly, of the Intelligence Service of the United States, spent much effort in trying to find the missing numbers of *Alexander's Weekly Messenger,* in order to read Poe's articles. I feel naturally incompetent to settle the question of Poe's ability. Poe continued the discussion through August, October, and December, 1841, and discontinued his offers when he felt they no longer were serving to attract readers to the

---

[30] *Graham's Magazine,* XVIII (April, 1841), 203. One of the "characters" in Walsh's article, incidentally, was named "Dupin."

[31] See "Edgar Allan Poe, Cryptographer," by William F. Friedman, Office of the Chief Signal Officer, War Department, Washington, D. C., *American Literature,* VIII (January, 1937), 266-280. Mr. Friedman states that this cryptogram which Poe described as so difficult was solved in thirty-five minutes by persons who had had exactly ten days' study of cryptography. He also seems to prove that the difficulty of the cipher sent to Poe by F. W. Thomas, and composed by Dr. Charles S. Frailey, was due not to its complexity but to the outrageous character of its diction. He also called attention to Poe's misquotation of Lord Bacon's remarks on ciphers in *De Augmentis,* and suggested the probability that Poe was quoting at second hand.

[32] Autograph Ms. Letter, Thomas to Poe, May 12, 1845, Griswold Collection, Boston Public Library.

magazine. If he did not rise to professional levels, he certainly was far above the average reader in his knowledge of the subject. The principal result was to lead him to the writing of "The Gold Bug."

In November, 1841, Poe published "A Chapter on Autography," which he continued in December and in January, 1842. In the *Southern Literary Messenger* he had used the autographs of well known authors in a humorous way by representing them as replying to a letter which was entirely imaginary. In *Graham's* he presented the autographs, followed by a brief paragraph, in which he described the literary, and, at times, the personal characters of about one hundred American writers. It was a journalistic device and was probably of some interest to readers of the magazine. Today it is valuable partly to inform us who these writers were, for outside of elderly biographical dictionaries it would be hard to find any information about some of them. It is also interesting to see Poe's early opinions of men like Lowell, Longfellow, and Emerson. Longfellow, whom Poe placed in "the chair of Moral Philosophy" at Harvard, "is entitled to the first place among the poets of America, certainly to the first place among those who have put themselves prominently forward as poets." Here Poe was probably filing, as it were, a reservation against the day when *he* would once more resume the art he held for a time in abeyance. Lowell is placed second only to Longfellow, "and perhaps one other," who again is not named. Emerson is placed among "a class of gentlemen with whom we have no patience whatever—the mystic for mysticism's sake." Poe, however, selected among Emerson's poetry "The Sphynx" [sic], "The Problem" and "The Snowstorm" for favorable comment and, on the whole, treated his contemporary more justly than did Emerson, who dismissed Poe much later with the phrase, "the jingle-man." Poe treated Burton very gently, and Griswold with high praise. In turning over the pages of the "Autography," one is struck with the large number of writers who were editors. Some of these were given sly digs, others praised generously, a few of the paragraphs like that upon Lewis Gaylord Clark, of the *Knickerbocker*, were later to rebound on Poe's head.

Poe did not limit himself to *Graham's* so far as his creative work was concerned. In the *Gift* for 1842 [33] which was out in the fall of

[33] "Eleonora" was printed in the *New York Weekly Tribune*, Vol. I, No. 1, Saturday, September 18, 1841, columns four and five, as "From the Gift for 1842." It appeared even earlier with a similar note, in the Boston *Notion* for September 4, 1841. Annuals seem usually to have come out about October, but in this instance a publication date of about September 1, 1841, is suggested for the *Gift* for 1842.

1841, appeared "Eleonora," one of his finest stories. It is the idealized, the spiritualized version of the theme of spiritual integrity, made concrete by its association with the death of a beautiful woman. In "Morella" and "Ligeia" the changes in the identity of the woman who is loved and lost are wrought in a mood of terror. But in "Eleonora" the atmosphere is conceived in terms of peace and beauty. "Eleonora" and her lover have always dwelt together, with her mother, in the "Valley of the Many-Colored Grass." Love comes to them when he is twenty, and she fifteen, and it is a passionate love, which deepens the tints of the green carpet, and changes the white daisies to ruby red asphodels. Eleonora's beauty is of the ethereal kind: "In stature she was tall, and slender even to fragility; the exceeding delicacy of her frame, as well as of the hues of her cheek, speaking painfully of the feeble tenure by which she held existence. The lilies of the valley were not more fair. With the nose, lips and chin of the Greek Venus, she had the majestic forehead, the naturally-waving auburn hair, and the large luminous eyes of her kindred. Her beauty, nevertheless, was of that nature which leads the heart to wonder not less than to love." [34]

When Eleonora dies, her one grief is a fear that her lover will replace her image in his heart. He vows never to do so, and for years lives "with the aged mother of Eleonora." [35] When he marries Ermengarde, there is no struggle. The voice of Eleonora comes to him as an immaterial sigh, absolving him "for reasons which shall be made known to thee in Heaven, of thy vows unto Eleonora." Perhaps it was Poe's way of telling Virginia that no matter what happened, she was his mate for eternity.

A sentence in "Eleonora" is of great help in understanding the differences in Poe's treatment of the same underlying theme: "The question is not yet settled—whether madness is or is not the loftiest intelligence —whether much that is glorious, whether all that is profound—does not spring from disease of thought—from moods of mind, exalted at the expense of the general intellect."

When the mood is spiritual, as in "Eleonora," the intellect yields to its guidance and the result is ideal. When the mood is horrible, as in "Berenice," the thought becomes diseased, and the intellect, being subverted to the mood, has no restraining influence. This accounts for the wildness, the undue emphasis of horror in some of Poe's

[34] This description in the story as it appeared in the *Gift* was omitted in the *Broadway Journal*, and is not given in the usual reproductions.
[35] This phrase is also omitted from the later versions.

stories, even for the lapse from artistic sanity in "The Facts in the Case of M. Valdemar."

"A Succession of Sundays" was published on November 27, 1841, in the *Saturday Evening Post*. It is one of the Grotesques—in which a crusty guardian promises to permit two lovers to marry when "Three Sundays came together in a week." The story is hardly more than an incident, although the explanation of the travellers whose arrival proves the possibility of the occurrence, is carried on in conversation more lively than is usual with Poe.[36]

According to an editorial statement in the December issue of 1841, the subscription list of *Graham's* had grown from 5,500 to 25,000. The editorial staff was increased by "two lady editors," Mrs. Ann S. Stephens and Mrs. E. C. Embury, while George R. Graham, Charles J. Peterson and Edgar A. Poe also remained. John Sartain quite naïvely attributed this success to the appeal of his engravings, which decorated a number of the issues.

The policy of an editor can be reflected in a monthly magazine only after a certain interval, and the third volume, the last one of which Poe was editor, showed a decided advance. The magazine was increased from fifty-three to seventy-two pages. Longfellow appears in January, 1842, for the first time, with his "Goblet of Life." He also contributed a paper on Heinrich Heine in March, 1842. Lowell sent verse with regularity, better in quality than before, even if in "Rosaline" he spoke of "cold worms" crawling about a dead woman. Perhaps he had been affected by Poe's earlier use of the same unpleasant phrasing in "Irene"!

In March, 1842, a new contributor, Frances Osgood, appeared as the author of a sentimental story, "May Evelyn." It was the first association of Poe and Mrs. Osgood, to lead later to a warm friendship, unpleasant complications, and a spirited defence of Poe after his death. Mrs. Osgood's verse, which appeared in later issues of *Graham's*, was better than her fiction. Indeed, her dramatic narrative, "The Daughters of Herodias" can be read even now without apology. It did not appear until July, but Poe had probably arranged for it before he gave up the editorship in May of 1842.

Poe gave to *Graham's* two fine stories during his final months with the magazine. "Life in Death," which later became "The Oval Por-

[36] Those interested will find the source of this story in the Philadelphia *Public Ledger*, October 29, 1841, when "Three Thursdays in One Week" appeared anonymously. See F. N. Cherry, *American Literature*, II (November, 1930), 232-235.

trait," appeared in April, 1842. It is a brief pastel, told by a desperately wounded man who seeks refuge in an unoccupied château, and sees the portrait of a young and beautiful girl, which startles him by its likeness to life. Finding an old volume that describes the paintings, he learns her story. She had given her life to please her husband, an artist, who, as he painted into his picture her marvellous beauty, drained from her her health and spirits. Finally, when he gazed on his completed work and cried out, "This is indeed Life itself," he beheld his bride dead before him. The similarity of theme to Hawthorne's "The Birthmark" which was to appear in *The Pioneer* in March, 1843, is apparent, but Hawthorne's treatment is so different that there can be no question of plagiarism.

"The Mask of the Red Death," which was published in May, represents Poe at his height in that form of the Arabesques in which he let his fancy create a mood of terror wrought out of the symbolism of color. The description of the luxurious chambers of Prince Prospero leads, step by step, to the flaming scarlet of the last room, which throws its weird light against the ebony blackness of the velvet curtains. But no paraphrase can give an idea of the effect of Poe's language, when each sentence seems so inevitable. The resources of rhetoric have rarely been so marvellously employed. At the very outset the contrast between the interest of the Abbey and the outside world, where the pestilence rages, is established with finality:

"The external world could take care of itself. In the meantime, it was folly to grieve, or to think. The prince had provided all the appliances of pleasure. There were buffoons, there were improvisatori, there were ballet dancers, there were musicians, there was Beauty, there was wine. All these and security were within. Without was the 'Red Death.'"

The phantom figure of the Red Death touches no one, and when at last the revellers find courage to attack him, there is nothing tangible within the ghastly cerements, dabbled with blood, which had apparently shrouded his form. With a restraint that is one of the surest marks of genius, Poe gives no hint of the great moral the tale tells to those who can think. For the others, he had no message.

There was no poetry by Poe in this last volume, except "To One Departed," which was in process of being transferred from "Mary (?)," its original inspiration, by way of a "Seraph," to Mrs. Osgood. The stanzas are inverted in *Graham's*.

Poe's theory of criticism as distinguished from his critical theory is expressed in his "Exordium," which began the review columns in

Graham's in January, 1842. He sounded his protest against the undue emphasis upon a national literature—"as if any true literature could be national—as if the world at large were not the only proper stage for the literary histrio." Poe was objecting not to a national point of view, but to a parochial one, a limitation of our writers to "American themes" which Longfellow was to criticize in 1848 in *Kavanagh*. It is a limitation which is still urged upon our creative artists, and which has never been imposed upon any other race. If it had, we should not possess *Hamlet* or the *Merchant of Venice*.

Poe next called attention to the habit of certain critics of neglecting the book reviewed in order to tell all they know about the subject. This manner has also persisted until today. In order to make his point, he confines criticism to a comment upon Art, and apparently objects to a discussion of the material of the book. Fortunately, he did not limit himself so strictly. He concludes with a description of the perfect critic: "And of the critic himself what shall we say?—for as yet we have spoken only the *proem* to the true *epopea*. What *can* we better say of him than, with Bulwer, that 'he must have courage to blame boldly, magnanimity to eschew envy, genius to appreciate, learning to compare, an eye for beauty, an ear for music, and a heart for feeling.' Let us add, a talent for analysis and a solemn indifference to abuse."

Poe lived up to his standard in his lengthy review of Dickens' *Barnaby Rudge* in February, 1842. His elaborate retelling of the plot was probably due to his desire to call attention to his own skill in foretelling the solution of the murder mystery as early as May 1, 1841, in the *Saturday Evening Post*. Poe was not overly modest in this reference to his solution. The earlier review in the *Post* states that he had Parts I, II, and III, of *Barnaby Rudge* before him, in other words, eleven chapters.[37] He did see that Rudge was the murderer, but he made mistakes in other prophecies, announcing that Geoffrey Haredale had been instrumental in his brother's murder, and that Barnaby would be instrumental in bringing on his father's arrest. Neither turned out to be correct.[38] Poe did not establish any profound critical

[37] Part II contained Chapters IV to VII, Part III, Chapters VIII to XI. Part I appeared March 10, 1841. The remaining numbers were dated simply 1841.

[38] The review in the *Post* is not easy to find. It is reprinted complete in the *New York Times Literary Supplement* for June 1, 1913, Magazine Section, Part V, under title of "Famous Dickens-Poe Mystery Solved at Last." The *Post* review is quoted entire in *The Dickensian*, II (London, 1913), 174-178, evidently from the *Times*.

principles in either review, and he yielded to temptation in printing destructive criticisms like that on Cornelius Mathews' *Wakondah*. Some years later he apologized to Mathews for this review, in a manly and self-respecting letter.

But Poe signalized his departure from the editorial staff of *Graham's* by two remarkable pieces of constructive criticism, both dealing with American writers. The first was an extended critique of Longfellow's *Ballads*. In March, he compared Longfellow and Lowell, and placed them at the head, so far as America went, of the new school of poetry which had the ideal as its aim. In the April number, he continued his critique and used the occasion to re-state his theory of poetry with an enthusiasm and an eloquence which proves conclusively that it is as a poet that Poe must ultimately be judged:

> An important condition of man's immortal nature is thus, plainly, the sense of the Beautiful. This it is which ministers to his delight in the manifold forms and colors and sounds and senti- ments amid which he exists. And, just as the eyes of Amaryllis are repeated in the mirror, or the living lily in the lake, so is the mere *record* of these forms and colors and sounds and sentiments —so is their mere oral or written repetition a duplicate source of delight. But this repetition is not Poesy. He who shall merely sing with whatever rapture, in however harmonious strains, or with however vivid a truth of imitation, of the sights and sounds which greet him in common with all mankind—he, we say, has yet failed to prove his divine title. There is still a longing unsatisfied, which he has been impotent to fulfil. There is still a thirst unquenchable, which to allay he has shown us no crystal springs. This burning thirst belongs to the *immortal* essence of man's nature. It is equally a consequence and an indication of his perennial life. It is the desire of the moth for the star. It is not the mere apprecia- tion of the beauty before us. It is a wild effort to reach the beauty above. It is a forethought of the loveliness to come. It is a passion to be satiated by no sublunary sights, or sounds, or sentiments, and the soul thus athirst strives to allay its fever in futile efforts at creation. Inspired with a prescient ecstasy of the beauty beyond the grave, it struggles by multiform novelty of combination among the things and thoughts of Time, to anticipate some por- tion of that loveliness whose very elements, perhaps, appertain solely to Eternity. And the result of such effort, on the part of souls fittingly constituted. is alone what mankind have agreed to denominate Poetry.

After discussing the various elements out of which Poetry is created, he arrived at its definition:

> To recapitulate, then, we would define in brief the Poetry of words as the *Rhythmical Creation of Beauty*. Beyond the limits of Beauty its province does not extend. Its sole arbiter is Taste. With the Intellect or with the Conscience it has only collateral relations. It has no dependence, unless incidentally, upon either Duty or *Truth*.

Poe used truth in a special sense, of course. He was opposed to the didactic, but there is no essential untruth in Poe's poetry. Indeed, in selecting the best of Longfellow's ballads for comment, he says, "We would mention as poems *nearly true*, 'The Village Blacksmith,' 'The Wreck of the Hesperus' and especially 'The Skeleton in Armor.' " It is striking that Poe should have celebrated "the beauty of simple mindedness" in "The Village Blacksmith," and answered fifty years in advance the sophisticated criticism which relegates Longfellow to a lower rank because he dared to deal with the fundamental relations of life.

Poe found in "The Skeleton in Armor" a pure and perfect thesis, artistically treated. He defended Longfellow from a recent criticism in the *Democratic Review*, which objected to his having "but one idea" in each poem. Poe rightly dwelt here upon the unity in Longfellow's poetry, although he had not always recognized it.[39] This appreciation of Longfellow is important because it represented Poe's sane judgment before personal and unworthy considerations began to sway him. It also proved that Poe was broad minded enough to find great beauty in the work of a poet "whose conception of the aims of poesy is all wrong"—according to Poe's standards.

The second constructive criticism was the now famous review of Hawthorne's *Twice Told Tales*, which began with a brief notice in April and was continued in May of 1842. Poe began the May number with the recognition that many of the *Twice Told Tales* were not short stories, but, rather, essays, and he placed them above similar familiar essays in the *Spectator*, on account of their originality. Poe's understanding of his great rival is in some ways extraordinary, but is explainable. We have only to call up the picture of Poe as he wrote this sentence: "These effusions of Mr. Hawthorne are the product of a truly imaginative intellect, restrained, and in some measure repressed, by fastidiousness of taste, by constitutional melancholy and by in-

---

[39] See p. 295.

dolence." While we are trying to fit the words to the brooding artist in Salem, the thought must occur to us—how well they describe the writer himself as he pens them in Philadelphia.

Poe made clear that he believed the highest expression of genius lay in "the composition of a rhymed poem, not to exceed in length what might be perused in an hour." But he continues:

> Were we called upon, however, to designate that class of composition which, next to such a poem as we have suggested, should best fulfil the demands of high genius—should offer it the most advantageous field of exertion—we should unhesitatingly speak of the prose tale, as Mr. Hawthorne has here exemplified it. We allude to the short prose narrative, requiring from a half-hour to one or two hours in its perusal. . . .
>
> A skilful literary artist has constructed a tale. If wise, he has not fashioned his thoughts to accommodate his incidents; but having conceived, with deliberate care, a certain unique or single *effect* to be wrought out, he then invents such incidents—he then combines such events as may best aid him in establishing this preconceived effect. If his very initial sentence tend not to the outbringing of this effect, then he has failed in his first step. In the whole composition there should be no word written, of which the tendency, direct or indirect, is not to the one pre-established design. And by such means, with such care and skill, a picture is at length painted which leaves in the mind of him who contemplates it with a kindred art, a sense of the fullest satisfaction. The idea of the tale has been presented unblemished, because undisturbed; and this is an end unattainable by the novel. Undue brevity is just as exceptionable here as in the poem; but undue length is yet more to be avoided.

This passage has often been reprinted, beginning with Poe's own repetition in his review of *Mosses from an Old Manse*, in *Godey's Lady's Book* in November, 1847. It belongs, however, in any study of Poe, for it represents him at his best critical form. This is really constructive criticism, for all later writers on the art of fiction have had to quote it, and it has become the standard definition of a short story. Poe then proceeded to classify prose tales, speaking of the ratiocinative, the humorous and the sarcastic. He did not mention, however, the short stories of character.

Poe's praise of Hawthorne is all embracing, and in view of his later criticism of the *Mosses* for lack of originality, it is interesting to find him saying in 1842, "Mr. Hawthorne is original at all points."

One delightful slip Poe made. He thought he detected a plagiarism from himself in Hawthorne's "Howe's Masquerade," and he quoted the passage in which General Howe faces the figure in the cloak and drops his own mask and cloak on the floor. Poe then compares this scene with a similar one in "William Wilson," and establishes the deadly parallel. He would not have been so explicit had he known that "Howe's Masquerade" had been published in the *Democratic Review* for May, 1838, over a year before "William Wilson" appeared in the *Gift!*

In August, 1841, Poe made an attempt to publish another collection of his short stories. He wrote to his former publishers:

Mess. Lea & Blanchard,
     Gentlemen,
            I wish to publish a new collection of my prose Tales with some such title as this—

"The Prose Tales of Edgar A. Poe, Including "The Murders in the Rue Morgue," The "Descent into The Maelström," and all his later pieces, with a second edition of the "Tales of the Grotesque and Arabesque." The "later pieces" will be eight in number, making the entire collection thirty-three—which would occupy two *thick* novel volumes.

I am anxious that your firm should continue to be my publishers, and, if you would be willing to bring out the book, I should be glad to accept the terms which you allowed me before —that is—you receive all profits, and allow me twenty copies for distribution to friends.

Will you be kind enough to give me an early reply to this letter, and believe me
         Yours very resp'y.,

               EDGAR A POE

Philadelphia,
Office Graham's Magazine,
  August 13/41.[40]

Lea and Blanchard declined the request promptly on August 16th, on the ground that the original edition had not yet been sold. Poe did not give up the idea, however. Sometime during 1842 he prepared a new edition, to be called *Phantasy Pieces,* in two volume. In addition to the twenty-five tales included in *Tales of the Grotesque and Ara-*

[40] Original Autograph Ms., Drexel Institute Library, Philadelphia.

besque, there were eleven, which had already appeared in magazines. Only the first volume of this revision is in existence,[41] the second having apparently disappeared. Fortunately, the table of contents for this entire proposed revision is given in the first volume.

Contents

The Murders in the Rue Morgue, The Man that was Used Up, A Descent into the Mäelström, Lionizing, The Colloquy of Monos and Una, The Business Man, The Mask of the Red Death, Never Bet your Head, Eleonora, A Succession of Sundays, The Man of the Crowd, ~~The Pit and the Pendulum,~~ King Pest, Shadow—A Fable Parable, Bon-Bon, Life in Death, The Unparralleled [sic] Adventure of one Hans Pfaal, The Homocamelopard, Manuscript found in a Bottle, Mystification, The Horse-Shade, The Assignation, Why the Little Frenchman wears his hand in a sling, The Teeth, Silence—A Fable, Loss of Breath, The Island of the Fay, The Devil in the Belfry, Morella, A Pig Tale, ~~The Mystery of Marie Rogêt,~~ The Duc de L'Omelette, Ligeia, The Fall of the House of Usher, How to write a Blackwood Article, A Predicament, William Wilson, The Conversation of Eiros and Charmion.

To Printer—In printing the Tales preserve the order of the Table of Contents.

It will be noticed, first, that the order of the *Phantasy Pieces* is not the order of the *Tales of the Grotesque and Arabesque.* Ten out of the first eleven tales are taken from the most recent of Poe's stories, and the final ten had been published in the earlier volume. Otherwise the principle of selection seems to be simply that of variety. There are no unpublished or unknown stories. "The Horse-Shade" is "Metzengerstein," "The Teeth" is "Berenice," "A Pig Tale" is "A Tale of Jerusalem," and in each of these instances the new title is not an improvement and was not retained.[42]

Several changes of title, however, were preserved in later printings.

[41] In the library of Mr. Henry Bradley Martin, where I have examined it through his courtesy. Mr. George Blumenthal, who once owned the book, had some reproductions made in facsimile, and generously donated one to the Library of the University of Pennsylvania.

[42] These stories are not included in the text of the revised first volume, but my identification of the titles seems to me to be justified. None of Poe's biographers have apparently seen the *Phantasy Pieces,* except Dr. John W. Robertson, and he speaks of "The Horse Shade" and "The Teeth" as being "unknown stories."

PHANTASY-PIECES

by

Edgar Allan Poe.

[Including all the author's late tales with a new edition of the "Grotesque and Arabesque"]

Seltsamen tochter Jovis,
Seinem schosskinde,
Der Phantasie.

Göthe

Two
~~Three~~ Volumes.

TITLE PAGE OF THE *Phantasy Pieces*, PREPARED BY POE FOR A
SECOND EDITION OF THE *Tales of the Grotesque and Arabesque*,
BUT NEVER PUBLISHED

Reproduced from a facsimile of the unique original through the courtesy of Mr. George Blumenthal, and by permission of the present owner, Mr. H. Bradley Martin.

Contents

To Printer — be imitating the Tales preserve the order of the Table of Contents

TABLE OF CONTENTS OF THE *Phantasy Pieces*

"Epimanes" became "The Homocameleopard" and this was retained
as the subtitle of "Four Beasts in One." "Von Jung" became "Mystification"; "The Visionary," "The Assignation"; "Siope," "Silence,—a Fable";
"Signora Zenobia," "How to Write a Blackwood Article"; "The Scythe
of Time," "A Predicament."

Poe's deliberate crossing out of "The Pit and the Pendulum" and
"The Mystery of Marie Rogêt" provides an interesting subject of
speculation. It could hardly have been owing to his lack of appreciation of them. They were the two latest of this group of stories to
appear, in October, November, and December, 1842, and perhaps he
thought he saw a chance to publish his volumes which might have
been jeopardized by waiting for their publication. The first two tales
on the list were those selected for the edition of 1843, consisting of
but two stories.[43]

Many reasons have been suggested for Poe's resignation from the
staff of *Graham's Magazine*. His own statement, given in his letter to
Thomas, of May 25, 1842, is to be preferred to the melodramatic
stories concerning his leaving the office without a word, upon seeing
Rufus W. Griswold in his chair:

> Philadelphia, May 25, 1842.
>
> My dear Thomas,—Through an accident I have only just now
> received yours of the 21st. Believe me, I never dreamed of doubt-
> ing your friendship, or of reproaching you for your silence. I
> knew you had good reasons for it; and, in this matter, I feel that
> you have acted for me more judiciously, by far, than I should
> have done for myself. You have shown yourself, from the first
> hour of our acquaintance, that *rara avis in terris*—"a true friend."
> Nor am I the man to be unmindful of your kindness.
>
> What you say respecting a situation in the Custom House here
> gives me new life. Nothing could more precisely meet my views.
> Could I obtain such an appointment, I would be enabled thor-
> oughly to carry out all my ambitious projects. It would relieve me
> of all care as regards a mere subsistence, and thus allow me time
> for thought, which, in fact, is action. I repeat that I would ask
> for nothing farther or better than a situation such as you mention.
> If the salary will barely enable me to live I shall be content. Will
> you say as much for me to Mr. Tyler, and express to him my sin-
> cere gratitude for the interest he takes in my welfare?

[43] For detailed description of changes in *Phantasy Pieces* see Appendix.

The report of my having parted company with Graham is correct; although in the forthcoming June number there is no announcement to that effect; nor had the papers any authority for the statement made. My duties ceased with the May number. I shall continue to contribute occasionally. Griswold succeeds me. My reason for resigning was disgust with the namby-pamby character of the Magazine—a character which it was impossible to eradicate. I allude to the contemptible pictures, fashion-plates, music, and love-tales. The salary, moreover, did not pay me for the labour which I was forced to bestow. With Graham, who is really a very gentlemanly, although an exceedingly weak man, I had no misunderstanding. I am rejoiced to say that my dear little wife is much better, and I have strong hope of her ultimate recovery. She desires her kindest regards—as also Mrs. Clemm.

I have moved from the old place—but should you pay an unexpected visit to Philadelphia, you will find my address at Graham's. I would give the world to shake you by the hand; and have a thousand things to talk about which would not come within the compass of a letter. Write immediately upon receipt of this, if possible, and do let me know something of yourself, your own doings and prospects: see how excellent an example of egotism I set you. Here is a letter nearly every word of which is about myself or my individual affairs. You saw White—little Tom. I am anxious to know what he said about things in general. He is a *character* if ever one was. God bless you—

Edgar A. Poe.[44]

The fashion plates were everything that Poe said about them, and more, and certainly some of the stories fully justified Poe's strictures. The very liberality of Graham's payments for popular authors, although Poe undoubtedly approved of it, must have been a bit galling to an editor who received eight hundred dollars a year for his services.[45] By the end of the second year of *Graham's* the circulation

[44] Attributed by Woodberry, *Century Magazine*, XLVIII (September, 1894), 732-733, to "Griswold Mss.," among which it is not at present. Harrison prints it without reference. It was sold at auction December 16-17, 1929.

[45] According to Poe's editorial on "The Pay for Periodical Writing," *Weekly Mirror*, I (October 19, 1844), 28, Graham paid prose writers from $2 to $12 a page, and poets from $5 to $50 an "article."

rose to 40,000,[46] and Graham made a fortune from it. How much, if anything, Poe was paid in addition for his short stories and criticisms, has not been definitely settled. Poe's duties on *Graham's* apparently consisted of writing the reviews, reading the last ·proofs and contributing one tale a month. He expressly denies that he has any of the "drudgery" of the magazine—which evidently fell to the lot of Charles Peterson. The tone of a letter [47] written at this time, which apologizes for the action of Peterson in printing a poem which Lewis J. Cist had sent to Poe for the abortive "Penn" project, may indicate some ill feeling between Poe and Peterson. The following passage from Graham's defence of Poe after his death belongs here, for it not only, by implication, indicates that Poe received additional payment only for extraordinary articles, but it also reveals the cordial relations between Graham and himself:

> For three or four years I knew him intimately, and for eighteen months saw him almost daily; much of the time writing or conversing at the same desk; knowing all his hopes, his fears, and little annoyances of life, as well as his high-hearted struggle with adverse fate—yet he was always the same polished gentleman— the quiet, unobtrusive, thoughtful scholar—the devoted husband —frugal in his personal expenses—punctual and unwearied in his industry—*and the soul of honor,* in all his transactions. This, of course, was in his better days, and by them *we* judge the man. But even after his habits had changed, there was no literary man to whom I would more readily advance money for labor to be done. He kept his accounts, small as they were, with the accuracy of a banker. I append an account sent to me in his own hand, long after he had left Philadelphia, and after all knowledge of the transactions it recited had escaped my memory. I had returned him the story of "The Gold Bug," at his own request, as he found that he could dispose of it very advantageously elsewhere.

[46] Poe claimed this figure was reached before he left *Graham's*, see his letter to Bryan, July 6, 1842. John Sartain, who engraved the plates, and therefore knew the amounts printed, checks with this figure, but places it at the end of the second year. See his *Reminiscences of a Very Old Man,* p. 198.

[47] Poe to Lewis J. Cist, September 18, 1841. I have only a facsimile of the original which was sold in 1927. Poe did contribute a story each month from April, 1841, until September, 1841, but did not continue to publish every month in *Graham's.*

"We were square when I sold you the 'Versification' article;
for which you gave me first 25, and afterward 7—in
all $32.00
Then you bought 'The Gold Bug' for................   52.00
                                                     ———
I got both these back, so that I owed.............. $84.00
You lent Mrs. Clemm 12.50
                                                     ———
Making in all $96.50
The Review of 'Flaccus' was 3¾ pp., which,
     at $4, is   15.00
Lowell's poem is   10.00
The review of Channing, 4 pp. is 16,
     of which I got 6, leaving   10.00
The review of Halleck, 4 pp. is 16,
     of which I got 10, leaving   6.00
The review of Reynolds, 2 pp.   8.00
[48] The review of Longfellow, 5 pp. is
     20, of which I got 10, leaving   10.00
                                                ———
So that I have paid in all   59.00
                                                      ———
Which leaves still due by me $37.50"

This I find was his uniform habit with others, as well as myself
—carefully recalling to mind his indebtedness, with the fresh
article sent. And this is the man who had "no moral susceptibility," and little or nothing of the "true point of honor." It may
be a very plain, business view of the question, but it strikes his
friends that it may pass as something, as times go.

I shall never forget how solicitous of the happiness of his wife
and mother-in-law he was, whilst one of the editors of Graham's
Magazine—his whole efforts seemed to be to procure the comfort
and welfare of his home. Except for their happiness—and the
natural ambition of having a magazine of his own—I never heard
him deplore the want of wealth. The truth is, he cared little for
money, and knew less of its value, for he seemed to have no
personal expenses. What he received from me in regular monthly
instalments, went directly into the hands of his mother-in-law
for family comforts—and *twice* only, I remember his purchasing
some rather expensive luxuries for his house, and then he was
nervous to the degree of misery until he had, by extra articles,
covered what he considered an imprudent indebtedness.[49]

[48] Probably the review of Longfellow's *Spanish Student* which Graham
did not publish. The other reviews were published in 1843 and 1844, after
Poe left *Graham's*.

[49] "The Late Edgar Allan Poe," *Graham's Magazine,* XXXVI (March,
1850), 224-226.

It must, of course, be remembered that the purchasing power of eight hundred dollars was probably three times what it is today. Longfellow received two thousand dollars as the Smith Professor of Modern Languages at Harvard in 1839, and the normal salary of the full professors at the University of Pennsylvania in 1840 was twenty-three hundred dollars. They can hardly be said to have been overpaid, and yet Poe might easily have thought his recompense was relatively meagre.

It is evident that no quarrel could have taken place between Poe and Graham. But Poe still had his magazine in project, and Graham's unwillingness to join him was certainly one of the reasons for the break.

In the July issue appeared this note:

"The connection of E. A. Poe, Esq., with this work ceased with the *May Number*. Mr. P. bears with him our warmest wishes for success in whatever he may undertake." [50]

How much Poe shared in the combination of literary and social life which tradition attributes to the hospitality of George Graham, can be only a matter of conjecture. Graham lived during Poe's editorship in a fairly large house at the corner of Franklin and Buttonwood Streets, in the northern section of Philadelphia, but in 1843 he moved to 191 Mulberry Street, or as it later became, 521 Arch Street, a distinctly more fashionable part of the city. He drove a good team of horses and he evidently enjoyed life fully.

Contemporary evidence however places Poe among the leaders in what literary life there was in Philadelphia. Horace W. Smith, the son of Richard Penn Smith, a playwright and short story writer well known at that time, speaks of his father's associates: "Well do I remember how proud I was of him: he took me with him wherever he went, and his associates and companions (child as I was) became mine. James N. Barker, Robert M. Bird, Joseph C. Neal, Edwin Forrest, James Goodman, Edgar A. Poe, Louis A. Godey, William E. Burton, Robert T. Conrad, Joseph C. Chandler and Morton McMichael were the literary magnates of Philadelphia." [51]

Horace Smith was writing in 1879, his memory may not have been very accurate, and his omission of Graham's name from this group may have been accidental. But it may also indicate that Poe had won

[50] *Graham's Magazine*, XXI, 60.
[51] Horace W. Smith, *Life and Correspondence of Reverend William Smith* (Philadelphia, 1879-80), II, 529.

his position in Philadelphia before he became editor of *Graham's*. Poe was never a "magnate" but it is clear that he was known favorably to the journalistic group of the better sort in Philadelphia. If he was ever to launch his magazine, he thought, the time had come.

CHAPTER XIII

Following the Illusion

In contrast to the cloudy and often doubtful course of Poe's professional career, there was one shining certainty. Whatever might be thought or said of him by the men with whom he came in contact and conflict, there was always the love of Virginia, steadfast and unalterable. As she matured, the adoration of the child he had married grew into the devotion of the woman, and the physical attraction for the handsome young cousin she worshipped blossomed into a spiritual passion which his love had nurtured and which, in its turn, sent its roots deeper and deeper into his life. How deeply those roots were planted can be measured only in terms of "Eleonora," of "The Raven," of "Ulalume" and of "Annabel Lee." His constant presence has deprived us of the letters which might have told us of their mutual affection, but Poe's distraught appeal from Richmond in 1835 tells us clearly what they would have been. To a husband who was always hovering over her to protect her from the threatening dangers of her illness, she had no need to write.

So much emphasis has been placed upon Virginia, the "child wife," that biographers have apparently forgotten that children grow up and that the woman of twenty might possibly be a little girl no longer. While Mrs. Clemm's statement that Virginia was an accomplished musician and spoke Italian like a native of Italy must be taken with several grains of salt, like all her utterances, it is correct at least concerning Virginia's competence in music. When Thomas sent Poe a song he hoped to publish, Poe replied, "I have delayed answering [your letter] in hope that I might say your song was out, and that I might give you my opinion and Virginia's about its merits." [1]

Captain Mayne Reid, the Irish novelist, was a constant visitor to the Poe home in 1843, and later painted a vivid portrait of her. In speaking of pleasant hours spent at Poe's cottage, he said: "They were passed in the company of the poet himself and his wife—a lady angelically beautiful in person and not less beautiful in spirit. No one who

[1] Poe to Thomas, October 27, 1841. Lewis Chase, "A New Poe Letter," *American Literature*, VI (March, 1934), 67.

remembers that dark-eyed, dark-haired daughter of Virginia—her *own* name, if I rightly remember—her grace, her facial beauty, her demeanour, so modest as to be remarkable—no one who has ever spent an hour in her company but will endorse what I have above said. I remember how we, the friends of the poet, used to talk of her high qualities." [2]

In speaking of Poe's attraction for women, which Reid thought overestimated, he added, "It was enough for one man to be beloved by one such woman as he had for his wife." Even Thomas Dunn English, who heartily disliked Poe, spoke of Virginia's "air of refinement and good breeding." [3] Although some of the feminine visitors to the Poe home did not estimate so highly the charm or mentality of Virginia, that is, perhaps, only more conclusive proof that her attraction for the men friends like Thomas and Reid was shared by her husband.

This love of Poe for Virginia brought soon its tragedy. Some time in January, 1842, Virginia, while singing at her piano in the Coates Street house, broke a blood-vessel. Poe's own words tell best of the event, and of its consequence. Six years later he wrote to George Eveleth:

> January 4, 1848
>
> You say—"Can you *hint* to me what was the terrible evil which caused the irregularities so profoundly lamented?" Yes; I can do more than hint. This "evil" was the greatest which can befall a man. Six years ago, a wife, whom I loved as no man ever loved before, ruptured a blood-vessel in singing. Her life was despaired of. I took leave of her forever & underwent all the agonies of her death. She recovered partially and I again hoped. At the end of a year the vessel broke again—I went through precisely the same scene. Again in about a year afterward. Then again—again—again & even once again at varying intervals. Each time I felt all the agonies of her death—and at each accession of the disorder I loved her more dearly & clung to her life with more desperate pertinacity. But I am constitutionally sensitive—nervous in a very unusual degree. I became insane, with long intervals of horrible sanity. During these fits of absolute unconsciousness I drank, God only knows how often or how much. As a matter of course, my

---

[2] Mayne Reid, *Edgar Allan Poe*. Taken from a Memoir of Mayne Reid, written by Elizabeth Reid, his widow, and published in London, 1890. Edited by Vincent Starrett (Ysleta, Texas, 1933), pp. 3-4. First printed as "A Dead Man Defended" in Reid's Magazine, *Onward*, for April, 1869.

[3] *Independent*, XLVIII (1896), 1,415.

enemies referred the insanity to the drink rather than the drink to the insanity. I had indeed, nearly abandoned all hope of a permanent cure when I found one in the *death* of my wife. This I can & do endure as becomes a man—it was the horrible never-ending oscillation between hope & despair which I could *not* longer have endured without total loss of reason. In the death of what was my life, then, I receive a new but—oh God! how melancholy an existence.[4]

If ever drinking were excusable, it was certainly in this desperate effort to forget. A sorrow can be borne, when it is final, by any one who pretends to be a man. But the daily load of apprehension, which one takes on at waking, and from which even sleep is no refuge, is hardest to bear. Yet in one sense Virginia was Poe's protector, as we shall see. And no matter how hard life was for them all, a great devotion filled it with beauty. The impression it made upon Graham was a lasting one:

His love for his wife was a sort of rapturous worship of the spirit of beauty which he felt was fading before his eyes. I have seen him hovering around her when she was ill, with all the fond fear and tender anxiety of a mother for her first-born—her slightest cough causing in him a shudder, a heart-chill that was visible. I rode out one summer evening with them, and the remembrance of his watchful eyes eagerly bent upon the slightest change of hue in that loved face, haunts me yet as the memory of a sad strain. It was this hourly *anticipation* of her loss, that made him a sad and thoughtful man, and lent a mournful melody to his undying song.[5]

There were intervals, naturally, when Virginia's health seemed restored. In August, 1842, Poe despaired of her recovery; in September her health was "slightly improved," and he wrote Thomas "my spirits are proportionably good." In these brighter days there were no doubt picnics in Fairmount Park and on the Wissahickon, and there were visits from friends who have left testimony as to the neatness and self-respecting atmosphere, for which all three of the family were responsible.

[4] Ms. of original letter in possession of Dr. A. S. W. Rosenbach, through whose courtesy it is reproduced here in part. For the complete letter, see Chapter XVII.

[5] "The Late Edgar Allan Poe," *Graham's Magazine*, XXXVI (March, 1850), 225.

PHILADELPHIA ABOUT THE TIME OF POE'S RESIDENCE

Showing the Schuylkill River and the region of Fairmount Park near his house in Coates Street. On the left is the Reservoir, where Poe took Sartain in July, 1849.

Reid's description of Poe "during two years of intimate, personal association" speaks of his "analytic reasoning such as few men possess," of his "original character" and of his personal habits:

I feel satisfied that Edgar A. Poe was not, what his slanderers have represented him, a rake. I know he was not; but in truth the very opposite. I have been his companion in one or two of his wildest frolics, and can certify that they never went beyond the innocent mirth in which we all indulge when Bacchus gets the better of us. With him the jolly god sometimes played fantastic tricks—to the stealing away his brain, and, sometimes, too, his hat—leaving him to walk bareheaded through the streets at an hour when the sun shone too clearly on his crown, then prematurely bald.

While acknowledging this as one of Poe's failings, I can speak truly of its not being habitual; only occasional, and drawn out by some accidental circumstance—now disappointment; now the concurrence of a social crowd, whose flattering friendship might lead to champagne, a single glass of which used to affect him so much that he was hardly any longer responsible for his actions.

Reid adds how he knew Poe to be a whole month in his own house, working hard at his writing.

Some of these visitors, unlike Reid, were to bring trouble to Poe in his lifetime and to cloud his memory after death. Dr. Thomas Dunn English, a Philadelphian who graduated from the School of Medicine of the University of Pennsylvania in 1839, met Poe in the same year. English contributed verse to *Burton's*, and his graduation thesis upon phrenology, in which he defended the theories of Gall and Spurzheim, gave him mutual interests with Poe, who had been reading up on phrenology for some time. English, however, was only twenty years old when he met Poe first on the corner of Sixth and Chestnut Streets, and since his description of their cottage tallies most definitely with the house in Spring Garden, his intimacy must have been later in the Philadelphia period. He was a tall, well built man, and when I met him in 1895 at a gathering of Pennsylvania alumni, he was of rather distinguished appearance. Unfortunately, I lost the opportunity to obtain his informal opinion of Poe, for Du Maurier had just published *Trilby,* and revived interest in English's sentimental ballad, "Ben Bolt." Dr. English would talk of nothing but the harm that song had done his reputation as a poet. An examination of his *Select Poems,* however, will confirm Poe's unfavorable strictures upon them, though the manner of his attack was hardly justified. English published in 1896 his

Reminiscences of Poe[6] a fairly clever account written with apparent frankness, which, by hinting at scandals that he was too much of a gentleman to reveal, gave a worse impression than if he had presented the supposed facts for possible refutation. In view, however, of his general tone of animosity, the testimony of Dr. English concerning the much discussed question of Poe's use of drugs is valuable: "Had Poe the opium habit when I knew him (before 1846) I should both as a physician and a man of observation, have discovered it during his frequent visits to my rooms, my visits at his house, and our meetings elsewhere—I saw no signs of it and believe the charge to be a baseless slander." [7] He and Poe were probably companions on occasions when Poe yielded to temptation to drink the one glass which was too much for him, but in view of English's comparative youth, the blame can hardly be allotted to him. Their relations are of much greater importance during the later period in New York.

It was also in Philadelphia that Poe met his evil genius, the Reverend Rufus Wilmot Griswold. Griswold was born in Rutland, Vermont, in 1815. He was a printer and a newspaper man, and was licensed in 1837 as a Baptist clergyman, though he seems not to have had any permanent charge. After editorial work in New England and New York, where he made influential friends like Horace Greeley and Park Benjamin, he came to Philadelphia on November 27, 1840, to join the staff of the *Daily Standard,* and while he returned to Boston for a few months, he was once more in Philadelphia in September, 1841.[8]

Griswold at this time was one of those unattached writers who are called "free lances" by those they praise and "literary scavengers" by those whom they attack. His *Biographical Annual,* containing memoirs of thirty-six "eminent persons recently deceased," and his *Gems from American Female Poets, With Brief Biographical Notices,* will indicate how he was living on the work of others, with a definite slant toward the desire of human beings to see themselves or their dead friends given publicity. Griswold had the sense for publicity well developed. For some years he was planning the first of his major anthologies, *The Poets and Poetry of America.* He was not troubled by the woes of

[6] *Independent,* XLVIII (October 15, 22, 29, November 5), 1,381-82; 1,415-16; 1,448; 1,480-81.

[7] *Independent,* XLVIII (October 15, 1896), 1,382.

[8] For information concerning Griswold's career, see W. M. Griswold, *Passages from the Correspondence . . . of Rufus W. Griswold* (Cambridge, 1898); J. L. Neu, "Rufus Wilmot Griswold," *University of Texas Studies in English,* V (1925), 101-165. Also, D. A. B.

the anthologists of today in this field. Poets, who had usually been paid nothing for their verses by the magazines, were only too willing to give Griswold *carte blanche* to select from their works. By this anthology, which appeared in April, 1842, and by his later *Prose Writers of America*, and *Female Poets of America*, he acquired a position as a species of literary dictator, whose favor it was advisable to seek and whose power to hurt the vanity of literary aspirants steadily grew.

Griswold met Poe first, according to his own statement,[9] in the spring of 1841 in connection with the *Poets and Poetry of America*. In a letter of March 29, 1841, Poe offered several poems to Griswold, and said he would be proud to see "one or two of them in the book." [10] He also sent a memorandum of his biography, containing, incidentally, several errors. Griswold selected "The Coliseum," "The Haunted Palace," and "The Sleeper" for the anthology, devoting two pages to Poe, including a brief biographical notice. Since he gave three to Lowell, four to Longfellow, nineteen to Whittier, twelve to Charles Fenno Hoffman, seven to J. G. C. Brainard, eight to Lydia Sigourney, and ten to R. C. Sands, Griswold's critical taste in poetry or his impartiality cannot be ranked very high.

Poe spoke of Griswold in his "Autography" in December, 1841, as "a gentleman of fine taste and sound judgment," and in the *Boston Miscellany* for November, 1842, he published a favorable review of *The Poets and Poetry of America*, although he differed with Griswold as to certain of his selections.

Poe quoted with approval Griswold's definition of poetry, which agreed with his own, stated that, "The book should be regarded as *the most important addition which our literature has for many years received,*" and concluded that Griswold had shown himself "a man of taste, talent, and *tact.*" [11]

---

[9] Preface to "Memoir," Griswold's edition of *The Literati—by Edgar A. Poe* (New York, 1850), p. v.

[10] Original Autograph Ms., Griswold Collection, Boston Public Library.

[11] "Griswold's American Poetry," "By Edgar A. Poe." *Boston Miscellany*, II (November, 1842), 218-221. This review contains a list of the authors treated by Griswold, usually omitted in reproductions. There was a very brief but laudatory notice of the book in the May number of *Graham's*. There is also a review of the book in *Graham's* for June, 1842, which has been attributed to Poe. It does not have any marked characteristics of his style. Since Poe had left *Graham's* and since he repudiated the leading review in the June number, on Bulwer's *Zanoni*, in a letter to Snodgrass of June 4, 1842, Poe's authorship of these two reviews is doubtful.

Griswold's appointment to the staff of *Graham's* was announced in the July number,[12] although he had probably been employed before then. In writing to Thomas in May, Poe had expressed no resentment at Griswold's becoming his successor. But in Poe's letters during the summer there are cutting remarks about Griswold's book. On June 4th, he wrote to Snodgrass, "Have you seen Griswold's Book of Poetry? It is a most outrageous humbug, and I sincerely wish you would 'use it up.' " [13]

In a letter to Thomas of September 12, 1842, Poe relates an incident which, if true, points to growing ill feeling. The letter contains other information of importance:

My Dear Thomas,

I did not receive yours of the 2d until yesterday—why God only knows, as I either went or sent every-day to the P. Office. Neither have I seen Mr. Beard, who, I presume, had some difficulty in finding my residence—since you were here I have moved out in the neighborhood of Fairmount. I have often heard of Beard, from friends who knew him personally, and should have been glad to make his acquaintance.

A thousand sincere thanks for your kind offices in the matter of the appointment. So far, nothing has been done here in the way of *reform*. Thos. S. Smith is to have the Collectorship, but it appears has not yet received his commission—a fact which occasions much surprise among the quid-nuncs.

Should I obtain the office—and of course I can no longer doubt that I shall obtain it—I shall feel that to you alone I am indebted. You have shown yourself a true friend, and I am not likely to forget it, however impotent I may be, now or hereafter, to reciprocate your many kindnesses. I would give the world to clasp you by the hand & assure you, personally, of my gratitude. I hope it will not be long before we meet.

In the event of getting the place, I am undetermined what *literary* course to pursue. Much will depend upon the salary. Graham has made me a good offer to return. He is not especially pleased with Griswold—nor is any one else, with the exception of the Rev. gentleman himself, who has gotten himself into quite a hornet's nest by his "Poets & Poetry." It appears you gave him personal offence by *delay* in replying to his demand for informa-

---

[12] *Graham's Magazine*, XXI (1842), 60.
[13] Original Autograph Ms., Pierpont Morgan Library.

tion touching Mrs. Welby, I believe, or somebody else. Hence his
omission of you in the body of the book; for he had prepared
quite a long article from my MS. and had selected several pieces
for quotation. He is a pretty fellow to set himself up as an *honest*
judge, or even as a capable one.—About two months since, we
were talking about the book, when I said that I had thought of
reviewing it in full for the "Democratic Review," but found my
design anticipated by an article from that ass O'Sullivan, and
that I knew no other work in which a notice would be readily
admissible. Griswold said, in reply—"You need not trouble yourself about the *publication* of the review, should you decide upon
writing it; for I will attend to all that. I will get it in some repu-
table work, and look to it for the usual pay; in the meantime
handing you whatever your charge would be." This, you see, was
an ingenious insinuation of a bribe to puff his book. I accepted
his offer forthwith, wrote the review, handed it to him and received from him the compensation:—he never daring to look over
the M. S. in my presence, and taking it for granted that all was
right. But that review has not yet appeared, and I am doubtful
if it ever will. I wrote it precisely as I would have written under
ordinary circumstances; and be sure there was no predominance
of praise.

Should I go back to Graham I will endeavor to bring about
some improvements in the general appearance of the Magazine,
& above all, to get rid of the quackery which now infects it.

If I do *not* get the appt. I should not be surprised if I joined
Foster in the establishment of a Mag. in New-York. He has made
me an offer to join him. I suppose you know that he now edits
the "Aurora."

Touching your poem. Should you publish it, Boston offers the
best facilities—but I feel sure that you will get no publisher to
print it, except on your own account. Reason—Copy-Right Laws.
However, were I in your place, and could contrive it in *any* way,
I would print it at my own expense—of course without reference
to emolument, which is not to be hoped. It would make only a
small volume, & the cost of publishing it even in such style as
Hoffman's best poems, could not be much, absolutely. It should be
handsomely printed or not at all.

When is Rob. Tyler to issue his promised poem?

Have you seen how Benjamin & Tasistro have been playing
Kilkenny cats with each other? I have always told Graham that

Tasistro stole everything, worth reading, which he offered for sale.

What is it about Ingraham? He has done for himself, in the opinion of all honest men, by his chicaneries.

I am happy to say that Virginia's health has slightly improved. My spirits are proportionably good.   Perhaps all will yet go well. Write soon & believe me ever your true friend

EDGAR A. POE.[14]

It is hard to see how the two men could have remained friends after such an incident. According to C. F. Briggs, Griswold told him "shocking bad stories" about Poe, which Poe's "whole demeanor contradicts." [15] These may have been of later occurrence. Poe and Griswold were both suspicious, and both had caustic tongues. On January 28, 1843, in the Philadelphia *Saturday Museum* appeared a review of the *Poets and Poetry of America,* unsigned. It is a blistering attack upon Griswold as a poet and an anthologist, and if he believed it to be by Poe, anyone of his vindictive nature would have long remembered it. There are sharp differences of opinion concerning its authorship.[16]

In the criticism are certain traces of Poe, such as the elaborate analysis of the rules of versification, and the definition of poetry, which make it clear that if he was not the author of the entire review, he was at least a collaborator. The most striking sentence is the last, which, in view of Griswold's treachery as Poe's literary executor,

[14] Original Autograph Ms., Anthony Collection, New York Public Library. According to Thomas's endorsement, he did not receive the letter until he returned to Washington.

[15] Briggs to Lowell, quoted by Woodberry, II, 123, as of January 6, 1845.

[16] Woodberry and Harrison accept it on internal evidence. Killis Campbell does not. He lays stress upon the fact that Poe does not mention it among the articles he states he has written upon Griswold's work. But since that list is given in a letter from Poe to Griswold, "undated, but in 1849" printed in Griswold's "Preface" but not found among the Griswold Mss., that evidence, unsupported, is not important. Campbell thinks it might be by Hirst, and there is a certain plausibility here, as Hirst is not mentioned among the Philadelphia poets who should have been treated. Dr. Mabbott believes it is a collaboration between Poe and Hirst, mostly by the former. He has called my attention to the suggested substitution for "In the greenest of our valleys" of "In a sunny, smiling valley," which is in a poem by Hirst, "To a Ruined Fountain," *Snowden's Ladies' Companion,* September, 1842. Poe would hardly have made such a suggestion, unless of course, he did it to throw people off the scent.

sounds like a prophecy: "Forgotten, save only by those whom he has injured and insulted, he will sink into oblivion, without leaving a landmark to tell that he once existed; or, if he is spoken of hereafter, he will be quoted as the *unfaithful servant who abused his trust.*"

The two men saw little of each other for two years, and it was inevitable that a breach should occur. With the evangelical abolitionist, Poe had no intellectual kinship.

Poe's resignation from Graham's did not interrupt his creation of fiction, but he found it more difficult to place his stories. A letter to Snodgrass reveals this, and also his method of writing, and how strong was his desire for publicity:

Philadelphia—June 4. 1842.

My Dear Snodgrass,

How does it happen that, in these latter days I never receive an epistle from yourself? Have I offended you by any of my evil deeds?—if so how? Time was when you could spare a few minutes occasionally for communion with a friend.

I see with pleasure that you have become sole proprietor of the "Visiter;" and this reminds me that I have to thank your partiality for many flattering notices of myself. How is it, nevertheless, that a *Magazine* of the highest class has never yet succeeded in Baltimore? I have often thought, of late, how much better it would have been had you joined me in a Magazine project in the Monumental City, rather than engage with the "Visiter"—a journal which has never yet been able to recover from the *mauvais odeur* imparted to it by Hewitt. Notwithstanding the many failures in Baltimore, I still am firmly convinced that your city is the best adapted for such a Magazine as I propose, of any in the Union. Have you ever thought seriously upon this subject.

I have a proposition to make. You may remember a tale of mine published about a year ago in "Graham" and entitled the "Murders in the Rue Morgue." Its *theme* was the exercise of ingenuity in detecting a murderer. I am just now putting the concluding touch to a similar article, which I shall entitle "The Mystery of Marie Rogêt—a Sequel to 'The Murders in the Rue Morgue.'" The story is based upon that of the real murder of Mary Cecilia Rogers, which created so vast an excitement, some months ago, in New York. I have handled the design in a very singular and entirely *novel* manner. I imagine a series of nearly exact coincidences occurring in Paris. A young grisette, one *Marie Rogêt,* has been

murdered under precisely similar circumstances with *Mary
Rogers*. Thus under pretence of showing how Dupin (the hero of
the Rue Morgue) unravelled the mystery of Marie's assassination,
I, in fact, enter into a very rigorous analysis of the *real* tragedy
in New-York. *No point* is omitted. I examine, each by each, the
opinions and arguments of our press on the subject, and show (I
think satisfactorily) that this subject has never yet been *approached*. The press has been entirely on a wrong scent. In fact, I
really believe, not only that I have demonstrated the falsity of the
idea that the girl was ~~not~~ the victim of a gang ~~as supposed,~~ but
have *indicated the assassin*. My main object, however, as you will
readily understand, is the analysis of the *principles of investigation* in cases of like character. Dupin *reasons* the matter throughout.

The article, I feel convinced, will be one of general interest,
from the nature of its subject. For reasons which I may mention to
you hereafter, I am desirous of publishing it in *Baltimore,* and
there would be no channel so proper as the paper under your
control. Now the tale is a long one—it would occupy twenty-five
pages of Graham's Magazine—and is worth to me a hundred dollars at the usual Magazine price. Of course I could not afford to
make you an absolute present of it—but if you are willing to take
it, I will say $40. Shall I hear from you on this head—if possible
by return of mail?

Have you seen Griswold's Book of Poetry? It is a most outrageous humbug, and I sincerely wish you would "use it up."

If you have not yet noticed my withdrawal from Graham's
Magazine, I would take it as a great favor if you would do so
in something like the following terms. Even if you *have* noticed
it, this might go in.

We have it from *undoubted authority* that Mr. Poe *has* retired
from the editorship of "Graham's Magazine," and that his withdrawal took place with the *May* number, notwithstanding the
omission of all announcement to this effect in the number for
June. We observe that the "Boston Post" in finding just fault with
an exceedingly ignorant and flippant review of "Zanoni" which
appears in the June number, has spoken of it as from the pen of
Mr. Poe. We will take it upon ourselves to say that Mr. P. neither
did write the article, nor could have written any such absurdity.
The slightest glance would suffice to convince us of this. Mr. P.
would never be guilty of the grammatical blunders, to say nothing

of the mere twattle, which disgrace the criticism. When did he ever spell *liaison, liason*, for example, or make use of so absurd a phrase as *"attained to"* in place of attained? We are also fully confident that the criticism in question is not the work of Mr. Griswold, who (whatever may be his abilities as the compiler of a Book of Poetry) is at all events a decent writer of English. The article appears to be the handiwork of some underling who has become imbued with the fancy of *aping* Mr. Poe's peculiarities of diction. A pretty mess he has made of it! Not to announce Mr. P's withdrawal in the June number, was an act of the rankest injustice; and as such we denounce it. A man of talent may occasionally submit to the appropriation of his articles by others who *insinuate* a claim to the authorship, but it is a far different and vastly more disagreeable affair when he finds himself called upon to father the conceit, ignorance and flippant impertinence of an ass.

Put this in editorially, my dear S., and oblige me eternally. You will acknowledge that it will be an act of justice.

Write immediately and believe me your friend.

EDGAR A. POE.

If you put in the paragraph send me the No. of the Visiter.[17]

Poe must have been in desperate need for money, for he offered the story on the same day to the Boston *Notion*, one of the mammoth weeklies of that time, for fifty dollars.[18] Neither magazine accepted the offer, for "Marie Rogêt" was published in *Snowden's Ladies' Companion* in November and December, 1842, and February, 1843.

Poe's own explanation in his letter to Snodgrass of his method in writing "The Murder of Marie Rogêt" is clear. By placing the murder in Paris, he could alter details, since he does not claim to solve the Mary Rogers case, but only to show how such a case should be approached. He kept quite close to the facts as known.[19] Mary Cecelia Rogers, a clerk in the tobacconist's shop of John Anderson, 114-116

---

[17] Original Autograph Ms., Pierpont Morgan Library.

[18] Poe to George Roberts, June 4, 1842. Original Autograph Ms., Collection of J. K. Lilly, Jr.

[19] Mary's betrothed, Daniel C. Payne, of 47 John Street, probably killed himself at the supposed site of the murder, in October, 1841. He had been drinking and death may have been caused by laudanum or exposure. Dr. T. O. Mabbott quotes *Brother Jonathan*, October 16, 1841, in sending me these facts.

Liberty Street, New York, was murdered in August, 1841.[20] She was last seen alive at the Lossburg Steps in Weehawken, New Jersey, with a man, apparently a naval officer. Her body was found floating in the Hudson River, and the mystery of her death baffled the police. Poe made clear that his principal interest was the character study of Dupin, his detective, and Dupin sleeps behind dark glasses while the Prefect of Police is explaining *his* theory of the crime, and then proceeds to examine all the newspapers for accidental and collateral information. He has become the model for detectives in fiction, whose contempt for official sources has hardened into a convention. Dupin analyses the statements of police and press and destroys them. His main effort is to prove that the murder was not the action of a gang of ruffians as the press indicated, but was the work of one man. Several years later Poe stated to Eveleth that " 'The naval officer' who committed the murder (or rather the accidental death arising from an attempt at abortion) confessed it." [21]

"Marie Rogêt" while ingenious, is not as interesting as any of the three other great stories of ratiocination. It is too long and too much time is spent on upsetting false theories. Poe probably recognized that it was growing out of proportion, for he did not follow out the clues suggested by Dupin. In a paragraph attributed to the editors of the magazine, the statement is made that the portion of the Ms. dealing with the following up of the clues was omitted. But, of course, as Poe admitted to Eveleth, that paragraph is part of the story. Here really lies the reason for the comparative failure of Marie Rogêt. It is just in Dupin's method of solution, step by step, from the clues he has discovered, that Poe is supreme. Again the fact that he was following a real case hampered him. It was only when his imagination had complete sway that he excelled.

"The Landscape Garden" had been published in October, 1842,

---

[20] See *New York Mail and Express,* April 19, 1900, where a picture of the store is given. The steps have only recently been destroyed through the widening of the road between Nineteenth and Gregory Streets, a W. P. A. project.

[21] Poe to Eveleth, January 4, 1848, Chapter XVII. In a footnote to the story as it appeared in the *Tales* of 1845, Poe claimed that the confession of *two* persons established the truth of his deduction. See, however, R. V. Costello, "Poe and Marie Rogêt," *New York Evening Post,* January 10, 1920, who claims the gang really committed the murder. W. K. Wimsatt, Jr., in *Proceedings of the Modern Language Association,* LVI (March, 1941), 230-248, collects the newspaper accounts and reviews the situation. but arrives at no conclusion.

in the *Ladies' Companion.* In "The Landscape Garden," Poe expressed again his love of natural beauty. There is something pathetic in Poe's creation of a hero, Seabright Ellison, who, owing to the inheritance of a vast fortune,[22] can indulge his love of beauty by devoting himself to landscape gardening, on a large scale. Poe took occasion to present his theory that while the loveliness of natural objects cannot be improved by art, the *composition* or arrangement of the elements of the landscape may well add greatly to the beauty of the whole. Poe was consistent in his theory of beauty—the landscape artist who merely restored the scene to its original beauty was not as great an artist as the man who added creatively a new charm. One can be taught—the other must spring from the flame of inspiration. "The Landscape Garden" ended abruptly with the plans of Ellison; later Poe amplified the story as "The Domain of Arnheim."

"The Pit and the Pendulum" belongs also to 1842, since it appeared in the *Gift* for 1843, which came out in the fall. It is a remarkable study of the effect of terror upon a man imprisoned in a dungeon of the Inquisition. Of greatest interest is the analysis of the different strata of dreams through which we pass from sleep into waking. Any competent dreamer will recognize the truth of Poe's statement: "In the return to life from the swoon there are two stages: first, that of the sense of mental or spiritual; secondly, that of the sense of physical existence." Any one who has lain, powerless to move, in the first of these stages, will remember how every faculty of his mental powers struggled to attain the second stage.

"The Pit and the Pendulum" is a fine example of Poe's use of several sources in a combination of his own. In Brockden Brown's *Edgar Huntly* (1799) the hero falls in a pit, believes he is a victim of a tyrant and is to be buried alive, is tormented by thirst, and is especially stricken with fear because, like Poe's hero, he is deprived through darkness and unfamiliar surroundings of his usual experiences. The Inquisition probably came from Poe's reading Leonard Gallois' translation of Juan Antonio Llorente's *Critical History of the Spanish Inquisition,*[23] in which a prisoner lies tightly bound in the path of a slowly descending pendulum. From "The Iron Shroud," by the author of "First and Last,"[24] Poe may have taken the idea of a

[22] Poe called attention to the Thelluson will, which suggested the accumulation of "ninety million pounds."

[23] See Margaret Alterton, *Modern Language Notes,* XLVIII (June, 1933), 349-356.

[24] *Blackwood's Magazine,* XXVIII (August, 1830), 364-371. See D. L.

dungeon whose walls become heated and close in on the victim. But, as before, the best way to appreciate Poe's excellence in the creation of a mood is to note his superiority in the combination of these incidents into something new, and his own.

Poe continued his efforts to obtain a government post, this time in the Custom House in Philadelphia. He had some encouragement from Thomas,[25] who engaged the interest of Robert Tyler, the son of the President. Poe as usual began to consider the appointment as already made. Two letters to Poe's friend, James Herron,[26] a civil engineer in Washington, reveal not only Poe's optimism concerning the appointment but also his despairing mental condition. In the first letter, an undated fragment, he speaks of his abandonment of all mental exertion and his determination to take advantage of the Bankruptcy Act. After mentioning the appointment as certain, Poe concludes, "Mrs. Poe is again dangerously ill with hemorrhage from the lungs. It is folly to hope."

The second letter speaks for itself:

Philadelphia, June 30, 1842.

My dear Mr. Herron,

Upon return from a brief visit to New York, last night, I found here your kind letter from Washington, enclosing a check for $20, and giving me new life in every way. I am more deeply indebted to you than I can express, and in this I really mean what I say. Without your prompt and unexpected interposition with Mr. Tyler, it is by no means improbable that I should have failed in obtaining the appointment which has become so vitally necessary to me; but now I feel assured of success. The $20, also, will enable me to overcome other difficulties—and, I repeat, that I thank you from the bottom of my heart. You have shown yourself a true friend.

My wife's health has slightly improved and my spirits have risen in proportion, but I am still *very* unwell—so much so that I shall be forced to give up and go to bed.

Clark, *Modern Language Notes*, XLIV (June, 1929), 349, whose other suggestions I do not follow.

[25] Thomas to Poe, May 21, 1842. Original Autograph Ms., Griswold Collection, Boston Public Library.

[26] Herron was well known for his inventions, among them a trellis railway structure. He won the gold medal of the American Institute in 1846. The Philadelphia Directory for 1844 shows he was a resident of that city.

Your own brilliant prospects *must* be realized; for it is not Fate which makes such men as yourself. You make your own Fate. There is such a thing as compelling Fortune, however reluctant or averse. As regards myself—I will probably succeed too. So let us both keep a good head.

Wishing you the high success which you deserve,

I am your sincere friend,

EDGAR A. POE.

Jas. Herron Esqre [27]

Even in his despair, in both letters Poe congratulates his friend on his own success. Herron evidently did what he could, but nothing happened. Then on September 2nd, Thomas evidently wrote to Poe reopening the question and Poe replied on September 12th.[28] Before Thomas received this letter, he had come to Philadelphia[29] and visited the family at the Coates Street home. Poe wrote to Thomas apologizing for his failure to meet him:

Philadelphia, Sep. [21?] 1842.

My dear Thomas,

I am afraid you will think that I keep my promises but indifferently well, since I failed to make my appearance at Congress Hall on Sunday, and I now, therefore, write to apologise. The will to be with you was not wanting—but, upon reaching home on Saturday night, I was taken with a severe chill and fever—the latter keeping me company all next day. I found myself too ill to venture out, but, nevertheless, would have done so had I been able to obtain the consent of all parties. As it was I was quite in a quandary, for we keep no servant and no messenger could be procured in the neighborhood. I contented myself with the reflection that you would not think it necesary to wait for me very long after 9 o'clock, and that you were not quite as implacable in your resentments as myself. I was much in hope that you would have made your way out in the afternoon. Virginia & Mrs. C. were much grieved at not being able to bid you farewell.

I perceive by DuSolle's paper that you saw him. He announced your presence in the city on Sunday, in very handsome terms.

[27] Both letters, Autograph Mss., are in the W. H. Koester Collection.

[28] See letter on pp. 352-354, in connection with Griswold.

[29] Thomas's notation on the letter—"Did not get this until my return. Saw Poe in Philadelphia."

I am about going on a pilgrimage, this morning, to hunt up a copy of "Clinton Bradshaw" & will send it to you as soon as procured.

Excuse the brevity of this letter, for I am still very unwell, & believe me most gratefully & sincerely your friend,

EDGAR A. POE.

F. W. Thomas, Esq.[30]

On November 19th, however, he wrote Thomas again showing how little fitted Poe was to cope with a politician:

Philadelphia, November 19, 1842.

My Dear Friend,—Your letter of the 14th gave me new hope— only to be dashed to the ground. On the day of its receipt, some of the papers announced four removals and appointments. Among the latter I observed the name—Pogue. Upon inquiry among those behind the curtain, I soon found that no such person as—Pogue had any expectation of an appointment, and that the name was a misprint or rather a misunderstanding of the reporters, who had heard *my own* name spoken of at the Custom House. I waited two days, without calling on Mr. Smith, as he had twice told me that "he would send for me when he wished to swear me in." To-day, however, hearing nothing from him, I called. I asked him if he had no good news for me yet. He replied, "No, I am instructed to make no more removals." At this, being much astonished, I mentioned that I had heard, through a friend, from Mr. Rob Tyler, that he was requested to appoint me. At these words he said roughly,—"From *whom* did you say?" I replied, "From Mr. Robert Tyler." I wish you could have seen the scoundrel,—for scoundrel, my dear Thomas, in your private ear, *he is*,—"From *Robert* Tyler!" says he—"Hem! I have received orders from *President* Tyler to make no more appointments, and shall make none." Immediately afterward, he acknowledged that he had made one appointment *since* these instructions.

Mr. Smith has excited the thorough disgust of every Tyler man here. He is a Whig of the worst stamp, and will appoint none but Whigs if he can possibly avoid it. People here laugh at the idea of his being a Tyler man. He is notoriously not such. As for me, he has treated me most shamefully. In my case, there was no need of any political shuffling or lying. I proffered my willingness to

[30] Original Autograph Ms., Huntington Library.

postpone my claims to those of political claimants, but he told me, upon my first interview after the election, that if I would call on the fourth day he would swear me in. I called and he was not at home. On the next day I called again and saw him, when he told me that he would send a messenger for me when ready: this without even inquiring my place of residence, showing that he had, from the first, no design of appointing me. Well, I waited nearly a month, when, finding nearly all the appointments made, I again called. He did not even ask me to be seated—scarcely spoke— muttered the words "I will *send* for you, Mr. Poe"—and that was all. My next and last interview was to-day—as I have just described. The whole *manner* of the man, from the first, convinced me that he would not appoint me if he could help it. Hence the uneasiness I expressed to you when here. Now, my dear Thomas, this insult is not *to me,* so much as to your friend Mr. Robert Tyler, who was so kind as to promise, and who requested, my appointment.

It seems to me that the only way to serve me *now* is to lay the matter once again before Mr. Tyler, and, if possible through him, to procure a few lines *from the President,* directing Mr. Smith to give me the place. With these credentials he would scarcely again refuse. But I leave all to your better judgment.

You can have no idea of the low ruffians and boobies—men, too, without a shadow of political influence or caste—who have received office over my head. If Smith had the feelings of a gentleman, he would have perceived that, from the very character of my claim,—by which I mean my *want* of claim,—he should have made my appointment an early one. It was a gratuitous favor intended me by Mr. Rob Tyler, and he (Smith) has done *his* best to deprive this favor of all its grace by delay. I could have forgiven all but the innumerable and altogether *unnecessary* falsehoods with which he insulted my common sense day after day.

I would write more, my dear Thomas, but my heart is too heavy. You have felt the misery of hope deferred, and will feel for me.

Believe me ever your true friend,

EDGAR A. POE.[31]

---

[31] Woodberry, *Century Magazine,* XLVIII (September, 1894), 733-734, quotes from a Ms. in possession of C. W. Frederickson. Harrison checks through independent copying of a letter said to be in the Lenox Library. It is not now in the New York Public Library, which absorbed the Lenox.

It is pleasant to turn from these "hopes deferred" to Poe's early association with Lowell. Several of Lowell's poems had been printed in *Graham's* while Poe was an editor, and when Poe heard that Lowell was about to found *The Pioneer*, a monthly magazine, he wrote to him:

> Dr Sir,—Learning your design of commencing a Magazine in Boston, upon the first of January next, I take the liberty of asking whether some arrangement might not be made by which I should become a regular contributor.
>
> I should be glad to furnish a short article each month—of such character as might be suggested by yourself—and upon such terms as you could afford "in the beginning."
>
> That your success will be marked and permanent I will not doubt. At all events, I most sincerely wish you well; for no man in America has excited in me so much admiration—and, therefore, none so much of respect and esteem—as the author of "Rosaline."
>
> May I hope to hear from you at your leisure? In the meantime, believe me
>
> Most Cordially yours,
>
> EDGAR ALLAN POE.
>
> James Russell Lowell, Esqre.
> 　　Philadelphia, November 16, 1842.[32]

Lowell in reply offered ten dollars for any article Poe sent him, promising more if his venture succeeded and asking especially for stories. The prospectus for the *Pioneer* [33] is not unlike those which Poe issued for the *Penn Magazine* or the *Stylus*. It emphasizes the need for a "natural" rather than a "national" literature. Lowell and Carter, his partner, owned as well as edited the *Pioneer*.

Poe had evidently sent "The Tell-Tale Heart" to the *Boston Miscellany*, which had printed his review of Griswold's anthology, but H. T. Tuckerman had become its editor and declined it, possibly because Poe's description of him in his "Autography" as "insufferably tedious and dull" did not appeal to him. He turned the story over to Lowell who printed it in the first number of the *Pioneer* in January, 1843. Lowell's letter telling Poe of this transfer closes with the words "Wishing you all happiness, I remain your true friend." [34]

[32] Original Autograph Ms., Harvard College Library.
[33] See Horace E. Scudder's *James Russell Lowell*, I, 103-105.
[34] Woodberry, I, 347.

Poe sent Lowell on December 23rd,[35] his poem, "Lenore," a revision of "A Pæan," with some caustic remarks on Tuckerman, and Lowell printed it in the issue of February, 1843, with the short lines which spread it over two pages. It was greatly improved by the changes, which are so many as to forbid retelling here. How careful Poe was concerning the appearance of his verses is shown in a letter to Lowell:

My dear Sir,
  If not too late, I would be glad to substitute the lines here given, for what I sent you some days since.
  Should the long line "To friends above etc." not come conveniently within the breadth of the page, it may be made to commence farther to the left, so as to correspond with "But waft the angel &c."

Most truly yours,

EDGAR POE.

James Russell Lowell, Esqr.
  Dec. 27. 42.[36]

Poe wrote a letter of congratulation to Lowell concerning the *Pioneer:*

Philadelphia, February 4, 1843.
  My dear Mr. Lowell,—For some weeks I have been daily proposing to write and congratulate you upon the triumphant début of the "Pioneer," but have been prevented by a crowd of more worldly concerns.
  Thank you for the compliment in the footnote. Thank you, also, for your attention in forwarding the Magazine.
  As far as a $3 Magazine can please me at all, I am delighted with yours. I am especially gratified with what seems to me a certain coincidence of opinion and of taste, between yourself and your humble servant, in the minor arrangements, as well as in the more important details of the journal. For example,—the poetry in the same type as the prose—the designs from Flaxman—&c. As regards the contributors our thoughts are one. Do you know that when, some time since, I dreamed of establishing a Magazine of my own, I said to myself—"If I can but succeed in engaging, as

[35] Autograph Ms., Harvard College Library. This letter has the signature and possibly the date torn off. The postmark is December 25th. C. E. Norton noted "December 23, 1842," on the letter.
[36] Original Autograph Ms., W. H. Koester Collection.

permanent contributors, Mr. Hawthorne, Mr. Neal, and two others, with a certain young poet of Boston, who shall be nameless, I will engage to produce the best journal in America." At the same time, while I thought, and still think highly of Mr. Bryant, Mr. Cooper, and others, I said nothing of *them.*

You have many warm friends in this city—but the reforms you propose require time in their development, and it may be even a year before "The Pioneer" will make due impression among the Quakers. In the meantime, persevere.

I forwarded you, about a fortnight ago I believe, by Harnden's Express, an article called "Notes upon English Verse." A thought has struck me, that it may prove too long, or perhaps too dull, for your Magazine—in either case, use no ceremony, but return it in the same mode (thro' Harnden) and I will, forthwith, send something in its place.

I duly received, from Mr. Graham, $10 on your account, for which I am obliged. I would prefer, however, that you would remit directly to myself through the P. Office.

I saw, not long ago, at Graham's, a poem without the author's name—but which for many reasons I take to be yours—the chief being that it was *very* beautiful. Its title I forget, but it slightly veiled a lovely Allegory—in which "Religion" was typified, and the whole painted the voyage of some wanderers and mourners in search of some far-off isle. Is it yours?

Truly your friend,

E. A. POE.[37]

Alas, the *Pioneer* died with the March issue. Lowell's severe disease of the eyes, which took him to New York for treatment for some time, and the rather impossible conditions of the contract with his printers were the immediate causes of the failure. But the general conditions which operated against the success of the *Pioneer* were those which defeated Poe. The "Notes on English Verse" appeared in the March number, but I shall postpone discussion of them until Poe's theories of versification are treated in connection with "The Rationale of English Verse."

Poe's intercourse with Charles Dickens in Philadelphia in March, 1842, was also pleasant, but led to nothing definite. Dickens evidently tried to secure the publication of a volume of Poe's stories in England, but was unsuccessful. Poe must have made a favorable impression

[37] Original Autograph Ms., Harvard College Library.

upon Dickens, for on the British novelist's second trip to the United States, he hunted up Mrs. Clemm and made a contribution to her support.

During the Philadelphia period there developed also a correspondence between Poe and a strange being whose importance, except as it contributes to our knowledge of Poe, seems to me to have been greatly exaggerated. Thomas Holley Chivers was a Georgian, born in 1807, who wrote poetry which is thought by some to resemble Poe's work, and even to anticipate it. Poe asked him to obtain subscriptions for the *Penn Magazine* in 1840, and Chivers replied with an assurance of support, but no definite financial aid.[38]

In his "Autography" [39] Poe gave him more than adequate notice:

Dr. Thomas Holley Chivers, of New York, is at the same time one of the best and one of the worst poets in America. His productions affect one as a wild dream—strange, incongruous, full of images of more than arabesque monstrosity, and snatches of sweet unsustained song. Even his worst nonsense (and some of it is horrible) has an indefinite charm of sentiment and melody. We can never be sure that there is *any* meaning in his words,— neither is there any meaning in many of our finest musical airs,— but the effect is very similar in both. His figures of speech are metaphor run mad, and his grammar is often none at all. Yet there are as fine individual passages to be found in the poems of Dr. Chivers as in those of any poet whatsoever.

The correspondence lapsed, at least on Poe's part, but in July, 1842, seeing possibly a chance to interest Chivers in his projected periodical, Poe wrote him, giving what could hardly have been a sincere tribute, and Chivers resumed the correspondence. Poe's letter in September is illuminating in revealing undaunted his hopes for the magazine:

Philadelphia
Sep. 27. 1842.

My Dear Sir,

Through some accident, I did not receive your letter of the 15th inst: until this morning, and now hasten to reply.

[38] His letter of August 27, 1840, in the Boston Public Library may be consulted by the curious. One sentence will suffice, "He who has never wandered amid the labyrinthine vistas of the flower-gemmed solitudes of thought knows nothing of the capabilities of the soul in its aspirations after the Beautiful in Natural Truth."

[39] *Graham's Magazine*, XIX (December, 1841), 284-285.

Allow me, in the first place, to thank you sincerely for your kindness in procuring me the subscribers to the Penn Magazine. The four names sent will aid me most materially in this early stage of the proceedings.

As yet I have taken no overt step in the measure, and have not even printed a Prospectus. As soon as I do this I will send you several. I do not wish to announce my positive resumption of the original scheme until about the middle of October. Before that period I have reason to believe that I shall have received an appointment in the Philadelphia Custom House, which will afford me a good salary and leave the greater portion of my time unemployed. With this appointment to fall back upon, as a certain resource, I shall be enabled to start the Magazine without difficulty, provided I can make an arrangement with either a practical printer possessing a small office, or some one not a printer, with about $1000 at command. It would, of course, be better for the permanent influence and success of the journal that I unite myself with a gentleman of education & similarity of thought and feeling. It was this consciousness which induced me to suggest the enterprise to yourself. I know no one with whom I would more readily enter into association than yourself.

I am not aware what are your political views. My own have reference to no one of the present parties; but it has been hinted to me that I will receive the most effectual patronage from Government, for a journal which will admit occasional papers in support of the Administration. For Mr. Tyler personally, & as an honest statesman, I have the highest respect. Of the government patronage, upon the condition specified, *I am assured* and this alone will more than sustain the Magazine.

The only real difficulty lies in the beginning—in the pecuniary means for getting out the two (or three) first numbers; after this all is sure, and a great triumph may, and indeed *will* be achieved. If you can command about $1000 and say that you will join me, I will write you fully as respects the details of the plan, or we can have an immediate interview.

It would be proper to start with an edition of 1000 copies. For this number, the monthly expense, including paper (of the finest quality) composition, press-work & stitching will be about 180$. I calculate *all* expenses at about $250—which is $3000 per annum —a *very* liberal estimate. 1000 copies at $5 = 5000$—leaving a nett profit of 2000$, even supposing we have only 1000 subscribers. But I am sure of *beginning* with at least 500, and make no doubt of obtaining 5000 before the expiration of the 2d year. A Magazine, such as I propose, with 5000 subscribers will produce us each an income of some $10,000; and this you will acknowledge is a game worth playing. At the same time there is no earthly reason why such a Magazine may not, eventually, reach a circulation as great as that of "Graham's" at present—viz. 50,000.

I repeat that it would give me the most sincere pleasure if you would make up your mind to join me. I am sure of our community of thought & feeling, and that would accomplish *much*.

In regard to the poem on Harrison's death,[40] I regret to say that nothing can be done with the Philadelphia publishers. The truth is that the higher order of poetry is, and always will be, in this country, unsaleable; but, even were it otherwise, the present state of the Copy-Right Laws will not warrant any publisher, in *purchasing* an American book. The only condition, I am afraid, upon which the poem can be printed, is that you print at your own expense.

I will see Griswold and endeavour to get the smaller poems from him. A precious fellow is he!

Write as soon as you receive this & believe me

Yours most truly

EDGAR A. POE.[41]

The magazine, as we know, did not appear in October. Chivers' personal association with Poe belongs more definitely to the later period.[42]

As this letter indicates, Poe was never forgetful of his project for a magazine of his own. On January 31, 1843, he entered into an agreement with Thomas C. Clarke and Felix O. C. Darley concerning the publication of a magazine to be called "The Stylus." Darley was to furnish the illustrations at seven dollars apiece. This document, which seems to be in Poe's handwriting,[43] betrays a certain familiarity with

[40] The Mighty Dead. [Note inscribed in Chivers' hand, on the Ms. letter.]
[41] Original Autograph Ms., Huntington Library.
[42] Woodberry printed Poe's letters to Chivers in the *Century*, LXV (1903), 435-447; 545-558, and reprinted this account in part in the *Life of Poe* (1909) in the *Appendix*. Harrison had in the meantime published the letters of Chivers in the Virginia Edition. S. Foster Damon, in *Thomas Holley Chivers, Friend of Poe* (New York, 1930), wrote the standard biography.
[43] Original agreement is in the Huntington Library.

legal terms, although it may have been dictated by his friend Henry B. Hirst, who was completing his law studies at this time.

In order to secure Clarke's interest in the *Stylus*, Poe permitted the announcement to be made that he had joined the staff of the *Saturday Museum* of Philadelphia, a weekly paper published by Clarke and Company at 101 "Chesnut" Street. In the issue of February 25, 1843, an extensive biography of Poe with his portrait and with reproductions of many of his poems, was published in this sheet.[44]

This biography was reprinted in the issue of March 4th [45] together with an editorial note:

EDGAR A. POE, Esq.

The Spirit of the Times, of Friday, says:—"The Saturday Museum of this week contains a very fair likeness of our friend, Edgar A. Poe, Esq. with a full account of his truly eventful life. We look upon Mr. Poe as one of the most powerful, chaste, and erudite writers of the day, and it gives us pleasure to see him placed, through the public spirit of our neighbor of the Museum, in his proper position before the world."

We are glad to hear so good a paper as the Times speak thus highly of Mr. Poe, not only from the justice which it renders that powerful writer, but because we have been so fortunate as to secure his services as assistant Editor of the Saturday Museum. We have the pleasure of announcing this week, this association, from which our paper cannot fail to reap the most brilliant advantages. The arrangement will be commenced with some splendid typographical improvements, that we are about introducing, and which will put the Museum where we intend it shall be placed—beyond the reach of competition.

So great was the interest excited by the Biography and Poems of Mr. Poe, published in the Museum of last week, that to supply those who were disappointed in obtaining copies, we shall be at the expense of an extra Museum, in which the whole article will be re-printed, with corrections and additions. Of this extra we

[44] An issue of February 25th, apparently unique, was in possession of the late Mr. J. H. Rindfleisch, of Richmond, to whose courtesy I owe a photostat of the original. It does not contain Poe's "Song of the Newly Wedded" (Bridal Ballad), which was added in the reprint of March 4th, and there are other verbal differences. The dates have been cut out. It may have been a dummy for the printer, who was to fill in the new dates.

[45] For this issue, I am indebted to Dr. James S. Wilson, who owns one of the rare copies, and to Mr. John C. Wyllie, also of the University of Virginia, for the photostat in enlarged type which enabled me to read it. Mr. J. H. Rindfleisch also sent me a photostat copy of this issue.

shall publish an edition on fine white paper. It will be ready for delivery at this office on Saturday morning.[46]

The biography fills the entire first page of the large sheet, fifteen by twenty inches, printed in that infinitesimal type with which our ancestors tried their eyes. It is stated to be based on information given by T. W. White, of the *Messenger*, and F. W. Thomas, but as will be seen, it was really by Henry B. Hirst. Thomas wrote Poe on February 1st, excusing himself on the grounds of his labors at the Department from compiling the article from the memoranda Poe had sent him.[47]

Thomas sent Poe a letter of introduction to Robert Tyler on February 8, 1843,[48] explaining that he was too ill to present Poe in person. Poe did not go down to Washington, however, in February, but his letter to Thomas makes a number of points clear:

Philadelphia, February 25, 1843.

My dear Thomas,—Herewith I forward a "Saturday Museum" containing a Biography and caricature, both of myself. I am ugly enough, God knows, but not *quite* so bad as that. The biographer is H. B. Hirst of this city. I put into his hands your package, as returned, and he has taken the liberty of stating his indebtedness for memoranda to yourself—a slight extension of the truth for which I pray you to excuse him. He is a warm friend of yours, by the by—and a warm friend is a matter of moment at all times, but especially in this age of lukewarmness. I have also been guilty of an indiscretion in quoting from a private letter of yours to myself—I could not forego the temptation of letting the world know how well you thought of me.

On the outside of the paper you will see a Prospectus of "The Stylus"—my old "Penn" revived and remodelled under better auspices. I am anxious to hear your opinion of it. I have managed *at last* to secure, I think, the great object—a partner possessing ample capital, and, at the same time, so little self-esteem, as to allow me entire control of the editorial conduct. He gives me, also, a half interest, and is to furnish funds for all the business

[46] Page 2 of the issue of March 4, 1843. This editorial does not mention the reprinting on its own first page. There was an Extra which contained a reprint of the notice concerning the *Stylus*, but not the biography. This is in the American Antiquarian Society. There were probably two Extras, but I have not found the one announced in the notice in the *Museum*.

[47] Original Autograph Ms., Griswold Collection, Boston Public Library.

[48] Original Autograph Ms., Griswold Collection, Boston Public Library.

operations—I agreeing to supply, for the first year, the literary matter. This will puzzle me no little, but I must do my best—write as much as possible myself, under my own name and pseudonyms, and hope for the casual aid of my friends, until the first stage of infancy is surpassed. The articles of copartnership have been signed and sealed for some weeks, and I should have written you before, informing you of my good luck, but that I was in hope of sending you, at the same time, a specimen-sheet. Some little delay has occurred in getting it out, on account of paper. In the mean time, all arrangements are progressing with spirit. We shall make the most magnificent Magazine as regards externals, ever seen. The finest paper, bold type, in single column, and superb wood-engravings (in the manner of the French illustrated edition of "Gil Blas" by Gigoux, or "Robinson Crusoe" by Grandville).

There are three objects I would give a great deal to accomplish. Of the first I have some hope—but of the two last exceedingly little, unless you aid me. In the first place, I wish an article from yourself for my opening number—in the second, one from Mr. Rob Tyler—in the third, one from Judge Upshur. If I could get all this, I should be made—but I despair. Judge Upshur wrote some things for "The Messenger" during my editorship, and if I could get him interested in the scheme he *might,* by good management, be induced to give me an article, I care not how brief, or on what subject, *with his name.* It would be worth to me at least $500, and give me *caste* at once. I think him, as a reasoner, as a speaker, and as a writer, absolutely unsurpassed. I have the *very highest* opinion of his abilities. There is no man in America from whom I so strongly covet an article. Is it procurable?

In a few weeks, at farthest, I hope to take you by the hand. In the mean time write, and let me know how you come on.

About a week since I enclosed an introductory letter to yourself in one to a friend of mine (Professor Wyatt) now in Washington. I presume you have seen him. He is much of a gentleman, and I think you will be pleased with him.

Virginia and Mrs. Clemm beg to be remembered.

Truly your friend,

EDGAR A. POE.[49]

P.S. Smith not rejected yet. Ah if I could only get the inspectorship, or something similar, *now*—how completely it would put me out of all difficulty.

[49] Original Autograph Ms., Griswold Collection, Boston Public Library

This biography in the Philadelphia *Museum* has, therefore, unusual importance since Poe furnished the material and evidently edited the poems. It included, and in some cases, was the primary source of information, correct and incorrect, concerning Poe's ancestry and personal history. The myths concerning the elopement of Poe's parents, their death "on a visit to Richmond," Poe's journey to Greece and St. Petersburg, his return from Europe on the night after Mrs. Allan's burial, are mingled with more authentic accounts of the West Point episode, and the University of Virginia. No mention of the army service is made. Poe's connection with the *Messenger* is correctly stated, and the account proceeds:

> With Mr. Graham (with whom he has always maintained the most friendly relations) he remained as critical editor, for a period of some fourteen or fifteen months; but is not to be considered responsible, (as some have held him) either for the external appearance, or the general internal character of that periodical.
>
> It has often been a subject for wonder that with the pre-eminent success which has attended his editorial efforts, Mr. Poe has never established a magazine, in which he should have more than a collateral interest, and we are now happy to learn that such is at length, his intention. By reference to another page of our paper, it will be seen that he has issued the Prospectus of a Monthly, to be entitled "The Stylus," for which, it is needless to say, we predict the most unequivocal success. In so saying, we but endorse the opinion of every literary man in the country.

The account then proceeds with thirty-two laudatory criticisms of Poe's stories, including quotations from all the leading writers of the day. Poe did not hesitate to quote from private letters like those from Irving or Longfellow, turning them into the third person, as though they had been printed. From Hawthorne he quoted the passage from "The Hall of Fantasy" as it first appeared in the *Pioneer* in February, 1843: "Mr. Poe gained ready admission [into the Hall of Fantasy] on account of his imagination, but was threatened with ejection as belonging to the obnoxious class of critics." This passage was omitted in later versions of the "Hall of Fantasy."

Of greater significance, however, is that portion of the article which deals with Poe's poetry. Those who, like the present writer, believe that it is as a poet that Poe will ultimately be remembered, are supported by the statement: "But notwithstanding his success as a prose writer, it is as a poet we now wish chiefly to consider him."

Although Poe had constantly made changes in his poems for the magazines in which he republished them since the appearance of his volume of 1831, the *Saturday Museum* text is important because it contains an extensive revision of his poetry up to that time.[50]

Poe did not make these changes merely for the sake of more pleasing sounds. On the most important of the poems, like "To Helen" and "Israfel," Poe lavished the care which still further enhanced the beauty of verses that might have seemed perfect to a lesser poet. In "To Helen" by changing "that shadowy window niche" in which Psyche stands, to "yon brilliant window niche" and the "folded scroll" which she holds to "the agate lamp," Psyche becomes not a shrouded figure, but a shining beacon to light the "weary way worn wanderer" back to his "native shore." In "Israfel" "He might not sing one half so well" became "He might not sing so wildly well." In "Romance," the long passage of the *Poems* of 1831 referring to "the idle boy, who read Anacreon and drank wine" was omitted. Poe had probably begun to feel the criticisms of his habits, and thought it discreet to give his enemies no support. The lines themselves are not self-revelation, but an early and Byronic assumption of the easy distinction of dissipation. The textual changes were usually preserved in the 1845 edition of Poe's poems with the exception of those in "Al Aaraaf," where Poe reverted to the 1829 version.[51]

The biography lists among Poe's works "a work of fiction, in two volumes, under a *nom-de-plume*, never acknowledged;—also two papers, on American topics, for a Parisian critical journal—with one or two anonymous articles in a British periodical, and several also anonymous, in an American Quarterly." The novel and the foreign articles have so far baffled research.

The biography closes with a description of Poe:

> He is now but little more than thirty years of age; in person, he is somewhat slender, about five feet, eight inches in height, and

[50] Revised versions of the following poems: "To Helen," "Al Aaraaf" (partially), "Sonnet—To Science," "Romance," "To the River," "The Conqueror Worm," "Lenore," "Sonnet to Zante," "The Sleeper," "To One in Paradise," "Sonnet—Silence," "Israfel," "Song of the Newly Wedded (Bridal Ballad)," "To One Departed," "The Coliseum," and "The Haunted Palace." The omitted poems of importance are, "Tamerlane," "A Dream Within a Dream," "The Lake," "Fairyland," "The City in the Sea," "The Valley of Unrest," and the "Hymn."

[51] For a detailed textual comparison, which would be out of place here, see Dudley Hutcherson, "The Philadelphia Saturday Museum Text of Poe's Poems," *American Literature*, V (March, 1933), 38-48.

well proportioned; his complexion is rather fair; his eyes are grey and restless, exhibiting a marked nervousness; while the mouth indicates great decision of character; his forehead is extremely broad, displaying prominently the organs of Ideality, Casualty [sic], Form, Constructiveness, and Comparison, with small Eventuality and Individuality. His hair is nearly black, and partially curling. Our portrait, conveys a tolerably correct idea of the man.

The Prospectus of the *Stylus* resembled closely in some of its paragraphs the announcement of the *Penn Magazine*, and so these need not be repeated. There are, however, a few remarks pertaining only to the new magazine:

Prospectus

of

THE STYLUS:

A Monthly Journal of General Literature

to be edited by

EDGAR A. POE

And Published, in the City of Philadelphia, by

CLARKE & POE.

———unbending that all men
Of thy firm Truth may say—"Lo! this is writ
With the antique *iron pen*."
Launcelot Canning.

To the Public.—The Prospectus of a Monthly Journal to have been called "The Penn Magazine," has already been partially circulated. Circumstances, in which the public have no interest, induced a suspension of the project, which is now, under the best auspices, resumed, with no other modification than that of the title. "The Penn Magazine," it has been thought, was a name somewhat too local in its suggestions, and The STYLUS has been finally adopted. . . .

As, for many reasons, it is inexpedient to commence a journal of this kind at any other period than the beginning or middle of the year, the first number of "The Stylus" will not be regularly issued until the first of July, 1843. In the meantime, to insure its perfect and permanent success, no means will be left untried which *long* experience, untiring energy, and the amplest capital, can supply. The price will be *Five Dollars* per annum, or *Three Dollars* per single volume, in advance. Letters which concern only the Editorial management may be addressed to Edgar A. Poe, individually; all others to Clarke & Poe. . . .

The new journal will endeavor to be at the same time more varied and more unique;—more vigorous, more pungent, more original, more individual, and more independent. It will discuss not only the Belles-Lettres, but, very thoroughly, the Fine Arts, with the Drama; and, more in brief, will give, each month, a Retrospect of our Political History. It will enlist the loftiest talent, but employ it not always in the loftiest—at least not always in the most pompous or Puritanical way. It will aim at affording a fair and not dishonorable field for the *true* intellect of the land, without reference to the mere prestige of celebrated names. It will support the general interests of the Republic of Letters, and insist upon regarding the world at large as the sole proper audience for the author. It will resist the dictation of Foreign Reviews. It will eschew the stilted dulness of our own Quarterlies, and while it *may*, if necessary, be no less learned, will deem it wiser to be less anonymous, and difficult to be more dishonest, than they.

An important feature of the work, and one which will be introduced in the opening number, will be a series of *Critical* and *Biographical Sketches* of *American Writers*. These Sketches will be accompanied with full length and characteristic portraits; will include every person of literary note in America; and will investigate carefully and with rigorous impartiality, the individual claims of each.

It shall, in fact, be the chief purpose of "The Stylus," to become known as a journal wherein may be found, at all times, upon all subjects within its legitimate reach, a sincere and a fearless opinion. It shall be a leading object to assert in precept, and to maintain in practice, the rights, while, in effect, it demonstrates the advantages, of an absolutely independent criticism;—a criticism self-sustained; guiding itself only by the purest rules of Art; analyzing and urging these rules as it applies them; holding itself aloof from all personal bias; and acknowledging no fear save that of outraging the Right.

CLARKE & POE [52]

[52] *Saturday Museum*, March 4, 1843, p. 3.

In another part of the *Museum* the statement is made that Poe will begin his connection with the paper on May 1, 1843, "at a high salary," but no record of his salary has come down to us, because, apparently, there was none.

Notwithstanding all the trumpeting in the *Saturday Museum*, Poe did not join the staff [53] at least in any active way, although he did write occasionally for it. He republished his "Conversation of Eiros and Charmion" as "The Destruction of the World," and printed some conundrums.[54] He went to Washington early in March, unfortunately as it proved, partly to solicit subscriptions for the *Stylus* and partly to keep an open eye upon an appointment under the Tyler Administration. Two letters tell sufficiently the story of this visit. The first was to T. C. Clarke:

Washington—March 11. 1843.

My Dear Sir,

I write merely to inform you of my will [sic]—doing—for, so far, I have done nothing. My friend Thomas, upon whom I depended, is sick. I suppose he will be well in a few days. In the meantime, I shall have to do the best I can. I have not seen the President yet.

My expenses were more than I thought they would be, although I have economised in every respect, and this delay (Thomas' being sick) puts me out sadly. *However* all is going right. I have got the subscriptions of *all* the Departments—President, [erasure] &c I believe that I am making a *sensation* which will tend to the benefit of the Magazine.

Day after to-morrow I am to lecture.

Rob. Tyler is to give me an article—also Upsher. Send me $10 by mail, as soon as you get this. I am grieved to ask you [erasure] for money, in this way.—but you will find your account in it— twice over.

Very truly yours

EDGAR A. POE.

Thos. C. Clarke Esqre.[55]

---

[53] See his letters to Lowell, March 27 and October 19, 1843.

[54] April 1, 1843. I owe these two items to Dr. T. O. Mabbott, who examined this issue in the Library of the University of North Carolina.

[55] Original Autograph Ms., Young Collection, New York Public Library. The handwriting of this letter shows that Poe was not himself when he wrote it.

Poe did not lecture, however, for on the next day his friend, J. E. Dow, wrote to Clarke:

Washington, March 12, 1843.

Dear Sir,—I deem it to be my bounden duty to write you this hurried letter in relation to our mutual friend E.A.P.

He arrived here a few days since. On the first evening he seemed somewhat excited, having been over-persuaded to take some Port wine.

On the second day he kept pretty steady, but since then he has been, at intervals, quite unreliable.

He exposes himself here to those who may injure him very much with the President, and thus prevents us from doing for him what we wish to do and what we can do if he is himself again in Philadelphia. He does not understand the ways of politicians, nor the manner of dealing with them to advantage. How should he?

Mr. Thomas is not well and cannot go home with Mr. P. My business and the health of my family will prevent me from so doing.

Under all the circumstances of the case, I think it advisable for you to come on and see him safely back to his home. Mrs. Poe is in a bad state of health, and I charge you, as you have a soul to be saved, to say not one word to her about him until he arrives with you. I shall expect you or an answer to this letter by return of mail.

Should you not come, we will see him on board the cars bound to Phila., but we fear he might be detained in Baltimore and not be out of harm's way.

I do this under a solemn responsibility. Mr. Poe has the highest order of intellect, and I cannot bear that he should be the sport of senseless creatures who, like oysters, keep sober, and gape and swallow everything.

I think your good judgment will tell you what course you ought to pursue in this matter, and I cannot think it will be necessary to let him know that I have written you this letter; but I cannot suffer him to injure himself here without giving you this warning.

Yours respectfully,

J. E. Dow.

To Thomas C. Clarke, Esq.,
    Philadelphia, Pa.[56]

Poe was in good enough shape to return to Philadelphia alone, but the vigilant Mrs. Clemm met him at the train. His letter to his two

[56] Gill's *Life*, pp. 120-122.

friends in Washington is that of a man deeply mortified and trying to believe that he had not disgraced himself:

Philadelphia
March 16. 1843.

My Dear Thomas, & Dow

I arrived here, in perfect safety, and *sober,* about half past four last evening—nothing occurring on the road of any consequence. I shaved and breakfasted in Baltimore and lunched on The Susquehannah, and by the time I got to Phila. felt quite decent. Mrs. Clemm was expecting me at the car-office. I went immediately home, took a warm bath & supper & then went to Clarke's. I never saw a man in my life more surprised to see another. He thought by Dow's epistle that I must not only be dead but buried & would as soon have thought of seeing his Great-great-great grandmother. He received me, therefore, very cordially & made light of the matter. I told him what had been agreed upon—that I was a little sick & that Dow, knowing I had been, in times passed, given to spreeing upon an extensive scale, had become unduly alarmed &c. &c.—that when I found he had written I thought it best to come home. He said my trip had improved me & that he had never *seen me looking so well!!!*—and I don't believe I ever did.

This morning I took medicine, and, as it is a snowy day, will avail myself of the excuse to stay at home—so that by to-morrow I shall be *really* as well as ever.

Virginia's health is about the same—but her distress of mind had been even more that I had anticipated. She desires her *kindest* remembrances to both of you—as also does Mrs. C.

Clarke, it appears, wrote to Dow, who must have received the letter this morning. Please re-inclose the letter to me, here—so that I may know how to guide myself.—and, Thomas, do write immediately as proposed. If *possible,* enclose a line from Rob. Tyler—but I fear, under the circumstances, it is not so—I blame no one but myself.

The letter which I looked for & which I wished returned, is not on its way—reason, no money forthcoming—Lowell had not yet sent it—he is ill, in N. York of opthalmia. Immediately upon receipt of it, or before, I will forward the money you were both so kind as to lend—which is 8 to Dow and 3½ to Thomas—What a confounded business I have got myself into, attempting to write a letter to two people at once!

However—this is for Dow. My dear fellow—Thank you a thousand times for your kindness & great forbearance, and don't say a word about the cloak turned inside out, or other peccadilloes of that nature. Also, express to your wife my deep regret for the vexation I must have occasioned her. Send me, also, if you can the letter to Blythe. Call, also, at the barber's shop just above Fuller's and pay for me a levy which I believe I owe. And now God bless you—for a nobler fellow never lived.

And this is for Thomas. My dear friend. Forgive me my petulance & don't believe I think all I said. Believe me I am very grateful to you for your many attentions & forbearances and the time will never come when I shall forget either them or you. Remember me most kindly to Dr. Lacey—also to the Don, whose mustachios I *do* admire after all, and who has about the finest figure I ever beheld—also to Dr. Frailey. Please express my regret to Mr. Fuller for making such a fool of myself in his house, and say to him (if you think it necessary) that I should not have got half so drunk on his excellent Port wine but for the rummy coffee with which I was forced to wash it down. I would be glad, too, if you would take an opportunity of saying to Mr. Rob. Tyler that if he *can* look over matters and get me the Inspectorship, I will join the Washingtonians forthwith. I am as serious as a judge —& much [more] so than many. I think it would be a feather in Mr. Tyler's cap to save from the perils of mint julap [sic]—& "Port wines"—a young man of whom all the world thinks so well & who thinks *so* remarkably well of himself.

And now, my dear friends, good bye & believe me

Most truly yours

EDGAR A. POE.

Mess. Dow & Thomas.

Upon getting here I found numerous letters of subscribers to my Magazine—for which no canvass has yet been made. This was unexpected & cheering. Did you say, Dow that Commodore Elliot had desired me to put down his name? Is it so or did I dream it? At all events, when you see him present my respects and thanks. Thomas, you will remember that Dr. Lacey wished me to put him down—but I don't know his first name—please let me have it.[57]

---

[57] Original Autograph Ms., Griswold Collection, Boston Public Library. There is another form in the Pratt Library, Baltimore, which is probably a first draft. It does not contain the annotation by Thomas, and there is no sure indication that it was sent through the mail.

On this letter Thomas wrote a note of sympathetic understanding.

This letter explains itself. While his friends were trying to get Poe a place he came on to Washington in the way he mentions. He was soon quite sick, and while he was so Dow wrote to one of his friends in Philadelphia about him. Poor fellow, a place had been promised his friends for him, and in that state of suspense which is so trying to all men, and particularly to men of imagination, he presented himself in Washington certainly not in a way to advance his interests. I have seen a great deal of Poe, and it was his excessive and at times marked sensibility which forced him into his "frolics," rather than any mere morbid appetite for drink, but if he took but one glass of weak wine or beer or cider, the Rubicon of the cup was passed with him, and it almost always ended in excess and sickness. But he fought against the propensity as hard as ever Coleridge fought against [it], and I am inclined to believe, after his sad experience and suffering, if he could have gotten office with a fixed salary, beyond the need of literary labour, that he would have redeemed himself— at least at this time. The accounts of his derelictions in this respect when I knew him were very much exaggerated. I have seen men who drank bottles of wine to Poe's wine-glasses who yet escaped all imputations of intemperance. His was one of those temperaments whose only safety is in total abstinence. He suffered terribly after any indiscretion. And, after all, what Byron said of Sheridan was truer of Poe:—

"... Ah, little do they know
That what to them seemed vice might be but woe."

And, moreover, there is a great deal of heartache in the jestings of this letter.

T.

Clarke seems not to have been unduly disturbed by the incident, and Thomas wrote Poe on March 27th that he was still trying to interest President Tyler. But nothing came from his efforts.

Poe sent his poem "Eulalie" to Carter on February 16, 1843, but was too late, as the *Pioneer* died in March.[58]

[58] Original Autograph Ms., Collection of J. K. Lilly, Jr. This early version of "Eulalie" differs from the first printed form in the *American Review* for July, 1845, in the second stanza:

"And ah! less bright
The stars of the night
Than the eyes of the radiant girl,

Lowell wrote to Poe on March 24, 1843, apologizing for his failure to pay Poe for his contributions to the *Pioneer*, and Poe, while depending upon this money to repay Dow and Thomas, replied:

Philadelphia, March 27, '43.

My Dear Friend,—I have just received yours of the 24th and am deeply grieved, first that you should have been so unfortunate, and, secondly, that you should have thought it necessary to offer me any apology for your misfortunes. As for the few dollars you owe me—give yourself not one moment's concern about *them*. I am poor, but must be very much poorer, indeed, when I even think of demanding them.

But I sincerely hope all is not so bad as you suppose it, and that, when you come to look about you, you will be able to continue "The Pioneer." Its decease, just now, would be a most severe blow to the good cause—the cause of a Pure Taste. I have looked upon your Magazine, from its outset, as the best in America, and have lost no opportunity of expressing the opinion. Herewith I

> And never a flake
> Their lustre can make
> Of the vapor and gold and pearl,
> Can vie with the sweet young Eulalie's most humble and
>   careless curl—
> Can compare with the bright-eyed Eulalie's most vagrant
>   and careless curl."

The sixth line of the third stanza read:

"The Moon in the purple sky,"

but "the Moon" was crossed out and "Astart" [sic] inserted. This may mean that Astarté was substituted for the moon, and represented Venus, or it may help settle the question whether Astarté in "Ulalume" meant Venus or the moon. Another Ms. of "Eulalie," in the W. H. Koester Collection, is identical with this early form, except that the line

"Astarté within the sky,"

indicates that it is a stage between the first form and the later one. The number of manuscripts of "Eulalie" probably reflect the difficulty Poe had in placing it. These early forms also do away with several supposed "sources" of "Eulalie," which appeared in 1845—and are a warning to those who attribute to Poe inspiration from others' work without knowing the date of *first* composition of his poems.

send a paper, "The Phil. Sat. Museum," in which I have said a few words on the topic.

I am *not* editing this paper, although an announcement was prematurely made to that effect; but have the privilege of inserting what I please editorially. On the first of July next I hope to issue the first number of "The Stylus," a new monthly, with some novel features. I send you, also, a paper containing the Prospectus. In a few weeks I hope to forward you a specimen sheet. I am anxious to get a poem from yourself for the opening number, but, until you recover your health, I fear that I should be wrong in making the request.

Believe me, my dear friend, that I sympathize with you *truly* in your affliction. When I heard that you had returned to Boston I hoped you were entirely well, and your letter disappoints and grieves me.

When you find yourself in condition to write, I would be indebted to you if you could put me in the way of procuring a brief article (also for my opening number) from Mr. Hawthorne —whom I believe you know personally. Whatever you gave him, we should be happy to give. A part of my design is to illustrate, whatever is fairly susceptible of illustration, with finely executed wood-engravings—after the fashion of Gigoux's "Gil Blas" or "Grandville's Gulliver" [sic]—and I wish to get a tale from Mr. Hawthorne as early as possible (if I am so fortunate as to get one at all), that I may put the illustration in the hands of the artist.

You will see by the Prospectus that we intend to give a series of portraits of the American literati, with critical sketches. I would be glad if I could so arrange matters as to have you *first,* provided you yourself have no serious objection. Instead of the "full-length portraits" promised in the Prospectus (which will be modified in the specimen sheet), we shall have medallions about three inches in diameter. Could you put me in possession of any likeness of yourself?—or would you do me the same favor in regard to Mr. Hawthorne?—You perceive I proceed upon the ground that you are intimate with Mr. H., and that making these inquiries would not subject you to trouble or inconvenience.

I confess that I am by no means so conversant with your own compositions (especially in prose) as I should be. Could you furnish me with some biographical and critical data, and tell me when or how I could be put in possession of your writings generally?—but I fear I am asking altogether too much.

If the 4th number of "The Pioneer" is printed, I would be obliged if you would send me an early copy through the P. O.

Please remember me to Mr. Carter, and believe me

Most sincerely your friend,

EDGAR A. POE.

J. Russell Lowell, Esqre.[59]

In view of the insistence upon Poe's applications for loans, this generosity should be remembered in his behalf. Lowell tried to secure the story from Hawthorne, sent one of his own poems, and signed his letters as an "affectionate friend." Poe's note to him on June 20, 1843, tells him that the *Stylus* had to be abandoned:

Philadelphia, June 20, 1843.

My Dear Friend,—I owe you fifty apologies for not having written you before—but sickness and domestic affliction will suffice for all.

I received your poem, which you undervalue, and which I think truly beautiful—as, indeed, I do all you have ever written—but alas! my Magazine scheme has exploded—or, at least, I have been deprived, through the imbecility, or rather through the idiocy of my partner, of all means of prosecuting it for the present. Under better auspices I may resume it next year.

What am I to do with the poem? I have handed it to Griswold, subject to your disposition.

My address is 234 North Seventh St., above Spring Garden, West Side. Should you ever pay a visit to Philadelphia, you will remember that there is no one in America whom I would rather hold by the hand than yourself.

With the sincerest friendship I am yours,

EDGAR A. POE.[60]

This letter gives Poe's address for the first time as 234 North Seventh Street, now 530. It was in the district known as Spring Garden. This cottage has a special interest, since it is the only actual

---

[59] Original Autograph Ms., Harvard College Library.

[60] Copy of letter, Griswold Collection, Boston Public Library. Harrison XVII, 149, prints it as to J. T. Fields from the Fields Collection.

POE'S HOME IN "SPRING GARDEN," PHILADELPHIA

Still standing. Now the back building of 530 North 7th Street. Photograph, taken in 1909, by the courtesy of Joseph Jackson.

home of Poe, maintained as a Poe museum, which contains any large amount of associated literary material.[61]

This house, on the corner of Seventh Street and Brandywine Alley, a small street running parallel to Spring Garden Street, was a three-story brick cottage, with a garden toward the east, and a porch in the rear. The garden is now occupied by the front buildings on Seventh Street, which were added after Poe left Philadelphia. Even now when the cottage is simply the back building of a larger house, it is not hard to picture a comfortable home in 1843. The living room and kitchen have good light and open fireplaces, where Poe sat with Virginia and Mrs. Clemm, reading and writing. There are pleasant rooms on the second and third floors, although the roof is low.

We do not know exactly when the family moved to North Seventh Street. Poe told Thomas in September, 1842, that he had moved out "in the neighborhood of Fairmount" and since the Directory for 1843, gave him as a resident of the Coates Street house, it was probably for only one year or less that he lived at North Seventh Street.[62]

They were probably settled there in the spring of 1843, and Virginia's health was good enough to permit her to take care of the flower garden, even if the "rose-covered cottage" as it is often called, must have been an exaggeration. While it was still on the outskirts of the city, is was much nearer the centre than Fairmount. As Poe went down Seventh Street, he passed the houses of respectable families whose names are still well known today, although the neighborhood has radically changed, and they have moved away. Poe passed Buttonwood Street next, where Graham had lived; but just about the time Poe moved to Spring Garden, Graham departed to Arch Street. At the next street, Callowhill, Poe could see the home of George Lippard, the novelist of scandal and history who was later to help save him from disaster. Continuing down to High or Market Street, he was near

[61] It was purchased in 1933 by Mr. Richard Gimbel, who has collected a large library of magazines containing articles by Poe, all the well known biographies, and works dealing with Poe, including manuscript material. An attractive brochure, *The Rose Covered Cottage* by Mr. Anthony Frane, Custodian of the house, gives full information concerning its history.

[62] The descriptions given by Graham and Griswold evidently refer to the Coates Street residence. Mayne Reid's description of "a lean-to of three rooms (there may have been a garret with a closet) of painted plank construction, supported against the gable of the more pretentious dwelling" can apply to neither the Coates Street nor the Spring Garden Street houses, both of which were built of brick. The Directory for 1844 reads "Poe, E. A., editor 7th ab. S. Garden."

the publishing house of Haswell, Barrington and Haswell, who had printed his *Conchologist's First Book*. Turning left at Chestnut Street, he was within a block of the law office of his friend Henry B. Hirst, at 40 South Sixth Street. One of Poe's biographers states that he registered for the study of law, with Hirst as a sponsor, at the University of Pennsylvania.[63] I should be delighted to claim Poe as an alumnus of my own University, but, unfortunately, the old Law School, founded in 1790, had lapsed temporarily before Poe came to Philadelphia, and was revived only in 1850.

It would be pleasant to imagine that the comparative comfort in the appearance of the house on Seventh Street reflected some measure of prosperity for the Poe family. On the contrary, there was evidently the spectre of care ever present. Though Poe wrote bravely to Lowell, there is a letter to Griswold on June 11, 1843, which it must have galled him to send, if indeed he did write it:

> Dear Griswold:—Can you not send me $5? I am sick, and Virginia is almost gone. Come and see me. Peterson says you suspect me of a curious anonymous letter. I did not write it, but bring it along with you when you make the visit you promised to Mrs. Clemm. I will try to fix that matter soon. Could you do anything with my *note?*
>
> > Yours truly,
> >
> > E. A. P.[64]

After having written as Poe did to Lowell in June, it must have been dire want which made him appear to dun his friend in September:

> Philadelphia, September 13, 1843.
>
> My Dear Friend,—Since I last wrote you I have suffered much from domestic and pecuniary trouble, and, at one period, had nearly succumbed. I mention this by way of apology to the request I am forced to make—that you would send me, if possible, $10—which, I believe, is the amount you owe me for contribution. You cannot imagine how sincerely I grieve that any necessity can urge me to ask this of you—but I ask it in the hope

---

[63] Mary E. Phillips, *Poe the Man*, p. 289.

[64] The original letter, so far as I can ascertain, is not in existence. It was printed in Griswold's "Preface" to his "Memoir" of Poe, in *The Literati, etc.*, of 1850, p. v. In view of Griswold's forgeries, such unsupported evidence is not trustworthy.

that you are now in much better position than myself, and can spare me the sum without inconvenience.

I hope ere long to have the pleasure of conversing with you personally. There is no man living with whom I have so much desire to become acquainted.

Truly your friend,

EDGAR A. POE.

J. R. Lowell, Esqre.[65]

Poe's letter to Lowell in October shows that Carter and Lowell were dividing the debts of the *Pioneer*. It has other interesting information:

Philadelphia, October 19, 1843.

My Dear Friend,—I was upon the point of fulfilling a long neglected duty and replying to Mr. Carter's letter, enclosing $5, when I received yours of the 13th, remitting $5 more. Believe me I am sincerely grateful to you both for your uniform kindness and consideration.

You say nothing of your health—but Mr. C. speaks of its perfect restoration, and I see, by your very MS., that you are well again, body and mind. I need not say that I am rejoiced at this—for you must know and feel that I am. When I thought of the possible loss of your eyesight, I grieved as if some dreadful misfortune were about happening to myself.

I shall look with much anxiety for your promised volume. Will it include your "Year's Life," and other poems already published? I hope that it may; for these have not yet been fairly placed before the eye of the world. I am seeking an opportunity to do you justice in a review, and may find it in "Graham," when your book appears. No poet in America has done so much. I have maintained this upon all occasions. Mr. Longfellow has genius, but by no means equals you in the true spirit. He is moreover so prone to imitation that I know not how to understand him at times. I am in doubt whether he should not be termed an arrant plagiarist. You have read his "Spanish Student"? I have written quite a long notice of it for Graham's December number. The play is a poor composition, with some fine poetical passages. His "Hymn to the Night," with some strange blemishes, is glorious.—How much I should like to interchange opinions with you upon poems and

[65] Original Autograph Ms. Letter, Norton Collection, Harvard College Library. Norton wrote on the margin that the money was paid.

poets in general! I fancy that we should agree, usually, in results, while differing frequently, about principles. The day may come when we can discuss everything at leisure, in person.

You say that your long poem has taught you a useful lesson,— "that you are unfit to write narrative—unless in a dramatic form." It is not you that are unfit for the task—but the task for you—for any poet. Poetry must eschew narrative—except, as you say, dramatically. I mean to say that the *true* poetry—the highest poetry —must eschew it. The Iliad is *not* the highest. The connecting links of a narrative—the frequent passages which have to serve the purpose of binding together the parts of the story, are necessarily prose, from their very explanatory nature. To color them— to gloss over their prosaic nature—(for this is the most which can be done) requires great skill. Thus Byron, who was no artist, is always driven, in his narrative, to fragmentary passages, eked out with asterisks. Moore succeeds better than any one. His "Alciphron" is wonderful in the force, grace, and nature of its purely narrative passages:—but pardon me for prosing.

I send you the paper with my life and portrait. The former is true in general—the latter particularly false. It does not convey the faintest idea of my person. No one of my family recognized it. But this is a point of little importance. You will see, upon the back of the biography, an announcement that I was to assume the editorship of the "Museum." This was unauthorized. I never did edit it. The review of "Graham's Magazine" was written by H. B. Hirst—a young poet of this city. Who is to write your life for "Graham"? It is a pity that so many of these biographies were entrusted to Mr. Griswold. He certainly lacks independence, or judgment, or both.

I have tried in vain to get a copy of your "Year's Life" in Philadelphia. If you have one, and could spare it, I would be much obliged.

Do write me again when you have leisure, and believe me,
                         Your most sincere friend,
                                            EDGAR A. POE.

J. R. Lowell, Esqre.[66]

If Poe wrote the review of Longfellow's "Spanish Student" it did not appear in *Graham's* in December, and this episode may prove that Poe was not able to place his criticisms at will. Lowell tried to help

[66] Original Autograph Ms., Harvard College Library.

him obtain lectures in Boston. Poe proposed to him a scheme for a new form of magazine:

Philadelphia, March 30, 1844.

My Dear Friend,—Graham has been speaking to me, lately, about your Biography, and I am anxious to write it at once, always provided you have no objection. Could you forward me the materials within a day or two? I am just now quite disengaged —in fact positively idle.

I presume you have read the Memoir of Willis, in the April number of G. It is written by a Mr. Landor—but I think it full of hyperbole. Willis is *no* genius—a graceful trifler—no more. He wants force and sincerity. He is very frequently far-fetched. In me, at least, he never excites an emotion. Perhaps the best poem he has written is a little piece called "Unseen Spirits," beginning "The Shadows lay—Along Broadway."

You inquire about my own portrait. It has been done for some time—but is better as an engraving, than as a portrait. It scarcely resembles me at all. When it will appear I cannot say. Conrad and Mrs. Stephens will certainly come before me—perhaps Gen. Morris. My Life is not yet written, and I am at a sad loss for a Biographer—for Graham insists upon leaving the matter to myself.

I sincerely rejoice to hear of the success of your volume. To sell eleven hundred copies of a bound book of American poetry, is to do wonders. I hope everything from your future endeavors. Have you read "Orion"? Have you seen the article on "American Poetry" in the "London Foreign Quarterly"? It has been denied that Dickens wrote it—but, to me, the article affords so strong internal evidence of his hand that I would as soon think of doubting my existence. He tells much truth—although he evinces much ignorance and more spleen. Among other points he accuses myself of "metrical imitation" of Tennyson, citing, by way of instance, passages from poems which were written and published by me long before Tennyson was heard of:—but I have at no time made any poetical pretension. I am greatly indebted for the trouble you have taken about the lectures, and shall be very glad to avail myself, next season, of any invitation from the "Boston Lyceum." Thank you, also, for the hint about the "North American Review";—I will bear it in mind. I mail you, herewith, a "Dollar Newspaper," containing a somewhat extravagant tale of my own. I fear it will prove little to your taste.

How dreadful is the present condition ot our Literature! To what are things tending? We want two things, certainly:—an International Copy-Right Law, and a well-founded Monthly Journal, of sufficient ability, circulation, and character, to control, and so give tone to, our Letters. It should be, externally, a specimen of high, but not too refined Taste:—I mean, it should be boldly printed, on excellent paper, in single column, and be illustrated, not merely embellished, by spirited wood designs in the style of Grandville. Its chief aims should be Independence, Truth, Originality. It should be a journal of some 120 pp. and furnished at $5. It should have nothing to do with Agents or Agencies. Such a Magazine might be made to exercise a prodigious influence, and would be a source of vast wealth to its proprietors. There *can* be no reason why 100,000 copies might not, in one or two years, be circulated; but the means of bringing it into circulation should be radically different from those usually employed.

Such a journal might, perhaps, be set on foot by a coalition, and, thus set on foot, with proper understanding, would be irresistible. Suppose, for example, that the élite of our men of letters should combine secretly. Many of them control papers, &c. Let each subscribe, say $200, for the commencement of the undertaking; furnishing other means, as required from time to time, until the work be established. The articles to be supplied by the members solely, and upon a concerted plan of action. A nominal editor to be elected from among the number. How could such a journal fail? I would like very much to hear your opinion upon this matter. Could not the "ball be set in motion"? If we do *not* defend ourselves by some such coalition, we shall be devoured, without mercy, by the Godeys, the Snowdens, *et id genus omne.*

Most truly your friend,
Edgar A. Poe.[67]

This plan has been described as absurd, and it has not been tried. But the Playwrights' Theatre, recently established, in which five of the leading American playwrights combined successfully to produce their own plays, may indicate that Poe's idea was not so chimerical.

The year 1843 was more fruitful of quality than quantity in Poe's poetry and fiction. "The Conqueror Worm," the only new poem by Poe during this period, appeared first in *Graham's Magazine* in Janu-

[67] Original Autograph Ms., Harvard College Library.

ary, 1843. The association of the worm with death had appeared in "The Sleeper" and is, of course, an ancient idea. The title was probably suggested by "The Proud Ladye," a poem by Spencer Wallis Cone, which was reviewed in *Burton's* in June, 1840. This contained the lines

> "Let him meet the conqueror worm
> With his good sword by his side." [68]

The poem is very uneven in its merit. The conception of the tragedy of mankind, conquered by the Worm, who symbolizes the Serpent, the spirit of evil, is powerful. But in its expression, the fourth stanza transcends the limits which separate the horror that is awe-inspiring from the horror that becomes banal through its excess. In the last stanza Poe explains the meaning of the poem so carefully that it seems as though he were afraid we should miss the moral. This flavor of the didactic is alien to his poetry.

"The Conqueror Worm" is important, however, historically, as marking one step in the poetic treatment in America of the relations of God and man. Here the "mimes, in the form of God on high," that is, human beings, are destroyed by the Serpent, and the "Angel throng" are helpless to prevent the tragedy.

Many years later, William Vaughn Moody, in his "Masque of Judgment" took the next step. God is no longer simply indifferent to the struggle. Having failed to make the best use of the good in man, He also is attacked by the Serpent, and the Angelic host fight to the last in His defence, but are defeated. Man is justified by Moody in his struggle for free will, whether he sin or not. Eugene O'Neill went further, in his own words,[69] in treating "the one eternal tragedy of Man in his glorious, self-destructive struggle to make the Force (God, or his biological past) express him, instead of being, as an animal is, an infinitesimal incident in its expression." O'Neill has gone further even than this, in *Lazarus Laughed,* where he pictures dying as a return to a full communion with Eternal Life, in which, however, the individual human will is preserved. Poe was ahead of his time, as usual, in his conception of this relation between God and man, but it was not in "The Conqueror Worm," but rather in his later story, "Mesmeric Revelation," that he shows his undoubted influence on later writers. In this story, he rejected the idea of the absorption of

[68] Killis Campbell, *Poems of Poe,* p. 242, quoting Ingram's article in London *Bibliophile,* May, 1909.

[69] See his letter to the present writer in 1925. *History of the American Drama from the Civil War to the Present,* II, 199.

the individual in God. That would be "an action of God returning upon itself—a purposeless and futile action. Man is a creature. Creatures are thoughts of God. It is in the nature of thought to be irrevocable."

While there are differences in their treatment of this problem, Poe, Moody, and O'Neill, each in his own way, insist on the essential dignity of man, through the freedom of his will. Their kinship is only one of the many instances which prove Poe to be in the main stream of American thought. That he was one of the fountainheads of that stream has unfortunately caused him to be dubbed an "exotic" by those who have not traced the stream to its sources.

Poe also sent *Graham's* his most famous story of this year. Graham paid Poe fifty-two dollars for "The Gold Bug." Poe learned, however, that the *Dollar Newspaper,* one of the blanket sheets, was offering a prize of one hundred dollars for the best short story, so he asked Graham to return it. That friendly editor did so, and evidently took his repayment in reviews. As the first of these, "Flaccus," appeared in March, 1843, "The Gold Bug" must have been written quite early in that year. It won the prize and was published in the *Dollar Newspaper,* June 21 and 28, 1843. It was reprinted in *The Saturday Courier* of Philadelphia on June 24th, July 1st, and July 8th, the last installment including the two woodcuts by F. O. C. Darley.[70] This reprint, which must have been arranged before the story was published, indicates Poe's growing reputation in Philadelphia. It was the first time that one of his stories received practically simultaneous publication in two journals. The positions of the story in the *Courier* indicate the immediate popularity of "The Gold Bug." On June 24 it appeared on the third page. On July 1, it was promoted to the first page, where it remained on July 8. The *Dollar Newspaper* also reprinted it on July 12th, evidently to meet a continuous demand. It was dramatized by Silas S. Steele, a prolific playwright of Philadelphia, and played on August 8th, at the Walnut Street Theatre. As Steele's three-act verse drama, *Clandare,* was also given, *The Gold Bug; or, the Pirate's Treasure,* was probably a short melodrama. The play has not survived, but we know that it had four characters.[71] "Friendling" is the name given by Steele to the narrator of the story,

[70] In collection of William H. Koester, of Baltimore. A copy of "The Gold Bug," also in this collection, is a pamphlet published in London, without date, but apparently early. It contains thirty-six pages, and was "No. 1" of a projected issue of "The Thousand and One Romances."

[71] See A. H. Wilson, *A History of the Philadelphia Theatre, 1835 to 1855* (Philadelphia, 1935).

whom Poe left nameless, and who was evidently the chief character, since he was played by the leading man, J. S. Charles. In addition to Legrand and Jupiter, Steele gave the old woman who led Legrand to the high seat the name of "Old Martha."

I have already discussed the setting of "The Gold Bug" on Sullivan's Island.[72] The continued popularity of the story has been due to Poe's skill in building up the anticipation of the finding of the treasure and by the very immensity of the sum. At once the reader begins to speculate, consciously or unconsciously, upon what he would do with so much money. When Legrand begins his explanation of the parchment which has led him to the discovery, the reader is again held by the thought that all this wealth might have been lost except for an accident. If the narrator had not brought the parchment near the fire, the secret drawing of the skull and the cipher which had lain so long concealed from the eyes of man might never have been discovered. In the solution of the cipher, Poe again shows his constant effort to limit the strain on the attention of the reader. He chose a very simple form of cipher, that in which a letter is represented always by the same character. His explanation and substitutions are clear, and he stops when he has secured ten letters and wisely remarks that it is unnecessary to proceed further with the details of the solution. Legrand finds the tree by the same power of analysis that had solved the cipher. There is even more connection between the characters and the incidents than in the "Murders in the Rue Morgue," or in "Marie Rogêt." Legrand is an enthusiast, and a visionary, and both the narrator and Jupiter become real characters.

When "The Gold Bug" was reprinted in the *Tales* of 1845, Poe made some verbal changes,[73] and later in the Lorimer Graham copy [74] of the *Tales* he added two paragraphs toward the end of the story, defending his choice of a skull on the ground that the "object, if small, should be *white*," and that a skull would increase its whiteness when exposed to the weather. Evidently he was feeling some criticism! He also changed the elevation of the glass from forty-one to twenty-one degrees, with that careful attention to reality which even in his wildest dreams did not desert him.[75]

[72] See Chapter VI.
[73] A detailed comparison by T. O. Mabbott of the text in the *Dollar Newspaper* and in the *Tales* may be found in a special edition of "The Gold Bug," New York, 1929.
[74] Now in the Century Association in New York City.
[75] The source hunters have been busy, of course, with "The Gold Bug."

"The Tell Tale Heart," which Lowell welcomed for *The Pioneer* in January, 1843, is in one sense a companion piece to "The Pit and the Pendulum." It is also a study of terror, but this time it is related, partially, in terms of the memory of terror. The madman who tells the story of his murder of the old man whose eye is so repellent to him, paints a remarkable picture of the fright of his victim. But it is vivid because he has himself suffered causeless terrors in the night and he enters, therefore, with sympathy into those of the old man, even as he is preparing to murder him. The transition to the supernatural takes place, also, in the imagination of the narrator. With his faculties keyed up beyond the mental register, he believes he hears the old man's heart beating, first when he is alive, and finally when he is dead. The complete unity of the story disarms the critical faculties until the imagination of the madman seems for the moment reality. It is an almost perfect illustration of Poe's own theory of the short story, for every word contributes to the central effect.

Poe may have read Charles Dickens' story of "The Clock-Case," included in *Master Humphrey's Clock* [76] in 1840-1841, in which a retired lieutenant kills his nephew, a child whose death would enrich him and whose gaze maddens him. The murderer even sits on the child's grave when visitors come. But the discovery is made not by the conscience of the murderer, but by bloodhounds who scent the concealed corpse. Here, as usual, if Poe took a suggestion he wove it into his own pattern.

"The Black Cat," which appeared in August [77] is even more closely related to "The Tell-Tale Heart" than the latter is to "The Pit and the Pendulum." Again the preservation of the tone makes the tale a complete unity. The narrator is afflicted with that spirit of perverseness, of which Poe himself was so aware. His sadistic passion tortures the very animal he loves best, and he murders his wife in a fit of

---

There may have been some remembrance of his friend, Dr. Robert M. Bird's *Sheppard Lee*, which Poe had reviewed in *The Messenger* in September, 1836. In that novel a Negro, Jim Jumble, dreams three nights of finding a treasure at the foot of a beech tree in a swamp and his master digs for it. But since Jupiter in "The Gold Bug" does *not* dream, and his master does not dig on account of anything the Negro says or does, the connection between *Sheppard Lee* and "The Gold Bug" seems very uncertain.

[76] See E. S. Krappe, "A Possible Source for Poe's 'The Tell-Tale Heart' and 'The Black Cat,'" *American Literature*, XII (March, 1840), 84-88.

[77] Published August 19, 1843, in the *United States Saturday Post*, a temporary substitution for its old title, *The Saturday Evening Post*.

maniacal rage. The disclosure of the crime, as in "The Tell-Tale Heart," is caused by the conscience of the murderer. "The Black Cat" is one of the most powerful of Poe's stories, and the horror stops short of the wavering line of disgust.

From this mood of horror, Poe turned to his satirical treatments of cheats and impostures in "Raising the Wind; or, Diddling Considered as One of the Exact Sciences," published in the *Saturday Courier* on October 14, 1843. It is another of his grotesque trifles and is simply a succession of incidents whose only unity consists in their portraying of the success of clever scoundrels in preying upon the unsuspecting. Poe is said with some reason to have been lacking in humor. Still, I heard recently one of the episodes in this story told over the radio as a new joke!

Another tale of 1843 represents Poe in his quest for beauty, and he found it in Philadelphia in one of its loveliest forms. He may have been attracted to the Wissahickon River by Fannie Kemble's *Journal,* or by some verses which had appeared in *Burton's,* or he may have discovered the stream in one of his many walks. When he first saw it we do not know, but certainly on more than one summer day, Poe left the Coates Street house and struck across Fairmount Park until he joined the Ridge Road. This is one of the long avenues which defied Philadelphia's love of rectangles and insisted upon leading the pedestrian or coach rider by a shorter route to the country. Poe has given us his own impressions in the sketch, "Morning on the Wissahiccon," as it was then spelled, which appeared in *The Opal* for 1844, ornamented by a picture of an elk, standing on a rock overlooking the stream. But Poe's own words are better than any paraphrase. After a general discussion of American scenery, he proceeds:

> I have already said, or should have said, that the brook is narrow. Its banks are generally, indeed almost universally, precipitous, and consist of high hills, clothed with noble shrubbery near the water, and crowned at a greater elevation, with some of the most magnificent forest trees of America, among which stands conspicuous the *liriodendron tulipiferum.* The immediate shores, however, are of granite, sharply-defined or moss-covered, against which the pellucid water lolls in its gentle flow, as the blue waves of the Mediterranean upon the steps of her palaces of marble. Occasionally in front of the cliffs, extends a small definite *plateau* of richly herbaged land, affording the most picturesque position for a cottage and garden which the richest imagination could conceive. The windings of the stream are many and abrupt, as is

usually the case where banks are precipitous, and thus the impression conveyed to the voyager's eye, as he proceeds, is that of an endless succession of infinitely varied small lakes, or, more properly speaking, tarns. The Wissahiccon, however, should be visited, not like "fair Melrose," by moonlight, or even in cloudy weather, but amid the brightest glare of a noonday sun; for the narrowness of the gorge through which it flows, the height of the hills on either hand, and the density of the foliage, conspire to produce a gloominess, if not an absolute dreariness of effect, which, unless relieved by a bright general light, detracts from the mere beauty of the scene.

Not long ago I visited the stream by the route described, and spent the better part of a sultry day in floating in a skiff upon its bosom. The heat gradually overcame me, and, resigning myself to the influence of the scenes and of the weather, and of the gently moving current, I sank into a half slumber, during which my imagination revelled in visions of the Wissahiccon of ancient days—of the "good old days" when the Demon of the Engine was not, when pic-nics were undreamed of, when "water privileges" were neither bought nor sold, and when the red man trod alone, with the elk, upon the ridges that now towered above. And, while gradually these conceits took possession of my mind, the lazy brook had borne me, inch by inch, around one promontory and within full view of another that bounded the prospect at the distance of forty or fifty yards. It was a steep rocky cliff, abutting far into the stream, and presenting much more of the Salvator character than any portion of the shore hitherto passed. What I saw upon this cliff, although surely an object of very extraordinary nature, the place and season considered, at first neither startled nor amazed me—so thoroughly and appropriately did it chime in with the half-slumberous fancies that enwrapped me. I saw, or dreamed that I saw, standing upon the extreme verge of the precipice, with neck outstretched, with ears erect, and the whole attitude indicative of profound and melancholy inquisitiveness, one of the oldest and boldest of those identical elks which had been coupled with the red men of my vision.

I say that, for a few moments, this apparition neither startled nor amazed me. During this interval my whole soul was bound up in intense sympathy alone. I fancied the elk repining, not less than wondering, at the manifest alterations for the worse, wrought upon the brook and its vicinage, even within the last few years, by the stern hand of the utilitarian. But a slight movement of the animal's head at once dispelled the dreaminess which invested me, and aroused me to a full sense of the novelty of the adventure. I arose upon one knee within the skiff, and, while I hesitated whether to stop my career, or let myself float nearer to the object of my wonder, I heard the words "hist! hist!" ejaculated quickly but cautiously, from the shrubbery overhead. In an instant afterwards, a negro emerged from the thicket, putting aside the bushes with care, and treading stealthily. He bore in one hand a quantity of salt, and, holding it towards the elk, gently yet steadily approached. The noble animal, although a little fluttered, made no attempt at escape. The negro advanced; offered the salt; and spoke a few words of encouragement or conciliation. Presently, the elk bowed and stamped, and then lay quietly down and was secured with a halter.

Thus ended my romance of the elk. It was a *pet* of great age and very domestic habits, and belonged to an English family occupying a villa in the vicinity.

Poe really saw an elk, and the "villa" still stands.[78] On the rock where the elk was poised, a statue of William Penn, erected by John Welsh, with the words "Toleration" cut deep in it, crowns the east bank of the stream. Poe was evidently floating down from the northwest, and the morning sun lit up his favorite tulip poplars, which must have carried his thoughts back to the luxuriant woods near Charleston. On the Wissahickon, however, they were set against a contrast of the evergreens which line the shores. Little has been done to spoil the beauty of the Wissahickon, and if Poe should return today, he could look up or down the stream from the spot past which he was drifting, and find it hard to decide which view is the lovelier.

Undiscouraged by his failure to secure a publisher for his *Phantasy Pieces*, Poe attempted to issue his tales in pamphlet form. William H. Graham, a Philadelphia publisher, printed in 1843 *The Prose Romances of Edgar A. Poe*, in what was hopefully described on the title page as a "Uniform Serial Edition." "No. 1" contained "The Murders in the Rue Morgue" and "The Man That Was Used Up." These were

[78] The house, known as "Spring Bank" was in 1838 a sanitarium conducted by Samuel Mason, who kept a number of pets for the amusement of his patients. While the house was sold in May, 1838, to George Wilson, a farmer, he, in turn, sold it in 1840 to Dr. Edward Lowber, who also had a sanitarium and probably inherited the elk with the property. The rock was known as "Mom Rinker's Rock," in honor of an American spy who sat on it and dropped her letters over the brink, concealed in a ball of yarn, which found its way to Washington at Valley Forge. John Welsh purchased the place in 1870 and his descendant, Mr. J. Somers Smith, still owns it. I am indebted to him and to my colleague, Dr. Cornelius Weygandt, for facts concerning "Spring Bank," and also to the *Portrait of a Colonial City*, by H. D. Eberlein and C. Van D. Hubbard (Philadelphia, 1939), pp. 200-203.

Francis J. Grund Esqre
with Mr Poe's respects
U. S. Hotel

THE
PROSE-ROMANCES OF EDGAR A. POE.
AUTHOR OF "THE GOLD-BUG," "ARTHUR GORDON PYM," "TALES
OF THE GROTESQUE AND ARABESQUE,"
ETC. ETC. ETC.

UNIFORMLY SERIAL EDITION.

EACH NUMBER COMPLETE IN ITSELF.

No. I.

CONTAINING THE

MURDERS IN THE RUE MORGUE.

AND THE

MAN THAT WAS USED UP.

PHILADELPHIA:
PUBLISHED BY WILLIAM H. GRAHAM.
NO 98 CHESTNUT STREET
1843.

Price 12½ cents

TITLE PAGE OF *The Prose Romances of Edgar A. Poe*
Reproduced from the original autograph presentation copy through the
courtesy of the Library of Congress.

the two stories which had led the Table of Contents in the *Phantasy Pieces*, and if the first issue had been successful, Poe would probably have proceeded in that order to continue the publication of his stories. But no further issues appeared, and the pamphlet has become one of the rarest of all Poe's publications. The volume in the Library of Congress, which Poe gave to Francis J. Grund, the Bohemian traveller and writer upon American life, is insured for $50,000. On the same title-page on which his autograph has enhanced the present value, there is clearly printed—"Price 12½ Cents."

Poe revised the stories with his usual care. A comparison with the earlier versions shows constant verbal alterations, usually improvements, which were generally retained in the edition of 1845.[79]

Notwithstanding Poe's retirement, *Graham's* continued to be his principal outlet for criticism, some of which was repayment for the sum Graham had paid for "The Gold Bug." Reviews of "The Poetry of Rufus Dawes" in October, 1842, of "Flaccus" (Thomas Ward) in March, 1843, and of William Ellery Channing, the younger, in August, were examples of that destructive criticism which was so easy for Poe and which, at least in the case of Channing, was undeserved. He closed the castigation of Dawes with the sentence: "The laudation of the unworthy is to the worthy the most bitter of all wrong." But Poe could have permitted time to take care of Dawes and "Flaccus." They were harmless, and, indeed, Dawes' "Athenia of Damascus," a play in verse, is not bad. But the review of Ellery Channing's poetry represents Poe at his worst in criticism. Stickler for accuracy as he was, he begins and ends with the mistaken idea that Ellery Channing was the son of the essayist of the same name, while, of course, he was his

[79] There are fifty-two alterations in "The Murders in the Rue Morgue" of the text as given in *Graham's*. The quotation from Sir Thomas Browne is inserted, at the beginning, and the reference of the last quotation to Rousseau's *Nouvelle Héloïse* is added. The most interesting text addition occurs in the last paragraph. As this edition is so rare that Harrison could not collate the changes in the Virginia Edition, I give it here: "Nevertheless, that he [the Prefect] failed in the solution of the mystery, is by no means, that matter for wonder which he supposes it. *Nil sapientiae odiosius acumine nimio,* is, perhaps, the only line in the puerile and feeble Seneca not absolutely unmeaning; and, in truth, our friend the Prefect is somewhat too cunning to be profound." In Graham's the Prefect had been "too cunning to be acute." The quotation from Seneca was omitted in the 1845 revision. "The Man That Was Used Up" contains for the first time in print the motto from Corneille which Poe wrote into the *Phantasy Pieces.* It has fifteen corrections of the 1840 text, but the trivial nature of the story makes any comparison superfluous.

nephew. Then Poe tears the verses apart and subjects the poetry to that unfair test of demanding a realistic explanation of individual lines of poetry separated from their context. It would seem that Poe had a sadistic delight in torturing a poet somewhat akin to the spirit in which the hero of "The Black Cat" maltreated his equally innocent victim.

The account of Fitz-Greene Halleck in September is in better taste. It repeats, however, much of the matter in Poe's earlier review. In his discussion of Cooper's *Wyandotté*, in November, he showed unusual lack of discrimination in placing Cooper among those writers who are popular but will not achieve fame, while he placed Brockden Brown, John Neal, Simms, and Hawthorne, in a group above Cooper in permanent appeal. On the other hand, he anticipated W. C. Brownell for many years in his appreciation of Cooper's women, and rightly placed Maud Meredith among those characters that have reality. In his lengthy review of *Orion*, by the English poet R. H. Horne, he lost control of his critical faculties and pronounced portions of that poem the most "sublimely imaginative in the wide realm of poetical literature." In the same number of *Graham's* for March, 1844, he was on surer ground in his brief criticism of Lowell's second volume of verse, for he revealed his insight into qualities in Lowell which had hardly as yet been recognized.

The two stories which appeared in the spring of 1844 were of quite different calibre. "The Spectacles," which found a market in the *Dollar Newspaper* for March 27, 1844, is one of the most absurd of the Grotesques. The story of Mr. Talbot, who is so near-sighted that he falls in love with his great-great-grandmother, defies criticism. "A Tale of the Ragged Mountains" which appeared in *Godey's* for April, 1844, has much more significance. For the setting Poe returned to Charlottesville, and the strange adventure of Bedloe takes place in the mountains toward the South. But the University of Virginia does not enter into the story. Before taking a walk in the mountains, Bedloe has swallowed his usual morning dose of morphine, which, combined with the fact that Dr. Templeton, his attendant physician, has been hypnotising Bedloe for neuralgia, leaves a possible natural explanation for what follows. Bedloe sees an Eastern city in insurrection, believes that he takes part in the defence of a citadel held by British soldiers, and is killed while leading a sally. Then his spirit returns to the place in the mountains where he had begun the vision, and he resumes his natural body and his normal faculties. The skill of Poe is shown first in the handling of Bedloe's dream, which is quite in keeping with the normal dream state. In creating dreams in fiction, the authors, if they are not competent dreamers, are unaware that they may describe the strangest of incidents, provided that these incidents are consistent with themselves. One must also preserve the dreamer's belief in the validity of the dream. Poe truly says: "When one dreams, and in the dream suspects that he dreams, the suspicion never fails to confirm itself, and the sleeper is almost immediately aroused." Bedloe's dream proceeds in accordance with these rules. Poe succeeds also in preserving an atmosphere of the supernatural through the tale of Dr. Templeton, who reveals his knowledge of Bedloe's dream before he tells it. Templeton has taken part in this very defence of Benares under Hastings in 1780, and the reader may believe if he likes, that Bedloe was the re-incarnation of Oldeb, the officer whom Templeton knew, and who had led the disastrous sally. The realistic treatment of the supernatural was rarely better done by Poe.

In this period we see, as usual, the two natures in Edgar Poe coming out in response to circumstances. On one side there is Poe's demand of his correspondent, John Tomlin, a poet of Tennessee, that he break the seal of confidence in which Lambert Wilmer had written to Tomlin, and send Wilmer's letter to Poe. Tomlin did so, requesting Poe in a postscript to "return Wilmer's letter." Wilmer's note has rarely been quoted fully, only the paragraph concerning Poe being given. But the entire letter retails gossip of an unfavorable character, and his description of Poe must be read in that light:

Philadelphia, May 20, 1843.

Dear Sir:

I have not heard from you for several weeks. I sent on in various packages, a dozen copies of Recantation which I hope came to hand. Any number of that, or the "Quacks" always at your service.

Literary affairs are at a very low ebb in this city at present. Sumner Lincoln Fairfield, who once ranked high among the writers of our country, has become a common loafer about the streets. It is distressing to view such a change.

Edgar A. Poe (you know him by character, no doubt, if not personally), has become one of the strangest of our literati. He and I are old friends,—have known each other since boyhood, and it gives me inexpressible pain to notice the vagaries to which he has lately become subject. Poor fellow! he is not a teetotaller by any means, and I fear he is going headlong to destruction, moral, physical and intellectual.

T. S. Arthur, another old friend of mine, has acquired great popularity by a certain kind of writing and is getting along prosperously.

The "Philadelphia Clique" as it is called, composed of Robt. C. Conrad, R. Morris, J. C. Neale and several others, has seen its palmiest days and is falling into disrepute;—their association to hold each other up will not avail them. Jos. C. Neale, neverthe-less, is a man of splendid talents, and Conrad has some excellent points; but the political unpopularity of the latter affects his literary reputation. Neale is indolent.

My next publication will be "Preferment," a political satire, not partisan or very slightly so. Much of it is already written and I expect to bring it out sometime within the present year. Favor me with a few lines whenever you have time to waste.

Your obliged and sincere friend,

L. A. WILMER.[80]

What Poe did with the letter, we do not know. When we remember Wilmer's account of Poe's sobriety in Baltimore, and his defence of Poe after his death, this letter evidently points to some lapses of Poe, caused by anxiety and poverty. On the other hand, a letter which Poe wrote to Cornelius Mathews in March, 1844, represents the other Poe, manly in his apology for a mistake and written in the clear, firm hand of a man quite in control of himself:

Philadelphia

March 15, 1844.

Dr. Sir,

I have a letter and small parcel for Mr. Horne, your friend, and the author of "Orion." Would you be so kind as to furnish me with his address?—and put me in the best way of forwarding the package securely?

I am reminded that I am your debtor for many little attentions, and embrace this opportunity of tendering you my especial thanks for your able pamphlet on the International Copy-Right Question, and for the admirable Adventures of Puffer Hopkins.

Could I imagine that, at any moment, you regarded a certain impudent and flippant critique as more than a matter to be laughed *at*, I would proffer you an apology on the spot. Since I scribbled the article in question, you yourself have given me fifty good reasons for being ashamed of it.

With the Highest Respect & Esteem

Yr Ob St.

EDGAR A. POE.

To Cornelius Mathews Esqre.[81]

[80] Original Autograph Ms., Boston Public Library.
[81] Original Autograph Ms., Huntington Library.

Poe referred to his review of Mathews' *Wakondah* in *Graham's Magazine* for February, 1842, in which he had described the poem as "trash."

What determined Poe to leave Philadelphia for New York in April, 1844, may never be known. It seems idle to recount the vague rumors of scandal hinted at by those who retailed them at second hand. Even to deny them is to dignify them. Among other qualities which made Edgar Poe unfit to cope with the world was his inability to see that the best way to kill a scandal is to ignore it. This is all the more noteworthy since he could give to a friend good advice in this regard which he was unable to profit by himself.[82] On February 18, 1844, Poe wrote to George Lippard the novelist—

> And as for these personal enemies, I cannot see that you need put yourself to any especial trouble about THEM. Let a fool alone —especially if he be both a scoundrel and a fool—and he will kill himself far sooner than you can kill him by any active exertion. Besides—as to the real philosophy of the thing—you should regard small animosities—the animosities of small men—of the literary animalculae (who have their uses, beyond doubt)—as so many tokens of your ascent—or, rather, as so many stepping stones to your ambition. I have never yet been able to make up my mind whether I regard as the higher compliment, the approbation of a man of honor and talent, or the abuse of an ass or a blackguard. Both are excellent in their way—for a man who looks steadily up.
>
> If my opinion of "The Ladye Annabel" can be of *any* service to you whatever, you have my full permission to publish this letter, or any portion of it you may deem proper.
>
> With respect and friendship,
>
> Yours,
>
> EDGAR A. POE.

There need, perhaps, be no other reason given for the change of residence than Poe's constant restlessness and his realization of the steadily growing importance of New York. His six years in Philadelphia marked the summit of his achievement as a man of letters. Thirty-one of his short stories had been published while he was living

[82] Lippard published the letter of which this is a part, on pages 167 and 168 of his novel *Herbert Tracy, or the Legend of the Black Rangers* (Philadelphia, 1844). Lippard quoted the letter in "A Word to the Reader," in which he refers to Poe as "universally confessed one of the most gifted men in the land." The novel is in the William H. Koester Collection.

there, and among them "Ligeia," "The Fall of the House of Usher," "William Wilson," "Eiros and Charmion," "The Murders in the Rue Morgue," "Eleonora," "The Masque of the Red Death," "The Tell-Tale Heart," and "The Gold Bug." He had been the Editor of the foremost monthly journal in the United States, and had published there some of the few pieces of constructive criticism that this country had so far seen. While little new poetry had come from him, he had perfected his earlier poems in many cases through his revisions, and in "The Haunted Palace" at least had reached the heights. He had become widely known, and if he had made enemies, he also had made friends. For part of his stay in Philadelphia he was even happy, and when he left it, it is not too much to say that he left happiness behind him.

CHAPTER XIV

New York—"The Raven" and Other Matters

It was with his usual optimism that Poe took Virginia to a city where he had met disappointment in 1837. It was, he hoped, to be different, and yet it is difficult to see what was the basis for that hope. It is true that the book trade was more flourishing. Poe succeeded in having both his *Tales* and his *Poems* published in 1845. But so far as the magazines, to which he must look for support, were concerned, there was no improvement in the situation, which New York had not yet begun to dominate. The leading magazines, the *Knickerbocker,* the *New Mirror,* the *Democratic Review,* were no more prosperous than *Graham's* and *Godey's.* He could hardly have expected to be helped by the *Knickerbocker Magazine,* considering what he had said concerning Lewis Gaylord Clark, its editor, and yet it set the tone in New York more than any other periodical. It may be, indeed, that Poe, sensing this lack of leading magazines, hoped to find the opportunity to found his own.

Perhaps it was the atmosphere of the growing metropolis that attracted Poe, rather than any specific advantage. New York had more than 300,000 inhabitants, and had become the great port of entry from Europe. Notwithstanding its poorly paved and poorly lighted streets, the endless throng of people on Broadway, the luxurious dresses of the women, the evidences of wealth, the hurry-scurry that Willis and Dickens described, all these gave an appearance of prosperity. Poe had visited New York during his residence in Philadelphia and like many thousands since his day, he saw opportunity there. He was to experience both the readiness of New York to treat a visitor with open arms if he has any wares to sell, and equal willingness to close its doors to the aspirant who remains to storm the citadel. It was, however, the best place to attract foreign recognition, and in this respect it widened the reputation for which Poe always longed.

Poe's letter to Mrs. Clemm describing the journey of himself and Virginia from Philadelphia reveals again how much his own vivid account is to be preferred to any paraphrase:

(New York, Sunday Morning,
(April 7, just after breakfast.
([1844]

My dear Muddy,

We have just this minute done breakfast, and I now sit down to write you about everything. I can't pay for the letter, because the P. O. won't be open to-day.—In the first place, we arrived safe at Walnut St. wharf. The driver wanted to make me pay a dollar, but I wouldn't. Then I had to pay a boy a levy to put the trunks in the baggage car. In the meantime I took Sis in the Depôt Hotel. It was only a quarter past 6 and we had to wait till 7. We saw the Ledger and Times—nothing in either—a few words of no account in the Chronicle.—We started in good spirits, but did not get here until nearly 3 o'clock. We went in the cars to Amboy, about 40 miles from N. York, and then took the steamboat the rest of the way.—Sissy coughed none at all. When we got to the wharf it was raining hard. I left her on board the boat, after putting the trunks in the Ladies' cabin, and set off to buy an umbrella and look for a boarding house. I met a man selling umbrellas, and bought [o]ne for 62 cents. Then I went up Greenwich St. and soon found a boarding-house. It is just before you get to Cedar St., on the west side going up—the left-hand side. It has brown stone steps, with a porch with brown pillars. "Morrison" is the name on the door. I made a bargain in a few minutes and then got a hack and went for Sis. I was not gone more than ½ an hour, and she was quite astonished to see me back so soon. She didn't expect me for an hour. There were 2 other ladies waiting on board—so she wasn't very lonely.— When we got to the house we had to wait about ½ an hour before the room was ready. The house is old & looks buggy—[The signature on the reverse side was cut out so there is a break here] [T]he landlady is a nice chatty ol[d soul—g]ave us the back room on th[e third floor—]e night & day & attendance, f[or 7$ the] cheapest board I ever knew, taking into consideration the central situation and the *living*. I wish Kate [the cat Catterina] could see it—she would faint. Last night, for supper, we had the nicest tea you ever drank, strong & hot,—wheat bread & rye bread —cheese—tea-cakes (elegant), a great dish (2 dishes) of elegant ham, and 2 of cold veal, piled up like a mountain and large slices —3 dishes of the cakes, and everything in the greatest profusion. No fear of starving here. The landlady seemed as if she

couldn't press us enough, and we were at home directly. Her
husband is living with her—a fat, good-natured old soul. There
are 8 or 10 boarders—2 or 3 of them ladies—2 servants.—For
breakfast we had excellent-flavored coffee, hot & strong—not
very clear & no great deal of cream—veal cutlets, elegant ham
& eggs & nice bread and butter. I never sat down to a more
plentiful or a nicer breakfast. I wish you could have seen the
eggs—and the great dishes of meat. I ate the first hearty breakfast I have eaten since I left our little home. Sis is delighted,
and we are both in excellent spirits. She has coughed hardly any
and had no night sweat. She is now busy mending my pants
which I tore against a nail. I went out last night and bought a
skein of silk, a skein of thread, 2 buttons, a pair of slippers, &
a tin pan for the stove. The fire kept in all night.—We have now
got 4$ and a half left. Tomorrow I am going to try & borrow
3$, so that I may have a fortnight to go upon. I feel in excellent
spirits, & haven't drank a drop—so that I hope so[on] to get out
of trouble. The very instant I scrape together enough money I
will send it on. You can't imagine how much we both do miss you.
Sissy had a hearty cry last night, because you and Catterina
weren't here. We are resolved to get 2 rooms the first moment
we can. In the meantime it is impossible we could be more comfortable or more at home than we are. It looks as if it were going
to clear up now. Be sure and go to the P. O. & have my letters
forwarded. As soon as I write Lowell's article, I will send it to
you, & get you to get the money from Graham. Give our best
loves to Catterina.

Be sure and take home the Messenger, [to Hirst] We hope to
send for you *very* soon.

[Signature cut out.] [1]

How much they depended upon Mrs. Clemm, who had been left
behind to sell such books as she could, how pitiful was Poe's narrow
margin, how almost childlike was his attitude toward the bitter reali-
ties of life, this letter makes clear.

Let us hope that the house at 130 Greenwich Street was a more
cheerful home than it is today. The brownstone steps and the porch
have gone, but the old staircase, now unused, remains, also the dingy

---

[1] The Original Autograph Ms. letter has been mutilated for the signature.
It is now in the Enoch Pratt Library, Baltimore. I have inserted probable
words in brackets.

rooms, uninhabited now, over the more cheerful ground floor, adorned by the "Old Brokers' Café." In 1844 the nearby river on which Virginia looked while she waited for her mother to join them and the more open spaces would have improved the situation of the house, located almost at the lowest point of Manhattan. The old Planters' Hotel, a few houses below, claims a Poe tradition with much less certainty. It was a well known place in 1844 and would have strained his pocketbook unduly.

The postscript of Poe's letter to Mrs. Clemm refers to a matter which was later to plague him. Poe had wished to see a volume of the *Southern Literary Messenger* and Henry B. Hirst had borrowed one for his use from William Duane. Either through dire need or carelessness Mrs. Clemm did not return the *Messenger* to Hirst, but sold it with other books to Leary, the Philadelphia bookseller. When Duane, some months later, asked for the return of the book, Mrs. Clemm evidently did not tell her nephew the facts, for he wrote to Duane as follows:

New York,
Octo. 28. 44.

My dear Sir,

Owing to my absence from this city (where I am now residing) I did not receive your letter of the 15th until this morning.

I regret exceedingly that circumstances should have led you to think me negligent, or uncourteous, in not returning the volume of the "Messenger"—for one or the other (perhaps both) you must long since have considered me. The facts are these: some eight months ago, I believe, I chanced to mention, in Mr. Hirst's hearing, that I wished to look over a particular article in the "Messenger." He immediately volunteered to procure me the desired volume from you. I would much rather have borrowed it personally—but he seemed to make a point of the matter, and I consented. Soon afterwards he handed me the book, which I retained a very short time. It is now certainly more than seven months since I returned it to Mr. Hirst, through my mother-in-law (Mrs. Clemm) who informs me that she left it at his office, with one of his brothers. Most probably it was deposited in a book-case, and thus overlooked and forgotten. May I trouble you to send for it?

Very truly yours,
EDGAR ALLAN POE

William Duane, Esq.

When Duane showed this letter to Hirst, the latter replied that it was "a damned lie." Duane found out soon after that Leary had sold the volume to a bookseller in Richmond, who sold it to the publishers of the *Messenger*, who in turn sold it to a friend of Duane, through whom it was recovered. When Duane called Poe's attention to these facts, Poe replied, with a marked change in the tone of his note:

New York,
Jan. 28. 45.

Sir,

Richmond is the last place in which I should have hoped to find a copy of either the 1st 2d or 3d volumes of the Messenger. For this reason I did not apply there. I have been putting myself, however, to some trouble in endeavouring to collect among my friends here the separate numbers of the missing volume. I am glad that your last letter relieves me from all such trouble in future. I do not choose to recognize you in this matter at all. To the person of whom I borrowed the book, or rather who insisted upon forcing it on me, I have sufficient reason to believe it was returned. Settle your difficulties with him, and insult me with no more of your communications.

EDGAR A. POE

Mr. Duane

On this letter Duane endorsed the words: "Bombastes Furioso Poe. Dated Jan. 28. 1845. Received, Jan. 31, 1845. Not to be answered." Then after retailing the events given above, he continues: "Poe had the grace to be ashamed of himself, when he heard of the manner in which I had had to repurchase my own book. He remarked to H. B. Hirst Esqr: 'What must Mr. Duane think of me?'" [2]

I have given this correspondence, not on account of the importance of the incident itself, but because it reveals between the lines one of those occasions in which Mrs. Clemm brought upon Poe lasting trouble. For many years this story, magnified, of course, shadowed his reputation in Philadelphia. But Duane misinterpreted Poe's second letter. It was written by a man who had been permitted by a woman he loved to place himself in a false position, and who defended her at the cost of his own reputation. Mrs. Clemm might have sold the

[2] The original autograph letters are in the Dreer Collection, Historical Society of Pennsylvania.

book by accident before Poe's letter of April 7th reached her, but with the postscript before her, she should have reclaimed it. Instead, she concealed the sale from Poe, and let him write the letters to Duane. She could by no stretch of imagination confuse a trip to Leary's with a visit to Hirst's office. Poe's remark to Hirst was not a confession of guilt; it was an assumption of the blame for an action of which he was innocent. He could not even have the satisfaction of returning the five dollars it had cost Duane to buy his own property back, for Poe never had it to spare.[3]

Poe's first activity, after reaching New York City, was to publish in the *New York Sun* on April 13, 1844, what is now known as the "Balloon-Hoax." It appeared under the caption, "Astounding News by Express, via Norfolk! The Atlantic Crossed in Three Days, Signal Triumph of Mr. Monck Mason's Flying Machine! Arrival at Sullivan's Island, near Charleston, S. C.—After a Passage of Seventy-Five Hours, etc."

The effect of this clever bit of imaginary narrative is best told in Poe's own words, written by him to the *Columbia Spy*, and published on May 25th:

> The "Balloon-Hoax" made a far more intense sensation than anything of that character since the "Moon-Story" of Locke. On the morning (Saturday) of its announcement, the whole square surrounding the "Sun" building was literally besieged, blocked up —ingress and egress being alike impossible, from a period soon after sunrise until about two o'clock P. M. In Saturday's regular issue, it was stated that the news had been just received, and that an "Extra" was then in preparation, which would be ready at ten. It was not delivered, however, until nearly noon. In the meantime I never witnessed more intense excitement to get possession of a newspaper. As soon as the few first copies made their way into the streets, they were bought up, at almost any price, from the news-boys, who made a profitable speculation beyond doubt. I saw a half-dollar given, in one instance, for a single paper, and a shilling was a frequent price. I tried, in vain, during the whole day, to get possession of a copy. It was excessively amusing, however, to hear the comments of those who had read the "Extra."[4]

[3] The Duane copy of the *Messenger* is now in the collection of Mr. Henry Bradley Martin. There are some notes in Poe's hand, but none which identify his own work.

[4] Letter II, New York, May 21, 1844, *Doings of Gotham*, p. 33.

Poe's letters to the *Columbia Spy* are of unusual importance. They reveal how dependent he was upon some immediate if small return, for the paper was limited in circulation. It was published at Columbia, Pennsylvania, by Bowen and Gossler, while Poe was a correspondent.[5]

The letters give us, at first hand, Poe's impressions of New York from the time of his arrival until June 25th. The power of description which he often employed in purely imaginative flights, he spent here on reality:

I have been roaming far and wide over this island of Mannahatta. Some portions of its interior have a certain air of rocky sterility which may impress some imaginations as simply *dreary* —to me it conveys the sublime. Trees are few; but some of the shrubbery is exceedingly picturesque. Not less so are the prevalent shanties of the Irish squatters. I have one of these *tabernacles* (I use the term primitively) at present in the eye of my mind. It is, perhaps, nine feet by six, with a pigsty applied externally, by way both of portico and support. The whole fabric (which is of mud) has been erected in somewhat too obvious an imitation of the Tower of Pisa. A dozen rough planks, "pitched" together, form the roof. The door is a barrel on end. There is a garden, too; and this is encircled by a ditch at one point, a large stone at another, a bramble at a third. A dog and a cat are inevitable in these habitations; and, apparently, there are no dogs and no cats more entirely happy.

On the eastern or "Sound" face of Mannahatta (*why* do we persist in *de-euphonizing* the true names?) are some of the most picturesque sites for villas to be found within the limits of Christendom. These localities, however, are neglected—unimproved. The old mansions upon them (principally wooden) are suffered to remain unrepaired, and present a melancholy spectacle of decrepitude. In fact, these magnificent places are doomed. The spirit of Improvement has withered them with its acrid breath. Streets are already "mapped" through them, and they are no longer suburban residences, but "town-lots." In some thirty years every noble cliff will be a pier, and the whole island will be densely desecrated by

---

[5] Copies of this journal are rare. Woodberry published the Letter of June 18th (II, 81-87) from the manuscript in the Ridgeway Library, Philadelphia, without, however, identifying the paper. The Letter of June 4th was published in the *New York Times*, January 14, 1912, as from the *Columbia Spy*. It remained for Mr. Jacob E. Spannuth to discover the file containing the seven letters, which he published under the title *Doings of Gotham*, with Introduction and Comments by Thomas O. Mabbott (Pottsville, 1929).

buildings of brick, with portentous *facades* of brown-stone, or brown-*stonn*, as the Gothamites have it.[6]

A vivid touch this, of the district in which Edward Harrigan was to lay the scene of his delightful comedy of *Squatter Sovereignty*. Later, Poe reveals how he sought exercise and pleasure as he had done on the Wissahickon:

> When you visit Gotham, you should ride out the Fifth Avenue, as far as the distributing reservoir, near Forty-third Street, I believe. The prospect from the walk around the reservoir is particularly beautiful. You can see, from this elevation, the north reservoir at Yorkville; the whole city to the Battery; with a large portion of the harbor, and long reaches of the Hudson and East rivers. Perhaps even a finer view, however, is to be obtained from the summit of the white, light-house-looking shot-tower which stands on the East river, at Fifty-fifth Street, or thereabouts.
>
> A day or two since I procured a light skiff, and with the aid of a pair of *sculls* (as they here term short oars, or paddles) made my way around Blackwell's Island, on a voyage of discovery and exploration. The chief interest of the adventure lay in the scenery of the Manhattan shore, which is here particularly picturesque. The houses are, without exception, *frame*, and antique. Nothing very modern has been attempted—a necessary result of the subdivision of the whole island into streets and town-lots. I could not look on the magnificent cliffs, and stately trees, which at every moment met my view, without a sigh for their inevitable doom— inevitable and swift. In twenty years, or thirty at farthest, we shall see here nothing more romantic than shipping, warehouses, and wharves.[7]

Poe found the city thronged with strangers, and wearing an aspect of intense life. From the point of cleanliness, it was far below Philadelphia. The change in administration of the city brought reprisals from the officials about to be removed and plunged Third Avenue, "One of the most important thoroughfares," in darkness. Poe objected from purely constitutional grounds to the new Mayor, Harper, closing the "Rum Palaces" and "Rum Hovels" on the Christian Sabbath. Why, he asks, with connotations of which he could not have been aware, should they not be closed on Saturday also? The Magazines, he remarks, "are dragging their slow length along." Of the *Knickerbocker* he "hears little and sees less," probably because of his relations with

[6] Letter I, May 14, 1844, *Doings of Gotham*, pp. 25-26.
[7] Letter III, May 27, 1844, *Doings of Gotham*, pp. 40-41.

Lewis Gaylord Clark, the Editor. The *Ladies' Companion,* which had bought "Marie Rogêt" was "the *ne plus ultra* of ill-taste, impudence and vulgar humbuggery." He scoffs at the winner of a ten-mile race, in an hour and four minutes; remarking that he had done it himself in less time and that at least a thousand men in the West could do twelve miles an hour. His constant impatience with the dogmatic speculations of science comes to the surface in his account of Wilkes' expedition to the Antarctic region:

> Let Mr. Wilkes say what he will, the Expedition was a failure. This is the gentleman who picked up, on an iceberg at sea, a few morsels of rock, and brought them home (wrapped in Cotton) as specimens of an Antarctic Continent—after the fashion of the *skolastikos* in Hierocles. By the examination of these specimens, a committee, appointed by Mr. W., will determine the soil, climate, extent, geological condition, population, governmental policy, religion, and literature of the new country, which is to be entitled "Wilkesland," after its illustrious discoverer.[8]

By June 12th he had become a regular New Yorker for the letter is devoted to a scathing criticism of the architecture of Brooklyn. The street cries in New York and the noise of the wagons over the cobblestones drive him mad, and his sane suggestions about street paving prove again how close his observation was of things near at hand. His keen critical sense shows in his notice of Willis's poems, when he regrets that Willis had to leave Glen Mary "and the tranquility and leisure he might there have found. In its retirement he might have accomplished much, both for himself and for posterity; but, chained to the oar of a mere weekly paper, professedly addressing the frivolous and the fashionable, what can he now hope for but a gradual sinking into the slough of the Public Disregard?" [9]

Was it his own situation Poe had in mind when he was writing about the man who chose to be the most popular writer in the United States in 1844, and is now almost forgotten? Poe devotes much of the next letter to Willis, and to *Graham's*. Then the letters cease. It was not his forte to be a columnist, but they give a valid pen picture of New York of a century ago, as well as a revelation of Poe's interests. They also indicate other contributions by Poe that have not been reprinted. In the letter of May 21st, Poe speaks of the biography of

[8] Letter IV, June 4, 1844, *Doings of Gotham,* p. 49.
[9] Letter VI, June 18, 1844, Original Autograph Ms., Library Company of Philadelphia, *Doings of Gotham,* p. 68.

Robert T. Conrad in *Graham's* for June, 1844, which was "already out"—as being "by a friend of yours" and doing Conrad no more than justice. The review has a resemblance to Poe's critical style, but if it was by him, it is curious that he should speak of Judge Conrad's *Jack Cade* or *Aylmere*, as it was variously called, as "perhaps the best American play." For in a later article on the American drama he does not mention Conrad. Why he should not have signed the article is not clear.

Poe may also have contributed three editorials to the *Public Ledger* of Philadelphia on July 17, 18, 19, 1844, of a satirical nature, two on the "Omnibus" and one on "Cats." The second was reprinted in the *Columbia Spy* of August 14th, with a note by Eli Bowen, which implied it was by Poe. The articles are pleasant reading, but are of interest mainly as evidence of his dependence upon newspapers for support.[10]

In one of his strolls in upper New York, Poe saw the home of Patrick Brennan, surrounded by a farm of two hundred and sixteen acres, extending from the Hudson River to a point about two hundred feet west of the Bloomingdale Road, later called the Boulevard, and now Broadway. If the house were standing today, it would be in the neighborhood of 84th Street between Amsterdam Avenue and Broadway. It was a comfortable "double framed" dwelling of two stories. With Virginia's health in mind, Poe asked Mrs. Brennan to take the family to board. Although the neighborhood had some reputation as a summer resort, they were the first guests Mrs. Brennan received, and she became much attached to them. She always denied the charges concerning Poe's drinking, and insisted that she never saw him under the influence of liquor. She also paid tribute to his devotion to Virginia.

Poe was in the habit of taking long rambles in the neighborhood, especially to a rock overlooking the Hudson, known as "Mount Tom," where he would spend hours gazing at the river. He was fond of children and took some of the Brennan family, especially Thomas, one of the boys, with him at times to the river side, where he would draw figures of all sorts to amuse them.

One of the Brennan girls, later Mrs. James R. O'Beirne, was a witness of his long hours of work, when she was permitted to sit in his room while he was composing. She seems to have made the most acute test of a writer's patience by rearranging his manuscripts in accord-

---

[10] For other unsigned articles in the *Columbia Spy*, which may be by Poe, see *Doings of Gotham*.

ance with her own feminine sense of order. So far, the traditions rest on solid foundation.[11]

General O'Beirne's identification of a room in the Brennan house as the identical one described by the poet in "The Raven," and the arrangement of a plaster cast of Pallas, on a high shelf in front of a few smoky panes of glass, seem fanciful, notwithstanding Poe's own statement about the plaster cast. If Poe read the poem to Mrs. Brennan, she said nothing about it to Gill, who was keen to pick up matters of that sort. There can be little doubt, however, that "The Raven" was completed, if not begun, in the Brennan home.

Poe's only new poem to be published in 1844 was "Dreamland," in *Graham's* for June, but it is one of his finest creations. Dangerous as subjective interpretations are, it is hard to believe that this poem does not reflect Poe's own remarkable power of projection "Out of Space— Out of Time." He produces the effect of vastness and desolation by his usual methods of denying limitations:

> "Bottomless vales and boundless floods
>
> . . . .
>
> Mountains toppling evermore
> Into seas without a shore.
>
> . . . .
>
> Lakes that endlessly outspread
> Their lone waters, lone and dead."

Notwithstanding its unholy aspect, and the shrouded forms that greet the traveller:

> "For the heart whose woes are legion
> 'Tis a peaceful, soothing region,—
> For the spirit that walks in shadow
> 'Tis—oh, 'tis an Eldorado!"

These shrouded figures are not to return, and by comparison with this life they are progressing apparently to a happier state:

---

[11] Gill talked to Mrs. Brennan and gave a first-hand account in his *Life*, pp. 148-150. General James R. O'Beirne, Mrs. Brennan's son-in-law, added some facts in an interview, "Poe and 'The Raven,'" in the *N. Y. Mail and Express*, April 21, 1900. Through the good offices of Dr. T. O. Mabbott, I have checked the personal accounts with Mr. H. Mott Brennan, whose grandfather was the Thomas Brennan whom Poe took with him to Mount Tom.

"But the traveller, travelling through it
May not—dare not, openly view it;
Never its mysteries are exposed
To the weak human eye unclosed."

And so the dreamer returns:

"By a route, obscure and lonely,
Haunted by ill angels only,
Where an Eldolon, named NIGHT,
On a black throne reigns upright.
I have wandered home but newly
From this ultimate dim Thule." [12]

Every phrase tends to the one effect, the description of the reaction of a human traveller to this land between Death and Life. As ever, the vowels and consonants are chosen by a master of sounds and the poet strikes with the fingers of harmony a note that resounds in any understanding ear with the inevitability of great poetry.

A letter from Poe to Lowell deals with the projected biography of Poe to be written by Lowell and gives a list of Poe's still unpublished stories:

New York, May 28, '44.

My dear Friend,—I received yours last night, forwarded from Philadelphia to this city, where I intend living for the future. Touching the Biography—I would be very proud, indeed, if you would write it, and did, certainly, say to myself, and I believe to Graham—that such was my wish; but as I fancied the job might be disagreeable, I did not venture to suggest it to yourself. Your offer relieves me from great embarrassment, and I thank you sincerely. You will do me justice; and that I could not expect at all hands.

Herewith, I mail you a Life written some time since by Hirst, from materials furnished principally by Thomas and Mr. T. W. White. It is correct, I think, in the main (barring extravagant eulogy), and you can select from it whatever you deem right. The limit is 6 pp. of Graham—as much less as you please. Besides the Tales enumerated in the foot-note, I have written "The Spectacles"; "*The Oblong Box*"; "A Tale of the Ragged Mountains";

[12] In *Graham's* these six lines are repeated three times, but in later versions they occur only at the beginning and ending of the poem.

*"The Premature Burial"; "The Purloined Letter"; "The System of
Doctors Tar and Fether";* "The Black Cat"; "The Elk"; "Diddling
Considered as one of the Exact Sciences"; *"Mesmeric Revelation";*
"The Gold Bug"; *"Thou art the Man";* about 60 altogether, including the "Grotesque and Arabesque." Those italicized are as yet
unpublished—in the hands of different editors. Of the "Gold Bug"
(my most successful tale), more than 300,000 copies have been
circulated.

There is an article on "American Poetry" in a late number of
the "London Foreign Quarterly," in which some allusion is made
to me, as a poet, and as an imitator of Tennyson. I would like
you to say (in my defense) what is the fact: that the passages
quoted as imitations were written and published, in Boston,
before the issue of even Tennyson's first volume. Dickens (I
know) wrote the article—I have private personal reasons for
knowing this. The portrait prepared does not in the least resemble
me.

I wrote you a long letter from Philadelphia about seven weeks
since—did you get it? You make no allusion to it. In great haste,

Your most sincere friend,

EDGAR A. POE.[13]

Poe was evidently having difficulties in placing his fiction. He had
offered "The Oblong Box" to Willis for the *New Mirror,* but Willis
had suggested that the *Opal* would be a better place to print it. Poe's
letter of May 29th to Mrs. Hale, who was the editor both of the *Opal*
and *Godey's,* urges her to accept an article from him, and "to take it
unseen, upon Mr. Willis's testimony in its favor. It cannot be improper
to state, that I make the latter request to save time, because I am as
usual, exceedingly in need of a little money." [14]

Mrs. Hale evidently gave him encouragement, for he wrote on
May 31st:

New-York
May 31st 44.

My Dear Madam,
    I hasten to reply to your kind and very satisfactory letter,
and to say that, if you will be so good as to keep open for

[13] Original Autograph Ms., Harvard College Library.
[14] Ms. Letter, Sales Catalogue of Anderson's Galleries, January 25, 26,
1917.

me the ten pages of which you speak, I will forward you, in 2 or 3 days, an article which will about occupy that space, and which I will endeavour to adapt to the character of "The Opal." The price you mention—50 cts per page—will be amply sufficient; and I am exceedingly anxious to be ranked in your list of contributors.

Should you see Mr. Godey very soon, will you oblige me by saying that I will write him in a few days, and forward him a package?

With sincere respect,
Yr Ob. St.
Edgar A. Poe

Mrs. Sarah J. Hale.[15]

Poe probably referred to "A Chapter of Suggestions" which appeared in the *Opal* for 1845. In this "Chapter of Suggestions" Poe repeated his earlier views on Dickens, Bulwer, and Macaulay, and discussed his favorite subject of dreams. He also paid his respects to "those little people who habitually sneer at greatness." It hardly needs comment that Poe, already well known, was more than glad to write for fifty cents a page and that he was still depending upon a Philadelphia editor to take his contributions. Mrs. Hale also bought "The Oblong Box" and "Thou Art the Man" for *Godey's*.

Notwithstanding the slowness of editors in accepting or publishing his contributions, Poe kept on hard at work with his fiction, some of which must have been written before he left Philadelphia. "The Premature Burial" which the *Dollar Newspaper* printed on July 31, 1844, was another story of terror. Poe began by establishing the general truth that in a tale of horror the recital of actual fact is more impressive than any fictional treatment, because the reader believes it. Then by reciting certain actual cases of premature burial,[16] he built up that willingness to believe which prepared the reader to accept the main story. Poe's narrator has suffered from catalepsy, and returns to consciousness slowly through an intermediate stage of helplessness.

---

[15] Original Autograph Ms., Huntington Library.

[16] One of these, at least, that of Mdlle. Victorine Lafourcade, had been reported in *The Philadelphia Casket* for September, 1827 (Campbell's *Mind of Poe*, p. 167). Another, possibly imaginary, of a "Mr. Stapleton," has parallels in a tale "Buried Alive" in *Blackwoods*, October, 1821 (King, *Texas Studies in English*, X, 128). As usual, the sources were only incidental to Poe's story.

He goes through all the terrors of one who is buried alive, especially acute because the many precautions he has taken against such an event seem to have been neglected by those who should have seen to them. When he is awakened to find that he is lying in a berth in a small sloop, and the coffin lid he has imagined is really the bottom of the berth, above him, the story does not become burlesque. The active violent terror has driven the shadows of fear of imaginary danger away, and he is cured of his disease.

"Mesmeric Revelation" which appeared in the *Columbian Magazine* in August, 1844, is a prelude to *Eureka*. Poe assumes the validity of mesmerism and tries through placing of a man, ill with phthisis, under such a trance, to ascertain the truth of immortality. Mr. Van Kirk asks to be mesmerized, hoping that the consequent exaltation will permit him to perceive a train of reasoning which has convinced him while in his trance, but of which, when he awakes, he is aware only of the effect, and not of the cause. He asks, therefore, that the narrator who is also the mesmerizer should ask him questions while he is in the trance, thereby noting the origin of Van Kirk's beliefs. I have already spoken in another connection of this story as an expression of Poe's certainty of man's free will and the persistence of his individuality after death.[17]

Van Kirk's answers tell us that "what we call 'death,' is but the painful metamorphosis. Our present incarnation is progressive, preparatory, temporary. Our future is perfected, ultimate, immortal." Poe bases the distinction between inorganic life and organic beings upon a Creator. Opposed to Emerson's conception of spirit being the only creator, God, with all the powers attributed to spirit, is but the perfection of matter. If God had so willed it, law could have been inviolate, with its result, perfection. But in order to produce violation of law, impediments, afforded by the number, complexity, and substantiality of the laws of organic life and matter, have been created. Thus pain is produced. Pain is reality and is necessary to happiness. "All things are either good or bad by comparison.—*Positive* pleasure is a mere idea. To be happy at any one point we must have suffered at the same. Never to suffer would have been never to have been blessed.... The pain of the primitive life of Earth is the sole basis of the bliss of the ultimate life of Heaven." Thus Poe in 1844-45 [18] ex-

---

[17] See pp. 391-392.
[18] Poe added a long passage in the revision of this story for the *Tales* of 1845. In order to avoid confusion, I have dealt with the story in its final form, including quotations which were not printed in 1844.

pressed the idea of relativity in human happiness. It was, of course, not original with him, but he put it forcibly. He also made clear that the future life cannot even be described by our terms. We will have to create terms before we can describe it. It was in this essay also that he suggested the indivisibility of matter.

Poe wrote to George Bush, then Professor of Hebrew Language and Literature at New York University, concerning this story:

> New York
> Jan. 4, 45.
>
> Dear Sir;
>
> With this note I take the liberty of sending you a newspaper—"The Dollar Weekly"—in which there is an article, by myself, entitled "Mesmeric Revelation." It has been copied into the paper from a Monthly Magazine—"The Columbian"—in which it originally appeared in July last.
>
> I have ventured to send you the article because there are many points in it which bear upon the subject-matter of your last admirable work on the Future Condition of Man [19] and therefore I am induced to hope that you will do me the honor to look over what I have said.
>
> You will, of course, understand that the article is purely a fiction;—but I have embodied in it some thoughts which are original with myself & I am exceedingly anxious to learn if they have claim to absolute originality, and also how far they will strike you as well based. If you would be so kind as to look over the paper and give me, in brief, your opinion, I will consider it a high favor.
>
> Very Respy. Yr. Ob. St.
>
> EDGAR A. POE.
>
> Please reply thro' the P. Office. [20]

What Bush replied is not known. But the reproduction of the story in the *Dollar Newspaper* of Philadelphia is intriguing, to say the least. The readers who expected another "Gold Bug" must have been puzzled. Perhaps the editor of the *Columbian* may have asked Poe for a

[19] Poe probably referred to Bush's *Anastasis; or, The Doctrine of the Resurrection of the Body, Rationally and Scripturally Considered* (1844).

[20] Copy of Original Autograph Ms. Through the courtesy of Mrs. Thomas F. Madigan. The journals interested took the matter seriously. See Poe's comment on *The Regenerator, Broadway Journal*, II (September 20, 1845), 174.

lighter story, for he published "The Angel of the Odd" in October. This is as absurd as "Mesmeric Revelation" is thought-provoking, and is, as Poe said "an Extravaganza." Viewed even from that point of view, its humor is tiresome and the dialect which the "Angel" speaks, was not spoken anywhere on the globe.

"The Purloined Letter" belongs to this group of stories, mentioned by Poe to Lowell as still in the hands of editors in May, 1844, although it found a place in the *Gift* for 1845. It is the most unified of the stories of ratiocination, and in motive it is the best. Dupin is given the problem by the Prefect of Police at a point where the detective story usually ends. The robber is known; the problem lies in securing the letter, for its possession by the Minister D——— gives him a power over the owner of the letter, a royal personage, and a woman, which he has been using for political blackmail. Poe scorns the usual obvious details of a search, in which his imitators have revelled. Through the conversation of the Prefect we learn that all known methods have been employed. Dupin proceeds upon his knowledge of the *character* of the Minister D———, because he, unlike most detectives of fiction, is also a character. He knows that the robber is both a mathematician and a poet, therefore he is a master of mathematical processes of reasoning and also aware of their limitations. Through Dupin, Poe shows that mathematical axioms are not universally, but only relatively, true, and once more announces his doctrine of relativity, a prelude in a sense to *Eureka*.

Identifying himself with the imaginative processes of such a man as D———, Dupin decides that the Minister will employ the simplest method of concealment, because that will baffle the police. Dupin visits the apartments of D———, notices a letter, soiled and half torn, standing conspicuously on a rack, and decides it is the letter which the police have disregarded. Their reasoning, without imagination, has led them to believe no one would leave exposed such a valuable letter. Here a lesser artist would have concluded the story. But Dupin dislikes the Minister, for an evil turn he has done him. Dupin leaves, prepares a facsimile of the letter, and returns, after arranging that a disturbance shall be created in the street which attracts the Minister's attention. He then substitutes the false letter for the real one. Thus the Minister D———, believing that he still retains his power, will try to use it, will be defied and will be ruined. Poe created, therefore, two characters, Dupin and the Minister D———. Both of them have characteristics of Poe, the power of analysis and the imagination that transcends analysis. Like Dupin, Poe could long remember an injury;

like D——— he could neglect to remember that he had injured a possible enemy.[21]

"The Oblong Box" was suited quite well to *Godey's*, where it appeared in September, 1844. Charleston is simply a place to leave for a boat trip to New York, and the devices by which a bereaved husband endeavors to carry secretly the corpse of his wife, are singularly uninteresting. In "Thou Art the Man," which appeared in *Godey's* for November, the great master of ratiocinative stories burlesqued that branch of fiction. There is no attempt to treat the murder seriously. The tale has more significance through Poe's use of the moral contrast, in which Dickens was so adept, and which they bestowed on Bret Harte as a heritage. The guilty man has the reputation of probity and good fellowship; the innocent party, who is convicted and saved from execution only at the last minute, is a rake.

Poe must have enjoyed writing "The Literary Life of Thingum Bob," which came out in his old magazine, the *Southern Literary Messenger*, in December, 1844. It is a grotesque of the better quality. There is the literary charlatan, who sends in contributions to the magazines, made up of quotations from famous authors, and the ignorant editors who fail to recognize them, but criticize such lines as

"Hail! Holy Light, Offspring of Heaven, first born"

on the ground that hail can *not* be *holy light* and an offspring at the same time. The absurd verses which are accepted, the log-rolling, the "tomahawking" of poor devil authors, while exaggerated, nevertheless have a verity that makes the satire effective. Of the few real names used, scarcely any were of living men, but in revising the story, Poe included Lewis Gaylord Clark which, of course, made his exclusion from the *Knickerbocker* secure.

Meanwhile, Poe never forgot his hopes for his magazine. A long letter to Professor Anthon in this connection is of great interest because Poe gives a summary of all his magazine experience up to this time and explains why he has devoted himself to this field. With the letter he sent one of the tales, which one, he does not say. Poe evidently built high hopes upon Anthon's influence with Harpers, for the

---

[21] "The Purloined Letter" was published in *Chambers' Edinburgh Journal* in November, 1844 (II, 343 f.) with extensive revision, principally in cutting down conversation. As Poe printed the longer version from *The Gift* in his *Tales* of 1845 he evidently preferred it, if indeed he had anything to do with the version as published in *Chambers'*.

manuscript draft was prepared with the greatest care, constant alterations giving it the appearance of a literary composition:

My Dear Sir,

Many years have elapsed since my last communication with
you, and perhaps you will be surprised at receiving a letter from
me now—if not positively vexed at receiving one of so great a
length and of such a character. But I trust to your goodness of
heart for a patient hearing, at the least.

You will have already seen that, as usual, I have a favor to
solicit. You have, indeed, been to me in many respects a good
genius & a friend—but the request I have to make now is one of
vital interest to myself—so much so that upon your granting it or
refusing it, depends, I feel, much if not all of the prosperity and
even comfort of my future life.

I have had few friends. I cannot flatter myself, that you have
felt sufficient interest in me to have followed in any respect my
literary career, since the period at which you first did me the
honor to address me a note while Editor of the Southern Messenger. A few words of explanation on this point will therefore be
necessary here.

As I am well aware that your course of reading lies entirely out
of the track of our lighter literature, and as I take it for granted
therefore that none of the papers in question have met your eye
—I have thought it advisable to send you with this letter—a single
tale as a specimen. This will no doubt put you in mind of the
trick of the skolastikos—but I could not think of troubling you
with more than one. I do not think it my best tale—but it is perhaps the best in its particular vein. Variety has been one of my
chief aims.

In lieu of the rest, I venture to place in your hands the published opinions of many of my contemporaries. I will not deny
that I have been careful to collect & to preserve them. They include, as you will see, the warm commendations of a great number of very eminent men, and of these commendations I should
be at a loss to understand why I have not a right to be proud.

Before quitting the Mess: I saw, or fancied that I saw, through
a long & dim vista, the brilliant field for ambition which a Magazine of bold & noble aims presented to him who should successfully establish it in America. I perceived that the country from
its very constitution, could not fail of affording in a few years, a

larger proportionate amount of readers than any upon the Earth. I perceived that the whole energetic, busy spirit of the age tended wholly to the Magazine literature—to the curt, the terse, the well-timed, and the readily diffused, in preference to the old forms of the verbose and ponderous & the inaccessible. I knew from personal experience that lying *perdus* among the innumerable plantations in our vast Southern & Western Countries were a host of well-educated men, singularly devoid of prejudice, who would gladly lend their influence to a really vigorous journal provided the right means were taken of bringing it fairly within the very limited scope of their observation. Now, I knew, it is true, that some scores of journals had failed (for indeed I looked upon the best success of the best of them as failure) but then I easily traced the causes of their failure in the impotency of their conductors, who made no scruple of basing their rules of action altogether upon what had been customarily done instead of what was now before them to do, but in the greatly changed & constantly changing condition of things.

In short, I could see no real reason why a Magazine, if worthy the name, could not be made to circulate among 20,000 subscribers, embracing the best intellect & education of the land. This was a thought which stimulated my fancy & my ambition. The influence of such a journal would be vast indeed, and I dreamed of honestly employing that influence in the sacred cause of the beautiful, the just, & the true. Even in a pecuniary view, the object was a magnificent one.

The journal I proposed would be a large octavo of 128 pp. printed with clear, bold type, in single column, on the finest paper, and disdaining everything of which is termed "embellishment" with the exception of an occassional [sic] portrait of a literary man, or some well-engraved wood design in obvious illustration of the text. Of such a journal I had cautiously estimated the expenses. Could I circulate 20 000 cop. at 5$ the cost wd be about $30.000, estimating all contingencies at the highest rate. There would be a balance of $70.000 per annum.

But not to trust too implicitly to *a priori* reasonings, and at the same time to make myself thoroughly master of all details which might avail me concerning the mere business of publication, I entered a few steps into the field of experiment. I joined the "Messenger" as you know, which was then in its 2d year with 700 subscribers & the general outcry was that because a Magazine had never succeeded South of the Potomac therefore a Magazine never c'd succeed. Yet in despite of this & in despite of the wretched taste of its proprietor which hampered & controlled me at all points I (in 15 months) increased the circulation in 15 months to 5,500 subscribers paying an annual profit of 10,000 when I left it. This number was never exceeded by the journal which rapidly went down & may now be said to be extinct. Of "Graham's Magazine" you have no doubt heard. It had been in existence under the name of the "Casket" for 8 years, when I became its editor with a subscription list of about 5000. In about 18 months afterward its circulation amounted to no less than 50.000—astonishing as this may appear. At this period I left it. It is now 2 years since, and the number of subscribers is now *not more* than 25.000—but possibly very much less. In 3 years it will be extinct. The nature of this journal, however, was such, that even its 50.000 subscribers could not make it very profitable to its proprietors. Its price was $3—but not only were its expenses immense owing to the employment of absurd steelplates & other extravagances which tell not at all, but recourse was had to innumerable agents who recd it at a discount of no less than 50 per cent & whose frequent dishonesty occasioned enormous loss. But, if 50 000 can be obtained for a 3$ Maga- among a class of readers who really read little, why may not 50.000. be procured for a $5 journal among the true and permanent readers of the land?

Holding steadily in view my ultimate purpose—to found a Magazine of my own, or in which at least I might have a proprietary right,—it has been my constant endeavour in the meantime not so much to establish a reputation great in itself as one of that particular character which should best further my special objects, and draw attention to my exertions as Editor of a Magazine. Thus I have written no books and have been so far essentially a Magazinist. ... bearing not only willingly but cheerfully sad poverty & the thousand consequent contumelies & other ills which the condition of the mere Magazinist entails upon him in America—where more than in any other region upon the face of the globe to be poor is to be despised.

The one great difficulty resulting from this course is that unless the journalist collects his various articles he is liable to be grossly misconceived & misjudged by men of whose good opinion he would be proud—but who see, perhaps, only a paper here & there, by accident.—often only one of his mere extravaganzas; written to supply a particular demand. He loses, too, whatever merit may be his due on the score of *versatility*—a point which can only be estimated by collection of his various articles in volume form and altogether. This is indeed a serious difficulty—to seek a remedy for which in my own case is my object in writing you this letter.

Setting aside, for the present, my criticisms poems & miscellanies (sufficiently numerous) my tales a great number of which might be termed Phantasy Pieces, are in number sixty-six. They would make, perhaps, 5 of the ordinary novel volumes. I have them prepared in every respect for the press; but, alas, I have no money, nor that influence which would enable me to get a publisher—although I seek *no* pecuniary remuneration. My sole immediate object is the furtherance of my ultimate one. I believe that if I could get my Tales fairly before the public, and thus have an opportunity of eliciting foreign as well as native opinion respecting them—I should by their means be in a far more advantageous position than at present in regard to the establishment of a Magazine. In a word, I believe that the publication of the work would lead forthwith either directly through my own exertion or indirectly with the aid of a publisher to the establishment of the journal I hold in view.

It is very true that I have no claims upon your attention—not even that of personal acquaintance. But I have reached a crisis of my life, in which I sadly stand in need of aid, and without being able to say why,—unless it is that I so earnestly desire your friendship—I have always felt a half-hope that if I appealed to you you would prove my friend. I know that you have unbounded influence with the Harpers—& I know that if you would exert it in my behalf you could procure me the publication I desire.[22]

Anthon did not reply until November 2nd:

[22] Woodberry prints a letter, dated "June, 1844" (II, 72-79), crediting it to the Griswold Collection. It is not signed and is not at the Boston Public Library. Since Anthon makes no mention in his reply of the delay of five months, I question the date Woodberry assigns to Poe's Letter, especially since Poe states that he has written "sixty-six tales." The manuscript draft, now in the Huntington Library, is not dated or signed, and bears no writing on the verso of any of the sheets. I have printed from the Huntington Ms., but have not attempted to print the many crossed-out words, or repetitions, except in one case, "in 15 months," where it is not clear which phrase Poe intended to omit.

New York, November 2, 1844.

Dear Sir,—I have called upon the Harpers, as you requested, and have cheerfully exerted with them what influence I possess, but without accomplishing anything of importance. They have *complaints* against you, grounded on certain movements of yours, when they acted as your publishers some years ago; and appear very little inclined at present to enter upon the matter which you have so much at heart. However, they have retained, for a second and more careful perusal, the letter which you sent to me, and have promised that, if they should see fit to come to terms with you, they will address a note to you forthwith. Of course, if you should not hear from them, their silence must be construed into a declining of your proposal. My *own advice* to you is to call in person at their store, and talk over the matter with them. I am *very sure* that such a step on your part will remove many of the difficulties which at present obstruct your way.

You do me injustice by supposing that I am a stranger to your productions. I subscribed to the "Messenger" solely because you were connected with it, and I have since that period read and, as a matter of course, admired very many of your other pieces. The Harpers also entertain, as I heard from their own lips, the highest opinion of your talents, but—I remain very sincerely,

Your friend and well-wisher,

CHARLES ANTHON.

P. S. The MSS. which you were kind enough to send can be obtained by you at any time on calling at my residence.

C. A.[23]

The disappointment must have been great, but Poe did not abandon his hopes.

Poe's correspondence with Lowell and others continues to reveal his personal as well as his literary experiences during 1844. Lowell apologized for his delay in writing the biography of Poe for *Graham's* and asked Poe for "a sort of spiritual biography," written "as to a friend." [24] Poe replied, in an important letter, in which he combined some of the scientific ideas which he had already written in "Mesmeric Revelation" with his own estimates of his poems and stories:

New York, July 2, '44.

My dear Mr. Lowell,—I can feel for the "constitutional indolence" of which you complain—for it is one of my own besetting

[23] Original Autograph Ms., Griswold Collection, Boston Public Library.
[24] Woodberry, II, 87-89, attributing it to the Griswold Ms., among which it is not at present.

sins. I am excessively slothful and wonderfully industrious—by fits. There are epochs when any kind of mental exercise is torture, and when nothing yields me pleasure but solitary communion with the "mountains and the woods,"— the "altars" of Byron. I have thus rambled and dreamed away whole months, and awake, at last, to a sort of mania for composition. Then I scribble all day, and read all night, so long as the disease endures. This is also the temperament of P. P. Cooke, of Virginia, the author of "Florence Vane," "Young Rosalie Lee," and some other sweet poems—and I should not be surprised if it were your own. Cooke writes and thinks as you—and I have been told that you resemble him personally.

I am *not* ambitious—unless negatively. I now and then feel stirred up to excel a fool, merely because I hate to let a fool imagine that he may excel me. Beyond this I feel nothing of ambition. I really perceive that vanity about which most men merely prate, —the vanity of the human or temporal life. I live continually in a reverie of the future. I have no faith in human perfectibility. I think that human exertion will have no appreciable effect upon humanity. Man is now only more active—not more happy—nor more wise, than he was 6000 years ago. The result will never vary—and to suppose that it will, is to suppose that the foregone man has lived in vain—that the foregone time is but the rudiment of the future—that the myriads who have perished have not been upon equal footing with ourselves—nor are we with our posterity. I cannot agree to lose sight of man the individual in man the mass.—I have no belief in spirituality. I think the word a *mere* word. No one has really a conception of spirit. We cannot imagine what is not. We deceive ourselves by the idea of infinitely rarefied matter. Matter escapes the senses by degrees—a stone—a metal—a liquid—the atmosphere—a gas—the luminiferous ether. Beyond this there are other modifications more rare. But to all we attach the notion of a constitution of particles—atomic composition. For this reason only we think spirit different; for spirit, we say, is unparticled, and *therefore* is not matter. But it is clear that if we proceed sufficiently far in our ideas of rarefaction, we shall arrive at a point where the particles coalesce; for, although the particles be infinite, the infinity of littleness in the spaces between them is an absurdity.—The unparticled matter, permeating and impelling all things, is God. Its activity is the thought of God—which creates. Man, and other thinking beings, are individualizations of the unparticled matter. Man exists as a "person," by being clothed with matter (the particled matter) which individualizes him. Thus habited, his life is rudimental. What we call "death" is the painful metamorphosis. The stars are the habitations of rudimental beings. But for the necessity of the rudimental life, there would have been no worlds. At death, the worm is the butterfly—still material, but of a matter unrecognized by our organs—recognized occasionally, perhaps, by the sleep-walker directly—without organs—through the mesmeric medium. Thus a sleep-walker may see ghosts. Divested of the rudimental covering, the being inhabits *space*,—what we suppose to be the immaterial universe,—passing everywhere, and acting all things, by mere volition, cognizant of all secrets but that of the nature of God's volition—the motion, or activity, of the unparticled matter.

You speak of "an estimate of my life,"—and, from what I have already said, you will see that I have none to give. I have been too deeply conscious of the mutability and evanescence of temporal things to give any continuous effort to anything—to be consistent in anything. My life has been *whim*—impulse—passion— a longing for solitude—a scorn of all things present, in an earnest desire for the future.

I am profoundly excited by music, and by some poems—those of Tennyson especially—whom, with Keats, Shelley, Coleridge (occasionally), and a few others of like thought and expression, I regard as the *sole* poets. Music is the perfection of the soul, or idea, of Poetry. The *vagueness* of exaltation aroused by a sweet air (which should be strictly indefinite and never too strongly suggestive) is precisely what we should aim at in poetry. Affectation, within bounds, is thus no blemish.

I still adhere to Dickens as either author, or dictator, of the review. My reasons would convince you, could I give them to you, but I have left myself no space. I had two long interviews with Mr. D. when here. Nearly everything in the critique, I heard from him, or suggested to him, personally. The poem of Emerson I read to him.

I have been so negligent as not to preserve copies of any of my volumes of poems—nor was either worthy of preservation. The best passages were culled in Hirst's article.[25] I think my best poems "The Sleeper," "The Conqueror Worm," "The Haunted Palace," "Lenore," "Dreamland," and the "Coliseum,"—but all

[25] In the Philadelphia *Saturday Museum*, March 4, 1843.

have been hurried and unconsidered. My best tales are "Ligeia,"
the "Gold-Bug," the "Murders in the Rue Morgue," "The Fall of
the House of Usher," the "Tell-Tale Heart," the "Black Cat,"
"William Wilson," and "The Descent into the Maelström." "The
Purloined Letter," forthcoming in the "Gift," is perhaps the best
of my tales of ratiocination. I have lately written for Godey "The
Oblong Box" and "Thou art the Man,"—as yet unpublished. With
this I mail you the "Gold-Bug," which is the only one of my tales
I have on hand.

Graham has had, for nine months, a review of mine on Longfellow's "Spanish Student," which I have "used up," and in which
I have exposed some of the grossest plagiarisms ever perpetrated.
I can't tell why he does not publish it.—I believe G. intends my
Life for the September number, which will be made up by the
10th August. Your article should be on hand as soon as convenient.

Believe me your true friend,

E. A. Poe.[26]

This letter contains one of Poe's most striking epigrams: "Man is
now only more active—not more happy—nor more wise, than he was
6000 years ago." Perhaps it is as true today as it was in 1844.

Poe repeated this phrase, with many others, in a letter to Chivers
on July 10, 1844, and also urged the latter to join him in the *Stylus.*
"You will find me here—at New York—where I live at present, in
strict seclusion, buried with books and ambitious thoughts. ..." Poe
was evidently uncertain about his address, for he asks Chivers to "put
a letter to my address [which he does not give] in the P. Office, and
we will thus find each other." Poe also tells him that he has been
lecturing on American Poetry.[27]

Poe was working hard on his projected *Critical History of American
Literature,* which never was completed, and he wrote to Lowell on
August 18th, telling him of it and sending him "Mesmeric Revelation" asking him to get it reprinted in some paper. "I am living so
entirely out of the world, just now," he continues, "that I can do
nothing of the kind myself." [28]

This seclusion had evidently been constant, for in his letter to
Thomas of September 2, 1844, he emphasizes it:

[26] Autograph Ms. Letter, Harvard College Library.
[27] Original Autograph Ms., Huntington Library.
[28] Original Autograph Ms., Harvard College Library.

New York, September 8, 1844.

My dear Thomas,—I received yours with sincere pleasure, and nearly as sincere surprise; for while you were wondering that I did not write to *you*, I was making up my mind that you had forgotten *me* altogether.

I have left Philadelphia, and am living, at present, about five miles out of New York. For the last seven or eight months I have been playing hermit in earnest, nor have I seen a living soul out of my family—who are well and desire to be kindly remembered. When I say "well," I only mean (as regards Virginia) as well as usual. Her health remains excessively precarious.

Touching the "Beechen Tree," I remember it well and pleasantly. I have not yet seen a published copy, but will get one forthwith and notice it as it deserves—and it deserves much of high praise—at the very first opportunity I get. At present I am so much out of the world that I may not be able to do anything *immediately*.

Thank God! Richard (whom you know) is himself again. Tell Dow so: but he won't believe it. I am working at a variety of things (all of which you shall behold in the end)—and with an ardor of which I did not believe myself capable.

You said to me hurriedly, when we last met on the wharf in Philadelphia, that you believed Robert Tyler really wished to give me the post in the Custom House. This I also really think; and I am confirmed in the opinion that he could not, at all times, do as he wished in such matters, by seeing ———— ———— at the head of the "Aurora"—a bullet-headed and malicious villain who has brought more odium upon the Administration than any fellow (of equal littleness) in its ranks, and who has been more indefatigably busy in both open and secret vilification of Robert Tyler than any individual, little or big, in America.

Let me hear from you again very soon, my dear Thomas, and believe me *ever*   Your friend,   POE.[29]

Poe received the critical biography from Lowell, shortly after the receipt of a letter from his friend written on September 27, 1844.[30]

[29] Woodberry, *Century Magazine*, XLVIII (October, 1894), 863. "The Beechen Tree" was a poem by Thomas. The editor of the *Aurora* at this time was probably Thomas Dunn English.

[30] Original Autograph Ms. Anthony Collection, New York Public Library.

Poe's acknowledgment contains two important paragraphs. The first makes clear that he felt authorized to alter the biography before he gave it to *Graham's*, and the second refers to his happiness in his own married life:

New York, October 28, '44.

My dear Friend,—A host of small troubles growing from the *one* trouble of poverty, but which I will not trouble you with in detail, have hitherto prevented me from thanking you for the Biography and all the well-intended flatteries which it contains. But, upon the principle of better late than never, let me thank you now, again and again. I sent it to Graham on the day I received it—taking with it only one liberty in the way of modification. This I hope you will pardon. It was merely the substitution of another brief poem for the last you have done me the honor to quote.

I have not seen your marriage announced, but I presume from what you said in your penultimate letter, that I may congratulate you now. Is it so? At all events I can wish you no better wish than that you may derive from your marriage as substantial happiness as I have derived from mine.[31]

Lowell's critical article on Poe is one of the best appraisals he received during his lifetime. Although it did not appear until February, 1845, in *Graham's*, it was written as we have seen, in 1844, before "The Raven" was published. Lowell pronounced Poe "the most discriminating, philosophical, and fearless critic upon imaginative works who has written in America. It may be [he continued], that we should qualify our remark a little and say that he *might be,* rather than that he always *is,* for he seems sometimes to mistake his phial of prussic-acid for his inkstand. If we do not always agree with him in his premises, we are, at least, satisfied that his deductions are logical, and that we are reading the thoughts of a man who thinks for himself, and says what he thinks, and knows well what he is talking about. His analytic power would furnish forth bravely some score of ordinary critics. We do not know him personally, but we suspect him for a man who has one or two pet prejudices on which he prides himself. These sometimes allure him out of the strict path of criticism,

[31] Original Autograph Ms., Harvard College Library. The remainder of the letter repeats the long account of his projected coöperative scheme for a magazine.

but, where they do not interfere, we would put almost entire confidence in his judgments. Had Mr. Poe had the control of a magazine of his own, in which to display his critical abilities, he would have been as autocratic, ere this, in America, as Professor Wilson has been in England; and his criticisms, we are sure, would have been far more profound and philosophical than those of the Scotsman. As it is, he has squared out blocks enough to build an enduring pyramid, but has left them lying carelessly and unclaimed in many different quarries."

In speaking of Poe's early poems Lowell said with an insight only a poet critic possesses: "They display what we can only express by the contradictory phrase of *innate experience.*" He dwelt also upon the grace and symmetry of "To Helen." "There is," he said, "the smack of ambrosia about it." He also selected one of the exquisite lyric passages in "Al Aaraaf." Then he proceeded, "Mr. Poe has that indescribable something which men have agreed to call genius." [32]

Lowell selected unerringly the two qualities that made Poe a genius—"a faculty of vigorous, yet minute analysis, and a wonderful fecundity of imagination." These led to a combination of "two faculties which are seldom found united; a power of influencing the mind of the reader by the impalpable shadows of mystery, and a minuteness of detail which does not leave a pin or a button unnoticed."

The closest rival Edgar Poe had among the critics of that period saw how Poe's realistic method corrected and held in check the treat-

---

[32] This striking phrase is curiously like Poe's own expression in "The Literary Life of Thingum-Bob, Esq." "After all what is it?—this indescribable something which men will persist in terming genius?" This story was published in *The Southern Literary Messenger* in December, 1844, while Lowell's article appeared in *Graham's* in February, 1845. But Poe had Lowell's biography by October 1, 1844. Did he appropriate the phrase from a manuscript entrusted to him? *The Messenger* was probably in print by November 15th, and Poe's stories often lay unpublished for some time in editorial hands. Moreover, his letter to Anthon, if not written in June, 1844, was certainly sent before he received Lowell's article, and Poe speaks of having written "sixty-six stories," which would have included "The Literary Life of Thingum-Bob." The phrase may have been in both men's minds from an earlier source. Lowell, in his essay on Dryden published in 1868, said, "Cowper, in a letter to Mr. Unwin (5th January, 1782) expressed what I think is the common feeling about Dryden, that with all his defects, he had that indefinable something we call Genius." I thought the puzzle was solved. But the letter of Cowper, to which Lowell referred, does not contain the phrase! Nor does any other letter of Cowper to Mr. Unwin published in Hayley's edition (1806), so far as I can see.

ment of the romantic material in which he delighted. Lowell paid his tribute also to the form of Poe's art, selected "The Fall of the House of Usher," and "The Haunted Palace" for especial praise and one other poem for which Poe, according to his letter of October 28th, substituted "Lenore."

Poe's desire for seclusion and the time to write could not be gratified. There was soon urgent need for regular income, and Poe found it with Nathaniel Parker Willis and George Pope Morris, who had revived the *New York Mirror*, a weekly literary magazine. This became the *Weekly Mirror*. The high postage rates for magazines caused it to become a daily newspaper, the *Evening Mirror*, with a weekly supplement, the *Weekly Mirror*. Poe contributed to both papers, joining the staff either directly or by correspondence in October, 1844. Willis has given clearly the picture of Poe at this time:

"Some four or five years since, when editing a daily paper in this city, Mr. Poe was employed by us, for several months, as critic and sub-editor. This was our first personal acquaintance with him. He resided with his wife and mother, at Fordham, a few miles out of town, but was at his desk in the office, from nine in the morning till the evening paper went to press. With the highest admiration for his genius, and a willingness to let it atone for more than ordinary irregularity, we were led by common report to expect a very capricious attention to his duties, and occasionally a scene of violence and difficulty. Time went on, however, and he was invariably punctual and industrious. With his pale, beautiful, and intellectual face, as a reminder of what genius was in him, it was impossible, of course, not to treat him always with deferential courtesy, and to our occasional request that he would not probe too deep in a criticism, or that he would erase a passage colored too highly with his resentments against society and mankind, he readily and courteously assented,—far more yielding than most men, we thought, on points so excusably sensitive. With a prospect of taking the lead in another periodical, he, at last, voluntarily gave up his employment with us, and, through all this considerable period, we had seen but one presentment of the man,—a quiet, patient, industrious, and most gentlemanly person, commanding the utmost respect and good feeling by his unvarying deportment and ability.

"Residing as he did in the country, we never met Mr. Poe in hours of leisure; but he frequently called on us afterwards at our place of business, and we met him often in the street,—invariably the same sad-mannered, winning and refined gentleman, such as we had always known him. It was by rumor only, up to the day of his death, that we knew of any other development of manner or character.[33]

Poe was not at Fordham, of course, at this time. His letter to Thomas, January 4, 1845, makes clear that he was still out of town at Brennan's, contrary to the usual statements that he had moved into town in November, 1844:

New-York
Jan. 4. 45.

Dear Thomas,

I duly received your two letters and "The Beechen Tree," for which let me thank you. My reason for not replying instanter was that I was just then making arrangements which, if fully carried out, would have enabled me to do you justice in a manner satisfactory to both of us—but these arrangements finally fell through, after my being kept in suspense for months—and I could find no good opportunity of putting in a word anywhere that would have done you service. You know I do not live in town—very seldom visit it—and, of course, am not in the way of matters and things as I used to be. As for Benjamin's criticism—although I made all kinds of inquiry about it, I could meet no one who had even heard of it. At the "New-World" Office no paper containing it was even on file. I am disposed to think you were misinformed, and that no such critique appeared, in that paper at least. At all events, if there did, Benjamin, I am assured, did not write it. At the epoch you speak of, he was unconnected with the "New-World."

In about three weeks, I shall move into the City, and recommence a life of activity under better auspices, I hope, than ever before. *Then* I may be able to do something.

Virginia & Mrs. Clemm are about as usual and beg to be remembered.

I am truly glad to hear of Dow's well-doing. If ever man deserved prosperity, he does. Give him my respects—in which one word I mean to include all descriptions of kind feeling.

I remain, Thomas, truly
Your friend,

POE.[34]

[33] N. P. Willis, "The Death of Edgar A. Poe." *Home Journal,* October 20, 1849.

[34] Original Autograph Ms., Huntington Library.

Poe's statement that he seldom visited the city seems to place his office work on the *Mirror* after January, 1845. Yet Willis could hardly have imagined Poe's coming to the office from the country, even if he had confused the two places.[35] In any event, Poe's distinctive note is seen in the editorial columns. His criticism of the relative returns to authors, publishers, and booksellers in his "Authors' Pay in America," and "The Pay for Periodical-Writing," [36] give interesting information on those subjects. According to Poe, the publisher never distributed profits until the printing and binding were paid for, thus playing safe, and the bookseller received from twice to five times as much as the author. In view of the frequent discussions as to what is the matter with the publishing business today, Poe might be called in as an expert. While publishers no longer require writers to wait for royalties until the initial cost has been repaid, booksellers still take forty per cent of the sales' price as compared with the authors' ten or fifteen. Perhaps Poe was not so unpractical as he seemed, but there is no evidence that his protest was effective.

Poe continued this theme in January and February, 1845, hammering away at the lack of international copyright. Those who minimize his interest in American affairs have evidently not read his protest that "irreparable ill is wrought by the almost exclusive dissemination among us of foreign, that is to say of monarchical or aristocratical sentiment, in foreign books." [37] Poe also stated that "Any American for eight dollars, may receive any four of the British periodicals for a year." This was an early example of the "club rate," and had naturally a discouraging effect upon native periodicals.

In November, 1844, Poe published the first installment of his "Marginalia" in the *Democratic Review*. These are short or long paragraphs of the familiar or expository essay type, usually culled from his reading. Frequently they are repetitions of earlier reviews. Poe continued to publish these "Marginalia" in the *Democratic Review*, in *Godey's, Graham's* and finally in the *Southern Literary Messenger* in 1849. From their nature they defy any individual critical appraisement, but Poe treated them quite seriously. There have recently come

[35] Poe's letter to Griswold, written January 16, 1845, and one of the authentic notes, invites Griswold to call at the *Mirror* office.

[36] *Weekly Mirror,* I (October 12, 1844), 15, and (October 19), 28. These were reprints of similar articles in the *Evening Mirror.*

[37] These articles are unsigned, but the passage quoted, from the *Weekly Mirror* of February 8, 1845, is in Ms. in the Historical Society of Pennsylvania.

it looks smaller than it should be — smaller than the
sun which sets.

of seems to be closer and, therefore, we
expect it to appear larger. In other way

is not corresponding

* Now eyron — Area since discovd.
17 — a March : 6 Astroids.

REVISED PAGES FROM THE *Democratic Review* SHOWING POE'S
CARE IN REVISIONS OF "MARGINALIA"

to light,[38] a number of the pages from the first chapters, which were evidently being prepared for a new printing, or perhaps even for book publication. How well Poe kept up with recent astronomical science, is illustrated by his adding to the list of the planets, in an article on the measurement of time, the name of "Astraea," the minor planet, discovered December 8, 1845.[39]

In the first installment Poe anticipated *Eureka* in his definition of a plot. In another passage he suggested that "The orange ray of the spectrum and the buzz of the gnat (which never rises above the second A) affect me with nearly similar sensations." This is one more illustration of his belief in the identification of the effects of the senses. A long passage concerning the limitations of our eyesight is still worth reading, wherever he obtained the information.

It was in the *Evening Mirror* that "The Raven" appeared, in the issue of January 29, 1845. It was prefaced by a note by Willis: "We are permitted to copy (in advance of publication) from the 2d No. of the *American Review*, the following remarkable poem by Edgar Poe. In our opinion, it is the most effective single example of 'fugitive poetry' ever published in this country, and unsurpassed in English poetry for subtle conception, masterly ingenuity of versification, and consistent sustaining of imaginative lift and 'pokerishness.'"

Poe had sold the poem to the *Review*, where it appeared as "The Raven. By — Quarles.",[40] with an introduction apparently by the editor of the *Review*, but bearing marks of Poe's metrical theories.

There has been a great deal of discussion concerning the priority of the publication dates of the *Mirror* and the *Review*. Willis's words seem clear enough, and he did not speak of an "advance copy" as has been suggested, but "in advance of publication." Poe's relation with

---

[38] In the papers of the late President Gilman of Johns Hopkins. Dr. J. C. French has kindly furnished me with photostats of the corrected pages. In the first two installments, there are more than twenty corrections. See his article "Poe's Revision of Marginalia" in *Ex Libris, Quarterly Leaflet issued by Friends of the Library,* IX (January, 1940), 2-3, containing a facsimile of page 493 of the *Democratic Review.*

[39] The "Marginalia" should be read in the Virginia Edition, Vol. XVI. Harrison omitted, however, the installments from the *Democratic Review* for July, 1846, and from *Graham's* for March, 1848. Griswold did not follow the arrangement of the text in the magazines, except for the introductory paragraphs. There is a good deal omitted in his third volume of the *Works* (1850), and his version was reprinted by Stoddard and others.

[40] *The American Review. A Whig Journal of Politics, Literature and Science,* I (February, 1845), 143-145.

Willis and the *Mirror* would have suggested his offering the poem in manuscript to his own paper. He evidently did not see the *Mirror* proof, for there were errors like the repetition of "he" in the fifth line of the tenth stanza. This error was carried over to the *Weekly Mirror* of February 8th, but it does not appear in the *Review*. On the other side of the argument it is true that magazines were published in advance of their dates, and the *Review* may have been out before January 29th. Inasmuch as the *Weekly Mirror* of February 8th solemnly repeats the statement that it is publishing the poem "in advance of publication," too much stress need not be laid on Willis's first notice. Evidently when matter was reprinted for the weekly edition it was simply copied verbatim. In any event, the honor of first accepting the poem belongs to George H. Colton, the editor of the *American Review*.

"The Raven" made an impression probably not surpassed by that of any single piece of American poetry. It was widely copied, parodied,[41] and one humorist even took over a page of the *Mirror* to suggest five alternatives as to the relation of Lenore to the poet.[42]

It seems almost certain that "The Raven" was a growth, that the first form began to shape itself before Poe left Philadelphia. Several of the stories about the earlier reading of the poem are undoubtedly apocryphal, but since none of them make any valid contribution to its interpretation or bear any credible testimony concerning vital changes, they are really of little consequence.

With our knowledge of Poe's methods in writing his other poems, the best argument for the gradual inception of "The Raven" lies in the few changes made by Poe in the many opportunities he had for revision, after publication. They are limited generally to slight verbal alterations. Three lines are materially altered—and these are improved; but there is no such radical progress as in "To Helen" or "Israfel." [43]

The arch enemy of plagiarism met during his lifetime many claimants for the honor of having provided him with ideas, words, metrical form, and even the raven himself. And since Poe's death, there have

[41] See the *Weekly Mirror*, II, 62 and 132.
[42] *Weekly Mirror*, II (April 26, 1845), 42-43.
[43] The eleventh stanza was changed by Poe in the *Broadway Journal* to read as we now have it. In the *American Review* it had read in part:

"Caught from some unhappy master whom unmerciful Disaster
Followed fast and followed faster—so, when Hope he would adjure,
Stern Despair returned, instead of the sweet Hope he dared adjure—
                That sad answer—'Nevermore'."

been many more such attributions. These may usually be disregarded. There is no doubt, however, that the bird was suggested by the raven in Dickens' *Barnaby Rudge,* especially since Poe called attention to the possible symbolic association between Barnaby and "Grip," of which Dickens had not made full use. The similarity of the verses in Mrs. Browning's "Lady Geraldine's Courtship,"

> "With a murmurous stir uncertain in the air the
> purple curtain"

and Poe's

> "And the silken, sad, uncertain rustling of each
> purple curtain,"

also the less striking resemblance of her

> "Ever evermore the while in a slow silence she kept
> smiling"

and Poe's

> "Then this ebony bird beguiling my sad fancy into
> smiling,"

have often been pointed out.

But as Stevenson remarked when he acknowledged his own indebtedness to Poe in the preface to *Treasure Island,* no one can have a corner in talking birds. And the theme of Mrs. Browning's rather turgid poem is quite different from that of "The Raven."

More important is the spiritual ancestry of "The Raven" and here Poe is clearly his own ancestor. Those who have dismissed his account of the construction of the poem in "The Philosophy of Composition," as an artificial deception, a hoax upon critics and public alike, are only superficially correct.[44] Poe did not write the poem in a series of logical and mathematical operations, of course. But there is no one of the various ideas he describes in his essay which might not have come to him. What his critics have not seen is that he did not have them all at once, in the preparation of *one poem,* or in the logical order in which he retails them in "The Philosophy of Composition."

With most of them he had long been familiar. Poe was an artist

[44] Notwithstanding Mrs. Weiss's statement, quoted by Gill, *Life,* p. 150.

in the short story, and his method of approach in this field is not at all unlike that which he describes in his account of the genesis of "The Raven." At the beginning, he looks within himself for an effect. He exceeds his usual number of lines because he has chosen an effect which demands a climax of a nature which takes time to establish. He desires critical as well as popular appreciation. So he chooses an effect which is universal in its appeal. He thinks deliberately of the most universal of all effects, and he decides it is Beauty, beauty of the soul. This choice to Poe is obvious. He had been talking and writing about it all his thinking life, and his first poem "Tamerlane" is based upon the tragedy which springs from the sorrow which comes to a lover on the death of the woman he loves.

His choice of a raven, Poe said, was due to his need for a "non-reasoning creature, capable of speech." Surely the success of "The Murders in the Rue Morgue" provided him with this suggestion. The choice of a refrain is also quite natural; he had already used it in "Lenore," and he knew its history in English poetry. "Nevermore," or its variant, "No more" was in the "Sonnet to Zante" and "The Haunted Palace," and the sonorous quality of the long "o" was an old story with him. Poe's use of the refrain "Nevermore," however it came to him, is masterly. His insight into the perverse nature of man suggested to him the mounting torture of the lover as he puts the questions. First, shall he find peace in forgetfulness; second, is there peace in the future, and at last he cries

> "Tell this soul with sorrow laden, if within the
>   distant Aidenn,
> It shall clasp a sainted maiden whom the angels
>   name Lenore.
> Clasp a rare and radiant maiden whom the angels
>   name Lenore."

He knows the answer beforehand, yet he cannot keep from asking the question. It is one of the most profound impulses of human nature.

Poe spoke of the stanza in which this final appeal to the raven is framed as the climax of the poem, and he said he wrote it first. This again is quite possible, and his remark that even if he had been able to construct more vigorous stanzas preceding this one, he would have purposely enfeebled them, may not have been an afterthought.

It will be noticed that Poe did not include the two final stanzas in this category. There was no enfeebling here. Within them, he said, he established the Raven as "The emblem of Mournful and Never-ending Remembrance." But Poe in his essay, did not make clear a quality in these two stanzas which marks the poem with greatness. The seventeenth stanza, no longer an appeal, but a defiance, is the climax of action:

> " 'Be that word our sign of parting, bird or fiend!' I
> shrieked, upstarting—
> 'Get thee back into the tempest and the Night's
> Plutonian shore!
> Leave no black plume as a token of that lie thy soul
> hath spoken!
> Leave my loneliness unbroken!—quit the bust above
> my door!
> Take thy beak from out my heart, and take thy form
> from off my door!'
> Quoth the Raven 'Nevermore.' "

A lesser artist would have ended the poem here. But Poe knew that *action* is transitory, so he wrote another, in which he lifted the poem into a climax of *feeling*:

> "And the Raven, never flitting, still is sitting, *still*
> is sitting
> On the pallid bust of Pallas just above my chamber
> door;
> And his eyes have all the seeming of a demon's that is
> dreaming,
> And the lamp-light o'er him streaming throws his
> shadow on the floor;
> And my soul from out that shadow that lies floating on
> the floor
> Shall be lifted—nevermore!"

And there he could safely leave it, for the rest of time.

Reams of print have dealt with the question of whether the sorrow of the poet was described objectively by Poe or whether he was dramatizing a real love. This controversy is really unnecessary. Poe's dread of the loss of Virginia, born of her recurring danger and nurtured by his devotion, had become a spiritual offspring, as concrete to him as the child he was denied could ever have been. In one sense, therefore, the poet was describing an emotional creation which had become objective to him, and the vivid reality of the poem is a consequence. But the primary inspiration was the abstract love of a beautiful woman—whether she was Helen, Eleonora, Lenore, or any other variant of the same name. Whether she was actually dead, or whether he feared her inevitable doom, is a detail.

There were critics in those days, of course, who found fault with the lamplight and the footfalls—Poe's own explanation to Eveleth is best:

> For the purposes of poetry, it is quite sufficient that a thing is possible—or at least that the improbability be not offensively glaring. It is true that in several ways, as you say, the lamp might have thrown the bird's shadow on the floor. *My* conception was that of the bracket candelabrum affixed against the wall, high up above the door and bust—as is often seen in the English palaces, and even in some of the better houses in New-York.
>
> Your objection to the *tinkling* of the footfalls is far more pointed, and in the course of composition occurred so forcibly to myself that I hesitated to use the term. I finally used it, because I saw that it had, in its first conception, been suggested to my mind by the sense of the *supernatural* with which it was, at the moment, filled. No human or physical foot could tinkle on a soft carpet— therefore the tinkling of feet would vividly convey the supernatural impression. This was the idea, and it is good within itself; but if it fails (as I fear it does) to make itself immediately and generally *felt* according to my intention—then in so much is it badly conveyed, or expressed.[45]

The weakest portion of "The Philosophy of Composition" is its discussion of metre. But that must be postponed until it is taken up in a later discussion of "The Rationale of Verse."

Prompted perhaps by his "Imp of the Perverse," Poe resumed in January, 1845 his relations with Griswold, who was preparing his *Prose Writers of America.* According to a letter printed in Griswold's "Preface," Poe made the first approaches on January 10, 1845, offering something for the *Prose Writers of America,* yet expressing doubt concerning Griswold's feelings for him.[46] As this letter is not extant in Poe's hand, it may never have been written—at least in this form. Griswold wrote Poe on January 14th. I print in parallel columns the correct text from the autograph Ms. in the Boston Public Library and the text as printed by Griswold in his "Preface":

[45] Poe to Eveleth, December 15, 1846. Original Autograph Ms., Berg Collection, New York Public Library.

[46] This letter is printed in Virginia Edition, XVII, 196, from the "Griswold Memoir."

[Confidential]

New York, Jan 14, 1845.

Although I have some cause of personal quarrel with you, which you will easily enough remember, I do not under any circumstances permit, as you have repeatedly charged, my private griefs to influence my judgment as a critic, or its expression.

I retain, therefore, the early formed and well founded favorable opinions of your works, wh[ich] in other days I have expressed to you, and in a new volume which I have in preparation, I shall endeavor to do you every perfect justice.

Hence this note. Carey & Hart are publishing for me "The Prose Authors of America, and their Works," and I wish, of course, to include you in the list, —not a very large one,—from whom I make selections. And I shall feel myself yr debtor if, there being any writings of yours with wh.[ich] I may be unacquainted, you will advise of their titles, and where they may be purchased; and if, in the brief biography of you in my Poets &c of America, there are any inaccuracies, you will point them out to me. If the trouble were not too great, indeed, I should like to receive a list of all your works, with the dates of their production.

Yours &c.

R. W. GRISWOLD

To

Edgar A. Poe, Esq.[47]

Philadelphia, January 11, 1845

Sir: — Although I have some cause of quarrel with you, as you seem to remember, I do not under any circumstances permit, as you have repeatedly charged, my personal relations to influence the expression of my opinions as a critic. *By the inclosed proof-sheets of what I had written before the reception of your note,* you will see that I think quite as well of your works as I did *when I had the pleasure of being Your friend,*

R. W. GRISWOLD.[48]

[47] Original Autograph Ms., Griswold Collection, Boston Public Library.
[48] Griswold's "Preface" to his "Memoir." *The Literati,* 1850, p. vi. I have

It will be noticed that there is nothing in the real letter to show that it is in response to a letter by Poe. Griswold introduces the subject of the anthology, which he would certainly not have done in a reply to an offer of a contribution. But since he could falsify Poe's letters, there is no reason to doubt his ability to invent one. Poe replied:

[Confidential]   New-York: Jan. 16. 45.

Dear Griswold—if you will permit me to call you so—Your letter occasioned me first pain and then pleasure:—pain because it gave me to see that I had lost, through my own folly, an honorable friend:—pleasure, because I saw in it a hope of reconciliation.

I have been aware, for several weeks, that my reasons for speaking of your book as I did (of *yourself* I have always spoken kindly) were based in the malignant slanders of a mischief-maker by profession. Still, as I supposed you irreparably offended, I could make no advances when we met at the Tribune office, although I longed to do so. I know of nothing which would give me more sincere pleasure than your accepting these apologies, and meeting me as a friend.

If you *can* do this and forget the past, let me know where I shall call on you—or come and see me at the Mirror Office, any morning about 10. We can then talk over the other matters, which, to me at least, are far less important than your good will.

Very truly yours,

EDGAR A POE.

R. W. Griswold.[49]

Poe would never have written a letter like this in reply to a curt note such as Griswold prints in his "Preface." Again, there is nothing in Poe's reply of January 16th which implies any previous note by him. Griswold wished to represent Poe as making the advances toward a reconciliation. As in the case of the forgery of the Burton letter,[50] Griswold knew that the most dexterous method was to print Poe's

---

italicized the words not in Griswold's real letter. It will be noticed that Griswold also changed the place and date of writing this letter, to make his account in the "Preface" of the meeting more probable.

[49] Original Autograph Ms., Griswold Collection, Boston Public Library. "Confidential" seems to be erased, but it is clearly in Poe's hand.

[50] See pp. 279-281.

letter of January 16th correctly, but to change its whole tenor by implication through his forgery of a letter by himself to which it was ostensibly a reply.

Shortly afterwards they met, superficially at least, on friendly terms, and Poe sent him material for selection. This letter is another specimen of Griswold's manipulation:

New-York. Feb. 24. 1845.
My Dear Griswold,

Soon after seeing you I sent you, through Zeiber, all my poems worth re-publishing, & I presume they reached you. With this I send you another package, also through Zeiber, by Burgess & Stringer. It contains in the way of Essay "Mesmeric Revelation" which I would like to go in, even if something else is omitted. I send also a portion of the "Marginalia," in which I have marked some of the most pointed passages. In the matter of criticism I cannot put my hand upon anything that suits me — but I believe that in "funny" criticism (if you wish any such) Flaccus will convey a tolerable idea of my style, and of my serious manner Barnaby Rudge is a good specimen. In "Graham" you will find these. In the tale line I send you "The Murders in the Rue Morgue" and "The Man that was Used Up"—far more than enough, you will say—but you can select to suit yourself. I would prefer having in the "Gold Bug" to the "Murders in the R. M," but have not a copy just now. If there is

February 24, 1845
My dear Griswold:—*A thousand thanks for your kindness in the matter of those books, which I could not afford to buy, and had so much need of.* Soon after seeing you, I sent you, through Zieber, all my poems worth republishing, and I presume they reached you. *I was sincerely delighted with what you said of them, and if you will write your criticism in the form of a preface, I shall be greatly obliged to you. I say this not because you praised me: everybody praises me now: but because you so perfectly understand me, or what I have aimed at, in all my poems: I did not think you had so much delicacy of appreciation joined with your strong sense; I can say truly that no man's approbation gives me so much pleasure.* I send you with this another package, also through Zieber, by Burgess & Stringer. It contains, in the way of essay, "Mesmeric Revelation," which I would like to have go in, even if you have to omit the *"House of Usher."* I send also corrected copies of (in the way of funny criticism, but you don't

New-York. Feb. 24. 1845.

My Dear Griswold,

Soon after seeing you I sent you, through Zeiber, all my poems worth re-publishing, & I presume they reached you.. With this I send you another package: also through Zeiber, by Burgess & Stringer. It contains in the way of Essay "Mesmeric Revelation" which I would like to go in, even if something else is omitted. I send also a portion of the "Marginalia" in which I have marked some of the most pointed passages. In the matter of criticism I cannot put my hand upon anything that suits me — but I believe that in "funny" criticism (if you wish any such) Flaccus will convey a tolerable idea of my style, and of my serious manner Barnaby Rudge is a good specimen. In "Graham" you will find these. In the tale line I send you "The Murders in the Rue chougre" and "The Man that was used up" — far more than enough, you will say — but you can select to suit yourself. I would prefer having in the "Gold Bug" to the "Murders in the R. M", but have not a copy just now. If there is no immediate hurry for it, however, I will get one & send it-you corrected. Please write & let me know if you get this. — I have taken a 3d interest in the "Broadway Journal" & will be glad if you could send me anything, at any time, in the way of "Literary Intelligence".

Truly yours. Poe.

AUTOGRAPH LETTER OF POE TO GRISWOLD, WHICH THE LATTER ALTERED RADICALLY IN HIS "MEMOIR."

Reproduced from the original through the courtesy of the Boston Public Library.

no immediate hurry for it, however, I will get one & send it you corrected. Please write & let me know if you get this.—I have taken a 3d interest in the "Broadway Journal" & will be glad if you could send me anything, at any time, in the way of "Literary Intelligence."

Truly yours.

POE.[51]

like this) "Flaccus," which conveys a tolerable idea of my style; and of my serious manner "Barnaby Rudge" is a good specimen. In the tale line, "The Murders of the Rue Morgue," "The Gold Bug," and the "Man that was Used Up,"—far more than enough, but you can select to suit yourself. I prefer the "G. B." to the "M. in the R. M." I have taken a third interest in the "Broadway Journal," and will be glad if you could send me anything for it. *Why not let me anticipate the book publication of your splendid essay on Milton?*

Truly yours,

POE [52]

Griswold's changes not only represent Poe in a fawning attitude to a man he wishes to please, but they portray him as conceited and Griswold as a fine critic.

After all this correspondence Griswold published only "The Fall of the House of Usher," in the prose anthology. Griswold was preparing a new edition of the *Poets and Poetry of America,* and Poe's next letter to him is important not only as providing material for another forgery but also because it proves that Poe permitted him to publish "The Raven" in short lines. Here Griswold omitted much of the letter but added another sentence which apparently convicts Poe out of his own mouth of injustice to the forger. The letter is not dated, but the postmark is "New York April 19," and the reference to the lecture puts it in 1845:

[51] Original Autograph Ms., Griswold Collection, Boston Public Library.

[52] Griswold's "Preface," *The Literati,* 1850, p. vi. I have italicized some of the important additions of Griswold. Notice that he has omitted much that Poe wrote, or has modified it.

Dear Griswold,

I return the proof, with many thanks for your attentions. The poems look quite as well in the short metre as in the long, and I am quite content as it is. You will perceive, however, that some of the lines have been divided at the wrong place. I have marked them right in the proof; but lest there should be any misapprehension, I copy them as they should be:

Stanza 11.

Till the dirges of his Hope the Melancholy burden bore

Stanza 12.

Straight I wheel'd a cushion'd seat in
Front of bird and bust and door;

Stanza 12—again

What this grim, ungainly, ghastly,
Gaunt and ominous bird of yore

Stanza 13.

To the fowl whose fiery eyes now Burn'd into my bosom's core;
Near the beginning of the poem you have *"nodded"* spelt *"nooded."* In the "Sleeper" the line
Forever with uncloséd eye
should read

Dear Griswold: — I return the proofs with many thanks for your attentions. The poems look quite as well in the short metres as in the long ones, and I am quite content as it is. In "The Sleeper" you have "Forever with unclosed eye" for "Forever with unopen'd eye." Is it possible to make the correction? I presume you understand that in the repetition of my Lecture on the Poets, (in N. Y.) I left out *all* that was offensive to yourself. *I am ashamed of myself that I ever said anything of you that was so unfriendly or so unjust; but what I did say I am confident has been misrepresented to you. See my notice of C. F. Hoffman's (?) sketch of you.*

Very sincerely yours,

POE.[53]

---

[53] Griswold's "Preface" to Memoir. *The Literati,* 1850, p. vi. Killis Campbell called attention in his *Mind of Poe,* page 91, to the fact that Poe's "Notice" of Hoffman's sketch did not appear until May 17th!

Forever with unopen'd eye.
Is it possible to make the alteration?
> Very sincerely Yours
> POE.

PS) I presume you understand
that in the repetition of my Lecture on the Poets (in N. Y.) I
left out *all* that was offensive to
yourself? [54]

One can smile at the vanity of a man who could thus steal some praise from the most acute critic of his day. But his alteration of the manly and self-respecting attempt of Poe to meet Griswold's advances, into fawning, sycophantic overtures to a critic whose good word was valuable, is unforgivable.

[54] Original Autograph Ms., Griswold Collection, Boston Public Library.

CHAPTER XV

The *Broadway Journal* and the *Poems* of 1845

Poe left the staff of the *Mirror* because he saw in a new journal a better opportunity. While still on the *Mirror's* staff he had become a welcome contributor to the *Broadway Journal*. This weekly had been founded in January, 1845, by Charles F. Briggs, as editor, and John Bisco as publisher. Briggs, a Massachusetts man, who had written a novel, *The Adventures of Harry Franco*, and was beginning to use the hero's name as a *nom de guerre*, met Poe through Lowell's written introduction. John Bisco was also a New England man, who had been at one time editor of the *Knickerbocker*. They were partners, sharing the profits, if there were any.[1]

Poe contributed to the first and second numbers of the *Broadway Journal* his critique of Elizabeth Barrett's *Drama of Exile and Other Poems*,[2] the American reprint of her *Poems* of 1844. His treatment of those poems which he believed to be mystical, was at times unsympathetic. But his glowing tribute to her "wild and magnificent genius" which rendered her book "a flame" and which he believed justified him in calling her "the greatest—the most glorious of her sex," pleased her, if she was somewhat embarrassed by it. R. H. Horne, with whom Poe kept up a correspondence, sent him on May 17, 1845, a note from Miss Barrett to Horne, in which she said in part: "But I am uncomfortable about my message to Mr. Poe, lest it should not be grateful enough in the sound of it. Will you tell him—what is quite the truth— that in my own opinion he has dealt with me most generously, and that I thank him for his candour as for a part of his kindness. Will you tell him also that he has given my father pleasure; which is giving it to *me* more than twice. Also, the review is very ably written, and the reviewer has so obviously and thoroughly *read* my poems, as to be a wonder among critics.—Will you tell Mr. Poe this, or to this effect, dear Mr. Horne—all but part of the last sentence which perad-

---

[1] Ms. contract between Bisco and Briggs, December 23, 1844, is in Collection of W. H. Koester.

[2] *Broadway Journal*, I (January 4 and 11), pp. 4-8, 17-20.

venture may be somewhat superfluous." [3] The most interesting portion of the review is that in which Poe traced the relationship of Shelley, Tennyson, and Miss Barrett. His criticism of "Lady Geraldine's Courtship" in the same month in which "The Raven" appeared is also worth remembering. As Poe received one dollar a column for contributions to the *Journal,* he made thirteen dollars for this extensive article. [4]

The *Broadway Journal* carried, as a feature, critical judgments on "American Prose Writers" and Poe contributed one on N. P. Willis to the issue of January 18th. [5] He devoted this paper largely to a discussion of Fancy and Imagination, in which he differed with Coleridge and also with his own earlier treatment of the subject [6] by insisting that "Fancy as nearly creates as the imagination, and neither at all." Yet he continues "The pure imagination chooses, *from either beauty or deformity,* only the most combinable things hitherto uncombined," and the result is something that shall have nothing of the qualities of either alone. If this is not creation, it is hard to see what that term means. But Poe was correct in attributing to Willis a brilliant fancy, to which his great popularity was due.

"The Raven" was reprinted in the issue of February 8th, [7] Poe having modified and improved the eleventh stanza and corrected the typographical error in the tenth stanza. Briggs remarked that it was for the benefit of his out-of-town readers. The same issue contained Poe's characteristic review of Bulwer's poems, in which Poe again showed Bulwer's limitations.

In the issue of February 22nd, "Readers and Correspondents" were told: "We have the pleasure of announcing that hereafter Edgar A. Poe and Henry C. Watson will be associated with the editorial department of our Journal. Mr. Watson will have entire control of the musical department." The notice also contained the statement "Personalities will always be avoided in our columns," which proved to be more of a hope than a prophecy.

The issue of March 8, 1845, was headed by the names of "C. F. Briggs, Edgar A. Poe, H. C. Watson, Editors. Briggs told Lowell that Poe was "only an assistant to me," and otherwise minimized Poe's position. [8] But the actual contract between Bisco and Poe, dated Feb-

[3] Unsigned Autograph Ms. in Boston Public Library.
[4] Letter, Briggs to Lowell. H. E. Scudder's *Life of Lowell,* I, 158.
[5] Vol. I, pp. 37-38.
[6] See Chapter X.
[7] Vol. I, p. 90.
[8] Briggs to Lowell, March 8, 1845. Woodberry, *Life,* II, 125-128.

ruary 21, 1845,[9] proves that Poe was given "one third of the profits," and had the right to inspect the books, and Bisco agreed to make a settlement with him every four weeks. For this compensation he was to allow his name to be published as an editor, which meant that it had value, to furnish at least a page of original matter each week, and "give his faithful superintendance to the general conduct of the paper." There is also a clause which provides that if Poe neglects any of the duties of assistant editor he shall forfeit all claim to the profits.

Poe carried over from the *Mirror* to the *Journal* one of the most unfortunate controversies of his career. On January 13 and 14, 1845, he had reviewed in the *Evening Mirror*, Longfellow's *Waif*, a selection of his favorite pieces, which Longfellow had edited for the Christmas trade. Poe began by speaking of Longfellow's "Proem," better known now as "The Day is Done," as the "worthiest composition in the volume." Since the compilation included poems by Shelley, Herrick, and Browning, Poe evidently felt this was high praise. He could not lose an opportunity to dwell on his favorite topic, and he accused James Aldrich of imitating Thomas Hood, with the amiable statement "Somebody is a thief." At the end of the review, he remarked that there appeared "in this exquisite little volume a very careful avoidance of all American poets who may be supposed especially to interfere with the claims of Mr. Longfellow." Poe, as usual, combined his real appreciation of Longfellow's verse with insinuations against his literary honesty. A friend of Longfellow, who signed himself "H," replied, and Willis printed this reply with a rather jocular preface and equally caustic "Post Notes by the Critic" by Poe.[10]

Willis evidently regretted that he had permitted the attribution of a "moral taint" to Longfellow, for he published in the *Mirror* a half hearted defence of Poe's review which was more of an apology to Longfellow.[11] Poe returned to the charge on February 15th in the *Evening Mirror*, in reply to a calm and sensible statement in the *Broadway Journal* by Charles F. Briggs, who objected to charges of plagiarism without foundation and stated that Aldrich's poem had been published in any event two years before Hood's. He also referred

[9] See Appendix for contract between Poe and Bisco. Original contract is in the W. H. Koester Collection.

[10] These attacks and replies can be read most conveniently in the *Weekly Mirror* of January 25, 1845, pp. 250-251, where they are grouped together. The identification of the portions written by Willis and by Poe is given in the *Broadway Journal*, I, 147.

[11] "Longfellow's Waif," *Weekly Mirror*, February 8, 1845, p. 287.

to a recent charge in *The Rover* that Longfellow had passed off a ballad of Motherwell's as a translation from the German.[12]

Poe replied rather feebly to Briggs' refutation, and in an editorial in the *Weekly Mirror* of February 22nd, made only a veiled allusion to Longfellow. So far the matter was a tempest in a teapot and since Briggs' article and Poe's reply to it were both printed on February 15th, I suspect that the matter was privately arranged between them as a scheme to call attention to their respective journals.

Unfortunately for Poe, a correspondent, "Outis," sent a long article to the *Mirror*, in which he tried to turn the tables on the author of "The Raven," by drawing a series of parallels between that poem and some sentimental verses, "The Bird of the Dream." This counter attack was written in a clever imitation of Poe's manner, and Outis then showed the absurdity of such charges of plagiarism. He praised "The Raven" highly, and denied that he knew Poe, although he was acquainted with Longfellow.[13] Poe seized upon this letter of Outis as an opportunity to stage a discussion that would be good publicity for the *Broadway Journal*, of which he had just become an editor.

Through five weekly numbers [14] of the *Broadway Journal*, Poe replied to the defence by Outis. These articles represent him at his worst. That keen, logical mind faltered into banalities, contradictions, and misrepresentations that make any admirer squirm. Poe put up straw men to knock down, charged Outis with implications that are not justified, and even denied that the dates of publication of two poems had any bearing on the matter of plagiarism. Poe then printed an elaborate comparison of Longfellow's "Spanish Student" with Poe's own drama of "Politian," which are as unlike as well can be imagined. He also repeated the charge that Longfellow had represented Motherwell's ballad of "Bonnie George Campbell" as his own translation from the German of Wolff. Longfellow had already disproved this charge, but that made no difference to Poe.

[12] "Thefts of American Authors," *Broadway Journal*, I (February 15, 1845), 109. Briggs was wrong, however, in his dates. Hood's poem appeared in 1831 and Aldrich's in 1841.

[13] *Weekly Mirror*, March 8, 1845, pp. 346-347.

[14] IMITATION—PLAGIARISM—MR. POE'S REPLY TO THE LETTER OF OUTIS.—A LARGE ACCOUNT OF A SMALL MATTER—A VOLUMINOUS HISTORY OF THE LITTLE LONGFELLOW WAR. March 8th, pp. 147-150; March 15th, pp. 161-163; March 22nd, pp. 178-182; March 29th, pp. 194-198; April 5th, pp. 211-212. They were reprinted by Griswold in the *Literati* Volume, under the title "Longfellow and Other Plagiarists," which incidentally Poe did not use.

Worse than the bitterness with which Poe pursued lines and stanzas of Longfellow to their supposed origins, was his vulgarity in his personal references to Longfellow. There can be no excuse for remarks like, "Now when we consider that many of the points of censure made by me in this *critique* were absolutely as plain as the nose upon Mr. Longfellow's face," [15] or "There can be no doubt in the world, for example, that Outis considers me a fool:—...and this idea is also entertained by Mr. Aldrich, and by Mr. Longfellow—and by Mrs. Outis and her seven children—and by Mrs. Aldrich and hers—and by Mrs. Longfellow and hers." [16]

Longfellow replied to none of Poe's attacks. That he was conscious of them is shown in a remark in his *Journal*, on December 10, 1845. In speaking of Lowell's "superb poem," "To the Past," he wrote: "If he goes on in this vein, Poe will soon begin to pound him." [17]

The result of this "Longfellow War" was the alienation of such friends as Lowell and a growing sense of irritation on the part of fair-minded critics with Poe. He defended himself in his "Editorial Miscellany," [18] claiming that he had been one of Longfellow's "warmest and most steadfast" defenders. But the facts were against him.

A more pleasant impression of Poe as an editor is given in the reminiscences of Alexander T. Crane, the office boy and mailing clerk of the *Broadway Journal*. Crane wrote as a very old man and some of his account is obviously incorrect, but the following incident could not have been imaginary:

> Poe was a quiet man about the office, but was uniformly kind and courteous to everyone, and, with congenial company, he would grow cheerful and even playful. I saw him every day, for, as you may imagine, our office rooms did not consist of a great many compartments, and office boy and editor were pretty close together. He came to the office every day about 9 o'clock and worked until 3 or 4 in the afternoon, and he worked steadily and methodically, too.
>
> Not a great while after I had gone to work on the paper, on a hot August afternoon while wrapping and addressing Journals, I was overcome with the heat and fainted dead away. Poe was writing at his desk. When I recovered consciousness I was

[15] *Broadway Journal*, March 8, 1845, p. 147.
[16] *Broadway Journal*, March 15, 1845, p. 163.
[17] *Life of Longfellow*, ed. by Samuel Longfellow, II, 26.
[18] *Broadway Journal*, II (August 16), 93-94.

stretched out on the long table at which I had been at work and Poe was bending over me bathing my wrists and temples in cold water. He ministered to me until I was able to stand up, and then he sent me home in a carriage.

This act of kindness, coupled with his uniform gentle greetings, when he entered the office of a morning, together with frequent personal inquiries and words of encouragement, made me love and trust my editor.

Crane also tells us that the circulation of the *Journal* was less than one thousand, of which half was on the mailing list.[19]

How seriously Poe took this crusade against plagiarism is seen in his long letter to J. Hunt, Jr., Editor of the *National Archives,* defending himself against the latter's criticisms of Poe's attack.[20] The defence is hardly successful, but one paragraph dealing with Poe's general policy of criticism is worth preserving: "Let me put it to you as to a frank man of honor—Can you suppose it possible that any human being could pursue a strictly impartial course of criticism for 10 years (as I have done in the S. L. Messenger and in Graham's Magazine) without offending irreparably a host of authors and their connexions?—but because these *were* offended, and gave vent at every opportunity to their spleen, would you consider my course an iota the less honorable on that account? Would you consider it just to measure my deserts by the yelpings of my foes, indepently [sic] of your own judgment in the premises, based upon an actual knowledge of what I have done?"

As soon as he had definitely joined the staff of the *Broadway Journal,* Poe proceeded to reprint his poems and stories in it.[21] Poe did not make as many changes in his poems as he did in his stories. He had revised a number of the poems for the *Saturday Museum* in 1843. Yet

---

[19] *Sunday World-Herald,* Omaha, July 13, 1902, p. 24. Photostat, Library of Congress.

[20] Poe to Hunt, March 17, 1845, Original Autograph Ms., Huntington Library. Hunt was editor of the short-lived *National Archives,* which lasted from February 6 to March 13, 1845. When Poe wrote his letter the *National Archives* had already stopped.

[21] During his term as associate editor he reprinted his poems "To F——," "The Sleeper," "To One in Paradise," "The Conqueror Worm," and "Dreamland." The stories reprinted were "Passages in the Life of a Lion," "Berenice," "Bon-Bon," "The Oval Portrait," "Three Sundays in a Week," "The Pit and the Pendulum," "Eleonora," "Shadow," "The Assignation," "The Premature Burial," "Morella." The essay "Philosophy of Furniture" was also a repetition of earlier work.

his constant care is shown in the replacement of two verses in "The Sleeper":

> "The wanton airs, from the treetop
> Laughingly through the lattice drop"

which he had omitted.

The stories were quite often extensively revised, as compared with their forms in the *Tales of the Grotesque and Arabesque.* The tales that had appeared in magazines since that volume are naturally not so much changed. The texts of the *Broadway Journal* have been generally adopted as the standard for his stories, since Poe had an opportunity to revise them. Usually there is an improvement. In "Berenice" he omitted the distressing passage in which the hero went to look at Berenice in her death chamber. In "Bon-Bon" he added the motto from French vaudeville. He changed the title of "Life in Death" to "The Oval Portrait," and omitted the passages describing the effect of the drugs taken by the hero. This omission has been urged both by those who believe in Poe's use of opium and by those who deny it, as proof of their theories.

In "Eleonora" the descriptions of Eleonora and Ermengarde were curtailed. The title of the "Visionary" was changed to the "Assignation," and the "Catholic Hymn" was omitted from "Morella," as in the *Phantasy Pieces,* and the other changes made in that revision were preserved.

As Willis proved later, his friendship with Poe remained unaltered after his assistant left the *Mirror.* Since the publication of "The Raven" Poe was good copy, too, and references to him in the *Mirror* are frequent. The *Evening Mirror* of February 27, 1845, announced his lecture on the "Poets and Poetry of America," for February 28th, and promised the audience "fine carving" from "the critical blade of Mr. Poe." The account in the *Weekly Mirror* of March 8th was written by Willis, who was pleased to hear his poem "Unseen Spirits" read as one of three pieces of poetry which had been neglected by the critics. According to Willis, Poe had "an audience of critics and poets— between two and three hundred of victims and victimizers—and he was heard with breathless attention."

After "gently waking up the American Poetesses," including Mrs. Frances S. Osgood, for whom Poe prophesied a rosy future, he demolished some who were afloat "on bladders in a sea of glory." Among the men, Poe treated only what Willis called the "Copperplate five," probably because they had ornamented the frontispiece of Griswold's *Poets*

and Poetry of America. Bryant was praised highly, but Poe emphasized his keeping within narrow limits. Longfellow had the greatest
genius of the five, but his alacrity at imitation made him borrow when
he had better inspiration at home. Poe praised Halleck and recited
"Marco Bozzaris." Sprague and Dana were dismissed summarily, the
former being described as "Pope and Water." [22] The lecture took place
at the New York Historical Society. Poe in his letter to J. Hunt, Jr.,
states that the lecture was so popular that he will repeat it, and he
evidently was looking toward lecturing as a means of support.[23]

He may have been prompted to this repetition by a favorable criticism in the weekly issue of the *New York Tribune*, which lamented
that only "three hundred of our four hundred thousand people" attended, while "the bare announcement should have crowded the
doors. Shall we not have a repetition?" The critic gave Poe some good
advice, however, about his obsession concerning plagiarism.[24] The
repetition in March, however, does not seem to have been a success,
partly on account of the weather. In speaking of this evening, the
office boy, Crane, admits that once, during his service on the *Journal*,
he saw Poe drunk:

> Poe had given a lecture in Society library in New York on "The
> Poets and Poetry of America." The lecture had proved a great
> success and he was finally induced to consent to repeat it. The
> night set for the second lecture was a very bad one. It stormed
> incessantly, with mingled rain and hail and sleet. In consequence
> there were scarcely a dozen persons present when Poe came upon
> the platform and announced that, under the circumstances, the
> lecture could not be given, and those in the audience would re-
> ceive their money back at the door. I was one of those present,
> as Poe had given me a complimentary ticket to the lecture, and
> badly as I was disappointed, I could see upon his face that my
> master was much more so. It was a little thing, it is true, but he
> was a man easily upset by little things. The next morning he came
> to the office, leaning on the arm of a friend, intoxicated with
> wine.[25]

Willis copied from Dr. T. D. English's *Aristidean* a column headed
"Notes about Men of Note" and Poe led the list. "He never rests," the

[22] *Weekly Mirror,* I (March 8, 1845), p. 347.
[23] Original Autograph Ms., Huntington Library. March 17, 1845.
[24] *New York Tribune,* Weekly Edition, March 8, 1845.
[25] *Sunday World Herald,* Omaha (July 13, 1902), p. 24. Photostat,
Library of Congress.

article said. "There is a small steam engine in his brain which not only sets the cerebral mass in motion, but keeps the owner in hot water. His face is a fine one, and well gifted with intellectual beauty." [26]

On July 19th the *Mirror* devoted three full pages to the commencement of the Rutgers Female Institute,[27] and Poe was announced as heading the committee which judged the compositions of the first or highest department. By some ironic chance, his old adversary, Henry T. Tuckerman, whom he was to immortalize in "An Enigma," served on the same committee. Poe read the prize composition by Miss Lisa O. Hunter, and I have no doubt he did it well. These public appearances of Poe are easy to identify. But the stories of his Bohemian associations at "Sandy Welsh's cellar on Ann Street," where he is supposed to have read "The Raven," and accepted aid in its composition, rest upon very shadowy foundations.[28] Like other men working in New York City he ate luncheon somewhere, and met his friends. These meetings were probably as unproductive of literary result as they are today.

But Poe's letters to Thomas continue to reveal that capacity for friendship which has often been denied him; also, his incessant industry, and his desire to repay money he owed by further labor:

[May 4, 1845.]

My Dear Thomas,

In the hope that you have not yet *quite* given me up, as gone to Texas, or elsewhere, I sit down to write you a few words. I have been intending to do the same thing ever since I received your letter before the last—but for my life and soul I could not find, or make, an opportunity. The fact is, that being seized, of late, with a fit of industry, I put so many irons in the fire all at once, that I have been quite unable to get them out. For the last three or four months I have been working 14 or 15 hours a day —hard at it all the time—and so, whenever I took pen in hand to write, I found that I was neglecting something that *would be* attended to. I never knew what it was to be a slave before.

---

[26] *Weekly Mirror*, II (July 5, 1845), p. 201.
[27] Vol. II, pp. 225-227.
[28] They go back to Francis G. Fairfield's "A Mad Man of Letters," *Scribner's Monthly*, X (October, 1875), 690-699. Since he places the writing of "The Raven" while Poe was at Fordham, and bases his remarks upon Colonel John du Solle, at second hand, no great stress can be laid upon his testimony.

And yet, Thomas, I have made no money. I am as poor now as ever I was in my life—except in hope, which is by no means bankable. I have taken a 3d pecuniary interest in the "Broadway Journal," and for everything I have written for it have been, of course, so much out of pocket. In the end, however, it will pay me well—at least the prospects are good. Say to Dow for me that there never has been a chance for my repaying him, without putting myself to greater inconvenience than he himself would have wished to subject me to, had he known the state of the case. Nor am I able to pay him now. The Devil himself was never so poor. Say to Dow, also, that I am sorry he has taken to dunning in his old age—it is a diabolical practice, altogether unworthy "a gentleman & a scholar"—to say nothing of the Editor of the "Madisonian." I wonder how he would like me to write him a series of letters—say one a week—giving him the literary gossip of New York—or something of more general character. I would furnish him such a series for whatever he could afford to give me. If he agrees to this arrangement, ask him to state the length & character of the letters—how often—and how much he can give me. Remember me kindly to him & tell him I believe that dunning is his one sin—although at the same time, I do think it is the unpardonable sin against the Holy Ghost spoken of in the Scriptures. I am going to mail him the "Broadway Journal" regularly, & hope he will honor me with an exchange.

My dear Thomas, I hope you will never imagine, from any seeming neglect of mine, that I have forgotten our old friendship. There is no one in the world I would rather see at this moment than yourself; and many are the long talks we have about you and yours. Virginia & Mrs. Clemm beg to be remembered to you in the kindest terms. Do write me fully when you get this, and let me know particularly what you are about.

I send you an early number of the "B. Journal" containing my "Raven." It was copied by Briggs, my associate, before I joined the paper. "The Raven" has had a great "run," Thomas—but I wrote it for the express purpose of running—just as I did the "Gold-Bug," you know. The bird beat the bug, though, all hollow.

Do not forget to write immediately, & believe me

Most sincerely your friend,

POE [29]

---

[29] Original Autograph Ms., Griswold Collection, Boston Public Library. Thomas notes on the letter that Dow is dead.

Poe met Lowell for the first time, probably, in May, 1845, when Lowell, who had been living in Philadelphia, passed through New York. A description of the meeting is contained in a letter to Woodberry, written by Lowell on March 12, 1884, from London:

> I saw Poe only once and that must have been, I think, in 1843 when I was in New York sitting to Page for my portrait. I suppose there are many descriptions of him. He was small; his complexion of what I should call a clammy-white; fine, dark eyes, and fine head, very broad at the temples, but receding sharply from the brows backwards. His manner was rather formal, even pompous, but I have the impression he was a little soggy with drink—not tipsy—but as if he had been holding his head under a pump to cool it.
>
> His mother-in-law I used to see after his death—a rather ordinary uncultivated woman. I believe I helped her as well as I could in those days when I was earning my bread with my pen. If I had not paid Poe, by the way, she would certainly have reminded me of it and I should have paid her. I have no recollection that I ever did.
>
> Faithfully yours,
>
> J. R. LOWELL [30]

It will be noticed that Lowell's memory of the occasion is not very clear, as he could not have met Poe in 1843, for even if Poe visited New York in that year, Mrs. Clemm, who was present at their interview, was in Philadelphia. That Poe had been drinking, however, is shown by a letter from Mrs. Clemm to Lowell in 1850:

> Lowell, 9th March. 1850
>
> Dear Sir.
>
> I have received a letter from Mr. Redfield. (The publisher of my dear sons E. A. Poes works) in which he states that I will not receive any thing from those works until the expenses are paid. I suppose this is right, but in the mean time I must be entirely destitute. Now dear sir I wish you would so far oblige me as to dispose of a few copies for me among your friends in Cambridge. I am very much in want of a little money and have been ill all winter. I am entirely unable to make any exertion for myself. Mr. Longfellow (at my request) has taken 5 copies and paid me for them! If you will so far oblige me let me know how

---

[30] This letter was published in two installments: Woodberry, *Life*, II, 137; and by M. A. DeWolfe Howe, *New Letters of James Russell Lowell*, p. 275. I have combined them.

many I shall send you, And if it will be perfectly convenient to yourself to advance me about 10 dollars. You little know how desolate it is to be alone in this world. I have no *home* no dear Eddie *now*. How much I wish I could see you, how quickly I could remove your wrong impression of my darling Eddie. The day you saw him in New York *he was not himself*. Do you not remember that I never left the room. Oh if you only knew his bitter sorrow when I told him how unlike himself he was while you were there you would have pitied him, he always felt particularly anxious to possess your approbation. If he spoke unkindly of you (as you say he did) rely on it, it was when he did not know of what he was talking.

He was noble, generous, affectionate, and most *amiable*, (Dr. *Griswolds* assertion notwithstanding). Poor poor Eddie, it matters little to *him* now, but it almost breaks *my* heart to hear him spoken of so unkindly and *untrue*.[31]

Poe's impression of Lowell is given in the report by Chivers of his conversations with Poe. According to Chivers, Poe said: "He called to see me the other day, but I was very much disappointed in his appearance as an intellectual man. He was not half the noble looking person that I expected to see." [32] While Chivers is quite untrustworthy as a witness, Poe probably said something like the quotation. It is rather a pity that this friendship was broken, but like so many meetings of creative artists, there is often a disappointment. It would have been much better if Lowell and Poe had confined their communications to writing. Lowell's activity in the abolition ranks probably irritated Poe, and Poe made an unfortunate statement in the *Broadway Journal* [33] concerning an alleged plagiarism of Lowell from Wordsworth, in which he was wrong. On the other hand, he defended Lowell zealously against the criticism of Wilson, the Editor of *Blackwood's*, and referred to him as "The noblest of our poets." [34] Finally, Lowell's lines on Poe in 1848 in his "Fable for Critics":

> "Here comes Poe with his Raven like Barnaby Rudge,
> Three fifths of him genius and two fifths sheer fudge"

[31] Original Autograph Ms., Harvard College Library. The last paragraph is concerned with instructions about sending the money.

[32] "Poe-Chivers Papers," edited by G. E. Woodberry, *Century Magazine*, LXV (January and February, 1903). The reference to Lowell is on p. 446; and in addition to the personal description, the conversation deals critically with Lowell's poetry. It is not important, however.

[33] Vol. II (August 16, 1845), p. 88. Signed by Poe in Huntington copy.

[34] *Broadway Journal*, II (October 4, 1845), 199.

called forth a sharp criticism of that poem from Poe, in the *Southern Literary Messenger* for March, 1849.

About the time of the meeting with Lowell, Poe moved to the second floor of 195 East Broadway. Little is known of this house, which was torn down long ago.[35] The situation was more open than Amity Street, but the family returned to that neighborhood in the fall. In his letter to Chivers of July 22, 1846, Poe explained his silence by the receipt of six letters addressed to 195 E. Broadway and continued: "Did you not know that I merely boarded at this house? It is a very long while since I left it, and as I did not leave it on very good terms with the landlady, she has given herself no concern about my letters." [36]

There was trouble brewing in the management of the *Broadway Journal*, and after the issue of July 5th had been omitted, the second volume began with Edgar A. Poe and Henry C. Watson as editors, Briggs having withdrawn or having been eliminated. It is impossible to reconcile his statements concerning his intention to drop Poe [37] with the actual terms of the contracts, for Poe made his with Bisco, and as Poe, Bisco, and Watson went on together, the weight of evidence seems to be against Briggs. Bisco's notice, which appeared in the *Journal* on July 12th, stated that "the editorial charge of 'The Broadway Journal' is under the sole charge of Edgar A. Poe—Mr. H. C. Watson as heretofore, controlling the Musical Department."

According to the Memorandum of Agreement, dated July 14, 1845, Bisco was to assume the sole financial and Poe the sole editorial responsibility, and they were to divide the "nett profits" evenly. Poe was to receive his share on the first of every month. He was also as Editor to be "uninterfered with by any party whatever." Poe drew up this contract and hopefully included a provision that it was "to be renewable by Mr. Poe, indefinitely from year to year." [38]

Briggs' departure evidently gave Poe more chance to reprint his own work, or perhaps made it necessary in order to fill the magazine. In some issues he would reprint one or two stories and one or two poems, write a criticism and probably most of the miscellaneous

---

[35] Richard Cramer, "Poe's City Homes," *Ledger Monthly*, LVII (January, 1901), 28.

[36] Original Autograph Ms., Huntington Library.

[37] See Briggs to Lowell, Woodberry, II, 144-147.

[38] Original Autograph Ms., Berg Collection, New York Public Library. See Appendix for Contract.

notes. He usually signed the stories although occasionally he used the pen name, "Littleton Barry." [39]

During these revisions, "The Song of the Newly Wedded" became the "Bridal Ballad," "Lenore" was printed in long lines, as it had been in *Graham's*, instead of the short lines in the *Museum*, which had not been so effective. Sometimes the poems must have been put in as "fillers" for they are not always signed, and to "Romance" and to "Catholic Hymn" is appended what seems to be the printers' sign, called a double dagger or double obelisk (‡) instead of a name.

Among the stories, "Silence," "How to Write a Blackwood Article," and "A Predicament" assumed their new titles in print for the first time, again preserving the changes made in the *Phantasy Pieces*. In "William Wilson," the birth date of his double was changed to 1813, making Poe by implication two years younger than he had been in *Phantasy Pieces*. "Ligeia" was extensively though verbally revised, including the passages added in the *Phantasy Pieces*. "The Conqueror Worm" was still included in "Ligeia," although it had been published in the *Broadway Journal* separately.

There were other and minor changes in the tales, and Poe did not always preserve the alterations he had made in the *Phantasy Pieces*, which may indicate that he was too busy or less careful.

On July 19, 1845, Wiley and Putnam announced in the advertising columns of the *Broadway Journal* [40] as the second number of its new *Library of American Books*, "*Tales* by Edgar A. Poe." This volume was by no means Poe's long hoped for edition of his stories. The book contained only twelve tales: "The Gold Bug," "The Black Cat," "Mesmeric Revelation," "Lionizing," "The Fall of the House of Usher," "The Descent into the Maelström," "The Colloquy of Monos and Una,"

---

[39] The poems republished from the first number of Vol. II until Poe purchased the *Journal* were "The Coliseum," "Sonnet to Zante," "Israfel," "Sonnet—Silence," "Bridal Ballad," "Eulalie," "Catholic Hymn," "Lenore," "A Dream," "Romance," "The City in the Sea," "The Valley of Unrest," "To the River," "To F——," "To ———" (The bowers whereat, etc.), "Song—— (I saw Thee on Thy Bridal Day)," and "Fairyland." The stories were "How to Write A Blackwood Article," "A Predicament," "The Masque of the Red Death," "The Literary Life of Thingum-Bob," "The Business Man," "The Man that Was Used Up," "Never Bet the Devil your Head," "The Tell-Tale Heart," "William Wilson," "Why the Little Frenchman Wears His Hand in a Sling," "Silence—A Fable," "Diddling Considered as One of the Exact Sciences," "The Landscape Garden," "A Tale of Jerusalem," "Ligeia," "The Island of the Fay," "Ms. Found in a Bottle," "The Duc de L'Omelette," and "King Pest."

[40] P. 415.

T A L E S

E D G A R A. P O E.

NEW YORK:
WILEY AND PUTNAM, 161 BROADWAY.

1845.

"The Conversation of Eiros and Charmion," "The Murders in the Rue Morgue," "The Mystery of Marie Rogêt," "The Purloined Letter," and "The Man of the Crowd."

Poe apparently had little to do with the selection of the stories. As he wrote Eveleth [41] later, "The collection of tales issued by W. & P. were selected by a gentleman whose taste does not coincide with my own, from 72 written by me at various times—and those chosen are *not* my best—nor do they fairly represent me—in any respect." Poe had indeed a right to criticize any selection from his tales which omitted "Ligeia," "Shadow," "Eleonora," "William Wilson," and "The Masque of the Red Death," to mention only a few of his Arabesque masterpieces, but which included "Lionizing." Evert Duyckinck, who chose the stories, was counting on the popularity of the ratiocinative tales, and outside of "Lionizing," he may be criticized rather for omissions than for those selected.

Poe must have consented to the publication through his constant need of money. He was to receive a royalty of eight cents a copy on a book which sold for fifty cents. This was a real advance upon the return he had received for the *Tales of the Grotesque and Arabesque*, and indicates the value of Duyckinck's services as his literary agent, as well as Poe's growing importance.

Poe evidently revised the stories carefully for this edition and for these twelve stories this text has become the standard, subject to some later revisions. [42]

One of the most important changes was the omission of the opening paragraph in "The Murders in the Rue Morgue" which suggested that phrenological science might lead to the discovery of an organ of analysis. Poe may have been beginning to lose his interest in phrenology. He added to "Mesmeric Revelation" two important passages, one dealing with the arguments for and against absolute coalescence of the ether, and the other with the relativity of pain. In "The Fall of the House of Usher" he added the quotation from Béranger:

"Son coeur est un luth suspendu:
Sitôt qu'on le touche il résonne."

If Poe owed his line in "Israfel," "Whose heartstrings are a lute" to this poem of Béranger's, as has been suggested, it would be a remark-

[41] Original Autograph Ms., Berg Collection, New York Public Library. Poe to Eveleth, December 15, 1846. J. M. Wilson's Edition, p. 9.
[42] Made by Poe in the volume known as the "Lorimer Graham Copy" now in the Century Association, New York.

able example of Poe's retention of an idea for fourteen years! The remaining changes though frequently appreciable, are largely improvements in verbal expression, wrought out of that passion for perfection which never left Poe.

The *Tales* were generally well received. The editor of the *American Review* printed the criticism as a special article,[43] in which the volume is said to be "one of the most original and peculiar ever published in the United States and eminently worthy of an extensive circulation." The article began, however, with a statement which illuminates the contemporary criticism of Poe: "We fear that Mr. Poe's reputation as a critic, will not add to the success of his present publication. The cutting scorn with which he has commented on many authors, and the acrimony and contempt which have often accompanied his acuteness, must have provoked enmities of that kind, which are kept warm by being assiduously 'nursed.' "

Colton, for it was probably he who wrote the review, ratifies here Poe's charges of conspiracy against himself, which have been thought by some to be prompted by persecution mania on his part. In an extended review in the *Aristidean*,[44] the new journal edited by English, the originality and ingenuity of the stories are especially noted. There are certain portions of this review, especially the reference to the old story of Longfellow's plagiarism and the rejection of "The Tell-Tale Heart" by Tuckerman, which make me suspect Poe had a hand in writing it.

Whoever wrote the review referred to the favorable foreign criticism of the *Tales*. An example of British moralistic criticism was furnished by the *Literary Gazette and Journal of the Belles Lettres* of London.[45] This review, written by Martin Farquhar Tupper, praised the stories of ratiocination highly, and then proceeded: "Let us turn now to other pages equally brightened by genius, while they are untarnished with the dread details of crime." A sympathetic criticism of "A Descent into the Maelström" and "Eiros and Charmion" follows. Poe must have read with mixed feelings that the latter story "is full of terror and instruction: true to philosophy and holy writ: it details the probable mode of the final conflagration." But even if "The Fall of the House of Usher" is dismissed as "juvenile"—an English reviewer had called him a "genius!"

More restrained in his admiration, a critic in *Blackwood's*, dealing

[43] *American Review*, II (September, 1845), 306-309.
[44] October, 1845, pp. 316-319.
[45] January 31, 1846, pp. 101-103.

with Poe, Hawthorne, Margaret Fuller, and Simms,[46] denied Poe any boldness of imagination, yet selected for extensive quotation passages from "Eiros and Charmion" and "The Man of the Crowd," [47] where Poe's imagination shows itself clearly. Poe's powers of analysis and his ability at realistic description are commented upon at length. This reception of the *Tales* abroad was only one evidence of his growing recognition.

Poe published six new stories during 1845. He depended for his market on *Godey's* and *Graham's*, or on the rival political monthlies, the *American* [*Whig*] *Review* and the *Democratic Review*. "The Thousand-and-Second Tale of Scheherazade" [48] continued the famous story of the Arabian Nights, with a deft ironic touch. Fired by her success in interesting the King so long and saving herself from the bowstring, the Queen told one tale too many. Her story of Sinbad's cruise around the world in an armored cruiser gave Poe a good chance to depict modern inventions of all kinds in terms of the wonder of a past age. Before the end of the story the King had become so impatient at the impossibilities Scheherazade was telling about that he decided after all to send her to the bowstring. This was a warning, perhaps, to those who overestimate the imaginative powers of their readers!

Poe used his story "Some Words with a Mummy" [49] as a vehicle for satire upon the methods of historians in their interpretation of the past. After a description of the mummy in which Poe used very naturally, the *Encyclopedia Americana*,[50] he gives a very amusing conversation between the revived mummy, "Count Allamistakeo" and a group of Egyptologists. Many of our most cherished scientific discoveries are shown to be overshadowed by the achievements of Egypt. I have already used the mummy's description of the tyranny of the mob,[51] in estimating Poe's attitude toward democracy. He had a similar dislike for the progress that proceeded by organizations for reform.

"We sent for a copy of a book called the 'Dial,' and read out of it a chapter or two about something which is not very clear, but which the Bostonians call the Great Movement of Progress.

[46] "The American Library," *Blackwood's Magazine*, LXII (November, 1847); references to Poe, 582-587.

[47] See further comment on this story, quoted pp. 309-310.

[48] *Godey's Lady's Book*, XXX (February, 1845), 61-67.

[49] *American Review*, I (April, 1845), 363-370.

[50] See Lucile King, "Notes on Poe's Sources," *University of Texas Studies in English*, X (1930), 130-134.

[51] See p. 94.

"The Count merely said that Great Movements were awfully common things in his day, and as for Progress, it was at one time quite a nuisance, but it never progressed."

"The Power of Words" is a prose poem far above these satires in merit, clever as they are. Poe faced in this story the problem of creation and took the position that God created only in the beginning. Through the conversation of Oinos and Agathos, he depicted the future life as a place where the soul's unquenchable desire to *know* is recognized as its greatest happiness, and therefore the soul's search for knowledge is never ceasing. He also expressed the idea of the conservation of force in poetic terms. As no thought can perish, so no act is without infinite result. Since every vibration once set in motion is eternal, the power of a word once spoken is also everlasting. He would be rash who speaks of the words of any writer as indestructible, but surely if we seek to establish the lasting quality of the utterances of American poets, Poe will serve as well as any to support our belief. Those who dismiss Poe's scientific ideas as fantastic might compare this story with the accomplishment of the radio waves.

One of the most interesting of Poe's stories, both for itself and because of its explanation of his own nature, is "The Imp of the Perverse."[52] Poe is seen in one of his ablest phases, the criticism in telling phrases of pseudo-science. Phrenology is taken as a means to lead to something more important.

"The intellectual or logical man," Poe remarks, "rather than the understanding or observant man, set himself to imagine designs—to dictate purposes to God. Having thus fathomed, to his satisfaction, the intentions of Jehovah, out of these intentions he built his innumerable systems of mind." Poe rightly queries "If we cannot comprehend God in his visible works, how then in his inconceivable thoughts, that call the works into being?"

Induction, Poe argues, would have brought phrenology to admit the principle of perverseness. Poe draws then with a skill which fascinates anyone who is honest with himself, that human weakness which leads men to do the very thing which they wish above all other things not to do. How often this impulse explains Poe's own actions needs no proof. He could fight for months against temptation and then in spite of every moral impulse, take the one glass that destroyed his faculties.

After lying in the hands of editors for months, "The System of Dr. Tarr and Professor Fether" finally saw the light in *Graham's* for November, 1845. It is no wonder that an editor hesitated, for while the

[52] *Graham's Magazine*, XXVII (July, 1845), 1-3.

story is a clever picture of the capture of a French insane asylum by its inmates, the tale is not important.

"The Facts of M. Valdemar's Case" as it was first called in *The American Review* for December, 1845, was an instance in which Poe created disgust by the very success of his methods. Probably no one else would have thought of mesmerizing a man about to die and preserving his life for seven months, with the result that upon being released from the trance he falls at once into the state of putrescence to which he would have advanced had there been no hypnotism. Poe's normally fine taste deserted him here. Yet his methods are remarkable. The frame of the story is realistic, the actions of the characters, with the exception of Valdemar, are possible; the result is impossible. But the critical faculties have been dulled by the influence of plausible details, and the story was taken seriously, especially in England when it was reprinted as a pamphlet in 1846.[53] There are remarkable touches, like the description of Valdemar's voice, which impressed the narrator as "gelatinous or glutinous matters impress the sense of touch." It is a pity that the art which Poe lavished in this story could not have had more worthy material.

The most significant group of Poe's criticisms during 1845 dealt with the drama. He evidently, as editor of the *Broadway Journal*, had access to the theatres and he seems to have attended them freely. In his criticism of *Fashion*, the delightful social satire by Anna Cora Mowatt, he said "So deeply have we felt interested in the question of 'Fashion's' success or failure, that we have been to see it every night since its first production.[54] As *Fashion*, opening on March 25th at the Park Theatre, had an uninterrupted run of twenty nights, Poe must have gone frequently, for this remark began his second review, on April 5th. He had made the mistake of writing most of his first review, for March 29th, without seeing the play, having based his judgment on Mrs. Mowatt's original manuscript. Mrs. Mowatt had sent it to him with a note dated vaguely "Thursday Evening," saying that his criticisms would be prized.[55] Poe's criticisms of *Fashion* illustrate how

[53] *Mesmerism, "In Articulo Mortis." An Astounding and Horrifying Narrative. Shewing the Extraordinary Power of Mesmerism in Arresting the Progress of Death.* By Edgar A. Poe, Esq. of New York. London, 1846. Price threepence.

[54] The reviews appeared in the *Broadway Journal*, I (March 29 and April 5), 203-205 and 219-220. They are signed by Poe in the Huntington Copy.

[55] Virginia Edition, XVII, 207-208. Attributed to Griswold Collection in Boston Public Library, where it is not at present.

little one can really judge of a play by reading it. His first review speaks of the improbability of the characters and incidents, but as anyone who has seen the play on the stage knows, they are redolent of reality.[56] Poe concluded, however, that it was probably the best American play, which it was not. After he saw it on the stage, he estimated the characters more justly, but spoke of them as "overpowering the moral," which he thought a mistake. Poe seemed unaware that the masterpieces of drama have been those in which the characters are remembered rather than the theme, or "moral," as he called it, while plays in which the characters are submerged in the theme are usually forgotten. Yet his plea for more natural acting, and for a form of drama which is untrammelled by theatrical rules and definitions, points forward to a freer technique that was not to come for many years.

Mrs. Mowatt did not act Gertrude, the heroine, when *Fashion* was first performed. Poe's criticism of her acting later in *The Lady of Lyons* and other plays, is competent—and his picture of this high hearted and courageous woman who did so much to ennoble the American theatre is singularly interesting.[57]

To the *American Review* for August, 1845, Poe contributed a survey of "The American Drama" as he knew it.[58] His general introductory remarks are still worth reading, for they contain some sensible suggestions, as well as some overstatements. He objected to the plays of Sheridan Knowles as "the most preposterous series of imitations of the Elizabethan drama, by which ever mankind were insulted or begulled," and continued, "The first thing necessary is to burn or bury the 'old models' and to forget, as quickly as possible, that ever a play has been penned." And he pleaded for a drama "conceived and constructed with Feeling and with Taste, but with Feeling and Taste guided and controlled in every particular by the details of Reason— of Common Sense—in a word, of a Natural Art."

Poe showed his openmindedness here, for he had imitated in his own drama "Politian," the romantic-idealistic type of play. This impulse in literature was still powerful, and in American drama was to produce in 1855 such a masterpiece as Boker's *Francesca da Rimini,*

---

[56] *Fashion* has often been revived. It ran for 235 consecutive performances February 3 to August 30, 1924, in New York.

[57] *Broadway Journal*, II (July 19 and 26, August 2), 29-30; 43; 60. They are signed by Poe in the Huntington Copy.

[58] Vol. II, pp. 117-131. It was to be the first of a series of articles, but these did not appear.

which survived into the twentieth century and could be played even today if we had any great romantic actors. Poe did not see, what he should have seen, that in every age, the poet is the hope of the drama, whether, like Maxwell Anderson, he writes in verse or, like Eugene O'Neill, in prose. But perhaps at that period, this law of the drama did not need emphasis so greatly as the thesis Poe wished to drive home. He was living in a time when the real American drama had to combat the artificial drama of intrigue, largely of French origin. He was right in denouncing this artificial drama for its inconsequence, and its injurious effect upon "that real *life-likeness* which is the soul of the drama of character." Poe also remarks "The truth is that *cant* has never attained a more owl-like dignity than in the discussion of dramatic principle ... the modern stage critic ... talks about 'stage business and stage effect' as if he were discussing the differential calculus. For much of all this, we are indebted to the somewhat over-profound criticisms of Augustus William Schlegel." This last sentence might, incidentally, give some pause to those who derive Poe's critical principles from Schlegel.

Poe selected Willis's *Tortesa the Usurer* and Longfellow's *Spanish Student* for detailed treatment. He was less happy here, for he could not resist the temptation to ride his old hobby of Longfellow's plagiarism, and to submit *Tortesa* to standards of probability which no romantic play could meet. All of the complications, he insists "might have been avoided by one word of explanation to the duke." Yes, indeed, but all the tragedy of *Romeo and Juliet* might have been avoided by one word of explanation at the right time. There would, in either case, have been no play. Poe tried to show his erudition by denouncing Willis for basing the rescue of his heroine upon a law of Florence which provided that if a woman were refused admittance to her home by her father, she became dependent upon the man who helped her. There was such a law, however.[59] Poe was on much safer ground in his criticism of the "asides" of that period as unnatural, and he recognized that there are many passages in *Tortesa* that "teem with the loftiest qualities of the dramatic art."

It is hard for a critic to recognize the newest contemporary developments in an art. Poe did not know, apparently, of the foundations which were being laid in the field of the rural or "Yankee"

---

[59] Such an incident is made the basis of a story, *La Sepolta Viva*, by Domenico Manni, translated by Roscoe in his *Italian Novelists* (1825), Vol. 4. Poe could easily have seen it.

drama, or the drama of low life in the cities, which were ultimately to lead to the natural plays of Augustin Daly and James A. Herne. But anyone familiar with our dramatic history will appreciate how far ahead of his time Poe sounded an appeal for simple natural drama in America.

Poe was not impressed by the performance of Sophocles' *Antigone* at Palmo's Opera House, and said so. His remarks upon the Greek drama in general are best forgotten, but the sequel to his visit, which he published in the *Journal* [60] reveals his proper resentment at the irate withdrawal of complimentary admission by Dinneford, the Manager. The student of the theatre can find amusement at Poe's description of the difficulties of the dramatic critic of that day who dared to say what he thought.

Outside of the articles on the drama, Poe's critical work while he was editor of the *Broadway Journal* did not include anything of great value. His lengthy reviews of the poetry of Hirst, of Chivers, of Mrs. Osgood, seem perfunctory, or were prompted by friendship. His discrimination shows, however, in his selection of "Grayling; or, Murder Will Out" for especial praise in his criticism of Simms' *The Wigwam and the Cabin.* He says it is the best ghost story he has ever read, and it certainly is one of the most powerful.

Poe's interest in "Anastatic Printing" on which he wrote an article,[61] is of some significance in proving his interest in all new discoveries for the reproduction of the written word. This method of reproducing manuscripts did not, of course, do away with printing as he suggested. But Poe's own print-like characters would have been fine material for experiment. Brief articles, under the heading of "Editorial Miscellany" are more significant at times than the longer ones. A spirited criticism of the unfairness of British criticism, and especially of *Blackwood's,* and of the timidity of American judges who wait for the opinion of "a sub-sub-Editor" of "The Spectator," "The Athenaeum" or the "London Punch," before they dare to have one of their own,[62] is still worth reading.

Poe did not limit his critical articles to the *Broadway Journal.* He wrote for the *Aristidean* an amusing bit of destructive criticism on

[60] I (April 19, 1845), 251-252.

[61] *Broadway Journal,* I (April 12), 229-230.

[62] *Broadway Journal,* II (October 4, 1845), 199-200. The article is signed by Poe in the Huntington Copy and in "Marginalia."

George Jones' *Ancient America,*[63] and an extended treatment of *Longfellow's Poems* [64] marred by the ascription of Longfellow's reputation as due to his chair at Harvard and "marriage with an heiress," and including a feeble discussion of Longfellow's translations. In an article on "American Poetry" [65] Poe objects to generalizations in criticism and insists that the critic should stick to the thing criticized. Considering that Poe's most valuable criticisms, like that on Hawthorne's short stories, are generalizations, this limitation is unfortunate. But Poe's remark "True criticism is the reflection of the thing criticized upon the spirit of the critic" is worth remembering.

Two installments of the "Marginalia" were published in *Godey's* for August and September, 1845. They were briefer than the earlier sections. Poe rode his hobby of plagiarism hard and contributed eleven striking parallels. It is dangerous to attribute the first printing of any important contribution to the "Marginalia." In September, 1845, Poe copied verbatim his warning concerning the dangers of the spread of monarchical ideas, published first in the *Mirror* for February 8th. He evidently considered the right of an author to repeat himself as all paramount.

A letter from Poe to Neilson Poe in August reveals in its formal yet courteous tone how little connection the family in New York maintained with that branch of the Poes in Baltimore. It also makes clear the precarious state of Virginia's health:

New-York: August 8, /45.

My Dear Sir,

It gave me sincere pleasure to receive a letter from you—but I fear you will think me very discourteous in not sooner replying. I have deferred my answer, however, from day to day, in hope of procuring some papers relating to my grandfather. In this I have failed. Mrs. C. has no memoranda of the kind you mention, and all of which I have any knowledge are on file at Annapolis.

I thank you for the kind interest you take in my welfare. We all speak very frequently of yourself and family, and regret that, hitherto, we have seen and known so little of each other. Virginia, in especial, is much pained at the total separation from her sisters.

[63] I (1845), 9-12.

[64] I (1845), 130-142. Although the article speaks of "Mr. Poe," the repetition of the charge of plagiarism from the *Broadway Journal,* I (March 29), p. 198, identifies the article as by Poe.

[65] I (November, 1845), 373-382.

She has been, and is still, in precarious health. About four years ago she ruptured a blood-vessel, in singing, and has never recovered from the accident. I fear that she never will. Mrs. Clemm is quite well:—both beg to be kindly remembered.

I regret that I had no opportunity of seeing you during my last visit to Baltimore. Virginia and myself, however, will very probably spend a few weeks in your city during the fall, when we hope to be with you frequently. When you see any of Mr. Herring's family, will you say that we are anxious to hear from them?

I rejoice to learn that you prosper at all points. I hear *of* you often. "The B. Journal" flourishes—but in January I shall establish a Magazine.

Very cordially Yours,
EDGAR A. POE.[66]

Poe's reference to his last visit to Baltimore implies that he had been in that city in 1844 or 1845. An undated and unpublished letter to Isaac Munroe, speaks of delivering a lecture at Odd Fellows Hall in Gay Street, and asks Munroe to put a notice in the *Patriot* about it.

Sometime in 1845 Poe began to move in that curious mélange known as literary society. As usual, his own letters give little information concerning his social life, and the various contemporary accounts, while insistent upon the brilliancy of the company, are delightfully inconsistent as to dates. It was probably after the family left the neighborhood of East Broadway and came to 85 Amity Street in the winter of 1845 to 1846 that Poe mingled with his fellow writers. This house is one of the three homes associated with Poe, in New York, that are still standing. The building, originally a three-story house, with one of those basement dining rooms and a "stoop" so reminiscent of the Dutch origin of New York, has been remodeled. Like the Greenwich Street house, it is now a restaurant, "Bertolloti's," but it is less depressing in appearance, and the Poe tradition is more direct in the minds of the present occupants. There was a good-sized yard and the neighboring open spaces of Washington Square gave Virginia at least a breathing place.

It was not far to walk from 85 Amity Street to the home of Miss Anne Charlotte Lynch, later to be Madame Vincenzo Botta, who lived at 116 Waverly Place, one block south of Eighth Street, a little

---

[66] Original Autograph Ms., Pratt Institute.

west of Washington Square North. Tall, slender and graceful, her "countenance at times full of intelligent expression," [67] she made a charming hostess. At her evening parties, she welcomed men like Willis, Griswold, Dr. J. W. Francis, and less frequently, Halleck and Morris, women like Mrs. Caroline Kirkland, whose scenes of Western life had struck a new note of realism in American fiction, and visitors from New England like Miss Catherine Sedgwick, whose standing among novelists was recognized even in New York.

Mrs. Whitman, who is the chief source of information,[68] quotes an anonymous friend, who was really Mrs. E. Oakes Smith, as saying: "It was in the brilliant circles that assembled in the winter of 1845-46 at the houses of Dr. Dewey, Miss Anna C. Lynch, Mr. Lawson, and others that we first met Edgar Poe. . . . He delighted in the society of superior women." James Lawson, who was described by Poe in "The Literati" in a short but friendly manner, which Poe afterwards modified, may have gathered a more definitely masculine group, and so may Orville Dewey, the well known Unitarian clergyman. Poe, however, was more likely to meet writers of distinction at 20 Clinton Place, the home of Evert A. Duyckinck, the former editor of *Arcturus* and the later editor and proprietor of *The Literary World,* and of many cyclopedias. Duyckinck, who was about thirty years of age, was a good friend to Poe and provided for a time what Poe needed, an adviser and manager.

Mrs. Whitman, at second hand, however, tells of Poe's reciting "The Raven" at the house of "an accomplished poetess"—probably Miss Lynch, in the autumn preceding its publication. In view of Poe's statement to Thomas in January, 1845, that he rarely went into the city and Willis's remark that he never met Poe outside the *Mirror* office while he was an assistant, I am inclined to doubt Poe's attendance at these parties so early. But there is no question about his later presence during the winter of 1845 to 1846, or that Virginia at times accompanied him. Mrs. Whitman, writing this time with more authority, speaks of Virginia's face "always animated and vivacious," [69] and pays her own tribute to Poe's unfaltering devotion to his wife.

It is easy, however, to idealize such gatherings. I fancy that most of the guests were women, poetesses like Mrs. Mary E. Hewitt, Mrs. E. F. Ellet, and others, who contributed to *Graham's, Godey's* and other

[67] Poe, "The Literati," *Godey's Lady's Book,* XXXIII (September, 1846), 133.

[68] See her *Edgar Poe and His Critics,* p. 23.

[69] *Edgar Poe and His Critics,* p. 26.

magazines, verses permeated with a pressed rose sadness, often teeming with unrequited love or apprehension of early death.

Among these guests, the graceful distinguished figure of Poe moved with the dignity which even anxiety and poverty could not crush and with a courtesy to which so many have left their tribute. Unlike Hawthorne, Poe did not shun social gatherings; he liked sympathy and admiration. When the host or hostess summoned courage to ask him to recite, he usually assented, and then even the chatterers must have listened while his remarkable interpretations of his own or of others' poetry gave some meaning to the occasion. Poe contributed infinitely more than he received, we may be sure, but in his quiet observant way he was gathering material for *The Literati*.

It was not, however, at one of these literary gatherings, but in the unromantic atmosphere of the Astor House, in March, 1845, that he met Mrs. Frances Sargent Osgood. She was the first of the literary women with whom he formed a warm friendship, which blossomed into one of those sentimental adventures that punctuate his later life. He had accepted her verses for *Graham's*, and when he mentioned her poetry in his lecture on February 28, 1845, the episode began. Her own account is vivid:

> My first meeting with the poet was at the Astor House. A few days previous, Mr. Willis had handed me, at the table d'hote, that strange and thrilling poem entitled "The Raven," saying that the author wanted my opinion of it. Its effect upon me was so singular, so like that of "weird, unearthly music," that it was with a feeling almost of dread, I heard he desired an introduction. Yet I could not refuse without seeming ungrateful, because I had just heard of his enthusiastic and partial eulogy of my writings, in his lecture on American Literature. I shall never forget the morning when I was summoned to the drawing-room by Mr. Willis to receive him. With his proud and beautiful head erect, his dark eyes flashing with the electric light of feeling and of thought, a peculiar, an inimitable blending of sweetness and hauteur in his expression and manner, he greeted me, calmly, gravely, almost coldly; yet with so marked an earnestness that I could not help being deeply impressed by it. From that moment until his death we were friends; although we met only during the first year of our acquaintance. And in his last words, ere reason had forever left her imperial throne in that overtasked brain, I have a touching memento of his undying faith and friendship.
>
> During that year, while traveling for my health, I maintained a correspondence with Mr. Poe, in accordance with the earnest en-

treaties of his wife, who imagined that my influence over him had a restraining and beneficial effect. It *had*, as far as this—that having solemnly promised me to give up the use of stimulants, he so firmly respected his promise and me, as never once, during our whole acquaintance, to appear in my presence when in the slightest degree affected by them. Of the charming love and confidence that existed between his wife and himself, always delightfully apparent to me, in spite of the many little poetical episodes, in which the impassioned romance of his temperament impelled him to indulge; of this I cannot speak too earnestly—too warmly. I believe she was the only woman whom he ever truly loved.[70]

Mrs. Osgood was an attractive woman of thirty-four, whose husband was an artist of some ability. She had been a protegée of Mrs. Norton in England, and had published volumes of verse in 1838 and 1842. Stoddard paid her an unusual tribute by saying that both men and women liked her, and she seems indeed to have been a charming person. Her poetry, while generally rather mild, was distinctly above that of the average magazine poetess of that time. I have already spoken of "The Daughters of Herodias." "Elfrida," a dramatic poem, has some fine moments, and lyrics like "She Comes, the Spirit of the Dance," Poe praised with reason.

Mrs. Osgood was not at all averse to Poe's advances and they conducted a literary courtship, principally in the *Broadway Journal*. She sent to the *Journal* verses entitled, "So Let it Be, To ——," printed on April 5th,[71] and signed "Violet Vane." Two of the seven stanzas will indicate the orthodox romantic approach:

> "Perhaps you think it right and just,
> Since you are bound by nearer ties,
> To greet me with that careless tone,
> With those serene and silent eyes.
>
> . . . .
>
> The fair fond girl, who at your side,
> Within your soul's dear light, doth live,
> Could hardly have the heart to chide
> The ray that Friendship well might give."

[70] Mrs. Osgood to Griswold, according to his "Memoir," *The Literati* (1850), p. xxxvii. Since there would have been no motive for Griswold to alter this account, it may be looked upon as authentic. I have not preserved the typographical errors, such as "wierd"; or "Elective" for "Electric."

[71] *Broadway Journal*, I, 217. Reprinted in Mrs. Osgood's *Poems* (Philadelphia, 1850), pp. 403-404.

Poe replied on April 26,[72] by verses which had already been addressed "To Mary," and "To One Departed," but which became "To F——." She returned to the charge on September 6th, with her "Echo Song," [73] beginning:

> "I know a noble heart that beats
>   For one it loves how "wildly well!"
> *I* only know for *whom* it beats;
>   But I must never tell!"

On September 13th Poe published another "To F——," [74] which had earlier been addressed to "Eliza." His poem, "A Valentine," seems to have been written for her alone, and to have been read at the home of Miss Anne Lynch, on February 14, 1846,[75] and it was published in the *Evening Mirror*, on February 21, 1846. If the first letter of the first line, the second of the second line, and so on, are selected, the name of Mrs. Osgood appears. It is difficult to take courtships like this very seriously. Poets have been dusting off their amatory verses for new occasions since time immemorial, but they usually outgrow the habit with fading adolescence. Perhaps the very publicity of the courtship, while it caused comment, made it more innocuous. Life in New York in those days, if we can believe the testimony of travellers and observers, was lived so often in hotels and boarding houses, that even poets were affected by the external quality of the channels of affection.[76]

Mrs. Osgood was a good friend of the family, and Virginia welcomed her influence over Poe which seemed to keep him from stimu-

[72] *Broadway Journal*, I, 260.

[73] *Broadway Journal*, II, 129. Other verses of hers like "Love's Reply," I (April 12), 231, or "Slander," II (August 30), 113, may belong to this series.

[74] *Broadway Journal*, II, 148. Poe's interest in the matter may be judged by the fact that only the first four lines of this poem were inserted as a "filler" to complete a page of his story of "Diddling, etc." The poem did not have the full title of "To F——s S. O——d," until it reappeared in *The Raven and Other Poems*.

[75] The poem, as read in 1846, is in Autograph Ms. at the Pratt Library. It is dated "St. Valentine's Eve, 1846." There are several differences between this 1846 form and that usually printed. Poe misspelled Mrs. Osgood's middle name "Sargent" as "Sergeant," so the nature of the poem required rewriting, the last four lines being entirely different in the 1849 version.

[76] See the descriptions by Charles Dickens, James Silk Buckingham, Francis J. Grund, and others, especially the latter's *Aristocracy in America*.

lants, at least while in her presence. One of the most vivid pictures of their home life in the spring of 1846, is due to Mrs. Osgood:

> It was in his own simple yet poetical home that, to me the character of Edgar Poe appeared in its most beautiful light. Playful, affectionate, witty, alternately docile and wayward as a petted child—for his young, gentle, and idolized wife, and for all who came, he had even in the midst of his most harassing literary duties, a kind word, a pleasant smile, a graceful and courteous attention. At his desk beneath the romantic picture of his loved and lost Lenore, he would sit, hour after hour, patient, assiduous and uncomplaining, tracing, in an exquisitely clear chirography and with almost superhuman swiftness, the lightning thoughts— the "rare and radiant" fancies as they flashed through his wonderful and ever wakeful brain. I recollect, one morning, towards the close of his residence in this city, when he seemed unusually gay and light-hearted. Virginia, his sweet wife, had written me a pressing invitation to come to them; and I, who never could resist her affectionate summons, and who enjoyed his society far more in his own home than elsewhere, hastened to Amity-street. I found him just completing his series of papers entitled "The Literati of New-York." "See," said he, displaying, in laughing triumph, several little rolls of narrow paper (he always wrote thus for the press), "I am going to show you, by the difference of length in these, the different degrees of estimation in which I hold all you literary people. In each of these, one of you is rolled up and fully discussed. Come, Virginia, help me!" And one by one they unfolded them. At last they came to one which seemed interminable. Virginia laughingly ran to one corner of the room with one end, and her husband to the opposite with the other. "And whose lengthened sweetness long drawn out is that?" said I. "Hear her!" he cried, "just as if her little vain heart didn't tell her it's herself!" [77]

The only new, unpublished poem that appeared in 1845 was "Eulalie—A Song," printed in the *American Review* in July.[78] This celebration of married love has already been discussed at the date of its composition in 1843.

The *Tales* sold well enough to encourage the publishers to issue a collection of Poe's poetry. Poe's letter to Duyckinck shows that he was permitted this time to make his own selection:

[77] Mrs. Osgood to Griswold, *The Literati* (1850), XXXVI.
[78] II (July, 1845), 79.

My Dear Duyckinck,

I leave for you what I think the best of my Poems. They are *very* few—including those only which have not been published in volume form. If they can be made to fill a book, it will be better to publish them alone—but if not, I can hand you some "Dramatic Scenes" from the S. L. Messenger (2d Vol) and "Al Aaraaf" and "Tamerlane," two juvenile poems of some length.

Truly yours

POE.

Wednesday 10th [Sept. 1845?] [79]

The Raven and Other Poems appeared early in November, 1845.[80] The volume contained thirty poems, divided into two groups.[81] The first began with "The Raven," very naturally, but there is no discernible principle in the arrangement of these nineteen poems. As a preface, Poe said:

> These trifles are collected and republished chiefly with a view to their redemption from the many improvements to which they have been subjected while going at random "the rounds of the press." If what I have written is to circulate at all, I am naturally anxious that it should circulate as I wrote it. In defence of my own taste, nevertheless, it is incumbent upon me to say, that I think nothing in this volume of much value to the public, or very creditable to myself. Events not to be controlled have prevented me from making, at any time, any serious effort in what, under happier circumstances, would have been the field of my choice.

[79] Original Autograph Ms., Duyckinck Collection, New York Public Library.

[80] Wiley and Putnam's Announcement. Advertisement in *Broadway Journal*, II (November 8, 1845), 280. Its price was "31 cents." Noted among Books Received, II (November 22), 307. Reviews begin in November. It was published as No. 8 of Wiley and Putnam's *Library of American Books*. Poe says (*Broadway Journal*, December 13, 1845) that he read the proofs the evening before he delivered the Boston lecture on October 16th.

[81] The poems in Poe's order were: "The Raven," "The Valley of Unrest," "Bridal Ballad," "The Sleeper," "The Coliseum," "Lenore," "Catholic Hymn," "Israfel," "Dream-land," "Sonnet—To Zante," "The City in the Sea," "To One in Paradise," "Eulalie—A Song," "To F——s S. O——d," "To F——," "Sonnet—Silence," "The Conqueror Worm," "The Haunted Palace," "Scenes from Politian." Then followed Poems Written in Youth: "Sonnet—To Science," "Al Aaraaf," "Tamerlane," "A Dream," "Romance," "Fairy-land," "To —— (The bowers, whereat in dreams, I see)," "To the River ——," "The Lake —— To ——," "Song (I saw thee on thy bridal day)," "To Helen."

With me poetry has been not a purpose, but a passion; and the passions should be held in reverence; they must not—they cannot at will be excited with an eye to the paltry compensations, or the more paltry commendations, of mankind.

This Preface is important because it shows that poetry was his first love. The "Poems Written in Youth" include selections from the volumes of 1827 and 1829, with one striking exception. "To Helen" had first appeared in the volume of 1831, and why Poe relegated it to the youthful poems while he included among the main group the five others also printed first in 1831, is a puzzle. As a footnote to the first page of the "Poems Written in Youth," Poe made a statement:

Private reasons—some of which have reference to the sin of plagiarism, and others to the date of Tennyson's first poems— have induced me, after some hesitation, to republish these, the crude compositions of my earliest boyhood. They are printed *verbatim*—without alteration from the original edition—the date of which is too remote to be judiciously acknowledged.

The poems were not printed "verbatim," from the original editions, but appear in their revised forms. Poe omitted six of the 1827 poems and one from 1829. Some of these may be spared, but why he left out "Spirits of the Dead," or "To ———," later "A Dream within a Dream," is not clear, especially since he reprinted the latter in 1849. There was an opportunity here to accuse Tennyson of plagiarism in "Locksley Hall," which Poe seems to have missed!

This text of the 1845 volume has usually become the standard, with alterations from the Lorimer Graham Copy. These are not very important, except perhaps in the case of "Lenore." [82]

The reviews of *The Raven and Other Poems* were on the whole inadequate. The critic of *The Aristidean* [83] called attention to the influence of Miss Barrett's "Lady Geraldine's Courtship," praised "The Raven," highly, but said "Israfel" was "fiddle-de-dee." Margaret

---

[82] Poe added two verses,

> "Here is a ring as token
> That I am happy now!—"

in "Bridal Ballad," rearranged and slightly altered the last stanza of "Lenore," changed the color of the eyes of "To One in Paradise" from "dark" to "grey" and made verbal alterations which have usually been adopted.

[83] November, 1845, pp. 399-403.

THE RAVEN

AND

OTHER POEMS.

BY

EDGAR A. POE.

NEW YORK:
WILEY AND PUTNAM, 161 BROADWAY.

1845.

Fuller in *The New York Tribune* [84] combined a singular ability to select for quotation the right poems, like "Israfel" and "To One in Paradise," and some of the best lines in other poems, with almost complete blindness as to the significance of Poe's poetry in general. Lewis Gaylord Clark, in the *Knickerbocker*,[85] revenged himself upon Poe for the latter's various criticisms [86] of his magazine by a bitter onslaught on Poe's character:

> If we were disposed to retort upon Mr. Poe for the exceedingly gross and false statements which, upon an imaginary slight, he made in his paper respecting this Magazine, we could ask for no greater favor than to be allowed to criticize his volume of poems. Surely no author is so much indebted to the forbearance of critics as Mr. Poe, and no person connected with the press in this country is entitled to less mercy or consideration. His criticisms, so called, are generally a tissue of coarse personal abuse or personal adulation. He has praised to the highest degree some of the paltriest writers in the country, and abused in the grossest terms many of the best.

Such an attack is, of course, not criticism, but the entire review would repay reading by anyone who desires to estimate rightly the difficulties under which Poe or any other independent critic labored in that period. In Clark's case, there was a personal feud of long standing. But it was in the same decade that Cooper sued the New York newspapers for libel until they ceased in their attacks, wiser but poorer.

The *London Literary Gazette* [87] which had praised his *Tales*, gave his poems scanty notice, on the ground that the *Gazette* had already assigned his genius to its proper place. It quoted, however, "The Conqueror Worm" and the passage of "The Sleeper" in which occurred the lines,

> "Soft may the worms about her creep!"

only to denounce them as "morbid." The London *Athenaeum* copied "The Raven" and "Dreamland," but repeated the usual banality of demanding that if Poe had to be mystical it should be a mysticism

---

[84] November 26, 1845; reprinted in Weekly Issue, November 29th.

[85] Vol. XXVII (January, 1846), pp. 69-72.

[86] See "The Magazines," *Broadway Journal*, II (July 12, 1845), 10-11. Article signed in Huntington Copy.

[87] March 14, 1846, pp. 237-238.

"caught up on his own mountains,—fed on the far prairie—watered by the mighty rivers of the land, etc." [88] If this owl-like critic had lived in Shakespeare's day he would probably have criticized that poet for wasting his energies on the ghostly battlements of Elsinore when there were perfectly good localities in England for ghosts to operate, to say nothing of kings like Ethelred II, who had been strangely neglected by British poets! But the same critical stupidity still resounds today, both in England and America.

There was no such quick recognition of the poems as there had been of the stories. Poe had dedicated the volume "To the Noblest of her Sex—Elizabeth Barrett Barrett." Her letter to him, while it conveyed her personal appreciation and her sense of the vividness of his writing, confined her comment to "The Raven." [89] She added, "I think you will like to be told that our great poet, Mr. Browning, the author of 'Paracelsus' and the 'Bells and Pomegranates' was much struck by the rhythm of that poem." The future Mrs. Browning also remarked that "there is a tale of yours which I do not find in this volume, but which is going the rounds of the newspapers, about Mesmerism ("The Valdemar Case"), throwing us all into——dreadful doubts as to whether it can be true, as the children say of ghost stories. The certain thing in the tale in question is the power of the writer, and the faculty he has of making horrible improbabilities seem near and familiar." [90]

It may have been the mental disturbance of which Poe speaks in his letter to Duyckinck on November 13th which prompted him to commit one of those unfortunate mistakes which was long remembered to his discredit. Lowell's efforts to obtain a lecture appointment bore fruit, and Poe was invited to read a poem before the Boston Lyceum on October 16, 1845. As he had said long before in "Romance," he could not write a poem to order. He read, therefore, "Al

[88] *The Athenaeum*, No. 957 (February 28, 1846), 215.

[89] It is interesting to compare Miss Barrett's letter as printed in the *Century*, XLVIII (October, 1894), 859, with Poe's quotations from it in his letter to Field, June 15, 1846, now in the Huntington Library.

[90] Miss Barrett's note of the omission of "The Facts in the Case of M. Valdemar," from "the volume" is explained by the fact that Wiley and Putnam were issuing the *Tales* and the *Poems* together under one cover. Poe's presentation copy to her, now in the New York Public Library, is bound in this way, also the "Lorimer Graham" copy, with Poe's Ms. corrections, now in the Century Association. A reproduction of *The Raven and other Poems* from the last, is announced for early publication with foreword by T. O. Mabbott.

Aaraaf," which must have been over the heads of his audience, who had already listened to an address by Caleb Cushing. This might have been forgiven if he had not taken a drink afterwards and expressed his frank opinion of Boston. His own statement, published in the *Broadway Journal* on November 1st, gives us a first hand account of the occasion. It added naturally fresh fuel to the fire:

Editorial Miscellany

We take the following paragraph from "The Sunday Times and Messenger" of October 26:

"Mr. Poe's Poem.—Mr. Poe was invited to deliver a poem before the Boston Lyceum, which he did to a large and distinguished audience. It was, to use the language of an intelligent hearer, 'an elegant and classic production, based on the right principle; containing the essence of true poetry, mingled with a gorgeous imagination, exquisite painting, every charm of metre, and graceful delivery.' And yet the papers abused him, and the audience were fidgetty—made their exit one by one, and did not at all appreciate the efforts of a man of admitted ability, whom they had invited to deliver a poem before them. The poem was called the 'Messenger Star.' We presume Mr. Poe will not accept another invitation to recite poetry, original or selected, in that section of the Union."

Our excellent friend Major Noah has suffered himself to be cajoled by that most beguiling of all beguiling little divinities, Miss Walters, of "The Transcript." We have been looking all over her article, with the aid of a taper, to see if we could discover a single syllable of truth in it—and really blush to acknowledge that we cannot. The adorable creature has been telling a parcel of fibs about us, by way of revenge for something that we did to Mr. Longfellow (who admires her very much) and for calling her "a pretty little witch" into the bargain.

The facts of the case seem to be these:—We *were* invited to "deliver" (stand and deliver) a poem before the Boston Lyceum. As a matter of course, we accepted the invitation. The audience was "large and distinguished." Mr. Cushing preceded us with a very capital discourse: he was much applauded. On arising, we were most cordially received. We occupied some fifteen minutes with an apology for not "delivering," as is usual in such cases, a didactic poem: a didactic poem, in our opinion, being precisely no poem at all. After some farther words—still of apology—for the "indefinitiveness" and "general imbecility" of what we had to offer —all so unworthy a *Bostonian* audience—we commenced, and, with many interruptions of applause, concluded. Upon the whole the approbation was considerably more (the more the pity too) than that bestowed upon Mr. Cushing.

When we had made an end, the audience, of course, arose to depart—and about one-tenth of them, probably, had really departed, when Mr. Coffin, one of the managing committee, arrested those who remained, by the announcement that we had been requested to deliver "The Raven." We delivered "The Raven" forthwith—(without taking a receipt)—were very cordially applauded again—and this was the end of it—with the exception of the sad tale invented to suit her own purposes, by that amiable little enemy of ours, Miss Walters. We shall never call a woman "a pretty little witch" again, as long as we live.

We like Boston. We were born there—and perhaps it is just as well not to mention that we are heartily ashamed of the fact. The Bostonians are very well in their way. Their hotels are bad. Their pumpkin pies are delicious. Their poetry is not so good. Their Common is no common thing—and the duck-pond might answer— if its answer could be heard for the frogs.

But with all these good qualities the Bostonians have no soul. They have always evinced towards us individually, the basest ingratitude for the services we rendered them in enlightening them about the originality of Mr. Longfellow. When we accepted, therefore, an invitation to "deliver" a poem in Boston—we accepted it simply and solely, because we had a curiosity to know how it felt to be publicly hissed—and because we wished to see what effect we could produce by a neat little *impromptu* speech in reply. Perhaps, however, we overrated our own importance, or the Bostonian want of common civility—which is not quite so manifest as one or two of their editors would wish the public to believe. We assure Major Noah that he is wrong. The Bostonians are well-bred—as *very* dull persons very generally are.

Still, with their vile ingratitude staring us in the eyes, it could scarcely be supposed that we would put ourselves to the trouble of composing for the Bostonians anything in the shape of an *original* poem. We did not. We had a poem (of about 500 lines) lying by us—one quite as good as new—one, at all events, that we considered would answer sufficiently well for an audience of Transcendentalists. *That* we gave them—it was the best that we had—for the price—and it *did* answer remarkably well. Its name was *not* "The Messenger-Star"—who but Miss Walters would ever think of so delicious a little bit of invention as that? We had *no* name for it at all. The poem is what is occasionally called a "juvenile poem"—but the fact is, it is anything but juvenile now, for we wrote it, printed it, and published it, in book form, before we had fairly completed our tenth year. We read it *verbatim,* from a copy now in our possession, and which we shall be happy to show at any moment to any of our inquisitive friends.

We do not, ourselves, think the poem a remarkably good one: —it is not sufficiently transcendental. Still it did well enough for the Boston audience—who evinced characteristic discrimination in understanding, and especially applauding, all those knotty passages which we ourselves have not yet been able to understand.

As regards the anger of the "Boston Times" and one or two other absurdities—as regards, we say, the wrath of Achilles—we incurred it—or rather its manifestation—by letting some of our cat out of the bag a few hours sooner than we had intended. Over a bottle of champagne, that night, we confessed to Mess. Cushing, Whipple, Hudson, Field, and a few other natives who swear not altogether by the frog-pond—we confessed, we say, the soft impeachment of the hoax. *Et hinc illae irae.* We should have waited a couple of days.[91]

Poe was severely criticized and the *Charleston Patriot,* ready to defend a Southern poet, had a long article which Poe reprinted in the *Broadway Journal.*[92] Through a quotation in this notice from the *Boston Courier,* it is evident that Poe's poem was highly thought of by some of the audience, since that journal compared it with the "Eve of St. Agnes" and "Paradise Lost"! Poe might have let this rather clever defence of his excursion into what the *Patriot* called the "purlieus of the Puritans," stand alone, but again, unfortunately, he commented upon it, revealing a New England persecution mania, a jealousy of Longfellow and an inability to keep from personalities which are almost childish. The account makes clear, however, that it was the "first edition" that he delivered and which he was just then publishing in *The Raven and Other Poems* of 1845.[93]

That the personalities were not altogether on Poe's side, however, was shown clearly by the contemptuous account of his contributions to the evening, by Miss Cornelia M. Walter, the Editor of the *Transcript.* In the leading editorial of October 17th under the heading "A Failure," she said:

[91] *Broadway Journal,* II (November 1, 1845), 261-262.
[92] II (November 22, 1845), 309-311.
[93] He spoke of the *Boston Star* reprinting the "third edition" of the poem, "revised and improved" with "two or three columns of criticism" evidently unfavorable. What he meant by the "third edition" is not clear, unless he referred to the *Saturday Museum* text, which is hardly an "edition." Poe reverted to the 1829 form for the 1845 text.

.... When the orator had concluded, an officer of the society introduced to the assembly a gentleman, who, as we understood him to say, possessed a *raven*-ous desire to be known as the author of a particular piece of poetry on a celebrated croaking bird well known to ornithologists. The poet immediately arose; but, if he uttered poesy in the first instance, it was certainly of a most prosaic order. The audience listened in amazement to a singularly didactic exordium, and finally commenced the noisy expedient of removing from the hall, and this long before they had discovered the style of the measure, or whether it was rhythm or blank verse. We believe, however, it was a prose introductory to a poem on the "Star discovered by Tycho Brahe," considered figuratively as the "Messenger of the Deity," out of which idea Edgar A. Poe had constructed a sentimental and imaginative poem. The audience now thinned so rapidly and made so much commotion in their departure that we lost the beauties of the composition. ... Another small poem succeeded. This was "The Raven"—a composition probably better appreciated by its author than by his auditory, and which has already gone the rounds of the press, followed by a most felicitous *parody* from another source. The parody, however, had not been announced as "part of the entertainment," and was "unavoidably omitted." [94]

Considering the tone of this editorial, Poe treated Miss Walter with restraint.[95]

In the issue of the *Broadway Journal* for October 18, 1845, under "Critical Notices," appeared the statement that "the editor's temporary absence from the city will account to our publishing friends for present neglect of several new works. They will be attended to on his return." [96]

This notice probably referred to his visit to Boston, or to a trip devoted to raising a fund to purchase the *Journal*. On October 24th, he signed a contract with John Bisco, by which he obtained control of the paper. He agreed to pay Bisco fifty dollars in cash, to give him a

[94] See Joseph E. Chamberlin, "Edgar A. Poe and his Boston Critic, Miss Walter," *Boston Evening Transcript*, January 26, 1924, Book Section, p. 2, in which is reproduced the entire criticism. Miss Walter in private life was Mrs. W. B. Richard.

[95] Miss Walter continued her attacks, punning on his name, and commenting on his request for the support of his friends for the *Broadway Journal*. "What a question to ask! Edgar A. Poe to be in a condition to require *support*. It is indeed remarkable!"—*Boston Transcript*, October 28, 1845.

[96] Vol. II, p. 227.

note at three months for the full amount of debts due the paper, and to assume the responsibilities to subscribers and advertisers.[97]

Poe evidently made strenuous efforts to raise the money to carry out this contract. He wrote to Kennedy:

New York: Octo. 26. 45.

My dear Mr. Kennedy,

When you were in New York I made frequent endeavors to meet you—but—in vain—as I was forced to go to Boston.

I stand much in need of your aid, and beg you to afford it to me, if possible—for the sake of the position which you already have enabled me to obtain. By a series of manoeuvres almost incomprehensible to myself, I have succeeded in getting rid, one by one, of all my associates in "The Broadway Journal" and have now become sole editor and owner. It will be a fortune to me if I can hold it—and if I can hold it for one month I am quite safe —as you shall see. I have exhausted all my immediate resources in the purchase—and I now write to ask you for a small loan— say $50. I will punctually return it in three months.[98]

Kennedy wrote a friendly letter on December 1, but could not help him. Horace Greeley loaned him fifty dollars, which Poe was not able to repay. Poe wrote to Griswold for fifty dollars on October 26th,[99] and Griswold claims that he loaned him twenty-five dollars.

Poe's appeal to Chivers reveals how brave a fight he was putting up, alone:

New-York: Nov. 15. 45.

My Dear Friend—Beyond doubt you must think that I treat you ill in not answering your letters—but it is utterly impossible to conceive how busy I have been. The Broadway Journals I now send, will give you some idea of the reason. I have been buying out the paper, and of course you must be aware that I have had a tough time of it—making all kind of maneuvres—and editing the paper, without aid from anyone, all the time. I have succeeded, however, as you see—bought it out entirely, and *paid for it all,* with the exception of 140$ which will fall due on the 1st of Janu-

---

[97] See Appendix, for contract, printed from Ms. in the collection of W. H. Koester.

[98] Original Autograph Ms., Peabody Institute.

[99] The Ms. letter from Poe, asking the loan, is in the Griswold Collection, Boston Public Library, but the letter of November 1, thanking Griswold, is not. It is printed in Griswold's "Preface" to his Memoir.

ary next—I will make a fortune of it yet. You see yourself what a host of advertising I have. For Heaven's sake, my dear friend, help me *now* if you can—*at once*—for now is my time of peril. If I live until next month I shall be beyond the need of aid. If you *can* send me the $45, for Heaven's sake do it *by return of mail*— or if not all, a part. Time with me now, is money & money more than time. I wish you were here that I might explain to you my hopes & prospects—but in a letter it is impossible—for remember that I have to do *everything* myself—edit the paper—get it to press—and attend to the multitudinous *business* besides.

Believe me—will you not?—my dear friend—that it is through no want of disposition to write you that I have failed to do so:— the moments I now spend in penning these words are gold them- selves—& more. By & bye I shall have time to breathe—and then I will write you fully.

You are wrong (as usual) about Archy̆tas & Orīon—both are as I accent them. Look in any phonographic Dictionary—say Bolles. Besides, wherever the words occur in ancient poetry, they are as I give them. What is the use of disputing an obvious point? You are wrong too, throughout, in what you say about the poem "Orion"—there is not the shadow of an error; in its rhythm, from α to ω.

I never dreamed that you did not get the paper regularly until Bisco told me it was not sent. You must have thought it very strange.

So help me Heaven, I have sent and gone personally in all the nooks & corners of Broker-Land & such a thing as the money you speak of—*is not to be obtained.* Write me soon—soon—& help me if you can. I send you my Poems.

God bless you—

E. A. P.

We *all* send our warmest love to yourself, your wife & family.[100]
Poe wrote his cousin, George Poe, for a loan of two hundred dollars on November 30th,[101] but apparently without result.
On December 1st Poe in desperation wrote to Fitz-Greene Halleck:

New York, Dec. 1, 1845.

My dear Mr. Halleck: On the part of one or two persons who are much imbittered against me, there is a deliberate attempt now

[100] Original Autograph Ms., Huntington Library.
[101] Original Autograph Ms., Enoch Pratt Library.

being made to involve me in ruin, by destroying *The Broadway Journal.* I could easily frustrate them, but for my total want of money, and of the necessary time in which to procure it: the knowledge of this has given my enemies the opportunities desired.

In this emergency—without leisure to think whether I am acting improperly—I venture to appeal to you. The sum I need is $100. If you could loan me for three months any portion of it, I will not be ungrateful.

Truly yours,

EDGAR A. POE.[102]

Halleck loaned him the money, but it was not sufficient, of course.

Let us hope that it was some satisfaction to him in his trouble to see "Edgar A. Poe, Editor and Proprietor" on the first page of Vol. II, No. 16 of the *Broadway Journal,* issued on Saturday, October 25, 1845. At last he had a journal entirely his own. But it was not a monthly magazine, costing five dollars and appealing to the class of readers he had in mind. Poe's satisfaction was, in any case, short lived. He could not keep the journal afloat alone, and on December 3, 1845, he sold to Thomas H. Lane one half of his interest, retaining sole charge as Editor and sharing the business management with Lane. Lane agreed to pay all the debts that did not antedate November 17th, provided they did not exceed forty dollars.[103] The office of the paper was moved to 304 Broadway, the corner of Duane Street.[104]

Even Lane's help was unavailing, and while Poe was writing desperately to his friends, he was fighting against a bad nervous depression. His letter to Duyckinck, dated "Thursday—13th," which brings it probably in November, 1845, makes this clear:

85 Amity St.

My dear Mr. Duyckinck,

For the first time during two months I find myself entirely myself—dreadfully sick and depressed, but still myself. I seem to have just awakened from some horrible dream, in which all was confusion, and suffering—relieved only by the constant sense of your kindness, and that of one or two other considerate friends. I really believe that I have been mad—but indeed I have had abundant reason to be so. I have made up my mind to a step

---

[102] J. G. Wilson, *Life of Halleck* (New York, 1869), p. 431.

[103] See Contract published from the Original Ms. in possession of John W. Garrett, by Kenneth Rede, *American Literature,* V (March, 1933), 53-54.

[104] *Broadway Journal,* II (December 27, 1845), p. 315.

which will preserve me, for the future, from at least the greater portion of the troubles which have beset me. In the meantime, I have need of the most active exertion to extricate myself from the embarrassments into which I have already fallen—and my object in writing you this note is, (once again) to beg your aid. Of course I need not say to you that my most urgent trouble is the want of ready money. I find that what I said to you about the prospects of the B. J. is strictly correct. The most trifling immediate relief would put it on an excellent footing. All that I want is time in which to look about me; and I think that it is your power to afford me this.

I have already drawn from Mr. Wiley, first $30—then 10 (from yourself)—then 50 (on account of the "Parnassus")—then 20 (when I went to Boston)—and finally 25—in all 135. Mr. Wiley owes me, for the Poems, 75, and admitting that 1500 of the Tales have been sold, and that I am to receive 8 cts a copy—the amount which you named, if I remember—admitting this, he will owe me $120. on them:—in all 195. Deducting what I have received there is a balance of 60 in my favor. If I understood you, a few days ago, Mr. W. was to settle with me in February. Now, you will already have anticipated my request. It is that you would ask Mr. W. to give me, to-day, in lieu of all further claim, a certain sum whatever he may think advisable. So dreadfully am I pressed, that I would willingly take even the $60 actually due, (in lieu of all farther demand) than wait until February:—but I am sure that you will do the best for me that you can.

Please send your answer to 85 Amity St. and believe me—with the most sincere friendship and ardent gratitude

Yours
EDGAR A. POE.[105]

Poe's situation was evidently desperate, whether the help was given or not. A letter dated vaguely "Thursday morning" reveals probably that Virginia's illness had become again acute:

Thursday Morning [Nov. 13? 1845?].

My dear Mr Duyckinck,

I am still dreadfully unwell, and fear that I shall be very seriously ill. Some matters of domestic affliction have also hap-

---

[105] Original Autograph Ms., New York Public Library. Poe's Letters to Duyckinck were printed in the *Bulletin of the New York Public Library*, VI (January, 1902), 7-11.

pened which deprive me of what little energy I have left—and I have resolved to give up the B. Journal and retire to the country for six months, or perhaps a year, as the sole means of recruiting my health and spirits. Is it not possible that yourself or Mr Matthews [sic] might give me a trifle for my interest in the paper? Or, if this cannot be effected, might I venture to ask you for an advance of $50 on the faith of the "American Parnassus"? —which I will finish as soon as possible. If you could oblige me in this manner I would feel myself under the deepest obligation. Will you be so kind as to reply by the bearer?

Most sincerely yours

EDGAR A. POE

E. A. Duyckinck Esq.[106]

The changes in the stories after Poe became both editor and proprietor were not very significant. "Four Beasts in One" and "Mystification" assumed their present titles. Poe signed the last two stories "Littleton Barry" to avoid the appearance of his own name so frequently.[107]

All his efforts failing, on January 3, 1846, Poe issued his Valedictory:

Unexpected engagements demanding my whole attention, and the objects being fulfilled, so far as regards myself personally, for which "The Broadway Journal" was established, I now, as its Editor, bid farewell—as cordially to foes as to friends.

Mr. Thomas H. Lane is authorized to collect all money due the Journal.[108]

Lane closed up the business with the help, it is said, of Thomas Dunn English, and the *Broadway Journal* expired.

Outside of Poe's condition, the main cause of the failure was the lack of capital. The advertisements in the *Journal* seem to be ample, and in fact increased from two to four pages after Poe had complete possession of the paper. No satisfactory figures concerning its circula-

---

[106] Original Autograph Ms., New York Public Library.

[107] The stories republished while Poe was both Editor and Proprietor were: "The Thousand-and-Second Tale of Scheherazade," "The Power of Words," "Some Words with a Mummy," "The Devil in the Belfry," "The Spectacles," "Four Beasts in One," "A Tale of the Ragged Mountains," "The Oblong Box," "The Facts in the Case of M. Valdemar," "Mystification," and "Loss of Breath."

[108] *Broadway Journal*, II (January 3, 1846), 407.

tion are available, but there were agents in twenty-three cities according to the last issue. Then as now, a magazine must lose money at first, if it is to win eventually, and Poe could not afford to lose even for a few months. That he did not know this seems inexplicable.

The year 1845 was a memorable one in Poe's life. He published his most famous poem, four of his best-known short stories, a volume of tales and the first collected edition of his poetry in book form since 1831. He had been editor and finally proprietor of a magazine. His recognition at home and abroad was growing. His labor was constant and intense. The revisions of his stories alone called for unremitting care, and for a time he carried on the *Broadway Journal* not only as editor but as contributor, almost alone. His estimate to Thomas that his working day lasted fifteen hours was not excessive. Yet he ended the year defeated and with no reward except the consciousness of his widening fame. But that would not provide support for Virginia and Mrs. Clemm, and the worry over his wife's decline faced him every day.

CHAPTER XVI

Widening Horizons—Friends and Enemies

As the new year broke it found Poe still at 85 Amity Street, with no definite means of support. He turned to Duyckinck again:

> Jan 8. 46.
>
> Dear Mr. Duyckinck,—For "particular reasons" I am anxious to have another volume of my Tales published before the 1st of March. Do you not think it possible to accomplish it for me? Would not Mr Wiley give me, say $50, in full for the copyright of the collection I now send? It is a far better one than the first—containing, for instance, "Ligeia," which is undoubtedly the best story I have written—besides "Scheherazade," "The Spectacles," "Tarr and Fether," etc.
>
> May I beg of you to give me an early answer, by note, addressed 85 Amity St?
>
> > Truly yours
> >
> > > Edgar A. Poe.
>
> E. A. Duyckinck Esq.[1]

No edition appeared, however. A letter to Mrs. Sarah J. Hale, written January 16, 1846 reveals in his clear firm handwriting that Poe, even in times of distress, was usually in control of his faculties. It is a courteous letter dealing with her play "Ormond Grosvenor," which she had sent him for his criticism. The postscript is of especial interest to us:

> The B. Journal had fulfilled its destiny—which was a matter of no great moment. I have never regarded it as more than a temporary adjunct to other designs. I am now busy making arrangements for the establishment of a Magazine which offers a wide field for literary ambition. Professor Chas. Anthon has agreed to take charge for me of a Department of Criticism on Scholastic

[1] Original Autograph Ms., Duyckinck Collection, New York Public Library.

Letters. His name will be announced. I shall have, also, a Berlin and a Parisian correspondent—both of eminence. The first No. may not appear until Jan. 1847.[2]

Poe must have had mental resiliency to a remarkable degree, for he remained undaunted after defeat. There was always comfort and devotion at home. A charming if pathetic evidence of the love of Virginia for him exists in the Valentine she wrote him on February 14, 1846. The initial letters of the lines spell his name:

> "Ever with thee I wish to roam—
> Dearest my life is thine.
> Give me a cottage for my home
> And a rich old cypress vine,
> Removed from the world with its sin and care
> And the tattling of many tongues.
> Love alone shall guide us when we are there—
> Love shall heal my weakened lungs;
> And Oh, the tranquil hours we'll spend,
> Never wishing that others may see!
> Perfect ease we'll enjoy, without thinking to lend
> Ourselves to the world and its glee—
> Ever peaceful and blissful we'll be." [3]

Conventional as the verses are, there are some that reflect their lives together. The "cottage" was soon to be their home, but the "tattling tongues" were not to be silent. It is the utterance of a wife who wants her husband for herself, and not of the child she is pictured as being by those who force her relations with Poe into a false theory concerning his own physical nature. She was shrewd enough to encourage his friendship with Mrs. Osgood because she recognized that Mrs. Osgood protected him from the literary women like Mrs. Ellet, whose advances were more harmful and whose anonymous letters plagued Virginia. She had to watch the painful later scene, at Fordham, when Mrs. Ellet, seeing a letter from Mrs. Osgood lying open, took it upon herself to supervise her rival's relations with Poe. How she persuaded Mrs. Osgood to permit her to interfere is a mystery, but she did send two other self-appointed guardians of morality to demand from Poe the return of Mrs. Osgood's letters. When these ladies, whom Mrs.

[2] Original Autograph Ms., Huntington Library.
[3] Facsimile published by Josephine Poe January, "Edgar Allan Poe's 'Child Wife'," *Century Magazine,* LXXVIII (October, 1909), 894-896.

Whitman identifies as Margaret Fuller and Anne C. Lynch,[4] came to the Poe cottage, Poe was naturally incensed and incautiously exclaimed "Mrs. Ellet had better come and look after her own letters." Poe's own account of what followed was given to Mrs. Whitman to warn her against Mrs. Ellet:

I will give you here but one instance of her baseness & I feel that it will suffice. When, in the heat of passion—stung to madness by her inconceivable perfidy & by the grossness of the injury which her jealousy prompted her to inflict upon *all of us*—upon both families—I permitted myself to say what I should not have said—I had no sooner uttered the words, than I *felt* their dishonor. I felt, too, that, although *she* must be damningly conscious of her own baseness, she would still have a right to reproach me for having betrayed, under *any* circumstances, her confidence. Full of these thoughts, and terrified almost to death lest I should again, in a moment of madness, be similarly tempted, I went immediately to my secretary—(when those two ladies went away—) made a package of her letters, addressed them to her, and with my own hands left them at her door. Now, Helen, you *can*not be prepared for the diabolical malignity which followed. Instead of feeling that I had done all I could to repair an unpremeditated wrong—instead of feeling that almost any other person would have retained the letters to make good (if occasion required) the assertion that I possessed them—instead of this, she urged her brothers & brother-in-law *to demand of me the letters*. The position in which she thus placed me you may imagine. Is it any wonder that I was driven *mad* by the intolerable sense of wrong? —If you value your happiness, Helen, beware of this woman! She did not cease her persecutions here. My poor Virginia was continually tortured (although not deceived) by her anonymous letters, and on her death-bed declared that Mrs. E. had been her murderer. Have I not a right to hate this fiend & to caution you against her? You will now comprehend what I mean in saying that the *only* thing for which I found it impossible to forgive Mrs. O. was her reception of Mrs. E.[5]

The friendship was interrupted and Mrs. Osgood and Poe seem not to have met after 1847. But she sprang to his defence on her own

[4] There is a question about the second woman. Gill states that Miss Lynch told him she never heard of the episode.

[5] Original Autograph Ms. Letter, Friday, November 24 [1848], J. K. Lilly, Jr. Collection. In this connection Mrs. Osgood's poem "Slander" in the *Broadway Journal*, II (August 30, 1845), 113, may refer to the rumors which hurt Virginia.

Ever with thee I wish to roam —
Dearest my life is thine.
Give me a cottage for my home
And a rich old cypress vine,
Removed from the world with its sin and care
And the tattling of many tongues.
Love alone shall guide us when we are there —
Love shall heal my weakened lungs;
And Oh, the tranquil hours we'll spend,
Never wishing that others may see!
Perfect ease we'll enjoy, without thinking to lend
Ourselves to the world and its glee —
Ever peaceful and blissful we'll be.

Saturday February 14. 1846.

A VALENTINE BY VIRGINIA

death bed in 1850. This eloquent tribute, from which I have already quoted, was printed, it is true, by Griswold, and the original has disappeared. Yet it rings true, and since it is in Poe's favor it is probably genuine.

There is an informal letter by Mrs. Osgood printed in the correspondence of Dr. Griswold [6] which is so different in its tone, as not to seem the work of the same woman. It is a defence of her actions, and seeks to prove that Poe sought her and that she did not descend to the tactics of the others: "It is too cruel that I, the only one of those literary women who did not seek his acquaintance,—for Mrs. Ellet asked an introduction to him and followed him everywhere, Miss Lynch begged me to bring him there and called upon him at his lodgings, Mrs. Whitman besieged him with valentines and letters long before he wrote or took any notice of her, and all the others wrote poetry and letters to him,—it is too cruel that I should be singled out after his death as the only victim to suffer from the slanders of his mother." In view of the *Broadway Journal* courtship, this sentence is rather quaint.

The echoes of his Boston episode did not prevent Poe from being invited in April to read a poem at the Anniversary of the Literary Societies of the University of Vermont in the following August, but he was unable to accept. He declined on the plea of ill health, and pressing engagements,[7] but he probably was too wise to risk another occasional poem, which he could not write. The same letter to Duyckinck asks for a number of autographs, which he was apparently planning to use in connection with the articles on the "Literati."

The year 1846 saw little of Poe's creative writing. "The Sphinx," a short story published in *Arthur's Ladies Magazine* in January, must have been written in 1845. It is a satiric story of a man who thinks he sees a huge animal on a distant hill, when in reality he has been looking at an insect of only one sixteenth of an inch in size, which is, however, barely one sixteenth of an inch distant from the pupil of his eye. The satiric purpose of the story is to call attention to the undue emphasis laid on Democracy by those who see it too near them. "The Sphinx" has its importance in revealing Poe's continued interest in the America of his own day, but the story is not in his best vein. One of his finest Arabesques, however, was probably written early in 1846,

[6] *Passages from the Correspondence of Rufus W. Griswold* (Cambridge, 1898), pp. 256-257.

[7] Poe to Duyckinck, April 28, 1846. Original Autograph Ms., New York Public Library.

although it did not appear in *Godey's* until the November issue. "The Cask of Amontillado" is a powerful tale of revenge in which the interest lies in the implacable nature of the narrator. By his apparent unwillingness to lead his enemy to his family vaults, he deepens his revenge. He hurls no reproaches at his victim, as he builds up the wall of masonry that will be Fortunato's tomb. For he knows that as Fortunato slowly dies, the thought of his rejected opportunities of escape will sting him with unbearable regret, and as he sobers with terror, the final blow will come from the realization that his craving for the wine has led him to his doom. There is not one word to spare in "The Cask of Amontillado."

Poe had been busy, however, in writing criticisms for *Godey's Lady's Book*. Poe's reviews in *Godey's* were dignified by being placed in a special department called "Literary Criticism" and were signed with his name, an unusual proceeding in those days. The only important utterance, however, in this department was his discussion of Bryant's poetry. While it owed somewhat to his earlier review in 1837 in the *Southern Literary Messenger,* Poe seized the occasion to publish a scathing description of the log-rolling methods of reviewing then in vogue. He defended Bryant against Griswold's criticism that Bryant was not versatile, had related no history, had not sung of the passion of love and had not described artificial life. Poe claimed that it was by these very omissions that Bryant proved he knew what were the legitimate themes of poetry. In *Graham's Magazine* for April, 1846, appeared one of Poe's major critical articles, his "Philosophy of Composition" in which he purported to describe the composition of "The Raven." I have already discussed this essay in connection with the poem itself.

The "Marginalia" in *Graham's* for March, 1846, were mainly trifles, but in one passage Poe developed his ideas on dreams in an interesting analysis of the fancies he was able to induce, just at the brink of sleep. To him the ecstasy which sprang from these fancies was "a glimpse of the spirit's outer world."

The *Democratic Review* was more hospitable to large installments of "Marginalia" than the other journals. In April, 1846, Poe discoursed at length on topics that varied from credulity and penance, to Longfellow and Carlyle. Poe inveighed also against hero-worship in literature, and observed that except for the inevitable reaction against Carlyle, "we might have gone on for yet another century Emerson-izing in prose, Wordsworth-izing in poetry, and Fourier-izing in philosophy." In the *Democratic Review* for July, 1846, there was a discussion of the decline of the drama, repeating some of Poe's essay [8] on the American Drama, but varying the language somewhat. Simms' volume of sonnets was highly praised and Christopher Pease [sic] Cranch was more tenderly treated than Poe's custom, when dealing with the Transcendentalists. This essay is a preliminary sketch for the article on Cranch which appeared among "The Literati" in the same month in *Godey's*.

In May, 1846, appeared in *Godey's* the first installment of "The Literati of New York City. Some Honest Opinions at Random Respecting their Autorial Merits, with Occasional Words of Personality." [9]

So much comment was occasioned by the May installment that Godey republished it in June, announcing that "the May edition was exhausted before the first of May, and we have had orders for hundreds from Boston and New York, which we could not supply." He also recorded the receipt of letters protesting against the criticisms by Poe, but asserted that he was not to be intimidated. To the reprint of the May number in June, Poe added some autographs, and the series belongs to the same division of his critical work as his earlier "Autography" papers. But he gave up this idea or could not obtain the necessary autographs, for no more appeared.

The perturbation on the part of the writers or their friends was in most cases unnecessary. Poe made clear in his introduction that he intended to reproduce the tone of conversation in literary circles in New York, while expressing his own unbiased opinions. He believed that oral judgments were more sincere than published criticism.

Nearly all of the thirty-eight authors of whom he spoke in *Godey's* have been forgotten, and of those who are now remembered, Poe's opinions have usually been ratified by the judgment of time. When he made a mistake it was more often on account of too great leniency, than of too great severity. The women generally were treated with gallantry, although there was some slight malice in his personal picture of Margaret Fuller. The accounts of Willis, Halleck, Catherine Sedgwick, Lydia M. Child, Anna Cora Mowatt, Caroline Kirkland, Christopher Pearse Cranch and Epes Sargent will remain valuable to the student of American literature.[10]

[8] *American Review*, II (August, 1845), 117-131.

[9] The six installments were published in: XXXII (May, 1846), 194-201; (June, 1846), 266-272, also reprint of May installment, 289-296; XXXIII (July), 13-19; (August), 72-78; (September), 126-133; (October), 157-162.

[10] For Poe's own opinion of "The Literati," see p. 523.

Considering Lewis Gaylord Clark's personal attack in his review of *The Raven and Other Poems,* Poe's picture of him, although a bit contemptuous, was mild. "Mr. Clark once did me the honor to review my poems, and—I forgive him. . . . He is noticeable for nothing in the world except for the markedness by which he is noticeable for nothing," [11] is the worst thing Poe said of his enemy. His statements concerning the *Knickerbocker,* Clark's magazine, are quite fair. But the *Knickerbocker* clique was the strongest in New York, and Clark was personally popular.

In a few cases Poe indulged in personal criticism unworthy of him. "Mr. Briggs," he remarked, "has never composed in his life three consecutive sentences of grammatical English. He is grossly uneducated." [12]

A letter from Poe to Field, the Editor of the St. Louis *Reveillé,* on June 15, 1846, shows that the first installment of "The Literati" papers had drawn an editorial attack from Hiram Fuller, the new Editor of the *Mirror* since Willis and Morris had left it. After a vitriolic account of Fuller's private life, which is of no interest to us here, Poe continued:

> All that I venture to ask of you in the case of this attack, however, is to say a few words in condemnation of it, and to do away with the false impression of my *personal* * appearance it *may* convey, in those parts of the country where I am not individually known. You have seen me and can describe me as I am. Will you do me this act of justice, and influence one or two of your editorial friends to do the same? *I know you will.*
>
> I think the "N. O. Picayune," which has always been friendly to me, will act in concert with you.
>
> There is, also, an incidental service of great importance, just now, which you have it in your power to render me. That is, to put the following, editorially, in your paper:
>
> "A long and highly laudatory review of his Tales, written by *Martin Farquhar Tupper,* author of 'Proverbial Philosophy,' 'The Crock of Gold,' etc., appeared in a late number of 'The London Literary Gazette.' 'The Athenaeum,' 'The British Critic,' 'The Spectator,' 'The Popular Record,' 'Churton's Literary Register,' and various other journals, scientific as well as literary, have united in approbation of Tales & Poems. 'The Raven' is copied in

[11] *Godey's Lady's Book,* XXXIII (September, 1846), 132.
[12] *Godey's Lady's Book,* XXXII (May, 1845), 295.

full in the 'British Critic' and 'The Athenaeum.' 'The Times'—the matter of fact '*Times!*'—copies the 'Valdemar Case.' " [13]

P. S. Please *cut out* anything you may say and en[close] it to me in a letter. A newspaper will not be likely to reach me.

I have been very seriously ill for some months * and, being thus utterly unable to defend myself, must rely upon the chivalry of my friends. Fuller knows of my illness & depends upon it for his security. I have never said a word about the vagabond in my life. Some person, I presume, has hired him to abuse me.[14]

* I am 33 years of age—height 5 ft. 8.
* Am now scarcely able to write even this letter.

Poe was also summoning aid, in preparation for the attack he knew was coming, in consequence of the "Literati" article on Thomas Dunn English. This article, published in the July number of *Godey's* [15] must have been out by June 20th, for English replied to it in the *Mirror* on June 23rd. Poe and English had been friends in Philadelphia and they had contributed to each other's journals. English claimed that he had loaned Poe thirty dollars to help buy the *Broadway Journal;* Poe claimed that English owed him money for an article on "American Poetry" for *The Aristidean*—this caused some feeling. Poe's explanation for the break is given in a letter to Hirst:

New: York—June 27. 46.

My Dear Hirst,

I presume you have seen what I said about you in "The New-York Literati" and an attack made on me by English, in consequence. *Vive la Bagatelle!*

I write now, to ask you if you can oblige me by a *fair* account of your duel with English. I would take it as a great favor, also, if you would get from Sandy Harris a statement of the fracas with *him.* See Du Solle, also, if you can & ask him if he is willing to give me, for publication, an account of his kicking E. out of his office.

I gave E. a flogging which he will remember to the day of his death—and, luckily, in the presence of witnesses. He thinks to

[13] Then follow quotations from Miss Barrett's letter, see Chapter XV, and minor details.
[14] Original Autograph Ms., Huntington Library.
[15] Vol. XXXIII (July, 1846), pp. 17-18.

avenge himself by lies—by [sic] I shall be a match for him by means of simple truth.

Is it possible to procure me a copy of E's attack on H. A. Wise?

Truly yours,

POE.[16]

Judging from these letters to Field and Hirst, Poe evidently felt that an organized attack was being made on him and that he had better strike first. His criticism of English even in its first form, in *Godey's*, was contemptuous and unfair. Poe referred to him as, "without the commonest school education . . . Mr. E. is yet young—and might with his talents, readily improve himself at points where he is most defective. No one of any generosity would think the worse of him for getting private instruction. . . . I do not personally know Mr. English." This was sufficiently galling to a man who had attended two good preparatory schools and graduated from the School of Medicine at the University of Pennsylvania, and Poe's denial of acquaintance with English was silly. Poe paid little attention to the writings of English except to accuse him of plagiarising from Hirst.

English replied in the *Evening Mirror* of June 23, 1846, in a vicious attack on Poe's morality and sanity, which even Griswold later said was unworthy of a man of his standing. It is fortunately unnecessary [17] to reprint it here. English repeated with additions all the unsavory details of the scandals circulated concerning the Ellet and other affairs, describing Poe as "thoroughly unprincipled, base and depraved, but silly, vain and ignorant, not alone an assassin in morals, but a quack in literature." He also made a definite charge that Poe had committed forgery.

Notwithstanding the vileness of English's language, Poe should have let the obvious intemperance of the attack defeat itself. But instead he sent to Godey a long reply, dated June 27th, which that editor declined to print. Godey secured its publication, however, in the Philadelphia *Spirit of the Times*, of July 10, 1846, paying ten dollars for the privilege. Poe literally tore English apart so far as his charge of cowardice was concerned. He had the manliness to admit the charge of intoxication and he gave an explanation which is of great value to his biographers.[18]

[16] Original Autograph Ms., Huntington Library.

[17] The entire controversy may be read in the Virginia Edition, XVII, 233-258.

[18] See Chapter I, in connection with his father's habits.

The specific charge of forgery Poe successfully disproved by publishing the letter of the merchant, E. J. Thomas, who had been the source of the rumor. Thomas cleared Poe fully of this charge. English published a second reply in the *Mirror* on July 13, 1846, daring Poe to sue him.

Poe instituted a suit for damages against Fuller and Clason, the editor and proprietor of the *Mirror*, in the Superior Court of New York City on July 23, 1846. English departed for Washington, fearing to be involved in a criminal action, and the Court appointed a commission to go to the Capitol and force him to make a deposition.[19] The defence could find no witnesses to establish the truth of English's charges, and Poe was awarded a verdict of $225.00 damages on February 17, 1847. It was a costly victory, however, from the point of view of his reputation. His own view of the matter was given later to Eveleth.[20]

A letter from E. J. Thomas to Mrs. Osgood shows the sordid level of the trial:

March 15, 1847.

You know the result of Poe's suit vs Fuller. It went as I thought it would for I always believed the article a *libel* in reality. I had strong apprehension that your name would come out under English's affidavit in a way I would not like, for I believed Poe had told him things (when they were friends) that English would swear to; but they left the names blank in reading his testimony so that a "Mrs ———" and "a merchant in Broad St" were all the Jury knew, except on the latter point which I made clear by swearing on the stand that I was "the merchant in Broad St." I got fifty cents as a witness for which sum I swore that Poe frequently "got drunk" and that was all I could afford to swear to for fifty cents.[21]

When Griswold published the *Literati* as Volume III of the *Complete Works* of Poe, in 1850, he substituted for five of the papers other versions, among them one on English entitled "Thomas Dunn Brown." This paper is more contemptuous than the actual version published in *Godey's*, stating that English's father was a ferryman on the Schuylkill, emphasizing English's supposed lack of education, and calling him "an ass." This paper was actually written by Poe and is now in manuscript in the Huntington Library. It is part of a projected book to be called *Literary America, Some Honest Opinion about our Autorial*

[19] The curious may find this in "A Close-Up of Poe," by Carl Schreiber, *Saturday Review of Literature*, III (October 9, 1926), 165-167.

[20] See Letter to Eveleth, January 4, 1848.

[21] Original Autograph Ms., Griswold Collection, Boston Public Library.

Merits and Demerits with Occasional Words of Personality, on which
Poe was working during 1846, 1847, and 1848. Griswold found this
manuscript and substituted it for the article in *Godey's.* Killis Campbell defended Griswold on the ground that Poe intended to publish
this paper in his *Literary America.* But the important point remains,
that he had *not* published it, and had not written the worst features
of it in 1846. Griswold's insertion of the later article as though it had
been published in 1846, makes English's reply apparently more jus-
tifiable. Poe's later article is dated 1848, and was written by him *after*
the charges of forgery made by English had been disproved and
English had become his bitter enemy. An author even of a foolish
paper, such as Poe's first sketch, is entitled to have it republished as
it was written on the date assigned to it.

According to a letter from Mary Hewitt to Poe, he had gone to
Baltimore early in 1846, probably to lecture, and had been ill while
there.[22] He had also been keeping his residence from her and the rest
of the literary society, for Mrs. Hewitt did not know where to address
him. There may have been method in his madness, however. There is
also a long and rambling letter from Dr. R. D'Unger to E. R. Reynolds,[23] which despite many obvious errors, seems to establish Poe's
presence in Baltimore in 1846, at least for a short time. D'Unger's
account of Poe's work on the *Patriot,* an evening paper, during 1846
cannot be reconciled with known facts, but his picture of Poe, mingling with the Bohemian crowd of newspapermen but always maintaining the reserve of a gentleman, can hardly be entirely imaginary.
D'Unger's statement, "The loss of his wife was a sad blow to him.
He did not seem to care, after she was gone, whether he lived an
hour, a day, a week or a year; she was his all," indicates that Poe was
in Baltimore in 1847 or 1848.

The family in New York spent a brief time at a farmhouse of Mrs.
John C. Miller, near what is now the foot of 47th Street. It was known
as Turtle Bay, and provided healthful surroundings for Virginia until
Poe could secure a home of their own.

This was found in a cottage at Fordham, in the district known as
West Farms, at that time thirteen miles out of the city.[24] When the
Poe family went there in May or June of 1846, there were farmhouses

---

[22] Original Autograph Ms., Mary E. Hewitt to Poe, April 15, 1846. Griswold Collection, Boston Public Library.

[23] Published by J. A. Harrison in the *Independent,* LXI (November 1,
1906), 1049-1050.

[24] Poe to Chivers, July 22, 1846.

THE POE COTTAGE AT FORDHAM

From a sketch by A. G. Learned, based on an old print. Reproduced
through the courtesy of the artist.

and cottages, lining at intervals the Kingsbridge highway. Near the present East 192nd Street, on the eastern side of the road, stood a small frame dwelling house of one story and an attic, surrounded by about an acre of ground. It was owned by John Valentine, who leased it to Poe for an annual rent of one hundred dollars. Valentine had bought it from Richard Corsa on March 28, 1846. The cottage during Poe's day stood close to the road, with lilac bushes and a cherry tree between them. There were three rooms, on the first floor, a sitting room, a small bedroom for Virginia and a kitchen. The attic was divided into two rooms, that were evidently unheated. From the piazza, Poe could look south and east over the grounds of St. John's College, and if he walked to the high point of the ledge nearby, he could even see the Long Island hills beyond the East River.

The cottage was an inspiration to him. In a letter to Mrs. Whitman, written in October, 1848, he paints a picture of an ideal life with her in a home which is a dramatization of the actual surroundings of the cottage, but is evidently inspired by them. In his published story, "Landor's Cottage," the picture of the house which attracted him on his walking trip begins: "The main building was about twenty-four feet long and sixteen broad—certainly not more. Its total height, from the ground to the apex of the roof, could not have exceeded eighteen feet. To the west end of this structure was attached one about a third smaller in all its proportions." These figures are close to the actual proportions of the Fordham Cottage, although Poe naturally did not limit himself to an exact photograph of the house. The surroundings, including the flowers and the birds in their cages enter, too, into the story. As was Poe's usual method, he idealized reality.[25]

A vivid contemporary description of the house and its occupants as they were in 1846 was given by Mrs. Mary Gove Nichols in 1863.[26]

[25] Owing to the encroachments of building operations, the cottage was moved in June, 1913, to its present location, about four hundred and fifty feet north, opposite Poe Park, the property of the city. The cottage is under the charge of the Bronx Society of Arts and Sciences. The old kitchen which had been destroyed was replaced in facsimile in 1917, and the cottage is well cared for. The history of the cottage, based on original search among the real-estate records is given in Henry N. MacCracken's "Poe at Fordham," read at the Poe Centenary Exercises, January 19, 1909, published in *Transactions of the Bronx Society of Arts and Sciences*, I (May, 1910), 21-36. This account is to be supplemented by *The Poe Cottage at Fordham* by Reginald P. Bolton (New York, 1927).

[26] *Six Penny Magazine*, February, 1863. Reprinted in full by the Union Square Book Shop, with an introductory letter by Thomas O. Mabbott (New York, 1931).

Mrs. Mary Gove, as she was known in 1846, before her divorce from her first husband, was described in "The Literati" as "a mesmerist, a Swedenborgian, a phrenologist, a homeopathist and a disciple of Priessnitz." [27] She and George Colton, who had accepted "The Raven," paid the Poes a visit:

We found him, and his wife, and his wife's mother—who was his aunt—living in a little cottage at the top of a hill. There was an acre or two of greensward, fenced in about the house, as smooth as velvet and as clean as the best kept carpet. There were some grand old cherry-trees in the yard, that threw a massive shade around them. The house had three rooms—a kitchen, a sitting-room, and a bed-chamber over the sitting-room.[28] There was a piazza in front of the house that was a lovely place to sit in in summer, with the shade of cherry-trees before it. There was no cultivation, no flowers—nothing but the smooth greensward and the majestic trees. . . .

Poe's voice was melody itself. He always spoke low, even in a violent discussion, compelling his hearers to listen if they would know his opinion, his facts, fancies, or philosophy, or his weird imaginings. These last usually flowed from his pen, seldom from his tongue.

On this occasion I was introduced to the young wife of the poet, and to the mother, then more than sixty years of age. She was a tall, dignified old lady, with a most ladylike manner, and her black dress, though old and much worn, looked really elegant on her. She wore a widow's cap of the genuine pattern, and it suited exquisitely with her snow-white hair. Her features were large, and corresponded with her stature, and it seemed strange how such a stalwart and queenly woman could be the mother of her almost petite daughter. Mrs. Poe looked very young; she had large black eyes, and a pearly whiteness of complexion, which was a perfect pallor. Her pale face, her brilliant eyes, and her raven hair gave her an unearthly look. One felt that she was almost a disrobed spirit, and when she coughed it was made certain that she was rapidly passing away.

The mother seemed hale and strong, and appeared to be a sort of universal Providence for her strange children.

The cottage had an air of taste and gentility that must have

[27] *Godey's Lady's Book*, XXXIII (July, 1846), 16. She was best known as an advocate of health reform, marrying in 1848 Thomas Low Nichols, a pioneer in that field. See *D. A. B.*, for interesting accounts of both.

[28] The house originally had two rooms on the first floor, but the third room must by all accounts have been added before Mrs. Gove's visit.

been lent to it by the presence of its inmates. So neat, so poor, so unfurnished, and yet so charming a dwelling I never saw. The floor of the kitchen was white as wheaten flour. A table, a chair, and a little stove that it contained, seemed to furnish it perfectly. The sitting-room floor was laid with check matting; four chairs, a light stand, and a hanging bookshelf completed its furniture. There were pretty presentation copies of books on the little shelves, and the Brownings had posts of honour on the stand.

After a walk in the nearby woods, Mrs. Gove Nichols tells how Poe split his shoes in leaping with some of the other men in the company. Mrs. Clemm was, as usual, equal to the occasion. She took the visitor aside and asked her to speak to George Colton about the poem which she had taken to him the week before. The practical nature of Mrs. Clemm led her to continue:

"If he will only take the poem, Eddie can have a pair of shoes. He has it—I carried it last week, and Eddie says it is his best. You will speak to him about it, won't you?"

We had already read the poem in conclave, and Heaven forgive us, we could not make head or tail of it. It might as well have been in any of the lost languages, for any meaning we could extract from its melodious numbers. I remember saying that I believed it was only a hoax that Poe was passing off for poetry, to see how far his name would go in imposing upon people. But here was a situation. The reviewer had been actively instrumental in the demolition of the gaiters.

"Of course they will publish the poem," said I, "and I will ask C—— to be quick about it."

The poem was paid for at once, and published soon after.

The poem was probably "Ulalume." Let us hope Mrs. Gove was more accurate in her statement concerning the payment than she was concerning the publication, for the poem did not appear until December, 1847.

The installments of the *Marginalia* which appeared in *Graham's* and the *Democratic Review* during the early part of 1846 had been written earlier, for Poe was too ill from February to July to write for the magazines.[29] He was not idle, however, when his illness permitted him to work. He spent the morning in what Mrs. Clemm called euphemistically "his study," and later worked in the garden or read aloud to Virginia and herself.[30]

[29] Poe to Chivers, July 22, 1846.
[30] Mrs. Clemm to Neilson Poe, Ingram, II, 89.

Two more installments of the "Marginalia" appeared in *Graham's* in November and December, 1846. A long passage on the principles that should guide translators has some valuable suggestions. Those critics who dwell heavily on the supposed influence of German literature upon Poe might read with advantage his judgment on German criticism, including his statement, "I am not ashamed to say that I prefer even Voltaire to Goethe, and hold Macaulay to possess more of the true critical spirit than Augustus William and Frederick Schlegel combined."

He was working on his projected book on "American Letters," preliminary extracts from it, such as the revised critique on Hawthorne and "The Rationale of Verse," appearing in 1847 and 1848. Magazine editors were evidently not printing his contributions as soon as he expected, for while he wrote Eveleth that the Hawthorne article was to appear in January, 1847, it was not published until November. How closely he kept secluded at Fordham, watching over Virginia, one of the two extant letters from him to his wife reveals:

June 12th, 1846

My Dear Heart—My Dear Virginia,—

Our mother will explain to you why I stay away from you this night. I trust the interview I am promised will result in some *substantial good* for me—for your dear sake and hers—keep up your heart in all hopefulness, and trust yet a little longer. On my last great disappointment I should have lost my courage *but for you*—my little darling wife. You are my *greatest* and *only* stimulus now, to battle with this uncongenial, unsatisfactory, and ungrateful life.

I shall be with you to-morrow [illegible] P. M., and be assured until I see you I will keep in *loving remembrance* your *last words* and your fervent prayer!

Sleep well, and may God grant you a peaceful summer with your devoted

EDGAR.[31]

What this business was is not clear. Perhaps it was the proposed publication of *The Literati* in book form, with autographs, simultaneously in this country and England, which is announced in an

---

[31] Ingram, II, 88-89. Mrs. Shew's copy of the letter, which she sent to Ingram, is now at the University of Virginia.

article accompanying a republication of "The Raven." [32] If so, it came to nothing.

What sacrifices he was making for Virginia are indicated by another interview with Mrs. Gove:

"Do reviewers sell their literary conscience thus unconscionably?" said I.

"A literary critic must be loth to violate his taste, his sense of the fit and the beautiful. To sin against these, and praise an unworthy author, is to him an unpardonable sin. But if he were placed on the rack, or if one he loved better than his own life were writhing there, I can conceive of his forging a note against the Bank of Fame, in favour of some would-be poetess, who is able and willing to buy his poems and opinions."

He turned almost fiercely upon me, his fine eyes piercing me, "Would you blame a man for not allowing his sick wife to starve?" said he.

This last sentence explains, perhaps, the charges that he was willing to substitute his own work for that of another if he were paid to do so.

If we accept his various statements concerning his health, Poe was too ill to do any work during 1846. He may have overstressed this condition, for he did not neglect his correspondence with other writers. A letter from Hawthorne shows what his closest rival in fiction thought of his judgment:

Salem, June 17, 1846.

My dear Sir,—I presume the publishers will have sent you a copy of "Mosses from an Old Manse"—the latest (and probably the last) collection of my tales and sketches. I have read your occasional notices of my productions with great interest—not so much because your judgment was, upon the whole, favorable, as because it seemed to be given in earnest. I care for nothing but the truth; and shall always much more readily accept a harsh truth, in regard to my writings, than a sugared falsehood.

I confess, however, that I admire you rather as a writer of tales than as a critic upon them. I might often—and often do—dissent from your opinions in the latter capacity, but could never fail to recognize your force and originality in the former.

Yours very truly,

NATH. HAWTHORNE.[33]

[32] *Philadelphia Saturday Courier*, July 25, 1846.
[33] Original Autograph Ms., H. B. Martin Collection.

A letter from Poe to Chivers gives some important personal information:

New-York, July 22 /46.

My Dear Friend,

I had long given you up (thinking that, after the fashion of numerous other *friends*, you had made up your mind to desert me at the first breath of what seemed to be trouble) when this morning I received no less than 6 letters from you, all of them addressed 195 East Broadway. Did you not know that I merely boarded at this house? It is a very long while since I left it, and as I did not leave it on very good terms with the landlady, she has given herself no concern about my letters—not one of which I should ever have received but for the circumstance of new tenants coming in to the house. I am living out of town about 13 miles, at a village called Fordham, on the rail-road leading north. We are in a snug little cottage, keeping house, and would be very comfortable, but that I have been for a long time dreadfully ill. I am getting better, however, although slowly, and shall get *well*. In the meantime the flocks of little birds of prey that always take the opportunity of illness to peck at a sick fowl of larger dimensions, have been endeavoring with all their power to effect my ruin. My dreadful poverty, also, has given them every advantage. In fact, my dear friend, I have been driven to the very gates of death and a despair more dreadful than death, and I had not even *one* friend, out of my family, with whom to advise. What would I not have given for the kind pressure of your hand! It is only a few days since that I requested my mother in law, Mrs. Clemm, to write to you—but she put it off from day to day.

I send you, as you request, the last sheet of the "Luciferian Revelation." There are several other requests in your letters which I know you would pardon me for not attending to if you only were aware of my illness, and how impossible it is for me to put my foot out of the house or indeed to help myself in any way. It is with the greatest difficulty that I write you this letter—as you may perceive, indeed, by the M. S. I have not been able to write *one line* for the Magazines for more than 5 months—you can then form some idea of the dreadful extremity to which I have been reduced. The articles lately published in "Godey's Book" were written and paid for a long while ago.

Your professions of friendship I reciprocate from the inmost depths of my heart. Except yourself I have never met the man for whom I felt that intimate *sympathy* (of intellect as well as soul) which is the sole basis of friendship. Believe me that never for one moment, have I doubted the sincerity of your *wish* to assist me. There is not one word you say that I do not *see* coming up from the depths of your heart.

There is one thing you will be glad to learn:—It has been a long while since any artificial stimulus has passed my lips. When I see you—should that day ever come—this is a topic on which I desire to have a long talk with you. I am done forever with drink —depend upon that—but there is much more in this matter than meets the eye.

Do not let anything in this letter impress you with the belief that I *despair* even of worldly prosperity. On the contrary although I feel ill, and am ground into the very dust with poverty, there is a sweet *hope* in the bottom of my soul.

I need not say to you that I rejoice in your success with the silk. I have always conceived it to be a speculation full of promise if prudently conducted. The revulsion consequent upon the silk mania has, of course, induced the great majority of mankind to look unfavorably upon the business—but such feelings should have no influence with the philosophic. Be cautious and industrious—that is all.

I enclose you a slip from the "Reveillée." You will be pleased to see how they appreciate me in England.

When you write, address simply "New-York City." There is no Post office at Fordham.

God Bless You
Ever your friend,
Edgar A. Poe.

P. S. I have been looking over your "Luciferian Revelation" again. There are some points at which I might dissent with you—but there [are] a 1000 glorious thoughts in [it].[34]

---

[34] Original Autograph Ms., Huntington Library. A notation, presumably by Chivers, probably refers to the English magazines noted by Poe in his letter to Field of June 15, 1846. There is also the title of an article from the *Reveillé*, copied from the *Home Journal*, dealing with Poe's fame "in Europe and America." This was probably the article "Edgar A. Poe" printed in the *Reveillé*, July 6, 1846. Dr. Mabbott has a copy of the original, now in the Jefferson Memorial, St. Louis.

Simms wrote him on July 30th from New York City where he was too busy reading proof to visit Poe, a long and friendly letter, giving him some good advice concerning the tone of his criticism, but declining to be drawn into any of the controversies.

A request from Poe to Cooke to continue Lowell's memoir on Poe brought a friendly discriminating letter from Cooke on August 4th. Poe, in reply, showed how well he could criticize his own work:

New York—August 9, 1846.

My Dear Sir, Never think of excusing yourself (to me) for dilatoriness in answering letters—I know too well the unconquerable procrastination which besets the poet. I will place it all to the accounts of the turkeys. Were I to be seized by a rambling fit— one of my customary *passions* (nothing less) for vagabondizing through the woods for a week or a month together—I would not —in fact I *could* not be put out of my mood, were it even to answer a letter from the Grand Mogul informing me that I had fallen heir to his possessions.

Thank you for the compliments. Were I in a serious humor just now, I would tell you frankly, how your words of appreciation make my nerves thrill—not because you praise me (for others have praised me more lavishly) but because I feel that you comprehend and discriminate. You are right about the hair-splitting of my French friend:—that is all done for effect. These tales of ratiocination owe most of their popularity to being something in a new key. I do not mean to say that they are not ingenious—but people think them more ingenious than they are—on account of their method and *air* of method. In the "Murders in the Rue Morgue," for instance, where is the ingenuity of unravelling a web which you yourself (the author) have woven for the express purpose of unravelling? The reader is made to confound the ingenuity of the supposititious Dupin with that of the writer of the story.[35]

Not for the world would I have had any one else to continue Lowell's memoir until I had heard from you. I wish *you* to do it (if you will be so kind) and nobody else. By the time the book appears you will be famous (or all my prophecy goes for nothing) and I shall have the éclât of your name to aid my sales. But, seriously, I do not think that any one so well enters into the

[35] This analysis of the ratiocinative stories is repeated almost verbatim, in Griswold's "Memoir," as Griswold's own criticism.

poetical portion of my mind as yourself—and I deduce this idea from my intense appreciation of those points of your own poetry which seem lost upon others.

Should you undertake the work for me, there is one topic—there is one particular in which I have had wrong done me—and it may not be indecorous in me to call your attention to it. The last selection of my Tales was made from about 70, by Wiley & Putnam's reader, Duyckinck. He has what he thinks a taste for ratiocination, and has accordingly made up the book mostly of analytic stories. But this is not *representing* my mind in its various phases—it is not giving me fair play. In writing these Tales one by one, at long intervals, I have kept the book-unity always in mind —that is, each has been composed with reference to its effect as part of *a whole.* In this view, one of my chief aims has been the widest diversity of subject, thought, & especially *tone* & manner of handling. Were all my Tales now before me in a large volume and as the composition of another—the merit which would principally arrest my attention would be the wide *diversity and variety.* You will be surprised to hear me say that (omitting one or two of my first efforts) I do not consider any one of my stories *better* than another. There is a vast variety of kinds and, in degree of value, these kinds vary—but each tale is equally good *of its kind.* The loftiest kind is that of the highest imagination—and for this reason only "Ligeia" may be called my *best* tale. I have much improved this last since you saw it and I mail you a copy, as well as a copy of my best specimen of analysis—"The Philosophy of Composition.". . . .

Touching "The Stylus":—this is the one great purpose of my literary life. Undoubtedly (unless I die) I will accomplish it—but I can afford to lose nothing by precipitancy. I cannot yet say when or how I shall get to work—but when the time comes, I will write to you. I wish to establish a journal in which the men of genius may fight their battles; upon some terms of equality, with those dunces the men of talent. But, apart from this, I have *magnificent* objects in view—may I but live to accomplish them!
Most cordially your friend,
EDGAR A. POE.[36]

[36] Original Autograph Ms., Young Collection, New York Public Library. The letter is not addressed, but several references make it clear that it is written to Cooke. I have omitted four paragraphs which repeat matters already treated in other letters such as Mrs. Browning's opinion of his work.

Poe naturally welcomed any recognition from abroad. On December 30, 1846, he wrote to Duyckinck:

> Dear Duyckinck,—Mrs. Clemm mentioned to me, this morning, that some of the Parisian papers had been speaking about my "Murders in the Rue Morgue." She could not give me the details— merely saying that you had told her. The "Murders in the R. M." was spoken of in the Paris "Charivari," soon after the first issue of the tale in Graham's Mag:—April 1841. By the enclosed letter from Stonehaven, Scotland, you will see that the "Valdemar Case" still makes a talk, and that a pamphlet edition of it has been published by Short & Co. of London under the title of "Mesmerism in Articulo Mortis." It has fairly gone the rounds of the London Press, commencing with "The Morning Post." "The Monthly Record of Science" &c gives it with the title "The Last Days of M. Valdemar. By the author of the Last Conversation of a Somnambule"—(Mesmeric Revelation).
>
> My object in enclosing the Scotch letter and the one from Miss Barrett, is to ask you to do me a favor which (*just at this moment*) may be of great importance. It is, to make a paragraph or two for some one of the city papers, stating the facts here given, in connexion with what you know about the "Murders in the Rue Morgue." If this will not give you too much trouble, I will be deeply obliged. If you think it advisable, there is no objection to your copying any portion of Miss B's letter. Willis or Morris will put in anything you may be kind enough to write; but as "The Home Journal" has already said a good deal about me, some other paper would be preferable.
>
> POE.[37]

Poe's reference to the *Charivari* was probably an error, but it is true that the first important analytical criticism of the *Tales* of 1845 came in 1846 from France. Poe's recognition in France began in 1845, when in the November issue of the *Revue Brittannique* appeared a translation of "The Gold Bug" entitled "Le Scarabée d'Or," and signed "A. B." Alphonse Borghers was, therefore, the first translator of Poe into French.[38] In September, 1846, the *Revue* also published "Une

[37] Original Autograph Ms., Duyckinck Collection, New York Public Library.
[38] *Revue Brittannique*, 5th Series, Vol. 30, pp. 168-212. Biographers have usually depended on the letter just quoted, or on Poe's statement in *Mar-*

Descente au Maelström," signed "O. N.," or "Old Nick," the pen-name of E. D. Forgues. In both cases, the stories were credited to Poe. In the meantime, *La Quotidienne,* a Paris newspaper, had published, on June 11, 12, and 13, 1846, "Un Meurtre sans exemple dans les Fastes de la Justice" a free version of "The Murders in the Rue Morgue," representing it as being found in the papers of an American. It was signed "G. B." and Poe was not mentioned. The rue Morgue became "rue de l'Ouest," Madame L'Espanye became Madame Duparc, "Dupin" was transformed into "Bernier," and there were changes tending to deepen the horror.[39] On October 12, 1846, E. D. Forgues published in *Le Commerce* a version of "The Murders" under the title of "Une Sanglante Enigme," without credit to Poe. Forgues had accused a rival paper, *La Presse,* of plagiarism and this journal seized the occasion to accuse Forgues of having copied his story from *La Quotidienne.* In his reply, he acknowledged that he had taken the story from Poe. *La Presse* refused to print his reply and he sued that journal, but lost the suit. The trial in December, 1846, and consequent discussion brought Poe's name prominently before the French public.

On October 15, 1846, E. D. Forgues published an extended criticism of Poe's *Tales* in *Revue des Deux Mondes.*[40] In a sympathetic and penetrating analysis, Forgues treated the *Tales* seriously and placed them for the first time in the great succession of English fic-

---

ginalia in *Graham's,* November, 1846, "Some years ago, 'The Paris Charivari' copied my story with complimentary comments," and his remark, "We have written paper after paper which attracted no notice at all until it appeared as original in 'Bentley's Miscellany' or the 'Paris Charivari.'" *Broadway Journal,* II (August 30, 1845), 125. A thorough search of the *Charivari* reveals no copy of the story or mention of Poe. The details of the law suit, incorrectly given by Griswold, have also been copied extensively, and the mythical "first volume of translations of Poe in French" by Madame Meunier in 1846, appears in a number of bibliographies. The correct facts were given by Louis Seylaz, *Edgar Poe et les Premiers Symbolistes Français* (Lausanne, 1923), pp. 37-45; more fully by Léon Lemonnier, *Les Traducteurs d'Edgar Poe en France de 1845 à 1875* (Paris, 1928), pp. 11-67, who gives interesting parallel passages of Poe's stories with the translations. C. L. Cambiaire, in *The Influence of Edgar Allan Poe in France* (New York, 1927), pp. 1-41, has also given the correct facts. All three seem to have worked independently, with the original sources.

[39] The searchers found the women's clothes in the bureau "tachés de sang." The bloody tracks led them to the chimney, where the body of the daughter had been thrust. Poe spared his readers such details.

[40] "Les Contes D'Edgar A. Poe" in "Études sur le Roman Anglais et Américain," XVI, new series (1846), 341-366.

tion. Instead of merely describing the stories, he tried to discover the underlying creative principle of Poe's fiction, and he found it in the triumph of logic over an apparent mystery, which is the basis of the novel and the drama. The Frenchman naturally was attracted by the logic of Poe, and it was this quality which maintained Poe's hold on French critics and readers. With Poe, Forgues pointed out, logic is the mistress, not the slave, and he weighs probabilities not by uniform precepts, but by an instinctive sagacity belonging to the man himself. Forgues analyzed first *Monos and Una*, the tale in which Poe took "au serieux" that brotherhood of sleep and death which so many poets have sung. He felt that Poe, probably for the first time, had given to the memories of a dead man the character of an exact definition and of a reasoned conviction.

"Eiros and Charmion" attracted Forgues through the verity of its scientific approach. He devoted three of the ample pages of the *Revue* to this "récit extraordinaire," retelling the growth of the terror as the comet relentlessly approached the earth, appreciating Poe's marvellous establishment of its effect by the sudden vividness of vegetable life, until the end comes in the flame of universal destruction.

Forgues did not know, of course, the dates of the first appearances of Poe's stories in magazines. But in his efforts to show a development in Poe's fiction, or at least to establish a classification, the French critic revealed a certain instinctive knowledge of a progress which later students of Poe, with more material to judge, still find interesting. Having attempted with success to deal with problems of the future life, Poe was drawn to seek a plausible explanation of the relations of the human soul and the divinity. To illustrate this phase, Forgues chose "Mesmeric Revelation," and showed his understanding of the lucidity of Poe's logic in the story, which I have discussed fully elsewhere.

Forgues was not always an understanding critic. His objection to the "paysan" who tells the story of the wreck in "A Descent into the Maelström," because he could not have thought out the theory of the cylinder which saved him, is beside the question. In the first place, he is not a "peasant" but a fisherman, and, in any event, the reader of that story has to swallow the initial improbability of the fisherman talking like a man of letters, and nobody bothers about it.

When it came to the stories of ratiocination, the Frenchman recognized that Dupin was not a name, but a human being, and prepared his readers by a description of Dupin's intellectual training for his analytic feats. Apply this perspicacity, Forgues said, resulting from a tension of mind almost superhuman, and from a marvellous instinct, to an "operation de police," and you have an investigator whom nothing escapes. He attributes this success to Poe's American tenacity. Forgues regretted that Poe should have chosen Paris for his scene of Dupin's exploits, although he recognized the valid reason why Poe placed them far away from Baltimore or Philadelphia. He remarked that of Paris Poe had not the least idea, and gave evidence of errors in localities which disprove the stories that place Poe at any time in Paris. Forgues was also bothered by the spectacle of the prefect of police visiting Dupin—again missing Poe's method. Indeed, Forgues' treatment of the ratiocinative stories is the least effective portion of his essay. He omitted any analysis of "The Murders in the Rue Morgue" possibly because of his own earlier translation, treated "The Purloined Letter" and "The Gold Bug" with scant mention, and selected for extensive treatment "Marie Rogêt," the weakest of the four. Even here he does not contribute much of value. But he recognized that "The Black Cat" and "The Man of the Crowd" represented Poe in another phase, that of poetic invention, though he neglected to treat "The Fall of the House of Usher," the greatest of all the stories in that category.

Forgues called attention to Poe's relation to Brockden Brown as a painter of obsessions of the soul and maladies of the spirit, and concluded by a comparison of the short story with the novel, to the advantage of the former. "La victoire," he said, "était hier aux gros bataillons. Elle appartiendra demain aux troupes d'élite." [41]

The *Tales* of 1845 continued to be the source of French translations. "The Black Cat," "The Murders in the Rue Morgue," "Eiros and Charmion" and "A Descent into the Maelström" were translated by Madame Isabelle Meunier in *La Democratie Pacifique* in 1847 and "The Gold Bug" in 1848. Baudelaire, whose relation to Poe would call for a separate volume, chose for his first translation "Mesmeric Revelation," which appeared as "Révélation Magnétique" in *La Liberté de Penser* in July, 1848. The first volume of Poe's stories to appear in France was the *Nouvelles Choisies d'Edgar Poe*, translated by Alphonse Borghers, Paris, 1853. Borghers reprinted his translation of the "Gold Bug" and added "Hans Pfaall" as "l'Aeronaute Hollandais." The great vogue of Poe in France belongs to the period after his death, but his foreign recognition was a source of unusual satisfaction

---

[41] *Revue des Deux Mondes*, p. 366. Forgues seems to have been unaware of the poetry or the critical work of Poe.

to him, even if he was not always exact in his knowledge or his statements regarding it.

Poe found intellectual and spiritual companionship during his life at Fordham with members of the Faculty of St. John's College. The College, opened formally in June, 1841, passed under the control of the Jesuit Order in the summer of 1846, just about the time Poe moved to Fordham. His cottage was not far from the grounds of the University, as it had just become, and Poe was a constant visitor, with the freedom of the College grounds. The Reverend Edward Doucet, S. J., afterwards President of the University and a young Scholastic in 1846, was a close friend of Poe and has left testimony concerning his habits at that time:

> "I knew him well," said Father Doucet, on one occasion. "In bearing and countenance, he was extremely refined. His features were somewhat sharp and very thoughtful. He was well informed on all matters. I always thought he was a gentleman by nature and instinct."
>
> Father Doucet always indignantly denied the statement so freely made that Poe looked like one worn out by dissipation and excess. The unfortunate poet had one weakness, a weakness that amounted almost to a malady, but against which he fought manfully and well. Poor Poe. His enemies, for he had many, made capital out of his weakness, and hounded him with an animosity and a persistency that would have broken a less sturdy spirit.[42]

Father Doucet was an accomplished musician, and no doubt Poe discussed with him the relations of music and poetry, and found pleasure in listening to his friend's playing on the College organ.

In the midst of his anxieties Poe found time to continue a correspondence with a young admirer, George W. Eveleth, of Phillips, Maine, to which we owe much first-hand information concerning his later years.[43]

---

[42] Thomas Gaffney Taaffe, A History of St. John's College, Fordham, N. Y. (New York, 1891), pp. 100-101. Mr. Taaffe, in speaking of Poe's cottage, then in its first location, made an earnest plea for its preservation, pp. 7-8.

[43] Eveleth's letters to Poe were printed for the first time by Thomas Ollive Mabbott, from the Mss. in the New York Public Library, in the Bulletin of the New York Public Library, March, 1922, pp. 3-27. A reprint was published separately in April, 1922, under the title of The Letters From George W. Eveleth to Edgar Allan Poe. I am indebted to Dr. Mabbott for the privilege of quoting them.

The letters represent Poe in one of his most attractive phases, that of a man taking the trouble to answer many questions of a young student of Medicine, who had no claim on Poe except his admiration of a great writer whom he never met. Sometimes Eveleth's criticisms are penetrating, but his main service lay in eliciting replies from Poe concerning points of importance.

Eveleth wrote Poe three letters, beginning December 21, 1845, before he received a reply, finally demanding the return of three dollars which he had sent for a subscription to the *Broadway Journal*. Poe replied:

New-York—April 16. 46.

My Dear Sir,

You seem to take matters very easily and I really wonder at your patience under the circumstances. But the truth is I am in no degree to blame. Your letters, one and all, reached me in due course of mail—and I attended to them *as far as I could*. The business, in fact, was none of mine but of the person to whom I transferred the Journal and in whose hands it perished.

Of course, I feel no less in honor bound to refund you your money, and now do so, with many thanks for your promptness & courtesy.

Very cordially yours

G. W. Eveleth, Esqe.   EDGAR A. POE [44]

After a long silence, Poe replied to a number of his queries:

New-York: Dec. 15/46.

My Dear Sir,

By way of beginning this letter let me say a word or two of apology for not having sooner replied to your letters of

---

Poe's letters to Eveleth were published by Ingram in his *Life of Poe*, "as letters from a young friend." These were printed in part from copies sent by Eveleth to Ingram. These copies are now at the University of Virginia. They were published by James Southall Wilson in the *Alumni Bulletin of the University of Virginia*, January, 1924, and a reprint was published, under title of *The Letters of Edgar A. Poe to George W. Eveleth*. Dr. Wilson printed the letters complete for the first time. I am indebted to his courtesy for permission to quote from his copyrighted edition. The original autograph letters, in certain cases, have come to light, and I have printed from these when possible. When not otherwise indicated, the letters are quoted from Dr. Wilson's article.

[44] Original Autograph Ms., W. H. Koester Collection.

June 9th and Octo. 13th. For more than six months I have been ill
—for the greater part of that time dangerously so, and quite unable to write even an ordinary letter. My Magazine papers appearing in this interval were all in the publishers' hands before I
was taken sick. Since getting better, I have been, as a matter of
course, overwhelmed with the business accumulating during my
illness.

It always gives me true pleasure to hear from you, and I wish
you could spare time to write me more frequently. I am gratified
by your good opinion of my writings, because what you say
evinces the keenest discrimination. Ten times the praise you bestow on me would not please me half so much, were it not for
the intermingled scraps of censure, or of objection, which show
me that you well know what you are talking about.

Let me now advert to the points of your two last letters:

What you say about the blundering criticism of "the Hartford
Review man" is just. [For the next two paragraphs, see Chapter XIV, p. 443. They deal with "The Raven" and are therefore
printed in the appropriate place.]

Your appreciation of "The Sleeper" delights me. In the higher
qualities of poetry, it is better than "The Raven"—but there is not
one man in a million who could be brought to agree with me in
this opinion. "The Raven," of course, is far the better as a work of
art—but in the true basis of all art, The Sleeper is the superior.
I wrote the latter when quite a boy.

You quote, I think, the 2 *best* lines in "The Valley of Unrest"—
those about the palpitating trees. There *is* no more of "Politian."
It may be some years before I publish the rest of my Tales, essays,
&c. The publishers cheat—and I must wait till I can be my own
publisher. The collection of tales issued by W. & P. [Wiley and
Putnam] were selected by a gentleman whose taste does not
coincide with my own, from 72, written by me at various times—
and those chosen are *not* my best—nor do they fairly represent
me—in any respect.

The critique on Rogers is *not* mine—although, when it appeared,
I observed a similarity to my ordinary manner. The notice of
Lowell's "Brittany" *is* mine.[45] You will see that it was merely a
preparatory notice—I had designed speaking in full, but something prevented me. The criticism on Shelley is *not* mine; it is

---

[45] In *Graham's*, XXIV (March, 1844), 142-143.

the work of Parke Godwin. I never saw it. The critic alluded
to by Willis as connected with the Mirror, and as having found a
parallel between Hood & Aldrich *is* myself. See my reply to
"Outis" in the early numbers of The Broadway Journal. My reference to L. G. Clark, in spirit but not in letter, is what you suppose. He *abused* me in his criticism—but so feebly—with such a
parade of intention & effort, but with so little effect or power,
that I—forgave him:—that is to say, I had little difficulty in pardoning him. His strong point was that I ought to write well,
because I had asserted that others wrote ill—and that I *didn't*
write well because, although there had been a great deal of fuss
made about me, I had written so little—only a small volume of
100 pages. Why, he had written more himself!

You will see that I have discontinued "The Literati" in Godey's
Mag. I was forced to do so, because I found that people insisted
on considering them elaborate criticisms when I had no other design than critical gossip. The unexpected circulation of the series,
also, suggested to me that I might make a hit and some profit, as
well as proper fame, by extending the plan into that of *a book* [46]
on American Letters generally, and keeping the publication in my
own hands. I am now *at* this—body & soul. I intend to be thorough—as far as I can—to examine analytically, without reference
to previous opinions by *anybody*—all the salient points of Literature in general—e. g. Poetry, The Drama, Criticism, Historical
Writing, Versification, etc., etc. You may get an idea of the manner in which I propose to write the whole book, by reading the
notice of Hawthorne which will appear in the January "Godey,"
as well as the article on "The Rationale of Verse" which will be
out in the March or April no: of Colton's Am. Magazine, or
Review.

Do not trust, in making up your library, to the "opinions" in the
Godey series. I *meant* "honest"—but my meaning is not as fully
made out as I could wish. I thought too little of the series myself
to guard sufficiently against haste, inaccuracy, or prejudice. The
book will be *true*—according to the best of my abilities. As regards Dana—it *is* more than possible that I may be doing him
wrong. I have not read him since I was a boy, & must read him
carefully again. The Frogpondians (Bostonians) have badgered
me so much that I fear I am apt to fall into prejudices about

[46] This refers to his "Literary America," see pp. 560-561.

them. I have used some of their Pundits up, at all events, in "The Rationale of Verse." I will mail you the number as soon as it appears—for I really wish you to tell me what you think of it.

As regards the Stylus—that is the grand purpose of my life, from which I have never swerved for a moment. But I cannot afford to risk anything by precipitancy—and I *can* afford to wait— at least, until I finish *the book*. When that is out, I will start the Mag.—and then I will pay you a visit at Phillips. In the meantime let me thank you, heartily, for your name as a subscriber.

Please write—and *do not* pay the postage.

Truly your Friend,
EDGAR A POE [47]

As the winter of 1846 drew on, Poe faced the realization of the sorrow that had threatened him so long. Virginia was dying, and to his natural grief was added the bitterness of knowing that his poverty forbade him even to bring the great love of his life to an end in dignity and peace.

Once more Mrs. Gove's story draws a picture etched with sympathy:

> The autumn came, and Mrs. Poe sank rapidly in consumption, and I saw her in her bed chamber. Everything here was so neat, so purely clean, so scant and poverty-stricken, that I saw the sufferer with such a heartache as the poor feel for the poor. There was no clothing on the bed, which was only straw, but a snow white spread and sheets. The weather was cold, and the sick lady had the dreadful chills that accompany the hectic fever of consumption. She lay on the straw bed, wrapped in her husband's great-coat, with a large tortoise-shell cat on her bosom. The wonderful cat seemed conscious of her great usefulness. The coat and the cat were the sufferer's only means of warmth, except as her husband held her hands, and her mother her feet.
>
> Mrs. Clemm was passionately fond of her daughter, and her distress on account of her illness and poverty and misery, was dreadful to see.
>
> As soon as I was made aware of these painful facts, I came to New York, and enlisted the sympathies and services of a lady, whose heart and hand were ever open to the poor and miserable. A featherbed and abundance of bed-clothing and other comforts were the first fruits of my labour of love. The lady headed a subscription, and carried them sixty dollars the next week. From the day this kind lady first saw the suffering family of the poet, she

[47] Original Autograph Ms., Berg Collection, New York Public Library.

Virginia

From the drawing made by Arthur G. Learned from the water color painted by an unknown artist after Virginia's death. Reproduced through the courtesy of Mr. Learned, holder of the copyright.

watched over them as a mother watches over her babe. She saw them often and ministered to the comfort of the dying and the living.

Mrs. Marie Louise Shew, afterwards Mrs. Roland Houghton, was the new friend who came to the rescue of the family. She had some medical training, and was distinctly different from the "literary women" who plagued Poe. Her help was practical and timely.

Poe's necessities became public through a paragraph in the *New York Express* on December 15, 1846, which asked his friends and admirers to come to his assistance. Another, less cordial, in the *Saturday Evening Post* of Philadelphia began, "It is said that Edgar A. Poe is lying dangerously ill with the brain fever, and that his wife is in the last stages of consumption—they are without money and without friends, etc." [48] It was this last sentence which stung Poe and hurt Virginia.

These notices prompted Willis to write an Editorial in the *Home Journal,* in which he raised the very proper question why illness of those whose pride forbade them to ask for help must remain uncared for. He then continued:

> Mr. Poe lives out of the city, and we cannot ascertain before this goes to press, how far this report of his extreme necessity is true. We received yesterday a letter from an *anonymous hand,* mentioning the paragraph in question, expressing high admiration for Mr. Poe's genius, and enclosing a sum of money, with a request that we would forward it to him. We think it very possible that this, and other aid, may be timely and welcome, though we know, that, on Mr. Poe's recovery from former illnesses, he has been deeply mortified and distressed by the discovery that his friends had been called upon for assistance. The highly cultivated women who share his lot, his wife and mother, are, we also know, the prey of constant anxiety for him; and though he vigorously resumes the labours of his poorly paid profession with the first symptoms of returning strength, we have little doubt that a generous gift could hardly be better applied than to him, however unwilling he may be to have received it. We venture, therefore, while we acknowledge the delicate generosity of the letter of yesterday, to offer to forward any other similar tribute of sympathy with genius.
>
> In connection with this public mention of Mr. Poe's personal matters, perhaps it will not be thought inopportune, if we put on its proper footing, a public expression, which does him some in-

[48] Quoted by Eveleth without date in his letter to Poe, January 19, 1847.

justice. We have not seen nor corresponded with Mr. Poe for two years, and we hazard this delicate service without his leave, of course, and simply because we have seen him suffer for the lack of such vindication, when his name has been brought injuriously before the public, and have then wished for some such occasion to speak for him. We refer to conduct and language charged against him, which, were he, at the time, in sane mind, were an undeni-'able forfeiture of character and good feeling. To blame, in some degree, still, perhaps he is. But let charity for the failings of human nature judge of the degree. Mr. Poe was engaged with us in the editorship of a daily paper, we think, for about six months. A more considerate, quiet, talented, and gentlemanlike associate than he was for the whole of that time, we could not have wished. Not liking the unstudent-like necessity of coming every day into the city, however, he left us, by his own wish alone, and it was one day soon after, that we first saw him in the state to which we refer. He came into our office with his usual gait and manner, and with no symptom of ordinary intoxication, he talked like a man insane. Perfectly self-possessed in all other respects, his brain and tongue were evidently beyond his control. We learned afterwards that the least stimulus—a single glass of wine—would produce this effect upon Mr. Poe, and that, rarely as these instances of easy aberration of caution and mind occurred, he was liable to them, and while under the influence, voluble and personally self-possessed, but neither sane nor responsible. Now, very possibly, Mr. Poe may not be willing to consent to even this admission of any infirmity. He has little or no memory of them afterwards, we understand. But public opinion unqualifiedly holds him blameable for what he has said and done under such excitements; and while a call is made in a public paper for aid, it looks like doing him a timely service, to [at?] least partially to exonerate him. We run the risk of being deemed officious.

The subject of a *Retreat for disabled labourers with the brain,* we shall resume hereafter.[49]

Poe wrote to Willis denying his extreme privation and that he was without friends.[50]

How widely Poe had become known is proved by the republication of the appeal in Philadelphia papers and through them in Easton and

[49] *Home Journal,* Editorial Page, Saturday, December 26, 1846. Photostat from Library of Congress.

[50] Poe's letter is quoted by several biographers from Griswold's "Memoir," under date of December 30, 1846. I cannot locate the issue of the *Home Journal* in which it is supposed to have appeared, and to quote from Griswold unsupported is, of course, dangerous.

other Pennsylvania towns. Their tone is friendly, as indicated by a sentence like, "Mr. Poe has many friends in this city, and we have no doubt that they would willingly aid in so benevolent a design." [51]

The day before Virginia's death Poe wrote to Mrs. Shew, who, after many visits of friendship, had gone into the city to make some arrangements for her comfort:

> Kindest—dearest friend—My poor Virginia still lives, although failing fast and now suffering much pain. May God grant her life until she sees you and thanks you once again! Her bosom is full to overflowing—like my own—with a boundless—inexpressible gratitude to you. Lest she may never see you more—she bids me say that she sends you her sweetest kiss of love and will die blessing you. But come—oh come to-morrow! Yes, I *will* be calm—everything you so nobly wish to see me. My mother sends you, also, her "warmest love and thanks." She begs me to ask you, if possible, to make arrangements at home so that you may stay with us to-morrow night. I enclose the order to the Postmaster.
>
> Heaven bless you and farewell.
> EDGAR A. POE.
>
> Fordham.
> Jan. 29. 47. [52]

Before she left the cottage, Virginia gave Mrs. Shew a picture of her husband, and a little jewel case. She also took a worn letter and a fragment of one from a portfolio, which Mrs. Shew read at her request. They relieved Poe of blame for the break with John Allan. So far Mrs. Shew's memory, when she sent these reminiscences to Ingram in 1875 may be relied on. But as always, romance and rumor, twin sources of inaccuracy, surround the contents of these letters, which have disappeared. That they were written by the second Mrs. Allan, as Mrs. Shew stated, is hardly possible, as we know that lady's nature. Perhaps they were from Frances Allan, written after Poe's flight from Richmond. The story of "Poe's Mary" who says that on this day, Virginia joined her hand to Poe's may also be sent to join the other vagaries of that lady.

Virginia died on January 30, 1847, in the tiny bedroom on the first

[51] *Easton Star,* January 5, 1847, from "a Philadelphia paper." I have not been able to identify this paper.
[52] Original Autograph Ms., Huntington Library.

floor. She was clad in the "fine linen sheets" which gave Mrs. Clemm such comfort, and buried in the vault belonging to the Valentines, the owners of the cottage. Years later Virginia's body was taken to Baltimore and rests now beside the husband she adored. But as "Ulalume" tells us, her love, entrenched in his memory, guarded him even against himself.

Poe collapsed, as was natural, after the prolonged effort to meet his daily anxiety. Mrs. Clemm and Mrs. Shew took care of him, and the latter, whose medical knowledge was more reliable than her acquaintance with the Allan family, gave this explanation of their difficulties:

> I made my diagnosis, and went to the great Dr. Mott with it; I told him that at best, when Mr. Poe was well, his pulse beat only ten regular beats, after which it suspended, or intermitted (as doctors say). I decided that in his best health he had lesion of one side of the brain, and as he could not bear stimulants or tonics, without producing insanity, I did not feel much hope that he could be raised up from brain fever brought on by extreme suffering of mind and body—actual want and hunger, and cold having been borne by this heroic husband in order to supply food, medicine, and comforts to his dying wife—until exhaustion and lifelessness were so near at every reaction of the fever, that even sedatives had to be administered with extreme caution.... From the time the fever came on until I could reduce his pulse to eighty beats, he talked to me incessantly of the past, which was all new to me, and often begged me to write his fancies for him, for he said he had promised to many greedy publishers his next efforts, that they would not only say that he did not keep his word, but would also revenge themselves by saying all sorts of evil of him if he should die.[53]

Poe, like any nervous patient, had his ups and downs. He received a long letter from Eveleth in January, 1847, who unfortunately sent him word of the charge of plagiarism made in the *Saturday Evening Post* concerning *The Conchologist's First Book*. Poe replied on February 16, 1847, demanding more facts and evidently being wrought up about the matter.[54] Eveleth sent him, on February 21st, the date

[53] Ingram, *Life*, II, 115-116; Rev. Ed., 330. Dr. Valentine Mott was then one of the leading members of the School of Medicine of New York University.

[54] See pp. 275-277, where Poe's explanation is given in relation to the original publication.

of the publication of the charge, March 14, 1846. But Poe decided that the slander was not actionable.[55] He added:

> My suit against "The Mirror" has terminated by a verdict of $225 in my favor.—The costs and all will make them a bill of $492. Pretty well—considering that there was *no* actual "damage" done to me.
>
> I enclose you my reply to English, which will enable you to comprehend his accusations. The vagabond, at the period of the suit's coming on, ran off to Washington,—for fear of being crim- inally prosecuted. The "acknowledgment" referred to was not forthcoming, and "The Mirror" could not get *a single witness* to testify *one word* against my character.
>
> Thank you for your promise about "The Stylus." I depend upon you implicitly.
>
> You were *perfectly* right in what you said to Godey.
>
> I can not tell you why the review of Hawthorne [56] does not appear—but I presume we shall have it by and by. He paid me for it, when I sent it—so I have no business to ask about it.
>
> Most truly your friend
>
> EDGAR A. POE
>
> P. S. The "Valdemar Case" was a hoax, of course.

That Poe was still capable of writing vigorous English is revealed in a letter to Horace Greeley on February 21, 1847. On February 19th, *The Tribune* had contained an unfavorable editorial concerning the suit against *The Mirror,* and after stating the facts Poe continued:

> You are a man, Mr. Greeley—an honest and a generous man— or I should not venture to tell you so, and to your face; and as a man you must imagine what I feel at finding these paragraphs to my discredit going the rounds of the country, *as the opinions of Horace Greeley.* Everybody supposes that you have said these things. The weight of your character,—the general sense of your truth and love of justice—cause these few sentences (which in almost any other paper in America I would treat with contempt) to do me a vital injury—to wound and oppress me beyond measure.—

[55] Letter to Eveleth, March 11, 1847, J. S. Wilson's edition, pp. 13-14.

[56] The review of Hawthorne's *Twice Told Tales* of 1842 and *Mosses from an Old Manse,* of 1846, appeared in *Godey's Lady's Book,* November, 1847. It is reprinted in Harrison, XIII, 141-155.

In the printed matter I have underscored two passages. As regards the first:—it alone would have sufficed to assure me that *you* did not write the article. I owe you money—I have been ill, unfortunate, no doubt weak, and as yet unable to refund the money —but on this ground *you*, Mr. Greeley, would never have accused me of being habitually "unscrupulous in the fulfillment of my pecuniary engagements." The charge is *horribly false*—I have a hundred times left myself destitute of bread for myself and family that I might discharge debts which the very writer of this infamous accusation (Fuller) would have left undischarged to the day of his death.

The end passage underscored embodies a falsehood—and therefore *you* did not write it. I did *not* "throw away the quill." I arose from a sick bed (although scarcely able to stand or see) and wrote the reply which was published in the Phil. "Sp.[irit] of the Times," and a copy of which reply I enclose you. The "Columns of the Mirror" were tendered to me—with a proviso that I should forego a suit and omit this passage and that passage, to suit the purposes of Mr. Fuller.

[remainder unimportant]

With high respect,
Yours etc.

EDGAR A. POE.[57]

Among those who had helped the family in their distress was Mrs. Jane Ermina Locke, a poetess of Lowell, Massachusetts, who sent Poe verses and some financial assistance. His letter to her, dated March 10, 1847, is so evidently a draft, corrected and recorrected,[58] that it has been made by some an argument for Poe's nervous instability at this time. But a reference to a similar draft of the letter to Anthon in 1844, will show that Poe was simply taking pains to write a tactful but courteous letter of appreciation. It would have been better for his peace of mind if he had dropped the letter in the waste basket. Mrs. Locke was to plague him later.

Poe attempted to repay Mrs. Shew by his verses, "To M. L. S——," in the *Home Journal*, March 13, 1847. They bear evidence of the deepest sincerity, which the free medium of blank verse emphasizes. Poe thanked her

[57] Original Autograph Ms., J. P. Morgan Library.
[58] Original Autograph Ms., Griswold Collection, Boston Public Library.

"For the resurrection of deep buried faith
In Truth, in Virtue, in Humanity.

The closing lines written

"By him, who, as he pens them, thrills to think
His spirit is communing with an angel's,"

show that the poem was written after Virginia's death.

In the same month "The Domain of Arnheim" appeared in the *Columbian Magazine*. Poe revised and continued "The Landscape Garden," of 1842, by describing the voyages of Ellison in search of the most suitable spot on which to build his paradise of natural beauty. Poe's own habit of canoeing is reflected in the approach to Arnheim by the river, and the luxuriant dream, Oriental in its coloring, is a visual echo of his own imagining as he drifted on the Wissahickon or the Hudson, or looked down from the High Bridge over the Harlem valley.

Poe went to Philadelphia in August, 1847, to reestablish his magazine contacts. An unaddressed letter, probably to Judge Robert T. Conrad, who was one of the editors of the *North American* and who was assisting George Graham with his magazine, tells a story that was often to be repeated:

New-York
August 10. 1847.

Dear Sir,

Permit me to thank you, in the first place, very sincerely, for your considerate kindness to me while in Philadelphia. Without your aid, at the precise moment and in the precise manner in which you rendered it, it is more than probable that I should not now be alive to write you this letter. Finding myself exceedingly ill—so much so that I had no hope except in getting home immediately—I made several attempts to see Mr. Graham and at last saw him for a few minutes just as he was about returning to Cape May. He was very friendly—more so than I have ever known him, and requested me to write continuously for the Mag. As you were not present, however, and it was uncertain when I could see you, I obtained an advance of $10 from Mr. G. in order that I might return home at once—and thinking it, also, more proper to leave you time in which to look over the articles.

I would be deeply obliged if you could now give me an answer respecting them. Should you take both, it will render me, just now, the most important service. I owe Mr. G. about $50. The articles, at the old price ($4 per page) will come to $90—so that, if you write me that they are accepted, I propose to draw on Mr. G. for $40—thus squaring our account.

P. S. I settled my bill with Arbuckle before leaving Phil. but am not sure how much I owe yourself for the previous bill etc. Please let me know.

Very gratefully your friend
EDGAR A. POE.[59]

Poe's most important publication of 1847 was "Ulalume," one of his original and powerful poems. It was published anonymously in the *American Review* for December, 1847, as "To ———. Ulalume, A Ballad." According to Mrs. Whitman, it was written after Virginia's death,[60] although the description of the poem Mrs. Gove made Colton buy in 1846 tallies with "Ulalume." It may have been begun in 1846, sold to Colton and revised in 1847. Poe never considered the form of any of his poems as final, and he told Eveleth that he gave Colton "Ulalume" in return for "The Poetic Principle," which Colton could not print.

In "Ulalume" Poe depicts a struggle in the mind of a man between the human passion for one woman and the spiritual love he still cherishes for the memory of his "lost Ulalume." They are symbols of the tragic conflict in a human soul which has lost without knowing it, its spiritual integrity. The same conflict had been expressed in prose in "William Wilson," and in "The Fall of the House of Usher," and in poetry it had been suggested in "Silence," "The Haunted Palace" and "Eulalie," but it received its supreme expression in "Ulalume." Nothing is so terrible to the living soul as this loss of identity. "Psyche," who accompanies the poet is, of course, the spiritual aspect of this soul. She sees the danger which the poet does not wish to see. He tries to lull her terrors, to conquer "her scruples and gloom" and he has almost succeeded, but she points to the tomb of Ulalume, who preserves through her love for the poet that integrity, and he is saved.

It is dangerous always to read much of a poet's personal life into

[59] Original Autograph Ms., University of Virginia Library. There is a letter, addressed to Conrad, on August 31, 1847, in which Poe refers to these details. A facsimile of this letter is in Dr. Mabbott's Collection.

[60] *Edgar Poe and his Critics*, pp. 28-29.

his verse. But if "Ulalume" is to have a meaning in terms of Poe's emotional conflicts, that meaning is clear. Virginia had fulfilled both sides of his nature, the spiritual and the physical. She died and he was adrift. He turned to others for that support he needed in the endless struggle and was about to delude himself with the love that is merely passion, when the memory of Virginia came to his rescue. If there were any need to refute the theories which deny to Poe the normal experiences of a man, and to Virginia, those of a woman, "Ulalume" would be an answer. Perhaps in advance Poe foresaw what psychoanalysis, the naïveté of science, would suggest. Fortunately this struggle for identity is essentially a universal theme, and the symbolism makes it unnecessary to search too minutely for the living or dead women whom Poe meant to represent. One side of his nature is drawn by Astarté, the Phœnician form for the Babylonian Ishtar, the goddess of fertility. She is associated in Babylonian astrology with the planet Venus, later with the moon goddess Selene. In "Eulalie," Astarté clearly meant Venus, and the star in "Ulalume" represents passion of the flesh. She is contrasted with "Dian" who usually is represented by the moon—and chastity. In the endeavor to solve the perennial dispute as to whether Venus or the moon is meant, I asked many years ago my colleague in Astronomy, Eric Doolittle, which of these planets would have been crescent in the month of October, early in the morning and would have come up through the constellation of "the Lion." "Both," he replied. That Poe knew enough astronomy to place the pallid star in the right spot is not surprising, since he walked on the promenade at High Bridge, at all times of the day or night. It is also not surprising that he forgot the fact that a planet does not "flicker" like a fixed star, but shines with a steady light. Dr. Doolittle suggested that Venus could not be seen crescent with the naked eye, but that would not have worried Poe.

The form of "Ulalume" in general is peculiarly fitting to the thought. The repetition of verses is organic, for it represents the conflict in the poet's soul as he comes step by step to the tomb. How perfectly the measure glides along is seen when the last stanza suddenly goes to pieces. This was published, however, in the *American Review*, and is in the copy he sent to Miss Susan V. C. Ingram in 1849,[61] so that while Poe omitted it in other versions at Mrs. Whitman's suggestion, he evidently thought it necessary.

In this connection Poe's letter to Miss Ingram reveals his unwillingness to make any clearer the meaning of "Ulalume":

[61] Original Autograph Ms., J. P. Morgan Library.

Monday Evening
[Prob. Sept. 10, 1849]

I have transcribed "Ulalume" with much pleasure, dear Miss Ingram,—as I am sure I would do anything else, at your bidding —but I fear that you will find the verses scarcely more intelligible today in my manuscript than last night in my recitation. I would endeavor to explain to you what I really meant—or what I really fancied I meant by the poem, if it were not that I remembered Dr. Johnson's bitter and rather just remark about the folly of explaining what, if worth explanation, should explain itself. He has a happy witticism, too, about some book which he calls "as obscure as an explanatory note." Leaving "Ulalume" to its fate, therefore, & in good hands, I am,

Yours truly,

EDGAR A. POE.[62]

Poe has been criticized for using words like "Auber" and "Weir," simply to provide easy rimes for "October" and "year." But "Auber" he knew as a French composer [63] and "Weir" is a well known family name in Philadelphia—Dr. S. Weir Mitchell being named after a member of it. The words fit into the tone of the poem; that is the important matter.

If Poe had temporarily lost his grip on life, he had not lost his power to express a great theme in verse of haunting and inevitable phrases.

[62] Original Autograph Ms., Morgan Library.
[63] See "Foreign Intelligence" in *Broadway Journal,* II, 356. "Auber has been seriously indisposed—he was unable to preside at the last meeting of the Conservatoire."

CHAPTER XVII

Eureka

As the new year of 1848 opened, Poe grew better in health, revived his plan for a magazine, and began new projects. A letter to Eveleth tells of his hopes:

New York, Jan. 4, 1848.

My Dear Sir—Your last, dated July 26, ends with—"Write will you not?" I have been living ever since in a constant state of intention to write, and finally concluded not to write at all until I could say something definite about The Stylus and other matters. You perceive that I now send you a Prospectus—but before I speak farther on this topic, let me succinctly reply to various points in your letter. 1—"Hawthorne" is out—How do you like it? 2—"The Rationale of Verse" was found to come down too heavily (as I forewarned you it did) upon some of poor Colton's personal friends in Frogpondium—the "pundits," you know; so I gave him "a song" for it & took it back.[1] The song was "Ulalume—a Ballad," published in the December number of the Am. Review. I enclose it as copied by the Home Journal (Willis's paper), with the editor's remarks—please let me know how you like "Ulalume." As for the "Rat. of Verse," I sold it to "Graham" at a round advance on Colton's price, and in Graham's hands it is still—but not to remain even there; for I mean to get it back, revise or rewrite it (since "Evangeline" has been published) and deliver it as a lecture when I go South & West on my Magazine expedition. 3—I have been "so still" on account of preparation for the magazine campaign—also have been working at my book—nevertheless I have written some trifles not yet published—some which have been. 4—My health is better—best. I have never been so well. 5—I do not well see how I could have otherwise replied to English. You must know him, (English) before you can well

---

[1] This does not agree with Mrs. Gove's account of the purchase of a poem which seems to have been "Ulalume," in 1846.

New-York – Jan. 4, 1848.

My Dear Sir – Your last, dated July 26, ends with – "Write will you not"? I have been living ever since in a constant state of intention to write, and finally concluded not to write at all until I could say something definite about The Stylus and other matters. You perceive that I now send you a Prospectus – but before I speak farther on this topic, let me succinctly reply to various points in your letter. 1. – "Hawthorne" is out – how do you like it? 2 – "The Rationale of Verse" was found to come down too heavily (as I forewarned you it did) upon some of poor Colton's personal friends in Frogpondium – the "pundits" you know; so I gave him a song" for it & took it back. The song was "Ulalume a Ballad" published in the December number of the Am. Rev. I enclose it as copied by the Home Journal (Willis's paper) with the editor's remarks – please let me know how you like "Ulalume". As for the "Rat. of Verse" I sold it to "Graham" at a round advance on Colton's price, and in Graham's hands it is still – but not to remain even there; for I mean to get it back, revise or rewrite it (since "Evangeline" has been published) and deliver it as a lecture when I go South & West on my Magazine expedition. 3 – I have been "so still" on account of preparation for the magazine campaign – also have been working at my book – nevertheless I have written some trifles not yet published – some which have been. 4 – My health is better – best. I have never been so well. 5 – I do not well see how I could have otherwise replied to English. You must know him, (English) before you can well estimate my reply. He is so thorough a "blatherskite" that have replied to him with dignity would have been the extreme of the ludicrous. The only true plan – not to have replied to him at all – was precluded on account of the nature of some of his accusations – forgery for instance. To such charges, even from the Autocrat of all the Asses – a man is compelled to answer. Here he had me. Answer him I must. But how? Believe me there exists no such dilemma as that in which a gentleman placed when he is forced to reply to a blackguard. If he have any genius then is the time for its display. I confess to you that I rather like that reply of mine in a literary sense – and so do a great many of my friends. It fully answered its purpose beyond a doubt – would to Heaven every work of art did as much! You err in supposing me to have been "peevish" when I wrote the reply: – the peevishness was all "put on" as a part of my argument – of my plan: – so was the "indignation" with which I wound up. How could I be either peevish or indignant about a matter so well adapted to further my purposes? Were I able to accord so expensive a luxury as personal and especially as refutable abuse, I would willingly pay any man $2000 per annum, to hammer away at me all the year round. I suppose you know that I sued the Mirror & got a verdict. English eat it. 5 – The "common mind" referred to is Miss Frances S. Osgood, the poetess. 6 – I agree with you only in part as regards Miss Fuller. She has some general but no particular critical powers. She belongs to a school of criticism – the Göthean, æsthetic, eulogistic. The creed of this school is that, in criti-

AUTOGRAPH LETTER FROM POE TO EVELETH, JANUARY
Reproduced from the original through

circing an author you must imitate him, ape him, out-Herod Herod. She is grossly dishonest.
She abuses Lowell, for example, (the best of our poets, perhaps) on account of a personal quarrel
with him. She has omitted all mention of me for the same reason — although, a short time
before the issue of her book, she praised me highly in the Tribune. I enclose you her criticism
that you may judge for yourself. She praised "Witchcraft" because Mathews (who toadies her)
wrote it. In a word, she is an ill-tempered and very inconsistent old maid — avoid her.
7 — Nothing was omitted in "Marie Roget" but what I omitted myself: — all that is mystification. The story was originally published in Snowden's "Lady's Companion". The "naval officer"
who committed the murder (or rather the accidental death arising from an attempt at abortion) confessed it; and the whole matter is now well understood — but, for the sake of relatives
his is a topic on which I must not speak further. 8 — "The Gold Bug" was originally sent to
Graham, but he not liking it, I got him to take some critical papers instead, and sent
it to The Dollar Newspaper which had offered $100 for the best story. It obtained the premi-
um and made a great noise. 9 — The "necessities" were pecuniary ones. I referred to a
sneer at my poverty on the part of the Mirror. 10 — You say — "Can you hint to me what
was the terrible evil" which caused the irregularities so profoundly lamented?" Yes; I
can do more than hint. This "evil" was the greatest which can befall a man. Six years
ago, a wife, whom I loved as no man ever loved before, ruptured a blood-vessel in singing. Her
life was despaired of. I took leave of her forever & underwent all the agonies of her death. She recovered partially and I again hoped. At the end of a year the vessel broke again — I went through
precisely the same scene. Again in about a year afterward. Then again — again — again &
even once again at varying intervals. Each time I felt all the agonies of her death — and
at each accession of the disorder I loved her more dearly & clung to her life with more desperate pertinacity. But I am constitutionally sensitive — nervous in a very unusual degree.
I became insane, with long intervals of horrible sanity. During these fits of absolute uncon-
sciousness I drank, God only knows how often or how much. As a matter of course,
my enemies referred the insanity to the drink rather than the drink to the insanity.
I had indeed, nearly abandoned all hope of a permanent cure when I found one in the
death of my wife. This I can & do endure as becomes a man — it was the horrible
never-ending oscillation between hope & despair which I could not longer have
endured without total loss of reason. In the death of what was my life, then, I
receive a new but — oh God! how melancholy an existence.
    And now, having replied to all your queries let me refer to The Stylus. I am resolved
to be my own publisher. To be controlled is to be ruined. My ambition is great. If I succeed, I put
myself (within 2 years) in possession of a fortune & infinitely more. My plan is to go through the
South & West & endeavor to interest my friends so as to commence with a list of at least
500 subscribers. With this list I can take the matter into my own hands. There are some few
of my friends who have sufficient confidence in me to advance their subscriptions — but
at all events succeed I will. Can you or will you help me? I have room to say no more.
                                    Truly yours — E A Poe.

4, 1848, EXPLAINING THE REASON FOR HIS DRINKING (No. 10) [5]
the courtesy of Dr. A. S. W. Rosenbach.

estimate my reply. He is so thorough a "blatherskite" that to have replied to him with *dignity*, would have been the extreme of the ludicrous. The only true plan—not to have replied to him at all —was precluded on account of the nature of some of his accusations—forgery for instance. To such charges, even from the Autocrat of all the Asses—a man is *compelled* to answer. There he had me. Answer him I must. But how? Believe me, there exists no such dilemma as that in which a gentleman is placed when he is forced to reply to a blackguard. If he have any genius then is the time for its display. I confess to you that I rather *like* that reply of mine, in a literary sense—and so do a great many of my friends. It fully answered its purpose beyond a doubt— would to Heaven every work of art did as much! You err in supposing me to have been "peevish" when I wrote the reply;—the peevishness was all "put on" as a part of my argument—of my plan:—so was the "indignation" with which I wound up. *How* could I be either peevish or indignant about a matter so well adapted to further my purposes? Were I able to afford so expensive a luxury as personal and especially as *refutable* abuse, I would willingly pay any man $2,000 per annum, to hammer away at me all the year round. I suppose you know that I sued the Mirror & got a verdict. English eloped. 5 [2]—The "common friend" alluded to is Mrs. Frances S. Osgood, the poetess. 6—I agree with you only in part, as regards Miss [Margaret] Fuller. She has some general but no particular critical powers. She belongs to a *school* of criticism—the Göthean, aesthetic, eulogistic. The creed of this school is that in criticising an author you must imitate him, ape him, out-Herod Herod. She is grossly dishonest. She abuses Lowell, for example, (the best of our poets, perhaps) on account of a personal quarrel with him. She has omitted all mention of me for the same reason—although, a short time before the issue of her book, she praised me highly in the *Tribune*.[3] I inclose you her criticism, that you may judge for yourself. She praised "Witchcraft," [4] because Mathews (who toadies her) wrote it. In a word, she is an ill-tempered and very inconsistent old maid—avoid her. 7—Nothing was omitted in "Marie Roget" but what I omitted myself:—all *that* is mystification. The story was

[2] Poe made a mistake in the numbering, using "5" twice.
[3] November 26, 1845.
[4] Play by Cornelius Mathews, dealing with New England. One of the best of the early dramas.

originally published in Snowden's "Lady's Companion." The "naval officer," who committed the murder (or rather, the accidental death arising from an attempt at abortion) *confessed* it; and the whole matter is now well understood—but, for the sake of relatives, this is a topic on which I must not speak further. 8—"The Gold Bug" was originally sent to Graham, but he not liking it, I got him to take some critical papers instead, and sent it to The Dollar Newspaper, which had offered $100 for the best story. It obtained the premium and made a grea' noise. 9—The "necessities" were pecuniary ones. I referred to a sneer at my poverty, on the part of "The Mirror." [No. 10 omitted here.] [5]

And now, having replied to all your queries, let me refer to the Stylus. I am resolved to be my own publisher. To be controlled is to be ruined. My ambition is great. If I succeed, I put myself (within 2 years) in possession of a fortune and infinitely more. My plan is to go through the South & West and endeavor to interest my friends so as *to commence with a list of at least 500 subscribers*. With this list I can, take the matter into my own hands. There are some few of my friends who have sufficient confidence in me to advance their subscriptions—but at all events succeed *I will*. Can you or will you help me? I have room to say no more.

Truly yours—

E A Poe.[6]

During 1847 Poe had been working steadily upon *Eureka*, his prose poem dealing with the universe. He read it as a public lecture on February 3, 1848, at the Society Library in New York before a small audience, the weather being unpleasant. *Eureka* was in press early in June, Putnam having generously made Poe an advance payment of fourteen dollars! [7]

The lecture was favorably noticed by the press, and the accounts were in general written by hearers who seemed to find no difficulty in understanding its general purpose. The *Courier and Enquirer* spoke of it as "a nobler effort than any other Mr. Poe has yet given to the world." [8] This paper reprinted a notice in the *Home Journal:*

---

[5] Refers to drinking and Virginia's illness. See pp. 347-348, or facsimile.
[6] Original Autograph Ms. In Collection of Dr. A. S. W. Rosenbach.
[7] Poe to Bristed, June 7, 1848, see p. 566.
[8] February 11, 1848.

EUREKA:

A PROSE POEM

BY

EDGAR A. POE.

NEW-YORK:

GEO. P. PUTNAM,

OF LATE FIRM OF "WILEY & PUTNAM,"

155 BROADWAY.

MDCCCXLVIII.

TITLE PAGE OF *Eureka*

We understand that the purpose of Poe's lectures is to raise the necessary capital for the establishment of a magazine, which he proposes to call "The Stylus." They who like literature without trammels, and criticism without gloves, should send in their names forthwith as subscribers. If there be in the world a born anatomist of thought, it is Mr. Poe. He takes genius and its limitations to pieces with a skill wholly unequalled on either side of the water; and neither in criticism, nor in his own most singular works of imagination, does he write a sentence that is not vivid and suggestive. The severe difficulties with which Mr. Poe has been visited within the last year, have left him in a position to devote himself, self-sacrificingly, to his new task; and with energies that need the exercise, he will doubtless give it that most complete attention which alone can make such an enterprise successful.

"His remarks on the subject"—the *Tribune* observed, "were characterized by the strong analytical powers and intense capacity of imagination which distinguish him." [9]

The *Weekly Universe* of February 12th was enthusiastic in its report, but remarked that Poe took two hours! The *Evening Post* and the *Express* also commented intelligently and it is hard to see why Poe was not satisfied with the cordial reception of the lecture.

Since *Eureka* was to a certain extent the climax of Poe's creative achievement, to which he had devoted so much time and effort, it is of great importance in his biography. An analysis of it will decide whether Poe's mind was weakening during these last years or whether it was clear, active, and still creative. For the true life of Poe lay in the mind of Poe. In the Preface to *Eureka* Poe said:

> To the few who love me and whom I love—to those who feel rather than to those who think—to the dreamers and those who put faith in dreams as in the only realities—I offer this Book of Truths, not in its character of Truth-Teller, but for the Beauty that abounds in its Truth; constituting it true. To these I present the composition as an Art-Product alone:—let us say as a Romance; or, if I be not urging too lofty a claim, as a Poem.
>
> *What I here propound is true:*—therefore it cannot die:—or if by any means it be now trodden down so that it die, it will "rise again to the Life Everlasting."
>
> Nevertheless it is as a Poem only that I wish this work to be judged after I am dead. [10]

[9] February 4, 1848.
[10] Edition of 1848, p. 5.

Poe asked, therefore, that the work be considered as a poem, but his modern critics have refused to accept this limitation. They insist upon judging it as a scientific treatise, and with a certain amount of reason in their position. If the scientific ideas in *Eureka* are wild and incoherent, or were written without knowledge of what had been discovered in Poe's own day, the essay may be dismissed as unimportant so far as its thinking is concerned. If, on the other hand, it is based on accurate knowledge of the latest scientific discoveries of its *own time*, then it is entitled from that point of view to respect.

No one would, I fancy, claim that Poe has solved the riddle of the creation and the destiny of the universe. But then no one else, scientist or philosopher, has solved it. It is likewise unwise to claim that he has anticipated the mathematical systems of Einstein and other contemporary scientific philosophers. It is enough and quite enough to note in what respect certain of his ideas resemble the greater discoveries of modern times, and to hear what Emerson called in another connection "the far off gathering of the intuition."

Poe explained *Eureka* more than once, in letters to his correspondents, and these abstracts are consistent. The most inclusive explanation was sent to Eveleth on February 29, 1848:

> The General Proposition is this—Because Nothing was, *therefore* All Things are.
>
> 1—An inspection of the *universality* of Gravitation—i. e., of the fact that each particle tends, *not* to any one common point, but to *every other* particle—suggests *perfect* totality or *absolute* unity, as the source of the phenomenon.
>
> 2—Gravity is but the mode in which is manifested the tendency of all things to return into their original unity—is but the reaction of the first Divine Act.
>
> 3—The *law* regulating the return—i. e., the *law* of Gravitation —is but a necessary result of the necessary and sole possible mode of equable *irradiation* of matter through space: this *equable* irradiation is necessary as a basis for the Nebular Theory of Laplace.
>
> 4—The Universe of Stars (contradistinguished from the Universe of Space) is limited.
>
> 5—Mind is cognizant of Matter *only* through its two properties, attraction and repulsion: therefore Matter *is* only attraction and repulsion: a finally consolidated globe-of-globes, being but one particle, would be without attraction—i. e., gravitation: the existence of such a globe presupposed the expulsion of the separative

ether which we know to exist between the particles as at present diffused: thus the final globe would be matter without attraction and repulsion: but these *are* matter: then the final globe would be matter without matter—i. e., no matter at all: it must disappear. This Unity is *Nothingness.*

6—Matter, springing from Unity, sprang from Nothingness— i. e., was *created.*

7—All will return to Nothingness, in returning to Unity.[11]

This abstract obviously needs amplification. Poe's general proposition [12] is thus stated:

"In the Original Unity of the First Thing lies the Secondary Cause of All Things, with the Germ of their Inevitable Annihilation." It is necessary to remember that Poe uses the "Universe" in two senses: "By the term Universe, wherever employed without qualification in this Essay, I mean in most cases to designate the utmost conceivable expanse of space, with all things, spiritual and material, that can be imagined to exist within the compass of that expanse. In speaking of what is ordinarily implied by the expression, 'Universe' I shall take a phrase of limitation—'the Universe of Stars.'" [13] He then proceeds to discuss the *Cosmos* of Alexander von Humboldt, to whom he had dedicated *Eureka.* He praised its approach to the problem of the Universe, but remarked that its detail prevents "all individuality of impression."

With a mistaken sense of humor, Poe introduced at the outset a note of burlesque which has probably discouraged many from reading *Eureka.* Yet in the discussion which ensued he makes some valuable suggestions. Knowing my own limitations, I have asked for criticisms of *Eureka* from my scientific friends. From the reply of Dr. Paul R. Heyl, Physicist of the United States Bureau of Standards, I quote the portion dealing with this early section of the essay because he puts the matter so clearly:

[11] Original Autograph Ms., J. P. Morgan Library.

[12] *Eureka,* p. 8.

[13] *Eureka,* pp. 8-9. Quotations are from the First Edition, of 1848. In certain cases where Poe modified the statements in a copy which he was evidently preparing for a new edition, I have made use of these corrections. The quotations represent therefore Poe's latest thought on the subject. These revisions are given in Virginia Edition, XVI, 319-336. I have made my corrections from Poe's Ms. alterations in the volume of *Eureka* now in the library of Mr. H. B. Martin. The "Addenda" and Poe's "Notes" (see the Virginia Ed., pp. 337-354) are too technical for quotation here and sometimes are not correct.

Poe discusses deductive and inductive reasoning as typified by Aristotle and Bacon. ... Poe rebels against both methods as slow and crawling. He lays emphasis on intuition, regulated of course by consistency. In this he is right. The ancients guessed and theorized about nature, but stopped there. They did not check their guesses by experiment. We guess also, but our guesses in the first place are guided by past failures, of which we have a vast accumulation, and in the second place by experimental check.

Poe's discussion of axioms is interesting. In 1848 the axioms of geometry were still regarded as self-evident truths. Poe questions this [assumption]. Our whole concept of geometrical axioms has changed, due to the work of Lobachevsky and of Bolyai, which resulted in non-Euclidean geometry. We now regard the axioms of geometry as mere space definitions. By leaving out the parallel axiom it is possible to develop a geometry quite different from that of Euclid, but just as self-consistent. True, it is inconceivable, but inconceivability no longer troubles the mathematicians. Nothing but inconsistency can do that.

Lobachevsky's first publications antedate 1848, but were not translated from the Russian until much later. Bolyai (a Hungarian) published an abstruse article in Latin in 1831, but it attracted little attention until 1866 when it was translated into French. It is impossible that Poe should have heard of these men and their work.[14]

In discussing the Universe Poe remarks that there are two modes; to begin with the Earth and proceed indefinitely, or, to be more intelligible, to begin with Infinity and come down to Earth. He chooses the latter and first attacks the problem of Infinity.

To him Infinity is not a word that is capable of comprehension. Man needed a term to point out the direction of the effort to comprehend this "thought of a thought."

There follows a brief statement of the "inessentiality" of the solution of the kind of problem to which the conception of Infinity belongs. Poe believed that the Deity has not designed it to be solved. Poe states here that "We believe in a God," and he meets in advance the kind of scientific thinking which refuses to discuss a problem as soon as the conception of a Deity is brought into the discussion. There is, however, quite another school of scientific thought which is content to say "We are uneasy that there should be an apparently self-con-

[14] I am quoting certain portions of this letter verbatim, because it is only fair to Dr. Heyl to state that his opinions concerning the general theories of *Eureka* do not coincide with mine.

tained world in which God becomes an unnecessary hypothesis." [15]
Poe continues, "It may be said that no fog of the mind can well be
greater than that which, extending to the very boundaries of the
mental domain, shuts out even these boundaries themselves from comprehension." After this blow at the dogmatism of science, Poe proceeds with a certain humility to define his terms: "In using the phrase,
'Infinity of Space' I make no call upon the reader to entertain the
impossible conception of an absolute infinity. I refer simply to the
'*utmost conceivable expanse*' of space—a shadowy and fluctuating domain, now shrinking, now swelling, with the vacillating energies of
the imagination."

For obvious reasons, I take Einstein's doctrine of Relativity in a
diluted form. But it is interesting in connection with Poe's attitude
toward infinity to quote again from one of the foremost astronomers
of today: "I think Einstein showed his greatness in the simple and
drastic way in which he disposed of difficulties at infinity. He abolished infinity." [16]

Poe adopts the definition of Pascal for the Universe. "It is a sphere,"
he says, "of which the centre is everywhere, the circumference, nowhere." This is for Poe's Universe, the Universe of Space.

Poe adopts the Godhead as his starting point, and quoting from
Baron Bielfeld: "In order to comprehend what He is, we should have
to be God ourselves," he wonders whether "this present ignorance of
God is an ignorance to which the soul is everlastingly condemned."

It is striking that Poe, like Emerson, assuming God as "Spirit—that
is to say, as *not Matter*"—proceeds to state that Spirit created—*what?*
"*What* is it that we are justified—that alone we are justified in supposing to have been primarily *created?*" Here again, like Emerson,
Poe says, "We have attained a point where only *Intuition* can aid us."

Poe then states that his intuition forces him to the conclusion "that
what God originally created,—that that Matter which, by dint of his
Volition, he first made from his Spirit, or from Nihility, could have
been nothing but Matter in its utmost conceivable state of—what?—of
Simplicity."

Poe is certain of this intuition, but adds that the processes lie outside of the human analysis—at all events are beyond the utterance of
the human tongue. In the revised version, Poe inserted a sentence:

[15] Sir Arthur Eddington, *The Nature of the Physical World* (New York
and Cambridge, 1930), p. 281.

[16] Sir Arthur Eddington, *The Expanding Universe* (Cambridge and New
York, 1933), p. 31.

"If, however, in the course of this Essay, I succeed in showing that, out of Matter in its extreme of Simplicity, all things *might* have been constructed, we reach directly the inference that they *were* thus constructed, through the impossibility of attributing supererogation to omnipotence."

Poe considers then the nature of Matter in its simplicity. He decides that it must consist of "a particle—absolutely unique, individual, undivided, and not indivisible only because He who created it, by dint of his Will, can by an infinitely less energetic exercise of the same Will, as a matter of course, divide it." He then proposes to show "that this Oneness is a principle abundantly sufficient to account for the constitution, the existing phaenomena and the plainly inevitable annihilation of at least the material Universe."

Here Poe brings in his favorite principle of "variety out of unity." "The assumption of absolute Unity in the primordial Particle includes that of infinite divisibility." [17] "From the one Particle, as a centre, let us suppose to be radiated [18] spherically—in all directions—to immeasurable but still to definite distances in the previously vacant space— a certain inexpressibly great yet limited number of unimaginably yet not infinitely minute atoms."

Here is where Poe speaks first of the "utmost possible multiplicity of *relation* out of the emphatically irrelative *One*." He decides, however, that other forms of variety can be assumed from a *difference of form*, occurring at the first processes of mass-constitution. When the act of creation has been discontinued there comes at once "a reaction—in other words, a satisfiable tendency of the disunited atoms to return into One. But the diffusive energy being withdrawn, and the reaction having commenced in furtherance of the ultimate design—*that of the utmost possible Relation*—this design is now in danger of being frustrated, in detail, by reason of that very tendency to return which is to effect its accomplishment in general."

Poe here speculates upon the necessity of a repulsive force setting a limit to the coalition of atoms, up to a certain epoch. This I think is not very clear; and he acknowledges it. But he states that "Man neither employs, nor knows, a force sufficient to bring two atoms into contact. This is but the well established proposition of the impenetrability of matter."

Poe then develops the theory that electricity arises from the differ-

[17] In the revision Poe makes a note to "show this in another edition."
[18] In the original edition Poe used the term "irradiated" throughout.

ences in the respective sums of atoms of which the bodies are composed. He suggests that electricity may account for the physical appearance of light, heat and magnetism, but "far less shall we be liable to err in attributing to this strictly spiritual principle the more important phaenomena of vitality, consciousness and *Thought.*"

Poe, feeling perhaps that he was on less certain ground here, discards the terms "gravitation" and "electricity" and adopts the terms "Attraction" and "Repulsion." "The former is the Body; the latter the Soul; the one is the material; the other the spiritual, principle of the Universe. *No other principles exist.*" ... "So rigorously is this the case —so thoroughly demonstrable is it that Attraction and Repulsion are the sole properties through which we perceive the Universe—in other words, by which Matter is manifested to Mind—that for all merely argumentative purposes, we are fully justified in assuming that matter *exists* only as Attraction and Repulsion—that Attraction and Repulsion *are* matter;—there being no conceivable case in which we may not employ the term 'Matter' and the terms 'Attraction' and 'Repulsion' taken together, as equivalent, and therefore convertible, expressions in Logic."

Again Poe's idea is strangely modern. George Norstedt, quoting from Charles Nordman's "Einstein and the Universe," [19] says: "'All this [the result of Modern Research] irresistibly compels us to think that the inertia of the various component parts of atoms—that is to say of all matter—is exclusively electromagnetic in origin. There is now no matter. There is only electrical energy, which by the reaction of the surrounding medium upon it, leads us to the fallacious belief in the existence of this substantial and massive something which hundreds of generations have been wont to call "matter". . . . There is nothing but energy in the external universe. A strange—in a sense, an almost spiritual turn for physics to take.' This strange turn of modern physics Poe anticipated."

Poe then proceeds with a modification of the Newtonian law, saying that not only every body but *"every atom of every body, attracts every other atom, both of its own and of every other body, with a force which varies inversely as the squares of the distance between the attracting and attracted atom."* Believing that such a conception should not be limited to this planet, he claims that every earthly thing has "a tendency not only to the Earth's centre but in every conceivable

[19] See George Norstedt, "Poe and Einstein," *Open Court,* XLIV (1930), 173-180—passage quoted on p. 175.

direction besides." He shows his understanding of the logical consequences of this relation of the atoms, for it leads to influences beyond
the grasp of the imagination. "If I venture to displace, by even the
billionth part of an inch, the microscopical speck of dust which lies
now upon the point of my finger, what is the character of that act
upon which I have adventured? I have done a deed which shakes the
Moon in her path, which causes the Sun to be no longer the Sun, and
which alters forever the destiny of the multitudinous myriads of stars
that roll and glow in the majestic presence of their Creator." It is in
such a conception that Poe truly arrives at the imaginative scope of
a prose poem.

Those who smile at these visions, have not seen such a profound
and moving play as *Wings over Europe,* by Robert Nichols and Maurice Brown, which was based on a similar theory.[20] Some of the lines
read as though they had been taken out of Poe's essay.

The confidence of Poe in his theory is complete. "I am not so sure
that I speak and see,—that my heart beats and that my soul lives;—of
the rising of tomorrow's sun— ... as I am of the irretrievably bygone
Fact that 'All things and All Thoughts of Things with all their ineffable
Multiplicity of Relation, sprang at once into being from the primordial
and irrelative *One.*'"

Poe then takes up a difficulty of his theory, that of reconciling
radiation from a center, not continuous radiation, such as light usually
presumes, but of determinate radiation, that is, one finally discontinued, with generally equable distribution of Stars. It is interesting to
see that he speaks of this difficulty as a cloud which led him to the
ultimate solution, just as in *Murders in the Rue Morgue* apparent
difficulties led to a solution. Poe assumes a radiating force, emitting a
number of atoms and forcing them outward from a centre till they are
distributed loosely over the interior surface of a sphere—then another
exercise of the same force sending others out, in concentric strata, till
they come down at length to the central point. In the revision of
Eureka there is a note: "Here describe the process as one instanta-
neous flash." These atoms are equably distributed and the force by
which any individual atom was sent to its position in the sphere, was
directly proportional with the square of that atom's distance, while in
that position, from the centre of the sphere.

Frankly, I do not see why Poe's theory of a universe, starting from

[20] Produced first in the United States by the Theatre Guild at the Martin
Beck Theatre, New York, December 10, 1928.

nothing, and proceeding rapidly from an atom by radiation to a closed yet indeterminate sphere, is absurd. Eddington, in speaking of the start of things, objects to the theory of Einstein and de Sitter "that in the beginning all the matter created was projected wih a radial motion so as to disperse even faster than the present rate of dispersal of the galaxies." [21] I am not able to analyze the equations in which Einstein and de Sitter express this theory, and they do not state it in words. But as Eddington describes it, it suggests essential elements of Poe's theory of radiation. Eddington prefers a balanced universe, at the beginning, of homogeneous matter. And then he adds "To my mind *undifferentiated sameness* and *nothingness* cannot be distinguished philosophically." [22] Certainly I do not care to distinguish them, but at least Poe's "nothingness" has respectable company. I am more inclined to agree with another statement of Eddington: "The beginning seems to present innumerable difficulties unless we agree to look on it as frankly supernatural." [23]

Gravity, Poe claims, is a reaction, therefore, the desire of Matter to return to the Unity from which it came. He then takes up the tendency of the atoms to return to the centre,—not a centre in space but a *condition* of unity—because along the straight line joining the atom and the centre there are a greater number of atoms than along any other straight line. Poe concludes this branch of the subject with a restatement of his law: "I am fully warranted in announcing that *the Law which we have been in the habit of calling Gravity exists on account of Matter's having been radiated, at its origin, atomically, into a limited sphere of Space, from one, individual, unconditional, irrelative, and absolute Particle Proper, by the sole process in which it was possible to satisfy, at the same time, the two conditions, radiation, and generally-equable distribution throughout the sphere—that is to say, by a force varying in direct proportion with the squares of the distances between the radiated atoms, respectively, and the Particular centre of Radiation."*

The poetic interpretation of this law is that "the two principles, *Attraction* and *Repulsion*—the Material and the Spiritual—accompany each other, in the strictest fellowship, forever. Thus *The Body and The Soul walk hand in hand.*"

Poe then proceeds to take up one of the agglomerations of atoms, namely, our Solar System, and describes Laplace's Nebular Hypoth-

[21] *The Expanding Universe*, p. 80.
[22] *The Expanding Universe*, p. 82.
[23] *The Expanding Universe*, p. 178.

esis. His description of the hypothesis is clear, although his statement that it is "beautifully true" is not in accord with modern astronomy. Astronomers, nevertheless, treat it with the greatest respect.

Poe's presentation of astronomical phenomena was on the whole accurate. He was mistaken in believing the Moon self-luminous, but his scientific attitude is shown in his remark that the demonstration by Comte that the Nebular Hypothesis is in accord with the planetary system, does not prove the Hypothesis. It would be necessary to prove that no other series of data might equally as well account for the result.

Poe understood well the relative aspect of the Universe, although his conclusions concerning the Nebulae are not correct. He quotes Lord Rosse's supposed resolution of Orion Nebula into a simple collection of stars, now known to have been impossible. But his arguments against the existence of true nebulae, while incorrect, may be pardoned, since Poe could naturally not foresee the investigations which, through the spectroscope, show innumerable nebulae. One passage, however, has a strikingly modern quality:

> Of course, it will be immediately objected that since the light by which we recognize the nebulae now, must be merely that which left their surfaces a vast number of years ago, the processes at present observed, or supposed to be observed, are, in fact, *not* processes now actually going on, but the phantoms of processes completed long in the Past—just as I maintain all these mass-constitutive processes *must* have been.

Compare this with Sir Arthur Eddington's description:

> This brings us to the "theory of ghosts"—an idea developed more as a mathematical curiosity than as a serious physical speculation. In a perfectly spherical world rays of light emitted in all directions from a point will after travelling round the world converge to the same point; thus a real image is formed from which light will again diverge in all directions. Such an image might optically be mistaken for a substantial body. Owing to the time taken in circumambulating the world the image is not formed until at least 6000 million years later than its source. Other images would be formed after two circuits, three circuits, etc. We can thus imagine space to be populated not only with real stars and galaxies but with ghosts of stars which existed 6000 million, 12000 million, etc. years ago.[24]

[24] *The Expanding Universe*, p. 109-110.

Poe's description of the shape of our Galaxy and the Sun's position within it shows a keen perception of the vastness of the Galaxy. Although I cannot reproduce his lengthy description, it remains one more illustration of his ability at a brilliant portraiture of astronomical phenomena.[25]

Next comes one of the most interesting contributions of Poe, his conception of the Universe of Stars as not illimitable but finite. "Were the succession of stars endless, then the background of the sky would present us an uniform luminosity, like that displayed by the Galaxy—*since there could be absolutely no point, in all that background, at which would not exist a star.*"

Again Eddington, though with some difference of meaning, speaks of the whole volume of spherical space as finite. "It is," he says, " 'finite but unbounded'; we never come to a boundary, but . . . we can never be more than a limited distance away from our starting point. In the theory I am going to describe the galaxies are supposed to be distributed throughout a closed space of this kind." [26]

On the other hand, Poe saw no reason why there could not be other Universes, "each in the bosom of its own proper and particular God." He makes no attempt to prove this, believing it impossible of proof. Philosophers have usually treated this idea with the same detachment.[27]

Poe then proceeds to expound more definite conceptions of the solar system. He evidently knew the velocity of light and the general dimensions of the Solar System, and makes clear the immensity of the distances between the sun and the planets. He had also correct ideas of the distances of the stars. Poe quotes correctly and with judgment the great German astronomer, F. W. Bessel, on the distance of 61 Cygni, which Bessel had announced in 1838. Poe's explanation of parallax is clear and effective.

As the distances grow more vast, Poe rises to a high level of clarity in his interpretation to a lay audience of the wonders of the Universe of Stars:

And here, once again and finally, it seems proper to suggest that even as yet we have been speaking of trifles. Ceasing to wonder at the space between star and star in our own or in any

[25] See especially pages 96-99, 1848 ed.
[26] *The Expanding Universe*, p. 50. See also his *Nature of the Physical World*, p. 80.
[27] See Eddington, *The Expanding Universe*, p. 19.

particular cluster, let us rather turn our thoughts to the intervals between cluster and cluster, in the all comprehensive cluster of the Universe.

I have already said that light proceeds at the rate of 167,000 miles in a second—that is, about 10 millions of miles in a minute, or about 600 millions of miles in an hour:—yet so far removed from us are some of the "nebulae" that even light, speeding with this velocity, could not and does not reach us, from those mysterious regions, in less than 3 *millions of years*. This calculation, moreover, is made by the elder Herschell, and in reference merely to those comparatively proximate clusters within the scope of his own telescope. There *are* "nebulae," however, which, through the magical tube of Lord Rosse, are this instant whispering in our ears the secrets of *a million of ages* by-gone. In a word, the events which we behold now—at this moment—in those worlds—are the identical events which interested their inhabitants *ten hundred thousand centuries ago*. In intervals—in distances such as this suggestion forces upon the *soul*—rather than upon the mind—we find, at length, a fitting climax to all hitherto frivolous considerations of *quantity*.

This conception of the "Island Universe" distances which he tells us he obtained from the elder Herschell, is again held today after a long period of disbelief. The proof, which came about twenty years ago, through the resolution of the edges of the spiral nebulae into stars, is another instance of Poe's acceptance of a hypothesis, in which he judged correctly between different scientific schools of thought.

Poe then lets his imagination consider the difficulty experienced by astronomy in explaining the vast spaces apparently left void between stars. He explains this phenomenon by saying that *Space and Duration are one*. "That the Universe of Stars might endure throughout an aera at all commensurate with the grandeur of its component material portions and with the high majesty of its spiritual purposes, it was necessary that the original atomic diffusion be made to so inconceivable an extent as to be only not infinite." This identity Poe urges as a proof of the "absolute accuracy of the Divine *adaptation*," and proceeds to draw a distinction between Divine and human constructions, with respect to the reciprocity of adaptation between causes and effects. This is of interest because he reveals here his theory of plot construction in his purely literary work. To him, "the pleasure we derive from any display of human ingenuity is in the ratio of the *approach* to this species of reciprocity. In the construction of *plot*, for example, in fictitious literature, we should aim at so arranging the incidents that we shall not be able to determine, of any one of them, whether it depends from any one other or upholds it. In this sense, of course, *perfection of plot* is really, or practically, unattainable—but only because it is a finite intelligence that constructs. The plots of God are perfect. The Universe is a plot of God." It will thus be seen that the perfect plot to Poe was one in which cause and effect were so mutually adapted that it would be impossible for the reader to decide which is which. This attitude naturally led to the supernatural motive, where cause and effect did not operate.

Poe's acuteness of reasoning is shown in his rejection of the theory put forth by Mädler, of a central sun about which all systems revolve. This grandiose conception, now long since discredited by astronomical science, but considered and discussed by astronomers long after Poe's day,[28] might have appealed to a poet whose reason did not move in logical paths. But Poe showed how this central sun must be either luminous, in which case we should see it, or non-luminous, in which case it could not have thrown off luminous suns, or if it had, it would be seen by their light.

His discussion of the theory that the Universe is in a state of progressive collapse has not been without support from modern scientists. Eddington says: "It is true that the extrapolation foretells that the material universe will some day arrive at a state of dead sameness and so virtually come to an end." [29]

Poe rejects the necessity for a material ether as a resisting medium, showing knowledge of Lagrange's work on the configurations of the spheroids.

Another instance of Poe's keen analysis is shown in his distinguishing between mankind's love of symmetry, with which he deeply sympathizes, and the pursuit of superficial symmetry of forms and motions. "It is the poetical essence of the Universe—*of the Universe* which, in the supremeness of its symmetry, is but the most sublime of poems. Now symmetry and consistency are convertible terms:— thus Poetry and Truth are one.... *A perfect consistency, I repeat can be nothing but an absolute truth.*"

Toward the end of *Eureka* Poe rises to a contemplation not only of "the awful Present," but also of "the still more awful Future." An eloquent description of the End [30] follows, including the disappearance of Matter, which having served its purpose in the development

[28] It is still mentioned in such a treatise as Young's *Astronomy.*
[29] *The Expanding Universe,* p. 178.
[30] *Eureka,* p. 136.

of that *spiritual ether* in which Poe believed, would terminate and "God would remain all in all."

Poe does not stop with the end of this material Universe. "We can readily conceive that a new and perhaps totally different series of conditions may ensue ... another action and reaction of the Divine Will. Guiding our imaginations by that omniprevalent law of laws, the law of periodicity, are we not indeed more than justified in enter- taining a belief—let us say, rather, in indulging a hope—that the proc- esses we have here ventured to contemplate will be renewed forever, and forever, and forever; a novel Universe swelling into existence, and then subsiding into nothingness, at every throb of the Heart Divine? And now—this Heart Divine—what is it? *It is our own.*"

Poe goes back for proof of this theory to our "Memories of a Destiny more vast—very distant in the by-gone time, and infinitely awful." With a similarity to Wordsworth's *Intimations of Immortality*, he re- fers to our youthful belief in our memories, to the awakening of Reason which tells us that there was a time when we did not exist and that we were created by an Intelligence greater than our own. To Poe such a belief is incomprehensible, and therefore untrue, which is a curious limitation for him. He believes this limitation is inherent in our own nature, for "No thinking being lives who, at some luminous point of his life of thought, has not felt himself lost amid the surges of futile efforts at understanding, or believing, that anything exists *greater than his own soul.*"

Poe's own struggles with despondency, his bitterness and his pride, are reflected in the next sentence:

"The utter impossibility of any one's soul feeling itself inferior to another; the intense, overwhelming dissatisfaction and rebel- lion at the thought;—these, with the omniprevalent aspirations at perfection, are but the spiritual, coincident with the material, struggles towards the original Unity—are, to my mind at least, a species of proof far surpassing what Man terms demonstration, that no one soul *is* inferior to another—that nothing is, or can be, superior to any one soul—that each soul is, in part, its own God— its own Creator:—in a word, that God—the material *and* spiritual God—*now* exists solely in the diffused Matter and Spirit of the Univ∂rse; and that the regathering of this diffused Matter and Spirit will be but the re-constitution of the purely Spiritual and Individual God.

In this view, and in this view alone, we comprehend the riddles of Divine Injustice—of Inexorable Fate. In this view alone the existence of Evil becomes intelligible; but in this view it becomes more—it becomes endurable.

The ending of *Eureka* is purely imaginative, it deals poetically with the relations of a still existent Being and those creatures "which are really but infinite individualizations of Himself." They are conscious of a proper identity, "conscious, secondly and by faint indeterminate glimpses, of an identity with the Divine Being of whom we speak— of an identity with God." The former will grow weaker, the latter stronger, till Man "will attain that awfully triumphant epoch when he shall recognize his existence as that of Jehovah. In the meantime bear in mind that all is Life—Life—Life within Life—the less within the greater, and all within the Spirit Divine."

In the revision Poe added a note—"The pain of the consideration that we shall lose our individual identity, ceases at once when we further reflect that the process, as above described, is, neither more nor less than that of the absorption, by each individual intelligence, of all other intelligences (that is, of the Universe) into its own. That God may be all in all, each must become God."

Having quoted so freely from the work of Sir Arthur Eddington, Plumian Professor of Astronomy, at Cambridge University, I felt it proper to submit this analysis of *Eureka* to him, in order that I might not misinterpret his views. He was good enough to reply as follows:

1940 Sept 29

I am returning your typescript separately, as I think a letter is less likely to be delayed.

First, I raise no objections to any of your quotations from my writings. Opinions will naturally differ as to how far the resemblance between the ideas I am attempting to express and those of Poe to which the quotations are considered relevant should be stressed rather than the differences; but, whilst not always convinced of the appropriateness, I am not averse to their being used in your argument.

Secondly, I think you make out clearly that "Eureka" is not a work of dotage or disordered mind. It is, I think, the work of a man trying to reconcile the science of his time with the more philosophical and spiritual cravings of the mind. Poe, besides being fairly well-informed in science and mathematics, seems to have had the mind of a mathematician, and consequently was not to be put off with vague phrases; and made a creditable attempt to introduce precision of thought.

The correspondence between some of his ideas and modern

views is interesting; but, as bearing on his intellectual powers, one must view it with some detachment. Any one of independent mind,—a rebel against conventionally accepted views—is likely to hit the mark sometimes. That is particularly the case when it is a case of philosophical and spiritual intuition *versus* scientific progress. The idea of "unity in diversity and diversity in unity" is now becoming actually realised in scientific theory; but until science had reached a certain stage of development it was no more helpful to science than the doctrine of the Trinity which contains the same idea. I expect many believed that this must be an ultimate truth, but science must be left gradually to find it by its own pedestrian progress.

I should say then that regarded as an attempt to put forward a new physical theory, Eureka would rightly be regarded as a crank-theory by scientists of the time. (The trouble with cranks is usually, not that they are not far-seeing, but that they have no appreciation of the immediate obstacles in the road.) Poe's more definite suggestions (in the contemporary state of science) were not unintelligent but amateurish. But as a "poem" on the significance of things as partially revealed in the state of science of the time, I think it showed a fine penetration.

Yours sincerely,

A. S. EDDINGTON

If you should wish to quote any of these remarks, by all means do so.

I wish also to introduce at this point a statement made at my request by my colleague Dr. Charles P. Olivier, Flower Professor of Astronomy at the University of Pennsylvania:

Summing up I should say that Poe had read widely and with keen appreciation the general astronomy of the day. So long as he limited himself to choosing between rival hypotheses of others, he usually chose either the right one or the most probable in his day.

It is not, however, to be expected that anyone, a hundred years ago, could advance a theory of the Universe which today would be acceptable. Poe, of course, did not have the proper scientific training to make a very hopeful attempt. Further he tended to mix up religion, or at least a type of mysticism, with his hypotheses.

But even with these defects "Eureka" shows that its author had a keen intelligence and great ability in putting forward his ideas. One must admit the full mental vigor of its author without necessarily agreeing with his conclusions.

Poe was not, therefore, as has been frequently stated, entering in 1848 upon a period of mental decline. His mind was clear and his imaginative power was still capable of dealing with scientific problems that tax the best of modern thinkers. How far he might have proceeded had he possessed adequate technical training we can only surmise. That *Eureka* produced little effect upon the science of its own day is not surprising. Its concepts were in most cases, unusual, and the hospitality of science to unusual theories, especially those of men of letters, is not large.

And yet, ironically, the general reader must have the help of a scientist in reading the essay, for the ideas are not readily grasped. Even when they are, the mysticism of the essay is forbidding to those who are realistically inclined. Poe's message is not to these, and yet as Eddington says, "It is reasonable to inquire whether in the mystical illusions of man there is not a reflection of an underlying reality." [31]

Certainly as a prose poem *Eureka* rises to a lofty height. Poe's conception of the relations of God and man, of the Creator for the created, is one of the important steps taken during the Nineteenth and Twentieth Centuries in that spiritual succession in which William Vaughn Moody and Eugene O'Neill are other figures. When that spiritual progress is fully understood, then perhaps at last *Eureka* will come into its own. [32]

Eveleth sent another series of questions on January 11th, especially with regard to Poe's habits, of which he had read in the *Weekly Universe*. The editor of this sheet, incidentally, was a good prophet, for he remarked, "Mr. Poe will be more fairly judged after his death than during his life." Poe replied to Eveleth in another self-revealing letter:

New York—Feb. 29—48.

My dear Sir;

I mean to start for Richmond on the 10th March. Everything has gone as I wished it, and my final success is certain, or I abandon all claim to the title of Vates. The only contretemps of any moment, lately, has been Willis's somewhat premature announcement of my projects:—but this will only force me into action a little sooner than I had proposed. Let me now answer the points of your last letter.

[31] See the entire Chapter XV, "Science and Mysticism" of *The Nature of the Physical World.*

[32] Among recent discussions, see Clayton Hoagland, "The Universe of Eureka," *Southern Literary Messenger,* I (May, 1939), 307-313.

Colton acted pretty much as all mere men of the world act. I think very little the worse of him for his endeavor to succeed with you at my expense. I always liked him, and I believe he liked me. His "I understand the matter perfectly" amuses me. Certainly, then, it was the only matter he did understand. His intellect was *o*.

"The Rationale of Verse" will appear in "Graham" after all.[33] I will stop in Philadelphia to see the proofs.

The editor of the "Weekly Universe" speaks kindly, and I find no fault with his representing my habits as "shockingly irregular." He could not have had the "personal acquaintance" with me, of which he writes, but has fallen into a very natural error. The fact is thus:—my *habits* are rigorously abstemious, and I omit nothing of the natural regimen requisite for health—i. e., I rise early, eat moderately, drink nothing but water, and take abundant and regular exercise in the open air. But this is my private life—my studious and literary life—and of course escapes the eye of the world. The desire for society comes upon me only when I have become excited by drink. Then *only* I go—that is, at these times only I *have been* in the practice of going among my friends; who seldom, or in fact never, having seen me unless excited, take it for granted that I am always so. Those who *really* know me, know better. In the meantime I shall turn the general error to account. But enough of this: the causes which maddened me to the drinking point are no more, and I am done drinking forever. I do *not* know the editors and contributors of the "Universe," and was not aware of the existence of such a paper. Who are they? or is it a secret.

The "most distinguished of American scholars" is Prof. Chas. Anthon, author of the "Classical Dictionary."

I presume you have seen some newspaper notices of my late lecture on the Universe.[34] You could have gleaned, however, no idea of what the lecture was, from what the papers said it was. All praised it—as far as I have yet seen—and all absurdly misrepresented it. The only report of it which approaches the truth— is the one I enclose—from the "Express"—written by E. A. Hopkins, a gentleman of much scientific acquirement, son of Bishop Hopkins of Vermont; but he conveys only my general idea, and

---

[33] It did not appear in *Graham's,* but in the *Southern Literary Messenger.*
[34] *Eureka.*

his digest is full of inaccuracies. I enclose also a slip from the "Courier & Enquirer." Please return them. To eke out a chance of your understanding what I really *did* say, I add a loose summary of my propositions and results:—

[The summary of *Eureka* has been given on pages 542-543.]

After the summary Poe continued:

Read these items after the Report. As to the Lecture, I am very quiet about it—but, if you have ever dealt with such topics, you will recognize the novelty and *moment* of my view. What I have propounded will (in good time) revolutionize the world of Physical and Metaphysical Science. I say this calmly—but I say it.

I shall not go till I hear from you.

Truly yours,
E. A. POE.[35]

In a letter to George E. Isbell, of Binghamton, New York,[36] Poe sent a new prospectus of *The Stylus*. The language is somewhat changed, but the same principles of independence, and of devotion to "Literature, Drama and the Fine Arts" are expressed. It is not necessary to repeat the details; among the new ones were Poe's claim that he had established correspondents at London, Paris, Rome, and Vienna!

Poe paid his respects to the dogmatism of science in this letter:

"The Vestiges of Creation" I have not yet seen; and it is always unsafe and unwise to form opinions of books from reviews of them. The extracts of the work which have fallen in my way, abound in inaccuracies of fact:—still these may not materially

---

[35] Original Autograph Ms. in J. P. Morgan Library. It differs only slightly from the copy printed in J. S. Wilson's edition of the letters, except that it does not include the following postscript:

"By the bye, lest you infer that my views, in detail, are the same with those advanced in the *Nebular Hypothesis,* I venture to offer a few addenda, the substance of which was penned, though never printed, several years ago, under the head of—A Prediction."

[Here follow Poe's "Addenda," before noted.]

"How will *that* do for a postscript?"

[36] February 29, 1848. Letter and printed Prospectus of the *Stylus,* dated April, 1848, are in collection of J. K. Lilly, Jr. The letter is addressed to "George E. Irbey," but the surname is changed by an unknown hand to "Isbell." Since George E. Isbell appears in the directory of Binghamton in 1859, and a street is named after him, and since no "Irbey" appears to have lived in that town, the latter name is probably an error by Poe.

affect the general argument. One thing is certain; that the objections of *merely* scientific men—men, I mean, who cultivate the physical sciences to the exclusion, in a greater or less degree, of the mathematics, of metaphysics and of logic—are generally invalid except in respect to scientific details. Of all persons in the world, they are at the same time the most bigoted and the least capable of using, generalizing, or deciding upon the facts which they bring to light in the course of their experiments. And these are the men who chiefly write the criticisms *against* all efforts at generalization—denouncing these efforts as "speculative" and "theoretical."

There is also another abstract of "Eureka" somewhat more brief than that already quoted.

The "Marginalia" in Graham's for January, February, and March, 1848, include an interesting passage concerning the difficulty of anyone writing a book which could reveal his own heart. "No man ever will dare to write it. No man could write it, even if he dare. The paper would shrivel and blaze at every touch of the fiery pen." [37] What would Poe think of the women who dare to do this very thing today and emerge without a curl disturbed! There is an amusing account of the way in which the London *Popular Record of Modern Science* took "The Facts in the Case of M. Valdemar" seriously, and reprinted it under the title of "The Last Conversation of a Somnambule." [38]

Poe had been working during 1846 and 1847 on a critical account of American Literature. All that seems to be now extant is contained in a manuscript dated 1848.[39] What Poe hoped to publish is given best in his own words on the title page:

LITERARY AMERICA

Some Honest Opinions about our Autorial
Merits and Demerits

with

Occasional Words of Personality

by

Edgar A. Poe

[37] *Graham's*, XXXII (January, 1848), 24.
[38] *Graham's*, XXXII (March, 1848), 178-179.
[39] Now in the Huntington Library.

If I have in any point receded from what is commonly received, it hath been for the purpose of proceeding *melius* and not *in aliud.*

Lord Bacon.

Truth, peradventure, by force, may for a time be trodden *down,* but never, by any means whatsoever, can it be trodden out.

Lord Coke.

Prefaced with a Critical and Biographical sketch of the Author

by

James Russell Lowell and P. P. Cooke.

1848.

If the three articles which comprise the manuscript represent Poe's conception of a literary history, it is just as well that he did not publish it. They are substantially the same as the critical articles on Richard Adams Locke, "Thomas Dunn Brown," and Christopher Pearse Cranch,[40] published in Griswold's Edition of the *Literati* in 1850. Apart from the unfortunate nature of the article on English, this method of writing literary history is obviously not the proper one.

While the "Rationale of Verse" was not published until October and November, 1848, in the *Southern Literary Messenger,* it had been sold to Colton in 1847. Poe had published in 1843 his "Notes on English Verse" in the *Pioneer,* but he had rewritten these, not always to advantage. Both essays are now of interest in their revelation of how one of the most consummate masters of the art of poetry should have been so confused in his theories of versification. With his elaborate schemes of notation, his "bastard trochees" and other vagaries, we do not have to deal. Fortunately, they were not adopted, for they would only have added to the chapters of inaccuracy in the theoretical writings on English versification, to which he refers pungently at the opening of the essays. The trouble lay in Poe's ignorance of the history of English versification. He shared this ignorance, of course, with all those who wrote before Sievers' discoveries, fifty years later, of the real laws of Old English verse. But Coleridge had shown the way to truth in his discussion of "Christabel" and Poe deliberately refused to follow it. Curiously enough, he was closer to the truth in the earlier essay, for there he said: "[The versifier] should employ his syllables

[40] The three treatments of Cranch, in the *Democratic Review,* July, 1846, in "The Literati" in *Godey's* for the same month, and in *Literary America* (1848), illustrate Poe's methods in the repetition of the same material. That the articles in *Literary America* are later revisions is indicated clearly not only by the date, but also by the correct spelling of Cranch's middle name.

as nearly as possible, with the accentuation due in prose reading." Coleridge had recognized the accentual basis for English verse, but Poe floundered on with his conception of "long" and "short" syllables in English, and reached such absurdities as the rule that, "In a line, every long syllable must of its own accord occupy in its utterance, or must be *made* to occupy, precisely the time demanded for two short ones." There are, of course, no inherently long or short syllables in English verse. Our verse is not based on syllables at all.

Just as the English language absorbed the Latin, Danish and French influences and emerged still an English tongue, so our versification is still based on the fundamental laws of Old English verse. A number of accented elements, preferably four, are arranged at fairly even intervals in a line. Liberties are taken as to the number and stress of the unaccented elements. The rhythm is prevailingly rising or falling, that is, the unstressed elements either precede or follow the accented elements to which they belong rhetorically or etymologically. The rhythm may change even in the middle of a line. The governing element is the meaning—and whenever the meaning and any preconceived metrical rule conflict the latter always gives way. English poetry, unhampered by technical rules as in French poetry, has therefore become the greatest in the world.

Poe sensed some of the objections to the conventional theories. He denied the necessity of regularity in the succession of feet, recognized that "emphasis can make any syllable as long as desired" and in speaking of French verse, said that "it is without accentuation and, consequently without verse." If he had only gone a step further and seen that accent or stress and not quantity is the fundamental basis of English verse, he might have contributed definitely to our knowledge of that subject.

He quotes his own lines in "Al Aaraaf,"

> "When first the phantom's course was found to be
> Headlong hitherward o'er the starry sea"

as examples of the substitution of two "trochaic" for two "iambic" feet, when what he was really doing was to change from a rising to a falling measure, the entire second line being falling in its movement. The amazing thing is that as a poet, by using a falling measure, he produced a striking line describing the fall of the phantom, while as a critic, he solemnly tells us that he substituted "trochaic" feet for "iambic" feet, neither of which exist in English at all!

Mrs. Shew continued to befriend Poe and Mrs. Clemm, and Poe

published in the *Columbian Magazine* for March, 1848, his second poem to her, "To ———." It is again in blank verse, and while in part a composite of earlier lines, it has some striking verses like

"Unthought like thoughts that are the souls of thought"

It is also sincere, and quite different in quality from "An Enigma" which appeared in the same month in *Sartain's Union Magazine*. This was written for Mrs. Estelle Anna Lewis, whose pen name, Sarah Anna Lewis, is to be found in the verses. She was one of the women who paid in cash and in service to Mrs. Clemm for Poe's critical praises of her work and for his editing of her poems. A vivid picture of the loathing he felt for the position in which Mrs. Clemm put him is given in a letter written by Mrs. Shew (later Mrs. Houghton), to Ingram.[41]

"Mr. Poe expressed to me the *great mortification it was to him*, and I, childlike, I hated the fat, gaudily dressed woman whom I often found sitting in Mrs. Clemm's little kitchen, waiting to see the man of genius, who had rushed out to escape her, to the fields and forests —or to the grounds of the Catholic School in the vicinity. I remember Mrs. C— sending me after him in great secrecy one day. I found him sitting on a favorite rock, muttering his desire to die and get rid of *literary bores*."

Mrs. Shew seems to have suggested to Poe the writing of "The Bells," early in the summer of 1848. He came to her home, which was at 51 Tenth Street, near Broadway,[42] mentally exhausted, yet feeling that he had a poem to write. He was annoyed by the nearby bells, probably those of Grace Church at Tenth Street and Broadway. She gave him paper and wrote on it "The Bells, by E. A. Poe"—adding "The little silver bells." Poe finished the stanza in the first form, of seven lines. She then suggested "The heavy iron bells," and Poe wrote the first form of the second stanza of eleven lines. After he had slept for twelve hours in her brother's room, she took him home to Fordham.[43]

"The Bells" was rewritten at least three times before it reached the form in which it finally appeared in *Sartain's Magazine* in November, 1849. John Sartain also published the original brief form, in December, 1849, stating that it came to him "about a year since." "About six months after this," he continued, "we received the poem enlarged and

---

[41] April 3, [1875?]. Original Ms. now in Library of University of Virginia.
[42] H. N. MacCracken, *Poe at Fordham*, pp. 32-33.
[43] Ingram. *Life*, II, 155

altered nearly to its present size and form, and about three months since, the author sent another alteration and enlargement, in which condition the poem was left at the time of his death.[44]

He also denied Stoddard's charge that Poe had sold the poem three times. As Sartain said, "It came from Poe in three distinct forms, and at different intervals of time, and as each of the last two was a great improvement upon the preceding, it was but fair that the author should receive additional compensation each time.[45]

"The Bells" is one of the most successful verbal imitations of sound in the English language. The effect is secured largely by skillful contrast of close vowel sounds,

> "How they tinkle, tinkle, tinkle
> In the icy air of night."

with open vowels,

> "Hear the mellow wedding bells,
> Golden bells"

and, of course, by the apt creation of vivid phrases. Many and various have been the suggestions as to the sources for "The Bells"[46] but it is not the choosing of bells as a subject of a poem which is important. It is the way in which the sounds are chosen and combined which makes the poem a great one. Here Poe, as usual, was his own source.

Sometime later during 1848, Mrs. Shew wrote Poe that their friendship could not continue. As usual, much ink has been spent in conjecture. Her own words are the best testimony:

"Mr. Poe always treated me with respect and I was to him a friend in need and a friend indeed, but he was so excentric [sic] and so unlike others, and I was also, that I had to define a position I was bound to take and it hurt his feelings and after he was dead I deeply regretted my letter to him, as we all do when too late."[47] Poe made an appeal to her in 1849, which will come in its proper place.

On May 19, 1848, Poe wrote a long letter[48] to Mrs. Jane E. Locke,

[44] Editorial Page of *Sartain's Magazine*, V (December, 1849), 385-387.

[45] *Lippincott's Magazine*, XLIII (March. 1889), 411-415. See also Sartain's *Reminiscences of a Very Old Man* (New York, 1900), pp. 202-205.

[46] See especially Campbell's, Whitty's, and the Woodberry-Stedman Editions of the Poems.

[47] Mrs. Shew (Houghton) to Ingram, April 3, [1875?]. Original Autograph Ms., Library of University of Virginia. Mrs. Shew's ideas of punctuation are casual.

[48] Original Autograph Ms., W. H. Koester Collection. So far as I know, it has not been published in any of the biographies.

of Lowell, Massachusetts, evidently in reply to one of hers. It represents Poe in one of his least attractive roles, that of a man parrying the sentimental advances of a woman and yet encouraging her by the expression of an assumed interest. Some portions of the letter have collateral information:

But for duties that, just now, *will not* be neglected or even postponed—the proof reading of a work of scientific detail, [Eureka] in which a trivial error would involve me in very serious embarrassment—I would, ere this, have been in Lowell,—to clasp you by the hand—and to thank you personally for all that I owe you—and, oh, I feel that this is *very—very* much. . . . *Will* you remember that the hermit life which for the last three years I have led, buried in the woods of Fordham, has necessarily prevented me from learning *anything* of you, and will you still refuse to tell me at least *one* particular of your personal history? I feel that you cannot misunderstand me. Tell me nothing—I ask nothing—which has any reference to "worldliness" or the "fear of the world." Tell me only of the ties—if any exist—that bind you to the world:—and yet I perceive that I may have done very wrong in asking you this:—now that I have asked it, it seems to me the maddest of questions, involving, possibly, the most visionary of hopes.

Ermina Starkweather Locke, who for some reason unknown to her most authentic biographers,[49] prefixed "Jane" to her name, was a sentimental and occasional poetess and a kinswoman of Mrs. Osgood. Ill health and the care of a large family apparently gave her a pessimistic view of life. This was probably not brightened when Poe came to Lowell at her invitation to lecture on "The Poets and Poetry of America" at Wentworth Hall on June 10, 1848.[50]

[49] For personal information concerning Mrs. Locke and the Lowell episodes, I am indebted to Frederick W. Coburn, President of the Lowell Historical Society. See his paper on "Jane E. Locke," *Lowell Courier Citizen*, January 20 and 27, 1940, also "Lowell's Association with Edgar Allan Poe," January 20 and 27, February 3 and 10, 1941.

[50] Poe did not lecture in July, 1848, on "The Poetic Principle" as stated in Woodberry's *Life*, II, 269, Hervey Allen's *Israfel*, p. 763, etc. In the advertisements and advance notices of the lecture in the Lowell *Journal and Courier*, July 8 and 10, 1848, and the Lowell *Advertiser*, of July 8th, also in the account of the lecture in the *Advertiser* of July 11th, the title is given as "The Poets and Poetry of America." He intended to lecture on "The Poetic Principle" during the visit to Lowell in the fall of 1848 but apparently this lecture was not given.

Poe was apparently disappointed with his forty-three year old hostess at Wamesit Cottage, for he met her neighbor, Mrs. Nancy Locke Heywood Richmond, and was instantly attracted to her. She became the "Annie" of one of his most fervent affairs. Mrs. Locke, jealous of his attentions to her friend, contributed her version of that romance to the scandals of 1848 and 1849. Whether Poe saw her on his second visit, in the fall of 1848, is not very clear, but a letter of introduction to Mrs. Locke, which he gave to Mrs. Lewis in October, 1848, shows that he was still on good terms with her at that time.

Why Poe postponed his visit to Richmond in the interest of *The Stylus* is made clear from this letter, which does not appear in any of the biographies.

Fordham—June 7,—48.

Dr Sir,

I fear that, on reading this note, you will think me (what God knows I am not) most ungrateful for your former kindness—and that I presume upon it more than I should, in asking you to aid me again. My only excuse is, that I am desperately circum-stanced—in very bitter distress of mind and body—and that I look around me in vain to find any friend who both can and will aid me, unless it be yourself. My last hope of extricating myself from the difficulties which are pressing me to death, is in going personally to a distant connexion near Richmond, Va, and en-deavoring to interest him in my behalf. With a very little help all would go well with me—but even that little I cannot obtain; the effort to overcome one trouble only serving to plunge me in another. Will you forgive me, then, if I ask you to loan me the means of getting to Richmond? My mother in law, Mrs. Clemm, who will hand you this, will explain to you the particulars of my situation.

Truly & gratefully yours

C. A. Bristed Esqre EDGAR A. POE

Mr Putnam has my book in press, but he could make me no advance, beyond $14—some weeks ago.[51]

Charles Astor Bristed, then a young man of twenty-eight, was a grandson of John Jacob Astor, II, and a scholar and man of letters, although his publications came mainly after this period. Let us hope he helped Poe, as he could well have afforded some assistance. Poe

[51] Original Autograph Ms., W. H. Koester Collection.

EDGAR A. POE.

Will Mr Bristed honor Mr Poe with a few minutes private conversation?

POE'S VISITING CARD, MADE BY HIMSELF
Reproduced from the original through the courtesy of Mr. W. H. Koester.

had spoken favorably [52] of an article by him on "The Scotch School of Philosophy and Criticism" in *Colton's Review*, for October, 1845.

Mrs. Clemm's visit to Bristed may not have been fruitful for a letter to Bayard Taylor reveals Poe's effort to sell a poem, probably the second "To Helen," since it appeared in the *Union Magazine* in November, 1848:

June 15—48

Bayard Taylor Esq.
Dr Sir,
I would feel greatly indebted to you if you could spare time to look over the lines enclosed and let me know whether they will be accepted for "The Union"—if so, what you can afford to pay for them, and when they can appear.
Truly Yours,
EDGAR A. POE.

P. S. I feel that I have been guilty of discourtesy in not sooner thanking you for your picturesque and vigorous "Views A-Foot" —but when they reached me, and long afterwards, I was too ill to write—and latterly I have been every day hoping to have an

[52] "Marginalia," *Graham's*, January, 1848.

opportunity of making your acquaintance and thanking you in person.[53]

The correspondence with Chivers came to an end at this time, and helps to fix an important date:

> Fordham—Westchester Co—
> July 13, 48.

My Dear Friend,

    I have just returned from an excursion to Lowell:—this is the reason why I have not been to see you. My mother will leave this note at your hotel in the event of your not being in when she calls. I am *very* anxious to see you—as I propose going on to Richmond on Monday. Can you not come out to Fordham & spend tomorrow and Sunday with me? We can talk over matters, then, at leisure. The cars for Fordham leave the dépôt at the City Hall almost every hour—distance 14 miles.

> Truly yours
>
> POE.[54]

Across the top of this letter Chivers wrote, "The following is the last letter that I ever received from him."

John R. Thompson, then Editor of the *Southern Literary Messenger* was responsible for a distressing picture of Poe's habits at that time, and since his testimony has been given in detail in all the biographies it is necessary to test its validity. On October 17, 1848, he wrote to Philip Pendleton Cooke:

> Poe is not in Richmond. He remained here about 3 weeks, horribly drunk and discoursing "Eureka" every night to the audiences of the Bar Rooms. His friends tried to get him sober and set him to work but to no effect and were compelled at last to re-ship him to New York. I was very anxious for him to write something for me, while he remained here, but his lucid intervals were so brief and infrequent that it was quite impossible. "The Rationale of Verse" I took—more as an act of charity than anything else, for though exhibiting great acquaintance with the subject, it is altogether too bizarre and too technical for the general reader. Poe is a singular fellow indeed.[55]

More than a year later Thompson wrote to E. H. N. Patterson:

[53] Original Autograph Ms., W. H. Koester Collection.
[54] Original Autograph Ms., Huntington Library.
[55] Original Autograph Ms., W. H. Koester Collection.

Richmond, Va., 9 Nov., 1849.

My dear Sir,—Your letter making inquiries of a personal nature concerning poor Poe has been lying on my table some days. I avail myself of the first leisure moment to reply to it.

My first acquaintance with the deceased was in the spring of 1848, when I accidentally learned that a person calling himself Edgar A. Poe had been, for a fortnight, in a debauch, in one of the lowest haunts of vice upon the wharves in this City. If you have ever visited Richmond you may perhaps know that the business portion of the town and the sites occupied by residences exclusively are distant from the shipping by a mile and a half, so that very few persons not actually engaged in commercial affairs ever visit the landing at all. As soon as I heard the name of Poe in this connection my worst suspicions were excited, and I at once took a carriage and went to seek him. It was a very warm day in the latter part of May or early in June. When I reached the purlieus of this abandoned quarter, I learned that such a person had indeed been there, drunk, for two weeks, and that he had gone a few hours previous, without hat or coat, to the residence of Mr. John MacKenzie, some three miles distant in the country, alone & on foot. It was Poe. The next day he called on me with Mr. MacKenzie. From that time until his death we were much together and in constant correspondence. I did all I could to restrain his excesses and to relieve the pressure of his immediate wants (for he was extremely indigent) but no influence was adequate to keep him from the damnable propensity to drink and his entire residence in Richmond of late was but a succession of disgraceful follies. He spoke of himself as the victim of a pre-ordained damnation, as *l'âme perdue*, a soul lost beyond all hope of redemption. For three weeks previous to his departure from Richmond he had been sober—a Son of Temperance. But no confidence could be placed in him in any relation of life, least of all in antagonism to his fatal weakness. He died, indeed, of delirium from drunkenness; the shadow of infamy beclouded his last moments

> "And his soul from out that shadow
> Shall be lifted never more!"

But who shall judge harshly of the dead? Mercy benignly tempers the divine Justice, and to this Justice we commit his spirit.

Poe had spoken to me of your design with reference to the literary enterprise of which you speak. You were fortunate, I think, in not having embarked in it, for a more unreliable person that he could hardly be found. I have not, as yet, recovered his trunk, so that I cannot tell you whether or no he left any unpublished MSS. The day before he went North from Richmond, I advanced him a small sum of money for a prospective article which he probably never wrote. His complete Works will be brought out by the Rev. Dr. Griswold.

With much regard, I am Sir, yours,

JNO. R. THOMPSON.[56]

This later letter, which has been most often quoted, contradicts both itself and the earlier note. The "three weeks" has grown to a visit beginning "late in May or early in June." Poe did not leave New York until July 17, 1848, and if he spent two weeks "in one of the lowest haunts of vice" after his arrival in Richmond, it was not until August that Thompson saw him. Again, this second letter undoubtedly refers in part to the 1849 visit, yet Thompson writes as though he were speaking of one period. Both letters are couched in extravagant terms, and Poe's publications during August and September show that he was able to write,[57] and that Thompson was evidently an unreliable witness. Moreover, in Thompson's article on Poe in the *Messenger* for November, 1849, and in his *Genius and Character of Edgar Allan Poe*,[58] written some years later and only recently published, Thompson says nothing of this episode. In the last he says, "I love to think of him as he appeared during the two months preceding his death, a quiet, easy, seemingly contented and well-bred gentleman." That Poe was drinking when he was in Richmond in 1848 is quite probable, but that he lived in the state Thompson describes him, at second hand, is quite improbable. Poe did not seek the purlieus of the cities he visited, and unless he was drugged, he was not found there, until his last journey. Indeed there is something irritating in the romantic pictures of this 1848 visit. If Mr. Whitty's researches were correct, which is of course always open to question, there is no mention of Poe's visit in the Richmond newspapers of the time.[59] E. V. Valentine's "Notes" in the Valentine Museum, while giving many details concerning the 1849 visit, does not mention that of 1848. The

[56] Original Autograph Ms., Morgan Library.

[57] "The Literati of New York. S. Anna Lewis," *Democratic Review*, August, 1848. "Mrs. Lewis's Poems," *Southern Literary Messenger*, September, 1848. Of course, they may have been written before he reached Richmond.

[58] *The Genius and Character of Edgar Allan Poe*, by John R. Thompson, Ed. by James H. Whitty and James A. Rindfleisch (Privately Printed, 1929), p. 41.

[59] Memoir of Poe in the *Complete Poems of Edgar Allan Poe* (Boston and New York, 1917-19), p. lxv.

stories about Poe's duel with John M. Daniel are told in absolutely contradictory terms by equally competent and incompetent witnesses. He apparently did not meet Mrs. Shelton. Poe's own reference to Daniel "the man whom I challenged when I was here last year" [60] is the only evidence for the 1848 visit that seems authentic. When the lack of information concerning this 1848 visit is compared with the detailed and reliable information concerning his stay of 1849, it seems as though there might be some truth in Mrs. Clemm's statement that he did not visit Richmond from 1837 to 1849! [61] We shall, of course, accept Poe's own testimony in this case, but the visit must have been a minor episode.

[60] Poe to Mrs. Clemm, September, 1849. Original Autograph Ms., Griswold Collection, Boston Public Library.

[61] Mrs. Clemm to Mrs. Whitman, April 14th, 1859. Original Autograph Ms., J. K. Lilly, Jr. Collection.

CHAPTER XVIII

To Helen and For Annie

Poe was recalled from Richmond by a message from Mrs. Sarah Helen Whitman, a widow living in Providence, Rhode Island, whose relation to him is one of the most difficult for a biographer to make clear. Mrs. Whitman knew him in his loftiest and in his weakest moods. They became engaged to be married and their love story was broken in a manner painful to both. Poe's distress, according to his own story, led him even to attempt suicide. Yet although Mrs. Whitman broke the engagement, she defended him at all times, and she wrote in 1860 the first book in his defence—which still remains not only a convincing personal tribute but also one of the most sympathetic and brilliant interpretations of his poetry and fiction. So contradictory and at times so garbled have been many of the accounts of this relation, that it is necessary to give the details in full and to document each one.[1]

Sarah Helen Power Whitman was forty-five years old in 1848, an attractive woman, living with her mother and eccentric sister in Providence. Her poetry was not bad by any means. She had been publishing verse in the magazines since 1829, and was deeply impressed by the spiritualistic interest then rampant. She was an unworldly being, dressing with a distinctly individual taste and likely to drop her veils and scarfs in any spot, if the conversation grew tense. She was a favorite with both men and women, had a wide acquaintance here and later abroad, but there is a note of protecting fondness in those who have described her.[2]

Poe saw Mrs. Whitman first when he visited Providence with Mrs. Osgood in the summer of 1845, but he made no attempt at that time to meet her. She was standing on her front step as they passed, and

<hr>

[1] I am fortunate in being provided with photostats of the extensive collection of Poe-Whitman material, including Poe's letters to her, through the courtesy of J. K. Lilly, Jr.

[2] See especially the *Autobiography* of Elizabeth Oakes Smith, ed. by M. A. Wyman (Lewiston, 1924), pp. 100-102.

was not in her garden, which, incidentally, could hardly be recognized in Poe's later romantic description. Mrs. Whitman made the first move by sending, at Miss Lynch's request, a valentine to be read on February 14, 1848, at a party in New York. Mrs. Whitman wrote verses addressed to Poe, who was not present, entitled "The Raven," [3] closing:

> "Not a bird that roams the forest
> Shall our lofty eyrie share."

Through Miss Lynch and Mrs. Osgood the verses reached Poe, and were published in Willis's *Home Journal*, March 18, 1848. Poe sent her anonymously on March 2nd [4] a leaf torn out of his printed poems, containing his earlier "To Helen." Early in June [5] Poe sent her his new poem, "To Helen," and he offered it for publication to Bayard Taylor for the *Union Magazine* of New York on June 15, 1848. It was published in the November issue simply as "To ———."

The second "To Helen" is hardly in the same class of poetry as the masterpiece of 1831. It is in blank verse, and while it is not insincere, the tone is that of the idealized, overstressed emotion in which this courtship was carried on. The heartfelt adoration of Poe's early tribute to Mrs. Stanard, the more homely gratitude of the verses to Mrs. Shew, the pulsing passion of the later "For Annie," the profound tenderness of "Annabel Lee,"—they are not here. The beauty of the scenic background engages him:

> "The mossy banks and the meandering paths,
> The happy flowers and the repining trees,
> Were seen no more: the very roses' odors
> Died in the arms of the adoring airs."

The images are not fused into creation, they remain purely descriptive. The eyes of his beloved play a part somewhat like the conceits of the Caroline poets in England: the poet is playing with the idea of the eyes remaining after the rest of the vision has gone. It is dangerous business. Some years later "Lewis Carroll" was to satirize this type of

---

[3] For the poem as she sent it, see *Poe's Helen*, by Caroline Ticknor (New York, 1916), pp. 45-46. It is much changed in the edition of Mrs. Whitman's *Hours of Life and Other Poems* (Providence, 1853), pp. 66-69.

[4] The date is from the postmark on the letter, now in the collection of J. K. Lilly, Jr.

[5] Original Autograph Ms. letter of Friday [Nov.?] 24th. Poe to Mrs. Whitman, J. K. Lilly, Jr. Collection. Poe is incorrect in some of the dates in these letters, but Mrs. Whitman leaves this one uncorrected.

romance through the grin of the Cheshire Cat, which stayed after the cat had gone. But in the forties it was the accepted tone, and unless the wooing of Mrs. Whitman is understood as a literary adventure, in which two poets entered heartily and with their eyes wide open, it becomes an episode of folly or worse. And this certainly it was not. But it was as a poet rather than as a lover that Poe wrote of her eyes— incidentally they were her best feature—

"They fill my soul with Beauty (which is Hope)."

Mrs. Whitman did not reply at once, possibly because of Mrs. Osgood's warning: "I see by the *Home Journal* that your beautiful invocation has reached 'The Raven' in his eyrie and I suppose ere this he has swooped upon your little *dove-cot* in Providence. May Providence protect you if he has!—He is in truth, 'A glorious devil, with large heart and brain.' " [6]—

Poe meanwhile was making inquiries. On June 14th he wrote to Miss Anna Blackwell, whom he had known in Fordham: "Do you know Mrs. Whitman? I feel deep interest in her poetry and character. I have never seen her—but once - - - Her poetry is, beyond question, *poetry*, instinct with genius. Can you not tell me something about her —anything—everything you know—and *keep my secret*—that is to say let no one know that I have asked you to do so?" [7]

This letter found its way to Mrs. Whitman, through the feminine circle in Providence, and inspired Mrs. Whitman's communication to Poe at Richmond. This of course consisted of verses, concluding

"And gazing on night's starry cope,
I dwell with 'Beauty which is Hope.' "

She evidently liked the poem "To Helen" since she quoted from it. But this last stanza was omitted when she published the verses "A Night in August," in her volume of poems in 1853.

Late in August [8] or very early in September Poe returned to Ford-

---

[6] Caroline Ticknor, *Poe's Helen* (New York, 1916), p. 48.

[7] Original Autograph Ms., J. K. Lilly, Jr. Collection.

[8] Poe says in his letter of October 18th that he received her poem on September 10th, but Mrs. Whitman notes on the margin of the original letter, "It was earlier," and his letter of September 5th is good evidence that he was then at Fordham. Poe was often confused about his dates. It is best to accept his statements only when Mrs. Whitman leaves them undisturbed. She was not impeccable either.

EDGAR ALLAN POE IN 1848

From the photograph of a daguerreotype taken in Providence. Reproduced through the courtesy of Mr. Josiah K. Lilly, Jr.

ham, and resumed the campaign by writing under an assumed name. The script, while disguised, might have been recognized by her, as she had probably seen it, in New York.

New York—Sept. 5. 48

Dear Madam—Being engaged in making a collection of autographs of the most distinguished American authors I am, of course, anxious to procure your own, and if you would so far honor me as to reply, however briefly, to this note, I would take it as a *very especial* favor.

Res^y.

Yr. Mo. Ob. S^t.

EDWARD S. T. GREY [9]

Mrs. Sarah Helen Whitman

Mrs. Whitman did not reply, but Poe, armed with a letter of introduction from Miss M. J. McIntosh, dated September 15th, went to Providence and called on Mrs. Whitman on September 21st. His wooing was ardent, even though at least one interview was in a cemetery. But his own description of the first meeting is vivid with unreality:

And now, in the most simple words at my command, let me paint to you the impression made upon me by your personal presence.—As you entered the room, pale, timid, hesitating, and evidently oppressed at heart; as your eyes rested appealingly, for one brief moment, upon mine, I felt, for the first time in my life, and tremblingly acknowledged, the existence of spiritual influences altogether out of the reach of the reason. I saw that you were *Helen—my* Helen—the Helen of a thousand dreams—she whose visionary lips had so often lingered upon my own in the divine trance of passion—she whom the great Giver of all Good had preördained to be mine—mine only—if not now, alas! then at least hereafter and *forever,* in the Heavens.—You spoke falteringly and seemed scarcely conscious of what you said. I heard no words—only the soft voice, more familiar to me than my own, and more melodious than the songs of the angels. Your hand rested within mine, and my whole soul shook with a tremulous ecstasy. And then but for very shame—but for the fear of grieving or

[9] The original autograph Ms., J. K. Lilly, Jr. Collection, is dated, including postmark, September 5th. Yet the biographies give September 8th. On the back of the letter Mrs. Whitman wrote, "Sent by E. A. P. under an assumed name, in order to ascertain if I was in Providence."

oppressing you—I would have fallen at your feet in as pure—in as real a *worship* as was ever offered to Idol or to God. And when, afterwards, on those two successive evenings of all-Heavenly delight, you passed to and fro about the room—now sitting by my side, now far away, now standing with your hand resting on the back of my chair, while the preternatural thrill of your touch vibrated even through the senseless wood into my heart—while you moved thus restlessly about the room—as if a deep Sorrow or a more profound Joy haunted your bosom—my brain reeled beneath the intoxicating spell of your presence, and it was with no merely human senses that I either saw or heard you. It was my soul only that distinguished you there. I grew faint with the luxury of your voice and blind with the voluptuous lustre of your eyes.[10]

Poe asked her to marry him, but she sent him home, promising to write. Her message came on September 30th, and on the next day, he poured out his feelings to her in the long letter from which I have just quoted. In it he told her that "It is my diviner nature—my spiritual being—that burns and pants to commingle with your own." He acknowledged that she had not yet said she loved him. Unfortunately we do not have Mrs. Whitman's letter, but from the quotations which Poe incorporates in his own, she said to him: "Had I youth and health and beauty I would live for you and die with you. Now were I to allow myself to love you, I could only enjoy a bright brief hour of rapture and die." [11] Poe also hints here at a possible physical reason for her reluctance to remarry. Her health was apparently frail. Poe continues:

How selfish—How despicably selfish seems now all—*all* that I have written. Have I not, indeed, been demanding at your hands love which might endanger your life? [12] ... But oh, darling! if I *seem* selfish, yet believe that I truly, *truly* love you, and that it is the most spiritual of love that I speak, even if I speak it from the depths of the most passionate of hearts. Think—oh, think for *me*, Helen, and for yourself! *Is* there *no* hope?—is there *none?* May not this terrible [disease?] [13] be conquered? Frequently it *has*

[10] Original Autograph Ms., Poe to Mrs. Whitman, October 1, 1848. Collection of J. K. Lilly, Jr.

[11] These lines are crossed out, but Mr. Lilly has, I believe, restored the original words correctly. "Hour" may be "heaven."

[12] Another restoration of words of the original letter that had been crossed out.

[13] The word that has been cut out may be *disease*.

been overcome. And more frequently are we deceived in respect to its actual existence. Long-continued nervous disorder—especially when exasperated by ether or [word cut out]—will give rise to *all* the symptoms of heart—[sic]—di[sease an ¹⁴]d so deceive the most skillful physicians—as even in [my o ¹⁵]wn case they were deceived. But admit that this fearful evil *has* indeed assailed you. Do you not all the more really need the devotionate care which only one who loves you as *I* do, could or would bestow? On my bosom could I not still the throbbings of your own? Do not mistake me, Helen! Look, with your searching—your seraphic eyes, into the soul of my soul, and see if you can discover there one taint of an ignoble nature! At your feet—if you so willed it—I would cast from me, forever, all merely human desire, and clothe myself in the glory of a pure, calm, and *unexacting* affection. I would comfort you—soothe you—tranquillize you. My love—my faith—should instil into your bosom a praeternatural calm. You would rest from care—from all worldly agitation. You would get better, and finally well. And if *not*, Helen,—if not—if you *died*—then at least would I clasp your dear hand in death, and willingly —*oh, joyfully—joyfully—joyfully*—go down *with* you into the night of the Grave.

Write soon—soon—oh, *soon!*—But not *much*. Do not weary or agitate yourself for *my* sake. Say to me those coveted words which would turn earth into Heaven. If Hope is forbidden, I will *not* murmur if you comfort me with Love.—The papers of which you [speak ¹⁶] I will procure and forward immediately. They will cost me nothing, *dear* Helen, an[d] ¹⁷ I therefore re—enclose you what you so thoughtfully s[ent ¹⁸]. Think that, in doing so, my lips are pressed ferv[ently ¹⁹] and lingeringly upon your own. And now, in closing this long, long letter, let me speak last of that which lies nearest my heart—of that precious gift which I would not exchange for the surest hope of Paradise. It seems to me too sacred that I should even whisper *to you*, the dear giver, what it

¹⁴ The letters enclosed in square brackets have been cut out—they are thought to be *sease an*.
¹⁵ The letters enclosed in square brackets have been cut out—they are thought to be *my o*.
¹⁶ The letters that have been cut out are thought to be "speak."
¹⁷ The letter that has been cut out is thought to be *d*.
¹⁸ The letters that have been cut out are thought to be "ent."
¹⁹ The letters that have been cut out are thought to be "ently."

is. My soul, this night, shall come to you in dreams and speak to
you those fervid thanks which my pen is all powerless to utter.

Edgar.

P. S. *Tuesday Morning*—I beg you to believe, dear Helen, that
I replied to your letter *immediately* upon its receipt; but a most
unusual storm, up to this moment, precludes all access to the
City.[20]

Mrs. Whitman must have replied about the tenth of October, and
evidently told Poe of some of the accusations that had been made
against him, among others that he had "no principle—no moral sense."
Poe denied these naturally, but in his efforts to prove that he had
high, even quixotic—standards of honor, he descended pretty far in
the other direction.

I swear to you that my soul is incapable of dishonor—that, with
the exception of occasional follies and excesses which I bitterly
lament, but to which I have been driven by intolerable sorrow,
and which are hourly committed by others without attracting any
notice whatever—I can call to mind no act of my life which would
bring a blush to my cheek—or to yours. If I have erred at all, in
this regard, it has been on the side of what the world would call
a Quixotic sense of the honorable—of the chivalrous. The indulgence of this sense has been the true voluptuousness of my life.
It was for this species of luxury that, in early youth, I deliberately
threw away from me a large fortune, rather than endure a trivial
wrong. It was for this, at a later period, I did violence to my own
heart, and married, for another's happiness, where I knew that
no possibility of my own existed.[21]

Knowing how ardently, in his letter of August 29, 1835, he begged
Virginia to marry him,[22] this statement to Mrs. Whitman is a deliberate falsehood, and is no more to be believed than his statement concerning a fortune which John Allan had no intention of giving him.
But even if Poe's reference to Virginia had not been false, what excuse
can there be for a man who sacrifices the memory of a love as devoted
as Virginia's on the altar of a new idol?

Let us hope Poe was more sincere in his rejoicing to learn that

[20] Original Autograph Ms., Lilly Collection.

[21] Original Autograph Ms., October 18, 1848, Lilly Collection.

[22] See also Poe's letter to Lowell, p. 432, concerning the happiness of his
married life.

Mrs. Whitman was not wealthy but was wholly dependent upon her mother. He closes the letter of October 18th, acknowledging that he had been in Providence on "the Monday you mention," which must have been on October 9th or 16th, but had not gone to see her, fearing another farewell. On his way to Lowell to lecture later in October, he saw her and urged her to marry him. She declined to promise him, but agreed to write him at Lowell, in care of the Richmonds. She delayed writing, not wishing to hurt him, but being equally unwilling to agree to a marriage. The letter was indecisive when it came to Poe. The lecture had to be postponed on account of the excitement concerning the presidential election of 1848,[23] and he started for Providence, probably on November 2nd. According to Poe's letter to Mrs. Richmond on November 16th, he remembered nothing distinctly until he arrived in Providence.[24] After a bad night, he purchased two ounces of laudanum, took the cars back to Boston, swallowed half the laudanum, which was fortunately rejected, and he was ill in consequence.

Mrs. Whitman had expected him on Saturday, November 4th but he apologized in a brief note on November 7th.

> *Dearest* Helen—I have *no* engagements, but am *very* ill—so much so that I must go home, if possible—but if you say "stay," I will try & do so. If you cannot see me—write me *one word* to say that you *do* love me and that, *under all circumstances,* you will be mine. Remember that these coveted words you have never yet spoken—and, nevertheless, I have not reproached you. It was not in my power to be here on Saturday as I proposed, or I would undoubtedly have kept my promise. If you can see me, even for a few moments do so—but if not write—or send some message which will comfort me.[25]

Mrs. Whitman noted on the letter—"Written the day on which Mr. Poe returned from Lowell. I sent him word I would meet him in half an hour at the Atheneum."

After a painful interview, in which Mrs. Whitman showed him some letters which had been sent to her, warning her against him,

---

[23] Mrs. Whitman to Stoddard, September 30, 1872—Stoddard, *Life*, pp. 156-157.

[24] To avoid repetition, the reader is referred to this letter to Mrs. Richmond, p. 590. It should be read in connection also with Mrs. Whitman.

[25] Original Autograph Ms., J. K. Lilly, Jr. Collection.

Poe wrote her a letter of renunciation, which has apparently disappeared. He came to her home the next day, however, in an excited state, begging her to save him from a terrible doom. A physician was called and diagnosed the case as one of cerebral congestion. Poe was taken care of by William J. Pabodie, a common friend. Believing, she said, that Poe's salvation depended upon her, Mrs. Whitman, on November 13th, consented to an engagement, conditional upon his abstaining from drink.[26] On November 14th Poe wrote on board one of the Sound steamers, running between Providence and New York, that he had kept his promise to her.[27]

By an ironic chance Mrs. Whitman wrote him on November 17th, the day after Poe sent off his ardent epistle to "Annie," and Poe assured her on the 22nd that the "terrible excitement" had subsided and that no one but her could reassure him.[28] On November 24th, he wrote Mrs. Whitman a long letter, beginning:

> Friday the 24th
>
> In a little more than a fortnight, dearest Helen, I shall, once again, clasp you to my heart:—until then I forbear to agitate you by speaking of my wishes—of my hopes, and especially of my fears. You say that all depends on my own firmness. If this be so, all is safe—for the terrible agony which I have so lately endured —an agony known only to my God and to myself—seems to have passed my soul through fire and purified it from all that is weak. Henceforward I am strong:—this those who love me shall see—as well as those who have so relentlessly endeavored to ruin me. It needed only some such trials as I have just undergone, to make me what I was born to be, by making me conscious of my own strength.—But all does *not* depend, dear Helen, upon my firmness —all depends upon the sincerity of your love.
>
> You allude to your having been "tortured by reports which have all since been explained to your entire satisfaction." On this point my mind is fully made up. I will rest neither by night nor by day until I bring those who have slandered me into the light of day —until I expose them, *and their motives,* to the public eye. I *have* the means and I will ruthlessly employ them. On one point let

---

[26] Mrs. Whitman to Ingram—Autograph Ms., University of Virginia.

[27] This letter has apparently been lost. It is printed in Ingram, II, 178, and there is a copy in an envelope bearing Mrs. Whitman's statement that Mr. Pabodie had borrowed it. J. K. Lilly, Jr. Collection.

[28] Original Autograph Ms., J. K. Lilly, Jr. Collection.

me caution you, *dear* Helen. No sooner will Mrs. E.[llet] hear of my proposals to yourself, than she will set in operation every conceivable chicanery to frustrate me;—and, if you are not prepared for her arts, she will *infallibly* succeed—for her whole study, throughout life, has been the gratification of her malignity by such means as any other human being would die rather than adopt. You will be sure to receive anonymous letters so skillfully contrived as to deceive the most sagacious. You will be called on, possibly, by persons whom you never heard of, but whom she has instigated to call & villify me—without even *their* being aware of the influence she has exercised. I do not know *any* one with a more *acute* intellect about such matters than Mrs. Osgood—yet even she was for a long time completely blinded by the arts of this fiend & simply because her generous heart could not conceive how any woman could stoop to machinations at which the most degraded of the fiends would shudder.[29]

Poe was still hearing echoes of his visits to Mrs. Whitman's home.— "I confess, too, that the insults of your mother and sister still rankle in my heart." On November 26th he proposes to Mrs. Whitman "to establish in America the sole unquestionable aristocracy—that of intellect." And he does not forget to ask her for copies of his critical articles which he needs for his new lecture [The Poetic Principle], which he is writing. He also tells her that "Mrs. O's [30] 'Ida Grey' is in 'Graham' for August—45," which implies that Mrs. Osgood's career was still of interest to him. Poe also noted in this letter that the management of the lecture course wished him to appear on December 6th and that he could not be in Providence before December 13th. It has been assumed that Poe was in Providence again on December 15th, because on that day two legal documents were drawn, one a demand on the administrator of the Marsh estate, by Mrs. Anna [Marsh] Power to transfer the property to her, the second an agreement signed by Sarah Helen Whitman and her sister Susan Anna Power that the transfer should be made. To the first of these Poe's name is also signed, although legally it was not necessary. But following these is a brief note—

[29] Original Autograph Ms., Lilly Collection. Then follows the account of the Ellet episode, which I have given in its appropriate place, see p. 498.

[30] Reproductions of this letter, beginning with the *Last Letters*, give this as "Mrs. B," but the "O" is perfectly clear in the original letter in the Lilly Collection.

Whereas a Marriage is intended between the above named Sarah H. Whitman and the Subscriber Edgar A. Poe, I hereby approve of and assent to the transfer of the property in the manner proposed in the papers of which the preceding are Copies.

Providence, December 22, 1848

In presence of
William J. Pabodie   EDGAR A. POE.[31]

Since Poe was asked to sign or approve *copies*, it looks as though they had been sent to him, and that his final action took place after his arrival in Providence. Moreover, his next letter to Mrs. Whitman is dated,

> "New York City—
> Saturday, 2. P. M.

My *own dearest* Helen—Your letters—to my mother & myself— have just been received, & I hasten to reply, in season for this afternoons mail. I cannot be in Providence until Wednesday [Dec. 20] morning; and, as I must try and get some sleep after I arrive, it is more than probable that I shall not see you until about 2 P. M. Keep up heart—*for all will go well*. My mother sends her dearest love and says she will return good for evil and treat you *much* better than *your* mother has treated me. Remember me to Mr. P. & believe me

> *Ever* your own
>   EDGAR.[32]

Mrs. Whitman wrote on this letter "Dec. 17, 1848" and this date has been accepted by Poe's biographers. But December 17th did not fall on Saturday in 1848, but on Sunday, and the date therefore refers to the receipt by her. Poe therefore wrote on December 16th, acknowledging letters from Mrs. Whitman, which would not have been written had he been in Providence on December 15th. The issue is not simply a matter of the error of one day; it proves almost with certainty that he was keeping away from Providence until the date of his lecture on the 20th. The reference to Mrs. Power's treatment of him indicates clearly that he is referring to the legal documents which he has probably received, enclosed in Mrs. Whitman's letter. What emotions they raised in him we can only conjecture. Poe was never

[31] Original Ms., Lilly Collection.
[32] Original Autograph Ms., Lilly Collection.

grasping in money matters but the transaction showed not only a lack of confidence in him, but it also changed Mrs. Whitman's status from that of an heiress in her own right, to a daughter whose mother could cut her off from any share in the family estate. It is quite possible to attribute to Edgar Poe a selfish reluctance to proceed with a marriage to a woman without property. But it is just as possible to attribute his hesitancy to an unwillingness to ask Mrs. Whitman to share his poverty with himself—and Mrs. Clemm. On the afternoon of December 19th, the day he left New York for Providence, he called on Mrs. Mary Hewitt, and the following conversation occurred:

"Mr. Poe, are you going to Providence to be married?" "No, Madam," replied the poet, "I am not going to Providence to be married, I am going to deliver a lecture on Poetry." Then after a pause, and with a look of great reserve, he added, "That marriage may never take place." [33]

Poe lectured in Providence on December 20th on the "Poetic Principle" before an audience of about two thousand people.[34] He stayed at the Earl House, and fell in with a group of young men who persuaded him to drink. On one evening, he came to Mrs. Whitman's home partially intoxicated but was very quiet and made no such disturbance as Griswold afterwards described. This may have been on December 22nd, the day on which he signed his consent to the transfer of the property. Pabodie gives no definite dates but Mrs. Whitman is more explicit. Among the many letters she wrote afterwards concerning these events, one to Mrs. Hewitt on September 25 or 27, 1850, is to be preferred on account of its avoidance of dramatization:

[33] Mrs. Whitman's copy of Mrs. Hewitt's letter to her, pasted on the reverse of sheet three, of Griswold's letter to Pabodie, June 8, 1852. In the Lilly Collection. Another copy by Mrs. Whitman, dated October 2, 1850, is substantially identical except for the important difference in Poe's remark —"That marriage will never take place." The latter is among the Griswold Mss. in the Boston Public Library, and might be preferred, except that there is an allusion to the banns being published, which Mrs. Whitman asserts is incorrect.

[34] The best accounts of these few days come from the letters of William J. Pabodie, a friend of Mrs. Whitman and of Poe, who, however, did not wish the marriage to take place. His letter to the *New York Tribune*, written June 2, 1852, and his subsequent letter to Griswold (who unsuccessfully challenged his statements) on June 11, 1852, will impress any fair-minded person with their clarity and authenticity. There is a Ms. of this letter to Griswold in the Lilly Collection, probably the first draft. There is another in the Boston Public Library.

Our engagement was from the first a *conditional* one. My mother was inflexibly opposed to our union, and being in a pecuniary point of view entirely dependent upon her, I *could* not, if I would, have acted without her concurrence. Many painful scenes occurred during his several visits to Providence in consequence of this opposition. The story of the *"Police"* is without a shadow of foundation. Neither did Mr. Poe, *after* obtaining my mother's reluctant consent to our immediate marriage, commit any of those excesses which have been charged to him. This consent was not obtained until the evening of Dec. 22. On the 23 of December Mr. Poe wrote a note to the Rev. Dr. Crocker requesting him to publish our intention of marriage on the ensuing Sunday [Dec. 24]–he also wrote a letter to Mrs. Clemm informing her that we should be married on Monday and should arrive at Fordham on Tuesday in the second train of cars. We rode out together in the morning & passed the greater part of the day in making preparations for my sudden change of abode. In the afternoon, while we were together at one of the circulating libraries of the city, a communication was handed me cautioning me against this imprudent marriage & informing me of many things in Mr. Poe's recent career with which I was previously unacquainted. I was at the same time informed that he had *already* violated the solemn promises that he had made to me & to my friends on the preceding evening. I knew that, even had I been disposed to overlook these things myself, they must within a few hours come to the knowledge of my friends & would lead to a recurrence of the scenes to which I had been already subjected, and I felt utterly helpless of being able to exercise any permanent influence over his life. On our return home I announced to him what I had heard &, in his presence, countermanded the order, which he had previously given, for the delivery of the note he had addressed to Dr. Crocker. He earnestly endeavoured to persuade me that I had been misinformed, especially in relation to his having that very morning called for wine at the bar of the hotel where he boarded. The effect of this infringement of his promise was in *no degree perceptible,* but the authority on which I had received this & *other* statements concerning him, was not to be questioned. I listened to his explanations & his remonstrances without one word of reproach and with that marble stillness of despair so mercifully accorded to us when the heart has been wrought to its highest capacity of suffering. Nor was I, at that bitter moment, unsolaced by a sense of relief at being freed from the intolerable burden of responsibility which he had sought to impose upon me, by persuading me that his fate, for good or evil, depended upon *me*. I had now learned that my influence was un-availing. My mother on being informed of what had transpired had a brief interview with Mr. Poe which resulted in his deter-mination to return immediately to New York. In her presence & in that of his friend, Mr. Pabodie, I bade him farewell, with feelings of profound commiseration for his fate—of intense sorrow thus to part from one whose sweet & gracious nature had endeared him to me beyond expression, and whose rare & peculiar intellect had given a new charm to my life. While he was endeavouring to win from me an assurance that our parting should not be a final one, my mother saved me from a response by insisting upon the imme-diate termination of the interview. Mr. Poe then started up and left the house with an expression of bitter resentment at what he termed, the "intolerable insults" of my family. I never saw him more—[35]

The original letter to Dr. Crocker reads:

Will Dr. Crocker have the kindness to publish the banns of matrimony between Mrs. Sarah Helen Whitman and myself, on Sunday and on Monday. When we have decided on the day of the marriage we will inform you, and will thank you to perform the ceremony.

Resp^y Yr. Ob. S^t

EDGAR A. POE.[36]

It is undated, and if Mrs. Whitman's dates are correct, December 23rd being Saturday, the marriage could hardly have taken place on Mon-day, which would have been Christmas day. Moreover the note clearly states that the date is not yet decided upon.

Mr. Pabodie makes clear why the banns were not published:

He [Poe] was still urgently anxious that the marriage should take place before he left the City. That very morning, he wrote a note to Dr. Crocker, requesting him to publish the intended mar-riage, at the earliest opportunity, and intrusted this note to me, with the request that I should deliver it in person. The note is still in my possession. I delayed complying with his request, in the hope that the union might yet be prevented. Many of Mrs. W's friends deprecated this hasty and imprudent marriage; and it was their urgent solicitations, and certain representations, which were that afternoon made by them to Mrs. W. and her family,

---

[35] First printed in "New Letters About Poe," by Stanley T. Williams, *Yale Review*, N. S., XIV (1925), 761-763, from the original Ms.

[36] J. K. Lilly Collection.

that led to the postponement of the marriage, and eventually to a dissolution of the engagement. In the evening of that day Mr. Poe left for New York. These are the facts, which I am ready to make oath to, if necessary. You will perceive, therefore, that I did not write inadvisedly, in the statements published in the Tribune.[37]

Poe, however, was in earnest up to the last. His note to Mrs. Clemm, undated, reads: "My own dear Mother—We shall be married on Monday, and will be at Fordham on Tuesday in the first train."

Rumors, of course, began to spread at once. To kill two birds with one stone, Poe wrote to Mrs. Richmond, inclosing a letter to Mrs. Whitman, which "Annie" was to mail. "Annie" kept a copy of it which she sent to Ingram later. Some of this letter, dated January 25, 1849, is of importance; and since so many others have spoken, Poe is entitled to his day in court: It begins—"Dear Madam, In commencing this letter need I say to you after what has passed *between us*—no amount of procrastination on your part or on the part of your friends shall induce me to speak ill of you, even in my own defence?" Then after requesting equal forbearance on her part, he continues, "My object in now writing you is to place before you an extract from a letter recently addressed to myself." Poe then quoted part of a letter to him from Mrs. Richmond, which repeated some of the amiable scandals then circulating, but which I need not give since Pabodie's statement has already denied them. Poe and this gentleman were not entirely in accord, however, for Poe continues to Mrs. Whitman: "Mr. Pabodie who *at my request*, forbore to speak to the minister about publishing the *first banns* on the day I left....—Your simple disavowal is all that I wish—You will of course write me immediately on receipt of this—only in the event of my not hearing from you within a few days will I proceed to take more definite steps....I blame no one but your Mother. Mr. Pabodie will tell you the words which passed between us, while from the effects of those terrible stimulants you lay prostrate without even the power to bid me farewell." Here is evidence that Mrs. Whitman's dramatic picture of her throwing a handkerchief soaked in ether over her face has some foundation, but it disposes at the same time of the romantic conversation between them, which has brightened so many biographies! Poe then continues "So far I have assigned on[?] reason for *my* declining to fulfill our engagement. I had none but the suspicions and grossly insulting parsimony

---

[37] Original Autograph letter, Pabodie to Griswold, June 11, 1852, Lilly Collection.

of the arrangements into which you suffered yourself to be forced by your Mother. . . . It has been my intention to say simply, that our marriage was postponed on account of your ill health—Have you really said or done anything which can preclude our placing the rupture on such footing? If not, I shall persist in the statement and thus, this unhappy matter will die quietly away." [38]

On the contrary, it went sounding on for many years. Mrs. Richmond notes on the letter that, "Mrs. Whitman's reply exonerated him completely, yet I think they [Mr. Richmond's relatives in Providence] were inclined to discredit it and believe him still a very unprincipled man." How to reconcile Mrs. Richmond's note concerning "Mrs. Whitman's reply" with the latter's statement—"His letter I did not dare to answer" must be left to those capable of doing so. [39]

This episode was almost over. The evidence proves conclusively that Poe did not break the engagement or create a scene in order that it should be broken, as was for many years believed on Griswold's authority. That Mrs. Whitman was relieved and yet regretted the breach is also clear. All one has to do is to look at the grim countenance of Mrs. Power [40] to see that Poe had little chance.

Neither Poe nor Mrs. Whitman was heartbroken, however. He was solacing himself with thoughts of "Annie," and "Helen" was recovering from the great sentimental adventure of her life. Another letter to Mrs. Hewitt is illuminating:

"I could not have written to you so freely of these things my dear Mrs. Hewitt if the interest I feel in Mr. Poe had partaken of the character of what is usually termed *love*. It is something at once more intimate & more remote—a strange inexplicable enchantment that I can neither analyze nor comprehend." [41]

That was the real trouble!

While Poe was in the throes of the episode with Helen Whitman, he had turned for sympathy to Mrs. Richmond. Poe describes her in "Landor's Cottage."

[38] Mrs. Richmond's letter, copying Poe's to Mrs. Whitman, is in Ms. at the University of Virginia. Her Ms. reads clearly, "I have assigned on reason for my declining to fulfill our engagement." There is a blur which may indicate that the word is "one," or it may be her error for "no."

[39] See Mrs. Whitman's letter to Griswold, December 12, 1849, reprinted in part on p. 651.

[40] *Poe's Helen*, p. 120.

[41] "New Letters About Poe," Stanley T. Williams, *Yale Review*, N. S., XIV (1925), 770.

As no bell was discernible, I rapped with my stick against the door, which stood half open. Instantly a figure advanced to the threshold—that of a young woman about twenty-eight years of age—slender, or rather slight, and somewhat above the medium height. As she approached, with a certain *modest decision* of step altogether indescribable, I said to myself, "Surely here I have found the perfection of natural, in contradistinction from artificial *grace*." The second impression which she made on me, but by far the more vivid of the two, was that of *enthusiasm*. So intense an expression of *romance*, perhaps I should call it, or of unworldliness, as that which gleamed from her deep-set eyes, had never so sunk into my heart of hearts before. I know not how it is, but this peculiar expression of the eye, wreathing itself occasionally into the lips, is the most powerful, if not absolutely the *sole* spell, which rivets my interest in woman. "*Romance*," provided my readers fully comprehend what I would here imply by the word— "romance" and "womanliness" seem to me convertible terms; and, after all, what man truly *loves* in woman, is, simply, her *womanhood*. The eyes of Annie (I heard some one from the interior call her "Annie, darling!") were "spiritual gray"; her hair, a light chestnut: this is all I had time to observe of her.[42]

Poe stayed with the Richmonds at their home in "Westford" during his visits to Lowell to lecture, and the family, including Sarah Heywood, Annie's younger sister, and Carrie or Caddy, a child apparently, became his warm friends. Sarah has left a charming picture of his visits.

"I have 'in my mind's eye,' " she remarks, "a figure somewhat below medium height, perhaps, but so perfectly proportioned, and crowned with such a noble head, so regally carried, that, to my girlish apprehension, he gave the impression of commanding stature. Those clear sad eyes seemed to look from an eminence, rather than from the ordinary level of humanity, while his conversational tone was so low and deep, that one could easily fancy it borne to the ear from some distant height. I saw him first in Lowell, and there heard him give a Lecture on Poetry, illustrated by readings and recitations. His manner of rendering some of the selections constituted my only remembrance of the evening: it fascinated me, although he gave no attempt at dramatic effect. Everything was rendered with pure intonation and perfect enunciation, marked attention being paid to the rhythm: he almost *sang* the more musical versifications.

    ·   ·   ·   ·   ·   ·   ·   ·   ·   ·   ·   ·

[42] *Complete Works*, Virginia Edition, VI, 268-269.

"My memory photographs him again," the lady continues, "sitting before an open wood fire, in the early autumn evening, gazing intently into the glowing coal, holding the hand of a dear friend—'Annie'—while for a long time no one spoke, and the only sound was the ticking of the tall old clock in the corner of the room. (I wish I could tell you what he was thinking about during that rapt silence!)" [43]

Poe was evidently a privileged character, and his attachment to Mrs. Richmond was quite understood at the beginning of their friendship. Poe's relations with Mrs. Richmond need quite as much explanation as his episode with Mrs. Whitman, but for a different reason. It was not a literary adventure; it was a heartfelt love, in the sense in which they meant the word "love." Both used it, from our point of view, somewhat indefinitely. Mrs. Richmond, for example, spoke of "loving" Nat Willis, and Poe commented on her "loving" Willis, without jealousy. It must constantly be remembered that it was an age of overemphasis.

Poe's letters to Annie are too voluminous for them all to be quoted, but they must not be censored, as Ingram printed them, in the interest of later Victorian standards. In Mrs. Whitman's case, I felt that the episode should be treated as a unit, but Poe made such a confidant of Annie, pouring out his hopes and his successes and failures that his letters to her become a valuable source for other events than the love story, and it is better to weave them into the pattern of his later life.

Poe's first important letter to Mrs. Richmond was written while he was recovering from his disastrous visit to Providence on November 7, 1848. The letter is one which must be printed complete or not at all: [44]

Ah, Annie Annie! *my* Annie! What cruel thoughts about your Eddy, must have been torturing your heart during the last terrible fortnight, in which you have heard *nothing* from me—not even one little word to say that I still lived & loved you. But

[43] Ingram, II, 188-190; one vol. ed., pp. 389-390.
[44] It is here printed from the copy, made by Mrs. Richmond, which is in the Library of the University of Virginia. At the head of the letter she wrote the words, "Copy of a letter written at Fordham, November 16, 1848." The original letter has apparently disappeared. Ingram omitted several important passages. I am indebted to the courtesy of Dean James Southall Wilson for permission to print the letter as it was written by Poe.

Annie, I know that you *felt* too deeply the nature of my love for you, to doubt *that*, even for one moment, & this thought has comforted me in my bitter sorròw—I could bear that you should imagine *every other evil except that one*—that my soul had been untrue to yours. Why am I not *with* you now *darling* that I might sit by your side, press your dear hand in mine, & look deep down into the clear Heaven of your eyes—so that the words which I now can only *write*, might sink into your heart, and make you comprehend what it is that I would say—And yet Annie, *all* that I wish to say—all that my soul pines to express at this instant, is included in the one word, *love*—To be with you now—so that I might whisper in your ear the divine emotions which agitate me —I would willingly—oh *joyfully* abandon this world with all my hopes of another:—but you *believe* this Annie—you do believe it, & will always believe it—So long as I think that you *know* I love you, as no man ever loved woman—so long as I think you comprehend in some measure, the fervor with which I adore you, *so long*, no worldly trouble can ever render me absolutely wretched. But oh, *my darling, my* Annie, my own sweet *sister* Annie, my *pure* beautiful angel—*wife* of my soul—to be mine hereafter & *forever in the Heavens,* how shall I explain to you the *bitter, bitter* anguish which has tortured me since I left you? You saw, you *felt* the agony of grief with which I bade you farewell—you remember my expressions of gloom—of a dreadful horrible foreboding of Ill—Indeed—*indeed* it seemed to me that death approached me even then, & that I was involved in the shadow which went before him—As I clasped you to my heart, I said to myself—"it is for the last time, until we meet in Heaven"—I remember nothing distinctly, from that moment until I found myself in Providence. I went to bed & wept through a long, long, hideous night of despair—When the day broke, I arose & endeavored to quiet my mind by a rapid walk in the cold, keen air—but all *would* not do—the demon tormented me still. Finally I procured two ounces of laud[a]num & without returning, to my Hotel, took the cars back to Boston. When I arrived, I wrote you a letter, in which I opened my whole heart to you—to *you*—my Annie, whom I so madly, so distractedly love—I told you how my struggles were more than I could bear—how my soul revolted from saying the words which were to be said—and that not even for your dear sake, could I bring myself to say them. I then reminded you of that holy promise, which was the last I exacted from you in parting—the promise that, under all circumstances, you would come to me on my bed of death—I implored you to come *then*—mentioning the place where I should be found in Boston. Having written this letter, I swallowed about half the laud[a]num, & hurried to the Post-office—intending not to take the rest until I saw you—for, I did not doubt for one moment, that *my own* Annie would keep her sacred promise. But I had not calculated on the strength of the laudanum, for, before I reached the Post office my reason was entirely gone, & the letter was never put in. Let me pass over, my darling *sister*, the awful horrors which succeeded. A friend was at hand, who aided & (if it can be called easing) eased me, but it is only within the last three days, that I have been able to remember what occurred in that dreary interval. It appears that, after the laudanum was rejected from the stomach, I became calm, & to a casual observer, sane—so that I was suffered to go back to Providence—Here I saw *her*, & spoke, for *your* sake, the words which you urged me to speak—Ah Annie Annie! *my* Annie!—*is* your heart *so* strong?—is there *no* hope?—is there *none?*—I feel that I *must* die if I persist, & yet, how can I now retract with honor?—Ah *beloved*, think—think for *me* & for yourself—do I not *love* you Annie? do you not *love me?* Is not this *all?* Beyond this blissful thought, what other consideration *can* there be in this dreary world! It is not *much* that I ask, *sweet sister Annie*—my mother & myself would take a small cottage at Westford—oh *so* small—so *very* humble—I should be far away from the tumult of the world—from the ambition which I loathe— I would labor day & night, and with industry, I could accomplish *so* much—Annie! it would be a Paradise beyond my wildest hopes —I could see some of your beloved family *every* day, & you, often —oh *very* often—I would hear from you continually—regularly & *our* dear mother would be with us & love us both—ah *darling*— do not these pictures touch your inmost heart? Think—oh *think* for me—before the words—the vows are spoken, which put yet another terrible *bar*, between us—before the time goes by, beyond which there must be *no* thinking—I call upon you in the name of God—in the name of the holy love I bear you, to be *sincere* with me—*Can* you, *my* Annie, *bear* to think I am another's? *It would give me supreme—infinite bliss* to hear you say that you could *not* bear it—I am at home now with my dear muddie who is endeavoring to comfort me—but the sole words which soothe me, are those in which she speaks of *"my Annie"*—She tells me that she has written you, begging you to come on to Fordham—Ah beloved Annie, IS IT NOT POSSIBLE? I am so *ill*—so terribly, hopelessly ILL in body and mind, that I feel I CANNOT live, unless I can feel your sweet, gentle, loving hand pressed upon my forehead—Oh my *pure, virtuous, generous, beautiful, beautiful sister* Annie!—is it not POSSIBLE for you to come—if only for one little week?—until I subdue this fearful agitation, which if continued, will either destroy my life or, drive me hopelessly mad—Farewell—*here & hereafter—*

forever your own

EDDY—

This letter is only one of the evidences of the duality of Poe's nature. That he loved "Annie" as a man loves a woman, while he loved Helen Whitman as a poet loves a poetess, is clear. That he had not yet recovered from the Boston episode is also clear. Poe's attempt at suicide may be described correctly but in view of his statement that he remembered nothing of the trip from Boston to Providence, this is doubtful. If it is correct, it provides a definite proof that Poe was not in the habit of taking opium, for the drug would not have had such an effect upon an addict. Finally, his naïve suggestion of the cottage at Westford where, chaperoned by Mrs. Clemm, he could have seen constantly not only Annie, but also all her family, gives an unworldly flavor to the epistle.

It is not necessary, however, to delve deeply into psycho-analysis to explain this agony of indecision on Poe's part. Many a perfectly normal man has approached his engagement or his wedding with one woman, whom he loves well enough to marry, clouded by his knowledge that if another woman were free, he would be trying to win her instead. Poe's reluctance to "say the word" is quite understandable. Usually, the man keeps quiet about it, or tells a friend in those moments of confidence that precede important events in his life. Poe poured out his emotions to the woman whom, next to Virginia, he really loved. There is something curiously alike in the letter to Mrs. Clemm and Virginia of August 29, 1835, and this letter to Annie.

Mrs. Richmond did not reply to this epistle at once, for Poe wrote her sister, Sarah, on November 23rd, to know why, and assured her "If I did not love your sister with the *purest* and most unexacting love, I would not dare confide in you." [45]

[45] Ingram, *Life*, II, 195.

On December 28th [46] Poe wrote Annie concerning the success of his lecture at Providence, and during this fall and winter he did not let his sentimental excursions occupy all his attention. A letter to Mrs. Richmond, on January 25, 1849, in which he inclosed the missive to Mrs. Whitman,[47] reveals not only his sentiments for Annie, but also his literary engagements. After the customary assurances of devotion, Poe continued:

I deeply regret that Mr. R. should think ill of me. If you can, disabuse him—and at all times act for me as *you* think best. I put my honor, as I would my life and soul, implicitly in your hands; but I would *rather* not confide my purposes, *in that one regard,* to any one but your dear sister.

I enclose you a letter for Mrs. Whitman. Read it—show it only to those in whom you have faith, and then *seal* it with wax and mail it from Boston. . . . When her answer comes I will send it to you: that will convince you of the truth. If she refuse to answer I will write to Mr. Crocker. By the by, if you know his exact name and address send it to me. . . . But as long as you and yours love me, what need I care for this cruel, unjust, calculating world? . . . In all my present anxieties and embarrassments, I still feel in my inmost soul a *divine joy*—a happiness inexpressible—that nothing seems to disturb. . . .

I hope Mr. C. is well. Remember me to him, and ask him if he has seen my "Rationale of Verse," in the last October and November numbers of the *Southern Literary Messenger.* . . . I am *so* busy, now, and feel so full of energy. Engagements to write are pouring in upon me every day. I had two proposals within the last week *from Boston.* I sent yesterday an article to the *Am. Review.* about "Critics and Criticism." Not long ago I sent one to the *Metropolitan* called "Landor's Cottage:" it has something about "Annie" in it, and will appear, I suppose, in the March number. To the *S. L. Messenger* I have sent fifty pages of "Marginalia," five pages to appear each month of the current year. I have also made permanent engagements with every magazine in America (except Peterson's *National*) including a Cincinnati magazine, called *The Gentlemen's.* So you see that I have only to keep up my spirits to get out of all my pecuniary troubles. The

---

[46] This letter is dated only "Thursday Morning—28," but that would have been December, in 1848.

[47] See pp. 586-587.

least price I get is $5 per "Graham page," and I can easily average 1½ per day—that is $7½. As soon as "returns" come in I shall be out of difficulty.

But of one thing rest assured, "Annie"—from this day forth I shun the pestilential society of *literary women.* They are a heartless, unnatural, venomous, dishonorable *set,* with no guiding principle but inordinate self-esteem. Mrs. Osgood is the *only* exception I know. . . . Kiss little Caddy for me, and remember me to Mr. R. and to all.[48]

"Landor's Cottage" came back to him, however, and the article on "Critics and Criticism" was not published until after his death. But Poe was working hard and steadily and his mind was clearing. A letter dated vaguely "Thursday—8th" but evidently written in February, again proves how Poe was recovering his energies, and what rates he secured for his work:

[I have been so busy, dear "Annie," even since I returned from Providence—six weeks ago. I have not suffered a day to pass without writing from a page to three pages. Yesterday, I wrote five, and the day before a poem considerably longer than the "Raven." I call it "The Bells."] How I wish my Annie could see it! Her opinion is so dear to me on such topics. On *all* it is everything to me—but on poetry in especial. And Sarah, too.—I told her, when we were at Westford, that I hardly ever knew any one with a keener discrimination in regard to what is *really* poetical. The 5 prose pages I finished yesterday are called—what do you think?—I am sure you will never guess—*Hop-Frog!* Only think of *your* Eddy writing a story with *such* a name as "Hop-Frog"! You would never guess the subject (which is a terrible one) from the title, I am sure. It will be published in a weekly paper, of Boston, called "The Flag of Our Union"—not a *very* respectable journal, perhaps, in a literary point of view, but one that pays as high prices as most of the Magazines. The proprietor wrote to me, offering about 5$ a "Graham page" and as I was anxious to get out of my pecuniary difficulties, I accepted the offer. He gives $5 for a Sonnet, also. Mrs. Osgood, Park Benjamin, & Mrs. Sigourney are engaged. I think "The Bells" will appear in the "Am. Review."—I have got no answer yet from Mrs. W. who, I understand, has left Providence (*for the first time in her life*) and gone

[48] Ingram, II, 203-205; one vol. ed., pp. 401-403.

to New Bedford. My opinion is, that her mother (who is an old devil) has intercepted the [letter and will never give it to her].

Dear Muddy says she w[ill write a long letter in a day] or two & tell you *how good* I am. She is in high spirits at my prospects and at our hopes of soon seeing Annie. We have told our landlord that we will not take the house next year. Do not let Mr. R., however, make any arrangements for us in Lowell, or Westford —for, being poor, we are so much the slaves of circumstances. At all events, we will both come & see you & spend a week with you in the early spring or before—but we will let you know some time before we come. Muddy sends her dearest-dearest love to you & Sarah & to *all*. And now good bye, my *dear, darling, beautiful Annie.*

YOUR OWN EDDY.[49]

"Hop-Frog" is not only one of his most powerful stories, but it also illustrates in a striking manner, Poe's method of writing fiction. "Hop-Frog" is a story of the revenge of a court jester, a dwarf and cripple, who as a cruel joke is forced to drink wine by the king, although the jester hates it. Perhaps Poe's own reaction to those who urged him, against his will, to drink the one glass that took away his self-control, was the model for the behavior of the dwarf. But the king is not satisfied with this jest. A girl, Trippetta, a friend of the jester, begs the king to cease plying the dwarf with wine, and the monarch brutally throws the wine in her face. Hop-Frog plans his revenge. He is commanded to provide entertainment for the masquerade that evening. He suggests that the king and his seven councillors disguise themselves as ourang-outangs, and frighten the other guests. He dresses them in garments saturated with tar, covers them with flax, chains them together, and produces, to the king's delight, consternation among the guests as he and his companions rush into the room. By a clever trick, Hop-Frog drags them up in the air, sets fire to their coats, and soon they hang, amid his jibes, a burnt and hideous mass.

The source of this story is usually given as Lord Berners' translation of Froissart, but Froissart's tale merely relates an incident at the court of Charles VI of France. At the suggestion of a Norman squire, King Charles and five others, including the squire, dress as satyrs, with pitch and flax covering their clothes. They are accidentally

[49] Original Autograph Ms., Morgan Library. The letter is slightly torn and passages in brackets have been supplied from Ingram, *Life*, II, 206. Ingram "edited" the letter, as usual.

set on fire. The king not being chained to the rest, plunges into water and is saved.[50] But Poe must have seen an excerpt from this tale, printed in the *Broadway Journal* [51] and need not have read the original at all, for all the details he uses are in the *Journal*. What makes the story a great one, however, is the way Poe breathes into the jester the, incarnate spirit of a revenge taken by the physically weak but mentally alert cripple for a wrong done to the woman he loved. There is no jester and no revenge in Froissart. But there is a tale which may have given Poe a suggestion for the character of the jester. Poe certainly knew the story of "Monos and Daimonos" by Bulwer. In the same number of the *New Monthly Magazine* [52] in which this appeared, there was a story, "Frogère and the Emperor Paul," [53] which told of a trick played upon a jester by Emperor Paul of Russia, who apparently exiles the jester to Siberia, but really has him driven a long distance and returned to court. The jester is a party to the Emperor's death. The story, incidentally, is signed "P." Did Poe then combine these two incidents in "Hop-Frog"? The titles indicate it, but the point is that Poe contributed those elements which make the story important. The mere names become characters, the motive of revenge is not simply indicated, but is made the climax of the story. It is really a critical stupidity to speak of the "sources" at all; they are merely suggestions out of which a creative artist made something new.

Of the other stories of this period "Mellonta Tauta" [54] is a satirical narrative of a balloon journey in 2848, which has been thrown into the sea in a bottle just as the balloon collapses. Quite a large share of the bottle is filled with a modified form of the initial portions of Eureka. "Von Kempelen and his Discovery" [55] is one of those successful attempts of Poe to imitate a scientific report upon the supposed discovery of a method of turning lead into gold. In a letter to Duyckinck Poe suggested that the hoax would be believed "and that thus, acting as a sudden, although a very temporary, check to the gold-fever, it will create a stir to some purpose." [56] "X-ing a Paragrab" is a satiric

[50] *The Chronicles of Froissart,* translated out of French by Sir John Bourchier, Lord Berners. Cap. CXXXVIII, ed. London, 1903, VI, 96-100.

[51] I (February 1, 1845), 71.

[52] *New Monthly Magazine and Literary Journal,* XXVIII (1830), 387-392.

[53] Pp. 491-496.

[54] *Godey's Lady's Book,* February, 1849.

[55] *Flag of Our Union,* April 14, 1849.

[56] Poe to Duyckinck, March 8 [1849], Autograph Ms., New York Public Library.

trifle. "Landor's Cottage," Poe's last published story,[57] has already been discussed.

Poe was not to be left in his peaceful labors very long. Mrs. Locke, who felt herself aggrieved, stirred up her husband and both tried to break up the friendship between Poe and Annie. Poe's next letter to Mrs. Richmond must be read as an antidote to the letter of November 16, 1848. He was in better command of his faculties.

Fordham, Feb. 19, Sunday.[58]

Dear, dearest Annie, My sweet Friend and Sister—I fear that in this letter, which I write with a heavy heart, you will find much to disappoint and grieve you—for I must abandon my proposed visit to Lowell, and God only knows when I shall see you, and clasp you by the hand. I have come to this determination to-day, after looking over some of your letters to me and my mother, written since I left you. You have not *said* it to me, but I have been enabled to glean from what you *have* said, that Mr. Richmond has permitted himself (perhaps without knowing it) to be influenced against me by the malignant misrepresentations of Mr. and Mrs Locke. Now, I frankly own to you, dear "Annie," that *I am proud*, although I have never shown myself proud to you or yours, and never will. You know that I quarrelled with the Lockes *solely* on your account and Mr. R.'s. It was obviously my interest to keep in with them, and, moreover, they had rendered me some services which entitled them to my gratitude up to the time when I discovered they had been blazoning their favors to the world. Gratitude, then, as well as interest, would have led me not to offend them; and the insults offered to me individually by Mrs. Locke were not sufficient to make me break with them. It was only when I heard them declare that thru' their patronage alone you were admitted into society, that your husband was every thing despicable—that it would ruin my mother even to enter your doors, it was only when such insults were offered to *you*, whom I so sincerely and most purely loved, and to Mr. Richmond, whom I had every reason to like and respect, that I arose and left their house and incurred the unrelenting vengeance of that worst of all fiends, "a woman scorned." Now feeling all this, I cannot help thinking it unkind in Mr. Richmond, when I am absent and un-

[57] *Flag of Our Union*, June 9, 1849.
[58] February 19th fell on Monday in 1849, but the letter clearly belongs to that year.

able to defend myself, that he *will* persist in listening to what these people say to my discredit. I cannot help thinking it, more-over, the most unaccountable instance of weakness—of obtuseness —that ever I knew a *man* to be guilty of: women are more easily misled in such matters. In the name of God, what else had I to anticipate in return for the offence which I offered Mrs. Locke's insane vanity and self-esteem, than that she would spend the rest of her days in ransacking the world for scandal against me (and the falser the better for her purpose), and in fabricating accu-sations where she could not find them ready made? I certainly anticipated no other line of conduct on her part; but, on the other hand, I certainly did not anticipate that any man in his *senses* would ever listen to accusations from so suspicious a source. That any man could be really influenced by them surpasses my belief and the fact is "Annie," to come at once to the point, I cannot and *do* not believe it—The obvious prejudices of Mr. R.—cannot be on this ground. I much fear that he has mistaken the nature—the purity of that affection which I feel for you and have not scrupled to avow, an affection which first entered my heart, I believe, through a natural revulsion of feeling at discovering you, *you* the subject of the debased Mrs. L's vile calumnies, to be not only purer than Mrs. L. but finer and nobler, at all points, than any woman I have ever known or *could have imagined* to exist upon the earth. God knows dear, *dear* Annie with what horror I would have shrunk from insulting a nature so *divine* as yours, with any impure or earthly tone. But since it is clear that Mr. R. cannot enter into my feelings on this topic & that he even suspects *what is not,* it only remains for me beloved Annie to consult *your* hap-piness which under all circumstances will be and must be mine. Not only must I *not* visit you at Lowell, but I must discontinue my letters and you yours. I cannot and *will* not have it on my conscience, that I have interfered with the domestic happiness of the only being in the whole world, whom I have loved at the same time with truth and with purity—I do not *merely* love you, "Annie"—I admire and respect you even more—and Heaven knows there is no particle of selfishness in my devotion—I ask nothing for myself, but your *own* happiness—with a charitable interpre-tation of those calumnies which—for your sake, I am now endur-ing from this vile woman—and which, for your dear, *dear* sake, I would most willingly endure if multiplied a hundredfold. The calumnies, indeed, "Annie," do not materially wound me, except in depriving me of your society—for of your affection and respect I *feel* that they never can. As for any injury the falsehoods of these people can do *me*, make your mind easy about that. It is true that "Hell has no fury like a woman scorned," but I have encountered such vengeance before, on far higher grounds—that is to say, for a far less holy purpose, than I feel the defence of your good name to be. I scorned Mrs. Ellet, simply because she revolted me, and to this day she has never ceased her *anonymous* persecutions. But in what have they resulted? She has not deprived me of one friend who ever knew me and once trusted me—nor has she lowered me one inch in the public opinion. When she ventured too far, I sued her at once (through her miserable tools), and recovered exemplary damages—as I will unquestionably do, forthwith, in the case of Mr. Locke, if ever he shall muster courage to utter a single *actionable* word. It is true I shrink with a nameless horror from connecting my name in the public prints, with such unmentionable nobodies and blackguards as Locke and his *lady*—but they may provoke me a little too far —You will now have seen, dear Annie, how and why it is that my Mother and myself cannot visit you as we proposed. In the first place my presence might injure you in your husband's opinion— & in the second I could not feel at ease in *his* house, so long as he permits himself to be prejudiced against me, or so long as he associates with such persons as the Lockes. It had been my design to ask you and Mr. R—(or, perhaps, your parents) to board my Mother while I was absent at the South, and I intended to start after remaining with you a week, but my whole plans are now disarranged—I have taken the cottage at Fordham for another year—Time, dear, dear Annie, will show all things. Be of good heart, I shall never cease to think of you—and bear in mind the *two* solemn promises I have made you. The one I am now religiously keeping, and the other (so help me Heaven!) shall sooner or later be kept.—Always your dear friend and brother,

EDGAR.[59]

This is the letter of a self-respecting man and not of a philanderer. When Mrs. Richmond sent this letter to Ingram, she added a postscript:

[59] Copy by Mrs. Richmond, now in the Library of the University of Virginia.

In justice to my dear husband, I feel in duty bound to tell you, that he *never* suspected Mr. Poe of anything dishonorable, though the Locke's did their best to poison him in every way & make him believe their atrocious falsehoods—on receipt of this letter, he wrote them (the Lockes) denouncing them in the *strongest terms*, & the acquaintance ended there & then. He also requested me to *urge* Mrs. Clemm & Mr. Poe to come on & said she was welcome to stay as long as she wished. If I ever see you I shall have many many things to tell you and to explain.

Yours always

A. L. R.

On March 23rd, Poe sent the verses "For Annie" to Mrs. Richmond, telling her that they had been sold to the *Flag of Our Union*, where they appeared on April 28, 1849. Poe also sent them to Willis asking him to copy them in the *Home Journal*, where they appeared on the same day. Poe always considered his poetry as his own property which he could reprint anywhere he chose. Indeed his note to Willis indicates that Willis is doing him a favor by giving the verses wider publicity. Naturally some of the editors who paid him for the first insertion did not agree with this position. But considering how little they gave him, he had a certain amount of justice on his side. "For Annie" is one of Poe's finest poems, notwithstanding some curious lapses as in the second stanza. In "The Bells" he had imitated sounds by other sounds. In "For Annie" he did something much more difficult. He reproduced an emotional state by a short throbbing measure, in which the very incoherencies mirror perfectly the mood. The poet who wrote the lines

"And the fever called 'Living'
Is conquered at last"

had not ceased to possess the secret of the magnificent phrase.

While Poe was conducting this correspondence with Mrs. Richmond, he was not neglecting his editorial and literary associates. On January 13, 1849, he wrote to John R. Thompson, Editor of the *Southern Literary Messenger*, proposing a new series of "Marginalia" for two dollars a page.[60] Thompson accepted his offer and published installments from April to September, 1849 but evidently without any immediate payment.

Among these last installments of "The Marginalia" the best are Poe's discussion of songwriting; his defence of Bayard Taylor's

---

[60] Original Autograph Ms., Huntington Library.

Rhymes of Travel; his analysis of the feelings of a soul far superior to the race, who would in consequence have enemies at all points; the definition of art as the "reproduction of what the senses perceive in nature through the veil of the soul." While he used at times earlier material, there is no evidence of any falling off in his ability to write pungent paragraphs.

In the postscript of Poe's letter to Thompson, he said, "I am about to bestir myself in the world of letters rather more busily than I have done for three or four years past." Poe was evidently able to plan and to carry out a return to creative writing, if luck again had not been against him.

Poe's letter to F. W. Thomas, of February 14, 1849, strikes a fairly cheerful note:

Fordham, February 14, 1849

My dear Friend Thomas,—Your letter, dated November 27, has reached me at a little village of the Empire State, after having taken, at its leisure, a very considerable tour among the Post-Offices—occasioned, I presume, by your indorsement "to forward" wherever I might be—and the fact is, where I might *not* have been, for the last three months, is the legitimate question. At all events, now that I have your well-known MS. before me, it is most cordially welcome. Indeed, it seems an age since I heard from you, and a decade of ages since I shook you by the hand—although I hear *of* you now and then. Right glad am I to find you once more in a true position—in the field of Letters. Depend upon it, after all, Thomas, Literature is the most noble of professions. In fact, it is about the only one fit for a man. For my own part, there is no seducing me from the path. I shall be a *littérateur* at least all my life; nor would I abandon the hopes which still lead me on for all the gold in California. Talking of gold, and of the temptations at present held out to "poor-devil authors," did it ever strike you that all which is really valuable to a man of letters—to a poet in especial—is absolutely unpurchasable? Love, fame, the dominion of intellect, the consciousness of power, the thrilling sense of beauty, the free air of Heaven, exercise of body & mind, with the physical and moral health which result—these and such as these are really all that a poet cares for: then answer me this—*why* should he go to California? Like Brutus, "I pause for a reply"—which like F. W. Thomas, I take it for granted you have no intention of giving me. I have read the Prospectus of the "Chronicle," and like it much, especially the part where you talk about letting go the finger of that conceited booby, the East, which is by no means the East out of which came the wise men mentioned in Scripture. I wish you would come down on the Frogpondians. They are getting worse and worse, and pretend not to be aware that there *are* any literary people out of Boston. The worst and most disgusting part of the matter is that the Bostonians are really, as a race, far inferior in point of *anything beyond mere talent* to any other *set* upon the continent of North America. They are decidedly the most servile imitators of the English it is possible to conceive. I always get into a passion when I think about [it]. It would be the easiest thing in the world to use them up *en masse*. One really well-written satire would accomplish the business: but it must not be such a dish of skimmed-milk-and-water as Lowell's. I suppose you have seen that affair—the "Fable for Critics," I mean. Miss Fuller, that detestable old maid, told him once that he was "so wretched a poet as to be disgusting even to his best friends." This set him off at a tangent and he has never been quite right since—so he took to writing satire against mankind in general, with Margaret Fuller and her *protégé*, Cornelius Matthews [sic] in particular. It is miserably weak upon the whole, but has one or two good but by no means *original* things,—oh, there is "*nothing* new under the sun," and Solomon is right—for once. I sent a review of the "Fable" to the "S. L. Messenger," a day or two ago, and I only hope Thompson will print it. Lowell is a ranting abolitionist, and *deserves* a good using up. It is a pity that he is a poet. I have not seen your paper yet, and hope you will mail me one—regularly if you can spare it. I will send you something whenever I get a chance. With your coeditor, Mr. ———, I am not acquainted personally, but he is well known to me by reputation. Eames, I think, was talking to me about him in Washington once, and spoke very highly of him in many respects, so upon the whole you are in luck. The rock on which most new enterprises in the paper way split is namby-pambyism. It never did do & never will. No yea-nay journal *ever* succeeded. But I know there is little danger of your making the "Chronicle" a yea-nay one. I have been quite out of the literary world for the last three years, and have *said* little or nothing, but, like the owl, I have "taken it out in thinking." By and by I mean to come out of the bush, and then I have *some* old scores to settle. I fancy I see some of my *friends* already stepping up to the Captain's office. The fact is, Thomas, living buried in the country makes a man savage—wolfish. I am just in the humor for a fight. You will be pleased to hear that I am in better health than I ever knew myself to be—full of energy, and bent upon success. You shall hear of me again shortly—and it is not improbable that I may soon pay you a visit in Louisville. If I can do anything for you in New York, let me know. Mrs. Clemm sends her best respects, and begs to be remembered to your mother's family if they are with you. You would oblige me very especially if you could squeeze in what follows, editorially.[61] The lady [Mrs. Lewis] spoken of is a most particular friend of mine, and deserves *all* I have said of her. I will reciprocate the favor I ask, whenever you say the word, and show me how. Address me at N. York City as usual, and if you insert the following, please cut it out and enclose it in your letter.

Truly your friend,

EDGAR A. POE.[62]

Thompson did publish Poe's review of Lowell's *Fable for Critics,* in March, 1849. Poe criticized his former friend unmercifully for his omission of Southern writers, in which he was not entirely unjustified, since Poe was the only Southern author Lowell mentioned. Poe quoted the now famous lines beginning

> "Here comes Poe with his Raven, like Barnaby Rudge—
> Three-fifths of him genius, and two-fifths sheer fudge,"

which evidently rankled. Yet, in the same review, Poe defended Lowell and Longfellow from Margaret Fuller's criticism and spoke of them "as upon the whole, perhaps our best poets."

Mrs. Richmond's friendship for Poe, which was that of a self-respecting woman, who had no desire to break up her home, but who was truly devoted to Poe, did not come to an end. In a letter to her, undated, but belonging evidently to the spring of 1849, Poe told her of his illness and of his disappointments in his magazine contacts:

Annie,—you will see by this note that I am nearly, if not quite, well—so be no longer uneasy on my account. I was not so ill as my mother supposed, and she is so anxious about me that she

[61] This refers to an appended Ms. containing a rather pitiful example of Poe's praise of women poets. A note on it says it was not published.

[62] Autograph Ms., Griswold Collection, Boston Public Library.

takes alarm often without cause. It is not so much *ill* that I have been as depressed in spirits—I cannot express to you how terribly I have been suffering from gloom. I begin to have a secret terror lest I may *never* behold you again—Abandon all hope of seeing me soon. You know how cheerfully I wrote to you not long ago—about my prospects—hopes—how I anticipated being soon out of difficulty. Well! all seems to be frustrated—at least for the present. As usual, misfortunes never come single, and I have met one disappointment after another. The *Columbian Magazine*, in the first place, failed—then Post's *Union* (taking with it my principal dependence); then the *Whig Review* was forced to stop paying for contributions—then the *Democratic*—then (on account of his oppression and insolence) I was obliged to quarrel, finally, with—; and then, to crown all, the "——— ———" (from which I anticipated so much and with which I had made a regular engagement for $10 a week throughout the year) has written a circular to correspondents, pleading poverty and declining to receive any more articles. More than this, the *S. L. Messenger*, which owes me a good deal, cannot pay just yet, and, altogether, I am reduced to Sartain and Graham—both very precarious. No doubt, Annie, you attribute my *"gloom"* to these events—but you would be wrong. It is not in the power of any mere *worldly* considerations, such as these, to depress me.... No, my sadness is *unaccountable,* and this makes me the more sad. I am full of dark forebodings. *Nothing* cheers or comforts me. My life seems wasted—the future looks a dreary blank: but I will struggle on and "hope against hope" ... What do you think? I have received a letter from Mrs. L[ocke], and such a letter! She says she is about to publish a detailed account of *all* that occurred between us, under guise of romance, with fictitious names, &c.,—that she will make me appear noble, generous, &c. &c.—nothing bad—that she will "do justice to my motives," &c. &c. She writes to know if "I have any suggestions to make." If I do not answer it in a fortnight, the book will go to press as it is—and, more than all this—she is coming on immediately *to see me at Fordham.* I have not replied—shall I? and what? The "friend" who sent the lines to the "H. J." was the friend who loves *you* best—was myself. The *Flag* so misprinted them that I was resolved to have a true copy. The *Flag* has two of my articles yet—"A Sonnet to my Mother," and "Landor's Cottage." ... I have written a ballad called "Annabel Lee," which I will send you soon. *Why* do you not send the tale of which you spoke?" [63]

Poe does not mention in this letter to Annie his poem, "Eldorado," which was published in *The Flag of Our Union* on April 21, 1849, so the letter was probably written after this date. "Eldorado" is mainly interesting because it reveals once more Poe's inspiration for a poem through current American events. The gold rush was on, and though no mention is made of it, the symbolism is evident.

Far more important was Poe's sonnet "To My Mother," which appeared on July 7th in *The Flag of Our Union*.

> "Because I feel that, in the Heavens above,
>   The angels, whispering to one another,
> Can find, among their burning terms of love,
>   None so devotional as that of 'Mother,'
> Therefore by that dear name I long have called you—
>   You who are more than mother unto me,
> And fill my heart of hearts, where Death installed you,
>   In setting my Virginia's spirit free.
> My mother—my own mother, who died early,
>   Was but the mother of myself; but you
> Are mother to the one I loved so dearly,
>   And thus are dearer than the mother I knew
> By that infinity with which my wife
>   Was dearer to my soul than its soul-life."

The sincerity of feeling, and the exquisite taste of this tribute to Mrs. Clemm and to Virginia reveal Poe in that exaltation of soul which arises when gratitude to the living is rekindled by the memory of the beloved dead. Overlooking the occasions on which Mrs. Clemm had proved to be a handicap, he paid this tribute to her warm affection and her devotion, which are beyond question. But his tribute to his mother-in-law is only a means through which he rises to the loftier tribute to Virginia. Any theory that Poe was failing in 1849 in mental power is confuted by this poem, which shows his complete mastery of the sonnet structure. Poe wrote in the English sonnet form, which really consists of three quatrains and a couplet, but he also was aware of the power of the Italian form, with its rise to a climax at the end of

[63] Ingram, II, 213-15; one vol. ed., pp. 409-10. The fifth and sixth sentences are from Ingram's article in *Appleton's Journal*, May, 1878. He omitted them in the *Life*.

the octave. Combining these two forms, he brings to both the climax of the octave and the final climax of the Sonnet the expression of his undying love for his wife. How seldom in poetry the word "wife" has been happily used is known to every student of English verse. Even when a wife is celebrated, the word is avoided, probably on account of its domestic flavor. Only a great poet can overcome the danger that arises when the most intimate of all relations is exposed to the devastating test of print. But with his usual scorn of danger, Poe placed the word in the concluding couplet, the most conspicuous position in the poem.

Since Poe speaks of "Annabel Lee" in this same letter to Mrs. Richmond, it belongs in the spring of 1849. When it was published [64] after Poe's death, several claimants arose for the honor of being his inspiration. But the best judgment agrees with Mrs. Osgood, who spoke in her letter to Griswold of "the exquisite pathos of the little poem lately written, of which she [Virginia] was the subject, and which is by far the most natural, simple, tender and touchingly beautiful of all his songs. I have heard it said that it was intended to illustrate a late love affair of the author; but they who believe this, have in their dullness, evidently misunderstood or missed the beautiful meaning latent in the most lovely of all its verses—where he says,

'A wind blew out of a cloud, chilling
My beautiful Annabel Lee,
So that her high-born kinsmen came,
And bore her away from me.'"

I have already [65] called attention to the carrying over from "Tamerlane" of the idea expressed in "Annabel Lee" by the lines,

"With a love that the wingéd seraphs in Heaven
Coveted her and me."

Thus in Poe's first and in his last poem he struck a similar note of youthful love, lasting beyond death. The utter simplicity and unity of the poem do not reveal at first the artistic use of those elements of variety of which Poe was still a master. He called the poem a ballad, which it is not, in the historical sense, but he was probably thinking of the alternation of four and three stress rising measures, character-

[64] New York *Tribune,* October 9, 1849.
[65] P. 123.

Mrs. Maria Clemm

From a drawing made by Arthur G. Learned, of a daguerreotype taken
about 1849. Reproduced through the courtesy of Mr. Learned, owner
of the copyright.

istic of the ballad in its prime. Through a subtle variation of this arrangement Poe produced such marvellous effects as,

> "The angels, not half so happy in Heaven,
>   Went envying her and me—
> Yes! that was the reason (as all men know,
>   In this kingdom by the sea)
> That the wind came out of the cloud, chilling
>   And killing my Annabel Lee."

The word "chilling" in this stanza or in that quoted by Mrs. Osgood, while apparently due to a wrenching of accent, is really the one inevitable word in its place, and the meaning triumphs again over mere metrical rules.

Although "The Poetic Principle," Poe's last constructive criticism of importance, was not published until August 31, 1850 in the *Home Journal*,[66] it had been prepared as a lecture for the fall of 1848, and it probably underwent revision during 1849. It is on the whole the best of his critical articles on poetry. While he repeats frequently his earlier definitions, the essay is free from the artificial quality of the "Philosophy of Composition" and the incorrect theories of metre found in "The Rationale of Verse." Poe's style is almost beyond criticism, the cadences of the sentences rising and falling, not with a sing song monotony but with an effect varied and forcible. The essay is free also from those carping criticisms of individuals which disfigured so many of his reviews.

He sought in this essay to state the true function of poetry, and he found it, as before, in the "rhythmical creation of beauty." But while he still insisted that "unless incidentally, it has no concern whatever either with Duty or with Truth," he modified his earlier stand by saying:

"It by no means follows, however, that the incitements of Passion, or the precepts of Duty, or even the lessons of Truth, may not be introduced into a poem, and with advantage; for they may subserve, incidentally, in various way, the general purposes of the work:—but the true artist will always contrive to tone them down in proper subjection to that *Beauty* which is the atmosphere and the real essence of the poem."

[66] Probably from advance sheets of the Griswold Edition, as an introduction in the *Home Journal* states. It also appeared in Sartain's *Union Magazine* for October, 1850, "printed from the original manuscript." Sartain says he paid thirty dollars for it.

Poe's eloquence in defence of his worship of the beautiful rose to a height he had not previously reached:

An immortal instinct, deep within the spirit of man, is thus, plainly, a sense of the Beautiful. This it is which administers to his delight in the manifold forms, and sounds, and odors, and sentiments amid which he exists. And just as the lily is repeated in the lake, or the eyes of Amaryllis in the mirror, so is the mere oral or written repetition of these forms, and sounds, and colors, and odors, and sentiments, a duplicate source of delight. But this mere repetition is not poetry. He who shall simply sing, with however glowing enthusiasm, or with however vivid a truth of description, of the sights, and sounds, and odors, and colors, and sentiments, which greet *him* in common with all mankind—he, I say, has yet failed to prove his divine title. There is still a something in the distance which he has been unable to attain. We have still a thirst unquenchable, to allay which he has not shown us the crystal springs. This thirst belongs to the immortality of Man. It is at once a consequence and an indication of his perennial existence. It is the desire of the moth for the star. It is no mere appreciation of the Beauty before us—but a wild effort to reach the Beauty above. Inspired by an ecstatic prescience of the glories beyond the grave, we struggle, by multiform combinations among the things and thoughts of Time, to attain a portion of that Loveliness whose very elements, perhaps, appertain to eternity alone. And thus when by Poetry—or when by Music, the most entrancing of the Poetic moods—we find ourselves melted into tears—we weep then—not as the Abbate Gravina supposes—through excess of pleasure, but through a certain, petulant, impatient sorrow at our inability to grasp *now*, wholly, here on earth, at once and for ever, those divine and rapturous joys, of which *through* the poem, or *through* the music, we attain to but brief and indeterminate glimpses.

His selection of poems to illustrate his poetic theories, while limited almost entirely to love poetry, began however with Longfellow's "Proem" to "The Waif." Poe praised it for its natural quality. The old bitterness against Longfellow had gone, and no bad taste cropped out to stultify his criticism. Indeed the very selections Poe made for recitation are conspicuous examples of his good taste.

It seemed as though Poe's true self flashed out in the peroration of "The Poetic Principle":

We shall reach, however, more immediately a distinct conception of what the true Poetry is, by mere reference to a few of the simple elements which induce in the Poet himself the true poetical effect. He recognizes the ambrosia which nourishes his soul, in the bright orbs that shine in Heaven—in the volutes of the flower —in the clustering of low shrubberies—in the waving of the grain-fields—in the slanting of tall, Eastern trees—in the blue distance of mountains—in the grouping of clouds—in the twinkling of half-hidden brooks—in the gleaming of silver rivers—in the repose of sequestered lakes—in the star-mirroring depths of lonely wells. He perceives it in the songs of birds—in the harp of Æolus—in the sighing of the night-wind—in the repining voice of the forest—in the surf that complains to the shore—in the fresh breath of the woods—in the scent of the violet—in the voluptuous perfume of the hyacinth—in the suggestive odor that comes to him, at even-tide, from far-distant, undiscovered islands, over dim oceans, illimitable and unexplored. He owns it in all noble thoughts—in all unworldly motives—in all holy impulses—in all chivalrous, generous, and self-sacrificing deeds. He feels it in the beauty of woman—in the grace of her step—in the lustre of her eye—in the melody of her voice—in her soft laughter—in her sigh—in the harmony of the rustling of her robes. He deeply feels it in her winning endearments—in her burning enthusiasms—in her gentle charities—in her meek and devotional endurances—but above all —ah, far above all—he kneels to it—he worships it in the faith, in the purity, in the strength, in the altogether divine majesty—of her *love*.

He was describing here in words of compelling fitness the inspirations that had created his own standards. The charm of nature, the impulse of chivalry, the love of woman, these were the ideals he had cherished and which were never to desert him.

If the "Poetic Principle" represents Poe in the full command of his faculties, a letter to his friend Mrs. Shew written on June 19, 1849, reveals him in one of those moods of despair which alternated with his happier moments.

Can it be true, Louise, that you have the idea fixed in your mind to desert your unhappy and unfortunate friend and patient? You did not say so, I know, but for months I have known you were deserting me, not willingly, but none the less surely—my destiny—

"Disaster, following fast and following faster,"

& I have had premonitions of this for months. I repeat, my good spirit, my loyal heart! must this follow as a sequel to all the bene-

fits and blessings you have so generously bestowed? Are you to
vanish like all I love, or desire, from my darkened and "lost Soul"?
—I have read over your letter again and again, and cannot make
it possible with any degree of certainty, that you wrote it in your
right mind. (*I know you did not without tears of anguish and
regret.*) Is it possible your influence is lost to me? Such tender
and true natures are ever loyal until death; but you are not dead,
you are full of life and beauty! Louise, you came in with the
parson in your floating white robe—"Good morning, Edgar."
There was a touch of conventional coldness in your hurried manner, and your attitude as you opened the kitchen-door to find
Muddie, *is my last remembrance of you.* There was *love,* hope,
and *sorrow* in your smile, instead of love, hope, & *courage,* as
ever before. O Louise, how many sorrows are before you! Your
ingenuous and sympathetic nature will be constantly wounded in
contact with the hollow, heartless world; and for me, alas! unless
some true and tender, and pure womanly love saves me, I shall
hardly last a year longer alive! A few short months will tell how
far my strength—(physical and moral) will carry me in life here.
How can I believe in Providence when *you* look coldly upon me?
Was it not you who renewed my hopes and faith in God?—and
in humanity? Louise, I heard your voice as you passed out of my
sight—leaving me with the parson, "the man of God, the servant of
the Most High." He stood smiling and bowing at the mad man,
Poe. *But that* I had invited him to my house, I would have rushed
out into God's light and freedom! But I still listened to your voice.
I heard you say with a sob, "Dear Muddie." I heard you greet
my Catarina, but it was only as a memory ... nothing escaped
my ear, and I was convinced it was not your generous self that
was repeating words so foreign to your nature—to your tender
heart! I heard you sob out your sense of duty to my mother, and
I heard her reply "Yes, Loui ... yes!" *It was the mother of Alma,*
that child with the Madonna eyes. She is good and pure and
passably loving but she is of her father's type. She has not your
nature. Why sacrifice your angelic prerogative for a common-
place nature? Why turn your soul from its true work for the
desolate, to the thankless and miserly world? Why I was not a
priest is a mystery, for I feel I am now a prophet and I did then,
and *towered* in mind and body over my invited guest in spite of
the duties of hospitality and regard for your feelings, Louise,
when he said grace and you said a low "Amen." I felt my heart

stop, and I was sure I was then to die before your eyes. Louise, it is well—it is fortunate—you looked up with a tear in your dear eyes, and raised the window, and talked of the guava you had brought for my sore throat. Your *instincts* are better than a *strong man's reason for me*—I trust they may be for yourself. Louise, I feel I shall not prevail—a shadow has already fallen upon your soul, and is reflected in your eyes. It is *too late*—you are floating away with the cruel tide. I am a coward to write this to you, but it is not a common trial—it is a fearful one to me. Such rare souls as yours so beautify this earth! so relieve it of all that is repulsive and sordid, so brighten its toils and cares, it is hard to lose sight of them even for a short time. Again I say I am a coward to wound your loyal unselfish and womanly heart but you must know and *be assured* of my *regret* and my *sorrow* if aught I have ever written has hurt you. *My heart never wronged you.* I place you in *my esteem*—in all *solemnity*—beside the friend of my boyhood—the mother of my schoolfellow, of whom I told you, and as I have repeated in the poem, "The Beloved Physician," as the truest, tenderest of this world's most womanly souls, and an angel to my forlorn and darkened nature. I will not say "lost soul" again, for your sake. I will try to overcome my grief for the sake of your unselfish care of me in the past, and in life or death, I am ever yours gratefully and devotedly,

June 1849   EDGAR A. POE.[67]

Poe continued through 1849 the comparatively mild literary flirtation begun in 1848 with Mrs. Sarah Anna Lewis, who wrote under the pen name of "Estelle Anna Lewis," or "Stella." She had been of service to Mrs. Clemm, and Poe paid the price! He had written for her one of his feeblest poems, "An Enigma," [68] and for a consideration he edited her poems and wrote favorable reviews of them. In May, 1849, he tried to interest George P. Putnam in a new edition of Mrs.

[67] This letter is given without date in Ingram's *Life*, II, 157-159, but in his article in *Appleton's Journal*, in 1878, it is dated "June 1849." In Woodberry's *Life*, II, 261-264, and in later biographies it is undated but placed in 1848. It is clearly dated in Mrs. Shew—Houghton's copy, which she sent to Ingram, not only at the end of the letter, but also in her comments, as "1849." Copy is now in the Library of the University of Virginia, included in her letter of April 3 [1875?] to Ingram. I have corrected two obvious misspellings in Mrs. Houghton's extraordinary handwriting, and I have made no attempt to reproduce her punctuation.

[68] See Mrs. Shew's account of Poe's real opinion of Mrs. Lewis, p. 563.

Lewis's *Child of the Sea*.[69] There is something especially artificial in Poe's friendship with "Stella." She was evidently a vain woman, whose husband, Sylvanus D. Lewis, was able and willing to pay for her vanities. Later she took care of Mrs. Clemm.

Poe did his best for Mrs. Lewis, as this letter proves.

New York, June 28—49

Dear Griswold,—Since I have more critically examined your "Female Poets" it occurs to me that you have not *quite* done justice to our common friend, Mrs. Lewis; and if you could oblige me so far as to substitute, for your no doubt hurried notice, a somewhat longer one prepared by myself (subject, of course, to your emendations) I would reciprocate the favor when, where, and *as* you please. If you *could* agree to this, give me a hint to that effect, and the MS. is ready. I will leave it sealed with Mrs. L. who is unaware of my design—for I would rather she should consider herself as indebted to you for the favor, at all points. By calling on Mrs. L., and asking for a package to your address, you can at any moment get it. I would not, of course, put you to any *expense* in this matter:—all cost shall be promptly defrayed.

Truly yours,

EDGAR A. POE.[70]

That Poe thought of Griswold as his friend is easily seen in his desire to have the anthologist take the credit for the substitution.[71]

Poe was concerned during the spring of 1849 with another attempt at the publication of a magazine. He had kindled some interest in E. H. N. Patterson, who lived at Oquawka, or Yellow Banks, a town in Illinois on the Mississippi River. Poe wrote to Patterson in April, 1849, replying to a letter of December 18, 1848, and outlined once more his plans for a five dollar journal, hopeful as ever of a circulation of 20,000. Patterson wished to be the publisher in his own town, but Poe, naturally being dubious of Oquawka as a magazine metropolis, insisted on either New York or St. Louis. It is evident from Poe's

[69] Autograph Ms. letters to Mrs. Lewis, May 17, 1849, and to Putnam, May 18th, are in the W. H. Koester Collection.

[70] Original Autograph Ms., Griswold Collection, Boston Public Library.

[71] The letter that Griswold prints in his "Preface," without date, but as "early in 1849" contains also an appeal for Mrs. Lewis. Its contents however consist largely of praises of Griswold. Until I see the original Ms. I shall disbelieve in its existence—at least in the form in which Griswold gives it.

letters to John R. Thompson that he was becoming convinced that the section in which he could best hope to succeed was the South. He asked Patterson in May for fifty dollars to take a trip through the South and West in the interest of the proposed magazine. The letters between Poe and Patterson are detailed, but since the enterprise came to nothing, they are now of interest mainly because they tell us of Poe's movements at this time. He went to Boston and Lowell on May 23rd, to spend a week. It was the last time he saw Mrs. Richmond, and on June 16th he wrote his final letter to her:

Fordham,—June 16.

You asked me to write before I started for Richmond, and I was to have started last Monday (the 11th)—so, perhaps, you thought me gone, and without having written to say "good-bye"—but indeed, Annie, I *could not* have done so. The truth is, I have been on the point of starting every day since I wrote—and so put off writing until the last moment—but I have been disappointed—and can no longer refrain from sending you, at least, a few lines to let you see *why* I have been so long silent. *When* I can go now is uncertain—but, perhaps, I may be off to-morrow, or next day: —all depends upon circumstances beyond my control. Most probably, I will not go until I hear from Thompson (of the S. L. Messenger), to whom I wrote five days ago—telling him to forward the letter from Oquawka, instead of retaining it until he sees me. The reason of the return of my draft on *Graham's Magazine* (which put me to such annoyance and mortification while I was with you) was, that the articles I sent (by mail) did not come to hand. No insult (as I had half anticipated) was meant—and I am sincerely glad of this; for I did not wish to give up writing for *Graham's Magazine* just yet—I enclose the publisher's reply to my letter enquiry. The Postmaster here is investigating the matter, and, in all probability, the articles will be found, and the draft paid by the time you get this. So all this will be right. . . .

You see I enclose you quite a budget of papers: the letter of Mrs. L[ocke] to Muddy—Mrs. L[ocke's] long MS. poem—the verses by the "Lynn Bard," which you said you wished to see, and also some lines to me (or rather about me), by Mrs. Osgood, in which she *imagines me writing to her*. I send, too, another notice of "Eureka," from Greeley's *Tribune*. The letter of Mrs. L— you can retain if you wish it.

Have you seen the "Moral for Authors," a new satire by J. E.

Tuel?—who, in the name of Heaven, *is* J. E. Tuel? The book is miserably stupid. He has a long parody of the "Raven"—in fact, nearly the whole thing seems to be aimed at me. If you have not seen it and wish to see it, I will send it.... No news of Mrs. L[ocke] yet. If she comes here I shall refuse to see her. Remember me to your parents, Mr. R[ichmond], &c.—And now Heaven for ever bless you—

EDDIE.

I enclose, also, an autograph of the Mr. Willis you are so much in love with. Tell Bardwell I will send him what I promised very soon.... My mother sends you her dearest—most devoted love.[72]

Poe left Fordham by way of Brooklyn where he and Mrs. Clemm spent the night with Mr. and Mrs. Lewis. "Stella's" statement that as he parted from them all on June 30th, he asked her to write his life, may be doubted. But Mrs. Clemm's memory of his parting words to her on the steamboat ring more true.

" 'God bless you, my own darling Mother,' " he said; " 'do not fear for Eddy! See how good I will be while I am away from you, and [?] will come back to love and comfort you.' " [73]

She was never again to stand between him and weakness or temptation, or to place upon his shoulders the obligations which he had to satisfy at the expense of his critical integrity.

[72] Ingram, II, 216-217; one vol. ed., p. 411.
[73] Ingram, II, 221; one vol. ed., p. 415.

CHAPTER XIX

Richmond—The Last Appeal

Poe started for Richmond with his usual high hopes. His constant ambition to become the editor of a magazine had been renewed by his relations with Patterson, and though the cautious correspondent from Oquawka had not promised Poe complete control, he was prepared to furnish the sinews of war. Poe was also, in a real sense, going home. While he had not entirely abandoned the hope of locating his journal in New York, he had offered Patterson the alternative of St. Louis. The South was calling him in different ways. He had defended her men of letters in his criticisms, he had cooled the friendship of Lowell and other New Englanders by his attacks on the abolitionists, and he was feeling less and less happy in a region where New England dominated critical judgments and was insisting more and more upon her poetic supremacy. That Poe felt this keenly is seen in his comments upon Griswold's *Female Poets of America:* "He has been at the pains of doing what Northern critics seem to be at great pains *never* to do,—that is to say, he has been at the trouble of doing justice, in great measure, to several poetesses who have not had the good fortune to be born in the North." [1]

Poe had invaded the North in 1837 because he saw larger opportunities, and they were still larger in 1849, but not for him. In 1837, Bryant, Halleck, and Willis, who were looked upon as the leaders in American poetry, were New Englanders, it is true, but they had left New England for New York, and Halleck and Willis remained his friends. The New England group, Emerson, Longfellow, Whittier, Holmes, and Lowell, who in the twelve years from 1837 to 1849 had become dominant, remained in New England, and ruled from Boston, Cambridge, or Concord. Of this group Lowell alone had been enthusiastic in his critical judgment of Poe, and he had cooled decidedly by 1848.

Much of this mutual dislike was due, of course, to Poe's own caus-

[1] *Southern Literary Messenger,* XV (February, 1849), 126.

tic utterances, but in trying to understand the causes of his failure to make a satisfactory career, the fact that he was an alien to the North has not been sufficiently appreciated. He was the only important Southern man of letters in this period to leave his section and make his fight for fame in the North. Washington Allston did go to Boston after his long European stay, but he was a painter rather than a poet, and his creative power collapsed, in any event, after his return to the United States. Poe must have felt the growing sectional hatreds that were, twelve years later, to bring on the Civil War, and we may be sure he never hesitated to speak his mind. It was therefore quite natural that he should turn toward his own country and exchange commercial opportunity for the prospect of living in a section where people thought as he did. When two sections of a land dislike each other for their faults, trouble will ensue, but when they dislike each other for their virtues, the case is more serious. Poe's impulsive, excitable nature, his keen sense of personal honor and his contempt for purely material values, were not likely to endear him to the metropolis where standards were being based more and more upon commercial prosperity.

Unfortunately he stopped in Philadelphia, probably on business.[2] He may have taken a drink, for on Monday afternoon, which would have been July 2nd, or July 9th, he called on John Sartain, editor of the *Union Magazine*. Sartain's account, written forty years later, has some obvious inaccuracies but presents a vivid account of Poe's adventures. Looking pale and haggard, Poe begged Sartain for refuge from attack by two men who, he said, were on the train for New York, and were plotting to kill him. Poe therefore left the train at Bordentown and returned to Philadelphia. Either he or Sartain is in error in this statement, for he was not going to New York, unless he had determined to return to Mrs. Clemm's protection. He was suffering from a mania of persecution, and he persuaded Sartain to remove his moustache, which Sartain cut off with his scissors. Here once more, the account seems incorrect for Poe wore a moustache in Richmond shortly afterward.

> After tea [Sartain continued], it being now dark, he prepared to go out, and on my asking him where he was going, he said, "To the Schuylkill." I told him I would go too, to which he offered no objection. His shoes were worn down a good deal on the outer side of the heels, and he complained that his feet were chafed in

[2] See letter, Mrs. Clemm to Annie, July 9, 1849. Ingram, II, 222-223.

consequence, and hurt him, so I gave him my slippers to wear, as I had no second pair of shoes that would serve. When we had reached the corner of Ninth and Chestnut Streets we waited there for an omnibus, and among the things he said was that he wished I would see to it that after his death the painting Osgood had made of him should go to his mother (meaning Mrs. Clemm). I promised that as far as I could control it that should be done. We entered an omnibus and rode to its stopping-place, a tavern on the north side of Callowhill Street, on the bend it takes towards the northwest to reach the Fairmount bridge. At this place there was light enough, chiefly from what shone out through the door of the tavern, but beyond was darkness, and forward into the darkness we went.

I kept on his left side, and on nearly approaching the bridge I guided him off to the right by a gentle pressure until we reached the foot of the lofty flight of steep wooden steps that ascended almost to the top of the reservoir. Here was the first landing, and with seats, so we sat down.

Here on the old reservoir, now destroyed, but which some Philadelphians still remember, Poe told Sartain of his being in Moyamensing Prison, and of his dream of a radiant young female figure who stood on the topmost coping of the stone tower and spoke to him across a great distance. Sartain brought him home to Sansom Street, gave him a bed on the sofa and slept along side on three chairs to protect him. On the second morning [July 4th?] Poe had recovered sufficiently to go out alone. He soon returned telling Sartain that "the whole thing had been a delusion and a scare created out of his excited imagination."

Sartain then added:

> I asked him how he came to be in Moyamensing Prison, and he said he has been suspected of trying to pass a fifty-dollar counterfeit note; but the truth is it was for what takes so many there for a few hours only, the drop too much. When his turn came in the group before Mayor Gilpin, it was remarked, "Why, this is Poe the poet," and he was dismissed without the customary fine.[3]

Being now all right again, he was ready to go to New York.

[3] A careful search of the records of the Philadelphia County Prison, popularly known as "Moyamensing," made through the courtesy of Superintendent Frederick S. Baldi, by John D. Reid, Deputy Warden, shows no record of Poe having been imprisoned there. He may have given an assumed name, but a search in the records, kept alphabetically, under "Edward S. T. Grey," or "Edgar Perry," also proved fruitless.

He borrowed what was needful, and departed. I never saw him more.[4]

Poe repeated his account of the dream and the radiant figure to John R. Thompson, somewhat later. This time the vision took him on a flight over the housetops of Philadelphia, turning eventually into a black evil bird, which told Poe it was the cholera.[5] There was an epidemic of cholera in Philadelphia in July, 1849, and the episode is to be taken simply as an illustration of Poe's mental disturbance at this time. His letters from Philadelphia and Richmond about to be quoted tell the story better than any paraphrase. He was evidently in bad shape in Philadelphia [until July 13th] but fortunately he had friends in George Lippard, the novelist and Charles Chauncey Burr, the Editor of the *Nineteenth Century*.

On Saturday, July 7th, Poe wrote from Philadelphia in a despairing mood to Mrs. Clemm, misdating his letter as from New York.

New York, July 7. [Saturday]

My *dear, dear* Mother,—I have been *so* ill—have had the cholera, or spasms quite as bad, and can now hardly hold the pen.

The very instant you get this, *come* to me. The joy of seeing you will almost compensate for our sorrows. We can but die together. It is no use to reason with *me* now; I must die. I have no desire to live since I have done "Eureka." I could accomplish nothing more. For your sake it would be sweet to live, but we must die together. You have been all in all to me, darling, ever beloved mother, and dearest, truest friend.

I was never *really* insane, except on occasions where my heart was touched.

I have been taken to prison once since I came here for getting drunk; but *then* I was not. It was about Virginia.[6]

---

[4] "Reminiscences of Edgar Allan Poe," *Lippincott's Magazine*, XLIII (March, 1889), 411-415. Reprinted with some variations, in *Reminscences of a Very Old Man* (New York, 1900), pp. 206-212. Sartain makes no mention of Poe begging for laudanum, as Woodberry states, II, 309.

[5] Thompson's dramatized version may be found in his *Genius and Character of Edgar Allan Poe.* (Privately printed from his manuscript, by J. H. Whitty and J. H. Rindfleisch, 1929), pp. 23-25.

[6] Published first by C. Chauncey Burr in his quarterly journal, *The Nineteenth Century*, V (February, 1852), 29. He was given the letters by Mrs. Clemm, and incorporated them in his article, "Character of Edgar A. Poe," pp. 19-33.

Before this letter reached Mrs. Clemm, she had sent a pathetic note to Mrs. Richmond:

July 9, 1849

Eddy has been gone ten days, and I have not heard one word from him. Do you wonder that I *am distracted?* I fear everything. . . . Do you wonder that he has so little confidence in any one? Have we not suffered from the blackest treachery? Eddy was obliged to go through Philadelphia, and how much I fear he has got into some trouble there; he promised me *so* sincerely to write thence. I ought to have heard last Monday, and now it is Monday again and not one word. . . . Oh, if any evil has befallen *him* what can comfort me? The day after he left New York, I left Mrs. Lewis and started for home. I called on a rich friend who had made many promises, but never knew our situation. I frankly told her. . . . She proposed to me to leave Eddy, saying he might very well do for himself. . . . Any one to propose to *me* to leave my Eddy—what a cruel insult! No one to console and comfort him but me; no one to nurse him and take care of him when he is sick and helpless! Can I ever forget that dear sweet face [Virginia's], so tranquil, so pale, and those dear eyes looking at me so sadly, while she said, "Darling, darling Muddy, you will console and take care of my poor Eddy—you will *never, never* leave him? Promise me, my dear Muddy, and then I can die in peace." And *I did promise.* And when I meet her in heaven, I can say, "I have kept my promise, my darling." . . . If Eddy gets to Richmond safely and can succeed in what he intends doing, we will be relieved of part of our difficulties; but if he comes home in trouble and sick, I know not what is to become of us.[7]

Poe remained in Philadelphia until Friday, July 13, when he left for Richmond. On the way he wrote again to Mrs. Clemm, probably on Saturday,

Near Richmond.

The weather is awfully hot, and, besides all this, I am so homesick I don't know what to do. I never wanted to see any one half so bad as I want to see my own darling mother. It seems to me that I would make any sacrifice to hold you by the hand once more, and get you to cheer me up, for I am terribly depressed. I do not think that any circumstances will ever tempt me to leave you again. When I am with you I can bear anything, but when I am away from you I am too miserable to live.[8]

[7] Ingram, II, 222-223; one vol. ed., pp. 416-417.
[8] *Nineteenth Century,* V, 29.

He had scarcely arrived, on July 14, when he wrote again to Mrs. Clemm. In his agitation he lengthened the time he had been away from her from two weeks to three.[9] And his fastidious love of neatness shows strongly in his distress at his appearance:

> Richmond, Saturday Night. [July 14]
>
> Oh, my darling Mother, it is now more than three weeks since I saw you, and in all that time your poor Eddy has scarcely drawn a breath except of intense agony. Perhaps you are sick or gone from Fordham in despair, or dead. If you are but alive, and if I but *see you again,* all the rest is nothing. I love you better than ten thousand lives—so much so that it is cruel in you to let me leave you; nothing but sorrow *ever* comes of it.
>
> Oh, Mother, I am *so* ill while I write—but I resolved that come what would, I would not sleep again without easing your dear heart as far as I could.
>
> My valise was lost for ten days. At last I found it at the depot in Philadelphia, but (you will scarcely credit it) they had opened it and stolen *both lectures.* Oh, Mother, think of the blow to me this evening, when on examining the valise, these lectures were gone. All my object here is over unless I can recover them or re-write one of them.
>
> I am indebted for more than life itself to B[urr]. Never forget him, Mother, while you live. When all failed me, he stood my friend, got me money, and saw me off in the cars for Richmond.
>
> I got here with two dollars over—of which I inclose you one. Oh God, my Mother, shall we ever again meet? If possible, oh COME! My clothes are *so horrible,* and I am *so ill.* Oh, if you could come to me, *my mother.* Write instantly—oh *do* not fail. God forever bless you.
>
> EDDY.[10]

Poe's next letter proves that the episode was a temporary depression of a violent nature, rather than a permanent break down.

> Richmond, Thursday, July 19
>
> My Own Beloved Mother—
>
> You will see at once, by the handwriting of this letter, that I

---

[9] Though this letter is undated, it was evidently written before the letter of July 19th, and must therefore have been sent on Saturday, July 14th.
[10] *Nineteenth Century,* V, 30.

am better—much better in health and spirits. Oh, if you only knew how your dear letter comforted me! It acted like magic. Most of my suffering arose from that terrible idea which I could not get rid of—the idea that you were dead. For more than ten days I was totally deranged, although I was not drinking one drop; and during this interval I imagined the most horrible calamities.

All was hallucination, arising from an attack which I had never before experienced—an attack of mania-à-potu. May Heaven grant that it prove a warning to me for the rest of my days. If so, I shall not regret even the horrible unspeakable torments I have endured.

To L[ippard] and to C[hauncey] B[urr] (and in some measure, also, to Mr. S[artain]) I am indebted for more than life. They remained with me (L[ippard] and B[urr]) all day on Friday [July 13] last, comforted me and aided me in coming to my senses. L[ippard] saw G[odey], who said everything kind of me, and sent me five dollars; and [S. D.] P[atterson] sent another five. B[urr] procured me a ticket as far as Baltimore, and the passage from there to Richmond was seven dollars. I have not drank anything since Friday morning, and then only a little Port wine. *If possible,* dearest Mother, I *will* extricate myself from this difficulty for your *dear, dear sake.* So keep up heart.

All is not lost yet, and "the darkest hour is just before daylight." Keep up heart, my own beloved mother—all may yet go well. I will put forth all my energies. When I get my mind a little more composed, I will try to write something. Oh, give my *dearest,* fondest love to Mrs. L. Tell her that *never, while I live,* will I forget her kindness to my darling mother.[11]

Poe was well enough to write to E. H. N. Patterson and to Lippard on July 19th. He told Patterson that he had been "arrested in Philadelphia by the cholera." He promised to work again, "as soon as he

[11] *Nineteenth Century,* V, 30-31. The names are inserted on the evidence of Lippard's letter to Griswold, November 22, 1849.—"It is but just to state that C. C. Burr, John Sartain, L. A. Godey, S. D. Patterson, were the only persons in this city, whom (last summer) I could induce to give one cent to save Poe from starvation." Autograph Ms., Boston Public Library. Woodberry, II, 316, credits Graham and Peterson with the loans, but gives no supporting evidence, and Miss Phillips and Hervey Allen adopt his conclusions. Obviously Lippard is the best authority.

gathered a little strength" but his handwriting was clear and strong,[12] and Poe was probably overestimating his ill health. There was often a trace of the neurotic in his analysis of his own condition. He begged Lippard to find his lectures, but that good friend was not able to discover them.[13]

Poe put up in Richmond at the old Swan Tavern on the north side of Broad Street between Eighth and Ninth Streets,[14] a hotel which had once been fashionable and was even in 1849 a respectable house. It was near the home of Mrs. Jane MacKenzie, Duncan Lodge, an attractive house, built in 1843 [15] and still standing in 1940. His friend John MacKenzie was living there and Rosalie, his sister, whose attentions while natural, were often an embarrassment to her brother.

He was gradually recovering his health and he was received cordially by old and new friends. One of the latter, Susan Archer Talley, was then a young woman, whose verses Poe had praised and who had achieved the immortality of being included in Griswold's *Female Poets of America*. She has painted a picture of Poe's personal appearance which compensates us somewhat for the many errors of fact with which she has confused his biography.[16]

Rosalie took Poe to visit the Talley family soon after his arrival. Susan Talley's description of her meeting with Poe is vivid:

[12] Four of Poe's letters to Patterson are published in facsimile in *Some Letters to E. H. N. Patterson of Oquawka*, Illinois, with comments by Eugene Field (Chicago, the Caxton Club, 1898).

[13] Lippard to Griswold—November 22, 1849. Autograph Ms., Griswold Collection, Boston Public Library. We know of Poe's letter through Lippard's statement that he has the letter before him, dated July 19th.

[14] A mantelpiece from the hotel is now on the first floor of the Valentine Museum. Poe moved later to the Madison House.

[15] The usual statements in the biographies that Edgar and Rosalie Poe had played in this house as children is incorrect. It was in a much more modest house, built on the lots which William MacKenzie purchased in 1812. See Miss Mary Wingfield Scott's "Notes on Old Richmond Houses." Ms. in the Valentine Museum.

[16] Mrs. Weiss, as she became later, is one of the most irritating of the Poe biographers. Her article on "The Last Days of Edgar A. Poe," in *Scribner's Monthly*, XV (March, 1878), 707-716, is of real value. Her later contributions in *The Independent* May 5 and August 25, 1904, and her volume, *The Home Life of Poe* (New York, 1907), grow steadily more misleading. Mrs. Weiss was incapable of judging evidence and any accounts, except those based on her own first-hand knowledge, are untrustworthy. Griswold, in his introduction to her verses in the *Female Poets* states that she was completely deaf, and while this cannot, in the light of her conversations with Poe, be correct, yet her hearing may have been impaired!

Edgar Allan Poe

From the crayon portrait drawn by Flavius J. Fisher from a daguerreotype owned by John R. Thompson, editor of the *Southern Literary Messenger*, taken probably in September, 1849. Fisher gave the portrait in 1864 to E. V. Valentine, and it is reproduced through the courtesy of the Valentine Museum.

As I entered the parlor, Poe was seated near an open window, quietly conversing. His attitude was easy and graceful, with one arm lightly resting upon the back of his chair. His dark curling hair was thrown back from his broad forehead—a style in which he habitually wore it. At sight of him, the impression produced upon me was of a refined, high-bred, and chivalrous gentleman. I use this word "chivalrous" as exactly descriptive of something in his whole *personnel*, distinct from either polish or high-breeding, and which, though instantly apparent, was yet an effect too subtle to be described. He rose on my entrance, and, other visitors being present, stood with one hand resting on the back of his chair, awaiting my greeting. So dignified was his manner, so reserved his expression, that I experienced an involuntary recoil, until I turned to him and saw his eyes suddenly brighten as I offered my hand; a barrier seemed to melt between us, and I felt that we were no longer strangers.

I am thus minute in my account of my first meeting with Poe, because I would illustrate, if possible, the manner peculiar to him, and also the indescribable charm, I might almost say magnetism, which his eyes possessed above any others that I have ever seen.[17]

Mrs. Weiss made one observation concerning Poe which is illuminating: "His own insight into personal character was quick and intuitive, but not deep; and it struck me even then, with all my youthful inexperience, that in knowledge of human nature he was for a man of his genius, strangely deficient."[18]

It was just that inability to judge correctly the real nature of his acquaintances, that led Poe into so much trouble, and gave rise to charges of insincerity. His intimate friends he knew well, but he was led frequently into impulsive approaches to someone whom he believed to be his friend, but who was really not. Then on discovering a real or even fancied flaw, his bitter denunciation was partly caused by the recognition of his own error. His complete mistake concerning Griswold's supposed reconciliation is a case in point.

The perennial dispute over Poe's habits has, as usual, much material to feed on during this last visit to Richmond. Mrs. Weiss never saw him intoxicated, but learned afterward of two relapses, the second being serious. He was taken to Duncan Lodge by Dr. MacKenzie and Dr. Gibbon Carter and the latter warned Poe that another attack of the same nature would be fatal. Poe's reply was that if people would not tempt him, he would not fall.[19] Here Mrs. Weiss is probably to be relied on, even though her evidence is secondary.

Poe certainly made a strong fight to keep his word to his friends. William J. Glenn, the presiding officer of the Shockoe Hill Division, No. 54, of the Sons of Temperance, gives the details of Poe's reception into that body "sometime between July 1 and September 30, 1849," and continues, "There had been no intimation that Mr. Poe had violated his pledge before leaving Richmond in October." [20] How difficult it was for Poe to withstand that temptation in a society where conviviality was a matter of course, can well be imagined. To refuse to drink with an acquaintance was almost an insult, and few were good enough friends to help him in his struggle.

Poe was constantly occupied with his hopes for *The Stylus*. On August 7th he wrote again to Patterson, giving him good reasons why a three dollar magazine could not kindle Poe's enthusiastic cooperation. Patterson agreed on August 21 to support a five dollar journal if Poe could secure one thousand subscribers, and plans were made for a meeting in St. Louis for October 15th. To help on this project and to support himself Poe lectured on "The Poetic Principle" on August 17, 1849, in the Exchange Concert Rooms. The audience was large and enthusiastic, but since the tickets were sold at twenty-five cents,[21] Poe could hardly have profited greatly.

The Richmond *Whig* of August 21st, in a glowing editorial, remarked, "We were never more delighted in our lives," and stated that Poe manifested "an acquaintance with poets and their styles perfectly unique in this community. . . . We venture to ask Mr. Poe to make one more representation before us." The *Whig* published "Lenore" on September 18th. John M. Daniel, in a penetrating analysis, criticized unfavorably Poe's reading of poetry, although he approved of his critical theory.[22] This lecture may have led to Poe's revising for the *Examiner* several of his poems, only "The Raven," however, being published during his lifetime, in that paper. He may also have taken some informal part in the work of the office, but Daniel makes no

[19] *Scribner's Monthly*, XV, 712.

[20] Letter of William J. Glenn to E. V. Valentine, June 29, 1899, now in the Valentine Museum in Richmond.

[21] Advertisement in Richmond *Enquirer*, Friday, August 17th.

[22] "Edgar Allan Poe," *Southern Literary Messenger*, XVI (March, 1850), 177, reprinting his earlier account in the *Examiner*. Complete Article, 172-187.

mention of this in his article in the *Messenger*. Poe was at the time of his death, under an engagement to furnish literary articles for Daniel.[23]

Shortly after this first lecture Poe wrote to Mrs. Clemm telling of his renewed hopes. The first page is missing, but the remainder is one of the most important documents in Poe's correspondence:

possible. Every body says that if I lecture again & put the tickets at 50 cts, I will clear $100. I *never* was received with so much enthusiasm. The papers have done nothing but praise me before the lecture and since. I enclose one of the notices—the only one in which the slightest word of disparagement appears. It is written by Daniel—the man whom I challenged when I was here last year. I have been invited out a great deal—but could seldom go, on account of not having a dress coat. To-night Rose & I are to spend the evening at Elmira's. Last night I was at Poitiaux's— the night before at Strobia's, where I saw my dear friend Eliza Lambert (Gen. Lambert's sister). She was ill in her bed-room, but insisted upon our coming up, & we stayed until nearly 1 o'clock. In a word, I have received nothing but kindness since I have been here, & could have been quite happy but for my dreadful anxiety about you. Since the report of my intended marriage, the McKenzies [24] have overwhelmed me with attentions. Their house is so crowded that they *could* not ask me to stay.—And now, my own precious Muddy, the very moment I get a definite answer about everything, I will write again & tell you what to do. Elmira talks about visiting Fordham—but I do not know whether that would do. I think, perhaps, it would be best for you to give up everything there & come on here in the Packet. Write immediately & give me your advice about it—for you know best. Could we be happier in Richmond or Lowell?—for I suppose we could never be happy at Fordham—and, Muddy, I *must* be somewhere where I can see Annie.—Did Mrs. L. get the Western Quarterly Review? Thompson is constantly urging me to write for the Messenger, but I am so anxious that I cannot.—Mr. Loud, the husband of Mrs. S[t] Leon Loud, the poetess of Philadelphia, called on me the other day and offered me $100 to edit his wife's poems. Of

[23] *The Richmond Examiner during the War; or, the Writings of John M. Daniel,* with a Memoir of his Life, by his brother, Frederick S. Daniel (New York, 1868), p. 220.

[24] Poe's spelling of the name.

course, I accepted the offer. The whole labor will not occupy me 3 days. I am to have them ready by Christmas.—I have seen Bernard often. Eliza is expected but has not come.—When I repeat my lecture here, I will then go to Petersburg & Norfolk.— A Mr. Taverner lectured here on Shakspeare, a few nights after me, and had 8 persons, including myself & the doorkeeper.—I think, upon the whole, dear Muddy, it will be better for you to say that I am ill, or something of that kind, and break up at Fordham, so that you may come on here. Let me know immediately what you think best. You know we could easily pay off what we owe at Fordham & the place is a beautiful one—but I want to live *near Annie*.—And now, dear Muddy, there is one thing I wish you to pay particular attention to. I told Elmira when I first came here, that I had one of the pencil-sketches of her, that I took a long while ago in Richmond; and I told her that I would write to you about it. So, when you write, just copy the following words in your letter:

"I have looked again for the pencil-sketch of Mrs. S. but cannot find it anywhere. I took down all the books and shook them one by one, and unless Eliza White has it, I do not know what has become of it. She was looking at it the last time I saw it. The one you spoilt with Indian Ink ought to be somewhere about the house. I will do my best to [find?] it."

I got a sneaking letter to-day from Chivers.—Do not tell me anything about Annie—I cannot bear to hear it now—unless you can tell me that Mr. R. is dead—I have got the wedding ring.—and shall have no difficulty, I think, in getting a dress-coat.

Wednesday Night

[First line is torn—the only clear words are "night . . . own . . . dear Muddy." Then follows on the last page—] Also the letter. *Return the letter when you write.*[25]

[25] The original autograph letter, undated, is in the Griswold Collection, in the Boston Public Library. Someone, probably William M. Griswold, has written across the top—"Sept. 1849." Woodberry dates it September [5] but gives no authority. The postscript dated "Wednesday night," was probably written later than the letter. September 5th fell on Wednesday so the main letter was evidently not written on that date. It probably was written on a Tuesday, and the only Tuesdays would have been September 4th and 11th, for the letter of September 18th is evidently later. It may even have been earlier, if Mrs. Clemm's letter of September 4th refers to it, as seems probable.

With his resilient nature, Poe responded to the sympathy of his old friends. The visit to Poitiaux's took him back to the days in London in 1816 when his little sweetheart, Catherine Poitiaux, still living in 1849, had sent him her love. In that midnight chat with Eliza Lambert, the visits that the Allan family made to "Uncle Lambert's," the home of Eliza's father, called up the early days in Richmond when Poe was a handsome, petted child. Her brother, General Lambert, was Mayor of Richmond from 1841 until his death in 1853. Poe was also welcomed by his old friends, Robert Stanard, Robert Sully, the painter, and by Dr. Robert Henry Cabell and his wife, Julia Mayo Cabell, the cousin of the second Mrs. Allan. As he told Susan Talley, he found in their homes, "pictures, flowers, delightful music and conversation and a kindness more refreshing than all." His recognition by Mrs. Cabell is especially significant since it is evidence that the Allan family did not all take sides against him. The Richmond tradition of the Mayo family speaks of their wit and independence.

There must of course have been another side to the picture. As he passed his old home at the corner of Main and Fifth Streets he could not help a sardonic smile at the signs of prosperity and the two additional wings which Mrs. John Allan had found it necessary to build for the sons she had given her husband. Miss Nancy Valentine was still living with her, a woman of sixty-three, who was to die in the following January. She was out of the city nearly all the summer, visiting Mrs. Allan at Byrd Lodge, near Columbia, Virginia, or other friends. Perhaps this was the reason Poe did not try to see her. But in the letters she wrote to Mrs. Allan and the boys, she makes no mention of the lad who had never called her "Aunt Nancy" and for whose fame she apparently cared so little.[26] But there are constant references in her letters to John Allan, and she tells of her hopes that his sons will grow up to be like him, "who was the most noble and kind hearted soul in the world."

Perhaps some of these impressions gave rise to the mood of which Mrs. Weiss gives a vivid picture. It can hardly be imaginary, even though it is tinted with romance:

The only occasion on which I saw Poe really sad or depressed, was on a walk to the "Hermitage," the old deserted seat of the

[26] A bundle of Ann Valentine's letters has recently been discovered in the Valentine Museum. Even her letters to Elizabeth Valentine, who was in Richmond during July and August, 1849, and whose brother William heard Poe lecture, make no inquiries concerning Poe.

Mayo family, where he had, in his youth, been a frequent visitor.
On reaching the place, our party separated, and Poe and myself
strolled slowly about the grounds. I observed that he was unusually silent and preoccupied, and, attributing it to the influence
of memories associated with the place, forebore to interrupt him.
He passed slowly by the mossy bench called the "lovers' seat,"
beneath two aged trees, and remarked, as we turned toward the
garden, "There used to be white violets here." Searching amid the
tangled wilderness of shrubs, we found a few late blossoms, some
of which he placed carefully between the leaves of a note-book.
Entering the deserted house, he passed from room to room with
a grave, abstracted look, and removed his hat, as if involuntarily,
on entering the saloon, where in old times many a brilliant company had assembled. Seated in one of the deep windows, over
which now grew masses of ivy, his memory must have borne him
back to former scenes, for he repeated the familiar lines of Moore:

> "I feel like one who treads alone,
> Some banquet hall deserted"—

and paused, with the first expression of real sadness that I had ever
seen on his face.[27]

Poe's thoughts as he passed the scenes of his boyhood's love affair
with Sarah Elmira Royster were probably more pleasant, for the
affair was on again. Her own words to E. V. Valentine tell the story:

I was ready to go to church and a servant told me that a gentleman in the parlour wanted to see me. I went down and was amazed
to see him—but knew him instantly—He came up to me in the
most enthusiastic manner and said: "Oh! Elmira, is this you?"
That very morning I told him I was going to church, that I never
let anything interfere with that, that he must call again and when
he did call again he renewed his addresses. I laughed at it; he
looked very serious and said he was in earnest and had been
thinking about it for a long time. Then I found out that he was
very serious and I became serious. I told him if he would not take
a positive denial he must give me time to consider of it. And he
said a love that hesitated was not a love for him. But he sat there
a long time and was very pleasant and cheerful. He [continued?]
to visit me frequently but I never engaged myself to him. He
begged me when he was going away to marry him. Promised he
would be everything I could desire. He said when he left that

[27] *Scribner's Monthly*, XV, 712.

he was going to New York, to wind up some business and that he would return to Richmond as soon as he accomplished it, though he said at the same time that he had a presentment he never should see me any more.[28]

When Mr. Valentine pressed for an answer to his question "Were you engaged to Poe when he died?" her reply was elusive. "I was not engaged to Poe when he left here, but there was a partial understanding, but I do not think I should have married him under any circumstances."

There was evidently no great rapture in this mature love story. A letter from Elmira to her cousin, Dr. Philip Fitzhugh, written on December 11, 1848, indicates that she had not met Poe at that time. It is that of a woman rather bored with life and ready for another adventure. Yet her letter to Mrs. Clemm of September 22, 1849, clearly implies that she expected to marry Poe. Poe's engagement to Mrs. Shelton has usually been attributed to a desire to use her property in the publication of the *Stylus*. As human motives are rarely unmixed, he probably had some idea of profiting by the marriage. But there had been real if not undying affection between them, and on both sides there was a clutching at the memories of youth, as youth was slipping away from them. After all, each woman who has known a man intimately, keeps her own place in his heart, or at least in the chambers of his vanity.

Poe lectured at the Academy in Norfolk on the "Poetic Principle" on September 14, 1849. The *North American Beacon* of Norfolk made quite an occasion of Poe's lecture, quoting [29] in advance the editorials of the Richmond *Whig*, commenting on Poe's reputation in France and upon his lecture in Richmond. After the lecture, the *Beacon* published a favorable analysis of the "Poetic Principle," and spoke of the recitations, including "The Raven" as eliciting "rounds of applause from the intelligent audience." [30]

Poe had friends in Norfolk, one of whom, Miss Susan V. C. Ingram, gave, many years later, a charming picture of the group which gathered at the Hygeia Hotel at Old Point Comfort on Sunday evening, September 9th: [31]

[28] From E. V. Valentine's conversation with Mrs. Shelton, November 19, 1875. Ms. in Valentine Museum.
[29] Editorials, September 13 and 14, 1849, page 2.
[30] Editorial, September 17, page 2.
[31] *New York Herald*, February 19, 1905, third section, p. 4.

Mr. Poe sat there in that quiet way of his which made you feel his presence. After a while my aunt, who was nearer his age, said: "This seems to be just the time and place for poetry, Mr. Poe."

And it was. We all felt it. The old Hygiea stood some distance from the water, but with nothing between it and the ocean. It was moonlight and the light shone over everything with that undimmed light that it has in the South. There were many persons on the long verandas that surrounded the hotel, but they seemed remote and far away. Our little party was absolutely cut off from everything except that lovely view of the water shining in the moonlight and its gentle music borne to us on the soft breeze. Poe felt the influence. How could a poet help it? And when we seconded the request that he recite for us he agreed readily.

I do not remember all of the poems that he recited. There was "The Raven" and "Annabel Lee," and last of all he gave us "Ulalume," including the last stanza, of which he remarked that he feared that it might not be intelligible to us, as it was scarcely clear to himself, and for that reason it had not been published.[32]

I was not old enough or experienced enough to understand what the words really meant as he repeated:—

> "Said we, then, the two then. "Ah, can it
> Have been that the woodlandish ghouls—
> The pitiful, the merciful ghouls,
> To bar up our way and to ban it
> From the secret that lies in these wolds—
> From the thing that lies hidden in these wolds—
> Have drawn up the spectre of a planet
> From the limbo of lunary souls—
> This sinfully, scintillant planet
> From the hell of the planetary souls?"

I did, however, feel their beauty, and I said to him when he had finished, "It is quite clear to me, and I admire the poem very much."

He seemed pleased to have me speak so, and the next day I was greatly surprised to receive from him a manuscript copy of the poem. It made quite a scroll and must have taken him a long time to write out. The ten stanzas were written on five large sheets of paper pasted together in the neatest possible way, end to end. He wrote such a beautiful, fair hand it was a joy to look upon it. Not only did he acknowledge his appreciation of my apprecia-

[32] It *had* been published in the *American Review* for December, 1847.

tion by sending me this precious manuscript, but he accompanied it with the kindest sort of a note.[33]

This was only a little more than two weeks, as I remember, before Poe's death, but I saw him again before he went to Baltimore, where he died.

We went from Old Point Comfort to our home near Norfolk, Va., and he called on us there and again I had the pleasure of talking with him. Although I was only a slip of a girl and he what seemed to me then quite an old man, and a great literary one at that, we got on together beautifully. He was one of the most courteous gentlemen I ever have seen, and that gave a great charm to his manner. None of his pictures that I have ever seen look like the picture of Poe that I keep in my memory. Of course they look like him, so that any one seeing them could have recognized him from them, but there was something in his face that is in none of them. Perhaps it was in the eyes, perhaps in the mouth, I do not know, but any one who ever met him would understand what I mean.

There were no indications of dissipation apparent when we saw Poe in Virginia at that time. I think he had not been drinking for a long time. If I had not heard or read what was said about his intemperance I should never have had any idea of it from what I saw in Poe. To me he seemed a good man, as well as a charming one, very sensitive and very high minded.

I believe he was engaged at that time to be married to a widow, but he did not mention the matter to us.

I remember one little incident that illustrates how loyal he was to the memory of those who had been kind to him. I was fond of orris root and always had the odor of it about my clothes. One day when we were walking together he spoke of it. "I like it, too," he said. "Do you know what it makes me think of? My adopted mother. Whenever the bureau drawers in her room were opened there came from them a whiff of orris root, and ever since when I smell it I go back to the time when I was a little boy and it brings back thoughts of my mother." [34]

Meanwhile Mrs. Clemm was writing hysterically to Mrs. Richmond, begging for help to go to Poe's assistance. She also sent to Griswold a note which reveals her responsibility for some of Poe's lapses from critical independence.

[33] The note from Poe to Miss Ingram is given on pages 533-534, in the discussion of "Ulalume."

[34] In a rather pathetic note, written on May 26, 1913, Miss Ingram, then a woman of eighty, thanks the owner for permission to see the poem once again.

New York, September 4, 1849.

Dear Mr. Griswold,—I have tried so long to see you without success, that I have taken the liberty of addressing this note to you. I understand from Mrs. Lewis you received the package Mr. Poe left at her house for you. I wish you to publish it exactly as he has written it. If you will do so I will promise you a favorable review of your books as they appear. You know the influence I have with Mr. Poe. Not that I think he will need any urging to advance your interest. I have just heard from him; he writes in fine spirits and says his prospects are excellent—Will you be so kind as to let me know if you receive this? Please direct to me at N. Y., care of E. A. Poe.

Respectfully,

MARIA CLEMM.[35]

Poe returned to Richmond on September 17th. On the next day he wrote two letters, one to Mrs. Clemm, his last letter to her:

Richmond Va
Tuesday—Sep 18—49.

My own darling Muddy,

On arriving here last night from Norfolk I received both your letters, including Mrs. Lewis's. I cannot tell you the joy they gave me—to learn at least that you are well & hopeful. May God forever bless you, my *dear dear* Muddy—Elmira has just got home from the country. I spent last evening with her. I think she loves me more devotedly than any one I ever knew & I cannot help loving her in return. Nothing is as yet definitely settled—and it will not do to hurry matters. I lectured at Norfolk on Monday &[36] cleared enough to settle my bill here at the Madison House with $2. over. I had a highly fashionable audience, but Norfolk is a small place & there were 2 exhibitions the same night. Next Monday I lecture again here & expect to have a large audience. On Tuesday I start for Phila. to attend to Mrs. Loud's Poems—& *possibly* on Thursday I may start for N. York. If I do I will go straight over to Mrs. Lewis's & send for you. It will be better for me not to go to Fordham—don't you think so? Write immediately in reply & direct to Phila. For fear I should not get the letter, sign no name & address it to *E. S. T. Grey, Esqre. If possible* I

[35] Original Autograph Ms., Griswold Collection, Boston Public Library.
[36] A careful search of the *North American Beacon* for September, 1849, reveals no lecture except the one on Friday, September 14th.

will get married before I start—but there is no telling. Give my dearest love to Mrs. L. My poor poor Muddy I am still unable to send you even one dollar—but keep up heart—I hope that our troubles are nearly over. I saw John Beatty in Norfolk.

God bless & protect you, my own darling Muddy. I showed your letter to Elmira and she says "it is such a darling precious letter that she loves you for it already."

YOUR OWN EDDY.

Don't forget to write immediately to Phila. so that your letter will be there when I arrive.

The papers here are praising me to death—and I have been received everywhere with enthusiasm. Be sure & preserve all the printed scraps I have sent you & keep up my file of the Lit. World.[37]

On the same day he wrote to Mrs. Lewis, a rather cautious letter, —for him.

[Tuesday 18th Sept. 1849]

My dear, dear Mrs. Lewis—My dear sister Anna (for so you have permitted me to call you)—never while I live shall I forget you or your kindness to my mother. If I have not written you in reply to your first cherished letter, think anything of my silence except that I am ungrateful or unmindful of you—or that I do not feel for you the purest and profoundest affection—ah, *let* me say *love*. I hope very soon to see you and clasp your dear hand. In the meantime, may God bless you, my sweet sister.

Your always,

EDGAR.[38]

Something, however, was going on, for there is an undated fragment, hastily written.—

Dearest Anna,

Give the enclosed *speedily* to my darling ~~Anna~~ mother. It might get into wrong hands.[39]

[37] Original Autograph Ms. fragment, Pratt Library. From "and it will not do" on line eight, as far as "but keep" on line twenty-two, it is in Poe's own hand. The remainder is a copy, probably in the hand of Mrs. Clemm.

[38] The original autograph Ms. in the Koester Collection is undated, but Mrs. Lewis wrote on it "Tuesday, 18th Sept. 1849." This date may of course refer to the time she received it.

[39] Original Autograph Ms., Koester Collection.

The somewhat complicated plans by which Poe was to marry Mrs. Shelton and placate Mrs. Clemm apparently necessitated a diplomatic approach, for Elmira wrote to her prospective mother-in-law on September 22nd:

Richmond September 22nd 1849

My Dear Mrs. Clemm:

You will no doubt be much surprised to receive a letter from one whom you have never seen.—Although I feel as if I were writing to one whom I love very devotedly, and whom to *know,* is to *love*—   Mr. Poe has been very solicitous that I should write to you, and I do assure you, it is with emotions of pleasure that I now do so—I am fully prepared to *love* you, and I do sincerely hope that our spirits may be congenial—There shall be nothing wanting on my part to make them so—I have just spent a very happy evening with your dear Edgar, and I know it will be gratifying to you, to know, that he is all that you could desire him to be, sober, temperate, moral, & much beloved—He showed me a letter of yours, in which you spoke affectionately of me, and for which I feel very much gratified & complimented—You also mentioned your fears in regard to the influence Rose might have in predjudicing [sic] me against you. Be assured, that she has never attempted it, and if she had, she would have accomplished nothing, except a very decided disapprobation of such a course— Edgar speaks frequently & very affectionately of your daughter & his Virginia, for which I love him but the more—I have a very dear friend, (to whom I am much attached), by the name of *Virginia Poe,* she is a lovely girl in character, tho' not as beautiful in person as your beloved one—I remember seeing Edgar, & his lovely wife, very soon after they were married—I met them—I never shall forget my feelings at the time—They were indescribable, almost agonizing—"However in an instant," I remembered that I was a married woman, and banished them from me, as I would a poisonous reptile—

Edgar's lecture a few weeks since, on the Poetic Principle, was very beautiful, he had quite a full, and very fashionable audience —He will repeat his lecture on Monday next, when I sincerely hope he may be patronised by a very large attendance— It is needless (I know) for me to ask you, to take good care of him when he is, (as I trust he soon will be) again restored to your Arms—"I trust a kind Providence" will protect him, and guide him in the way of truth, so that his feet slip not—I hope my dear friend that you will write to me, and as Edgar will perhaps reach you as soon as this does, he will direct your letter— It has struck 12 O'Clock, and I am encroaching on the Sabbath, and must therefore conclude—"Good Night Dear Friend," May Heaven bless you, and shield you, And may your remaining days on earth, be peaceful and happy—And your eternity glorious and blissful— Thus prays your attached

tho unknown friend—ELMIRA.[40]

Poe was asked to repeat his lecture and he spoke again in Richmond on "The Poetic Principle" on September 24th. The Richmond *Examiner* said on the 25th: "Edgar A. Poe lectured again last night on the 'Poetic Principle' and concluded his lecture as before with his own celebrated poem of the 'Raven'. . . . We furnish our readers today with the only correct copy ever published which we are enabled to do by the courtesy of Mr. Poe himself." [41]

On Poe's last public appearance William Winston Valentine noticed the pallor which overspread his face, contrasted with the dark hair which fell from the summit of his forehead, with an inclination to curl. His brow was fine and expressive, but his eyes were dark and restless and while his mouth was firm, there hovered over it an expression of scorn and discontent. His gait was firm and erect but his manner was nervous and emphatic. Valentine also spoke of the great struggle for self-control in which Poe seemed to be constantly engaged, and the sadness in the intonations of his voice.[42]

From his letter to Mrs. Clemm on September 18th, it is clear that Poe planned to leave Richmond on Tuesday, September 25th. But apparently he spent that evening at "Talevara," the rather modest home of the Talleys, still standing on West Grace Street in 1940, but then in the suburbs. Here Susan Talley had a talk with him. He was as always, she says, hopeful of the future "seeming to anticipate it with an eager delight, like that of youth. He declared that the last few weeks in the society of his old and new friends had been the happiest that he had known for many years, and that when he again left New York he should there leave behind all the trouble and vexation of his past life. On no occasion had I seen him so cheerful and hopeful as on this evening. . . . In the course of the evening he showed me a letter just received from his 'friend, Dr. Griswold,' in

---

[40] Original Autograph Letter, Pratt Library. The passage describing her feelings on seeing Edgar Poe and Virginia was omitted by Ingram, and later biographers have followed him.

[41] E. V. Valentine's notes, Valentine Museum. The version of the "Raven" published in the *Examiner* has been accepted as the best text.

[42] From Edward V. Valentine's notes on his brother's impressions—sent to Ingram, September 28, 1874. Now in the Valentine Museum.

reply to one but recently written by Poe, wherein the latter had requested Dr. Griswold in case of his sudden death to become his literary executor. In this reply, Dr. Griswold accepted the proposal, expressing himself as much flattered thereby, and writing in terms of friendly warmth and interest. It will be observed that this incident is a contradiction of his statement that previous to Poe's death he had had no intimation of the latter's intention of appointing him his literary executor.... He was the last of the party to leave the house. We were standing on the portico, and after going a few steps he paused, turned, and again lifted his hat, in a last adieu. At the moment, a brilliant meteor appeared in the sky directly over his head, and vanished in the east. We commented laughingly upon the incident; but I remembered it sadly afterward." [43]

That night Poe stayed at Duncan Lodge, and spent the next day with Dr. Gibbon Carter, Dr. MacKenzie and other friends. On Wednesday evening, he called on Elmira, who wrote Mrs. Clemm about his visit:

"He came up to my house on the evening of the 26th Sept. to take leave of me. He was very sad, and complained of being quite sick. I felt his pulse, and found he had considerable fever, and did not think it probable he would be able to start the next morning (Thursday) as he anticipated. I felt so wretched about him all that night, that I went up early the next morning to inquire after him, when, much to my regret, he had left in the boat for Baltimore."

Yet John R. Thompson wrote to Griswold on October 10th, "The evening before his departure from Richmond he was with me and spoke in the highest spirits of his resolves and prospects for the future." Thompson gave Poe a letter to deliver to Griswold.

Late in the evening, Poe stopped at Dr. John Carter's office, looked over the papers, then, taking Dr. Carter's cane, he remarked that he would step across to Sadler's Restaurant on Main Street and eat supper. Meeting some acquaintances, he remained longer than he had probably expected and went at once to "the Baltimore boat," which left probably early in the morning of Thursday, the 27th. He seemed to these friends to be cheerful and sober. [44]

[43] *Scribner's Monthly*, XV (March, 1878), 713-714.

[44] Mrs. Weiss in *Scribner's Monthly* tells a straight story of these last days, but gives no exact dates. Thompson's autograph letter of October 10th, in the Historical Society of Pennsylvania, does not give the exact date of Poe's departure, but speaks of it as being "some three weeks since,"

Poe may have left his trunk and perhaps his valise at the Swan Tavern.[45] Since he expected to return soon it would not be surprising if he left his trunk behind. But with his constant care concerning his personal appearance, it is hard to believe that he started on his travels without any baggage. The matter is of importance since it has been made the basis of an argument that he was already in the grip of a mental seizure. Lippard, at Griswold's request, was looking for a valise in Philadelphia in November, which indicates that he believed Poe had some baggage with him.

But from the time Poe left Richmond until he was found in Baltimore on October 3rd, his progress has been overlaid with rumor and conjecture. He is said to have called on his friend, Dr. Nathan C. Brooks, in Baltimore, but found him not at home. If the boat to Baltimore arrived on Friday, September 28th, this leaves several days to account for. A statement made by Thomas H. Lane, the friend of Poe who had closed the affairs of the *Broadway Journal*, may fill a portion of this void. As he understood it, Poe came to Philadelphia on this last journey, and stopped off to see friends. He was brought home, ill, by James P. Moss of 70 South Fourth Street, who was the husband of Lane's aunt. He was a musician and a friend of Poe. The next morning, against their protests, Poe left, in poor condition, saying that he was going on to New York. Lane believed that Poe must have taken the wrong train, and gone back to Baltimore.[46]

Lane unfortunately in his memoranda gave no specific dates. Trains left Baltimore for Philadelphia at nine A.M. and eight P.M., arriving

obviously incorrect. The whole fabric of Poe's last few days in Richmond depends on the accuracy of Mrs. Shelton's statement that he spent the evening of Wednesday, September 26th with her. See letter, Mrs. Shelton to Mrs. Clemm, October 11, 1849, published by Woodberry in "The Poe-Chivers Papers," *Century Magazine*, N. S., XLIII (February, 1903), 551-552. Mrs. Weiss omits all mention of the visit to Mrs. Shelton but states that she read in the *Richmond Dispatch* a notice of Poe's death "three days" after the evening on which he left Richmond, which is obviously incorrect. I have attempted to reconcile the contradictory testimony of the two ladies, and have omitted some third-hand testimony. Woodberry states definitely that Poe left at 4 A.M. on Thursday, September 27th, but gives no authority. See Appendix, p. 755, for the schedules of boats from Richmond to Baltimore, none of which left at 4 A. M. on Thursday.

[45] See p. 463.

[46] This account is based on a letter of October 20, 1927, to me, from my college friend, the late Dallet Fuguet, a cousin of Lane. Fuguet says that Lane's mind was still "as keen as ever" when he took down the memoranda, and that Lane had often told him the story.

in Philadelphia at 2:45 P.M. and 2:15 A.M.[47] Poe could have taken either train, and would have arrived in Philadelphia on Saturday, September 29th or Sunday, September 30th.

Poe intended to stop in Philadelphia to see the poetess, Mrs. St. Leon Loud, whose verses he was to edit. He had asked Mrs. Clemm to address letters to him in Philadelphia under the name of "E. S. T. Grey," so that the evidence in favor of this visit cannot be dismissed lightly, even if it is not at first hand.[48]

If Poe did stop in Philadelphia, he returned to Baltimore by October 2nd or 3rd, for the next certain fact is the note sent to Dr. J. E. Snodgrass, his earlier friend and correspondent:

Baltimore City, Oct. 3, 1849

Dear Sir,—

There is a gentleman, rather the worse for wear, at Ryan's 4th ward polls, who goes under the cognomen of Edgar A. Poe, and who appears in great distress, & he says he is acquainted with you, and I assure you, he is in need of immediate assistance.

Yours, in haste,

Jos. W. WALKER

To Dr. J. E. Snodgrass.[49]

[47] *American Railway Guide and Pocket Companion for the United States,* for 1851. On Sundays the morning train was omitted in both directions.

[48] At that time the location of the railroad stations in Philadelphia would make a mistake on Poe's part improbable but not impossible. Passengers from Baltimore used the Philadelphia, Wilmington and Baltimore Railroad, whose main station was at Eleventh and Market Streets. There was also a station at Sixth and Chestnut Streets, connected by omnibus with the main station. This was only four blocks from 70 South Fourth Street. Passengers for New York had to take the ferries of the Camden and Amboy Railroad, from the foot of Federal Street or Walnut Street, to Camden, New Jersey, and thence went by rail to New York. The Walnut Street Ferry was also about four blocks from 70 South Fourth Street, which would have been near Walnut Street. It is quite possible that Poe, in his confused condition, walked up Fourth Street, instead of down Walnut Street. But on the other hand, he must have been in very poor shape not to notice that he was taking an omnibus instead of a boat!

[49] This note was copied from the original by William Hand Browne for Ingram. Letter of Browne to Ingram, October 25, 1880. It was in the possession of Dr. Snodgrass, later of his widow, and while on coarse paper it was well written. Letters of W. H. Browne to Ingram, February 2, 1900, and January 13, 1909. Letters now in the Library of the University of Virginia.

Walker was well known among the compositors on the *Baltimore Sun*. When he found Poe lying outside of Ryan's Fourth Ward polls, semi-conscious, he naturally sent for the friend whom Poe mentioned as the nearest to be found. The polling place was in a public house, known as Gunner's Hall,[50] at 44 East Lombard Street, a few doors east of High Street, and Dr. Snodgrass lived on High Street, not far away.

What had brought Poe into this condition is still a matter of conjecture. There was an election on Wednesday, October 3rd, for Members of Congress and House of Delegates,[51] and the fact that Poe was found in or near a polling place has given rise to vivid pictures, all problematical, of his having been drugged, taken from one polling place to another to be voted as a "repeater," and abandoned when his usefulness was over. There is no doubt that such practices were frequent in those days, but that Poe was made a victim of them has not been fully established.[52] The Baltimore papers made no mention of any violence at the polls. Perhaps the "cooping" was so well known that it was unnecessary to mention it!

When Dr. Snodgrass found Poe, his clothing had been taken and he was dressed in a poor suit of thin texture. He was still grasping the cane of Dr. Carter, which he had taken in Richmond.[53]

[50] The building was destroyed, probably in the fire of 1904.

[51] *Baltimore Sun*, October 3, 1849.

[52] Edward Spencer's account, *New York Herald*, March 27, 1881, found conveniently in Harrison's *Biography*, pp. 330-331, makes a good deal of Poe's Whig proclivities and the nearness of the Whig "Coop," where the repeaters were kept, to Ryan's polling place. W. Hand Browne quotes his friend Dr. James W. Alnutt as one who knew of the "cooping" of Poe; see his letter to Ingram, December 5, 1875. University of Virginia Library.

[53] The most coherent account of the last days is to be gained by a combination of the letters of William Hand Browne to Ingram, the account by Edward Spencer in 1881 in criticism of Dr. Snodgrass's account in *Beadle's Monthly*, March, 1867, and Dr. Moran's *first* statement, in his letter to Mrs. Clemm, November 15, 1849, before he began to dramatize the situation. The reason for the untrustworthy nature of the Rev. Dr. Snodgrass's version is explained by his first account, reproduced in *Life Illustrated*, New York, May 17, 1856, from the *Woman's Temperance Paper* of New York City. He was evidently using Poe's death as a warning to the intemperate, and consequently invented the "deep intoxication," which by 1867 had become "beastly intoxication." In this earlier account he did not accuse Poe of "scarcely intelligible oaths and other forms of imprecation" as he did in 1867. In 1856 he said, "The muscles of articulation seemed paralyzed to speechlessness, and mere incoherent mutterings." Probably the temperance lecturer repeated these choice bits of scandal so often that he came to believe them.

Dr. Snodgrass and Henry Herring, who had married Poe's aunt, Elizabeth Poe, took him to the Washington College Hospital, about five o'clock on the afternoon of Wednesday, October 3rd. He was placed in the second floor room in the tower facing the court.[54]

He remained unconscious until three o'clock the next morning, but even on regaining partial consciousness, he was unable to tell Dr. Moran, the attending physician, how he had come to the condition in which he was found. From this state of utter despair and self-reproach he passed into a violent delirium, which lasted until Saturday evening. He was carefully tended and Neilson Poe sent him changes of linen and called but could not see him.

On Saturday night he began to call loudly for "Reynolds!" Perhaps to his dim and tortured brain, he seemed to be on the brink of a great descending circle sweeping down like the phantom ship in the "Manuscript Found in a Bottle" into "darkness and the distance." In that first published story, Poe had written, "It is evident that we are hurrying onward to some exciting knowledge—some never to be imparted secret, whose attainment is destruction. Perhaps this current leads to the South Pole itself."

It would have been natural enough for his favorite theme, the terror of the opening chasm, to lead his thoughts to that other story, *Arthur Gordon Pym*, and from that to Jeremiah Reynolds, projector of the voyages to the South Seas, whose very language he had used in that tale. He could easily have known Reynolds, but what led to his wild cries for him must still remain uncertain.[55]

[54] The building is now occupied by the Church Home and Infirmary. A stairway was cut through Poe's room and destroyed it. A tablet states, "Here before alterations was the room in which Edgar Allan Poe died, October 7, 1849." The Washington College Medical School in 1849 was the Medical Department of Washington and Jefferson College at Washington, Pennsylvania.

[55] There is no absolute certainty that Poe had met Reynolds personally, but his account of the latter in the "Chapter on Autography" in the *Southern Literary Messenger* in 1836, and in *Graham's Magazine* in December, 1841, and Poe's many other laudatory references to his achievements in connection with expeditions of discovery in the South Seas indicate a meeting. There would have been opportunities in New York in 1837 to 1838 and in the later period. See for interesting accounts of Reynolds, R. F. Almy, "J. N. Reynolds: a Brief Biography," *Colophon*, II, N. S. (1937), 227-245, and Aubrey Starke, "Poe's Friend Reynolds," *American Literature*, XI (May, 1939), 152-166.

Toward three o'clock on the morning of Sunday, October 7th, Poe weakened and seemed to rest. About five o'clock he breathed a short prayer, "God help my poor soul!" Then the "fever called living was conquered at last," and the poet who had seen farthest into the dim region "out of space, out of time" went on his last journey, alone.

CHAPTER XX

The Recoil of Fate

It was on the cold raw afternoon of October 9, 1849, that the little funeral brought to the Presbyterian Cemetery at Fayette and Green Streets, where now stands the Westminster Church, the body of Edgar Poe. Of the four men who paid him this last tribute, Neilson Poe and Henry Herring were relatives by blood or inter-marriage, Dr. Snodgrass had been his friend and fellow craftsman and Z. Collins Lee showed by his presence the strength of the boyhood ties made at the University of Virginia. The Reverend W. T. D. Clemm, of the Caroline Street Methodist Episcopal Church in Baltimore, read the funeral service.

Poe was laid in a grave near his grandfather, to lie there until 1875 when his coffin was removed to the southeastern corner of the cemetery. There his monument now stands, and beneath it Virginia and Mrs. Clemm are once more united to him.

On the day of Poe's funeral, Mrs. Clemm, frantic with anxiety, wrote to Neilson Poe for news. She had evidently read a notice of Edgar's death. Neilson Poe replied at once:

October 11, 1849.

My dear Madam:
I would to God I could console you with the information that your dear Son, Edgar A. Poe is still among the living. The newspapers, in announcing his death, have only told a truth, which we may weep over & deplore, but cannot change. He died on Sunday morning, about 5 o'clock, at the Washington Medical College, where he had been since the Wednesday preceding. At what time he arrived in this city, where he spent the time he was here, or under what circumstances, I have been unable to ascertain. It appears that, on Wednesday, he was seen & recognised at one of the places of election in old town, and that his condition was such as to render it necessary to send him to the college, where he was tenderly nursed until the time of his death. As soon as I heard that he was at the college, I went over, but his physicians

642

did not think it advisable that I should see him, as he was very excitable—The next day I called & sent him changes of linen &c. And was gratified to learn that he was much better, & I was never so much shocked, in my life, as when, on Sunday morning, notice was sent to me that he was dead. Mr. Herring & myself immediately took the necessary steps for his funeral, which took place on Monday afternoon at four o'clock. He lies alongside his ancestors in the Presbyterian burying ground on Green Street—

I assure you, My dear Madam, that, if I had known where a letter would reach you, I would have communicated the melancholy tidings in time to enable you to attend his funeral—but I was wholly ignorant how to address you—The body was followed to the grave by Mr. Herring, Dr. Snodgrass, Mr. Z. Collins Lee, (an old classmate) and myself. The service was performed by the Rev. Wm. T. D. Clemm, a son of James L. Clemm. Mr. Herring & myself have sought, in vain, for the trunk & clothes of Edgar. There is reason to believe that he was robbed of them, whilst in such a condition as to render him insensible of his loss—

I shall not attempt the useless task of consoling you under such a bereavement—Edgar had seen so much of sorrow—had so little reason to be satisfied with life—that, to him, the change can scarcely be said to be a misfortune—If it leaves you lonely in this world of trouble, may I be allowed the friendly privilege of expressing the hope that, in the contemplation of the world to which he has gone & to which we are all hastening,—you will find consolations enduring & all sufficient—I shall be glad, at all times, to hear from you, & to alleviate, in every way in my power, the sorrows to which this dispensation may expose you—I only wish my ability was equal to my disposition.

My wife unites with me in expressions of sympathy.

truly your friend & servant

NEILSON POE [1]

This letter, which contains the best evidence concerning the funeral, indicates clearly how little credence can be placed on the many later accounts of the last days of Poe. If Neilson Poe could not find out from Dr. Snodgrass, who went with him to the cemetery, what had really occurred, much of the latter's later romantic pictures may be discounted. Neilson Poe ordered a tombstone for his cousin, but the fatality, which always accompanied Edgar Poe's living actions, followed him after death and the tombstone was broken before it could be erected.

[1] Original Autograph Ms., Pratt Library.

Poe's death attracted little attention in Baltimore. The *Sun* printed this notice:

Death of Edgar A. Poe. We regret to learn that Edgar A. Poe, Esq., the distinguished American poet, scholar and critic, died in this city yesterday morning, after an illness of four or five days. This announcement coming so sudden [sic] and unexpected, will cause poignant regret among all who admire genius, and have sympathy for the frailties too often attending it. Mr. Poe, we believe, was a native of this State, though reared by a foster-father at Richmond, Va., where he lately spent some time on a visit. He was in the 38th year of his age. [2]

Even more brief was the reference in the *Clipper*,

Died:—
On the 8th instant of congestion of the brain, Edgar A. Poe, Esq. aged 38 years. Mr. Poe was well known as a writer of great ability.[3]

Both papers gave Poe's age incorrectly, but for that error he was responsible. There was not a word in the Baltimore *American*, the *Patriot* or the *National Intelligencer*, even in the official death notices.[4]

In Philadelphia, the notice in the Baltimore *Sun* was copied in the *Public Ledger*,[5] and the *Pennsylvanian*,[6] and still briefer notices appeared in the *Pennsylvania Freeman*,[7] and McMakin's *Model American Courier*.[8]

The impression made in Richmond by Poe's last visit may be judged by the fact the newspapers there did not confine themselves to a few words, even in their immediate notices. The Richmond *Whig* reported his death on October 9th, with many laudatory remarks. "But the other day he was delighting our citizens with a lecture—he was walking our streets in the vigor of manhood, mingling with his acquaintances." The *Enquirer* in an editorial on October 12th, spoke of "his wonderful and

[2] *The Sun* (Baltimore), Monday, October 8, 1849, p. 2, col. 1.
[3] Baltimore *Clipper*, October 9, 1849, p. 2, col. 7.
[4] Mr. Louis A. Dielman, Executive Secretary and Librarian of the Peabody Institute of Baltimore, made for me a search of the newspapers from October 1st to 20th, with the above results.
[5] Vol. XXVIII (October 9th), p. 2, col. 1.
[6] Vol. XXXIII (October 9th), p. 2, col. 7.
[7] New Series, VI (October 11th), p. 3, col. 4.
[8] Vol. XIX (October 13th), p. 2, col. 2.

touching 'Raven,' which in his admirable and fascinating lectures in this city he recited with great beauty, pathos and effect."

On October 9th the New York *Journal of Commerce* commented in its Editorial Columns:

Edgar A. Poe—Our readers will observe, under our telegraphic head, the announcement of the death of this well known author. For some years past he has been more or less ill, and the announcement of his death is not unexpected, though none the less melancholy on that account.

Few men were his equals. He stands in a position among our poets and prose writers which has made him the envy of many and the admiration of all. His life has been an eventful and stormy one, and if any one shall be found to write its history, we venture to say that its simple truths will be of more thrilling interest than most romances.

During the early part of his life he wandered around the world, wasting the energies of a noble mind. Subsequently he returned to his native country, but his heart seemed to have become embittered by the experiences of life, and his hand to be against every man. Hence he was better known as a *severe* critic than otherwise; yet Mr. Poe had a warm and noble heart, as those who best knew him can testify. He had been sadly disappointed in his early years. Brilliant prospects had been dashed away from before him, and he wandered over the world in search of a substitute for them. During the latter part of his life it has seemed as if his really high heart had been weighed down under a heavy load, and his own words best express the emotions of his soul:

> "Alas, alas for me,
>   Ambition—all is o'er!
>   No more, no more, no more,
> (Such language hath the solemn sea
>   To the sands upon the shore,)
> Shall bloom the thunder blasted tree,
>   The stricken eagle soar."

It will not be denied, even by his enemies, that Mr. Poe was a man of great ability,—and all other recollections of him will be lost now, and buried with him in the grave. We hope he has found rest, for he needed it.

But the friendly and sensible wish of the Editor was not be be fulfilled. Almost at the very minute when the sods were falling on Poe's coffin, the fingers of slander were reaching for his fame. The Reverend

Rufus W. Griswold, who had accepted the responsibility of becoming Poe's literary executor, published in the Evening Edition of the *New York Tribune* of October 9th, a notice of his death and his career beginning:

> Edgar Allan Poe is dead. He died in Baltimore the day before yesterday. This announcement will startle many, but few will be grieved by it. The poet was known, personally or by reputation, in all this country; he had readers in England, and in several of the states of Continental Europe; but he had few or no friends; and the regrets for his death will be suggested principally by the consideration that in him literary art has lost one of its most brilliant but erratic stars.

Then followed an account of Poe's life. For some of the errors of fact Griswold was not responsible since he derived them from Poe's own autobiographical sketch. But he lost no opportunity of dwelling upon Poe's poverty. According to Griswold, when Poe called upon Kennedy, "a tattered frock-coat concealed the absence of a shirt, and the ruins of boots disclosed more than the want of stockings." Griswold dwelt, apparently with relish, on Poe's destitution in 1847. With that cleverness that marked the entire course of his attack on Poe he proceeded to win the reader's belief in his fairness by praising highly Poe's imaginative power and then altered the picture by charging that Poe "himself dissolved the spell, and brought his hearers back to common and base existence, by vulgar fancies or exhibitions of the ignoble passions."

When Griswold proceeded to a more definite analysis of Poe's character his own powers of destructive criticism evidently for the moment failed him. He claimed later that he wrote a few paragraphs "hastily" for the *Tribune*,[9] but he took the time to look up Bulwer's *The Caxtons* and make use of the description of Francis Vivian.[10] He began by a statement of his own that Poe's "harsh experience had deprived him of all faith, in man or woman." Next he paraphrased Bulwer for a few sentences and then after a reference to *The Caxtons*, gave Bulwer's language almost verbatim. In quoting this passage I am printing in italics the sentences in which he reproduced *The Caxtons*, without change:

> He had made up his mind upon the numberless complexities of the social world, and the whole system with him was an im-

[9] See his *Preface* to his *Memoir*.
[10] Part Eighth, Chapter III.

posture. This conviction gave a direction to his shrewd and naturally unamiable character. Still, though he regarded society as composed altogether of villains, the sharpness of his intellect was not of that kind which enabled him to cope with villainy, while it continually caused him by overshots to fail of the success of honesty. He was in many respects like Francis Vivian in Bulwer's novel of the "Caxtons." *"Passion, in him, comprehended many of the worst emotions which militate against human happiness. You could not contradict him, but you raised quick choler; you could not speak of wealth, but his [11] cheek paled with gnawing envy. The astonishing natural advantages of this poor boy—his beauty, his readiness, the daring spirit that breathed around him like a fiery atmosphere—had raised his constitutional self-confidence into an arrogance that turned his very claims to admiration into prejudices against him. Irascible, envious [12]—bad enough, but not the worst, for these salient angles were all varnished over with a cold repellent cynicism, his passions vented themselves in sneers. There seemed to [13] him no moral susceptibility; and, what was more remarkable in a proud nature, little or nothing of the true point of honor. He had, to a morbid excess, that desire to rise which is vulgarly called ambition, but no wish for the esteem or the love of his species; only the hard wish to succeed—not shine, not serve—succeed, that he might have the right to despise a world which galled his self-conceit."*

Griswold enclosed this passage in quotation marks in the *Tribune* article, but omitted them when he afterwards reprinted it in his "Memoir" of Poe. The veracity of a portrait so derived, it is hardly necessary to challenge. Yet it was extensively quoted as Griswold's own opinion, and it did much greater harm than if it had been recognized as a mere quotation. Griswold signed the article with the name of "Ludwig."

The damage this article did to Poe's reputation is incalculable. Printed in Horace Greeley's paper and republished in the *Weekly Tribune* on October 20th, it was accepted as authoritative, and it was copied, even in journals friendly to Poe. It appeared, for example, in the *Richmond Enquirer* on October 13th and it created that *first* impression, so hard to efface.

Meanwhile the women who had loved Poe were pouring out their sympathy to Mrs. Clemm. On October 10th Mrs. Richmond, with her

[11] "the" in *The Caxtons*.
[12] "arrogant" appears here in *The Caxtons*.
[13] "in" in *The Caxtons*.

usual emotional emphasis, begged her "darling mother" to come to her. "Oh, if I could only have laid down *my* life for his, that he might have been spared to you," Annie went on—"pardon me, if I add one pang to your grief, dear mother, but my own heart is breaking." Mrs. Richmond was, in the midst of her sorrow, practical in her sympathy. "Mr. R[ichmond] begs that you will come on here, soon as you can, and stay with us as long as you please." And on October 14th, she added another warm hearted invitation, coupled with a request to bring any writings of Poe. "Everything he has written is *so dear* to me," Annie continued: "Oh mother, darling, darling mother, is it possible, that he will never, *never* write to me again? I have waited *so long,* and now, *to know* it *never can be,* oh mother, is it wrong, I cannot bear it calmly." Mrs. Richmond added a postscript "If you have any letters of Mrs. Locke's, *do not destroy them,* but *be sure* and bring them with you, *for a very particular reason.*" [14] Perhaps Annie was anticipating an attack on her dead friend!

On October 11th, Mrs. Shelton wrote from Richmond:

Oh! how shall I address you, my dear, and deeply afflicted friend under such heart-rending circumstances? I have no doubt, ere this, you have heard of the death of our *dear Edgar!* yes, he was the *dearest object* on earth to me; and, well assured am I, that he was the pride of your heart. I have not been able to get any of the particulars of his sickness & death, except an extract from the *Baltimore Sun,* which said that he died on Sunday, the 7th of this month, with congestion of the brain, after an illness of 7 days.

Then, after telling of his last visit to her,[15] Elmira continued:

He expected, certainly, to have been with his "dear Muddy" on the Sunday following, when he promised to write to me; and after the expiration of a week, and no letter, I became very uneasy, and continued in an agonizing state of mind, fearing he was ill, but never dreamed of his death, untill it met my eye, in glancing casually over a Richmond paper of last Tuesday. Oh! my dearest friend! I cannot begin to tell you what my feelings were, as the horrible truth forced itself upon me! It was the most severe trial I have ever had; and God alone knows how I can bear it! [16]

[14] Quotations are from original autograph Ms. in Pratt Library.
[15] See p. 636.
[16] Woodberry, "The Poe-Chivers Papers," *Century Magazine,* N. S., XLIII (February, 1903), 551-552.

Mrs. Clemm accepted Annie's invitation promptly, and was soon at Lowell. Here Mrs. Whitman wrote her, in a more restrained tone than Annie or Elmira:

My dear Mrs. Clemm
    Every day since I recieved the heart-rending intelligence of Edgar's death I have been wishing to address you—Not knowing whether a letter directed to you at Fordham would reach you, I, this morning, commenced a letter to Mr. Griswold requesting him to assure you of my sympathy in your deep sorrow and of my unalterable affection for one whose memory is still most dear to me. I had not finished my long letter to him when I recieved your note—
    Its contents greatly surprised me because I have written to *no one* since your son's death, nor have I forwarded or *recieved* [sic] any communication of the kind to which you allude. I cannot but think there has been some misapprehension in relation to this affair—If I am well enough to write you again while you remain at Lowell I will do so. If *not* my letter to Mr. Griswold will inform you of much that I have been long wishing to communicate to you—in the mean time believe me dear madam
                    respectfully & affectionately
                            Your friend
                                    SARAH H. WHITMAN
Saturday evening
    October 28th [17]

Mrs. Whitman did not send her "long letter" to Griswold until December 12th.[18] It was written while she still believed Griswold to be Poe's friend, one to whom she could explain her refusal to answer Poe's letter of January 25, 1849, in the hope that Griswold would explain in turn to Mrs. Clemm, of whose address Mrs. Whitman seemed to be unaware:

    The tone of his letter was sad & reproachful—Yet he requested me to write to him immediately & to authorise him to say that our marriage was simply "postponed" on account of my ill health. —I would not have hesitated for a moment to have complied with his request had I not have [sic] feared that by so doing we might

[17] Original Autograph Ms., Pratt Library. October 28th was not Saturday in 1849—the letter was probably written on the 27th.
    [18] Original Autograph Ms., Historical Society of Pennsylvania. For complete letter see Howard P. Vincent, *American Literature*, XIII (May, 1941), 162-167.

both be involved in a recurrence of the unhappy scenes which had preceeded [sic] & attended our seperation [sic.]—Scenes, "when our happiness suddenly faded into horror & the most beautiful became the most fearful, as Hinnon became Ge-Henna" —With a heavy heart, & after the most dispassionate reflection, I resolved, for his sake rather than my own, not to reply to this letter, but to defer all painful reminiscences & explanations to a future day.

After a discussion of her unsuccessful attempt to find out from Mrs. Osgood news of Poe's health and welfare, Mrs. Whitman continued:

From the numerous efforts which have been made both before & since his death to prejudice me against *him* I cannot but infer that similar agencies have been employed to convince him that I had ceased to regard him with interest—

I trust Mrs. Clemm will believe the statement which I here make to you, that I have *never* spoken of him but in words of extenuation & kindness—*never* thought of him but with feelings of unutterable sympathy compassion & admiration. I am the more anxious that she should know this because I have reason to believe that others have sought to impress her with a contrary opinion—I also wish her to know that our seperation [sic] was not the result of any deliberate act of my own, far less of any change in my *feelings* towards him—I knew from the first that our engagement was a most imprudent one—I clearly foresaw all the perils & penalties to which it would expose us—but having consented to it (under circumstances which seemed to make life or death, happiness or misery alike indifferent to me) I resolved not to retract my promise—Nor would I have done so—The union to which I was so rashly urged, & to which I so rashly consented, was in the end prevented by circumstances over which I had no control—by a fatality which no act of mine could have averted.— And I can only account for the reproachful tone of Mr Poe's last letter by supposing (as he indeed therein suggested) that "some person equally *his* enemy & *mine*" had sought by the most false & groundless assertions to make him believe that my friendship for him was changed into disgust & abhorrence—Perhaps Mrs Clemm can tell me from whence these reports originated—but it is a matter of little moment now, for I trust that he *now* sees my heart & knows that I have never wronged him in thought word or deed.

Mrs. Whitman asked Griswold, "Can you tell me what has become of my letters to Mr. Poe?" But she asked in vain. After another denial of rumors sent abroad by a lady who had quoted Mrs. Whitman as her authority that Poe was "an intemperate and dissolute man," Mrs. Whitman continued:

> I was much interested by your eloquent sketch of his life published in the Tribune—I cannot doubt the justice of your remarks, although my *personal* experience would lead me to think his disposition more gentle and more gracious than you esteem it to be.

Griswold's reply of December 17, 1849, told Mrs. Whitman definitely that "I was not his friend, nor was he mine, as I remember to have told you." He then added more spice to the epistle:

> I do not wish, of course, to involve myself in any such private feuds as a knowledge that I so write to you would occasion, but I cannot refrain from begging you to be *very* careful what you say to, or write to, Mrs. Clemm, who is not your friend, nor anybody's friend, and who has no element of goodness or kindness in her nature—but whose whole heart and understanding are full of malice and wickedness. I *confide in you* these sentences, for your own sake only—for Mrs. C. appears to be a very warm friend to me. Pray destroy this note, and, at least, act *cautiously*, till I may justify it in a conversation with you.[19]

Griswold's first attack did not pass unchallenged. In the *Richmond Republican* of October 15th, an anonymous article, probably written by Susan Archer Talley,[20] begins:

> The recent death of Edgar A. Poe has already called forth numerous notices from the press. Among these we regret to observe several that, purporting to give an account of the poet's character, have, either from ignorance or prejudice against him, represented it in so unjust and distorted a view as to be almost unrecognizable to those who best knew him . . .

The article continues:

> He ever felt the impulse and desire of good within him, even while yielding to evil, and it was to him a source of constant anguish and remorse. It rendered him discontented and miserable. In his own words, spoken only a short time before his death, he

---

[19] Original Autograph Ms., Lilly Collection.

[20] At the bottom of the clipping from the *Republican*, now in the Valentine Museum, there is a note in pencil, "Written by Miss Susan Talley— Oct. 10." The handwriting is apparently that of Mann S. Valentine, a close friend of Miss Talley. The article does not mention Griswold's attack by name.

"felt as if his good angel had been grieved away, and a demon usurped its place." ...

With regard to Mr. Poe's real disposition, the writer can, from personal knowledge, speak confidently. His nature was more than usually warm and affectionate ... If quick to resent an injury, no one was ever more easily won by kindness ... and it seemed one of his greatest pleasures to do any thing in his power for those whom he considered as his friends.

On October 13th Willis published in the *Home Journal* a brief note, "Edgar Poe is no more. He died at Baltimore on Sunday last, in the fortieth year of his age. He was a man of genius and a poet of remarkable power. Peace to his manes." In the next issue, on October 20th, Willis printed his "Death of Edgar A. Poe." After stating that his own impressions of the nature of Poe differed from that generally conveyed in the death notices, Willis reprinted what he called "a graphic and highly finished portraiture from the pen of Dr. Griswold." But Willis continued: "Apropos of the disparaging portion of the above well written sketch, let us truthfully say"—and then he began his masterly defence of Poe. First came his picture of Poe as his patient, industrious and gentlemanly associate on the *Mirror*, already given in the discussion of Poe's relations with that journal.[21] Willis next spoke of the charges that Poe was "arrogant and bad hearted," and stated that "in this reversed character it was never our chance to see him." Then he concluded, with that delicate understanding and chivalric devotion to a fellow craftsman that should keep Willis's fame secure, to paint Poe's portrait in the warm light of the love the dead poet had inspired:

> But there is another, more touching and far more forcible evidence that there *was goodness* in Edgar Poe. To reveal it, we are obliged to venture upon the lifting of the veil which sacredly covers grief and refinement in poverty—but we think it may be excused if, so, we can brighten the memory of the poet, even were there not a more needed and immediate service which it may render to the nearest link broken by his death.
>
> Our first knowledge of Mr. Poe's removal to this city was by a call which we received from a lady who introduced herself to us as the mother of his wife. She was in search of employment for him, and she excused her errand by mentioning that he was ill, that her daughter was a confirmed invalid, and that their circumstances were such as compelled her taking it upon herself. The countenance of this lady, made beautiful and saintly with an

[21] See Chapter XIV, pp. 434-435.

evidently complete giving up of her life to privation and sorrow-
ful tenderness, her gentle and mournful voice urging its plea,
her long-forgotten but habitually and unconsciously refined manners, and her appealing and yet appreciative mention of the
claims and abilities of her son, disclosed at once the presence of
one of those angels upon earth that women in adversity can be.
It was a hard fate that she was watching over. Mr. Poe wrote with
fastidious difficulty, and in a style too much above the popular
level to be well paid. He was always in pecuniary difficulty, and,
with his sick wife, frequently in want of the merest necessaries of
life. Winter after winter, for years, the most touching sight to us,
in this whole city, has been that tireless minister to genius, thinly
and insufficiently clad, going from office to office with a poem, or
an article on some literary subject, to sell—sometimes simply
pleading in a broken voice that he was ill, and begging for him
—mentioning nothing but that "he was ill," whatever might be the
reason for his writing nothing—and never, amid all her tears and
recitals of distress, suffering one syllable to escape her lips that
could convey a doubt of him, or a complaint, or a lessening of
pride in his genius and good intentions. Her daughter died, a
year and a half since, but she did not desert him. She continued
his ministering angel—living with him—caring for him—guarding
him against exposure, and, when he was carried away by temptation, amid grief and the loneliness of feelings unreplied to, and
awoke from his self-abandonment prostrated in destitution and
suffering, *begging* for him still. If woman's devotion, born with a
first love and fed with human passion, hallow its object, as it is
allowed to do, what does not a devotion like this—pure, disinterested and holy as the watch of an invisible spirit—say for him
who inspired it? [22]

On the same day, October 20th, Henry B. Hirst spoke for Philadelphia, in McMakin's *Model American Courier:* [23]

Edgar A. Poe is no more. We knew him well, perhaps better
than any other man living, and loved him, despite his infirmities.
He was a man of great and original genius, but the sublime
afflatus which lifted him above his fellows, made him a shining
mark for the covert as well as open attacks of literary rivals, and,
alas! that it should be so, eventually proved his ruin.

After giving the best of the immediate post-mortem accounts of Poe's

---

[22] *Home Journal,* October 20, 1849, Editorial Page, Col. 4.
[23] Vol. XIX (Saturday, October 20, 1849), No. 33, p. 2. Signed "H. B.
H."—and Hirst is given as the author in the editorial preface to the account.

life, derived probably from Hirst's own biographical sketch in the *Saturday Museum* in 1843, he proceeded:

> Poe had his faults—who has not his errors? We are none of us infallible; but had his opportunities equalled his genius and his ambition, he would have died an universally esteemed great man. As it is, the world of authors and author-lovers, with some few pitiful exceptions, will mourn a departed brother. His name, under any circumstances, cannot be forgotten. His tales are without existing equals in English literature, and his "Raven," the personification of his own despair at the loss of his wife, has made him immortal.
>
> Poor Poe! Hour by hour have we listened to his delightful abstractions, poured forth in a voice so remarkable in the peculiarity of its intonation as to incline to the extraordinary in tone. He was unfortunate in every sense of the word. When miserable authors of still more miserable love stories and puling love poems, were winning gold from the Magazines of the day, he was rarely able to "sell an article," and was always suffering in the iron grasp of penury, and that, too, when the brilliant corruscations of his genius were eagerly sought for by the public *in vain....* We saw him twice and thrice a day, for two years. We sat night by night, a welcome guest at his often meagre, but, when fortune smiled on him, his well-filled board. In all that time, in all our acquaintance, we never heard him express one single word of personal ill-feeling against any man, not even in his blackest hours of poverty.

Hirst's account was not a reply to Griswold's attack, for it was received, according to the editor, before Griswold's article appeared.

Lambert Wilmer, under the caption "Edgar A. Poe and his Calumniators," denounced the writer of the Ludwig article:

> EDGAR A. POE AND HIS CALUMNIATORS.—There is a spurious biography of Edgar A. Poe which has been extensively published in newspapers and magazines. It is a hypocritical canting document, expressing much commiseration for the follies and "crimes" of that "poor outcast"; the writer being evidently just such an one as the Pharisee who thanked God that he was a better fellow than the publican. But we can tell the slanderous and malicious miscreant who composed the aforesaid biography (we know not and care not who he is,) that Edgar A. Poe was infinitely his superior, both in the moral and in the intellectual scale. The writer of this article speaks from his own knowledge when he says that Poe was not the man described by this anony-

mous scribbler. Some circumstances mentioned by the slanderous hypocrite we *know* to be false, and we have no doubt in the world that nearly all of his statements intended to throw odium and discredit on the character of the deceased are scandalous inventions.

We have much more to say on this subject, and we pledge ourselves to show that the article we speak of is false and defamatory, when the skulking author of it becomes magnanimous enough to take the responsibility by fixing his *name* to his malignant publication.[24]

In the November, 1849, issue of the *Southern Literary Messenger* John R. Thompson presented an appreciation of Poe's poetry and criticism, and assuming his infirmities as established, remarked that he would throw over them "in charity the mantle of forgetfulness." Thompson's article is of especial interest because he included in it a paragraph from a letter which Longfellow had written him in October: [25]

"What a melancholy death," says Mr. Longfellow, "is that of Mr. Poe—a man so richly endowed with genius! I never knew him personally, but have always entertained a high appreciation of his powers as a prose-writer and a poet. His prose is remarkably vigorous, direct and yet affluent; and his verse has a particular charm of melody, an atmosphere of true poetry about it, which is very winning. The harshness of his criticisms, I have never attributed to anything but the irritation of a sensitive nature, chafed by some indefinite sense of wrong."

The nobility of the last sentence of this letter is as striking as its penetration into the complex nature of Poe. It provides, also, a temptation to speculation. Longfellow evidently had Poe in his mind, after he heard of his tragic death. On September 22nd he had finished "The Building of the Ship." We know how carefully he revised his poems.

[24] Wilmer republished this letter in his *Our Press Gang* (1860), p. 385. He does not give the name of the "Philadelphia weekly paper" in which he printed it and the paper has not been found. His defence must have been written between October 9, 1849, when the Ludwig article appeared and the time when Griswold acknowledged the "Ludwig" article. The letter of Wilmer is reprinted by Dr. Mabbott in his *Merlin* (1941), pp. 25-26.

[25] The letter is not dated in Thompson's article. In the *Life of Longfellow* by Samuel Longfellow, II, 150, it is dated vaguely "October, 1849." But since it was printed in the November issue, it was probably received early in October.

Is it not possible that the death of Poe suggested as an addition the lines—

> "And in the wreck of noble lives,
> Something immortal still survives."

In any case, they provide a striking description of his great rival, which reads now like a prophecy.

In the meantime, Griswold lost no time in preparing to edit Poe's works. On October 15th, less than a week after Poe's death, he secured from Mrs. Clemm a power of attorney to make a contract with a publisher, for the editing and publishing of the writings of Poe, which she had placed in his hands.[26]

Griswold wrote to Thompson on October 25, 1849, asking for help in the preparation of the volumes. In the letter he said, "I heard of the death of Poe one evening at 7 [or 9] o'clock and wrote hastily for the next day's *Tribune* a notice of him." He added: "Mrs. Clemm has given me his MSS. &c. with full power of attorney, to act in her behalf, and she is to have all the profits that do not go to the booksellers.... Poe's *trunk* has not been recovered. Mr. Neilson Poe of Baltimore writes that from something said by Poe it was believed that he gave it into the hands of a porter at Baltimore to carry to the Philadelphia depot. Can you give any clue to it? It contained some important letters, and his *lectures* and I am very anxious to obtain the last, to print." [27]

Considering the mutual dislike of Mrs. Clemm and Rosalie, there must have been a vivid scene when Griswold brought to the former a letter to him from John R. Thompson, written November 3, 1849.[28] Acting as Rosalie's attorney, Thompson politely but firmly demanded for her as "the sister and *sole heir of* the deceased," the proceeds of the sale of the Collected Edition of Poe's works. Thompson concluded: "I have written to Mr. Neilson Poe, as Miss Poe's attorney, directing the trunk of the deceased to be forwarded to me. If it should come, I will be careful to secure for you the Ms. Lectures and whatever other literary contents may be found in it." [29]

[26] See Appendix, p. 754, for the complete document.

[27] Original Autograph Ms., Lilly Collection.

[28] Original Autograph Ms., Gratz Collection, Historical Society of Pennsylvania.

[29] The actual transit of the trunk is still a matter of dispute. If Thompson sent it to Neilson Poe by November 1st (Woodberry, II, 451) why did Thompson write to him on November 3rd demanding it? The trunk is now at the Poe Shrine in Richmond, transferred to the Shrine by Mrs. Jane

Griswold's reply of November 7th is known through Thompson's letter of November 11, 1849:

My dear Sir,
   The mail of to-night brings me your letter of the 7th, together with a letter from Mr. S. D. Lewis, Mrs. Clemm's Solicitor, on the subject of the Poe publication.
   Of course the sale of the Copy-right of "Tales and Poems" by the author himself to Wiley & Putnam puts an end to the claim of Miss Rosalie. . . .
   With regard to "Annabel Lee" I did not by any means attribute your publication of it to inconsideration or improper motives. The fact is simply this—Poe sold it to both of us, and for a high price too, and neither of us obtained anything by the transaction. I lost nearly as much by his death as yourself, as I paid him for a prose article *to be written,* and he owed me something at that time. . . . By the way, I have a lien on a copy of his "Tales & Poems," which contained full marginal notes & corrections in his own hand-writing. He was to give it to me, after a new edition had been published. If it has come into your hands, you will oblige me by sending it to me, after your labors are concluded. Pray recollect this." [30]

Thompson's reference to the copyright was based, of course, on Griswold's misrepresentation of the situation. Any sale of the copyright by Poe would have wiped out Mrs. Clemm's claims even more thoroughly than Rosalie's. As Poe's aunt, she came after his sister in her legal status and as his mother-in-law she had no standing. Her claim was based upon her care of Poe, and she had possession of the manuscripts!

Wiley and Putnam, who had published the *Tales* and the *Poems,* did not enter into the picture, unless they had sold their rights to Redfield, of which there is no record. In any case, their copyright of the *Tales* covered only twelve of the sixty-eight stories. If Thompson lost any money on "Annabel Lee," he amply made up for it later when he made a considerable sum out of his lecture on "The Genius and

---

MacKenzie Miller, granddaughter of Mrs. Jane Scott MacKenzie, who took Rosalie Poe into her home. Rosalie gave the trunk to Mrs. Miller, when she left the latter's home, so that she evidently had it in her possession. See Valentine Letters, p. 179, Mrs. Stanard's account there being checked by a written statement by Mrs. Miller, October 15, 1926, also in the Poe Shrine.

[30] Original Autograph Ms., Gratz Collection, Historical Society of Penn-sylvania.

Character of Edgar Allan Poe"! It is unlikely that Griswold had paid Poe anything—Griswold did not buy poetry. Since he published the poem in his "Ludwig" article, he was paid for it, indirectly. If the missing postscript in the "last letter" from Poe to Griswold ever existed, he was acting as Poe's agent in the matter of "Annabel Lee." If it is a forgery, Poe had presented the poem to him for a later edition of Griswold's anthology.

That Griswold really did not consider Mrs. Clemm as the heiress to Poe's rights, except for his own purposes, is indicated by his suggestion to Thompson later [31] that the latter secure the "Poetic Principle," print it and pay Rosalie for it! Griswold also states that Neilson Poe had not yet sent him any manuscripts.

If Griswold made any contract with Redfield, who published Poe's works, it has disappeared. Griswold stated several times that he had no remuneration for his editorial services, and that he accepted the task for Mrs. Clemm's benefit.[32] On her part she also stated positively that Redfield would pay her nothing until the expenses were all secured by the sale of the volumes. She was, however, given some sets of the books to sell, and she was still trying to dispose of them several years later.[33] Where this situation leaves Redfield is not clear.

Griswold wrote to Lowell two letters, one dated vaguely "Thursday Morning," [34] asking him to revise his sketch of Poe, printed first in *Graham's* in 1845, for the forthcoming volumes. In this note Griswold said:

> Poe was not my friend—I was not his—and he had no right to devolve upon me this duty of editing his works. He did do so, however, and under the circumstances I could not well refuse compliance with the wishes of his friends here. From his constant habit of *repeating himself,* and from his habits of *appropriation,*

[31] Griswold to Thompson, February 19, 1850, printed in *Genius and Character of Edgar A. Poe,* pp. 54-55.

[32] Letter to Lowell, October 31, 1849; to Thompson, October 25, 1849, etc.

[33] J. C. Derby, *Fifty Years Among Authors and Publishers* (New York, 1884), pp. 586-588, states that the sale reached about fifteen hundred sets a year. Derby adds, "The copyright was paid at first to Mr. Poe [!], and after his death to his mother-in-law, Mrs. Clemm, who received the copyright on several editions." In view of this remarkable statement, Derby's quotation from Redfield, defending Griswold's "Memoir," can hardly be considered good evidence.

[34] October 18 or 25, 1849. Original Autograph Ms., Harvard University Library.

particularly in the *Marginalia*, it is a difficult task; but I shall execute it as well as I can, in the short time that is allowed to me—that is, in *three weeks*.

On October 31st, Griswold wrote again, repeating his request, and telling Lowell that Willis would "rewrite, or make into one article, all that he has published in regard to Poe," Griswold contenting himself with the editing but "giving notice perhaps of an intention to prepare his life and correspondence hereafter." Griswold added "There are now six persons employed in setting up the copy, and I understand four others will be added next week—so that I shall probably need your Ms. the week after the next." [35] Someone was surely in a hurry to make money out of Poe's writings, now that he was dead. The publishers had expressed no such haste while he was alive.

Unfortunately we do not have Lowell's replies to these letters, for when the volumes appeared, his article was quite materially altered from its original form in *Graham's*. More than one-third was omitted, including his praise of Poe as "the most discriminating, philosophical and fearless critic upon imaginative works who has written in America." The last quarter of the sketch which contained "The Haunted Palace," with Lowell's enthusiastic comments, was omitted, together with the conclusion, "It is not for us to assign him his definite rank among contemporary authors, but we may be allowed to say that we know of none who has displayed more varied and striking abilities." In the place of these, three paragraphs were added of quite a different nature. While Poe's skill in employing the strange fascination of mystery and terror is acknowledged, this is stated to be not the province of "the great masters of imagination." [36] The high praise of Poe as a critic in *Graham's* becomes:

> As a critic, Mr. Poe was aesthetically deficient. Unerring in his analysis of dictions, metres, and plots, he seemed wanting in the faculty of perceiving the profounder ethics of art. His criticisms, are, however, distinguished for scientific precision and coherence of logic. They have the exactness and, at the same time, the coldness of mathematical demonstrations. Yet they stand in strikingly refreshing contrast with the vague generalisms and sharp personalities of the day. If deficient in warmth, they are also without the heat of partisanship. They are especially valuable as

[35] Original Autograph Ms., Harvard University Library.
[36] But see passage from the original article in *Graham's*, Chap. XIV, p. 433.

illustrating the great truth, too generally overlooked, that analytic power is a subordinate quality of the critic.

The essay then concludes with a mild statement:

On the whole, it may be considered certain that Mr. Poe has attained an individual eminence in our literature, which he will keep. He has given proof of power and originality. He has done that which could only be done once with success or safety, and the imitation or repetition of which would produce weariness.

Did Lowell cut down his sketch and write these concluding paragraphs, or did Griswold forge them, as he did the letters? In a letter to Thompson, on February 19, 1850, Griswold said, "Willis promised a new introduction, but did not give it; Lowell, a Memoir, but sent me only those old paragraphs." [37]

This statement apparently convicts Griswold out of his own mouth. The added paragraphs seem to be hastily written, and have not the finish of Lowell's original article. Griswold could imitate Lowell's style, as a comparison of his Introduction to Poe's stories in the *Prose Writers of America* with Lowell's original article on Poe easily establishes. But since Lowell never republished his article on Poe in his collected works, and did not protest publicly against the revision as it appeared in Griswold's edition, the matter can not be settled. Certainly the revised sketch was much less favorable in its estimate of Poe's work.

In January, 1850, Griswold's first two volumes appeared. Volume One contained the sketches by Willis and Lowell, and thirty-one of the short stories. The second volume was made up of the poems, omitting the greater "To Helen," and also included "The Rationale of Verse," "The Philosophy of Composition," and twenty-four more of the tales.

Poe's friends and enemies seized the opportunity in reviews of these two volumes, to pay tributes or to level attacks. Lewis Gaylord Clark in the *Knickerbocker* [38] for February, 1850, while acknowledging that "few of our American authors have possessed more of the creative energy or the constructive faculty," claimed that Poe was "destitute of moral or religious principle," charged him with plagiarism, and dismissed his criticisms as "worthless."

[37] Original letter is quoted in Appendix to *The Genius and Character of Edgar Allan Poe*, by J. R. Thompson, ed. by Whitty and Rindfleisch, p. 54.

[38] XXXV (February, 1850), 163-164.

The best of the early repudiations of Griswold came from Philadelphia, from George Graham, in his own magazine for March, 1850. It is so convincing, so clearly written from first-hand knowledge, that it becomes one of the most important of all Poe documents:

My DEAR WILLIS,—In an article of yours, which accompanies the two beautiful volumes of the writings of Edgar Allan Poe, you have spoken with so much truth and delicacy of the deceased, and with the magical touch of genius have called so warmly up before me the memory of our lost friend, as you and I both seem to have known him, that I feel warranted in addressing to you the few plain words I have to say in defense of his character, as set down by Dr. Rufus W. Griswold. Although the article, it seems appeared originally in the NEW YORK TRIBUNE, it met my eye for the first time in the volumes before me. I now purpose to take exception to it in the most public manner. I knew Mr. Poe well— far better than Mr. Griswold; and by the memory of old times, when he was an editor of "Graham," I pronounce this exceedingly ill-timed and unappreciative estimate of the character of our lost friend *unfair and untrue*. It must have been made in a moment of spleen, written out and laid aside, and handed to the printer, when his death was announced, with a sort of chuckle. It is Mr. Poe, as seen by the writer while laboring under a fit of the nightmare; but so dark a picture has no resemblance to the *living* man. Accompanying these beautiful volumes, it is an immortal infamy—the death's head over the entrance to the garden of beauty—a horror that clings to the brow of morning, whispering of murder. It haunts the memory through every page of his writings, leaving upon the heart a sensation of utter gloom, a feeling almost of terror. The only relief we feel, is in knowing that it is not true—that it is a fancy sketch of a perverted, jaundiced vision. The man who could deliberately say of Edgar Allan Poe, in a notice of his life and writings, prefacing the volumes which were to become a priceless souvenir to all who loved him—that his death might startle many, *"but that few would be grieved by it"*— and blast the whole fame of the man by such a paragraph as follows, is a judge dishonored. He is not Mr. Poe's peer, and I challenge him before the country, even as a juror in the case.

Graham then quoted the passage which Griswold had copied from *The Caxtons* [39] and proceeded:

Now, this is dastardly, and, what is worse, it is false. It is very adroitly done, with phrases very well turned, and with gleams of

[39] See p. 647.

truth shining out from a setting so dusky as to look devilish. Mr. Griswold does not feel the worth of the man he has under-valued—he had no sympathies in common with him, and has al-lowed old prejudices and old enmities to steal, insensibly perhaps, into the coloring of his picture. They were for years totally un-congenial, if not enemies, and during that period Mr. Poe, in a scathing lecture upon The Poets of America, gave Mr. Griswold some raps over the knuckles of force sufficient to be remembered. He had, too, in the exercise of his functions as critic, put to death, summarily, the literary reputation of some of Mr. Griswold's best friends; and their ghosts cried in vain for him to avenge them during Poe's life-time—and it almost seems, as if the present hack-ing at the cold remains of him who struck them down, is a sort of compensation for duty long delayed—for reprisal long desired but deferred. But without this—the opportunities afforded Mr. Gris-wold to estimate the character of Poe occurred, in the main, after his stability had been wrecked, his whole nature in a degree changed and with all his prejudices aroused and active. Nor do I consider Mr. Griswold *competent*—with all the opportunities he may have cultivated or acquired—to act as his judge—to dissect that subtle and singularly fine intellect—to probe the motives and weigh the actions of that proud heart. His whole nature—that distinctive presence of the departed which now stands impal-pable, yet in strong outline before me, as I knew him and *felt* him to be—eludes the rude grasp of a mind so warped and uncon-genial as Mr. Griswold's.

But it may be said, my dear Willis, that Mr. Poe himself deputed him to act as his literary executor, and that he must have felt some confidence in his ability at least—if not in his integrity—to perform the functions imposed with discretion and honor. I do not purpose, now, to enter into any examination of the appoint-ment of Mr. Griswold—nor of the wisdom of his appointment to the solemn trust of handing the fair fame of the deceased unim-paired to that posterity to which the dying poet bequeathed his legacy—but simply to question its faithful performance. Among the true friends of Poe in this city—and he had some such here—there are those I am sure that *he* did not class among *villains;* nor do *they* feel easy when they see their old friend dressed out, in his grave, in the habiliments of a scoundrel. There is some-thing to them in this mode of procedure on the part of the literary Executor, that does not chime in with their notions of "the true point of honor." It looks so much like a breach of trust, that, to their plain understandings, it is a proceeding that may very fairly be questioned. They may, perhaps, being plain business men, be somewhat unschooled in legacies, and obligations of this sort, but it shocks all their notions of fair dealing. They had been led to suppose, that thus to fritter away an estate was, to say the least of it, not of that high kind of integrity which courts of justice alone recognize in a settlement in ordinary affairs. As heirs, in part, to the inheritance left by their lost friend, they find the fairest part of the domain ravaged, and the strong castle battered down; and do not think because the hedges have been a little trimmed up, and the gateway set in fashion, that the property has been improved—on the contrary, they think the estate is ruined. They had all of them looked upon our departed friend as singularly indifferent to wealth for its own sake, but as very positive in his opinions that the scale of social merit was not of the highest—that MIND, somehow, was apt to be left out of the estimate altogether—and, partaking somewhat of his free way of thinking, his friends are startled to find they have entertained very unamiable convictions. As to his "quick choler" when he was contradicted, it depended a good deal upon the party denying, as well as upon the subject discussed. He was quick, it is true, to perceive mere quacks in literature, and somewhat apt to be hasty when pestered with them; but upon most other questions his natural amiability was not easily disturbed. Upon a subject that he understood thoroughly, he felt some right to be positive, if not arrogant, when addressing pretenders. His "astonishing natural advantages" had been very assiduously cultivated—his "daring spirit" was the anointed of genius—his self confidence the proud conviction of both—and it was with something of a lofty scorn that he *attacked*, as well as repelled, a crammed scholar of the hour, who attempted to palm upon him his ill-digested learning. Literature with him was religion; and he, its high-priest, with a whip of scorpions scourged the money-changers from the temple. In all else he had the docility and kind-heartedness of a child. No man was more quickly touched by a kindness—none more prompt to atone for an injury.

Graham then paid his tribute to Poe's honesty in money matters, already printed in connection with his editorship of the magazine,[40] painted a picture of Poe's devotion to Virginia and concluded:

It is true that later in life Poe had much of those morbid feelings which a life of poverty and disappointment is so apt to engender in the heart of man—the sense of having been ill-used, misunderstood, and put aside by men of far less ability, and of none, which preys upon the heart and clouds the brain of many a

[40] See pp. 342-343, Chapter XII.

child of song: A consciousness of the inequalities of life, and of the abundant power of mere wealth allied even to vulgarity, to over-ride all distinctions, and to thrust itself bedaubed with dirt and glittering with tinsel, into the high places of society, and the chief seats of the synagogue; whilst he, a worshiper of the beautiful and true, who listened to the voices of angels, and held delighted companionship with them as the cold throng swept disdainfully by him, was often in danger of being thrust out, houseless, homeless, beggared upon the world, with all his fine feelings strung to a tension of agony when he thought of his beautiful and delicate wife dying hourly before his eyes. What wonder, that he then poured out the vials of a long-treasured bitterness upon the injustice and hollowness of all society around him.

The very natural question—"Why did he not work and thrive?" is easily answered. It will not be *asked* by the many who know the precarious tenure by which literary men hold a mere living in this country. The avenues through which they can profitably reach the country are few, and crowded with aspirants for bread as well as fame. The unfortunate tendency to cheapen every literary work to the lowest point of beggarly flimsiness in price and profit, prevents even the well-disposed from extending anything like an adequate support to even a part of the great throng which genius, talent, education, and even misfortune, force into the struggle. The character of Poe's mind was of such an order, as not to be very widely in demand. The class of educated mind which he could readily and profitably address, was small—the channels through which he could do so at all, were few—and publishers all, or nearly all, contented with such pens as were already engaged, hesitated to incur the expense of his to an extent which would sufficiently remunerate him; hence, when he was fairly at sea, connected permanently with no publication, he suffered all the horrors of prospective destitution, with scarcely the ability of providing for immediate necessities; and at such moments, alas! the tempter often came, and, as you have truly said, *"one glass"* of wine, made him a madman. Let the moralist who stands upon tufted carpet, and surveys his smoking board, the fruits of his individual toil or mercantile adventure, pause before he lets the anathema, trembling upon his lips, fall upon a man like Poe! who, wandering from publisher to publisher, with his fine, print-like manuscript, scrupulously clean and neatly rolled, finds no market for his brain—with despair at heart, misery ahead for himself and his loved ones, and gaunt famine dogging at his heels, thus sinks by the wayside, before the demon that watches his steps and whispers, OBLIVION. Of all the miseries which God, or his own vices inflict upon man, none are so terrible as that of having the strong and willing arm struck down to a child-like inefficiency, while the Heart and Will, have the purpose and force of a giant's out-doing. We must remember, too, that the very organization of such a mind as that of Poe—the very tension and tone of his exquisitely strung nerves—the passionate yearnings of his soul for the beautiful and true, utterly unfitted him for the rude jostlings and fierce competitorship of trade. The only drafts of his that could be honored, were those upon his brain. The unpeopled air—the caverns of ocean—the decay and mystery that hang around old castles—the thunder of wind through the forest aisles—the spirits that rode the blast, by all but him unseen—and the deep metaphysical creations which floated through the chambers of his soul, were his only wealth, the High Change where only his signature was valid for rubies.

Could he have stepped down and chronicled small beer, made himself the shifting toady of the hour, and with bow and cringe, hung upon the steps of greatness, sounding the glory of third-rate ability with a penny trumpet, he would have been feted alive, and, *perhaps,* been praised when dead. But no! his views of the duties of the critic were stern, and he felt that in praising an unworthy writer, he committed dishonor.... Yet no man with more readiness would soften a harsh expression at the request of a friend, or if he himself felt that he had infused too great a degree of bitterness into his article, none would more readily soften it down, after it was in type—though still maintaining the justness of his critical views. I do not believe that he wrote to give pain; but in combating what he conceived to be error, he used the strongest word that presented itself, even in conversation. He labored, not so much to reform, as to *exterminate* error, and thought the shortest process was to pull it up by the roots....

But my object in throwing together a few thoughts upon the character of Edgar Allan Poe, was not to attempt an elaborate criticism, but to say what might palliate grave faults that have been attributed to him, and to meet by facts, unjust accusation—in a word, to give a mere outline of the man as he lived before me. I think I am warranted in saying to Mr. Griswold, that he must review his decision. It will not stand the calm scrutiny of his own judgment, or of time, while it must be regarded by all the friends of Mr. Poe as an ill-judged and misplaced calumny upon that gifted Son of Genius.

One of the best appreciations of Poe came from George W. Peck, in the *American Whig Review*,[41] for March, 1850. Peck was a critic of

[41] N. S., V, 301-315.

music, as well as a poet, and a man of wide culture. He considered Poe, "not as a phenomenon, *as an organic human being,*" and dismissed all his imperfections, since "it is only as a writer, born with a peculiar spirit, that the world has any concern with him."

It is most refreshing to see a critic in 1850, speaking of Poe as a man "who held his face upward while here, through much oppression and depression," who was "a pure-minded gentleman," and who "in the wildest of his extravagancies does not forget his native dignity." With a singular sympathy, Peck noticed that Poe found refuge from the weight of his emotions "in following out chains of thought in harmony with the gloom that enshrouded him. Instead of avoiding the shadow, he would boldly walk into it and analyze it." Peck recognized that the repetition in Poe's poetry was natural to him because it is the natural expression of intense feeling, and his valuable analysis of the relations of Poe's verse to music anticipate much that has been written upon that theme. Peck was evidently replying to the *Knickerbocker* attack, upon Poe's supposed lack of moral principle, and he prophesies that the world will agree with him, as it has done.

In sharp contrast with Peck's article is the long tirade against Abolitionists and things in general, which J. M. Daniel wrote for the *Southern Literary Messenger* in the same month of March, 1850.[42] Many of the errors of Griswold were perpetuated and Daniel hinted at a scandal too dark to be described, which is a cowardly way to attack a dead man. If he referred to the rumor concerning Poe's relations with the second Mrs. Allan, as he seems to do, he was simply spreading gossip without foundation. It is true that Daniel praised the work of Poe and predicted that "While the people of this day run after such authors as Prescott and Willis, speak with reverence of the Channings and Adamses and Irvings, their children, in referring back to our time in literary history, will say, 'this was the time of Poe.'" But Daniel left Poe's personal character sullied by an account written by a man who knew him, and who lived in Poe's own country. His quarrel with Poe in 1848, while obscure in its cause, discounts his testimony.[43]

Willis, meanwhile, was doing his best in the *Home Journal* to protect his dead friend. In the issue of March 16, 1850, he reprinted the

[42] XVI, 172-187.

[43] The Editor of the *Messenger* apologized in a note, p. 192 of the March issue, for the tone of the article—claiming it had been printed in his absence. His apology, however, was for the attacks on Willis and Griswold, as editors, rather than for the slanders upon Poe.

portions of Graham's article which dealt with Poe's love for Virginia, and his industry and the difficulties of his situation. On March 30 he printed a reply to Daniel's article in the *Southern Literary Messenger,* signed "Richmond" and written by some one who had known Poe both as a boy and a man. This correspondent denounced Daniel's picture of Poe as "a frightful caricature," in which Poe's moral character was blackened, and continued:

> The indictment (for it deserves no other name) is not true. It is full of cruel misrepresentations. It deepens the shadows into unnatural darkness, and shuts out the rays of sunshine that ought to relieve them. I do not deny that there were shadows. The wayward disposition and the checkered life, which are too often the heritage of genius, did indeed fall to the lot of this gifted man. But it is not true that he lived and died the wretch that he is painted; nor is it true that the unhappy results were those of character alone. Those who remember the admiration and flattery which sounded in his boyish ears—the mistaken fondness which indulged him in every caprice, and nourished his pride and wilfulness into a pernicious growth—cannot but know that education and circumstances had much to do with his career. And with the evidence before us of the devotion to him displayed by his wife's mother, and the fact that, even to the last, the hearts of his nearest kindred and friends still beat warmly for him, it is impossible to believe him so bad as he is here represented.[44]

John Neal, in his usual enthusiastic, if rambling manner, filled three columns of the *Portland Advertiser* of April 26, 1850, with a defence of Poe against Griswold's attack. Neal said that he had not known Poe personally, but added "I believe, too, that he was by nature, of a just and generous temper, thwarted, baffled, and self-harnessed by his own wilfulness to the most unbecoming drudgery.... The biographical notices are just and wise, and excellent, so far as they go, with one single exception, that of the Rev. R. W. Griswold; a book-wright and compiler by the cart-load, to whom the dying poet bequeathed his papers, and his character, to be hashed over, and served up, little by little, with a *sauce piquante,* resembling the turbid water, in which very poor eggs have been boiled to death."

Neal very shrewdly suggested that the most eloquent portions of Griswold's "Memoir" were probably paraphrased from Poe—but he did not select the right ones. By reprinting his earlier notices of Poe's

[44] "Estimates of Edgar A. Poe," *Home Journal* (Saturday, March 30, 1850), Editorial Page, Col. 7.

"Al Aaraaf," with Poe's letters to him at that time and later, he proved that Poe could take criticism, however unfavorable, in the right spirit, and could remember favors done him. He concluded: "But enough, the Poet is no more! yet his character is safe, notwithstanding the eulogy of his Executor."

Stung especially by the replies of Graham and Neal to his Ludwig article, Griswold prepared his defence, which, according to the rules of strategy, he made a further attack. First he collected, as was his proper duty, whatever manuscripts were available. Mrs. Clemm protested sharply to Griswold against any share of Poe's effects going to Rosalie:

Lowell April 29th. 1850

Dear Sir

On the receipt of your last letter, (in which you mentioned if I had my poor Eddies Lectures you could dispose of them for me,) I wrote again to Dr. Moran to make another application to Mr. Neilson relative to my dear sons trunk, in which I supposed the lectures were. I have received an answer, in which he states, that the trunk has been sent to you at your request, and for Miss Poe. I cannot understand this and wish you to let me know if there is any truth in it. Will you so much oblige me by so doing at your earliest convenience? Will you be so good as to enclose me a copy of the manuscript I left with Mrs. Lewis. I mean the "Literary [sic] of New York." A couple of sheets will be sufficient for my purpose. You know they have been all published in Godey you can if you need them refer to that magazine!

Yours respectfully,

MARIA CLEMM.[45]

Griswold published in the third volume "The Poetic Principle," "The Literati," the "Marginalia," and other critical articles by Poe.

In a "Preface," dated September 2, 1850, to his "Memoir" of Poe, he began by declaring that he had not written or published a syllable on Poe's life, since he knew that he was to be his literary executor. He also insisted that the task was not to his liking. He then denounced Graham for his "sophomorical and trashy but widely circulated letter," and accused him of hypocrisy "in his tenderness for the poor author (of whom in four years of his extremest poverty he had not purchased for his magazine a single line)." This was, of course, a rank falsehood, for Graham published something by Poe in every year

[45] Original Autograph Ms., Griswold Collection, Boston Public Library. Mrs. Clemm referred, of course, to the "Literati."

from 1840 to 1849, except 1847. Griswold then reviewed his acquaintance with Poe, largely by means of letters from Poe to himself. There are eleven of these, only six of which have been preserved. I have already called attention to forgeries by Griswold in the letters of February 24, 1845, and April 19, 1845. These forgeries have been known for many years, as well as Griswold's more subtle forgery of his own letter of January 14, 1845, which made Poe's reply of January 16 have quite a different meaning.[46] But it has not been realized that these forgeries throw doubt on the authenticity of Poe's supposed letter of January 10, 1845, which is non-extant.

The striking thing about these proved forgeries is that the portions interpolated by Griswold either praise his work highly, or express Poe's regret and even apology, for his unfavorable criticism of Griswold. Is it not logical to refuse to believe the statements or accept the tone of the letters, which Griswold quotes but which apparently do not exist? In the first, given as "undated," Griswold's *Poets and Poetry of America* is spoken of by Poe as "a better book than any other man in the United States could have made of the materials." The letter of "June 11, 1843," begs for a loan of five dollars and refers to an anonymous letter, of which Griswold suspects Poe to be the author. Poe's letter of October 26, 1845, asking for a loan of fifty dollars to keep the *Broadway Journal* alive, is extant and is practically correct in the "Preface." But the letter of November 1, thanking Griswold for twenty-five dollars, *is not extant,* and it promises Griswold to prepare "an article about you for the B. J., in which I do you justice— which is all *you* can ask of anyone."

The last non-extant letter is a long one, which Griswold says "is undated but appears to have been written early in 1849." It is primarily concerned with a request to give Mrs. Lewis more favorable notice, in Griswold's *Female Poets of America.* Now there is a letter [47] from Poe to Griswold dated June 28, 1849, which makes a similar request for Mrs. L——, but is quite different in tone. Griswold did not print this letter of June 28 in his "Preface," though he must have possessed it, for it is among the Griswold Mss. Is it not then reasonable to assume that this long letter, which gives Poe's list of his writings concerning Griswold, including a "Review in Pioneer," which Poe did not write, is again a forgery? In it Poe is made to say "I have never

[46] See pp. 443-450, for the letters printed in parallel columns comparing Griswold's forgeries with the originals.

[47] Autograph Ms., Boston Public Library. See p. 612 for the letter.

hazarded my own reputation by a disrespectful word of you," and the cringing tone of the epistle is not like Poe at all.

The last letter Griswold prints in the "Preface" contains, I believe, another forgery. It differs from the original autograph manuscript, now in the Wrenn Library at the University of Texas, by two clauses [48] of no great importance, and by the omission of the clause at the end of the letter—"but I fear I am asking too much." These are of interest only in proving that Griswold was tampering with the letter. But in his printed version there is an important postscript which is not in the manuscript.

"P. S.—Considering my indebtedness to you, can you not sell to Graham or to Godey (with whom, you know, I cannot with the least self respect again have anything to do directly)—can you not sell to one of these men, 'Annabel Lee,' say for $50, and credit me that sum? Either of them could print it before you will need it for your book. *Mem.* The Eveleth you ask about is a Yankee impertinent, who, knowing my extreme poverty, has for years pestered me with unpaid letters; but I believe almost every literary man of any note has suffered in the same way. I am surprised that you have escaped." [49]

Griswold evidently thought, by making Poe speak in an unfriendly manner of Graham and Godey, that he would discourage any further effort on Graham's part to defend Poe, and prevent Godey from coming to Poe's defence.[50] Poe could have had no motive in attacking Graham or Godey in the spring or summer of 1849, when the letter

[48] The insertion of "in your new edition" at the end of the first sentence, and "as here written" at the end of the second sentence instead of "thus."

[49] Killis Campbell spoke of this letter as "unhappily incomplete" (*Mind of Poe*, p. 88). The photostat, sent me through the courtesy of Dr. R. A. Law, Dr. R. H. Griffith, and Miss Fannie Ratchford, of the University of Texas, who carefully examined the framed letter, shows no indication of a postscript. Dr. Griffith thinks the letter was cut for framing both at the top and bottom, but it is inconceivable that a postscript of this importance should have been destroyed for such a purpose. The letter was folded three times, the first fold being 13/16 in. from the top; the second 3 1/16 from the top and the third, 5 4/16 in. from the top—the letter being 7 4/16 in. overall. These figures indicate that any cutting would have been at the top, where indeed, the date is omitted. The name of the person addressed might have been cut out at the bottom. Of course, there may have been a postscript concerning "Annabel Lee" in which Griswold inserted the sentences concerning Graham, Godey and Eveleth. Griswold did have a copy of "Annabel Lee" at Poe's death.

[50] See Griswold's forgery of a similar reflection upon Duyckinck, in Poe's letter to P. P. Cooke, p. 514.

was probably written. Graham published his "Fifty Suggestions" in May and June. Godey helped him in the black days of June 1849. Nor could he have had any reason for slurring Eveleth. Poe asked the latter not to pay the postage.[51] But the postmarks on Eveleth's letters almost invariably show that he prepaid them.[52] There is something especially dastardly in attempting by a forgery to deprive a dead man of his friends.

Griswold evidently believed that he had, through this "Preface," established himself in the eyes of a reader as the friend, and even as the patron, of Poe. He then proceeded with his main "Memoir," in which the deliberate altering of facts, and inventions or repetitions of slander, are many. These it is possible to disprove. But harder to combat without tediousness is the constant interpretation of rumor to Poe's discredit. For example, a petty story of John Allan's unreasoning support of Poe in the school room concludes, "Who can estimate the effect of this puerile triumph upon the growth of that morbid self-esteem which characterized the author in after life?"

Every dissipation of Poe's is overstressed. At Virginia "he was known as the wildest and most reckless student of his class," . . . until "his gambling, intemperance and other vices, induced his expulsion from the university," which we have seen to be a slander. The dark secret, concerning Poe's relation to the second Mrs. Allan, is repeated. The army service is placed after West Point, and Griswold states that Poe deserted, another falsehood.

When Griswold proceeds with the period of the *Southern Literary Messenger*, he cannot resist his favorite pastime of forgery. The letter from T. W. White to Poe, on September 29, 1835,[53] is much changed from its original form, with the effect of emphasizing Poe's derelictions. The break with White is laid entirely to Poe's irregularities, instead of to the combination of circumstances I have already discussed. Prompted either by a desire to appear fair to Poe, or by his own recognition of Poe's genius, Griswold interlarded his attacks on Poe's character with praise of his writings. His stories in 1838 belong to "a department of imaginative composition in which he was henceforth alone and unapproachable."

[51] Poe to Eveleth, December 15, 1846. Original Autograph Ms., Berg Collection, New York Public Library. Poe paid the postage on this letter, but did not pay it on his letter of February 16, 1847.

[52] See the *Letters of Eveleth to Poe*, edited by T. O. Mabbott.

[53] See pp. 228-229. Compare with Griswold's form, "Memoir," p. xiv, 1850 Ed.

Griswold's power to invent slanders seemed to grow as he progressed, for the account of Poe's connection with Burton represents him as "so unsteady of purpose and so unreliable that the actor was never sure when he left the city that his business would be cared for." Griswold's prize forgery, of Burton's letter to Poe, has been dealt with in detail.[54] Notwithstanding Graham's definite statements concerning Poe's real reason for severing his connection with *Graham's Magazine,* Griswold insisted that the sole cause was Poe's "infirmities."

Griswold did not hesitate to make use of the powers of expression of the man he was defiling. His analysis of Poe's tales of ratiocination at first glance seems acute until we recognize that he is repeating verbatim Poe's own description of his tales in his letter to P. P. Cooke, of August 9, 1846.

Griswold's bitter hostility is revealed in his treatment of Poe's manly acknowledgment of his lapses from sobriety, given in his reply to English.[55] Griswold prints it as "interesting" and then denies that Dr. Francis ever gave any such testimony, implying that Poe was lying. After charging Poe with blackmailing "a distinguished literary woman of South Carolina," from whom Poe had borrowed fifty dollars, Griswold quotes the notice in the *New York Express* concerning Poe's necessities, Willis's appeal for him, and Poe's reply. Anyone who knew the heartbreaking hardships which Poe was undergoing in 1846 to 1847, might have refrained from casting slurs upon his sincerity. But Griswold commented that Poe's article was written for effect, and that he had not been seriously ill. Griswold did at least acknowledge that Virginia was dead.

Griswold praised *Eureka* with discrimination, and then plunged into the episode with Mrs. Whitman. Seldom has anyone packed into brief form as many false statements as the following:

> They were not married, and the breaking of the engagement affords a striking illustration of his character. He said to an acquaintance in New York, who congratulated with him upon the prospect of his union with a person of so much genius and so many virtues—"It is a mistake: I am not going to be married." "Why, Mr. Poe, I understand that the banns have been published." "I cannot help what you have heard, my dear Madam: but mark me, I shall not marry her." He left town the same evening, and the next day was reeling through the streets of the city

---
[54] P. 280.
[55] See p. 49.

which was the lady's home, and in the evening—that should have been the evening before the bridal—in his drunkenness he committed at her house such outrages as made necessary a summons of the police. Here was no insanity leading to indulgence: he went from New York with a determination thus to induce an ending of the engagement; and he succeeded.

Poe's last days Griswold treated briefly. His death Griswold attributed to a drunken debauch in Baltimore and he gave as authentic, details which are imaginary, but which readers naturally took as correct, when given by an authorized biographer.

When Griswold turned to the summing up of Poe's character, it is easy to visualize the evangelical moralist who quotes, only to reject it, the advice to speak nothing but good of the dead. This would be impossible, he said, owing to the "notoriety of Mr. Poe's faults," and a career so "full of instruction and warning" cannot be neglected. Poe, he continued, "exhibits scarcely any virtue in either his life or his writings." Among other lacks is that of conscience—this with regard to the author of "William Wilson"!

Next it occurred to Griswold that to quote Poe as saying something unpleasant about Evert Duyckinck would remove any danger to Griswold from him. He returned, therefore, to the letter from Poe to P. P. Cooke which he had already used for the purpose of plagiarism. In printing it,[56] Griswold deftly inserted a phrase of which Poe was innocent. "The last selection of my tales was made from about seventy by [one of our great little cliquists and claquers] Wiley and Putnam's reader, Duyckinck." This insertion probably had its result, for Duyckinck retaliated, as we will see, on the man whom he had befriended. Griswold, unfortunately for himself, made the following accusation of bad faith concerning Poe's relation with Longfellow:

> I remember having been shown by Mr. Longfellow, several years ago, a series of papers which constitute a demonstration that Mr. Poe was indebted to him for the idea of "The Haunted Palace," one of the most admirable of his poems, which he so pertinaciously asserted had been used by Mr. Longfellow in the production of his "Beleaguered City." Mr. Longfellow's poem was written two or three years before the first publication of that by Poe, and it was during a portion of this time in Poe's possession; but it was not printed, I believe, until a few weeks after the appearance of "The Haunted Palace." "It would be absurd," as Poe himself said many times, "to believe the similarity of these

[56] See p. 514.

pieces entirely accidental." This was the first cause of all that malignant criticism which for so many years he carried on against Mr. Longfellow.

Longfellow hated discussions, but this was too much for him, and he promptly called Griswold to account:

Cambridge, Sept. 28, 1850.

Sir,—I think you must be mistaken in saying that I "showed you a series of papers" in reference to "The Haunted Palace," and "The Beleaguered City"; for I do not remember that I ever had any such papers in my possession, nor that Mr. Poe ever accused me of taking my poem from his.

I do remember showing you two letters from him to me, (dated May & June 1841) proving the different tone he assumed towards me in private and in public. Nothing is said in these letters about the point now at issue; and these are the only ones I ever received from him.

With regard to "The Beleaguered City," it was written on the nineteenth of September, 1839. I marked the date down at the time. It was first published in the "Southern Literary Messenger," November, 1839. I sent it to Mr. White, the Editor of that work, who had solicited a contribution from me. I do not believe Mr. Poe ever saw it till it was published; for he was not then, I think, connected with the Messenger, and could not have had this manuscript in his hands, for Mr. White did not, probably, receive it before the first of October; and it is the first article in the November No. of the Messenger.[57]

Griswold proceeded to attack Poe's honesty as a critic. We need not discuss his charges concerning Poe's changes in his estimates of contemporary writers. Poe may reasonably have altered his opinion in consequence of their later work. Griswold was on more tenable ground in his charge that Poe used private letters of Irving and Longfellow in his own account of his work, published in the *Saturday Museum* in 1843. Poe did change the comments from the first to the third persons, thus implying that Irving and Longfellow had published them. But here once more Griswold invented the worst elements in the situation. According to him, Irving had expressly prohibited Poe from using his letters publicly. There is nothing in Irving's second letter concerning "William Wilson" which either prohibits or permits its use, and he possibly did not care about the matter. The first letter, concerning the "House of Usher," has apparently disap-

[57] Original Autograph Ms., Boston Public Library.

peared. Poe, in his letter to Snodgrass, November 11, 1839, states definitely that "Irving desires me to make the passages public." The permission may have come in the first letter. In choosing between the accuracy of Poe and Griswold, there is little difficulty in making a selection.

Griswold's description of the relations between Poe, Graham and Godey, are so obviously incorrect that it is not worth the time to dispute them. He quotes Daniel's article in the *Southern Literary Messenger* as a "Defence of Mr. Poe," which it is not, either in title or substance, thereby giving the reader the impression that such sentences as "he believed in nobody, and cared for nobody," had been written by a friend.

In dealing with Poe's social qualities, Griswold played a clever trick. He published Mrs. Osgood's charming picture of Poe, from which I have already quoted, but he prefaced it by making Mrs. Osgood accept Griswold's own view of Poe's relations with men. Notice how adroitly he proceeds:

> Speaking of him one day soon after his death, with the late Mrs. Osgood, the beauty of whose character had made upon Poe's mind that impression which it never failed to produce upon minds capable of the apprehension of the finest traits in human nature, she said she did not doubt that my view of Mr. Poe, which she knew indeed to be the common view, was perfectly just, as it regarded him in his relations with men; but to women he was different, and she would write for me some recollections of him to be placed beside my harsher judgments in any notice of his life that the acceptance of the appointment to be his literary executor might render it necessary for me to give to the world. She was an invalid—dying of that consumption by which in a few weeks she was removed to heaven, and calling for pillows to support her while she wrote, she drew this sketch:

> "You ask me, my friend, to write for you my reminiscences of Edgar Poe. For you, who knew and understood my affectionate interest in him, and my frank acknowledgment of that interest to all who had a claim upon my confidence, for you, I will willingly do so. I think no one could know him—no one *has* known him personally—certainly no woman—without feeling the same interest. I can sincerely say, that although I have frequently *heard* of aberrations on his part from 'the straight and narrow path,' I have never *seen* him otherwise than gentle, generous, well-bred, and fastidiously refined. To a sensitive and delicately-nurtured woman, there was a peculiar and irresistible charm in the chiv-

alric, graceful, and almost tender reverence with which he invariably approached all women who won his respect. It was this which first commanded and always retained my regard for him.

"I have been told that when his sorrows and pecuniary embarrassments had driven him to the use of stimulants, which a less delicate organization might have borne without injury, he was in the habit of speaking disrespectfully of the ladies of his acquaintance. It is difficult for me to believe this; for to me, to whom he came during the year of our acquaintance for counsel and kindness in all his many anxieties and griefs, he never spoke irreverently of any woman save one, and then only in *my* defence, and though I rebuked him for his momentary forgetfulness of the respect due to himself and to me, I could not but forgive the offence for the sake of the generous impulse which prompted it. Yet even were these sad rumors true of him, the wise and well-informed knew how to regard, as they would the impetuous anger of a spoiled infant, balked of its capricious will, the equally harmless and unmeaning phrenzy of that stray child of Poetry and Passion. For the few unwomanly and slander-loving gossips who have injured *him* and *themselves* only by *repeating* his ravings, when in such moods they have accepted his society, I have only to vouchsafe my wonder and my pity. They cannot surely harm the true and pure, who, reverencing his genius and pitying his misfortune and his errors, endeavored, by their timely kindness and sympathy, to soothe his sad career." [58]

By printing this tribute from Mrs. Osgood, Griswold convinced many readers that he was a generous biographer, who had spared Poe many unfavorable facts. Fearing, however, to leave such a good taste in the mouths of those who had swallowed his tissue of falsehoods, he returned to his "Ludwig" article, and reprinted verbatim, its conclusion, the passages from *The Caxtons* included, which I have recently quoted.[59] The final view of Poe which the "Memoir" presented was that of a cynic "without faith in man or woman," and destitute of honor.

Griswold's treachery in blasting the reputation of the man whose work he was editing, was promptly criticized by an anonymous writer, in the Philadelphia *Saturday Evening Post* for September 21, 1850. If it was Henry Peterson, the editor, he certainly had no exalted opinion of Poe's nature, but his sense of fairness revolted at Griswold's action:

[58] "Memoir," *The Literati*, p. xxxvi.
[59] Pp. 646-647.

Now, this biography may be considered in two lights—first, as the production of a "literary executor," to be attached to the works of a deceased friend; secondly, as a simple biography. Considering it in the first light, we must say that a more cold-blooded and ungenerous composition has seldom come under our notice. Nothing so condemnatory of Mr. Poe, so absolutely blasting to his character, has ever appeared in print, as this work of his "literary *executor*." It is absolutely horrible (considering the circumstances under which Mr. Griswold writes) with what cool deliberateness he charges upon Mr. Poe the basest and most dishonorable actions. Writing as the "literary executor" of the deceased poet, we should have thought it would have suggested itself to any generous mind, that his part was that of a friendly counsel, rather than of a prosecuting attorney, or even of the judge sworn to do exact justice, to the extent of pronouncing the sentence of death. We have no desire to be uncharitable to Mr. Griswold, but really we are not able to find any excuse for him. He either knew that he was doing a most flagrantly ungenerous act, or else he did not know it—we think one horn of the dilemma quite as sharp as the other.

Unfortunately, in order to show how Griswold had "executed" Poe, the editor quoted some of the worst slanders, and while he characterized them as they deserved, he brought forward no evidence against them and probably hurt Poe as well as Griswold.

The malice of the "Memoir" soon began to bear fruit. Duyckinck in the *Literary World* for September 21, 1850, nettled probably by the forged sentence describing him as a "cliquist," spoke of Poe as "a literary attorney, who pleaded according to his fee." Yet Duyckinck asked pertinently why Griswold selected Poe's early unfortunate review of Cornelius Mathews, which Poe had repudiated, instead of later and more friendly ones, and why the third volume was carefully purged of any unhandsome references to Dr. Griswold.[60]

L. G. Clark, in the *Knickerbocker*, seized upon the worst slanders in the "Memoir," twisted them out of focus by omitting everything of a favorable nature, and by constantly referring to the "Memoir" as the work of Poe's own appointed biographer, showed how potent it was to be in the defamation of his character.[61]

Even those who desired to treat Poe fairly were handicapped. John

[60] *Literary World*, VII (September 21, 1850), 228.
[61] *Knickerbocker Magazine*, XXXVI (October, 1850), 370-372.

Savage, in the *Democratic Review*,[62] found it impossible to disregard Griswold's account and took refuge in a consideration of Poe's writings, which, after all, he said, were of more significance.

The first important defence of Poe, after the "Memoir" was published, came from his friend, C. Chauncey Burr, who had helped him in the black days in Philadelphia in 1849. In his own quarterly, the *Nineteenth Century*, Burr painted a striking analysis of one phase of Poe's character:

> I know that an attempt has been made by the enemies of Poe, to show that he was "without heart;" and even a contemporary whom we must acquit of any malice in the charge, has sung:
>
> > "But the heart somehow seems all squeezed out
> > by the mind." [63]
>
> Poe was undoubtedly the greatest *artist* among modern authors; and it is his consummate skill as an artist, that has led to these mistakes about the properties of his own heart. That perfection of horror which abounds in his writings, has been unjustly attributed to some moral defect in the man. But I perceive not why the competent critic should fall into this error. Of all authors, ancient or modern, Poe has given us the least of himself in his works. *He wrote as an artist.* He intuitively saw what Schiller has so well expressed, that it is an universal phenomenon of our nature that the mournful, the fearful, even the horrible, allures with irresistible enchantment. He probed this general psychological law, in its subtle windings through the mystic chambers of our being, as it was never probed before, until he stood in the very abyss of its center, the sole master of its effects.[64]

In presenting the letters from Poe to Mrs. Clemm, already printed, Burr apologized for laying bare "the agonies of a heart overflowing with kindness, gratitude and faith, yet cruelly dispossessed of every means of the blessing it would bestow."

The three volumes soon began to be noticed in England. In the *Westminster Review* for January, 1852, Poe heads the list of contemporary American authors. The review is brief and emphasizes his artistic powers, but dwells upon his moral deficiencies. The reviewer, who had been deceived into thinking "Mesmeric Revelation" and "The

---

[62] *United States Magazine and Democratic Review*, XXVII (December, 1850), 542-544; XXVIII (January and February, 1851) 66-69; 162-172.

[63] Lowell, *Fable for Critics.*

[64] *The Nineteenth Century*, V (February, 1852), 23-24.

Facts in the Case of M. Valdemar" were the accounts of real occurrences, praised the power of Poe to throw "an air of reality over his most imaginative productions." He quoted the scandal concerning Poe's deliberate breaking of the engagement with Mrs. Whitman, but also gave space to Mrs. Osgood's tribute. It is a fair treatment, so far as the critic was informed, but the result was, as usual, to depict Poe as Griswold had drawn him.[65]

The damage Griswold did is even better illustrated by the review in *Tait's Magazine*.[66] Vizetelly had published in London a selection of Poe's stories,[67] price one shilling. The "Memoir" was reprinted as an introduction, and was again accepted as correct. Although the reviewer tried in general to be fair, he dwelt on Poe's drinking, "for months he was regardless of anything but a morbid and insatiable appetite for the means of intoxication." The reviewer was evidently puzzled by the contradiction between Griswold's account and that of Willis, and acknowledged that "there must have been something noble in such a man." But he repeated the scandals about the scene at Mrs. Whitman's house and concluded:

> But without going further, we may as well return at once to the observations we made at starting; for the closest investigation of this man's character and abilities will only lead us to wonder and regret that so much intellectual power may coexist with so much moral weakness. In his character there existed at once strongest commonsense and wretchedest folly; it was steeped at once in depravity and poetry. For though to allow any literary excellence to our American brethren is considered a tolerably good proof of a low standard of taste, we yet venture to say that a half-dozen such poems as "The Raven" would have placed Edgar Poe in the foremost ranks of modern poetry. We hope to be forgiven if we have spoken too harshly of a dead man.

The articles in the *Westminster Review* and in *Tait's* Magazine called forth a restrained but effective protest from W. J. Pabodie, in the *New York Tribune* for June 2, 1852. He declared that there existed "not the shadow of foundation" for the scandals concerning Poe's

[65] *Westminster Review*, LVII (January, 1852), 162-164. American Edition, XXXIV, No. 1.
[66] "Edgar Poe," April, 1852. Reprinted in *Littell's Living Age*, XXXIII (May, 1852), 422-424.
[67] Readable Books, Vol. I, *Tales of Mystery, Imagination and Humor*, By Edgar A. Poe (London, Vizetelly, 1852).

rupture of his engagement with Mrs. Whitman. Pabodie then, in speaking of Poe's intemperance, continued:

> With the single exception of this fault, which he has so fearfully expiated, his conduct, during the period of my acquaintance with him, was invariably that of a man of honor and a gentleman; and I know that, in the hearts of all who knew him best among us, he is remembered with feelings of melancholy interest and generous sympathy.
>
> We understand that Dr. Griswold has expressed his sincere regret that these unfounded reports should have been sanctioned by his authority; and we doubt not, if he possesses that fairness of character and uprightness of intention which we have ascribed to him, that he will do what lies in his power to remove an undeserved stigma from the memory of the departed.

Pabodie's dextrous attempt to force Griswold into a retraction drew from that gentleman a violent epistle in which he demanded that Pabodie "explain his letter, in another, also in the *Tribune*," threatening unless he did so, to publish "such documents as will be infinitely painful to Mrs. Whitman and all those concerned." "For Mrs. Whitman," he continued, "I have great respect and sympathy. On this subject, however, if not on some others, she is insane."

The kind of mind Griswold possessed is shown by his next paragraph, which I print only because it proves his bitter feeling toward Poe:

> As to Poe's general conduct toward women, it is illustrated in the fact that he wrote to his Mother in Law (with whom it is commonly understood and believed, in neighborhoods where they lived, that he had criminal relations), that if he married the woman to whom he was engaged, in Richmond, for her money, he must still manage to live so near a creature whom he *loved* in Lowell, as to have intercourse with her as his mistress. Possessed of such letters, you may imagine how carefully and delicately I treated this whole subject, in my memoir. I suppressed everything that could be suppressed without the sacrifice of all truth in general effect.[68]

There were, of course, no such letters. Griswold may have been twisting a sentence in Poe's letter to Mrs. Clemm of September [4],

[68] This letter was published first by Gill, *Life*, p. 222, who omitted the paragraphs referring to Mrs. Whitman's "insanity" and to Poe's relations with Mrs. Clemm and Annie. The complete original Ms. is in the Lilly Collection.

1849, "I must be somewhere where I can see Annie." It is hardly necessary to say that the scandal concerning Mrs. Clemm and Poe arose from the fumes of Griswold's imagination. But if he put such foul trash on paper, what must he have been *saying* to his acquaintances in New York!

Mr. Pabodie was not the person to be bluffed by Griswold. In a long letter, which I have already used in describing Poe's last visit to Mrs. Whitman, he politely but firmly refused to modify anything he had published. "These are the facts," he wrote Griswold, "which I am ready to make oath to, if necessary." Apparently Griswold did not dare to carry out his threat to publish the "infinitely painful" documents in the *Tribune,* and left Pabodie in possession of the field.

In 1853, Richard Henry Stoddard published the first of the many articles he wrote on Poe.[69] He accepted Griswold's "Memoir" and while he praised Poe's poetry highly, he contributed no significant criticism. He concluded with an original poem on Poe. Curiously enough, Stoddard gave none of the stories he afterward told concerning his meetings with Poe. Why Stoddard wrote so often can only be explained by his desire to make some money, for he did not like Poe, nor did he appreciate his work.

Until 1854 the British critics had usually drawn on the "Memoir." But in that year, George Gilfillan, in the London *Critic,* added some savage denunciations of his own. According to him, "Poe was no more a gentleman than he was a saint, and of all the poetic fraternity, Poe was the most worthless and wicked." He was "a cool calculating deliberate blackguard" who broke his wife's heart. He was among other things, "a Yankee Yahoo," licentious and a habitual drunkard, without a conscience. In the midst of this tirade, the critic acknowledged that Poe's writing was "pure," "He has never save by his example (so far as we know his works) sought to shake faith, or sap morality." Gilfillan paid a high tribute to Poe's power of analysis, to his invention and to his imagination, but his picture of Poe's character is appalling. This article was reprinted in the *Southern Literary Messenger,*[70] and in *Littell's Living Age.*[71]

Graham, meanwhile, had not rested content with his first defence of Poe. In February, 1854, he published in his own magazine his "Genius

[69] *National Magazine,* II (March, 1853), 193-200. The article is unsigned.
[70] XX (April, 1854), pp. 249-253.
[71] XLI (April 22, 1854), 166-171.

and Characteristics of the Late Edgar Allan Poe." [72] After his lengthy disquisition on the nature of genius, with which the essay begins, Graham says:

> To these remarks we have been irresistibly led by a consideration of the various reviews of the life and writings of Edgar A. Poe, all of them, in our opinion, incomplete, and in some sort inapt, and many unjust, unkind, ungenerous and cruel. No sooner in fact had this brilliant but eccentric spirit passed away and been swallowed up in darkness, than the hand of almost every one was raised against him, every foible of his unhappy and ill-regulated life was hunted out and paraded before the censorious eyes of a world ever prone to lend a credulous ear to ill reports of those who stand eminent above the rest, it matters not for what, and eager, as it would seem, to take vengeance on them for their superiority in one respect by dwelling triumphantly on their inferiority in others.

Graham then proceeds logically:

> For mentioning his vices at all, except in the slightest and most casual manner, much less for dwelling on them pertinaciously and almost malignantly, there can be no earthly apology or justification; for they were in no wise reflected in or connected with his writings; neither were they in any respect seductive, amusing or fascinating vices, likely to court imitation, or lead astray a single individual from the path of sobriety or honor.

Graham very properly observes that in the cases of other poets who drank too much, like Sheridan and Burns, their fault has been condoned. But Poe's lapses have been held up to scorn. Graham put his finger on the reason. Poe was a critic and those he attacked while living, took their revenge when he was dead. Graham's analysis of Poe's nature is much too detailed for adequate quotation here, yet it is among the most sympathetic and penetrating that has been written.

He recognized Poe's constant struggles against temptation, and how his sensitive temperament reacted violently to injustice that a more phlegmatic nature would have disregarded. Of special significance was Graham's explanation of Poe's poverty:

> The sufferings caused by poverty to the sensitive, proud, educated gentleman are agonies indescribable, temptations irresistible; and Poe's poverty was at times excessive, extending to the want of the mere necessaries of life. Nor was this, we con-

---

[72] *Graham's Magazine,* XLIV (February, 1854), 216-225.

scientiously believe, in any considerable degree Poe's fault, for his genius, though of a very fine and high order, was not such as to command a ready or lucrative market. Pride, self-reproach, want, weariness, drove him to seek excitement, perhaps forgetfulness, in wine; and the least drop of wine, to most men a moderate stimulus, was to him literally the cup of frenzy.

Graham's estimate of Poe's criticism is valuable because of his association with Poe at a time when he was doing some of his best work. He rightly disliked Poe's obsession with plagiarism, or his treatment of Longfellow, and the following judgment is especially pertinent:

> We consider it a strong argument against the attribution of his sarcastic and cynical criticisms to personal jealousy or pique, and a preconceived determination to pull down reputations, that, with the exception of Mr. Longfellow, all those whom he has most cause to regard with envy, as possessing equal or higher reputations, are those whom he criticises most favorably and most fairly; while many of those on whom he uncorks the phials of his indignation, with a fury wholly disproportioned to the value of the offenders or the weight of the offenses, are often persons of so small consideration as to make one marvel at the amount of good vituperation wasted.

Graham's appraisement of Poe's writings is sound. He rightly judged that "it is on his tales, and on his poems yet more decidedly, that the reputation of Mr. Poe must stand." His classification of the stories into those of grotesque fancy, of ratiocination and of imagination, is still the best; and while his treatment of the poetry is not profound, it is sympathetic.

Quite different from the British portraits of Poe were those which Charles Baudelaire gave to France. Baudelaire had been, in 1848, one of the first to translate Poe,[73] but even before that he had haunted cafés where English was spoken, had sought the acquaintance of Americans, or anyone else who could give him information concerning Poe. He also purchased collected editions of Poe and periodicals containing his work.

In March and April of 1852, he published in the *Revue de Paris*, articles concerning Poe's life and work, which were republished, much changed, as the introductions to Baudelaire's translations of Poe's stories, the *Histoires Extraordinaires* of 1856 and the *Nouvelles Histoires Extraordinaires*, of 1857. The first of these he dedicated to Mrs.

[73] See p. 519.

Clemm, with a translation of the sonnet "To My Mother." [74] Even Baudelaire depended to a certain extent upon Griswold's "Memoir" for his account of Poe's life, and accepted the expulsion from the University of Virginia and other errors which he had no means of checking. But his deep sympathy with Poe's nature, based on his close study of his writing, and the innate affinity between them, led Baudelaire to reject the worst of the slanders.

For Griswold's treatment of Poe's character, Baudelaire had some vigorous phrases—"Does there not exist in America an ordinance which forbids to curs an entrance to the cemeteries?" Griswold, the most detestable of these animals, has committed "une immortelle infamie"; he is a "pedagogue vampire" who has defamed his friend. [75]

Baudelaire disposes of the irregularities of Poe by blaming them upon his American environment. His drinking was an escape from the "bourgeoisie" who surrounded him. An aristocrat by inheritance and breeding, Poe scorned the mob, who retaliated and drove him to solitude, poverty, and ruin. It is not necessary to retail all of Baudelaire's denunciations of the United States. He knew little about the country, and while he was quite correct in his belief that Poe was no democrat, he took many of Poe's satirical remarks, like those in "Some Words with a Mummy" as deadly serious, when, of course, Poe meant them as humorous—with a sting.

Baudelaire's picture of Poe living in a vast cage of mediocrity, a "Hop Frog" who amused his sovereign, the mob, while taking vengeance upon it, was not very helpful in establishing Poe's position as an artist in France. But Baudelaire's translations of Poe's works, made with a skill which places them among the great translations of the world's literature, accomplished that end in a large measure. The story of that influence does not belong, however, to this biography. [76]

In 1856, the most powerful and influential of the New England journals, *The North American Review*, made the publication of the fourth volume of Poe's works the occasion for an extended review of his life and writings. On the personal side, Griswold was followed,

[74] This dedication, together with the translations, appeared first in the columns of *Le Pays*, from July 25, 1854, to April, 1855. See Cambiare, pp. 33-37.

[75] *Histoires Extraordinaires, Traduit d'Edgar Poe* (Paris, 1891 ed.), p. 6.

[76] See pp. 514-520, for references to Poe's influence in France. The best analysis of Baudelaire's interpretation of Poe's character is found in Léon Lemonnier, *Edgar Poe et la Critique Française de 1845 à 1875* (Paris, 1928).

all the slanders being repeated. Griswold's forgery of Burton's letter
of May 30, 1839, led to charges against Poe of "sensationalism" and of
spreading "havoc" among literary men! The critic went out of his
way to conjure up a list of those who would support Griswold in his
charges—"Mr. Allan, the Faculty of Maryland University [sic]; the
President of the Academy at West Point; the officers of the regiment
from which he deserted; the publishers, White, Burton, Graham and
Godey, whose business he had injured or neglected." This after
Graham had published his "Defence"! The critic, although praising
his work in special cases, shows his animus in the concluding paragraphs when he prays for some "potent chemistry to blot out from
our brain—roll forever, beyond the power of future resurrection, the
greater part of what has been inscribed upon it by the ghastly and
charnel-hued pen of Edgar Allan Poe. Rather than remember all, we
would choose to forget all that he has written." [77]

Such falsification of facts was sufficiently unfortunate, but even
more unpardonable was the misquoting of those critics who defended
him. *Fraser's Magazine* [78] remarked "We are told by Mr. Willis that
the slightest indulgence in intoxicating liquor was sufficient to convert
Poe into a thorough blackguard," which of course Willis had not said.
This critic, like other British writers, had to depend upon Griswold,
and the power for evil which the "Memoir" possessed is shown clearly
in this extract:

> There is nothing of the *lues Boswelliana* about Mr. Griswold.
> He states with the greatest frankness the sins and scandals of the
> man who entrusted to him the vindication of a memory which
> sorely needed vindicating, if it were possible. It is curious, indeed,
> how little pains the biographer takes to conceal the shortcomings
> of his hero. He appears to have felt that any attempt to have done
> so would have been vain.

The British critic naturally was puzzled by the choice of Griswold,
evidenced by Mrs. Clemm's foreword. Well he might be, for such a
tragic happening as the selection of a man's bitterest enemy to be his
authorized biographer had never occurred, and was never to occur
again. But the critic added a few choice exaggerations, such as

[77] *North American Review*, LXXXIII (October, 1856), 427-455. This
article called forth rejoinders, in the *Cosmopolitan Art Journal* of New York,
I (March and June, 1857), 83, and 112. In this magazine occurred probably
the first agitation for a statue to Poe.
[78] *Fraser's Magazine for Town and Country*, LV (June, 1857), 686-690.

"Through his whole life there never was a time when, for more than two or three weeks, he promised to become anything better. . . . His envy of those more favored than himself by fortune amounted to raging ferocity."

Among the British reviews, that in the *Edinburgh Review* for April, 1858 [79] reached the climax of detraction. "Edgar Allan Poe," the critic began, "was incontestibly one of the most worthless persons of whom we have any record in the world of letters. . . . He outraged his benefactor, he deceived his friends, he sacrificed his love, he became a beggar, a vagabond, the slanderer of a woman, the delirious drunken pauper of a common hospital, hated by some, despised by others, and avoided by all respectable men." This was reprinted in the *Living Age*, and in the *Ladies' Repository*, and the mountain of slander rose, in this country and in England.

Today it seems hard to understand why the very over-statements of Poe's supposed crimes did not defeat themselves. The reason is given in one of the best of the articles on Poe, written by James Wood Davidson, the South Carolina teacher and writer, in *Russell's Magazine:* [80]

We are prepared by such an individuality, manifesting itself in such conditions, to see how it would and must produce such positive but antipodal opinions of the individual. His character was positive, intensely demonstrative, and the impression he created was therefore always unmistakable. He is said to have had "a fatal facility of making enemies." He secured more and more *bitter* enemies than any other American author has ever done, because he told more wholesome truths than any other author has dared to tell. And, if there is any one thing the exposition of which a man will not forgive, that thing is—*the truth.* A slandered man may find repose beneath the shade of his real or imaginary injuries, but the stern truth leaves no covert to flee to, save vengeance against the utterer. Poe allowed to quackery and stupidity no mercy; and now, his victims and their adherents, though they shrank to silence during his lifetime, have rallied like cowards to blurt their bravado over his too-early—but to them how timely!—grave. They have apparently exhausted even their

---

[79] *Edinburgh Review*, CVII (April, 1858), 420-421. Reprinted in *Living Age*, June 12, 1858, and in *Genius and Character of Edgar Allan Poe*, pp. 51-52.

[80] II (November, 1857), 161-173. The article is not signed, but Mrs. Whitman speaks of him as the author.

vast vocabularies of villifying epithets upon his name. They have beset him in every possible form and through every available medium, restrained by neither decency, truth, nor honor. . . .

On the other hand, Poe's brilliancy of mind, his independence, his princely poetical genius, his sensibility and suffering, his contempt of convention and manners, his instinctive appreciation of woman—these have secured him admirers, and have won him hearts whose tributes of affection are a world of proof in his favor. . . .

What was *true* the brilliant intellect of Edgar Poe never failed to perceive. What was *beautiful* his soul recognized at first blush, and loved for its kinship. Guided by these, his conscience was rarely in fault upon points of right. An instinctive self-respect, over which he had no control, forbade his ever seeking the lenient judgment of the many by explaining circumstances or appearances, which, unexplained, he knew must be construed against him. The world has little charity for any; for one who spurns its sympathy, none; and he who contemns its tribunal invariably receives the extreme visitations of its vengeance. As no judgment can be more erroneous, so none is more dictatorially given, or, when given, more persistently ultimate. Poe spurned that sympathy and received therefor the minimum of its meagre charity and the maximum of its profuse condemnation. A morbid sensibility impelled him to seek rather than avoid such occasions. He enjoyed the luxury of being misunderstood.

During the decade with which we must conclude this survey of the contemporary opinions of Poe, one of the women who loved him was preparing his defence in a more permanent form than that of the magazine articles of Graham and Hirst, of Burr and Davidson. Mrs. Whitman gathered from Mrs. Clemm details of his life and prepared first an article and later a small volume, *Edgar Poe and his Critics,* completed late in 1859 and published in 1860. During this decade she had fought off several attempts to shake her belief in her dead friend. Her own innate nobility is revealed in her letter to Mrs. Clemm, November 24 [1851]. Mrs. Locke had been pestering her with statements that Poe had spoken disrespectfully of Mrs. Whitman to her friends in Lowell.

"She then came to Providence," Mrs. Whitman wrote, "and passed a night with me. On her attempting to introduce the subject which she had so often touched upon in her letters, I interrupted her by saying that I did not wish to listen to any charges against one whose memory

was dear and sacred to me—That if *false* they could not be refuted—
If *true* I could understand and forgive them." [81]

Mrs. Whitman's article was offered to Lowell for the *Atlantic
Monthly,* but after detaining it for three months, he rejected it with-
out explanation.[82] Mrs. Whitman began her little book with this
Preface:

> Dr. Griswold's Memoir of Edgar Poe has been extensively read
> and circulated; its perverted facts and baseless assumptions have
> been adopted into every subsequent memoir and notice of the
> poet, and have been translated into many languages. For ten
> years this great wrong to the dead has passed unchallenged and
> unrebuked.
>
> It has been assumed by a recent English critic, that "Edgar Poe
> had no friends." As an index to a more equitable and intelligible
> theory of the idiosyncrasies of his life, and as an earnest protest
> against the spirit of Dr. Griswold's unjust memoir, these pages are
> submitted to his more candid readers and critics by
>
> One of his Friends.

While the volume is, therefore, a refutation of Griswold's "remorse-
less violations of the trust confided in him," Mrs. Whitman did not
reply to his charges by detailed examination of them. She proceeded,
instead, to paint a portrait of Poe with the brush of spiritual insight,
drawn in true perspective through her intimate knowledge of the man,
and made vivid by the colors of sympathy of which only a poet-
critic could know the values. When she had finished, Edgar Poe in
his real nature was there for the eyes of those who wish a true picture,
and to such as these, the scandals and half-truths drop, helpless to
blind or to confuse.

Mrs. Whitman put her finger at once on the puzzling differences
between the various portraits of Poe. They "are valueless as a portrait," she says, "to those who remember the unmatched glory of his
face when roused from its habitually introverted and abstracted look
by some favorite theme, or profound emotion." This inner light, noted

---

[81] Original Autograph Ms., Pratt Library. The year in which this letter
was written is not certain, but was probably 1851, since in it Mrs. Whitman spoke of receiving two years before a letter from Griswold concerning
her letters to Poe. This was probably the letter of December 17, 1849.

[82] Mrs. Whitman to Mrs. Clemm, April [?], [1859]. Original Autograph
Ms., Pratt Library. This letter is dated April 5th, but is evidently a reply
to Mrs. Clemm's letter from Alexandria, of April 22nd. in the Lilly Collection.

by Willis, Susan Talley, and others, shines for us only in his characters, in the lover of Eleanora, of Ulalume, of Annabel Lee.

Mrs. Whitman's tribute to Virginia, and to Poe's devotion to his wife, culminated in her sentence, often paraphrased, "It was to this quiet haven in the beautiful spring of 1846, when the fruit trees were all in bloom and the grass in its freshest verdure, that he brought his Virginia to die." Next comes the sympathetic interpretation of "Ulalume," which identifies the memory that challenges "Astarte's bediamonded crescent" with the spirit of Virginia.

Poe could not have asked for a better interpretation of his poems than Mrs. Whitman offered. Rejecting the criticism, not yet entirely hushed, that his creations were the results of mere artistic skill, and not genuine outgrowths of the inward life of a poet, she said:

> It is not to be questioned that Poe was a consummate master of language—that he had sounded all the secrets of rhythm—that he understood and availed himself of all its resources; the balance and poise of syllables—the alternations of emphasis and cadence —of vowel-sounds and consonants—and all the metrical sweetness of "phrase and metaphrase." Yet this consummate art was in him united with a rare simplicity. He was the most genuine of enthusiasts, as we think we shall presently show. His genius would follow no leadings but those of his own imperial intellect. With all his vast mental resources he could never write an occasional poem, or adapt himself to the taste of a popular audience. His graver narratives and fantasies are often related with an earnest simplicity, solemnity, and apparent fidelity, attributable, not so much to a deliberate artistic purpose, as to that power of vivid and intense conception that made his dreams realities, and his life a dream.

What other woman of that time could have given us this picture of Poe's personal powers:

> As a conversationist we do not remember his equal. We have heard the veteran Landor (called by high authority the best talker in England) discuss with scathing sarcasm the popular writers of the day, convey his political animosities by fierce invectives on the "pretentious coxcomb, Albert," and "the cunning knave, Napoleon," or describe, in words of strange depth and tenderness, the peerless charm of goodness and the naive social graces in the beautiful mistress of Gore House, "the most gorgeous Lady Blessington." We have heard the Howadji talk of the gardens of Damascus till the air seemed purpled and perfumed

with its roses. We have listened to the trenchant and vivid talk of the Autocrat; to the brilliant and exhaustless colloquial resources of John Neal, and Margaret Fuller. We have heard the racy talk of Orestes Brownson in the old days of his freedom and power, have listened to the serene wisdom of Alcott, and treasured up memorable sentences from the golden lips of Emerson. Unlike the conversational power evinced by any of these was the earnest, opulent, unpremeditated speech of Edgar Poe.

Like his writings it presented a combination of qualities rarely met with in the same person; a cool, decisive judgment, a wholly unconventional courtesy and sincere grace of manner, and an imperious enthusiasm which brought all hearers within the circle of its influence.

In several of her critical interpretations, it seems as though the author of "Eleonora" himself were speaking:

> It can hardly have escaped the notice of the most careless reader that certain ideas exercised over him the power of fascination. They return, again and again, in his stories and poems and seem like the utterances of a mind possessed with thoughts, emotions, and images of which the will and the understanding take little cognizance. In the delineation of these, his language often acquires a power and pregnancy eluding all attempts at analysis. It is then that by a few miraculous words he evokes emotional states or commands pictorial effects which live for ever in the memory and form a part of its eternal inheritance. No analysis can dissect—no criticism can disenchant them.

She reprinted the greater "To Helen," which Griswold had omitted, with singular stupidity, from his edition, and analyzed many of his poems with a judgment that still repays the student of Poe. A flash of inspiration, for example, concludes her study of his use of terror as a motive:

> Yet, as out of mighty and terrific discords noblest harmonies are sometimes evolved, so through the purgatorial ministries of awe and terror, and through the haunting Nemesis of doubt, Poe's restless and unappeased soul was urged on to the fulfilment of its appointed work—groping out blindly towards the light, and marking the approach of great spiritual truths by the very depth of the shadow it projected against them.

Mrs. Whitman, like a true critic, is not always in agreement with Poe's own beliefs. A masterly analysis of the growth of scepticism in English and American literature, gives Poe as its climax. It is too elaborate for quotation, and she goes too far in her statement that "the unrest and faithlessness of the age culminated in him." But this survey leads to a brilliant interpretation of the climax of *Eureka*, which was evidently not too much of a puzzle for *her*. The temptation to quote Mrs. Whitman must constantly be resisted, but who has better understood Poe's spiritual domain than the writer of these lines:

> Edgar Poe's dreams were assuredly often presageful and significant, and while he but dimly apprehended through the higher reason the truths which they foreshadowed, he riveted public attention upon them by the strange fascination of his style, the fine analytical temper of his intellect, and, above all, by the weird splendors of his imagination, compelling men to read and to accredit as *possible truths* his most marvellous conceptions. He often spoke of the imageries and incidents of his inner life as more vivid and veritable than those of his outer experience. We find in some pencilled notes appended to a manuscript copy of one of his later poems the words, "all that I have here expressed was actually present to me. Remember the mental condition which gave rise to Ligeia'—recall the passage of which I spoke, and observe the coincidence." With all the fine alchymy of his subtle intellect he sought to analyze the character and conditions of this introverted life. "I regard these visions," he says, "even as they arise, with an awe which in some measure moderates or tranquillizes the ecstacy—I so regard them through a conviction that this ecstacy, in itself, is of a character supernal to the human nature—*is a glimpse of the spirit's outer world.*"

With such an able defence of Poe in existence, how was it that the myths concerning his character persisted? Unfortunately, the circulation of Mrs. Whitman's volume was limited, although it was reprinted in 1885, and her method of defence, while admirable, did not meet categorically the slanders of Griswold. With nearly every set of Poe's works, went Griswold's "Memoir," while the magazine articles of Graham and others were after a time forgotten.

There has been an attempt in recent years, to find some excuse for Griswold, and the very enormity of his offence has been urged by one school of critics, as an argument for its incredibility. To meet this reaction in his favor, I have given in detail the forgeries, especially those I have newly discovered, because such accusations must be proved circumstantially. Forgery of this kind makes its perpetrator untrustworthy in every respect, and yet it is strangely persistent.[83]

[83] In a collection of the world's great letters, published in the year 1940, two of the worst slanders are repeated.

It has also been suggested that Griswold lacked sufficient motive for such actions. But Charles Godfrey Leland, who knew him well and liked him, admitted that he was one of the most vindictive of men when he had been attacked. Leland found in Griswold's desk, some years later, a mass of material to the discredit of Poe and of others, which Griswold evidently intended to publish. Fortunately, Leland burnt it all.[84] There is another possible explanation which Griswold's own words supply, in a letter to Carey and Hart:

> Gentlemen,
>
> I received a letter from you on Thursday and shall immediately proceed to the shipping of the "Poets and Poetry." I went at once to Harpers', and obtained the letter respecting the proposition to print Mrs. Osgood's Poems, and seeing from the first lines that the proposition was accepted, I read no farther, but started for Brooklyn, to exhibit it to Mrs. Osgood. In crossing the ferry, however, that letter, and a bundle of MSS. were lost, by my falling from the boat in a fit. The good people assisted me out of the water, after I had sunk twice; but were in too great a hurry to attend to their own business, to row about for the floating letters, or to dive after the pencil, knife, and small change that had escaped me.
>
> . . . .
>
> Yours very truly,
>
> Rufus W. Griswold.
>
> New York, March 17, 1849 [85]

Griswold was evidently not in normal health, either physically or mentally. It is perhaps idle to speculate on the effect of his disease upon his capacity for revenge, but it certainly invalidates his testimony or his judgments.

The Reverend Mr. Griswold was also, in a sense, a representative of his time. The forties and fifties saw a great wave of moralistic effort sweep over America. Reform movements were rampant. Advocates of temperance, of abolition, of slavery, of Graham bread, of spiritualism, of woman's rights, of the community life, were militant. To such a public, Poe's life as portrayed by Griswold, was a horrible but delicious bit of source material. Here was a great writer, who had insisted on living as he thought best, and the result was a tragedy.

[84] See C. G. Leland, *Memoirs* (New York, 1893), pp. 201-202.
[85] Original Autograph Ms., Gratz Collection, Historical Society of Pennsylvania. To my knowledge, it is unpublished.

That his dissipation had really been infrequent mattered little. Goodness, like happiness, has no history that is interesting to the reforming spirit.

The duality of Poe's nature will be apparent to anyone who has closely studied his life. It is reflected most concretely in his countenance. Take a full face daguerreotype of Poe, lay a card upon it, so that first one side and then the other will be concealed. On one side you will see a high forehead, an eye large and full, a firm mouth and a well shaped chin. On the other will appear a lower brow, a less lustrous eye, a mouth painfully drawn, and a chin less certain. That is why an artist like Sully chose to paint Poe's three-quarter face.

This duality accounts for the radically different opinions concerning his real nature. At times, under the influence of liquor, he undoubtedly said and did things to which his enemies could point without the possibility of contradiction. These incidents, magnified in that isolation which makes facts sometimes the most terrible of untruths, gave color to Griswold's slanders. But these actions were pitiable rather than dishonorable, and the bitter things he said concerning his enemies were often true, and therefore hurt the more.

That this weaker side of Poe was only the occasional aspect, has been established without the shadow of a doubt. He has given his own explanation for his use of liquor in words which defy any paraphrase.[86] These explanations were in private letters. In his reply to English,[87] he publicly hinted at family reasons which prevented him from being even more explicit, in connection with his drinking. The letter of David Poe, Jr., now first printed in a biography, explains indirectly but clearly, how Edgar Poe had inherited from his father a tendency to instability, due to liquor, which was a family failing.[88]

The testimony of unimpeachable quality has been given already to show that for long periods Poe was absolutely sober. His hard fight against a temptation, stronger to him than to normal people, and his remorse when he yielded, for the reasons he has given and for another which I have suggested,[89] leave much on the credit side to Poe.

Poe was not a drug addict. On this point we have direct testimony. Dr. English, who disliked him, gave his definite medical opinion to that effect.[90] Thomas H. Lane, who knew him for several years, while

---

[86] See pp. 347-348.
[87] See p. 49.
[88] See also letter of William Poe to Edgar Poe, June 15, 1843.
[89] See pp. 226-227.
[90] See p. 350.

acknowledging that "a drink or two" changed Poe from a mild man "in every way a gentleman" to a quarrelsome inebriate, insisted that Poe did not take drugs.[91] Indeed, the best negative argument lies in the fact that Poe was so little acquainted with the effect of laudanum that he either took or said he took at least an ounce of the drug in Boston in 1848,[92] which his stomach immediately rejected. "I had not calculated on the strength of the laudanum," are not the words of a drug addict. Those were days when opium was frequently given in small doses for pain, and Poe may well have taken it in that form.

There were failings of Edgar Poe, of course, which cannot be laid to drink. These I have made no attempt to conceal.

When his weaknesses have been catalogued, however, there rises above them the real Edgar Poe, the industrious, honorable gentleman whom Graham and Willis knew, the warm friend and courteous host whom Hirst, Mayne Reid and many others remembered. There was the brilliant thinker—whose charm came from that inner radiance that shone upon Helen Whitman and Susan Talley. Those who knew him best, loved him best. His wife and his mother adored the self-sacrificing, devoted husband and son. His friendships with Frances Osgood, Helen Whitman, Annie Richmond, Louise Shew, and Elmira Shelton, met the supreme test of separation under high emotional tension or even the embittered tongues of slander. Yet every one of them treasured the memory of his utter refinement and unfailing chivalry to her.

Of even more significance than Poe the man is Poe the artist. To bring to Virginia the few comforts she needed, he might harness his critical pen to drive a poetess, who could pay him, into temporary fame. But even the spectre of want could not force him into the prostitution of his genius as a poet and a writer of romance. Had he chosen to fill his pages with the sentimental twaddle then so popular, or to sully his creations of the beautiful with the suggestiveness that sells, he would have made a better living, and would now be forgotten. But he had his own lofty standards, and he lived up to them. For money he cared little, except as it provided for the wants of others. For fame he did care, but he was one of those souls who can see a prize, artistic, social, or financial, almost within their grasp, and, caring for something higher still, of which that prize is the price, can

[91] Letter of Dallet Fuguet to the present writer, October 20, 1927, containing memoranda of Lane, Fuguet's cousin.

[92] See letter to "Annie," November 16, 1848, pp. 589-590.

resolutely put it by. We can imagine him saying with Browning's Duke,

> "That would have taken some stooping—and I choose
> Never to stoop."

It is for this great refusal, for his willingness to lay all things upon the altar of his art, that Poe is most to be respected. He could hardly have done otherwise. A patrician to the fingertips, the carefulness of his dress, even in his poverty, was but an index to his devotion to those fields of effort in which he knew he was a master. After creating the detective story, he left it to others, who could not write the Arabesques of which he alone knew the secret. Limited as his field in poetry seems at first glance to be, it deals with great universal motives, with love, beauty, pride and death, and he carried those themes into lyric heights untouched before his time in America.

In his fiction, as well as his poetry, the pioneering spirit of the America of his day showed clearly in that restlessness which led him to dream "dreams no mortal ever dared to dream before," to test the outer limits of the human soul, and to attack even the citadel of the spirit's integrity, and the relations of God and His Universe.

His fame is now secure. The America in which he could find no adequate reward treasures every word he wrote, and in every city in which he lived, except the city of his birth, stands a lasting memorial to him. He has become a world artist and through the translations of his writings he speaks today to every civilized country. He has won this wide recognition by no persistent clamor of a cult, but by the royal right of preeminence. For today, nearly a hundred years since his death, he remains not only the one American, but also the one writer in the English language, who was at once foremost in criticism, supreme in fiction, and in poetry destined to be immortal.

Appendices

I. THE THEATRICAL CAREER OF EDGAR POE'S PARENTS

In a list of this extent, space will not permit argument concerning the conflicting testimony of different sources. In general the magazine or newspaper criticism published *after* the event is preferable to the advertisement. Owing to the constant changes of production on short notice, playbills are not as good evidence as newspaper notices of the succeeding day or even of the day of production. Where advertisements are the only available sources and differ from each other as to the parts assumed by the Poes, I have had to base my decision on their previous or later assumption of the parts, on the relative reliability of the newspapers, or on other factors. Where it is certain that the Poes took part in the play but no cast is given, their probable rôles are printed in brackets. Parts taken by Charles Hopkins are given only in connection with the Poes.

In preparing this list, its primary object, to show the variety and importance of the parts sustained by David and Elizabeth Arnold Hopkins Poe, has never been sacrificed to mere uniformity. When the part assumed by either of them is first played, the name of the play and its author are given, if possible. When the rôle is repeated, the author or play is given only when the part is difficult to identify or when, as in Poe's last season, it seemed important to have the full record immediately available. Repetitions of the play during a season are briefly indicated, either on its first production or on its repetition, but the completeness of the chronicle has never been impaired merely to save space.

PARTS ACTED BY ELIZABETH ARNOLD
1796-1797

Sources: James Moreland. "The Theatre in Portland in the Eighteenth Century," *New England Quarterly*, XI (June, 1938), 331-342; Search of *Eastern Herald and Gazette of Maine* by Miss Viola C. Hamilton, Secretary American Antiquarian Society; George O. Seilhamer, *History of the American Theatre*, Vol. III.

BOSTON THEATRE, April 15, 1796

Miss Arnold sings "The Market Lass." Her first appearance.

PORTLAND, MAINE, Assembly Room

Nov. 25, 1796. Miss Biddy Bellair in Garrick's *Miss in Her Teens*.
Nov. 28. Solomon Smack, in Yarrow's *Trick Upon Trick; or, The Vintner in the Suds*. Repeated Dec. 5.
Dec. 20. Benefit of Miss Arnold. Little Pickle in Bickerstaffe's *The Spoiled Child*.
Jan. 3, 1797. Miss Arnold sings "Listen to the Voice of Love," at the end of Home's *Douglas*.
Jan. 12. Miss Arnold's benefit. [Louisa or Jenny in Charles Dibdin's *Deserter*. Mrs. Bruin or Mrs. Sneak in *The Mayor of Garratt*.]
Jan. 17. Miss Arnold speaks Epilogue on closing night of the season.

NEWPORT, R. I.

April 5, 1797. Solomon Smack repeated.
April 12. Mrs. Tubbs' Benefit. Little Pickle repeated.

NEW YORK, John Street Theatre

Aug. 18, 1797. Maria in *The Spoiled Child*.

1797–1798

CHARLESTON, S. C. Sollee's Company at City Theatre, or
Charleston Theatre

Sources: *City Gazette and Daily Advertiser*. Searched by Miss E. A. Bull, checked by Miss Eola Willis's *The Charleston Theatre in the Eighteenth Century* (1924). Information concerning Wilmington furnished by Dr. Jay B. Hubbell.

Nov. 18, 1797. "A new song, called 'The Market Lass' by Miss Arnold, being her first appearance on this stage."
Nov. 27. A Page in Cross's *The Purse*.
Nov. 29. The Child [Boy] in Birch's *The Adopted Child*. Repeated Dec. 4, 1797; Jan. 12, 15, 16, Feb. 13, 1798.
Dec. 6. Duke of York in *Richard III*.
Dec. 23, 25. Cupid in Pantomime, *The Magic Chamber; or, Harlequin Protected by Cupid*.
Feb. 5, 1798. The Child, in Southerne's *Isabella; or, The Fatal Marriage*.

Feb. 9. Dancing Nymph in *Americana and Eleutheria; or, A New Tale of the Genii.*

Feb. 24, 26. Julia in Henry Siddon's *The Sicilian Romance.*

WILMINGTON, N. C.

Tubb's "Secession"—at Wilmington, North Carolina. The Company performed for "nine nights."

March 9, 1798. Lisette in Ballet, *Lisette and Annette;* Norah, in O'Keeffe's *A Poor Soldier.*

EDGAR'S COMPANY—the Charleston Comedians, at the Charleston Theatre.

April 9, 1798. Nancy in Murphy's *Three Weeks After Marriage.*

April 18. Miss Arnold Sings.

April 20. Pink in O'Keeffe's *The Young Quaker.*

April 23. Sings in Glee from Shakespeare—*Sigh no more, Ladies.*

April 27. Anna in *The Death of Major André; or, West Point Preserved.* [William Brown's lost play?]

April 30. Benefit of Mr. Tubbs and Miss Arnold. Sophia in Holcroft's *Road to Ruin.* Phoebe in Frances Brooke's *Rosina.* Speaks a Farewell Address.

Season closed May 2.

1799

PHILADELPHIA, Wignell's Company at the New Theatre

SOURCES: T. C. Pollock, *The Philadelphia Theatre in the Eighteenth Century* (1933). Search by E. Biddle Heg in Claypoole's *American Daily Advertiser.*

On account of the yellow fever, the New Theatre did not open for the season of 1798-1799 until February 5, 1799.

March 18, 1799. Miss Biddy Bellair. "Her first appearance on this stage."

March 23. Little Pickle. Repeated April 8.

April 1. Boy in *The Adopted Child.*

April 8. Little Pickle.

April 12. Poggie in Byrne's pantomimic ballet, *Highland Festivity.*

April 13. Lauretta in Moultru's *False and True.*

April 15. Sicilian Girl in Andrews' *Mysteries of the Castle.*

April 17. Norah in O'Keeffe's *The Poor Soldier.*

April 29. Moggy M'Gilpin in O'Keeffe's *The Highland Reel.*

May 8. Miss Biddy Bellair.

May 15. Fanny in S. J. Arnold's *The Shipwreck.*

May 20. Nina in John Rose's *The Prisoner*.
May 24, 25, 27. Beda in Colman's *Blue Beard*.

BALTIMORE, Wignell's Company at the New Theatre

Sources: Personal Search. *The Telegraph and Daily Advertiser.*

May 31, 1799. Miss Biddy Bellair. "Being her first appearance on this stage."

June 5. Lauretta in *False and True*.

June 7. "Miss Arnold's Night." Last appearance of Mr. Tubbs as "Master of Hotel" in Holcroft's *He's Much to Blame*.

June 10. Beda in Colman's *Blue Beard*.

Oct. 4, 1799. Molly Maybush in O'Keeffe's *The Farmer*.

Oct. 8. Beda in *Blue Beard*. Repeated Oct. 19, 21, 25; Nov. 4, 25, 26.

Oct. 9. "Principal character" in a ballet dance, given in connection with *The Constellation; or, A Wreath for American Tars*, with a representation of chase and action between the *Constellation* and *Insurgente* Frigates.

Oct. 16. Prince John of Lancaster in *Henry IV*, First Part.

Oct. 28. One of the "Females" in *The Mountaineers*.

Oct. 30. Catalina in O'Keeffe's *The Castle of Andalusia*.

Nov. 6. "Little Midshipman" in O'Keeffe's *The Rival Soldiers; or, Sprigs of Laurel*.

Nov. 8. Annette in MacNally's *Robin Hood; or, Sherwood Forest*.

Nov. 15. Indian Woman in *Columbus; or, A World Discovered*.

Nov. 23. Vocal part in the funeral procession in Act V of *Romeo and Juliet*.

1799-1800

PHILADELPHIA, Wignell's Company at the New Theatre

Sources: Search by E. Biddle Heg in *The True American Commercial Advertiser* and *The Philadelphia Gazette and Universal Daily Advertiser*.

Dec. 6, 1799. The Little Midshipman in O'Keeffe's *The Rival Soldiers; or, Sprigs of Laurel*.

Dec. 9. Annette in MacNally's *Robin Hood*.

Dec. 26. Sings in A Monody on Death of Washington, and is among the principal characters in a Ballet Dance, in *The Constellation*. Monody repeated Dec. 30.

March 14, 1800. Charles Hopkins in *She Stoops to Conquer*. "His first appearance on any stage."

April 7. Dolly in Prince Hoare's *Lock and Key*.

April 8. Dance composed by Mr. Francis, on naval victory. Miss Arnold one of the principal characters.

April 16. Maria in *The Sailor's Garland; or, The Family Picture.*

April 19. Prince John of Lancaster in *Henry IV, First Part.*

April 24, 25. Jane in Thomas Dibdin's *The Naval Pillar.*

April 28. "A Female Villager" in Allingham's *Fortune's Frolic.*

May 3. Belinda in O'Keeffe's *Modern Antiques; or, The Merry Mourners.* Hopkins as Joey.

May 9. Benefit of Mrs. Snowden, Miss Arnold and Miss Solomons.

May 14, 16. A Priestess and Virgin of the Sun in Kotzebue's *Pizarro,* probably Dunlap's adaptation.

May 17. Dances in Francis's *Shelty's Frolic; or, The Caledonian Fling.* Repeated May 19. "Positively the last night this season."

BALTIMORE, Wignell's Company, at the New Theatre

SOURCES: Personal Search. *The Telegraph and Daily Advertiser.* Also, *Federal Gazette and Baltimore Daily Advertiser.*

May 27, 1800. Boy in *The Adopted Child.*

May 28. Irish Lilt in Francis's arrangement of *Shelty's Frolic.* Repeated June 6 and 9.

May 30. Ellen in Kotzebue's *Sighs; or, The Daughter,* adapted by Prince Hoare.

June 2. *Macbeth.* The vocal parts by Miss Arnold and others.

June 3. Nancy in *The Naval Pillar; or, A Wreath for American Sailors.* Altered from Thomas Dibdin. Also, one of the "Females" in *The Mountaineers,* and a dancer in the ballet.

June 4. Sang in a Funeral Procession in Act V of *Romeo and Juliet.*

June 5. Benefit of Miss Arnold and Messrs. Hopkins and Blissett. Nancy in *The Naval Pillar.*

June 6. Cornelia (with a Song) in O'Keeffe's *The Positive Man; or, Sailors on Shore.*

June 7. Priestess, and Virgin of the Sun, in *Pizarro; or, The Spaniards in Peru.* Repeated June 9.

WASHINGTON, Wignell's Company at the United States Theatre in Blodgett's Hotel

SOURCES: Search by C. W. Hart in *Georgetown Centinel of Liberty.*

August 22, 1800. Little Pickle.

Sept. 5. A Minuet de la Cour in *A Masquerade* in Act I of *Romeo and Juliet.* Also sang in Funeral Procession in Act V.

Season closed September 19.

1800-1801

PHILADELPHIA, Wignell's Company, at the New Theatre

SOURCES: Search by Dr. Reese D. James, in Claypoole's *American Daily Advertiser*. See also Dr. James' *Old Drury of Philadelphia, A History of the Philadelphia Stage, 1800-35* (1932).

Oct. 8, 1800. A Female Villager in Allingham's *Fortune's Frolic*. Repeated Dec. 22.

Oct. 10. Irene in *Blue Beard*. Repeated Oct. 31, Dec. 17, Jan. 1, 1801, Feb. 18, April 7.

Oct. 17. A vocal part in An Epithalamium in Act III of *Isabella*.

Oct. 22. Priestess in *Pizarro*. Repeated Nov. 10, Dec. 22, Feb. 9. Also, Minuet de la Cour and a New Gavoto. Repeated Sept. 25, 1801.

Oct. 27. Dance in A Grand Masquerade in Act IV of Reynold's *Management*. Repeated Oct. 29, Nov. 21, 1800; Jan. 5, 1801.

Nov. 3. Vocal part in Lewis's *The Castle Spectre*. Repeated Nov. 14, Jan. 30, 1801.

Nov. 5. Ellen in *Sighs*.

Nov. 12. Norah in *The Poor Soldier*.

Nov. 14. Welsh Girl in *St. David's Day; or, The Honest Welshman*. Repeated Nov. 19, Nov. 28.

Nov. 17. Cupid in Garrick's *Cymon and Sylvia*.

Nov. 19. Attendant in *The Law of Lombardy*. Repeated Nov. 24, Dec. 3.

Dec. 1. Country Lass in Morton's *Speed the Plough*. Repeated Dec. 5, 10, 15, 26, Jan. 23, Feb. 16, March 18, April 7, 1801. Also Little Pickle.

Dec. 3. Celia in O'Keeffe's *A Trip to Fontainbleau*.

Dec. 5. Priscilla Tomboy in Bickerstaffe's *The Romp*. Repeated August 28, 1801; June 23, 1806.

Dec. 8. Catherine in Pearce's *Netley Abbey*. (Operatic farce.)

Dec. 15. Nelly in Prince Hoare's *No Song No Supper*.

Dec. 26. Lass in *Christmas Gambols; or, Harlequin Mariner*. Repeated Dec. 27, Jan. 2, Feb. 14, 1801.

Dec. 27. Indian Woman in Morton's *Columbus*.

Jan. 2, 1801. Prince of Wales in *Richard III*. Repeated Feb. 2.

Jan. 12. "Vocalist" in *Alexander the Great*. Repeated Jan. 14, 16, 19, 24, 26, Feb. 20.

Feb. 14. In a Spanish Fandango, composed by Mr. Francis. Also, Female in 2nd Act of *The Mountaineers*.

March 2. Zilia in Murphy's *Peru Revenged; or, The Death of Pizarro*. Also, Agnes in Holcroft's adaptation of Beaumarchais' *The Follies of a Day; or, The Marriage of Figaro*.

March 11. Nancy in *The Shakespeare Jubilee.*
March 13. Rosina in Kotzebue's *The Corsicans.*
March 14. In *Aladdin; or, The Wonderful Lamp.* Repeated April 6. In a New Strathspey with others.
March 21. Benefit of Mrs. Bernard and Miss Arnold. Miss Arnold in song at end of Kemble's *Point of Honour.*
March 25. In *A Treble Hornpipe.* Between play and farce.
Season ended April 11.

1801

BALTIMORE, Wignell's Company at the New Theatre

SOURCES: Dr. John C. French, quoting K. C. Rede. *Baltimore Sun,* Jan. 22, 1933. Search by W. D. Hoyt, Jr., in *The Telegraph and Daily Advertiser.*

April 20, 1801. A Country Lass in *Speed the Plough.* Repeated May 2, May 23.
April 22. Welsh Girl in *St. David's Day.* Repeated April 27.
April 24. Celia in *A Trip to Fontainbleau.* Repeated April 25, May 16.
April 29. Little Girl in Kotzebue's *The Count of Burgundy.* Also, a Villager in *Fortune's Frolic.*
May 4. Vocal Part in *The Castle Spectre.* Repeated May 11.
May 6. Laura in *Lock and Key.*
May 9. A Visiting Lady in *The Deaf Lover.*
May 13. Vocal Part in *Romeo and Juliet;* also danced Minuet de la Cour. Also, The Little Midshipman in *The Rival Soldiers.*
May 15. One of Females in *The Mountaineers.* Also, Belinda in *Modern Antiques.*
May 18. Fanny in *The Shipwreck.*
May 20. Ghita in William Cobb's *The Siege of Belgrade.*
May 25. A Vocal Part in *Macbeth.*
May 27. One of Principal Vocal Parts in *The Virgin of the Sun.* Repeated May 29.
June 4. Danced in pantomime, *Aladdin.*
June 5. Minuet de la Cour and New Gavot in *The Merchant of Venice.*
June 6. Lass in *The Highland Reel.* Also danced and sang.
June 8. Vocal Part in *Alexander the Great.* Repeated June 9.
June 10. Indian Woman in *Columbus.* Also, Irene in *Blue Beard.*

1801-1802

PHILADELPHIA, Wignell's Company, New Theatre, in July; Southwark
Theatre, August 14th to October 2nd; New Theatre, to April 7th

SOURCES: Claypoole's *American Daily Advertiser,* as for the season of
1800-1801.

July 17, 1801. Principal part in a Roundelay and Chorus in Act III
of *The Battle of Hexham; or, Days of Old.*
Aug. 14. Song after *The West-Indian.*
Aug. 28. Priscilla Tomboy in *The Romp.*
Sept. 7. Moggy in *The Highland Reel.*
Sept. 21. Miss Arnold in song.
Sept. 23. Ophelia in *Hamlet.*
Sept. 25. Minuet de la Cour.
Oct. 2. Song at end of *The Midnight Hour.*
Dec. 18. Camira [Selima] in Dibdin's *Il Bondocani.*
Dec. 26. Sam's Wife in *Obi; or, Three Fingered Jack.* Repeated Dec.
28, 30.
Feb. 24, 1802. Attendant nymph in *Hercules and Omphale,* grand his-
toric pantomime. Repeated Feb. 27, March 3, 4, 5.
March 19. "First actress" in *The Manager in Distress.*
March 22. "Favorite song" by Miss Arnold.
March 24. Pantomimical dance arranged by Mr. Francis, called *The
Scheming Milliner.* Miss Arnold in Reels, Strathspeys, and Waltz.
March 27. Grace Gaylove in Colman's *The Review, or The Wags of
Windsor.*
April 7. Benefit of Mrs. Snowden, Miss Arnold and Mr. Usher. *Speed
the Plough.* Miss Arnold in Song.

BALTIMORE, Wignell's Company at the New Theatre

SOURCES: Search by W. D. Hoyt, Jr., in *The Telegraph and Daily
Advertiser.*

April 22, 1802. Phoebe in *Rosina.*
April 26. Juba in Prince Hoare's *The Prize; or, 2,5,3,8.*
May 1. A "Principal part" in the chorus of George Colman's *The
Battle of Hexham; or, Days of Old.* Also, Grace Gaylove in *The
Review, or, The Man of All Trades,* also known as *The Wags of
Windsor.*
May 3. One of the Female Attendants in Robert Jephson's *The Law of
Lombardy.* Also, Mary in Knight's *The Turnpike Gate.* Repeated
May 10.
May 5. Camira in *Il Bondocani; or, The Caliph Robber.*

May 7. One of the vocal parts in *Macbeth*.

May 8. An Attendant Nymph in Act I of *Hercules and Omphale*, "a Grand Heroic Pantomime." Repeated May 12, 13, 17, June 7.

May 10. One of the Priestesses and Virgins of the Sun in *The Virgin of the Sun*.

May 14. Angelica in *The Shipwreck*.

May 19. Fatima in *Blue Beard*.

May 21. Page (Eugene) in Cumberland's adaptation of Kotzebue's *Joanna of Montfaucon*. Also, Molly Maybush in *The Farmer*.

May 22. First Actress in *The Manager in Distress*, a prelude in 1 act. Repeated May 28. Also, Sukey Starch in *Harlequin Hurry Scurry; or, A Rural Rumpus*, a pantomimical afterpiece.

May 24. One of the Lasses in O'Keeffe's *The Highland Reel*.

May 26. An Attendant in Congreve's *The Mourning Bride*. Also, Diana in O'Keeffe's *The London Hermit; or, Rambles in Dorsetshire*.

May 27. Vocal Part in *The Castle Spectre*.

May 30. One of the Lasses in *The Sailor's Landlady; or, Jack in Distress*, a pantomimical dance. Also, Belinda in *Modern Antiques; or, The Merry Mourners*.

June 1. An Attendant in *The Earl of Essex; or, The Unhappy Favorite*. Also, Nelly in *No Song No Supper*.

June 2. Vocal Part in *Alexander the Great; or, The Rival Queens*.

June 3. Nancy in *The Shakespeare Jubilee*, an entertainment in music, dialogue, and spectacle by David Garrick. In Act II a grand pageant exhibiting the most prominent characters in Shakespeare's plays, including Miss Arnold as Miranda in *The Tempest*.

June 4. Benefit performance for Mr. Usher, Mrs. Snowden, and Miss Arnold. Irene in *Blue Beard*.

June 5. Country Girl in *Lovers' Vows*. Also, Norah in *The Poor Soldier*. Also, one of Dancers in *The Scheming Milliner*.

June 8. One of the Circassians in *The Corsair; or, The Egyptian Robber*. Repeated June 9, 10.

June 10. Herman, a Page, in M. G. Lewis's *Adelmorn the Outlaw*.

June 12. A song, "Moggy, or the Highland Bell," in a Miscellaneous Entertainment.

ELIZABETH ARNOLD HOPKINS

1802

ALEXANDRIA, Green's Virginia Company, at the Alexandria Theatre

SOURCES: *Alexandria Columbian Advertiser*. Searched by Mrs. Lillian A. Hall, Harvard Theatre Collection, Robert H. Haynes, Assistant

Librarian, Harvard College Library, and Miss Viola C. Hamilton, of the American Antiquarian Society.

Theatre to open week of July 25, 1802. Notices begin August 2.

August 6, 1802. Hopkins as Father Philip in *The Castle Spectre*.

August 11. Hopkins as Sir Abel Handy in *Speed the Plough;* Mrs. Hopkins as Fanny in *The Shipwreck,* Hopkins as Stave. [First mention of "Mrs. Hopkins."]

August 14. Mrs. Hopkins as Little Pickle and Hopkins as John in *The Spoiled Child.* Hopkins as Orozembo in *Pizarro.*

Sept. 4. Hopkins as Major Domo, Mrs. Hopkins as Greek Slave in *The Corsair, or, The Egyptian Robber.*

Sept. 9. Minuet de la Cour and New Gavot by Mrs. Hopkins.

Sept. 11. Mrs. Hopkins danced a Spanish Fandango in *The Mountaineers.*

Sept. 13. Last Night. Mrs. Hopkins dances.

Sept. 16. A Grand Concert, at Gadby's Hotel. Mrs. Hopkins sang "The Lass of the Lake," "The Day of Marriage," and "Drink to Me Only with Thine Eyes." [1]

1803

NORFOLK, Green's Virginia Company. Norfolk or New Theatre

SOURCES: Search by Marshall W. Butt, Genealogist, in the *Norfolk Herald.*

March 9, 10, 1803. Hopkins as Tilman Totum and Mrs. Hopkins as Louisa in Prince Hoare's adaptation of Kotzebue's *Sighs.* Also, Rosina in *Rosina.*

March 12. Grace Gaylove in *The Review; or, The Wags of Windsor.* Repeated March 17.

March 16. Mary Tactic in *The Rival Soldiers; or, Sprigs of Laurel.* Repeated June 25.

March 21. Elmira in Bickerstaffe's *The Sultan.*

March 23. Zelina in J. D. Burk's *Oberon; or, The Siege of Mexico.*

April 1. Annette in *Robin Hood.* Also, Greek Slave in *Corsair.*

April 12. Mrs. Hopkins as Moggy McGilpin in *The Highland Reel.*

[1] Woodberry, Appendix, I, 360, states that Mrs. Hopkins was in Petersburg, Virginia, November 20—December 7, 1802, but gives no plays or casts. I can find no file of newspapers of Petersburg for those dates in Petersburg, Richmond, or any other depository. Scattered issues give no references to Mrs. Hopkins. They were probably playing, however, as *The Petersburg Republican* for Dec. 7, 1802, gives Hopkins in a recitation.

April 18. Beda in Colman's *Blue Beard*. Also, Miss Nancy in *Fortune's Frolic*.

April 23. Maria in *The Sailor's Garland*. Also, Jenny in *The Fruitless Precaution* (pantomimical Ballet).

April 25. Miss Nevile in *She Stoops to Conquer*. Also, Eliza Greville in Henry Bate's *The Flitch of Bacon*.

April 27, 28. Orilla in M. G. Lewis's *Adelmorn*.

April 30. Rose Sydney in Thomas Morton's *Secrets Worth Knowing*. Also, Rosina in *Rosina*.

June 6. Louisa in *Sighs*. Also, Wilelmina in Charles Dibdin's *The Waterman*.

June 8. Irene in *Blue Beard*. Also, Adelaide in O'Keeffe's *Prisoner at Large*.

June 23. Mary in Thomas Knight's *The Turnpike Gate*.

July 1. Benefit of Mr. and Mrs. Hopkins, Dance, A Pas Suel [sic] by Mrs. Hopkins after play *Columbus*.

July 8. Song by Mrs. Hopkins in *A Musical Olio*. Mr. and Mrs. Hopkins in a Triumphal Glee of the Red Knights, on their return from the Holy Land.

July 11. Song and Dance by Mrs. Hopkins.

July 13. [Emma] with song at end of Thomas Dibdin's *Reconciliation; or, The Birthday*, from Kotzebue.

DAVID POE, JR.

1803-1804

CHARLESTON, Placide's Company, The Charleston Theatre

SOURCES: Search by Miss Emma A. Bull in Charleston *City Gazette and Daily Advertiser*, Charleston *Courier*, the *Times, Carolina Gazette*. References in Robert A. Law, *Journal of English and Germanic Philology*, XXI (April, 1922), 344-346; Eola Willis, "The Dramatic Career of Poe's Parents," *Bookman*, 64 (Nov., 1926), 288-291; William S. Hoole, *A History of the Charleston Theatre* (Ms.); Emmett Robinson, Ms. notes on Charleston Stage.

Dec. 1, 1803. Officer in Faucet's Pantomime from Kotzebue's *La Peyrouse*. Repeated Feb. 25, 1804.

Dec. 5. Laertes in Brooke's *Gustavus Vasa*. "Being his second appearance on any stage."

Dec. 7. Harry Thunder in O'Keeffe's *Wild Oats*. Repeated Dec. 20.

Dec. 9. Donalbain in *Macbeth*.

Dec. 16. [Grimm] in Schiller's *The Robbers*. Also, an Indian in *Robinson Crusoe*.

The Company left for Savannah, Georgia, on December 23, 1803. The next notice of Poe in Charleston occurs on

Jan. 31, 1804. Falieri in Zschokke's *Abaellino.* Repeated Feb. 13, 1804.

Feb. 2. Stephano in Holcroft's *Tale of Mystery.* Repeated Feb. 14.

Feb. 10. Tressel in *King Richard III.* Repeated Feb. 27.

Feb. 14. Pedro in Dunlap's *The Voice of Nature,* adaptation of Caig-niez's *La Jugement de Salomon.* Repeated Feb. 21, March 2.

Feb. 15. Grimm in *The Robbers.*

Feb. 16. Young Woodland in Reynolds' *Cheap Living.* Repeated Feb. 20.

Feb. 18. Williams in *John Bull.*

Feb. 21. Allan A-Dale in *Robin Hood.* Repeated March 3, March 15.

Feb. 25. Don Pedro in *Much Ado About Nothing.*

March 5. Thomas in J. T. Allingham's *The Marriage Promise.* Repeated March 9.

March 7. Trueman in Lillo's *George Barnwell.*

March 12. Camillo in Jephson's *Julia; or, The Italian Lover.*

March 15. Trifle in M. G. Lewis's *Rivers; or, The East Indian.* Repeated March 21, April 9.

March 19. Dennis Crackskull in Sheridan's *Saint Patrick's Day.*

April 2. Don Garcia in Mrs. Cowley's *A Bold Stroke for a Husband.* Also, Mezetin in Dibdin and Garrick's *The Touchstone of Truth.*

April 4. Don Antonio Gaspard in Workman's *Liberty in Louisiana.*

April 9. A Hunter in *The Fatherless Children.*

April 12. Hortensio in *Catherine and Petruchio.*

April 19. Sebastian in Reynolds' *Charlotte and Werter.* Also, Lover in *The Old Soldier,* a pantomime.

MR. AND MRS. HOPKINS, DAVID POE, JR.

1804-1805

RICHMOND, Green's Virginia Company, at the Richmond Theatre

SOURCES: Search by Miss Mary F. Goodwin, Historiographer of the Diocese of Southern Virginia, in the *Virginia Gazette,* the *Richmond Enquirer,* the *Richmond Argus,* the *Impartial Observer,* the *Virginian,* the *Virginia Patriot.*

Season opened December 21, 1803.

Jan. 18, 1804. Hopkins as Sir Simon Rochdale in *John Bull.*

Feb. 13. Hopkins as Fulmer in *The West Indian.*

Feb. 14. Hopkins as Old Rapid in Morton's *A Cure for the Heart Ache.*

Feb. 18. Hopkins as Father Philip in *Castle Spectre* and Young Cockney in *The Romp.*

March 7. Hopkins as Sir Ralph Aspen in *Hear Both Sides.*

March 10. It is announced that $230 was raised at the benefit for the fire sufferers in Norfolk.

March 14. Hopkins as Apothecary and Peter in *Romeo and Juliet.*

March 21. Benefit of Mrs. Hopkins. [Bertha] in *The Point of Honor.* [Laura] in *The Agreeable Surprise.*

March 24. Hopkins as Mr. Sallus in *Every One Has His Fault.*

The Theatre was open only occasionally from April 7 to June 27, 1804. No mention of Mr. or Mrs. Hopkins until June 30. They may have been in Norfolk, but no file of Norfolk papers for the spring of 1804 is available.

June 30. Hopkins as Sir Abel Handy, Mrs. Hopkins as Susan Ashfield and Poe as Henry in *Speed the Plough.* "Mr. Poe, from the Charleston Theatre, will make his first appearance on our boards this evening."

July 17. Hopkins as Nicholas, Poe as Valet and Mrs. Hopkins as Rose Sidney in *Secrets Worth Knowing.* Also Poe as Selwyn, Hopkins as Stave and Mrs. Hopkins as Fanny in *The Shipwreck.*

July 21. Mrs. Hopkins in dance at end of *Christopher Columbus.*

July 25. Poe as Henry Morland, Hopkins as Dr. Pangloss and Mrs. Hopkins as Caroline Dormer in Colman's *The Heir at Law.* Original Epilogue, Mr. Poe, Mr. and Mrs. Hopkins.

July 27. Hopkins as Gov. Heartall, Poe as Timothy Quaint, Mrs. Hopkins as Mrs. Malford in *The Soldier's Daughter.*

Aug. 4. Hopkins as Goldfinch, Poe as Jacob, and Mrs. Hopkins as Sophia in *The Road to Ruin.* Also, Hopkins as Major Benbow, Poe as Nat Putty and Mrs. Hopkins as Eliza Greville in *Flitch of Bacon.*

Aug. 8. Hopkins as Shelty, Mrs. Hopkins as Moggy McGilpin in *Highland Reel.* Also, Joey and Belinda in *Modern Antiques.*

Aug. 11. Benefit of Mr. and Mrs. Hopkins. Poe as Lindorf, Hopkins as Dr. Cranium and Mrs. Hopkins as Stella in Boaden's *The Maid of Bristol.*

Aug. 15. Benefit for Miss Melford and Mr. Poe. Poe [George Barnwell] in *George Barnwell.*

Aug. 25. Poe as Duke of Buckingham in *Jane Shore.* Mrs. Hopkins in An Allemande.

Aug. 29. Mrs. Hopkins in Original Epilogue and [Julio] in *Deaf and Dumb.* Mr. Hopkins in Comic Song and Recitation.

Sept. 1. Mrs. Hopkins and Mr. Poe in an Allemande.

The Company may have been in Petersburg in November, but no file is available.

Dec. 8. Poe as Inkle, Hopkins as Trudge and Mrs. Hopkins as Narcissa in Colman's *Inkle and Yarico*. Also, Poe as Richard, Hopkins
as Sam and Mrs. Hopkins as Miss Peggy Plainway in Kenney's
Raising the Wind. Second cast repeated Jan. 5, 1805.

Dec. 19. Hopkins as Job Thornberry, Poe as Frank Rochdale, and Mrs.
Hopkins as Mary Thornberry in *John Bull*. Also, Poe as Charles in
The Village Lawyer.

Dec. 26. Poe as George Barnwell in *George Barnwell*. Also, Hopkins
as Billy Bluff, Poe as Tom Tough and Mrs. Hopkins as Sallie True-
heart in *Christmas Gambols,* comic ballet pantomime. Also, Mr.
and Mrs. Hopkins as Sharp and Melissa in *The Lying Valet*.

Jan. 3, 1805. Hopkins as Dr. Ollapod, Mrs. Hopkins as Emily Worth-
ington and Poe as Sir Charles Cropland in Colman's *The Poor
Gentleman*. Hopkins in Song and Minuet and Poe and Mrs.
Hopkins in A Strathspey. Also, Hopkins as Record, Mrs. Hopkins
as Clare and Poe as Le Sage in *The Adopted Child*. Cast of
Christmas Gambols repeated from Dec. 26, 1804.

Jan. 5. Hopkins as Sir Andrew Acid, Mrs. Hopkins as Honoria, and
Poe as Clairville in Reynolds' *Notoriety*. Also, Kenney's *Raising the
Wind*, repeated, with cast as on Jan. 5.

Jan. 18. Benefit of Mrs. Hopkins. Mrs. Hopkins in Song, Hornpipe and
Allemande.

1805

NORFOLK, Green's Virginia Company

Sources: *Norfolk Gazette and Public Ledger; Norfolk and Portsmouth
Herald,* as before.

April 6, 1805. Poe as Joey in Allingham's *Hearts of Oak*.

April 15. A Strathspey by Poe, Mrs. Green and Mrs. Hopkins after
George Barnwell.

May 1. Mrs. Hopkins as Annette in *Robin Hood*.

BALTIMORE, The Virginia Company at the Baltimore Theatre

Sources: *The Federal Gazette and Baltimore Daily Advertiser*.

June 7, 1805. David Poe as Young Norval in Home's *Douglas,* his first
appearance on the Baltimore stage.

RICHMOND, Haymarket Theatre

Source: *Virginia Gazette and Weekly Advertiser*.

Aug. 28, 1805. Mrs. Hopkins in a concert.

WASHINGTON, The Virginia Company at the Washington Theatre

SOURCES: *The National Intelligencer and Washington Advertiser.*

Sept. 9, 1805. Hopkins as Lord Priory in Mrs. Inchbald's *Wives as They Were and Maids as They Are.* Hopkins as Tiptoe and Mrs. Hopkins as Kitty in *Ways and Means; or, A Trip to Dover.*

Sept. 26. Poe as Joseph Surface and Hopkins as Sir Peter Teazle in *The School for Scandal.*

Oct. 2. Poe recites "Alonzo and Imogine" [sic]. Repeated Oct. 4.

Oct. 7. Mr. Hopkins' Benefit. *The Wife of Two Husbands,* parts not given.

Oct. 26. Hopkins dies.

Nov. 6. Mrs. Hopkins' Benefit. Lewis's *Adelmorn the Outlaw,* and Fielding's *Tom Thumb the Great,* parts not given.

Season closed December 21, 1805.

DAVID POE AND ELIZABETH HOPKINS

1806

RICHMOND, Green's Virginia Company, at the Richmond Theatre

SOURCES: Richmond newspapers, as before, especially *Virginia Gazette.*

Jan. 25, 1806. Mrs. Hopkins as Anna in Home's *Douglas.* A Hornpipe and Song by Mrs. Hopkins.

Jan. 29. Mrs. Hopkins as Charlotte in Moore's *The Gamester.*

Feb. 1. Poe as Mandeville and Mrs. Hopkins as Julia Clairville in Cumberland's *The Sailor's Daughter.* Mrs. Hopkins in song at end of play.

Feb. 5. Poe as Sir Larry M'Murragh and Mrs. Hopkins as Amy in Colman's *Who Wants a Guinea?* Also, Mrs. Hopkins as Miss Biddy Bellair. Repeated Feb. 8.

Feb. 8. Mrs. Hopkins as Nancy in Murphy's *Three Weeks After Marriage.*

Feb. 13. Mr. Poe as Villars and Mrs. Hopkins as Sophia Woodbine in Reynolds' *The Blind Bargain; or, Hear it Out.*

Feb. 15. Poe as Henry Morland and Mrs. Hopkins as Caroline Dormer in *The Heir at Law.*

Feb. 26, March 1. Poe as Harry Harebrain and Mrs. Hopkins as Miss Manly in Thomas Dibdin's *The Will for the Deed.* ("First time in America.") Also, Mrs. Hopkins as Julia in Mrs. Inchbald's *The Midnight Hour.*

March 29. Mrs. Hopkins' Benefit. Mrs. Hopkins as Matilda, Lady Randolph, in *Douglas.*

April 7. Mrs. Hopkins as Irene in *Blue Beard.*

DAVID AND ELIZABETH POE

April 10. Poe as Malford and Mrs. Poe as Mrs. Malford in *The Soldier's Daughter*.
Season lasted until May 18, but no casts given.

PHILADELPHIA, "New Theatre," Warren and Wood's Company

SOURCE: *American Daily Advertiser.*

June 20, 1806. Poe as Young Norval in *Douglas.* "His first appearance on this stage." Mrs. Poe as Rosina in *Rosina.*
June 23. Poe as Jack Analyse in *The Blind Bargain.* Mrs. Poe as Priscilla Tomboy in *The Romp.*
June 27. Poe as Fainwou'd in *Raising the Wind.*
June 30. Poe as Captain Loveit and Mrs. Poe as Biddy Bellair in *Miss in her Teens.*
July 4. Songs by Mrs. Poe.
July 7. Mrs. Poe as Agnes in *The Mountaineers.*
July 9. Poe as Switzer in *The Robbers.* Mrs. Poe as Miss Kitty Sprightly in Isaac Jackman's *All the World's A Stage.*

NEW YORK, The Summer Theatre, Vauxhall

SOURCE: G. C. D. Odell's *Annals of the New York Stage,* II, 272.

July 16, 1806. Mrs. Poe as Priscilla Tomboy.
July 18. Poe as Captain Belleville and Mrs. Poe as Rosina in *Rosina.* Also, Poe as Frank in Allingham's *Fortune's Frolic.*

1806-1807

BOSTON, Powell's Company at the Boston Theatre

SOURCES: For the three seasons in Boston, 1806-1809, search by Miss Mary S. Douglass through newspapers, *The Democrat, The Gazette, The Columbian Centinel, The Repertory, The Patriot, The New England Palladium, The Independent Chronicle,* all of Boston. These newspaper advertisements have been checked by *The Polyanthos,* III (Sept.-Nov., 1806), IV (Dec., 1806-March, 1807), V (April, 1807-July, 1807); *The Emerald,* I, II, N. S. I (1806-1808); Boston letters in *The Theatrical Censor and Critical Miscellany of Philadelphia,* Nos. 1-13 (Sept. 27, 1806-Dec. 30, 1806); also information furnished by Professor Milton Ellis and by Mrs. L. A. Hall, of the Harvard Theatre Collection. Article by W. K. Watkins, in *Boston Evening Transcript,* Jan. 13, 1909.

Oct. 13, 1806. Poe as Henry and Mrs. Poe as Miss Blandford in Morton's *Speed the Plough*. Also Mrs. Poe as Rosina in *Rosina*. First appearance of Poe in Boston, first appearance of Mrs. Poe there since 1796.

Oct. 15. Poe as Frederick and Mrs. Poe as Amelia Wildenhaim in Mrs. Inchbald's adaptation of *Lover's Vows*. Also, Mrs. Poe as Gillian in *The Quaker*.

Oct. 17. Poe as Charles Stanley, Mrs. Poe as Jessy Oatland in Morton's *A Cure for the Heart Ache*.

Oct. 20. Mrs. Poe sings "Just Like Love."

Oct. 22. Poe as George Barnwell in *George Barnwell*. Also, Mrs. Poe as Priscilla Tomboy.

Oct. 27. Poe as Sir George Touchwood in *The Belle's Stratagem*. Repeated Oct. 29. Also, Mrs. Poe as 1st Cottager in *Don Juan*. Repeated Nov. 10.

Oct. 29. Mrs. Poe as Leonora in Bickerstaffe's *The Padlock*.

Oct. 31. Mrs. Poe as Priscilla Tomboy.

Nov. 5. Poe as Valverde in Sheridan's adaptation, *Pizarro in Peru*.

Nov. 7. Mrs. Poe as Rose Sydney in *Secrets Worth Knowing*.

Nov. 10. Poe as Bellmour in Rowe's *Jane Shore*.

Nov. 12. Mrs. Poe as Fanny in Garrick's *Clandestine Marriage*. Also Virginia in *Paul and Virginia*.

Nov. 14. Poe as Maurice in Cobb's version of *The Wife of Two Husbands*.

Nov. 17. Poe as Bedemar in Otway's *Venice Preserved*. Repeated Nov. 26 and March 6, 1807. Also, Mrs. Poe as Maria in Burgoyne's *The Maid of the Oaks*.

Nov. 19. Poe as Frank Rochdale and Mrs. Poe as Mary Thornberry in *John Bull*. Also Mrs. Poe as Spring in *The Four Seasons*. Repeated Dec. 24.

Nov. 21. Poe as Armstrong and Mrs. Poe as Barbara in Colman's *The Iron Chest*. Repeated Nov. 24. Also Poe as Mr. Frank in *Fortune's Frolic*.

Dec. 1. Poe as Count Montalban in Tobin's *Honeymoon*. Mrs. Poe as Margaretta in *No Song No Supper*.

Dec. 3. Poe as Sir Harry in James Townley's *High Life Below Stairs*.

Dec. 10. Poe as Harry Stukely and Mrs. Poe as Kitty Sprightly in *All the World's A Stage*.

Dec. 17. Poe as Count Basset and Mrs. Poe as Miss Jenny in *The Provoked Husband*. Repeated Dec. 29. Also Poe as Dermot in *Dermot and Kathleen*. Repeated Dec. 22.

Dec. 31. Poe as Edward and Mrs. Poe as Laura Luckless in Thomas Dibdin's *Five Miles Off*. Also Poe as Khor and Mrs. Poe as Princess Lodoiska in Kemble's adaptation of *Lodoiska*.

Jan. 5, 1807. Poe as Altamont in Rowe's *The Fair Penitent*. Also Khor and Princess Lodoiska repeated.

Jan. 7. Poe as Frederick and Mrs. Poe as Mariana in *The Miser*, Fielding's adaptation of Molière.

Jan. 12. Poe as Harry Torrid in Edward Morris's *The Secret*. Mrs. Poe as Clorinda in *Robin Hood*.

Jan. 14. Poe as Osmyn in Turnbull's *The Maid of Hungary*.

Jan. 16. Poe as Beauchamp and Mrs. Poe as Sophy Pendragon in Mrs. Cowley's *Which is the Man?*

Jan. 19. Poe as Percy in *Castle Spectre*.

Jan. 21. Poe as Laertes to Cooper's *Hamlet*.

Jan. 26. Poe as Malcolm in *Macbeth*. Also Dermot in *Dermot and Kathleen*. See Dec. 17.

Jan. 28. Poe as Montano in *Othello*. Repeated Feb. 23.

Jan. 30. Poe as Tressel in *Richard III*. Also as Patie in *Patie and Peggy*.

Feb. 2. Poe as Frank in *Fortune's Frolic*.

Feb. 4. Poe as Duke of Medina in Beaumont and Fletcher's *Rule a Wife and Have a Wife*.

Feb. 11. Poe as Hassan in *The Castle Spectre*.

Feb. 16. Poe as Charles Surface in *The School for Scandal*. Also Ferdinand in Jephson's *Two Strings to your Bow*.

Feb. 25. Poe as Laertes to Fennell's *Hamlet*. Also Poe as Bagatelle and Mrs. Poe as Norah in *The Poor Soldier*.

March 2. Poe as George Barnwell in *George Barnwell*. [*King Lear* postponed on account of Fennell's illness. *Polyanthos IV*, 282.]

March 4. Mrs. Poe as Little Pickle.

March 6. Poe as Bedemar.

March 9. Poe as Sir Charles Freeman and Mrs. Poe as Cherry in *The Beaux Stratagem*.

March 11. Mrs. Poe as Cordelia to Fennell's *King Lear*. Repeated March 12. Also Little Pickle.

March 13. Poe as Duke of Austria and Mrs. Poe as Blanch in *King John*. Also Poe as Sergeant Jack and Mrs. Poe as Moggy in *The Highland Reel*.

March 16. Poe as Duke of Albany and Mrs. Poe as Cordelia in *King Lear*. Also Mrs. Poe as Lydia in Oulton's *The Sixty Third Letter*.

March 18. Poe as Blushenly in Cumberland's *The Natural Son*. Also Mrs. Poe as Leonora in *The Padlock*.

March 20. Poe as Colonel Raymond and Mrs. Poe as Fidelia, in Moore's *The Foundling*.

March 23. Poe as Francis in *The Stranger*. Also Mrs. Poe as Madame Peyrouse in *La Peyrouse*.

March 25. Poe as Orozimbo and Mrs. Poe as Cora in Morton's *Columbus*. Also Lenox and Mary in *The Rival Soldiers*.

March 26. Poe as Count Montalban and Mrs. Poe as Volante in Tobin's *Honeymoon*. Also Poe as Sir Harry in *High Life Below Stairs*.

March 30. Poe as Pylades in Ambrose Philips' *Distrest Mother*. Also Poe as Khor and Mrs. Poe as Princess Lodoiska.

April 1. Poe as Duke of Albany and Mrs. Poe as Cordelia in *King Lear*. Also Captain Loveit and Miss Biddy in *Miss In Her Teens*.

April 6. Poe as Decius Brutus in *Julius Caesar*. Mrs. Poe as Priscilla Tomboy.

April 8. Poe as Beef Eater and Mrs. Poe as Italian Girl in *The Critic*.

April 13. Poe as Sir Edward Specious and Mrs. Poe as Olivia in Reynolds' *The Delinquent*. Also Mrs. Poe as Lydia in Colman's *Love Laughs at Locksmiths*.

April 15. Mrs. Poe as Emily Worthington in Colman's *The Poor Gentleman*. Also Poe as Sir Bertrand and Mrs. Poe as Clara in *The Adopted Child*.

April 20. Mrs. Poe's Benefit. Poe as Young O'Donovan and Mrs. Poe as Sophia in O'Keeffe's *The Lie of a Day*. Also, Mrs. Poe as Sylvia in *Cymon and Sylvia*.

April 22. Mrs. Poe as Laura in Arnold's *The Agreeable Surprise*.

April 24. Poe as Ferdinand and Mrs. Poe as Ariel in *The Tempest*.

April 29. Poe as Marquis of Montague in Colman's *The Battle of Hexham*. Also Mrs. Poe as Spring in *The Four Seasons*. See Nov. 19, 1806.

May 1. Poe as Fernando in Cypriani's pantomime, *The Algerine Pirate*.

May 4. Poe as Melchior in M. G. Lewis's *Alfonso, King of Castile*. Also Jack Junk in *The Boston Sailors*. Also Mrs. Poe as Molly Maybush in *The Farmer*.

May 6. Poe as Bertrand in Tobin's *The Curfew*. Repeated May 15. Also Mrs. Poe as Betsey Blossom in *The Deaf Lover*.

May 8. Poe as Melville and Mrs. Poe as Sally Williams in Dunlap's *Glory of Columbia*. Also Mrs. Poe as Lydia in *Love Laughs at Locksmiths*.

May 11. Song by Mrs. Poe, dance by Poe.

May 15. Mrs. Poe as Fanny Atkins in *The Mogul Tale*.

May 18. Poe as Contarino and Mrs. Poe as Rosamonda in *Abaellino, the Great Bandit*. Also Doodle and Queen Dollalolla in Fielding's *The Tragedy of Tragedies*.

May 20. Mrs. Poe as Mrs. Malfort in *The Soldier's Daughter*. Also Josephine in *The Children in the Wood*.

May 22. Benefit of Mr. and Mrs. Poe. *The Curfew*. Poe as Bertrand. Also A Double Hornpipe by Mrs. Poe and Signor Cipriani. Also

The Tragedy of Tragedies. Poe as Doodle and Mrs. Poe as Queen Dollalolla.

May 25. Poe as Jack Junk in *The Bostc:.. Sailors.* Also Mrs. Poe as Eliza in *The Flitch of Bacon.*

Theatrical season closed with this performance.

1807-1808

BOSTON (continued)

Sept. 18, 1807. Mrs. Poe as Rosina in *Rosina;* also as Clorinda in *Robin Hood.*

Sept. 21. Mrs. Poe as Donna Clara in Sheridan's *The Duenna.* Poe as Captain Seymour in *The Irishman in London.*

Sept. 28. Poe as Bertrand in Tobin's *The Curfew.*

Oct. 2. Poe as Count Montalban and Mrs. Poe as Zamora in Tobin's *Honeymoon.*

Oct. 5. Mrs. Poe as Cordelia in *King Lear.*

Oct. 9. Poe as Captain Glenroy and Mrs. Poe as Rosalie Somers in Morton's *Town and Country.* Repeated Oct. 16.

Oct. 14. Mrs. Poe as Little Pickle in *The Spoiled Child.*

Oct. 22. Poe as Mandeville in *He Would be a Soldier;* also, Mrs. Poe as Peace, in a military and naval spectacle.

Oct. 26. Poe as Sir Richard Vernon in *Henry IV;* Mrs. Poe as Genevieve in Dimond's *The Hunter of the Alps.*

Oct. 30. Mrs. Poe as Ophelia in *Hamlet* and Leonora in *The Padlock.*

Nov. 2. Poe as Contarino and Mrs. Poe as Rosamonda in *Abaellino, the Great Bandit.*

Nov. 6. Poe as Salanio and Mrs. Poe as Jessica in *Merchant of Venice;* also Mrs. Poe as Narcissa in *Inkle and Yarico.*

Nov. 9. Poe as Francis in *The Stranger;* also, Poe as Khor and Mrs. Poe as the Princess in *Lodoiska.*

Nov. 16. Poe as Norfolk in *Henry VIII;* also, Mrs. Poe as Lydia in *The Sixty-Third Letter.*

Nov. 30. Mrs. Poe as Variella in Kenney's *The Weathercock.* Repeated Feb. 26, 1808.

Dec. 2. Poe as Altamont in *The Fair Penitent.*

Dec. 14 [or 16]. Mrs. Poe as Maria in Burgoyne's *Maid of the Oaks.*

Dec. 18. Mrs. Poe as Mrs. Malfort in *The Soldier's Daughter.*

Dec. 30. Poe as Henry Morland and Mrs. Poe as Cicely Homespun in *The Heir at Law.*

Jan. 4, 1808. Mrs. Poe as Maria in *Of Age Tomorrow.*

Jan. 8. Poe as Charles Stanley and Mrs. Poe as Jessy Oatland in *A Cure for the Heart Ache.*

Jan. 11. Poe as the Duke of Albany and Mrs. Poe as Cordelia in *King Lear.*

Jan. 15. Poe as Milford in *The Road to Ruin.*

Jan. 25. Poe as Tressel in *Richard III;* also Captain Heartwell in The *Prize.*

Jan. 29. Mrs. Poe as Ophelia in *Hamlet;* Poe as Sandford in *Who's The Dupe?*

Feb. 1. Poe as the Duke of Albany and Mrs. Poe as Cordelia in *King Lear;* Poe as Scruple in Colman's *Ways and Means.*

Feb. 5. Poe as Dawson in Moore's *The Gamester.*

Feb. 8. Poe as Volusius in *Coriolanus;* also Sandford in *Who's the Dupe?*

Feb. 15. Poe as Malcolm in *Macbeth.*

Feb. 18. Mrs. Poe as Mary Tactic in *The Rival Soldiers.*

Feb. 22. Mrs. Poe as Phoebe Whitethorn in *The Wags of Windsor.*

Feb. 26. Mrs. Poe as Variella in *The Weathercock.*

March 4. Mrs. Poe as Virginia in *Paul and Virginia.*

March 7. Mrs. Poe as Albina in Reynolds' *The Will.*

March 11. Mrs. Poe as Arabella in Mrs. Cowley's *More Ways Than One;* also Fatima in *Blue Beard.*

March 14. Poe as Brenno and Mrs. Poe as Herman in *Adelmorn the Outlaw;* also, Mrs. Poe as Clara in *The Adopted Child.*

March 16. Mrs. Poe sang a song in *The Sailor's Daughter.*

March 21. Benefit of Mr. and Mrs. Poe. Poe as Ataliba and Mrs. Poe as Cora in *The Virgin of the Sun;* Mrs. Poe as Selina in *A Tale of Mystery.*

March 25. Poe as Elvirus in *Such Things Are;* Mrs. Poe as Pleasure in *Harlequin's Choice.*

April 8, 11. Poe as Sir Arthur Tessel and Mrs Poe as Zelidy in Henry Siddons' *Time Tells a Tale.*

April 14. Poe as Claransforth and Mrs. Poe as Ellen Metland in Mrs. Inchbald's alteration of Kotzebue's *The Wise Man of the East.*

April 18. Benefit of Mr. and Mrs. Poe. Poe as Francis De Moor and Mrs. Poe as Amelia in Hodgkinson's adaptation of Schiller's *The Robbers;* also, Poe as Elector and Mrs. Poe as Ella in *Ella Rosenberg.*

April 25. Poe as Tourly and Mrs. Poe as Sophia Woodbine in *The Blind Bargain.*

1808

RICHMOND, The Haymarket Theatre

July 11, 1808. Mr. and Mrs. Poe in an Entertainment.

1808-1809

BOSTON, Powell's Company at the Boston Theatre

Oct. 19, 1808. Poe as Edmund and Mrs. Poe as Cordelia in *King Lear*. Poe as Captain Hartwell in *The Prize*.

Oct. 26. Poe as Montano in *Othello*. Also, Captain Le Brush in *The Register Office*.

Nov. 4. Mrs. Poe sings "Nobody Coming to Marry Me."

Nov. 9. Mrs. Poe in "A Favorite Song."

Nov. 14. Poe as Carlton and Mrs. Poe as Arabella in Mrs. Cowley's *More Ways Than One*.

Nov. 16. Poe as Henry in *Speed the Plough*.

Nov. 18. Mrs. Poe as Queen Dollalolla in *Life and Death of Tom Thumb the Great*.

Nov. 23. Poe as Ennui in *The Dramatist*.

Dec. 2. Poe as Freeman in *The Quaker's Wedding*.

Dec. 5. Poe as Grist the Miller in *Harlequin Dr. Faustus; or The Magician Tricked*.

Dec. 7. Poe as Hephestion in *Alexander the Great; or, The Rival Queens*.

Dec. 9. Poe as Saunders in *The Jew*.

Dec. 14. Poe as Dauntless in Kenney's *The World*. Repeated Dec. 19 and 28.

Dec. 23. Poe as Captain Standish in *The Pilgrims; or, The Landing of Our Forefathers at Plymouth Rock*. Repeated Jan. 2, 1809.

Jan. 4, 1809. Poe as Leczinsky and Mrs. Poe as a Peasant in *The Brazen Mask; or, Alberto and Rosabella*.

Jan. 6. Mr. Poe as Virolet in *The Mountaineers*. Also Poe and Mrs. Poe in *The Brazen Mask* as on Jan. 4.

Jan. 9. Poe as Leonard Melmouth in Reynolds' *Folly as it Flies*. Also *The Brazen Mask*, same cast as on Jan. 4.

Jan. 13. Poe as Duke of Medina in Beaumont and Fletcher's *Rule A Wife and Have A Wife*. Also *The Brazen Mask*, same cast as on Jan. 4.

Jan. 16. Poe as Dauntless in *The World*.

Jan. 18. Poe as Lover in *Don Juan*.

Jan. 20. *The Brazen Mask*. Poe as Leczinsky and Mrs. Poe [?] as a Peasant. [Announced in *Gazette* of Jan. 19.] See p. 30 for explanation.

Jan. 25. Poe as Belmour in *Jane Shore*.

Jan. 27. Poe as Theodore in *The Purse; or, Benevolent Tar*.

Feb. 3. Poe as Belville in Garrick's alteration from Wycherley's *The Country Wife*.

Feb. 10. Poe as Contarino and Mrs. Poe as Rosamonda in *Abaellino, the Great Bandit.*

Feb. 15. Mrs. Poe as Emily in Kenney's *False Alarms.* Repeated Feb. 24.

Feb. 22. Mrs. Poe as Antonia in Dibdin's *Two Faces Under a Hood.* Also, Charlotte in *The Apprentice.*

March 6. Mrs. Poe as Marcella in *A Bold Stroke for a Husband.*

March 15. Mrs. Poe as Christina in *Gustavus Vasa.*

March 17. Mrs. Poe as Female Volunteer in "A Military Interlude."

March 20. Mrs. Poe as Rachael in Colman's *Feudal Times.*

March 24. Mrs. Poe as Emma in Colman's *We Fly by Night.* Repeated April 3.

April 5. Mrs. Poe as Palmyra in Voltaire's *Mahomet* to Payne's Zaphna.

April 7. Mrs. Poe as Juliet to Payne's Romeo.

April 10. Mrs. Poe as Irene in John Brown's *Barbarossa,* to Payne's Achmet (Selim).

April 14. Mrs. Poe as Sigismunda to Payne's Tancred in James Thomson's *Tancred and Sigismunda.*

April 17. Payne's Benefit. Poe as Laertes and Mrs. Poe as Ophelia to Payne's Hamlet.

April 19. Benefit of Mrs. Poe. Poe as Alonzo and Mrs. Poe as Cora in *Pizarro* to Payne's Rolla. Also, Poe as Darina and Mrs. Poe as Abdalla in *Il Bondocani.*

April 21. Poe as Laertes and Mrs. Poe as Ophelia in *Hamlet.*

April 24. Mrs. Poe as Marianne in *The Miser.*

April 26. Mrs. Poe as a Female Volunteer. Repetition of March 17.

May 5. Mrs. Poe as Cordelia in *King Lear.*

May 10. Mrs. Poe as Marianna in Fennell's *Lindor and Clara.*

May 12. Mrs. Poe as Miss Marchmont in Kelly's *False Delicacy.*

1809-1810

NEW YORK, Price and Cooper's Company at The Park Theatre

SOURCES: Personal search in *New York Commercial Advertiser* and *New York Evening Post,* checked by G. C. D. Odell's *Annals of the New York Stage,* Vol. II; *The Ramblers' Magazine and New-York Theatrical Register,* for the Season of 1809-10, Vol. I. Dunlap's *History of the American Theatre,* Vol. II.

Sept. 6, 1809. Poe as Hassan and Mrs. Poe as Angela in M. G. Lewis's *The Castle Spectre.* Also, Captain Sightly and Priscilla Tomboy in *The Romp.*

Sept. 8. Poe as Davilla, Mrs. Poe as Cora in *Pizarro.* Also, Captain Belleville and Rosina in *Rosina.*

Sept. 11. Poe as Rosencranz and Bernardo, Mrs. Poe as Ophelia to Cooper's Hamlet. Also, Eugene and Laura in Arnold's *The Agreeable Surprise.*

Sept. 13. Poe as Sanchio in *Rule a Wife and Have a Wife,* and Lindorf in Prince Hoare's *Is He a Prince?*

Sept. 15. Poe as First Robber and Mrs. Poe as Morgiana in *The Forty Thieves; Is He a Prince?* repeated.

Sept. 18. Poe as Falieri and Mrs. Poe as Rosamonda to Cooper's *Abaellino.* Also Poe as Captain Sightly, Mrs. Poe as Priscilla Tomboy in *The Romp.*

Sept. 20. Same parts as on Sept. 15 in *Forty Thieves.*

Sept. 22. Poe as Julian, Mrs. Poe as Imma in M. G. Lewis's *Adelgitha.*

Sept. 25. Mrs. Poe as Desdemona; also Poe as Captain Sightly, Mrs. Poe as Priscilla Tomboy in *The Romp.*

Sept. 27. Poe as Alonzo in *Pizarro;* also Poe as Eugene and Mrs. Poe as Laura in *The Agreeable Surprise,* repetition of Sept. 11.

Sept. 29. Poe as Malcolm in *Macbeth,* also Poe as Almarick and Mrs. Poe as Elisena in Thomas Dibdin's *Princess and No Princess; or, The Forest of Hermanstadt.*

Oct. 2. Poe as Ratcliff and Mrs. Poe as the Prince [Edward] in *Richard III.* Also Poe as Almarick and Mrs. Poe as Elisena, as on September 29.

Oct. 4. Bertha in Charles Kemble's *The Point of Honor. Forty Thieves* repeated, no cast given.

Oct. 6. Poe as Amos in Mrs. Inchbald's *To Marry or Not to Marry.* Mrs. Poe as Phoebe Whitethorn in *The Wags of Windsor.*

Oct. 9. Poe as Amos, repetition of Oct. 6. Poe as Almerick and Mrs. Poe as Elisena, repetition of Sept. 29.

Oct. 11. Poe as Amos. Poe as First Robber and Mrs. Poe as Morgiana; both repetitions.

Oct. 13. Poe as Julian and Mrs. Poe as Imma in *Adelgitha.* Mrs. Poe as Josephine in *Children of the Wood.*

Oct. 16. Poe as Virolet in *The Mountaineers.* Poe as First Robber and Mrs. Poe as Morgiana, repetition.

Oct. 18. Poe as Capt. Cypress in Richard Leigh's *Grieving's a Folly.* [His last appearance on the stage.] Mrs. Poe as Josephine in *Children in the Wood.*

Oct. 20. Mrs. Poe as a Fisherwoman in *Don Juan.* Repeated Nov. 15.

Oct. 25. Little Pickle in *The Spoiled Child.*

Oct. 27. Rosina in *Rosina.*

Nov. 1. Jessica in *The Merchant of Venice.*

Nov. 3. [Charlotte] in Fielding's *Mock Doctor.* Repeated Nov. 8.

Nov. 4. [Little Pickle.]

Nov. 6. Mrs. Poe as Zamora (Eugenio) in Tobin's *Honeymoon.* Also
　　[Priscilla Tomboy].
Nov. 11. Emma in *We Fly By Night.* Repeated Dec. 1.
Nov. 17. Laura in *Lock and Key.*
Nov. 18. Peggy in *Raising the Wind.*
Nov. 20. Parisatis in Lee's *Alexander the Great; or, The Rival Queens.*
Nov. 22. Imma in *Adelgitha;* repetition of September 22.
Nov. 24. Prince of Wales in *Richard III.*
Nov. 25. Judith in *The Young Quaker.*
Nov. 27. Rosabelle in *The Foundling of the Forest.* Repeated Nov. 29,
　　Dec. 1, 22 [no cast].
Dec. 1. Emma in *We Fly By Night.*
Dec. 2. Elisena in *Princess and No Princess.*
Dec. 6. Teresa in M. G. Lewis's *Venoni.* Repeated Dec. 8, 15, 28.
Dec. 8. Dolly Bull in *John Bull at Fontainbleau.*
Dec. 11. Cora in *Pizarro.* Also Dolly Bull.
Dec. 13. Rosabelle in *Foundling of the Forest,* and Margaretta in
　　No Song No Supper.
Dec. 18. Miss Ogle in *The Belle's Stratagem.* [Dolly Bull.]
Dec. 26. Lucy in *George Barnwell.*
Jan. 12, 1810. Miss Ogle in *Belle's Stratagem.* Repeated Jan. 15.

The Park Theatre was closed from January 16 to February 22, 1810.

Feb. 23. Rosabelle and Dolly Bull repeated.
Feb. 28. Miss Ogle and [Little Pickle] repeated.
March 2. Rosabelle repeated. Peggy in *Raising the Wind.*
March 5. Cora in *Pizarro* to Payne's Rolla.
March 7. Ophelia to Payne's Hamlet.
March 9. Juliet to Payne's Romeo. Peggy in *Raising the Wind,* re-
　　peated also on April 4.
March 12. The Widow Bellair in Allingham's *The Widow; or, Who
　　Wins?* Repeated March 23.
March 14. Margaretta in *No Song No Supper.*
March 19. Elisena in *Princess and No Princess,* repeated. Dorothy in
　　Reynolds' *Laugh When You Can.*
March 21. Miss Godfrey in Foote's *The Lyar.*
March 26. Lucetta in Hoadly's *The Suspicious Husband.* Also, Gene-
　　vieve in *The Hunter of the Alps.*
March 28. Cherry in *Beaux Stratagem.* Phoebe Whitethorn in *Wags
　　of Windsor.*
April 6. Genevieve in *Hunter of the Alps,* repeated.
April 11. Juliet to Dwyer's Romeo.

April 16. Leonora in *Two Strings to Your Bow; or, A Servant with Two Masters.*

The Theatre was closed April 18 to April 27.

April 27. Catharine in Reynolds' *The Exile.* Repeated May 7.
May 4. Biddy Bellair.
May 9. Rosabelle in *Foundling of the Forest,* repeated.
May 14. Imma in *Adelgitha;* repeated.
May 16. Eliza in *Riches,* Burges's adaptation of *The City Madam.*
May 23. Ophelia to Cooper's Hamlet. Emily Melville in R. C. Dallas's *Not at Home.*
May 25. Valeria in Coriolanus. Emily Melville repeated, also on June 4 and June 8.
May 28. Regan to Cooper's Lear. Also, Ruth in Knight's *The Honest Thieves.*
May 30. Parisatis in *Alexander the Great.* Ruth repeated.
June 6. Zamora in *Honeymoon.*
June 8. Catharine in *The Exile.*
June 11. Taffline in *Town and Country.*
June 13. Ulrica in Reynolds' *The Free Knights; or, The Edict of Charlemagne.*
June 15. Josephine in *Children of the Wood,* repeated.
June 18. Edward in Mrs. Inchbald's *Every One Has His Fault.*
June 20. Mrs. Poe sings "Nobody Coming to Marry Me." [As a part of a long series of songs by the Company.]
June 22. Laura in *The Agreeable Surprise.*
June 25. Rosabelle in *The Foundling of the Forest.* Virginia in *Paul and Virginia.*
June 29. Rosa in Reynolds' *The Caravan.*
July 2. Benefit of Mrs. Poe. Rosamonda in *Abaellino.* Narcissa in Colman's *Inkle and Yarico.*
July 4. Ulrica in *The Free Knights* and Rosa in *The Caravan.*

1810

RICHMOND, Placide's Company at the Richmond Theatre

SOURCES: Search in newspapers as above.

Aug. 18, 1810. Mrs. Poe as Angela in *The Castle Spectre;* Maria in *Of Age Tomorrow.*
Aug. 24. Florence in Tobin's *The Curfew;* Emma Bastion in Colman's *We Fly By Night.*

Sept. 11. Little Pickle.

Sept. 21. Mrs. Poe's Benefit. [Letitia Hardy] in *The Belle's Stratagem.* Song by Mrs. Poe. Also, Allemande in Act 3 of *A Masquerade.*

1811

CHARLESTON, Placide's Company at Charleston Theatre

SOURCES: Search in *Charleston Courier,* as before.

Jan. 23, 1811. Angela in *The Castle Spectre;* Priscilla Tomboy in *The Romp.*

Jan. 28. Jacintha in Hoadley's *The Suspicious Husband.* Repeated March 9.

Jan. 30. Louisa Courtney in *The Dramatist.* Also, Little Pickle.

Feb. 1. Maria in *Of Age Tomorrow.* Repeated Feb. 20, March 1, May 7.

Feb. 4. Nymph in *Telemachus.* Repeated April 3.

Feb. 6. Rosina in *Rosina.* Repeated Feb. 8.

Feb. 9. Leonora in *The Padlock.*

Feb. 15. Lydia Languish in *The Rivals.* Also, Melissa in Garrick's *The Lying Valet,* repeated April 24.

Feb. 16. Agnes in Colman's *The Mountaineers.* Repeated Feb. 27.

Feb. 22. Letitia Hardy in *The Belle's Stratagem.* Josephine in *The Children in the Wood.*

Feb. 25. Lady Eleanor in Mrs. Inchbald's *Every One Has His Fault.*

Feb. 26. Susan Ashfield in Morton's *Speed the Plough.* Also, Louisa in *The Irishman in London.*

Feb. 27. Kitty in *Ways and Means.*

March 2. Lady Teazle in *School for Scandal.*

March 4. Jane in *Wild Oats.* Also, Miss Grantam in *The Lyar.*

March 6. Caroline Dormer in *The Heir at Law.*

March 9. Dimity in *Three Weeks After Marriage.*

March 13. Ismena in *The Sultan.*

March 15. Molly Maybush in O'Keeffe's *The Farmer.*

March 20. Rosabelle in *The Foundling of the Forest.* Repeated March 27. Also, Florella in Prince Hoare's *My Grandmother.*

March 21. At St. Cecelia's Society Concert Room. Song, "When Ruddy Aurora."

March 23. Christine in *Tekeli.*

March 25. Laura in *The Agreeable Surprise.* Repeated March 29.

March 27. Margaretta in *No Song No Supper.*

April 1. Mopsa in *A Winter's Tale.* Repeated April 17.

April 3. A Savoyard in *The Stranger*. (Sings.) Nymph in *Telemachus*.

April 15. Flora in Mrs. Inchbald's *The Midnight Hour*. Also, Dolly O'Daisy in Pocock's *Hit or Miss*. Also, Columbine in *Whim Upon Whim*.

April 16. At Sollee's Concert Room. Two songs by Mrs. Poe.

April 17. Donna Clara in Robert Jephson's *Two Strings to Your Bow*.

April 19. Francisca in *Don Juan*.

April 22. Nerissa in *The Merchant of Venice*. Also, Sally in Cross's *The Purse*.

April 26. "A Grace" in *Cinderella*.

April 29. Mrs. Poe's Benefit. Violante in *The Wonder*. Also, Lady (with a song) in *Hurry Scurry*. Also, Moggy McGilpin in *The Highland Reel*.

May 2. Fanny in Arnold's *Man and Wife*. Also, Irene in *Blue Beard*.

May 7. Nancy Joblin in W. C. White's *The Poor Lodger*; Maria, in *Of Age Tomorrow*; Columbine in pantomime.

May 14. Albina in *The Grandfather's Will*. Also, Nancy in T. C. Cross's *Blackbeard, The Pirate*.

May 16. Floribel in Dimond's *The Doubtful Son*. Nancy as on May 14.

May 18. A Song.

May 20. Emma in *The Birthday*. Almeida in *Blackbeard*. Lucy in *The Review; or, The Wags of Windsor*.

NORFOLK, Placide's Company at the Norfolk Theatre

July 26, 1811. Benefit of Mrs. Poe and Miss Thomas. [Donna Violante] in *The Wonder*. [Leonora] in *The Padlock*.

RICHMOND, Placide's Company at The Richmond Theatre. Season opened Aug. 16. A number of plays in which Mrs. Poe had acted are announced but no casts are given at first.

SOURCES: Richmond newspapers, as before, especially *The Patriot*.

Sept. 20, 1811. Mrs. Poe as one of the "Graces" in *Cinderella*.

Sept. 25. Bridget in Charles Kemble's *Budget of Blunders*.

Sept. 27. Emily Bloomfield in Dr. Ioor's *The Battle of Eutaw*.

Oct. 9. Mrs. Poe's benefit. Her name does not appear on the bills. She may have played her old parts, [Parisatis] in *Alexander the Great*; [Lydia] in *Love Laughs at Locksmiths*.

Oct. 11. Countess Wintersen in *The Stranger*.

[Her last appearance on the stage.]

II. ORIGINAL RECORDS OF THE POE AND CLEMM FAMILIES IN BALTIMORE [1]

Entries from First Presbyterian Church Record

John Hancock Poe, son of David and Elisabeth Poe, b. August 25, 1776; baptized 13 September, 1776.

David, son of David and Elisabeth Poe, b. July 18, 1784, bapt. 21 September 1784.

George Washington, son of David and Elisabeth Poe, b. August 21, 1782; bapt. Oct. 6.

William, son of David and Elisabeth Poe, b. March 2, 1780; bapt. April 14, 1780.

Samuel, son of David and Elisabeth Poe, b. Dec. 21, 1787; bapt. Feb. 17, 1788.

Mary, dau. of David and Elisabeth Poe, b. March 17, 1790; bapt. June 6, 1790.

Elisabeth, dau. of David and Elisabeth Poe, b. Sept. 26, 1792; bapt. Dec. 16, 1792.

Married, Jan. 4, 1803, Jacob Poe and Bridget Kennedy.

Married, May 1, 1804, William Clemm, Jr., and Harriet Poe.

Baptized March 3, 1816, Jacob Poe, born, Oct. 11, 1776.

Baptized, March 3, 1816, James Mosher Poe, born, January 3, 1812.

Buried, August 2, 1831, W. H. Poe, aged 24.

John, son of Jacob and Bridget Poe, b. March 24, 1805.

George, son of Jacob and Bridget Poe, b. March 20, 1807; bapt. August 2, 1807.

Amelia, dau. of Jacob and Bridget Poe, b. August 11, 1809.

Neilson, son of Jacob and Bridget Poe, b. August 11, 1809.

Entries from St. Paul's Protestant Episcopal Church Record

Harriet, wife of William Clemm, born March 29, 1785; bapt. June 14, 1809; buried, January 8, 1815.

---

[1] These records I owe to the courtesy of Mr. Louis H. Dielman, Secretary of the Peabody Institute of Baltimore, who obtained access to the original church records.

Georgianna Maria, dau. of William and Harriet Clemm, born, December 1, 1810; bapt. September 19, 1811.

Harriett Mary Elizabeth Clemm, dau. of William and Harriett Clemm, bapt. Oct. 2, 1816; born ———.

Josephine Emily, dau. of William and Harriet Clemm, b. August 13, 1808; bapt. June 14, 1809.

William Eichelberger, son of William and Harriet Clemm, born, Oct. 11, 1806; bapt. June 25, 1807.

William Clemm m. July 12, 1817, to Maria Poe.

William Clemm, buried, February 9, 1826, aet. 47.[2]

Henry Clemm, son of William and Maria Clemm, born, 10 Sept. 1818; bapt. 15 Nov. '18.

Josephine Emily, dau. of William and Harriet Clemm, born Aug. 13, 1808; baptized June 14, 1809.

Virginia Eliza, dau. of William and Maria Clemm, born Aug. 15, 1822; bapt. November 5, 1822.

Virginia Maria, dau. of William and Maria Clemm, born, Aug. 22, 1820, bapt. March 13, 1821.

Virginia *Sarah* Clemm, buried, Nov. 5, 1822, aged 2 years.

Virginia Maria and Virginia Sarah are probably identical persons; as the dates fit. They appear thus on the register.

[2] "Died this morning, William Clemm, in 47th year." *Baltimore Gazette*, Wednesday, 8 February, 1826.

III. EDGAR POE'S BIRTHPLACE

According to Walter K. Watkins—an antiquarian of Boston—Henry Haviland, a stucco worker, bought a tract of land on Carver, then Haskins Street, and built a brick house there and some wooden structures. Watkins found this information in the Suffolk Registry of Deeds, where he also discovered that the only land owned by Haviland was on Carver Street and no one of the name of Haviland owned land on Hollis Street. I found Henry Haviland in the City Directory for 1809 as living on Carver Street. In the Tax Records of 1808 I found the entry (shown on page 728) in the Ward 12 Street Book (which does not give streets or numbers). This was known as the "Taking Book."

This list seems to agree with Watkins' statement that the men lived in the house belonging to Henry Haviland. A similar entry in 1809 does not give David Poe's name. Since these lists were apparently made up in May, he may have been at the same residence in January, 1809, as in 1808.

The claim for 33 Hollis Street is based on the alphabetical index in the "Transfer Book" of 1808, made up from the above Occupational list in the "Taking Book." I was unable to check the alphabetical list for 1808 or 1809 in the Assessor's Office in Boston, since owing to the work then being done by the Works Projects Administration, they were not available. Assuming, however, that the facsimile of the "Transfer Book" given in the *Boston Herald* article on January 14, 1909, is correct there is an apparent error in the argument for Hollis Street. The entry reads:

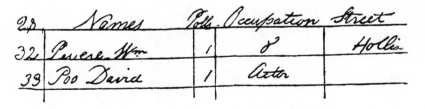

Those who believe in the Hollis Street house have concluded that "33" means the house number, and that the blank opposite David Poe's

ENTRIES IN THE "TAKING BOOK" IN THE BOSTON TAX RECORDS OF 1808

33	1808	Occupation	Polls	Real Estate	Per[sonal] Es[tate]	Owners	To Whom assessed	Remarks
H.P.	David Pow Poo [sic]	actor	1	800	600	H. Haviland	H	A
G.H.	Daniel Grover	actor	1	600	600	" "	:	A
B.H.	Joshua Barrett	rope maker	1	600	600	" "	:	A
A.H.	Moses Arden	rope maker	1	600	600	" "	:	ん
H.	Henry Haviland	stucco worker	1	1800	2000	H	H	

name under the column "Street" means "ditto." But the "33" refers not to the house number but to the page of the original "Taking Book" from which the extract has been made (see p. 728). The blank is not equivalent to a ditto mark. I examined records of other years, and repetitions of the names of streets are indicated by ditto marks and not by blanks. The omission of the name of the street was due to the fact that Carver Street was then unnamed, and was known unofficially as Haskins Street, from John Haskins, who had owned the land.[1] The evidence is not conclusive as to either house, but there seems less support for the Hollis Street number than for the other.

[1] See Walter K. Watkins' "Where Was Poe Born," *Boston Transcript,* January 13, 1909. Anonymous article, "Poe's Father Lived in Hollis Street," *Boston Herald,* January 14, 1909. The best summary is given by W. K. Watkins in the *Boston Transcript,* January 30, 1924, in which he replies to Joseph E. Chamberlin's article in the *Transcript* of January 26, 1924.

IV. THE POE FAMILY IN NORFOLK IN 1811

Much as I would like to establish the presence of David Poe, Jr., in Norfolk in 1811, as given by Mrs. Weiss, *Home Life of Poe*, pp. 1-4, her account, based upon the recollections of her mother, must be disregarded. Mrs. Weiss begins:

"'At this time,' continued my mother, 'we were living on Main Street, and my uncle, Dr. Robert Butt, of the House of Burgesses, lived close by, on Burmuda [sic] Street.'" She then proceeds to draw the picture of Mr. and Mrs. Poe, the two children, and an "old Welsh nurse," who she declares was Mrs. Poe's mother, as living next door to Dr. Butt.

Seldom has one sentence contained so many errors. The statement of Mr. Marshall W. Butt, Genealogist, of Portsmouth, Virginia, to the present writer, is conclusive:

(*a*) Virginia had no legislative body in the year 1811 known as the "House of Burgesses," this body having been succeeded, after the Revolution, by the "General Assembly." (See the journals of both bodies.)

(*b*) No person named Robert Butt sat as a member of the House of Burgesses of Virginia at any time. (See the "Journals of the House of Burgesses," published by the Virginia State Library, of which I have a complete set.)

(*c*) There is no family tradition and, to my knowledge, no official nor private record to the effect that a Robert Butt ever resided in Norfolk—Borough, Town or City. (My investigations of this name have been exhaustive.)

Robert Butt, my great, great, grandfather, died in 1803 (Nfk. County Will Bk. 4, pg. 18). He was not a doctor but a farmer living in Norfolk County (Nfk. County deeds and family records). He represented Norfolk County in the General Assembly of Virginia for the sessions of 1792, 1794, and 1799/1800. (See official records of this body.) He married first, Miss Tucker (from whom I descend) and secondly, Miss Sylvester, who was related to a family named Archer (family records). Mrs. Weiss' mother was, I believe, a Miss Archer. By his first wife, Robert Butt became father of one child, a son, Robert Bruce Butt, who was a physician but who, in 1811, was only twenty-two years old and unmarried. He was never a member of the General Assembly nor did he ever live in Norfolk. His home, in Portsmouth, is still standing. I am quite positive there were no other Robert Butts living in this vicinity at the time and must conclude that Mrs. Weiss or her mother or both were mistaken.

Very sincerely,

MARSHALL W. BUTT.

V. WHERE DID ELIZABETH POE DIE?

By Elizabeth Valentine Huntley and Louise F. Catterall,
of the Valentine Museum

Some recent biographers of Edgar Allan Poe have identified as the house in which his mother, Mrs. David Poe, died, a small brick building still standing in Richmond on the north side of Main Street between 22nd and 23rd. The building, now numbered 2220½ East Main Street, is set back from the street, in the rear of other houses. West of it, flush with Main Street, stands a row of three brick tenements, back of which are several small brick buildings, formerly kitchens. East of it, occupying the northwest corner of Main and 23rd Streets, is a large brick building, with the remains of a blocked-up archway still visible on the 23rd Street side. According to the Poe biographers, the three brick tenements were formerly actors' boarding houses, and the big corner building was the old Indian Queen Tavern. Carriages are said to have driven through the arched entrance on 23rd Street. The little house in which Mrs. Poe is said to have died, on December 8, 1811, is stated to have been occupied by a milliner whose name is variously given as Mrs. Fipps, Mrs. Phepoe, or Mrs. Phillips.

Susan Archer Weiss, in *The Home Life of Poe,* says that Mrs. Poe "was boarding at Mrs. Fipps', a milliner on Main Street." Her authority for this is Miss Mackenzie, Rosalie Poe's foster sister; but she gives no authority for the further statement that Mrs. Fipps's shop was between 15th and 17th Streets.

Hervey Allen's *Israfel* and Mary E. Phillips's *Edgar Allan Poe—the Man* go into much greater detail. Both give photographs showing the present appearance of the buildings in question. See *Poe the Man,* pp. 83-85, and *Israfel,* through Chapter I.

The accuracy of these theories about the location of Mrs. Poe's deathplace is open to serious question. They are based largely, we believe, on information given to Miss Phillips and Mr. Allen by the late James H. Whitty. We were led to question the theories through a study of the late Edward V. Valentine's manuscripts on old Richmond, which are now a part of the Valentine Museum collection. Detailed study of the tax books of the city of Richmond, the Richmond and Henrico County deed books, the fire insurance records of the Mutual Assurance Society, and advertisements in the 1811 Richmond newspapers substantiate the evidence of Mr. Valentine's notes.

In order for the theories to be true, the half-block in question, constituting Lot 38 in the old plan of the city of Richmond, must have contained in 1811 the following buildings: three undetached brick "actors' boarding houses," the small brick house said to have been Mrs. Phillips's shop, and the brick building said to have been the Indian Queen Tavern. All of them are still standing today, approximately as follows:

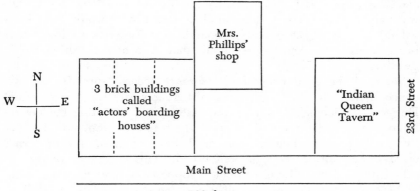

Main Street

132 feet

The first objection to this theory is found in the tax records for real property in the city of Richmond. In 1811 Richard Adams owned the whole of Lot 38, running 132 feet on Main Street. The property appears in the tax books as follows:

Lot	Proprietor	Tenants	Valuation	
38	Richard Adams	Oliver Peck		
"	"	John Wood	$5,500	Year: *1810* (p.5)
"	"	James, a negro		
38	Richard Adams	Oliver Peck		
"	"	&	5,500	Year: *1811* (p.6)
"	"	others		
38	Richard Adams	Oliver Peck, etc.	5,500	Year: *1812* (p.6)

From the way in which the proprietor's and tenants' names are listed, it *looks* as if Lot 38, in 1810, 1811, and 1812, contained not more than three buildings. A comparison of the tax record for Lot 38 with that for the adjoining Lot 37 shows that, whatever buildings may have been on Lot 38, they were not valued sufficiently high to have included a thriving tavern, three brick boarding houses and a two-story brick shop:

Lot	Proprietor	Tenants	Valuation	Year:
37	Thos. Pulling	Himself	$6,000	1810 & 1811
	R. Thompson est.	Mrs. Thompson	4,000	(p. 5 & 6)
	Rich. Adams	D. Doroghty	3,000	

The building owned and occupied by Thomas Pulling and valued at $6,000 was the Court House Tavern, on the north*east* corner of Main and 22nd Street.[1] If Lot 37, containing a Tavern and two other houses, was valued at $13,000, it seems unlikely that Lot 38 would have been valued at only $5,500 if it had contained a Tavern and four other brick houses. It seems more likely that it contained three single dwellings.

Study of the deed books and insurance records supports the evidence of the tax lists. In 1813, Richard Adams sold Lot 38 to Samuel Dutton and Benajah Dunham, the eastern half (fronting 66 feet on Main) going to Dutton and the western 66 feet to Dunham.[2] The tax list for 1814 [3] lists a house, owned by Dutton, at the north*west* corner of Main and 23rd Streets, as "unfinished." This is the site of the so-called Indian Queen Tavern, which is supposed to have been operating in 1811. By 1816 Dutton had died and the corner house is listed as being owned by the Dutton estate and occupied by "Mrs. Dutton and others."[4]

While this new building was in progress on the eastern half of Lot 38, improvements were also being made on the western half, owned by Benajah Dunham. In April, 1816, Dunham sold to Thomas Pulling (owner of the nearby Court House Tavern) the western third of his land, 22 feet, including a brick house 20 feet wide and a two foot alley to the west.[5] This was the house now numbered 2214 East Main Street, and is the farthest west of the three undetached brick houses said to have been the actors' boarding houses in 1811. Inspection of the three houses today shows that they were designed as a unit and must have been built at about the same time. This is proved

[1] M. A. S., No. 248, 1811; No. 1149, 1812.
[2] D. B., 7, p. 460, R. C. C.
[3] T. R. P., 1814, p. 5.
[4] T. R. P., 1816, p. 6.
[5] D. B., 15, p. 217, H. C. C.

by the records. The same tax book [6] which shows Mrs. Dutton occupying the house at the corner of 23rd and Main Streets also shows Thomas Pulling owning and occupying his house (just purchased from Dunham) valued at $2,000, on the western 22 feet of Lot 38; and further lists, on the adjoining 44 feet of the lot, an "unfinished house" owned by Benajah Dunham, valued at $3,000. The following tracing of an insurance plat, made November 4, 1816,[7] shows the three contiguous buildings as they are today:

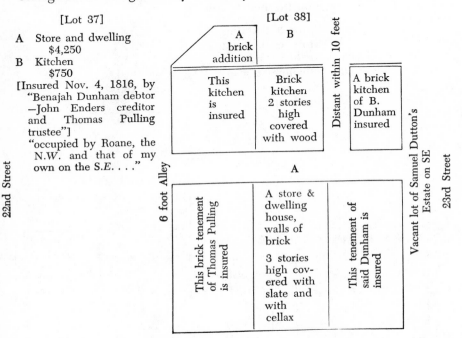

[Lot 37]

A   Store and dwelling
      $4,250
B   Kitchen
      $750
[Insured Nov. 4, 1816, by "Benajah Dunham debtor —John Enders creditor and Thomas Pulling trustee"]
"occupied by Roane, the N.W. and that of my own on the S.E. . . . ."

22nd Street

6 foot Alley

[Lot 38]

Distant within 10 feet

A
brick
addition

B

This kitchen is insured

Brick kitchen 2 stories high covered with wood

A brick kitchen of B. Dunham insured

A

This brick tenement of Thomas Pulling is insured

A store & dwelling house, walls of brick

3 stories high covered with slate and with cellar

This tenement of said Dunham is insured

Vacant lot of Samuel Dutton's Estate on SE

23rd Street

Main or E. Street

This plat is interesting, not only because it shows that the center building was insured for the first time in November, 1816 (thus bearing out the 1816 tax record of the house as "unfinished" or just finished at that time), but especially because it describes the land immediately *east* of the three tenements as "*vacant* lot of Samuel Dutton's estate." This lot is the one on which *now* stands the house in which Mrs. Poe is said to have died in 1811.

[6] T. R. P., 1816, p. 6.
[7] M. A. S., No. 683.

Returning to the building at the northwest corner of Main and 23rd Streets, which the 1814 tax list shows as "unfinished" and untenanted, we find this eastern half of Lot 38 changing hands several times after Samuel Dutton's death. In September, 1825, it was purchased by Thomas Pulling.[8] In October, 1825, he insured "my 6 bldgs. on part of Lot 38 now occupied by no person, situated between the property of Benajah Dunham's creditors on the N.W. and 23rd St. on the S.E." [9] The six buildings are insured for $4,500 and their location and character are shown on the plat as follows:

A	Store & dwelling house	$1,250.
B	Store & dwelling house	1,250.
C	Dwelling house	850.
D	Dwelling house	850.
E	Kitchen	150.
F	Kitchen	150.
		$4,500.

22nd Street

E Street	B Store & dwelling house, 3 stories high Walls brick Roof wood	C Dwelling house— 3 stories walls brick roof wood	E Brick kitchen covered with wood
	A Store & dwelling house 3 stories high walls brick roof wood	D Dwelling house 3 stories walls brick roof wood	F Brick kitchen covered with wood

23rd Street

8 D. B., 28, p. 219, H. C. C.
9 M. A. S., No. 3558, 1825.

This plat indicates that the building at the corner of Main and 23rd Streets, said by Poe biographers to have been the Indian Queen Tavern, was in 1825 actually four buildings, with each of the front two designated as a combined "store & dwelling," separated from the back two by a passage-way. This passage accounts clearly for the bricked-in arch, still visible. Examination of the present building agrees with this 1825 insurance tracing: the Main Street side of the building can be seen to have been originally two buildings, and the bricked-in arch on 23rd Street appears much too small ever to have allowed carriages to drive through. It was obviously the foot passage connecting the front and rear buildings—an architectural plan often used at that time, notably in the three "actors'" tenements on the western half of Lot 38.

This tracing also indicates that the little house, No. 2220½, associated with Mrs. Poe, was not there in 1825. The house is separated from the corner buildings only by a five foot alley, and the land on which it stands was part of Pulling's property. If the house had been there in 1825 it seems certain that it would have been insured along with the others, or its presence at least indicated on the plat.

The first actual appearance of the little house is in 1830, on a map accompanying the deed which transferred the eastern half of Lot 38 to Peter Joseph Chevallie.[10] It appears on this plat as "E":

In addition to the evidence that the buildings associated with Mrs. Poe and now standing on Lot 38 were in fact not built until after her death in 1811, we have evidence that the corner building was never the Indian Queen Tavern, and, so far as the deed books show, was never a tavern at all.

As early as 1806 the building on Lot 39, on the north*east* corner of 23rd and Main Streets, was known as the Indian Queen Tavern.[11] In 1811 this property was owned by John Cunningham and occupied by John Glynn. In 1813 the tavern was owned by Benjamin Duval, whose dwelling house and tile factory were on the adjoining Lot 40.[12] The property, running 66 feet on Main Street from the corner of 23rd Street eastward, and containing six buildings, was again insured as "Benj. Duval's Indian Queen Tavern" in 1816, when the value was increased, three buildings having been added since 1813.[13] In 1821 the tavern

[10] D. B., 29, p. 400; 98c, pp. 632, 633, R. C. C.
[11] M. A. S., No. 639, 1806.
[12] M. A. S., No. 24, 1813; D. B., 7, p. 469, R. C. C.
[13] M. A. S., Nos. 1195 and 1150, March 18, 1816.

$20' = 1''$

Richard Young—S.C.R. (for Wm. Williams)

Dec. 29, 1830.   D. B. 98c   633R

Dividing line of lots Nos. 38 and 52

Alley 20' wide

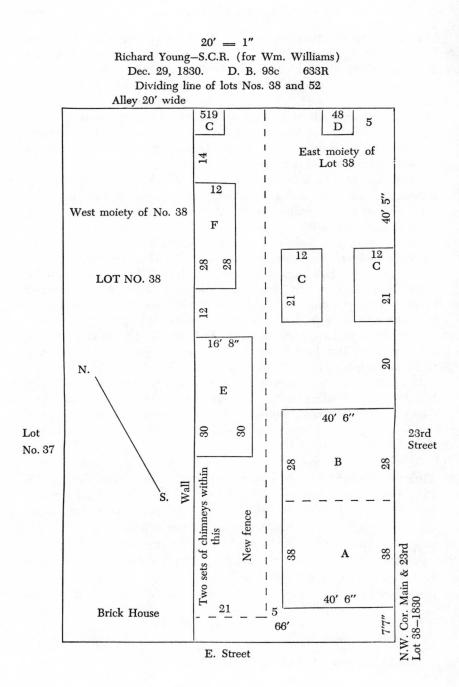

was destroyed by fire.[14] Deeds to this property, however, as late as 1838, refer to the northeast corner of Main and 23rd Streets as "the lot on which the Indian Queen Tavern was situated." There is absolutely no doubt that this and not the north*west* corner, was the site of the Indian Queen Tavern from 1806 to 1821.[15]

There obviously would not have been two Indian Queen Taverns at the same time on opposite corners of 23rd Street. Since deeds and insurance records constantly mention the east corner as being the site of this tavern, and since none of the records for the property at the west corner ever mention the presence there of any tavern at all, it seems perfectly clear that in the years after 1821, when the Indian Queen burned, its exact location was forgotten and it was only remembered that it had been at "the corner of Main and 23rd."

Turning to the Richmond newspapers of 1811, we find that none of the notices concerning performances of Placide's Company at the Richmond Theatre, or benefits given by the Company for Mrs. Poe during her last illness, or finally the accounts of her death, ever state where Mrs. Poe lived or where she died.[16] Neither are we able to identify any Mrs. Phillips (or Fipps, or Phepoe, as it sometimes appears), or even any milliner at all with a shop on Main Street between 22nd and 23rd Streets, in 1811. In 1802 a Mrs. Phepoe had a millinery shop at Mrs. Turner's Tavern, corner of 14th and Main Streets;[17] in 1819 a Mrs. Dolly Phillips is listed in the Richmond Directory as living on E (later Main) Street, between 4th and 5th Streets—no other Phillips, Fipps, or Phepoe appearing in this directory; in the 1845 and 1852 directories Mrs. C. Philip, milliner, is on Main Street between 15th and 17th; and in 1855 Lucy Phillips' boarding house is on Main between 22nd and 23rd—at last the right address, but forty-four years after Mrs. Poe's death. We are at a loss to know what Mr. Hervey Allen means when he says that he identified the proper Mrs. Phillips from "the Richmond directories of the time." There *were* no Richmond directories for the first third of the nineteenth century except the one in 1819, and that one had only one Phillips—and she was not listed as a milliner.

This, of course, is not absolutely conclusive proof that there was not

[14] *Compiler*, April 4, 1821.

[15] D. B., 23, p. 549, H. C. C.; 25, pp. 106, 107, 108, 263, 395, 396, H. C. C.; 38, p. 172, R. C. C.

[16] *Enquirer*, Aug. 13, Sept. 6, Oct. 8, Oct. 25, Oct. 29, Nov. 22, Dec. 10, 1811; *Va. Patriot*, Aug. 20, Nov. 19, Nov. 29, Dec. 10, 1811.

[17] *Examiner* May 1, 1802.

a Mrs. Phillips, milliner, on Main Street between 22nd and 23rd in 1811. Not every milliner could afford to advertise in the papers, and there is no 1811 directory. But there certainly seems to be no proof that there *was* such a Mrs. Phillips. It is also true that Mrs. Poe could have died on Lot 38 in a small brick house. There were buildings on Lot 38 in 1811, and the Indian Queen Tavern would, as claimed, have been nearby, though not on the location as given by Mr. Allen and Miss Phillips. But the records do seem to show that this Indian Queen Tavern burned to the ground in 1821, that the so-called actors' boarding house was not built until 1816, and that Mrs. Poe did not die in the particular small brick house now standing at 2220½ East Main Street.

It is possible to form an alternative theory as to where she did die. We give it here, purely as a theory. There is no proof.

In 1811 the Washington Tavern stood at the northwest corner of 9th and Grace Streets, on the site of the present Hotel Richmond. Before 1797 this tavern had been known as the Indian Queen, but by 1802 it had become the Washington.[18] In 1811 it might still have been referred to as "the old Indian Queen." Moreover, this neighborhood is known to have been frequented by the actors of Mr. Placide's Company, who played at the Richmond Theatre on Broad Street below 12th, just four and a half blocks from the Tavern. The following advertisement appeared in the *Virginia Patriot*, November 19, 1811:

Richmond Theatre

A meeting of the subscribers to the Richmond Theatre is requested on Thursday evening, 5 o'clock at the Washington Tavern, at which time and place, the Managers will be prepared to pay the interest upon the subscriptions for the present year.

Mon. 18th Nov. 1811." [19]

Another advertisement connected with the Company of which Mrs. Poe was a member appeared in the *Enquirer*, November 22, 1811: [20]

For Rent, and immediate possession given, the Tenement near the Washington Tavern, now in the occupancy of Mr. Placide. For terms apply to

EDWARD HALLAM.

[18] D. B., 43, p. 232, R. C. C.; also Title Insurance Co., abstract of title, Hotel Richmond.
[19] *Virginia Patriot,* Tuesday, November 19, 1811, Vol. II, No. 212, page 3, col. 4.
[20] Vol. 8, No. 57, p. 1, col. 1.

A similar advertisement of Hallam's had been in the *Enquirer* a year before (November 9, 1810), offering for rent the houses "now in the occupancy of Mr. Placide and Mr. Young, fronting the Capitol Square and adjoining the Washington Tavern." Placide was, of course, the manager of the Company to which Mrs. Poe belonged, and brought his actors to Richmond every year for a season at the Richmond Theatre. Edward Hallam had acquired in 1803 the property which Placide rented, fronting 42 feet on Ninth Street, back of the Washington Tavern.[21] There were a number of other houses on the adjoining lots where actors could doubtless have secured rooms. Moreover, a number of rooms were available at the Tavern itself. An advertisement by Curtis R. Moore in the *Enquirer* (Tues., Aug. 27, 1811) announcing a change in the management of the Tavern, assures the public that

> every attention shall be devoted to render the Establishment agreeable to Travellers and others who may favor him with their custom. Private apartments, suitable for the reception of families travelling and as convenient and agreeable as any in this city, separate from that part of the establishment devoted to public entertainment, can always be furnished.
>
> Thirty-five members of the next State Legislature, can be comfortably accommodated on application. . . .

It seems probable that Mrs. Poe would have found a room in or near the Washington Tavern, four and a half blocks from the Theatre, where others of the Company are proved by Hallam's advertisements to have stayed, rather than in a house fifteen blocks away, near 23rd and Main Streets. Incidentally, she would then have been just across Capitol Square from the house on the northeast corner of Thirteenth and Main Streets, where John Allan is said to have lived in 1811. Mrs. Allan's first sight of Poe may have been of him playing in the Square.

KEY TO REFERENCE ABBREVIATIONS

D. B., Deed Book.
H. C. C., Henrico Circuit Court.
R. C. C., Richmond Chancery Court.
T. R. P., Tax, Real Property (City of Richmond).
M. A. S., Mutual Assurance Society of Virginia.

[21] D. B., 15, p. 203; 60, p. 695, R. C. C.

VI. POE'S RECORD IN THE ARMY AND AT WEST POINT

WAR DEPARTMENT

The Adjutant General's Office

Washington

December 15, 1939

Dear Sir:

Receipt is acknowledged of your letter of December 6, 1939 in which you request the complete military record of Edgar Allan Poe, known in the Army as Edgar A. Perry.

The records show that Edgar Allan Poe enlisted May 26, 1827 at Boston, Massachusetts, under the name of Edgar A. Perry, and was assigned to Battery H, 1st U. S. Artillery, then stationed at Fort Independence, Boston Harbor. The battery changed station about October 31, 1827 to Fort Moultrie, South Carolina, and remained there until October 31, 1828, when it changed to Fort Monroe, Virginia. Perry served as an artificer from May 1, 1828 to the date of his appointment as sergeant major January 1, 1829, at Fort Monroe, Virginia. On the muster roll of the battery dated February 28, 1829, he is reported present for duty at Fort Monroe, Virginia, and on the muster roll of the battery next on file, he is reported as discharged April 15, 1829, by substitute, under S. O. #28 from Eastern Department dated April 4, 1829. On a return of the 1st Regiment U. S. Artillery for the month of April, 1829, Sergeant Samuel Graves of Company H, is shown to have enlisted April 17, 1829 and to have "Re-enlisted substitute for Sgt. Major Perry." However, no record of any financial arrangement between the two men has been found, and if such a financial transaction was made it was no doubt a private affair between the two men of which no record would be kept by the military authorities.

At date of enlistment May 26, 1827, Perry gave his age as 22 years; birthplace, Boston, Massachusetts; occupation, clerk; height, 5 feet 8 inches; eyes, grey; hair, brown; and complexion, fair.

The records further show that Edgar A. Poe was admitted to Military Academy July 1, 1830, and was dismissed March 6, 1831 by sentence of Court Martial per Military Academy Orders No. 7, Engineer Dept., February 8, 1831.

The copies of application for discharge and recommendations, herewith returned, have been compared with the originals, and are correct as to wording.

Very truly yours,

E. S. ADAMS
Major General,
The Adjutant General.

Records of the trial of E. A. Poe and of the approval by the Secretary of War of the action of the Court Martial.

Engineer Department
Washington, February 8, 1831.

Military Academy Order, No. 7.

3. The Court next proceeded to the trial of Cadet E. A. Poe of the U. S. Military Academy on the following Charges and Specifications.

Charge 1st. . . . Gross neglect of duty.

Specification 1st. . . . In this, that he the said Cadet Poe did absent himself from the following parades and roll calls between the 7th of January and 27th January 1831, Viz. absent himself from evening parade on the 8, 9, 15, 20, 24 & 25 January 1831; absent from reveille roll call on the 8, 16, 17, 19, 21, 25 & 26 Jan'y 1831, absent from Class parade on the 17, 18, 19, 20, 24 & 25 Jan'y 1831, absent from guard mounting on the 16 Jan'y 1831, and absent from Church parade on the 23d. Jan'y 1831; all of which at West Point N. Y.

Specification 2d. . . . In this, that he the said Cadet E. A. Poe, did absent himself from all his Academical duties between the 15th & 27 Jan'y 1831, viz. absent from Mathematical recitation on the 17, 18, 19, 20, 21, 22, 24, 25 & 26th Jan'y 1831, all of which at West Point N. Y.

Charge 2d. . . . Disobedience of Orders.

Specification 1st. . . . In this, that he the said Cadet Poe, after having been directed by the officer of the day to attend church on the 23d January 1831, did fail to obey such order, this at West Point.

Specification 2d. . . . In this, that he the said Cadet Poe did fail to attend the Academy on the 25 Jany. 1831, after having been directed to do so by the officer of the day: This at West Point N. Y.

To which charges and specifications the prisoner pleaded as follows, to the 1st specification of the first charge "Not Guilty", to the 2nd specification of the 1st charge "Guilty," and "Guilty" to the second charge and specification.

The court after mature deliberation on the testimony adduced find the prisoner "Guilty" of the 1st specification of 1st charge and confirm his plea to the remainder of the charges and specifications, and adjudge that he Cadet E. A. Poe be *dismissed* the service of the United States.

· · · · · · ·

7. . . . The proceedings of the General Court Martial of which Lieut. Thomas J. Leslie of the Corps of Engineers is President in the cases of Cadets *L. Jones, H. Swartwont, E. A. Poe, Thomas W. Gibson, W. A. Parker, and Henry Minor* have been laid before the Secretary of War and approved.

· · · · · · ·

Cadet E. A. Poe will be dismissed the service of the United States and cease to be considered a member of the Military Academy after the 6th March 1831.[1]

[1] From the Records of the War Department, Office of the Adjutant General, which are now in the National Archives. From photostat sent through the courtesy of Dr. P. M. Hamer, Chief, Division of Reference. January 4, 1940.

VII. THE *TALES OF THE FOLIO CLUB*

There has been much dispute concerning the tales which are to be included under this title. According to the editorial statement in the *Southern Literary Messenger* for August, 1835, including a quotation from the judges of the *Visiter* contest, there were sixteen stories, one of which seems to have been lost when they were returned by Carey and Lea. In Poe's letter to Hall the publisher in Philadelphia, of September 2, 1836, he says: "There has appeared in the *Messenger* a series of Tales, by myself—in all seventeen." Only fourteen stories by Poe had appeared in the *Messenger* at that time. Originally, however, there were eleven tales, corresponding to the eleven members of the Club. These were:

The members generally, were most remarkable men.

There was, first of all, Mr. Snap, the President, who is a very lank man with a hawk nose, and was formerly in the service of the Down-East Review.

Then there was Mr. Convolvulus Gondola, a young gentleman who had travelled a good deal.

Then there was De Rerum Naturâ, Esqr., who wore a very singular pair of green spectacles.

Then there was a very little man in a black coat with very black eyes.

Then there was Mr. Solomon Seadrift who had every appearance of a fish.

Then there was Mr. Horribile Dictu, with white eyelashes, who had graduated at Göttingen.

Then there was Mr. Blackwood Blackwood who had written certain articles for foreign magazines.

Then there was the host, Mr. Rouge-et-Noir, who admired Lady Morgan.

Then there was a stout gentleman who admired Sir Walter Scott.

Then there was Chronologos Chronology who admired Horace Smith, and had a very big nose which had been in Asia Minor. . . .

Here follows in the MS. the fragment of the piece now entitled "Silence: A Fable." [1]

[1] Virginia Edition, II (Tales I), pp. xxxviii-xxxix.

Obviously, the five stories published in the *Philadelphia Saturday Courier*, "Metzengerstein," "The Duc de L'Omelette," "A Tale of Jerusalem," "Loss of Breath" and "Bon Bon" are to be included. "The Manuscript Found in a Bottle," which won the *Visiter* prize, "Siope" ("Silence") which formed part of the manuscript book submitted to the judges, "Epimanes" ("Four Beasts in One") which was sent to the *New England Magazine* in 1833, "Lionizing," mentioned by Poe in his letter to White July 20, 1835, "The Visionary" ("The Assignation") given with "Lionizing" in the *Messenger* account in August 1835, are certain also. Latrobe stated definitely in his account of the meeting of the judges that there was a difficulty in choosing the best. "Portions of the tales were read again and finally the committee selected the 'Ms. Found in a Bottle.' One of the stories was called 'A Descent into the Maelström' and this was at one time preferred." Owing to the publication of the latter story in 1841, several authorities have concluded that Latrobe was confusing the two stories. This would be reasonable if he were mentioning only one of them. But how he could speak of them together and still confuse them is difficult to understand. Of the other early stories, "Berenice," "Morella," "King Pest," "Shadow" and "Mystification" have usually been accepted, largely on internal evidence, and their dates of publication. "Hans Pfaall" is stated by Poe in his letter to White of July 20, 1835, to have been written especially for the *Messenger*, where it had appeared in June. Therefore, it may not have been one of the *Tales of the Folio Club*, although it clearly belongs to the early period.

VIII. POE'S REVISION OF THE *PHANTASY PIECES*

Poe's method of revision of the *Phantasy Pieces* illustrates his meticulous care and also his point of view. In "Morella" the principal change lay in the omission of the "Catholic Hymn" which had been published separately in *Burton's.* There is a toning down of some of the expressions. The narrator no longer "shrieked" the name "Morella" at the baptism; he "whispered" the name. A similar modification came in the love Morella's father feels for his daughter. In the Huntington Ms. it was "more fervent and more holy." In the *Tales of the Grotesque and Arabesque* it became "more fervent and more intense." In the *Phantasy Pieces,* "more intense" was omitted, and this reading Poe preserved. In "Lionizing" Poe had represented his hero, who had become John Smith, as having collected all that could be said on the subject of "Nosology" by Pliny, Aristotle, Alexander Ross, Minutius Felix, Hermanus Pictorius, Del Rio, Villarêt, Bartholinus, and Sir Thomas Browne. Poe added a footnote, in the *Phantasy Pieces,* "The authors here named have all really treated, at some length, of the nose." This note was not printed in the *Broadway Journal* or the *Tales* of 1845, obviously because the queer jumble of Greek philosophers, a Scottish poet, a Roman advocate, a Danish physician, and so on, was omitted. The note was, of course, an added element of satire on pretended accuracy of reference.

In "William Wilson," Poe changed the wording of a significant sentence, and also the date of his birth, to read—"for after leaving Dr. Bransby's, I casually learned that my namesake was born on the nineteenth of January, 1811—a somewhat remarkable coincidence; for the day is precisely that of my own nativity." [1] Poe omitted a phrase, "To the moralist fully acquainted with the minute spirings [sic] of human action," which may reflect his dislike of the introduction of moral teaching into fiction. He restored it, however, partially in later versions. Two alterations in the climax of "William Wilson," strengthened it. When Wilson faces his conscience, the text had simply said, "A large mirror, it appeared to me." For the last phrase Poe substituted "(so at first it appeared to me in my confusion)." The change of the natural

---

[1] The date was 1809 in *Tales of the Grotesque and Arabesque.*

into the supernatural is thereby made more gradual. Finally, the picture of Wilson is made more distinct by the introduction of "Not a thread in all the raiment" before the sentence "Not a line in all the marked and singular lineaments of that face which was not, even identically, *mine own.*" Both insertions were preserved by Poe.

In "The Man that was Used Up," Poe inserted a motto:

> "Pleurez, pleurez, mes yeux, et fondez vous en eau!
> La moitié de ma vie a mis l'autre au tombeau,—Corneille."

The first time it was printed was in the *Prose Romances* of 1843. There is no change of importance in the text in this story.

In "The Fall of the House of Usher" Poe included as usual "The Haunted Palace" but changed the last line of the third stanza to read: "The ruler of the realm was seen." He had also discovered, or had been told of, an amusing error in the list of works that Roderick Usher and his friend pored over. In the *Tales* of 1840, one of these was given as "the Subterranean Voyage of Nicholas Klimm de Holberg." Poe corrected "de" to "by," depriving Ludwig von Holberg of his title, but restoring to him his famous *Nicolai Klimii iter subterraneum.*

One sentence in "The Duc de L'Omelette" reflects Poe's changing ideas. In the original form in the *Saturday Courier* it read, "There was a chain of an unknown blood-red metal—its upper end lost like Col-e, *parmi les nues.*" In the *Tales* of 1840, this reference became C——. In the *Phantasy Pieces,* Poe inserted "Carlyle." Later on, in the *Broadway Journal,* it became "the city of Boston."

Poe's tendency toward moderation showed in his change from "one hundred times" to "fifty times" in contrasting the altitude of the spectral vessel with that of the hulk on which the narrator of "A Manuscript Found in a Bottle" is floating. However Poe did not preserve the alteration. He did keep the change from "the snow drifted down bodily in enormous masses" to "It snowed fiercely" in "Bon-Bon." There are quite a few interpolations in this story. The devil's remark, "But my conscience smote me for the lie," became "But my conscience smote me for having uttered a truth, even to aid a friend." This is in better keeping with the tone of the story. This correction Poe preserved, but there are two alterations in another script, which were not followed. Evidently some one else was trying his hand at corrections. "Shadow" had practically no alteration, being very properly looked upon by Poe as in perfect form. He introduced a motto, however, "Yea! though I walk through the valley of the SHADOW—*Psalm of David.*"

In "Ligeia" Poe interpolated a striking clause. To the description of the repeated revivification of the corpse of Rowena and her lapse into death, he added: "how each agony wore the aspect of a struggle; and how each struggle was succeeded by I know not what of wild change in the personal appearance of the corpse." This clause prepares the way for the final assumption by Ligeia of the body of her rival, without appearing to do so. The poem of "The Conqueror Worm" is not included in "Ligeia" as it was later, so that the date of its first publication, January, 1843, fixes the preparation of the *Phantasy Pieces* as not later than 1842.

In "King Pest" there are again two sets of alterations, and, once more, while the printlike characters of Poe represent corrections that have been preserved, the others, at times illegible, and even ungrammatical, have been discarded. The only significant change is the substitution of "Plague" for "Pest" as the "fearful cry" sounding through the city.

"How to Write a Blackwood Article" appears for the first time with that title, in *Phantasy Pieces*, followed by a motto,

> "In the name of the Prophet,—figs!!"
> —*Cry of the Turkish Fig-Pedler.*

In this story there is a sheet carefully written and pasted on what had been page 221 of the *Tales of the Grotesque and Arabesque:* "To Printer—Substitute this for what is marked out in pencil. No. ¶"

Talk of the Ionic and Eleatic Schools—of Archytas, Gorgias and Alcmaeon. Say something about objects and subjects. Be sure and abuse a man called Locke. Turn up your nose at things in general; and when you let slip anything very unconscionably absurd, you need not be at the trouble of scratching it out, but just put in a foot-note and say you are indebted for the above profound observation to the "Kritik der reinen Vernunft" or to the "Metaphysische Anfangsgrunde der Naturwissenschaft." This will look erudite and at the same time *frank.*

This passage was substituted for "Talk of the Academy and the Lyceum and say something about the Ionic and Italic Schools, or about Bossarion,[2] and Kant, and Schelling, and Fichte, and be sure you abuse a man called Locke, and bring in the words *a priori* and *a posteriori.*" The new passage certainly sounds more learned, but since its satiric intent is clear, it can be only a matter of conjecture why Poe made this

[2] Probably an error for Cardinal Johannes Bessarion (c. 1395-1472), and not a typographical slip, for Poe refers to him as Bossarion in "Bon-Bon."

careful alteration. In any event, he preserved it in the *Broadway Journal*. The pendant story, "A Predicament," had as a motto "What chance, good lady, hath bereft you thus?—*Comus.*"

In addition to these more significant changes, there are verbal alterations which in Poe's judgment, added to the rhetorical strength, and there is a constant changing of punctuation marks.

IX. CONTRACTS FOR THE *BROADWAY JOURNAL*

Memorandum of an agreement entered into between John Bisco and
Edgar A. Poe Feby 21st 1845—

Edgar A. Poe agrees to assist C. F. Briggs in the editorship of the
"Broadway Journal" published by John Bisco, to allow his name to be
published as one of the Editors of said paper, to furnish each and every
week original matter to the amount of, at least, one page of said paper,
and to give his faithful superintendence to the general conduct of the
same—

John Bisco agrees to pay Edgar A. Poe as compensation for his
services—one-third of the profits arising from the said "Broadway
Journal" and to allow him to inspect the Books of the same whenever
he may wish to do so to ascertain said profits, provided that said Books
be inspected in the publishing office—The said Bisco also agrees to
make a settlement with the said Poe as often as every four weeks—

This agreement shall bind the parties for the space of one year from
date—after which should they wish to continue their relations, new
arrangements shall be made—the said Poe having the privelege [sic]
to retain the same terms—but should the said Poe break the agreement
before the end of one year by neglecting any of the duties of assistant
editor of said paper then he shall forfeit all claim to any part of the
profits of said paper—

> JOHN BISCO
> EDGAR A. POE

Witnesses
Ferg. Robinson
Edward N. Mead [1]

Memorandum of an Agreement between John Bisco and Edgar A.
Poe, July 14th, 1845.

John Bisco is to publish at New-York, on Saturday of each week,
regularly, in good style, a quarto newspaper under the title of "The

[1] Original Autograph Ms. Contract, apparently in Bisco's handwriting,
W. H. Koester Collection.

Broadway Journal," uniform with the number of the 12th inst., at his sole cost and charge; to pay the expenses of the said publication, and to have therefor one half of the nett [sic] profits of said publication.

Edgar A. Poe is to be the sole editor of the said "Broadway Journal," furnishing the matter therefore, from week to week, uninterfered with by any party whatever, and to receive, for said editorial conduct, one half of the entire profits over and above all the reasonable costs and charges of said publication; to be at liberty in himself, or by a person deputed by him, to inspect at all times the books and accounts of said Journal, provided that he inspects them or causes them to be inspected, in the office of the said Journal; the said books to be kept by the said Bisco. And the said Poe is to receive from the said Bisco, on the first day of each month, a monthly account of the said Journal, and be then paid his share of the profits thereof. This contract is to run for one year, and is to be renewable by Mr. Poe, indefinitely, from year to year, so long as he is satisfied with said undertaking; his interest in said paper being at all times an absolute lien and charge thereon.

JOHN BISCO

EDGAR A. POE

Witness

Cornelius Mathews [2]

Memorandum of an agreement entered into between John Bisco and Edgar A. Poe this 24th day of October 1845.

John Bisco agrees to dispose of his entire right and title to the weekly paper entitled the "Broadway Journal" to Edgar A. Poe on the following terms to wit.

The said paper to be transfered free from all encumbrances except such as enumerated—and deliver ten complete sets of the same to the said Poe—from the commencement in January last to the present time the said Bisco to have the right to settle with the following named agents up to the present date the Journals unsold in their possession being the property of the said Bisco—Colon & Adriance Phila. Geo. Jones Albany R. G. H. Huntington Hartford.

Edgar A. Poe agrees to pay the said Bisco Fifty Dollars in cash on Signing agreement, to give the said Bisco his note at three months for the full amount of debts due the paper up to date as ascertained by a

[2] Original Autograph Ms. in Poe's handwriting, Berg Collection, New York Public Library.

bill made out by the said Bisco—the note not to be subject to any contingencies as to collecting said accounts—to deliver to the address of the said Bisco ten copies of the Said paper each and every week from date to the close of the third volume to serve all subscribers who have paid in advance for the paper and fulfil all contracts with all advertisers who have paid in advance for advertising without charge to the said Bisco; also to bear the expenses of the 16th No. of Vol. 2.

JOHN BISCO
EDGAR A. POE

In presence of
Samuel Fleet [3]

[3] Ms. in unknown hand, in William H. Koester Collection.

X. GRISWOLD'S POWER OF ATTORNEY FROM MRS. CLEMM FOR THE PUBLICATION OF POE'S WORKS

To all to whom these presents shall come—Know ye

Whereas I the undersigned, Maria Clemm, am the sole owner and lawful possessor of the writings and Literary Remains of the late Edgar A. Poe.

And whereas it is desirable that his works both in prose and poetry should be published in connection in a uniform Edition. And whereas it was the express wish and injunction of the Author before his death that Dr. Rufus W. Griswold should compile and edit the same in case of their publication.

Now therefore this Indenture witnesseth, that I have placed said writings in the hands of the said Dr. R. W. Griswold for the purpose of such compilation, editing and publication as aforesaid.

And I do hereby constitute and appoint him my true and lawful attorney and agent to make such contract with a publisher or publishers and others, in my name, as may be necessary and as he may deem proper for the purpose of consummating in each and every particular the object aforesaid—hereby ratifying all that he has done or may lawfully do in these premises.

In Witness whereof I have hereunto set my hand and seal this fifteenth day of October one thousand eight hundred and forty nine.

Signed Sealed and delivered

MARIA CLEMM

in presence of

[No witnesses]

State of New York

City of Brooklyn Kings County Gr: On this 20th day of October 1849, personally appeared before me Mrs. Maria Clemm to me known to be the same individual described in and who executed the within Power of Attorney, and acknowledged the execution thereof by her for the uses and purposes therein expressed

S. D. LEWIS
Commr. of Deeds [1]

[1] Original Ms., Richard Gimbel Collection. "Stella's" husband drew up the power of attorney.

XI. POE'S LAST JOURNEY

The traveller from Richmond to Baltimore had a choice of several routes depending on the day of the week he wished to make the trip. There was the all water route via Norfolk; rail to Frederick and boat to Baltimore; rail to Acqua Creek and boat to Baltimore; also the all rail route, changing trains at Washington. The persistent tradition is that Poe went by boat.

Woodberry's statement that Poe left Richmond at four A.M. on September 27, 1849, which would have been Thursday, has been accepted by later biographers. He gives no supporting evidence, however. A thorough investigation of the earliest authoritative sources, especially the *American Railway Guide and Pocket Companion for the United States,* for 1851, was made at the request of my brother, Francis McD. Quinn, General Passenger Agent of the Pennsylvania Railroad, by Mr. M. L. Bickel, of the Passenger Department. This information was supplemented by an examination of the Richmond newspapers by Mrs. Ralph T. Catterall of the Valentine Museum, and of the Baltimore papers by Mr. Richard H. Hart.

Poe might have taken one of several routes, but among the many boats scheduled, there are none indicated as leaving at 4 A.M. on a Thursday. The steamer *Pocahontas* left Richmond every Tuesday at 4 P.M. for Baltimore, and at various times the Richmond *Whig* and the *Enquirer* list six other boats as leaving Richmond for Baltimore, but not during the week of September 23, 1849.

A careful check of the Baltimore *Sun* and the *American* shows that on Friday, the 28th of September, the steamer *Pocahontas*, Captain Parrish, arrived from Richmond, but no hour is given. As the running time from Richmond to Baltimore was about twenty-five hours, Poe could have taken this boat, if it left Richmond on Thursday, the 27th. It is not advertised to do so, but it is hardly likely that the boat made only one trip a week. Woodberry might easily have misread 4 P.M. for 4 A.M.

Poe may have broken the journey at Norfolk. The Norfolk, Portsmouth and Old Point Line's steamer *Augusta,* left Richmond on Monday, Wednesday, and Friday at 6 A.M. No arriving time at Norfolk is given in the *Guide,* but the distance being approximately one hundred miles, the down trip with the flow of the river would require about eight hours. In the W. H. Koester Collection there is a copy of Thomas Moore's *Irish Melodies* (1819) in which Dr. John F. Carter wrote a statement that Poe had left the volume in his office in 1849. At the top of the title page the word "Augusta" is written, not in Poe's hand. The book may have been a parting gift, and the notation may indicate the boat on which Poe left Richmond. But in that case he did not leave on Thursday, September 27th. From Norfolk the steamers *Georgia, Herald* and *Jewess* of the Baltimore and Norfolk U. S. Mail Line made daily trips to Baltimore, leaving at 4 P.M. and arriving at Baltimore about 7 A.M.

These boats connected at Norfolk with the *Curtis Peck, Mt. Vernon* or *Augusta*. It is possible that Poe left Richmond on a Thursday morning by one of the two first named, but there is no evidence in the *Guide* that they left Richmond on that day.

The *Sun* and the *American* record the arrivals at Baltimore from Norfolk of the *Jewess* on September 28th and the *Herald* on the 29th. Poe could have been on either boat.

XII. A POSSIBLE NEW POE SATIRE

It is possible that Poe had spent a portion of his apparently unfruitful time during 1837 and 1838 in composing a satire which appeared in the *Museum* under the title of "The Atlantis, a Southern World—or a wonderful Continent discovered, by Peter Prospero, L.L.D.; M.A., P. S."

The evidence for Poe's authorship is largely internal. "The Atlantis" begins in the first volume of the *Museum* and continues in the second. Toward the end [1] occur several passages which are distinctly in Poe's manner:

> Thus far we have endeavored by solid argument and just considerations, to correct the several errors and abuses to which we have alluded; but a friend who sent us the following parody or pasquinade, has taken the most advisable expedient to sink those follies into utter disrepute and contempt. Upon an occasion in which one of these lecturers upon phrenology and interpreters of heads, sent him a card indicating the time and place in which he would display his gifts, and as usual, extolled the powers of his art, and the encouragement he and his productions had met with in many countries, this friend of mine published in the paper, which contained the advertisement comprised in the card, the following exact parody, confining himself strictly to the original as to all the particulars of thought and language, to which reference is made:
>
> RINOSOPHIA, OR NOSE-OLOGY.—A great discovery in the science of phrenology, which will be explained to the public in a series of lectures upon Noseology, or as the Greeks call it, Rinosophia, accompanied by an examination of noses, as a practical test and demonstration of the truth of the science: by Horatius B. Scriblerus, a practical Nose-ologist, and lineal descendant of the celebrated Martinus and Cornelius Scriblerus.
>
> The first of the series of lectures, will be delivered in the State House of this town, upon the approaching festival of the church, to commence at 8 o'clock in the evening.

[1] *The American Museum of Science, Literature and the Arts* (Baltimore, September, 1838 to June, 1839), II, 39-41.

Suffice it for the present, that Mr. Scriblerus should inform the inhabitants of the city of Saturnia, that the science of Rinosophia or Noseology, is an attempt to simplify that of phrenology, or rather craniology, and instead of deducing its principles from an examination of the whole head and brain, the interior machinery of which nature has naughtily hidden from the eye of the philosopher, very wisely confines its researches to the observation of that external organ which is proverbially exposed to the inspection of all observers. Mr. Scriblerus will undertake to show that from the organic structure of the nose, together with the lines and angles, may be determined all the propensities, faculties, affections and prevailing dispositions of the heart and mind. In fact, the fundamental principles of this science, have been long recognized in the republic of letters, though never before, as Mr. Scriblerus flatters himself, so fully unfolded and happily applied to practical purposes. Who has not heard of the Grecian nose, the Roman nose, the aquiline, the pug, the flat nostril, and the sharp projecting bill, which indicates the scolding woman, with various other modifications of structure too tedious to enumerate, and which language inadequately distinguishes? These several forms are known to present significant indications of either the great and virtuous, or the ignoble and debasing properties of our nature, insomuch that Lavater might well pronounce of Cicero's, that it was worth a kingdom. But we have not time in this brief address, to discuss the merits of this newly discovered science, or illustrate and recommend its maxims. For confirmation of its truth, and to satisfy an enlightened community that it is deeply founded in the Baconian method of investigation, we need only refer those who are inclined to incredulity, to the celebrated Nose that made its appearance in the town of Strasburg, and awoke such pother and confusion in the schools of science, and if we may credit the veritable history of Tristram Shandy, set all the philosophers of that age most keenly by the ears. Should not this single instance prove entirely satisfactory, we would direct our readers to the more authentic history of the learned Taliacotius, as related in the Hudibras, who adopted as wise as it was an extraordinary expedient, to supply to his patients this important organ of perception, when they were deprived of it, from the most honorable pieces of flesh out of the bodies of Porters.

It may be proper to add to the foregoing brief statement, that in order to gratify the literary curiosity of the good people of Saturnia, it is the intention of Mr. Scriblerus, during his course of lectures, to exhibit to them enormous fossil remains of Noses, derived from Dr. Buckland's collection, which afford undoubted

indications that they are vestiges of a former world which sub-
sisted millions of years anterior to the formation of the present
race of animals. He will show, moreover, upon the noses of Noah
and his family, which are in his possession, the most incontestible
proofs, by ornithicknological demonstration, or from the prints of
birds' feet which may be clearly deciphered, that birds must
have lighted upon the noses of this patriarchal family, during their
residence in the Ark, which were as high at least as the steeple of
St. Paul's Church. Mr. Scriblerus will conclude these interesting
lectures, by demonstrating that not only is the nose of man the
great seat and organ of sensation and thought, and not the pineal
gland as Des Cartes dreamed, but that with this organ, also, we
can taste, hear and see; and of consequence, that it was with this
instrument and not with the lower stomach, as stated in our
journals, that the celebrated French lady, who lately occasioned
so much conversation in Paris, was enabled to perform such wonders in hearing and in vision. That our magnetized sleeping
beauties in like manner, are led by the nose, through all their
spiritual peregrinations and somnambular visions, any one may
prove to his satisfaction, by only giving a tolerably stout pinch of
that organ, during their artificial slumbers.

N. B. Mr. Scriblerus has taken a room in Mr. Combe's residence,
Washington St. in which he will receive visitors for the examination of their noses. Should any person have been unfortunately
deprived of this invaluable feature of the human face divine, like
Tycho Brahe of old, it is suggested that our porters Tiberius,
Caligula, and Nero, are ready to submit to the Talicotian operation to accommodate ladies and gentlemen with supplemental
noses. Treatises upon noseology may be purchased at the same
time for a few cents, that have reached an hundred editions, in
Germany and France. It is earnestly requested that ladies will refrain from snuff on the day in which they present their noses for
inspection and examination.

The opening of "Lionizing," is distinctly in the same tone:

The first action of my life was the taking hold of my nose with
both hands. My mother saw this and called me a genius; my father
wept for joy and presented me with a treatise on Nosology. This
I mastered before I was breeched.

I now began to feel my way in the science, and soon came to understand that, provided a man had a nose sufficiently conspicuous,
he might, by merely following it, arrive at a Lionship. But my
attention was not confined to theories alone. Every morning I gave

my proboscis a couple of pulls and swallowed a half dozen of drams.

When I came of age my father asked me, one day, if I would step with him into his study.

"My son," said he, when we were seated, "what is the chief end of your existence?"

"My father," I answered, "it is the study of Nosology."

"And what, Robert," he inquired, "is Nosology?"

"Sir," I said, "it is the science of noses."

"And can you tell me," he demanded, "what is the meaning of a nose?"

"A nose, my father," I replied, greatly softened, "has been variously defined by about a thousand different authors." (Here I pulled out my watch.) "It is now noon, or thereabouts, we shall have time enough to get through with them all before midnight."

Poe's frequent creation of characters who pulled their enemies' noses is well known.

The references to Martinus and Cornelius Scriblerus are especially significant. Poe was familiar with the "Memoirs of Martin Scriblerus," that satire on the abuses of learning which was the joint work of Arbuthnot, Swift and Pope, for in "The Psyche Zenobia," [2] he appropriated from it a quotation from Demosthenes and its translation in *Hudibras*.[3] The tone of both "The Psyche Zenobia" and "Lionizing" resembles the "Memoirs"—and there can be little doubt that Poe was under the influence of Swift and Pope at this time.

In "The Atlantis," which is the account of a journey to a country called "Saturnia," Dean Swift is introduced as speaking of Scriblerus,[4] and there are several other references to the "Scribleri" family. Martin Scriblerus, according to this account, had four children, Horatius B. ——, Josephus R. J. ———, Nicholas B. ——, and Nathaniel D. ——— —all of whom settled in the United States.

Several of Poe's favorite writers are introduced into "Saturnia." Coleridge is credited with "glittering paradoxes," and speaks of Kepler as more important than Newton because of the "intuitive, generative constitution of his mind." Coleridge is to be condemned to read the works of Horatius B. Scriblerus.[5]

[2] Afterwards "How to Write a Blackwood Article."

[3] Cf. quotation in Chapter VI in "Memoirs of Scriblerus" (Pope's works, ed. by Roscoe, 1824, VII, 43) with *Tales of the Grotesque and Arabesque*, I, 225, or *Virginia Edition*, II, 280.

[4] I, 239. Another reference on p. 335.

[5] I, 244.

Certain of Poe's scientific ideas, later to be developed, are foreshadowed in this account. Martinus Scriblerus had a strong predilection for the craniology of Gall, Spurzheim and Combe.[6] Animal magnetism is discussed, and a journey to the moon in a balloon. Of even more significance is the discussion of the conflicting views of the foundation of the Universe by Aristotle and Bacon,[7] perhaps a precursor of the introductory passages of "Eureka," and later the question is raised whether Aristotle was acquainted with the Baconian Method.[8] The reference to Tycho Brahe, in the quoted passage, is reminiscent of "Al Aaraaf."

If Poe wrote "The Atlantis," his failure to sign the series of installments might be due to the Editors' reluctance to have so many relative contributions by one author. Or Poe might well have hesitated to sign a satire so different in tone from "Ligeia" or "The Haunted Palace." If he wrote "The Atlantis" he probably looked upon it as a piece of hackwork, written to make a little money. Yet it has some very amusing conceptions, such as the marriage of Dr. Franklin, the writer's guide, to Madame Helvetius, and the union of Dr. Johnson with Hannah More. It may be of course that Poe added the passages dealing with Nose-ology to the work of some one else.

[6] I, 440.
[7] I, 55-56.
[8] I, 248.

Bibliography

Space limitations have prevented me from publishing an extended Bibliography. As I have indicated in the text or footnotes the date of publication of practically every poem and short story, and of the most important criticisms by Poe, these may be found through the Index. Lists of biographical and critical books and articles concerning Poe, assembled in the hope of publication, I have included in the card files of the Bibliography of American Literature, in preparation through the Works Progress Administration, under the direction of Mr. E. H. O'Neill, at the University of Pennsylvania. This Bibliography is open to all qualified workers in the field. Duplicate files of the Poe section will be furnished by the University of Pennsylvania to any research library, on films, upon application.

Under these circumstances, it seemed best to publish a selective working Bibliography for quick reference. Preference has been given to collections and reprints of Poe's own work. Under "Biographical and Critical Works," I have listed only books, and have omitted articles, except in a few cases of unusual importance, chiefly historical. All articles quoted in the text have been referred to by full titles in the footnotes.

BIBLIOGRAPHIES

CAMPBELL, KILLIS, in *Cambridge History of American Literature* (New York, 1918), II, 452-468. Accurate and still useful.
————, in *Short Stories of Edgar Allan Poe* (New York, 1927). [Contains an excellent bibliography of the various printings of the stories.]
HARRISON, JAMES A., in Virginia Edition of Poe, XVI, 355-379.
HEARTMAN, CHARLES F., and REDE, KENNETH, *A Census of First Editions and Source Materials by Edgar Allan Poe in American Collections*, 2 vols. (Metuchen, New Jersey, 1932).
HEARTMAN, C. F., and CANNY, J. R., *A Bibliography of First Printings of the Writings of Edgar Allan Poe* (Hattiesburg, Mississippi, 1940). [Owing to errors, must be checked.]
ROBERTSON, JOHN W., *A Bibliography of the Writings of Edgar A. Poe*, 2 vols. (San Francisco, 1934).
STEDMAN, E. C., and WOODBERRY, G. E., in their edition of Poe's *Works*, X, 267-281.
WOODBERRY, G. E., in his *Life of Poe*, II, 399-417.
In *More Books*, the Bulletin of the Boston Public Library, beginning March, 1941, the complete list of the autograph letters of the Griswold Collection has been published.

WORKS—COLLECTED EDITIONS

The Works of the Late Edgar Allan Poe. With a Memoir by Rufus Wilmot Griswold and Notices of his Life and Genius by N. P. Willis and J. R. Lowell, 4 vols. (New York, 1850-1856). The Griswold "Memoir" was first published in Vol. III in 1850 and was afterwards transferred to Vol. I.

The Works of Edgar Allan Poe, edited by John H. Ingram, 4 vols. (Edinburgh, 1874-1875, 1880, etc.).

The Works of Edgar Allan Poe, edited by R. H. Stoddard, 6 vols. (New York, 1884, 1894).

The Works of Edgar Allan Poe, edited by E. C. Stedman and G. E. Woodberry, 10 vols. (Chicago, 1894-1895; New York, 1914).

The Complete Works of Edgar Allan Poe, Virginia Edition, edited by James A. Harrison, 17 vols. (New York, 1902). Reprinted as the Monticello Edition, Large Paper (New York, 1902). [The most complete edition, unfortunately out of print.]

The Complete Works of Edgar Allan Poe, edited by C. F. Richardson, 10 vols. (New York, 1902).

The Complete Works of Edgar Allan Poe, with Biography and Introduction by Nathan Haskell Dole, 10 vols. (London and New York, 1908).

The Complete Poems of Edgar Allan Poe, edited by J. H. Whitty (Boston, 1911); Revised Edition (Boston, 1917).

The Poems of Edgar Allan Poe, edited by Killis Campbell (Boston, 1917). [The best edition of the Poems.]

Selected Poems of Edgar Allan Poe, edited by Thomas Ollive Mabbott (New York, 1928).

SEPARATE WORKS

Tamerlane and Other Poems. By a Bostonian (Boston, 1827).

Al Aaraaf, Tamerlane, and Minor Poems (Baltimore, 1829).

Poems. By Edgar A. Poe. Second Edition (New York, 1831).

The Narrative of Arthur Gordon Pym, of Nantucket. Comprising The Details of a Mutiny and Atrocious Butchery on Board the American Brig Grampus, on her Way to the South Seas, in the Month of June, 1827. (New York, 1838; London, 1838). Published anonymously.

The Conchologist's First Book; or, A System of Testaceous Malacology (Philadelphia, 1839; 1840, revised; 1845).

Tales of the Grotesque and Arabesque, 2 vols. (Philadelphia, 1840).

The Prose Romances of Edgar A. Poe, Uniform Serial Edition. Each Number Complete in Itself. No. 1 (Philadelphia, 1843). Contains "The Murders in the Rue Morgue" and "The Man That Was Used Up." The only number issued.

Tales (New York, 1845; London, 1845, New York, 1849).

The Raven and Other Poems (New York, 1845; London, 1846). The *Tales* and the *Poems* were also published in one volume (New York, 1845).

Mesmerism "in Articulo Mortis" (London, 1846) (pirated).

Eureka: A Prose Poem (New York, 1848).

In addition the following broadsides and leaflets are known:

Prospectus of the Penn Magazine (Philadelphia [June, 1840], [August 1840], [September, 1840], January 1, 1841).

Prospectus of the Stylus (New York, January, 1848, April, 1848). It is uncertain whether a Philadelphia 1843 issue appeared separately or not; no specimen is known.

REPRINTS AND SELECTIONS

The most useful reprints of Poe's works are as follows:

Tamerlane and Other Poems, reproduced in facsimile from the edition of 1827 with an Introduction by Thomas Ollive Mabbott (New York, Facsimile Text Society, 1941).

Al Aaraaf, Tamerlane and Minor Poems, reproduced from the edition of 1829, with a Bibliographical Note by Thomas O. Mabbott (New York, Facsimile Text Society, 1933).

Poems, reproduced from the edition of 1831, with a Bibliographical Note by Killis Campbell (New York, Facsimile Text Society, 1936).

Politian, an unfinished Tragedy by Edgar A. Poe, edited and published complete for the first time, by Thomas O. Mabbott (Richmond, 1923).

Doings of Gotham in a Series of Letters by Edgar Allan Poe as Described to the Editors of the Columbia Spy; Together with Various Editorial Comments and Criticisms by Poe, now first collected by Jacob E. Spannuth; with a Preface, Introduction and Comments by Thomas O. Mabbott (Pottsville, Pennsylvania, 1929).

The Gold Bug, with a Foreword by Hervey Allen and Notes on the text by Thomas O. Mabbott (Garden City, New York, 1929).

Poe's Short Stories, edited with an Introduction by Killis Campbell (New York, 1927).

Tales of Edgar Allan Poe, edited by James Southall Wilson (New York, 1927). [Interesting Introduction.]

Selections from the Critical Writings of Edgar Allan Poe, edited by F. C. Prescott (New York, 1909). [Good Introduction.]

Tales, with an Introduction by Carl Van Doren (New York, 1932).

Edgar Allan Poe and the Philadelphia Saturday Courier. Facsimile Reproductions of the First Texts of Poe's Earliest Tales and "Raising the Wind," with an Introduction by John Grier Varner (Charlottesville, Virginia, 1933).

Edgar Allan Poe: Representative Selections, with Introduction, Bibliography, and Notes, edited by Margaret Alterton and Hardin Craig (New York, 1935).

Complete Tales and Poems of Edgar Allan Poe, with Introduction by Hervey Allen (New York, 1938). [One-volume edition for popular use.]

The revived *Southern Literary Messenger*, edited by F. Meredith Dietz, is constantly reprinting articles by Poe published in that journal.

LETTERS

Ingram and Gill printed many letters of Poe. W. M. Griswold sold to the *Century Magazine* the right of publication of a large number of letters, and G. E. Woodberry edited them in his "Selections from the Correspondence of Edgar Allan Poe," *Century Magazine,* XLVIII (1894), 572-583; 725-737; 854-866. He also published "The Poe-Chivers Papers," *Century,* LXV (1903), 435-447, 545-558, and included many of these letters in his *Life of Poe* in 1909. Much new material was included in J. A. Harrison's Virginia Edition, Vols. I and XVII (Biography and Letters, 1902). The following publications of special groups of letters often contain material not to be found in Harrison or Woodberry:

Some Letters of Edgar Allan Poe to E. H. N. Patterson of Oquawka, Illinois, with comments by Eugene Field (Chicago, 1898).

"Letters of E. A. Poe, 1845-49," *Bulletin of the New York Public Library,* VI (New York, 1902), 7-11.

Last Letters of Edgar Allan Poe to Sarah Helen Whitman, edited by J. A. Harrison (New York, 1909).

Some Edgar Allan Poe Letters, printed for private distribution only, from originals in the collection of W. K. Bixby (St. Louis, Missouri, 1915).

"The Letters from George W. Eveleth to Edgar Allan Poe," edited by Thomas O. Mabbott in *Bulletin of the New York Public Library* (New York, 1922). Reprinted separately, 1922.

"The Letters of Edgar A. Poe to George W. Eveleth," edited by James S. Wilson in *Alumni Bulletin,* University of Virginia, XVII (January, 1924), 34-59. Reprinted separately, 1924.

Edgar Allan Poe Letters Till Now Unpublished, in the Valentine Museum, Richmond, Virginia, with an Introductory Essay and Commentary by Mary Newton Stanard (Philadelphia, 1925).

"Letters from Mary E. Hewitt to Poe," edited by Thomas O. Mabbott, in *Christmas Books* (New York, Hunter College, 1937), pp. 116-121.

Edgar Allan Poe Letters and Documents in the Enoch Pratt Library, edited by A. H. Quinn and R. H. Hart (New York, Scholars' Facsimiles and Reprints, 1941).

CONCORDANCE

BOOTH, BRADFORD A., and JONES, CLAUDE E., *A Concordance of the Poetical Works of Edgar Allan Poe* (Baltimore, 1941).

BIOGRAPHICAL AND CRITICAL

ALLEN, HERVEY, *Israfel. The Life and Times of Edgar Allan Poe,* 2 vols. (New York, 1926). Revised edition, 2 vols. in one (1934). [Written with spirit, but largely secondary, and with a tendency toward the romantic and the acceptance of unchecked evidence.]

————, and Mabbott, Thomas O., *Poe's Brother. The Poems of William Henry Leonard Poe* (New York, 1926).

Alterton, Margaret B., *Origins of Poe's Critical Theory* (Iowa City, 1925).

Baudelaire, Charles, "Edgar Poe, sa vie et ses oeuvres" in *Histoires Extraordinaires, traduit D'Edgar Poe* (Paris, 1856), Vol. VI of *Oeuvres Complètes de Ch. Baudelaire* (Paris, 1891).

————, "Notes Nouvelles sur Edgar Poe" in *Nouvelles Histoires Extraordinaires, traduit D'Edgar Poe* (Paris, 1857), Vol. VII of *Oeuvres Complètes de Ch. Baudelaire* (Paris, 1892).

Bewley, Sir Edmund, *The Origin and Early History of the Family of Poë or Poe* (Dublin, 1906).

The Book of the Poe Centenary, edited by C. W. Kent and J. S. Patton (Charlottesville, University of Virginia, 1909).

Brownell, W. C., "Poe," in *American Prose Masters* (New York, 1909).

Cambiaire, Célestin P., *The Influence of Edgar Allan Poe in France* (New York, 1927).

Campbell, Killis, "Poe," in *Cambridge History of American Literature* (New York, 1918), II, 55-69.

————, *The Mind of Poe, and Other Studies* (Cambridge, 1932). [One of the most significant studies of Poe. Contains "The Mind of Poe," "Contemporary Opinion of Poe," "The Poe-Griswold Controversy," "The Backgrounds of Poe," "Self-Revelation in Poe's Poems and Tales," "The Origins of Poe," and "The Poe Canon."]

————, "Poe Documents in the Library of Congress," *Modern Language Notes,* XXV (April, 1910), 127-128. [First study of Ellis-Allan Letters.]

————, "Some Unpublished Documents Relating to Poe's Early Years," in *Sewanee Review,* XX (April, 1912), 201-212.

————, "New Notes on Poe's Early Years," *The Dial,* LX (February 17, 1916), 143-146.

————, "Poe's Reading," *University of Texas Studies in English,* V (October, 1925), 166-196.

————, "Poe's Treatment of the Negro and of Negro Dialect," *University of Texas Studies in English,* XVI (July, 1936), 106-114.

Canby, Henry S., "Edgar Allan Poe," in *Classic Americans* (New York, 1931).

Cobb, Palmer, *The Influence of E. T. A. Hoffmann on the Tales of Edgar Allan Poe* (Chapel Hill, North Carolina, 1908).

Damon, Samuel Foster, *Thomas Holley Chivers, Friend of Poe* (New York, 1930).

Didier, Eugene L., *The Poe Cult and Other Poe Papers* (New York, 1909).

Englekirk, John E., *Edgar Allan Poe in Hispanic Literature* (New York, 1934).

Evans, May Garrettson, *Music and Edgar Allan Poe* (Baltimore, 1939).

Facts About Poe. Portraits and Daguerreotypes of Edgar Allan Poe. By Amanda P. Schulte, with a sketch of the Life of Poe, by James S. Wilson, University of Virginia Record Extension Series, X, No. 8, April, 1926. [A very useful book.]

FERGUSON, J. DELANCEY, *American Literature in Spain* (New York, 1916), 55-86; 229-236.

FOERSTER, NORMAN, *American Criticism: A Study in Literary Theory from Poe to the Present* (Boston and New York, 1928).

FRENCH, JOHN C., "Poe and the Baltimore Saturday Visiter," *Modern Language Notes*, XXXIII (May, 1918), 257-267.

————, "Poe's Literary Baltimore," *Maryland Historical Magazine*, XXXII (June, 1937), 101-112.

GILL, WILLIAM F., *The Life of Edgar Allan Poe* (New York, Philadelphia, and Boston, 1877; London, 1878). [Some first-hand information and facsimiles, but not discriminating.]

HARRISON, JAMES A., *Life and Letters of Edgar Allan Poe*, 2 vols. (New York, 1903). Revision of Vols. I and XVII in Virginia Edition. [Enthusiastic and at times valuable, especially the letters.]

INGRAM, JOHN H., *Edgar Allan Poe, His Life, Letters, and Opinions*, 2 vols. (London, 1880; revised editions, 1 vol., 1884, 1891). [Historically interesting, and usually discriminating.]

JACKSON, DAVID K., *Poe and the Southern Literary Messenger* (Richmond, 1934).

————, *The Contributors and Contributions to the Southern Literary Messenger* (Charlottesville, Virginia, 1936).

KRUTCH, JOSEPH WOOD, *Edgar Allan Poe, A Study in Genius* (New York, 1926). [Based on a mistaken theory of Poe's physical constitution.]

LAUVRIÈRE, ÉMILE, *Edgar Poe. Sa vie et son oeuvre*, 2 vols. (Paris, 1904). [One of the modern pioneers in French criticism of Poe.]

————, *L'étrange Vie et les étranges Amours d'Edgar Poe* (*Paris*, [1935]) Translated by Edwin G. Rich as *The Strange Life and the Strange Loves of Edgar Allan Poe* (Philadelphia, 1935).

————, *Le Génie Morbide D'Edgar Poe. Poèsies et Contes* (Paris, n.d., [1935]). [This volume of criticism is better than the above biography by Lauvrière. He lays too much stress upon Poe's relations with women.]

LEMONNIER, LÉON, *Edgar Poe et la Critique Française de 1845 à 1875* (Paris, 1928).

————, *Les Traducteurs d'Edgar Poe en France de 1845 à 1875: Charles Baudelaire* (Paris, 1928).

————, *Edgar Poe et les Poètes Français* (Paris, 1932). [Lemonnier is one of the most prolific of the French critics of Poe. Several of his articles are included in the volumes given above. See also below.]

————, "Edgar Poe et le Roman scientifique Français," *La Grande Revue*, XXXIV (August, 1930), 214-223.

————, "L'influence d'Edgar Poe sur les conteurs Français symbolistes et décadents," *Revue de littérature comparée*, XIII (Paris, 1933), 102-133.

LOWELL, JAMES RUSSELL, "Our Contributors, No. XVII, Edgar Allan Poe," *Graham's Magazine*, XXVII (February, 1845), 49-53.

MABBOTT, THOMAS OLLIVE, Editor, *Merlin, Baltimore, 1827, Together with Recollections of Edgar A. Poe by Lambert A. Wilmer* (New York, 1941).

MAUCLAIR, CAMILLE (Faust), *Le Génie d'Edgar Poe; la légende et la vérité—la méthode—la pensée—l'influence en France* (Paris, c. 1925). [More sensible than the usual French treatment of Poe. Useful also in the discussion of Poe's influence on French literature.]

MORRIS, G. D., *Fenimore Cooper et Edgar Poe d'après la critique française du dix-neuvième siècle* (Paris, 1912).

NICHOLS, MARY GOVE, "Reminiscences of Edgar Allan Poe," *Sixpenny Magazine*, February, 1863. Privately printed, with introductory letter by T. O. Mabbott (New York, 1931).

PHILLIPS, MARY E., *Edgar Allan Poe, the Man*, 2 vols. (Philadelphia, 1926). [The product of much labor, but poorly organized. Profusely illustrated.]

POPE-HENNESSY, UNA, *Edgar Allan Poe, a Critical Biography* (London, 1934). [Conservative, secondary, and contributes little original material.]

PRITCHARD, JOHN P., "Horace and Edgar Allan Poe," *Classical Weekly*, XXVI (March 6, 1933), 129-133.

————, "Aristotle's Influence upon American Criticism," *Proceedings of the American Philological Association*, LXVII (1936), 341-362.

ROBERTSON, JOHN W., *Edgar A. Poe, a Psychopathic Study* (New York, 1923). [Quite sensible, for a book of this nature.]

SEYLAZ, LOUIS, *Edgar Poe et les premiers symbolistes français* (Lausanne, 1923).

SHANKS, EDWARD, *Edgar Allan Poe* (London and New York, 1937). [Inaccurate in biography, no real contribution.]

SMITH, C. ALPHONSO, *Edgar Allan Poe: How to Know Him* (Indianapolis, 1921).

STANARD, MARY NEWTON, *The Dreamer, The Life Story of Poe* (Philadelphia, 1925). [An imaginary biography.]

STEDMAN, E. C., "Edgar Allan Poe," *Scribner's Monthly*, XX (May, 1880), 107-124. Also in book form (Boston, 1881). Revised in *Poets of America* (Boston, 1898). See also his introductions to the *Works*, I, 91-121; VI, xi-xxvi and X, xiii-xxxv.

STOVALL, FLOYD, "Poe's Debt to Coleridge," *University of Texas Studies in English*, X (1930), 70-127. [Studied and not always correct, but scholarly.]

THOMPSON, JOHN R., *The Genius and Character of Edgar Allan Poe*, edited and arranged by James H. Whitty and James H. Rindfleisch (Richmond, Virginia, privately printed, 1929).

TICKNOR, CAROLINE, *Poe's Helen* (New York, 1916).

WEISS, SUSAN ARCHER, *The Home Life of Poe* (New York, 1907). [See comment in text.]

WHITMAN, SARAH HELEN, *Edgar Poe and his Critics* (New York, 1860). Second edition (Providence, 1885).

WILLIS, NATHANIEL PARKER, "Death of Edgar A. Poe," *Home Journal* (October 20, 1849).

WILSON, JAMES SOUTHALL, "The Young Man Poe," *Virginia Quarterly Review*, II (April, 1926), 238-253.

WOODBERRY, GEORGE E., *Edgar Allan Poe* (Boston, 1885). American Men of Letters.

——, *The Life of Edgar Allan Poe, Personal and Literary, with his Chief Correspondence with Men of Letters*, 2 vols. (Boston, 1909). [Revision and expansion of the earlier biography. Scholarly and usually accurate, but written before certain important material was available, and leaning too much upon Griswold.]

Index

The Index is arranged alphabetically not only as to the main heads, but also *within* the heads, so far as the principal items are concerned. Minor page references follow these in order of pages. Then come letters from and to individuals. Letters to and from Poe are placed under "Poe, Edgar Allan," and letters concerning Poe under the writers' names. Volumes by Poe are in capitals and small capitals; all other volumes and all periodicals in italics, and all poems, stories and criticisms in roman type quoted.

Adams, Major General E. S., letters from, to present writer, 119n, 167, 743

Adams, John Quincy, 254

Adams, Samuel, 2

"L'Aeronaute Hollandais," French translation of "Hans Pfaall," 519

AL AARAAF, TAMERLANE AND MINOR POEMS, analysis of, 156-164; contemporary criticism of, 165-166; publication of, 152, 156; title page of, 155

"Al Aaraaf," analysis of, 156-161; criticism of by Neal, 152-154, by Lowell, 433; Poe's explanation of, 138-143, 153-154; publication of, 156; republished, 481n; 171, 175, 180, 182, 183, 185, 194, 269, 374, 374n, 485-486, 487, 562, 668

Aldrich, James, 453, 455, 523

Alexander, Charles W., impression of Poe, 296-297

Letter from, to T. C. Clarke, 296-297

Alexander's Weekly Messenger, 326, 326n, 327

Alexandria, Poe's mother in, 12

Allan, John, adoption (?) of Poe, 61-63; ambitions to write, 57; ancestry of, 54; attitude toward Poe, 60, 66, 71, 77, 89, 113, 116-117, 136-137, 172-173; birth of, 52; children of, by second marriage, 30n, 207n; Collier, Edward, pays bills for, 61; commercial standing of, 71; cost of Poe's education, in London, 69-73, in Richmond, 60, 82-84, at University of Virginia, 109-113, furnishing Poe with equipment for West Point, 167; death of, 52n, 207; England, in (with family), 64-80; financial difficulties of, 79; homes of, in London, 67, 77, in Richmond, 53, 81, 82, 88-89, 92-93; illegitimate children of, 168-169; inherits from uncle, 92; impression of, by Ann Valentine, 627; marriage of (to Frances Keeling Valentine), 531, (to Louisa G. Patterson), 30n, 170, 207n; partner in firm of Ellis and Allan, 51; refuses Poe permission to return to University of Virginia, 109; refuses to pay Poe's debts at University of Virginia, 112-113; returns to America 81; Richmond, comes to, 52, in, 52-64, 81-95, social standing of, in, 55; will of, 168-169; will of, effect of, 207; 51, 117, 132, 133, 134, 135, 148, 151, 152, 166, 186, 191, 194, 198, 206, 527, 578, 671, 685

Allan, John, *continued*
  Letters (and extracts) from Allan
    to, John H. Eaton, 136-137;
    Charles H. Ellis, 59, 60, 64, 65,
    66, 67, 71, 133, 205; James
    Nimmo, 56-57; Margaret Nimmo,
    55-56; W. H. Poe, 89
  Letters (and extracts) to Allan
    from, Rosanna Dixon, 57-58;
    George W. Spotswood, 111-112
  Letters from and to Poe, see Poe,
    Edgar Allan, *Letters*
Allan, Mrs. John (Frances Keeling
  Valentine), death of, 133; descrip-
  tion of, 58; illness of, in London,
  67-68; marriage of, 52; takes
  Edgar, 46; 51, 57, 66, 77, 79, 81,
  90, 91, 93, 116-117, 134, 169,
  373, 527, 631
  Letters from, to John Allan, 58-59,
    77-78
Allan, Mrs. John (Louisa G. Patter-
  son), marriage to John Allan, 30n,
  170; 167, 169, 189, 195, 196, 205,
  206, 207, 627, 666
Allan, Mary, 63, 66, 79
Allan, Nancy, 63
Allan, William, 63
Allen, Hervey, 196n, 227n, 255n,
  277n, 296n, 565n, 621n, 732
Allston, Washington, 616
American authors, difficulties of,
  305-306, 436
American drama, Poe's survey of,
  471-473; 283-284, 501
"American Letters," projected book
  on, 510
American Monthly Magazine, 266
American Museum (Baltimore), 269,
  271, 272, 290, 292
American Poetry, Specimens of, 128,
  503
American Quarterly Review, 243,
  268
American (Whig) Review (Editor,
  G. H. Colton), appreciation of
  Poe in, 665-666; 381n, 438, 439,
  467, 468, 523, 532, 533, 535, 593,
  594, 604, 630n

Amity Street, Baltimore, No. 3, Poe's
  home, 205, 218
Amity Street, New York, No. 85,
  Poe's home, 463, 475-476, 480,
  493, 496
Anderson, Maxwell, 472
"Angel of the Odd, The," publication of, 420-421
"Annabel Lee," analysis of, 606-607;
  carrying over from "Tamerlane" of
  idea expressed in lines of, 123; inspiration for, 606; Poe speaks of,
  604-605; publication of, 606,
  606n; 255, 346, 573, 630, 657,
  658, 670, 670n
"Annie." See Richmond, Mrs.
  Charles
Anthon, Charles, 433n, 496-497, 530,
  558
  Letters from and to Poe, see Poe,
    Edgar Allan, *Letters*
Aristidean, The, Poe's objections to
  generalizations in criticism in, 474;
  reviews by Poe in, 473-474; reviews of Poe in, 467, 482; 503
Aristotle, 544
Army, United States, Poe, at Fort
  Independence, 119; at Fort Moultrie, 129; at Fortress Monroe, 129-
  135; Poe, enlists in, 119, promoted,
  133, withdraws with honorable
  discharge, 134-135; Poe's record
  in, 742-744; testimonial letters
  from officers concerning Poe, 135-
  136; 174, 671
Arnold, Mrs. Elizabeth Smith (Mrs.
  Charles Tubbs), debut of, in Boston, 3; last record of, 9; marriage
  of, to Henry Arnold, 2, to Charles
  Tubbs, 4; theatrical career of, in
  America, 4, 6-9, in England, 1-3
Arnold, Henry, 2
Arnott, Dr. N., impressions of Poe,
  82
ARTHUR GORDON PYM, analysis of,
  264-266; publication of, 260, 263;
  reception of, 263, 264; sources of,
  264; 262, 267, 294, 640
Arthur's Ladies' Magazine, 499